BLACK+DECKER

Complete Guide to Wiring

WIRING

Updated 9th Edition

Current with 2023–2026 Electrical Codes

COOL
SPRINGS
PRESS

T0377766

Quarto.com

8th Edition, 2022; 7th Edition, 2017; 6th Edition, 2014; 5th Edition, 2011; 4th Edition, 2008; 3rd Edition, 2005; 2nd Edition, 2003

First Published in 2001 by Creative Publishing international, now Cool Springs Press, an imprint of The Quarto Group, 100 Cummings Center, Suite 265-D, Beverly, MA 01915, USA. T (978) 282-9590 F (978) 283-2742

Cool Springs Press titles are also available at discount for retail, wholesale, promotional, and bulk purchase. For details, contact the Special Sales Manager by email at specialsales@quarto.com or by mail at The Quarto Group, Attn: Special Sales Manager, 100 Cummings Center, Suite 265-D, Beverly, MA 01915, USA.

29 28 27 26 25   1 2 3 4 5

ISBN: 978-0-7603-9784-8

Digital edition published in 2025

eISBN: 978-0-7603-9785-5

Library of Congress Cataloging-in-Publication Data avail

Photography: Quarto Publishing Group USA Inc., except p. 177 © Mike Clarke/istock.com; p. 202 © George Peters/istock.com; p. 206 courtesy of Broan NuTone; p. 209 courtesy of Acuity Brands Lighting, Inc., acuitybrands.com 800-922-9641, featuring Juno Switchable White Flat LED Wafer Canless Fixture; p. 218 (top right) courtesy of Kohler; p. 220 courtesy of Ikea; p. 250 © George Peters /istock.com; p. 251 © David Ross /istock.com; p. 263 (top right) © Steve Harmon/istock.com, (lower right) courtesy of SieMatic; p. 266 © Jeff Chevrier/istock.com; p. 267 (top right & lower) courtesy of Generac Power Systems, Inc.; p. 278 courtesy of Cabin Fever, featuring McMaster Carr vapor-tight light fixtures
Illustrations: Ada Keesler

Printed in China

Black + Decker: The Complete Guide to Wiring, 9th Edition
Created by: The Editors of Cool Springs Press, in cooperation with BLACK+DECKER. BLACK+DECKER and the BLACK+DECKER logo are trademarks of The Black + Decker Corporation and are used under license. All rights reserved.

NOTICE TO READERS

For safety, use caution, care, and good judgment when following the procedures described in this book. The publisher and BLACK+DECKER cannot assume responsibility for any damage to property or injury to persons as a result of misuse of the information provided.

The techniques shown in this book are general techniques for various applications. In some instances, additional techniques not shown in this book may be required. Always follow manufacturers' instructions included with products, since deviating from the directions may void warranties. The projects in this book vary widely as to skill levels required: some may not be appropriate for all do-it-yourselfers, and some may require professional help.

Consult your local building department for information on building permits, codes, and other laws as they apply to your project.

The Complete Guide to Wiring **9th Edition**

Introduction	7

WORKING SAFELY WITH WIRING	**9**
How Electricity Works	10
Glossary of Electrical Terms	14
Understanding Electrical Circuits	16
Grounding + Polarization	18
Home Wiring Tools	20
Wiring Safety	22

WIRE, CABLE + CONDUIT	**25**
Wire + Cable	26
NM Cable	34
Conduit	42

BOXES + PANELS	**49**
Electrical Boxes	50
Installing Boxes	56
Electrical Panels	64

SWITCHES	**73**
Wall Switches	74
Types of Wall Switches	76
Specialty Switches	84
Testing Switches	88

RECEPTACLES	**93**
Types of Receptacles	94
Receptacle Wiring	100
GFCI Receptacles	104
Testing Receptacles	108

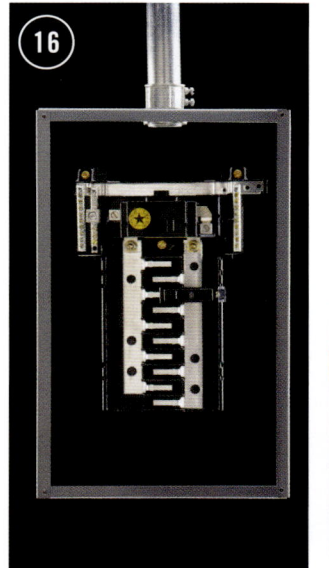

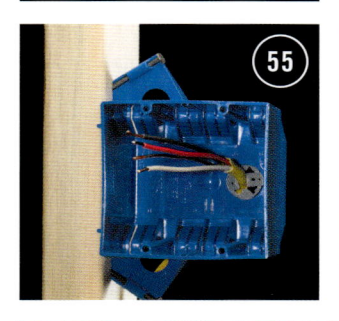
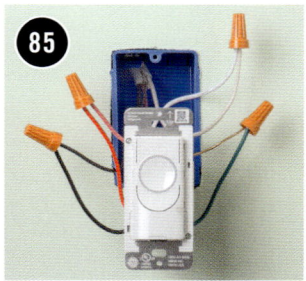

PLANNING + PREP — 111

Planning Your Project	112
Highlights of the National Electrical Code	120
Room by Room Wiring	134

CIRCUIT MAPS — 149

Common Household Circuits	150

COMMON WIRING PROJECTS — 167

GFCI + AFCI Breakers	168
Surge-Protective Devices	172
Service Panels	174
Grounding + Bonding a Wiring System	182
Subpanels	188
120/240-Volt Dryer Receptacles	192
120/240-Volt Range Receptacles	193
Dryer and Range Cords	194
Adding an Outdoor Receptacle	198
Ceilings Lights	202
Recessed Ceiling Lights	206
Track Lights	212
Vanity Lights	216
Hardwired Smoke + CO Alarms	218
Low-Voltage Pathway + Patio Lighting	220
Doorbells	224

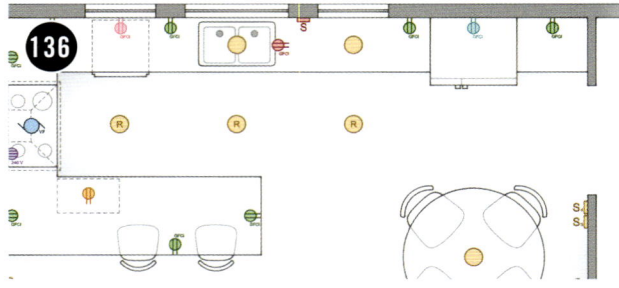

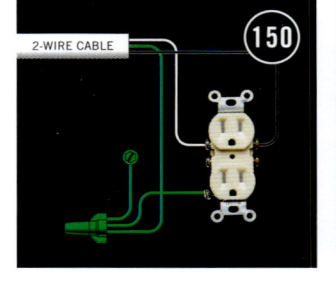

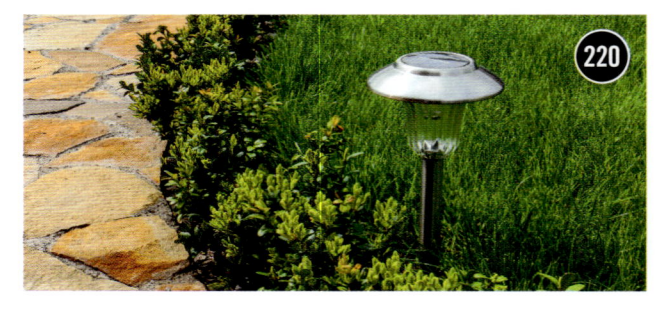

Wireless Switches	228
Baseboard Heaters	232
Underfloor Radiant Heat Systems	236
Ceiling Fans	242
Remote-Control Ceiling Fan Retrofit	246
Bathroom Exhaust Fans	250
Installing and Using a Whole-House Fan	254
Range Hoods	260
Backup Power Supply	264
Installing a Transfer Switch	270
Outbuildings	276
Motion-Sensing Floodlights	284

COMMON REPAIR PROJECTS, WIRING PROBLEMS + SOLUTIONS	**289**
Troubleshooting Light Fixtures	290
Repairing Chandeliers	294
Repairing Ceiling Fans	296
Replacing Plugs + Cords	298
Service Panels + Grounding	302
Cables + Wires	305
Boxes	309
Cords	312
Receptacles + Switches	314

Conversions	**316**
Resources	**316**
Index	**317**

Introduction

This 9th edition of *Black + Decker The Complete Guide to Wiring* has been updated to reflect current technology and techniques and the National Electrical Code (NEC) of 2023. Because the information is based on the current, nationally accepted electrical code, it's important to understand what it is and how it's implemented, as well as the changes mandated in the most recent version.

The code is maintained and updated by the National Fire Protection Agency in an ongoing process. The Agency publishes an updated version every three years. The NEC is the standard on which state and local codes are based. The goal is to create uniform rules with a focus on the latest safety practices. Many DIYers are surprised to learn, on their first trip to the local building department, that not all states have implemented the 2023 code. In fact not all of them have even implemented the 2020 code (one state is operating from the 2008 code!). Bureaucracies work slowly and experts in many states study changes for long periods prior to accepting and implementing them.

However, homeowners are well served by following the most recent code. (Even in states that have yet to adopt the latest version, inspectors will generally consider work done to the current code as overkill, rather than unacceptable.) That said, it's imperative to consult your local building department and electrical inspector whenever you're tackling an electrical project beyond the simple removal and replacement of a switch, receptacle, or light fixture.

Changes of note in the NEC 2023 include:

Electric Vehicle Charging Outlets
Outlets intended for electric vehicle charging equipment (EVCE) must be on a dedicated circuit if the circuit is more than 16 amps or 120 volts. This applies to both plug-and-cord connected, and hardwired EVCEs. It doesn't apply to general-purpose garage receptacles.

Kitchen Island and Peninsula Receptacles
You are no longer required to install a receptacle at kitchen islands and peninsulas. You must, however, prewire for a receptacle at these locations. However, receptacles for islands and peninsulas are highly recommended as a safety feature.

GFCI Receptacles
GFCI protection is required for outlets rated less than 150 volts and 60 amps serving microwave ovens, wall ovens, cooktops, ranges, sump pumps, and clothes dryers.

Receptacle Installation
Some receptacles allow wires to be inserted into the back of the receptacle, called *push-in* or *back-stabbing*. This procedure is now limited to 15-amp circuits and #14 copper wire, with some exceptions. It is not recommended, in any case.

Wet-Area Receptacle Covers
Receptacles that are exposed to water are required to have covers that can be closed when a plug is inserted. These covers are now required to open at least 90 degrees, or as far as designed, whichever is less.

Working Safely with Wiring

In a sense, this entire book is about the title of this section. When it comes to electricity, the greater your knowledge, the lower your risk. Safety should always come first in home improvement, but no more so than in working with electrical issues. Where plumbing mishaps can lead to some fairly gross situations, many electrical repairs pose potentially deadly risks.

Even if it doesn't hurt you, miswiring or an error in an electrical repair can cost you mightily—including losing a home to fire. Obviously, caution and attention to detail should be your watchwords no matter what repair you tackle.

This book will help you build a knowledge base and skills. It's wisest to go through the book from start to finish so that your expertise is well rounded. You'll find a commonsense explanation of how electricity works in a home, how to stop or redirect it, and many individual projects that give you a chance to see those principles in action.

However, should you ever feel overwhelmed—even if that happens after you've begun an electrical project—stop and contact a licensed, insured electrician. The only electrical project you should tackle is one with which you feel totally comfortable.

In this chapter:

- How Electricity Works
- Glossary of Electrical Terms
- Understanding Electrical Circuits
- Grounding + Polarization
- Home Wiring Tools
- Wiring Safety

How Electricity Works

A household electrical system can be compared with a home's plumbing system. Electrical current flows in wires in much the same way that water flows inside pipes. Both electricity and water enter the home, are distributed throughout the house, do their "work," and exit.

In plumbing, water first flows through the pressurized water supply system. In electricity, current first flows along hot wires. Current flowing along hot wires also is pressurized. Electrical pressure is called voltage.

Large supply pipes can carry a greater volume of water than small pipes. Likewise, large electrical wires carry more current than small wires. This electrical current-carrying capacity of wires is called ampacity.

Water is made available for use through the faucets, spigots, and showerheads in a home. Electricity is made available through receptacles, switches, and fixtures.

Water finally leaves the home through a drain system, which is not pressurized. Similarly, electrical current flows back through neutral wires. The current in neutral wires is not pressurized and is at zero volts,

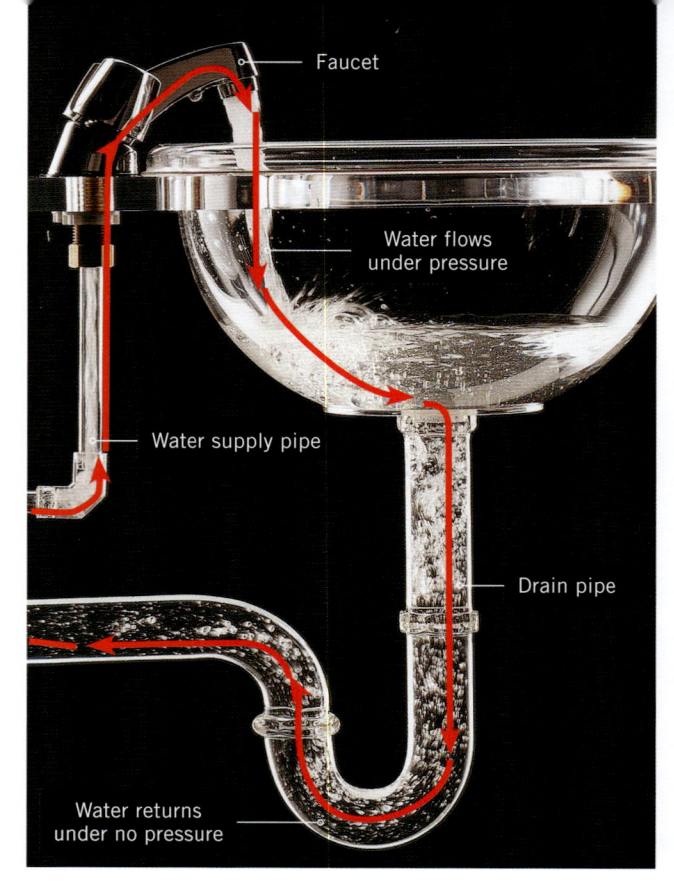

Water and electricity both flow. The main difference is that you can see water (and touching water isn't likely to kill you). Like electricity, water enters a fixture under high pressure and exits under no pressure.

when everything is functioning as intended. Do not assume, however, that the neutral is at zero volts. Several defects can put voltage on the neutral, so treat the neutral as a hot wire until demonstrated otherwise.

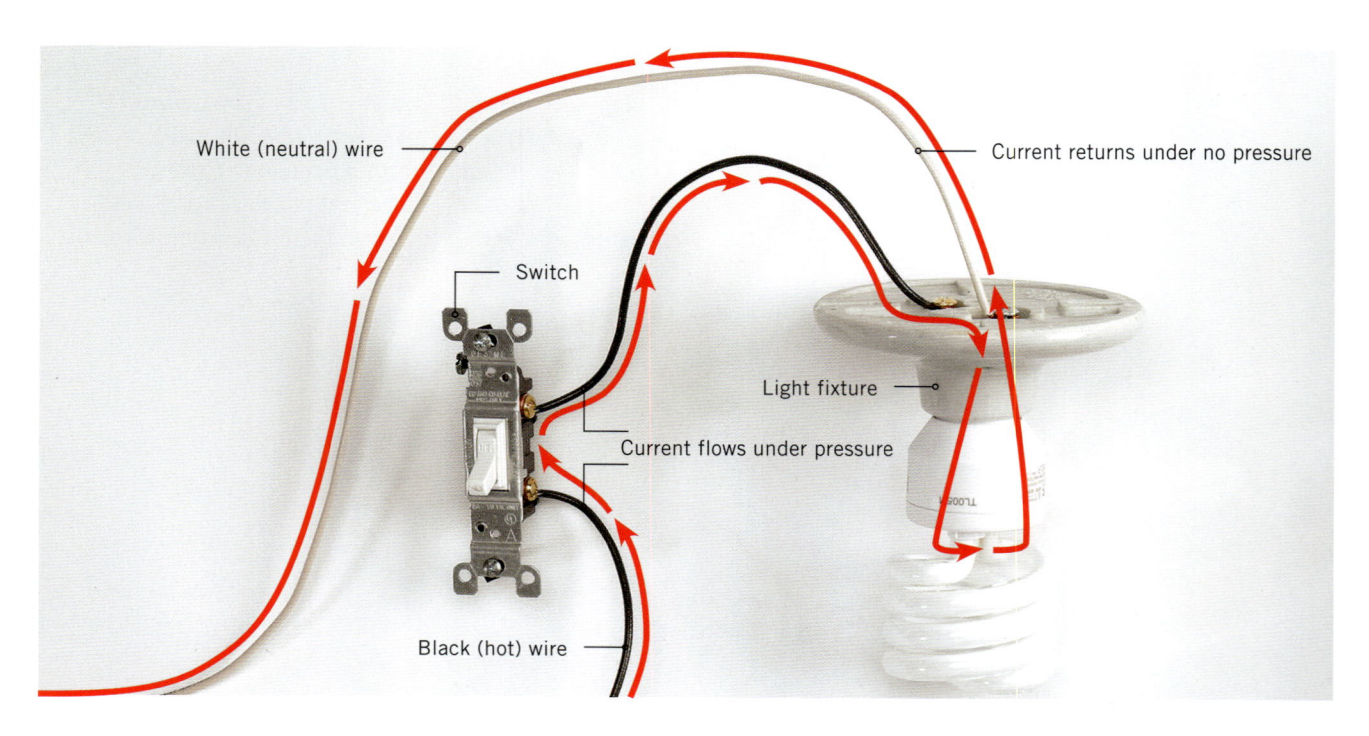

The Delivery System

Electricity that enters the home is produced by large power plants. Power plants are located in all parts of the country and generate electricity with generators fueled by the Sun, water, wind, or steam. From these plants electricity enters large "step-up" transformers that increase voltage to half a million volts or more.

Electricity flows at these high voltages and travels through high-voltage transmission wires to communities that can be hundreds of miles from the power plants. "Step-down" transformers located at substations then reduce the voltage for distribution along street wires. On utility power poles, smaller transformers further reduce the voltage to ordinary 120-volt electricity for household use.

Wires carrying electricity to a house either run underground or are strung overhead and attached to a piece of conduit called a service mast. Most homes built after 1950 have three wires running to the service head: two power wires, each carrying 120/240 volts, and a grounded neutral wire. Electricity from the two 120-volt wires may be combined at the service panel to supply electricity to large 240-volt appliances such as clothes dryers or electric water heaters.

Incoming electricity passes through a meter that measures electricity consumption. Electricity then enters the service panel, where it is distributed to circuits that run throughout the house. The service panel also contains circuit breakers or fuses that shut off power to the individual circuits in the event of a short circuit or an overload. Certain high-current appliances, such as microwave ovens, are usually plugged into their own individual circuits to prevent overloads.

Voltage ratings determined by power companies and manufacturers have changed over the years. These changes do not affect the performance of new devices connected to older wiring. For making electrical calculations, use a rating of 120 volts or 240 volts for your circuits.

Power plants supply electricity to thousands of homes and businesses. Step-up transformers increase the voltage produced at the plant.

Substations are located near the communities they serve. A typical substation takes electricity from high-voltage transmission wires and reduces it for distribution along street wires.

Electrical transformers reduce the high-voltage electricity that flows through wires along neighborhood streets. A utility pole transformer— or ground transformer—reduces voltage from 10,000 volts to the normal 120/240-volt electricity used in households.

Parts of the Electrical System

Current flows to the home from the utility service

The service mast (metal conduit) and the weatherhead create the entry point for electricity into your home. The mast is supplied with three wires, two of which (the insulated wires) each carry 120 volts and originate at the nearest transformer. In some areas, electricity enters from below ground as a lateral instead of the overhead drop shown above.

The meter measures the amount of electricity consumed. It is usually attached to the side of the house and connects to the service mast. The electric meter belongs to your local power utility company. If you suspect the meter is not functioning properly, contact the power company.

Surges in current flow to grounding rod

A grounding wire connects the electrical system to the earth through a metal grounding rod driven next to the house or through another type of grounding electrode.

Current flows back to neutral at service mast

Light fixtures attach directly to a household electrical system. They are usually controlled with wall switches.

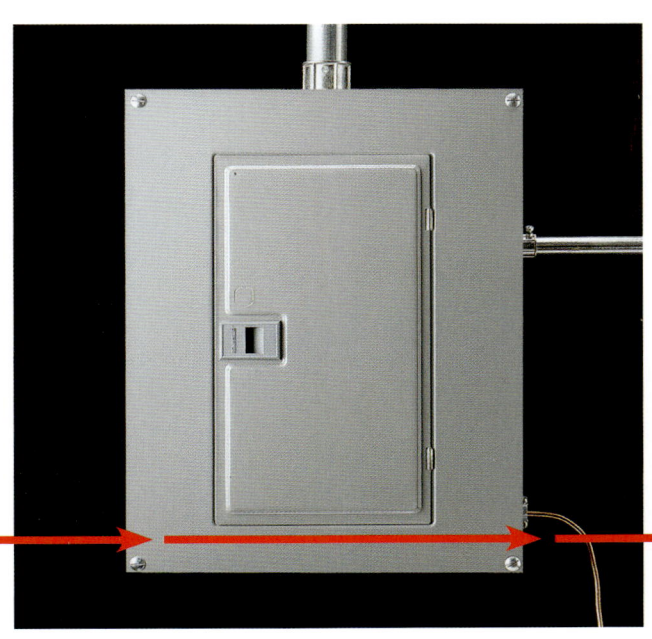

The main service panel, or "breaker box," distributes power to individual circuits. A circuit breaker protects each circuit from short circuits and overloads. Circuit breakers also are used to shut off power to individual circuits while repairs are made. Older homes may have fuses instead of circuit breakers.

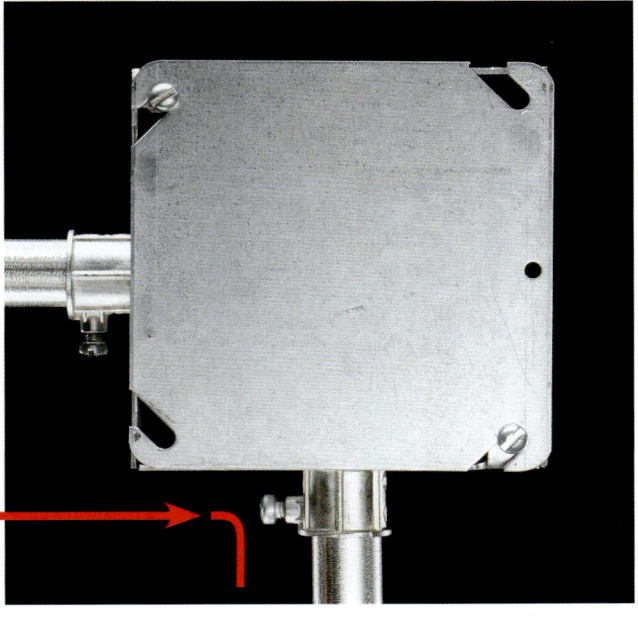

Electrical boxes enclose wire connections. According to the National Electrical Code, all wire splices and connections must be contained entirely in a covered plastic or metal electrical box. This box must be accessible for inspection and for service.

Switches control electricity passing through hot circuit wires. Switches can be wired to control light fixtures, ceiling fans, appliances, and receptacles.

Receptacles, sometimes called outlets, provide plug-in access to electricity. A 120-volt, 15-amp or 20-amp receptacle with a grounding hole is the most typical receptacle in wiring systems installed after 1965. Most receptacles have two plug-in locations and are called duplex receptacles.

Ampere (or amp): Refers to the rate at which electrical current flows to a light, tool, or appliance.

Armored cable: An assembly of insulated wires enclosed in a flexible, interlocked metallic armor. Abbreviated "AC."

Box: A device used to contain wiring connections.

Cable: Two or more wires that are grouped together and protected by a covering or sheath.

Circuit: A continuous loop of electrical current flowing along wires.

Circuit breaker: A safety device that interrupts an electrical circuit in the event of an overload or short circuit.

Conductor: Any material that allows electrical current to flow through it. Copper wire is an especially good conductor.

Conduit: A metal or plastic pipe used to protect wires.

Continuity: An uninterrupted electrical pathway through a circuit or electrical fixture.

Current: The flow of electricity along a conductor.

Duplex receptacle: A receptacle that provides connections for two plugs.

Flexible metal conduit (FMC): Hollow, coiled steel or aluminum tubing that may be filled with wires (similar to armored cable, but AC is prewired).

Fuse: A safety device, usually found in older homes, that interrupts electrical circuits during an overload or short circuit.

Greenfield: A brand name for an early type of flexible metal conduit. The current term is *flexible metal conduit*. Note: flexible metal conduit is different from armored cable.

Grounded wire: See neutral wire.

Grounding wire: A wire used in an electrical circuit to conduct current to the service panel in the event of a ground fault. The grounding wire often is a bare copper wire or a green insulated wire.

Hot wire: Any wire that carries voltage. In an electrical circuit, the hot wire usually is covered with black or red insulation.

Insulator: Any material, such as plastic or rubber, that resists the flow of electrical current. Insulating materials protect wires and cables. Also called the ungrounded wire.

Junction box: See Box.

Meter: A device used to measure the amount of electrical power being used.

Neutral wire: A wire that returns current at zero voltage to the source of electrical power. Usually covered with white or light gray insulation. Also called the grounded wire.

Nonmetallic sheathed cable: NM cable consists of two or more insulated conductors and, in most cases, a bare ground wire housed in a durable PVC casing.

Outlet: A place where electricity is taken for use. A receptacle is a common type of outlet. A box for a ceiling fan is another type of outlet.

Overload: A demand for more current than the circuit wires or electrical device was designed to carry. This should cause a circuit breaker to trip or a fuse to blow.

Pigtail: A short wire used to connect two or more wires to a single screw terminal.

Polarized receptacle: A receptacle designed to keep hot current flowing along black or red wires and neutral current flowing along white or gray wires. The wider slot is neutral.

Power: The work performed by electricity for a period of time. Use of power makes heat, motion, or light.

Receptacle: A device that provides plug-in access to electricity.

Romex: A brand name of plastic-sheathed electrical cable that is commonly used for indoor wiring. Commonly known as nonmetallic, or NM, cable.

Screw terminal: A place where a wire connects to a receptacle, switch, or fixture.

Service panel: A metal box usually near the site where electricity enters the house. In the service panel, electrical current is split into individual circuits. In residences the service panel has a circuit breaker or a fuse to protect each circuit.

Short circuit: An accidental and improper contact between two current-carrying wires or between a current-carrying wire and a grounding conductor.

Switch: A device that controls electricity passing through hot circuit wires. Used to turn lights and appliances on and off.

UL: Formerly known as Underwriters Laboratories, this organization tests electrical devices and manufactured products for safety.

Voltage (or volts): A measurement of electricity in terms of pressure.

Wattage (or watts): A measurement of electrical power in terms of total work performed. Watts can be calculated by multiplying the voltage times the amperage.

Wire connector: A device used to connect two or more wires together. Also called a wire nut.

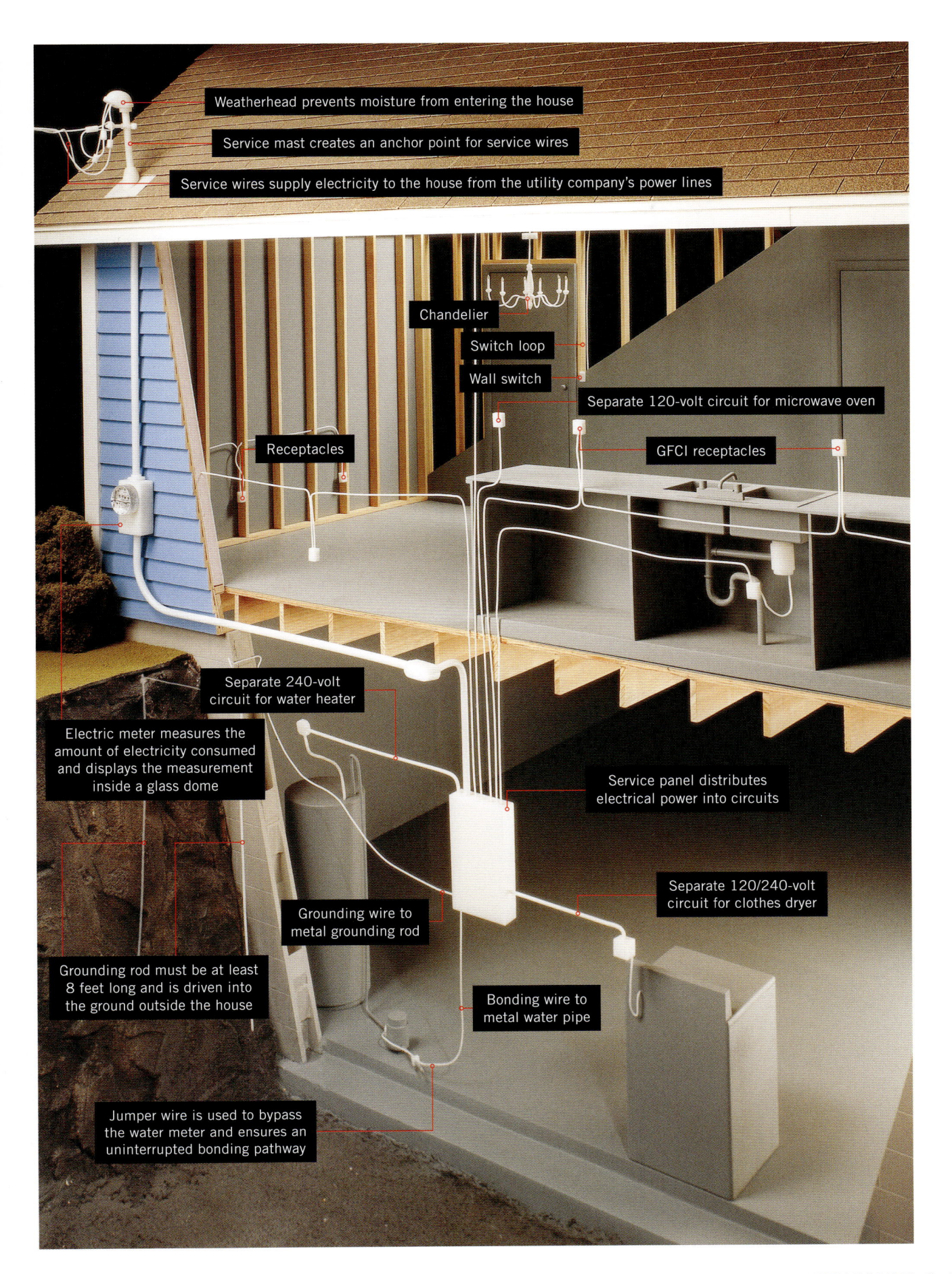

Weatherhead prevents moisture from entering the house

Service mast creates an anchor point for service wires

Service wires supply electricity to the house from the utility company's power lines

Chandelier

Switch loop

Wall switch

Separate 120-volt circuit for microwave oven

Receptacles

GFCI receptacles

Separate 240-volt circuit for water heater

Electric meter measures the amount of electricity consumed and displays the measurement inside a glass dome

Service panel distributes electrical power into circuits

Grounding wire to metal grounding rod

Separate 120/240-volt circuit for clothes dryer

Grounding rod must be at least 8 feet long and is driven into the ground outside the house

Bonding wire to metal water pipe

Jumper wire is used to bypass the water meter and ensures an uninterrupted bonding pathway

Understanding Electrical Circuits

An electrical circuit is a continuous loop. Household circuits carry electricity from the main service panel, throughout the house, and back to the main service panel. Several switches, receptacles, light fixtures, or appliances may be connected to a single circuit.

Current enters a circuit loop on hot wires and returns along neutral wires. These wires are color coded for easy identification. Hot wires are black or red, and neutral wires are white or light gray. For safety, all modern circuits include a bare copper or green insulated grounding wire. The grounding wire conducts current in the event of a ground fault (see page 18) and helps reduce the chance of severe electrical shock. The service panel also has a bonding wire connected to a metal water pipe and a grounding wire connected to a metal grounding rod, buried underground, or to another type of grounding electrode.

If a circuit carries too much current, it can overload. A fuse or a circuit breaker protects each circuit in case of overloads.

Current returns to the service panel along a neutral circuit wire. Current then leaves the house on a large neutral service wire that returns it to the utility transformer.

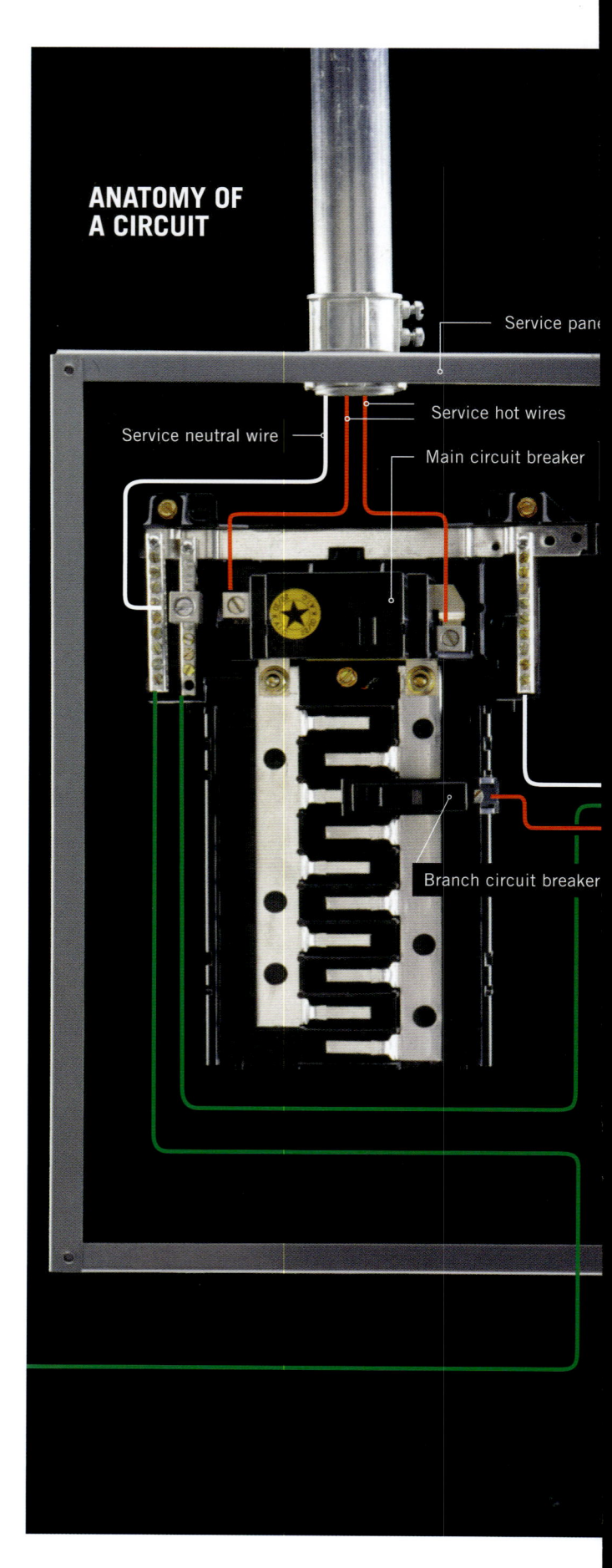

ANATOMY OF A CIRCUIT

Service pan[el]

Service hot wires

Service neutral wire

Main circuit breaker

Branch circuit breaker

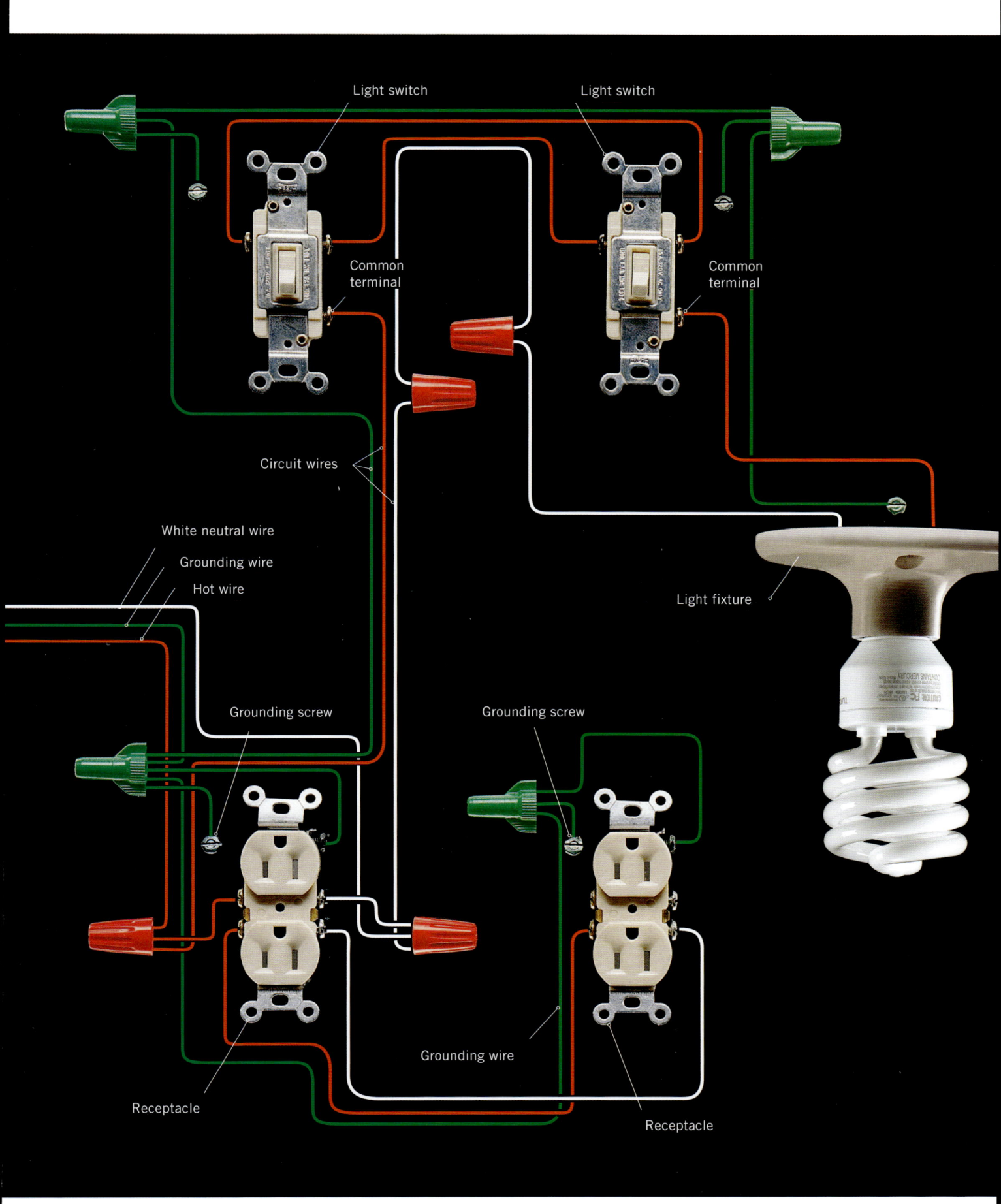

Light switch

Light switch

Common terminal

Common terminal

Circuit wires

White neutral wire

Grounding wire

Hot wire

Light fixture

Grounding screw

Grounding screw

Receptacle

Grounding wire

Receptacle

Grounding + Polarization

Electricity always seeks to return to its source and complete a continuous circuit. Contrary to popular belief, electricity will take all available return paths to its source, not just the path of lowest resistance. In a household wiring system, this return path is provided by white neutral wires that return current to the main service panel. From the service panel, current returns along the uninsulated neutral service wire to a power pole transformer.

You will see the terms *grounding* and *bonding* used in this and other books about electricity. These terms are often misunderstood. You should understand the difference to safely work on electrical circuits.

Bonding connects the noncurrent-carrying metal parts of the electrical system, such as metal boxes and metal conduit, in a continuous low-resistance path back to the main service panel. If this metal becomes energized (a ground fault), current travels on the bonded metal and quickly increases to an amount that trips the circuit breaker or blows the fuse. The dead circuit alerts people to a problem.

Other metal that could become energized also must be bonded to the home's electrical system. Metal water and gas pipes are the most common examples. A metal water and gas pipe could become energized by coming in contact with a damaged electrical wire. Metal gas pipe could become energized by a ground fault in a gas appliance such as a furnace.

Bonding is a very important safety system. A person could receive a fatal shock if he or she touches energized metal that is improperly bonded, because that person becomes electricity's return path to its source. Bonding is also a fire safety system that reduces the chance of electrical fires.

Grounding connects the home's electrical system to the earth. Grounding's primary purpose is to help stabilize voltage fluctuations caused by lightning and other problems in the electrical grid. Grounding also provides a secondary return path for electricity in case there is a problem in the normal return path.

Grounding is accomplished by connecting a wire between the main service panel and a grounding electrode. The most common grounding electrode is a buried copper-coated steel rod. Other grounding electrodes include reinforcing steel in the footing, called a ufer ground.

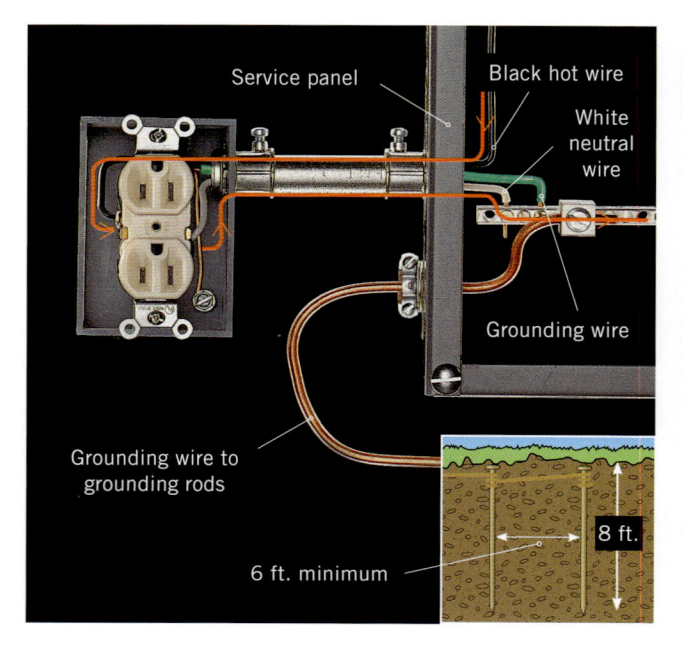

Service panel · Black hot wire · White neutral wire · Grounding wire · Grounding wire to grounding rods · 6 ft. minimum · 8 ft.

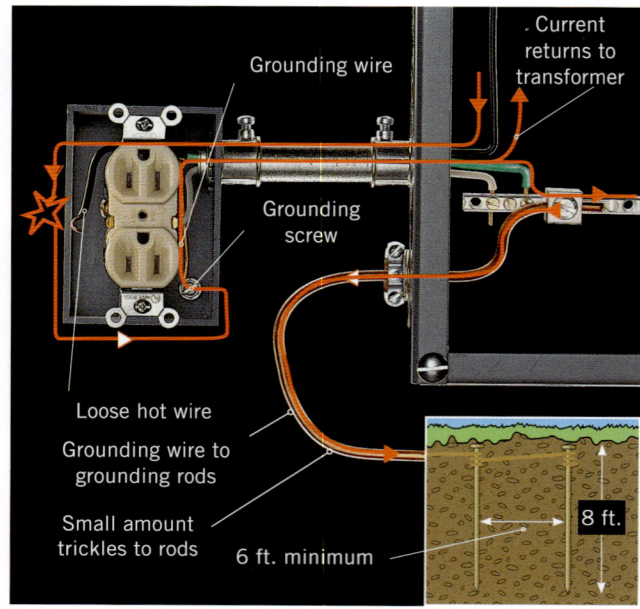

Current returns to transformer · Grounding wire · Grounding screw · Loose hot wire · Grounding wire to grounding rods · Small amount trickles to rods · 6 ft. minimum · 8 ft.

Grounding of the home electrical system is accomplished by connecting the household electrical system to the metal water service pipe, if any, between your house and the street and to another grounding electrode such as metal grounding electrodes that are buried in the earth.

After 1920 most American homes included receptacles that accepted polarized plugs. The two-slot polarized plug and receptacle was designed to keep hot current flowing along black or red wires and neutral current flowing along white or gray wires.

The metal jacket around armored cable and flexible metal conduit, widely installed in homes during the 1940s, provided a bonding path. When connected to metal junction boxes, it provided a metal pathway back to the service panel. Note,

however, that deterioration of this older cable may decrease its effectiveness as a bonding conductor.

Modern cable includes a green insulated or bare copper wire that serves as the bonding path. This bonding wire is connected to all three-slot receptacles and metal boxes to provide a continuous pathway for any ground-fault current. By plugging a three-prong plug into a grounded three-slot receptacle, people are protected from ground faults that occur in appliances, tools, or other electric devices.

Use a receptacle adapter to plug three-prong plugs into two-slot receptacles, but use it only if the receptacle connects to a grounding wire or grounded electrical box. Adapters have short grounding wires or wire loops that attach to the receptacle's coverplate mounting screw. The mounting screw connects the adapter to the grounded metal electrical box.

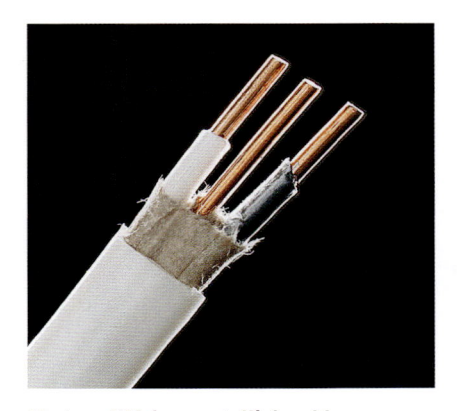

Modern NM (nonmetallic) cable, found in most wiring systems installed after about 1965, contains a bare copper wire that provides bonding for receptacle and switch boxes.

Armored cable has a flexible metal jacket and contains hot and neutral wires. It may contain a grounding wire or it may use the metal jacket to provide the grounding path. Flexible metal conduit (not shown) is sold empty.

Polarized receptacles have a long slot and a short slot. Used with a polarized plug, the polarized receptacle keeps electrical current directed for safety.

Tamper-resistent three-slot receptacles are required by code for new homes and when replacing existing receptacles. They are usually connected to a standard two-wire cable with ground.

A receptacle adapter allows three-prong plugs to be inserted into two-slot receptacles. The adapter should be used only with receptacles mounted in a bonded metal box, and the grounding loop or wire of the adapter must be attached to the coverplate mounting screw.

Double-insulated tools have nonconductive plastic bodies to prevent shocks caused by ground faults. Because of these features, double-insulated tools can be used safely with ungrounded receptacles.

Home Wiring Tools

To complete the wiring projects shown in this book, you need a few specialty electrical tools as well as a collection of basic hand tools. As with any tool purchase, invest in quality products when you buy tools for electrical work. Keep your tools clean, and sharpen or replace any cutting tools that have dull edges.

The materials used for electrical wiring have changed dramatically in the last 20 years, making it much easier for homeowners to do their own electrical work. The following pages show how to work with the following components for your projects.

Hand tools you'll need for home wiring projects include a stud finder/laser level (A) for locating framing members and aligning electrical boxes; tape measure (B); a cable ripper (C) for scoring NM sheathing; standard (D) and Phillips (E) screwdrivers; a utility knife (F); side cutters (G) for cutting wires; channel-type pliers (H) for general gripping and crimping; linesman pliers (I) that combine side cutter and gripping jaws; needlenose pliers (J); wire strippers (K) for removing insulation from conductors.

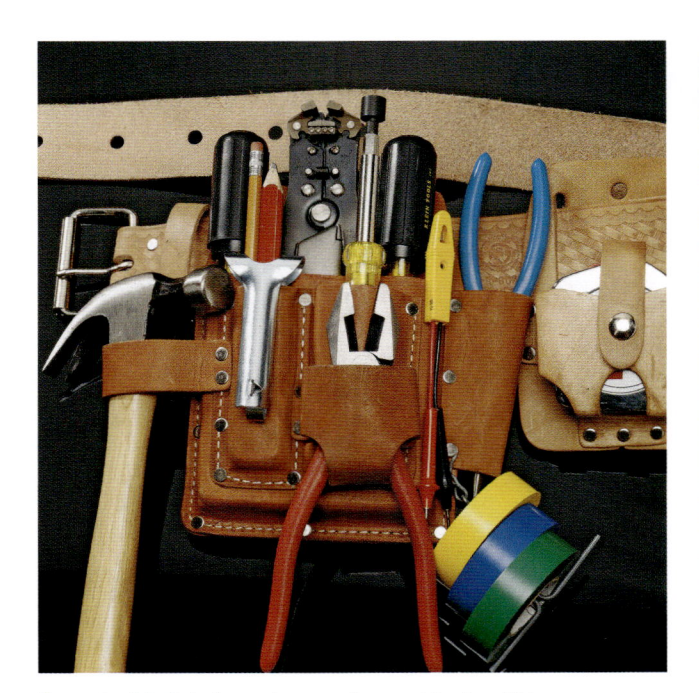

Use a tool belt to keep frequently used tools within easy reach. Electrical tapes in a variety of colors are used for marking wires and for attaching cables to a fish tape.

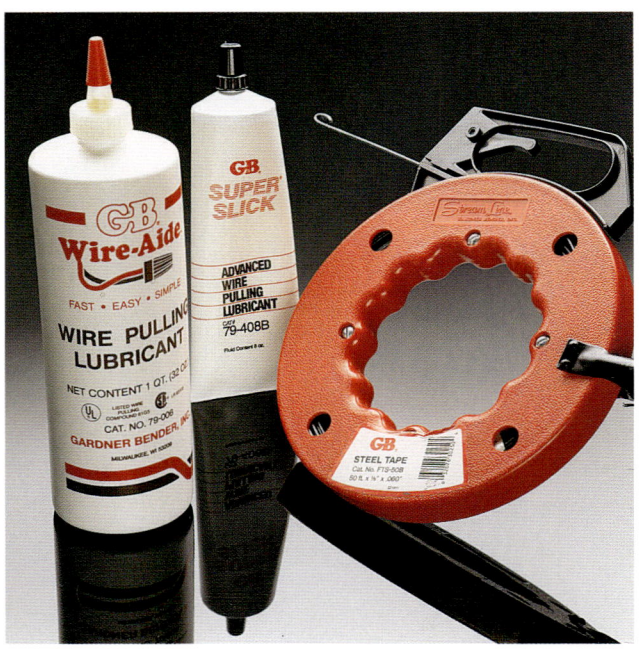

A fish tape is useful for installing cables in finished wall cavities and for pulling wires through conduit. Lubrication products reduce friction and make it easier to pull cables and wires.

Diagnostic tools for home wiring use include a noncontact voltage tester (A) to safely check wires for current and confirm that circuits are dead; a plug-in tester (B) to check receptacles for correct polarity, grounding, and circuit protection; a multimeter (C) to measure AC/DC voltage, AC/DC current, resistance, capacitance, frequency, and duty cycle (model shown is an auto-ranging digital multimeter with clamp-on jaws that measure through insulation).

Wiring Safety

Safety should be the primary concern of anyone working with electricity. Although most household electrical repairs are simple and straightforward, always use caution and good judgment when working with electrical wiring or devices. Common sense can prevent accidents.

The basic rule of electrical safety is always turn off power to the area or device you are working on. At the main service panel or at the subpanel (as applicable), shut off the circuit breaker or remove the fuse that controls the circuit you are servicing. Then check to make sure the power is off by testing for power with a voltage tester.

TIP: Test a live circuit with the voltage tester to verify that it is working before you rely on it.

Restore power only when the repair or replacement project is complete.

Follow the safety tips shown on these pages. Never attempt an electrical project beyond your skill or confidence level.

Shut power OFF at the main service panel or subpanel where the circuit originates before beginning any work.

Create a circuit index and affix it to the inside of the door to your main service panel. Update it as needed.

Confirm power is OFF by testing at the outlet, switch, or fixture with a voltage tester.

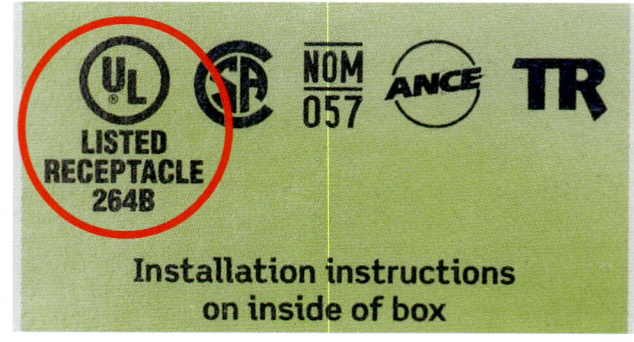

Use only UL-approved electrical parts or devices. These devices have been tested for safety by Underwriters Laboratories.

Wear rubber-soled shoes while working on electrical projects. On damp floors, stand on a rubber mat or dry wooden boards.

Use fiberglass or wood ladders when making routine household repairs near the service mast.

Extension cords are for temporary use only. Cords must be rated for the intended usage.

Breakers and fuses must be compatible with the panel manufacturer and match the circuit capacity.

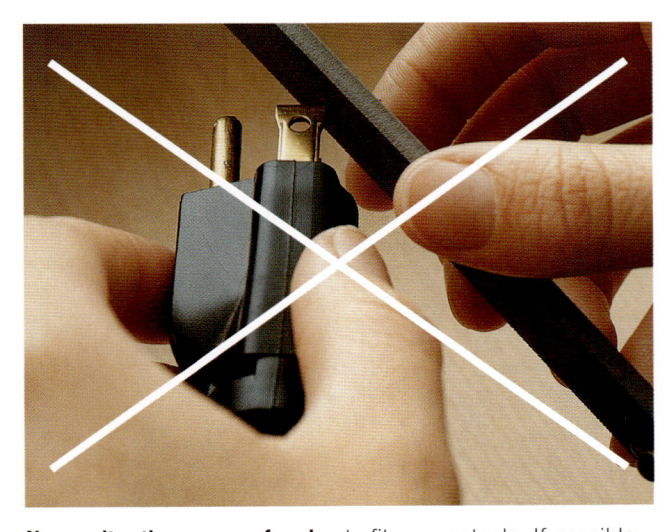

Never alter the prongs of a plug to fit a receptacle. If possible, install a new grounded receptacle.

Do not penetrate walls or ceilings without first shutting off electrical power to the circuits that may be hidden.

Wire, Cable + Conduit

Wire, cable, and conduit comprise the electrical infrastructure in your home. Selecting the appropriate size and type and handling it correctly is absolutely necessary to a successful wiring project that will pass inspection.

Copper or aluminum wires are the primary conductors of electricity in any home. The electricity itself travels on the outer surfaces of the wire, so insulation is added to the wires to protect against shock and fires. The insulated wires are frequently grouped together and enclosed in sheathing according to gauge and function. Multiple wires enclosed in sheathing form a cable. In some cases, the wires are enclosed in metal or plastic tubes known as conduit. Conduits and tubing (also known as raceways) are used primarily in situations where the cables or wires are exposed, such as in open garage walls.

This chapter introduces some of the many varieties of wire, cable, and conduit used in home construction and explains which types to use where. It also will demonstrate the essential skills used to run new cable, install conduit, strip sheathing, make wire connections, and more.

In this chapter:
- Wire + Cable
- NM Cable
- Conduit
- Surface-Mounted Wiring

Wire + Cable

Wires (known as conductors) are made of copper or aluminum in most houses. Copper is a better conductor of electricity and is used in most houses. Copper-coated aluminum wires may be found in a few houses built in the early 1970s, but this wire is uncommon. "Tin"-coated copper wires may be found in houses built in the 1940s and 1950s.

A group of two or more wires enclosed in a metal, rubber, cloth, or plastic sheathing is called a cable (see photo, opposite page). The sheathing protects the wires from damage and protects people from electrical shock. Conduit also protects wires, but it is not considered a cable.

Individual wires are covered with rubber or plastic insulation. An exception is a bare copper grounding wire, which does not need insulation. The insulation is color coded (see chart, below left) to identify the wire as a hot wire, a neutral wire, or a grounding wire. New cable sheathing is also color coded to indicate the size of the wires inside. White means #14 wire, yellow means #12 wire, and orange means #10 wire.

In most wiring systems installed after 1965, the wires and cables are insulated with PVC. This type of insulation is very durable and can last as long as the house itself.

Before about 1965, wires and cables were insulated with rubber or cloth. Rubber and cloth insulation has a life expectancy of about 25 to 30 years. Old insulation that is cracked or damaged can be reinforced **temporarily** by wrapping the wire with plastic electrical tape. However, old wiring with cracked or damaged insulation should be inspected by a qualified electrician to make sure it is safe. Homeowner insurance companies may refuse to provide coverage for houses with cloth-covered and knob-and-tube wiring.

Wires must be large enough for the amperage rating of the circuit. A wire that is too small can become dangerously hot. Wire sizes are categorized according to the American Wire Gauge (AWG) system. To check the size of a wire, use the wire stripper openings of a combination tool as a guide.

WIRE COLOR CHART

WIRE COLOR		FUNCTION
	White or gray	Neutral wire carrying current at zero voltage
	Black	Hot wire carrying current at full voltage
	Red	Hot wire carrying current at full voltage
	White, black markings	Hot wire carrying current at full voltage
	Green	Serves as a bonding pathway
	Bare copper	Serves as a bonding pathway

Individual wires are color-coded to identify their function. In some circuit installations, the white wire serves as a hot wire that carries voltage. If so, this white wire may be labeled with black tape or paint to identify it as a hot wire.

WIRE SIZE CHART

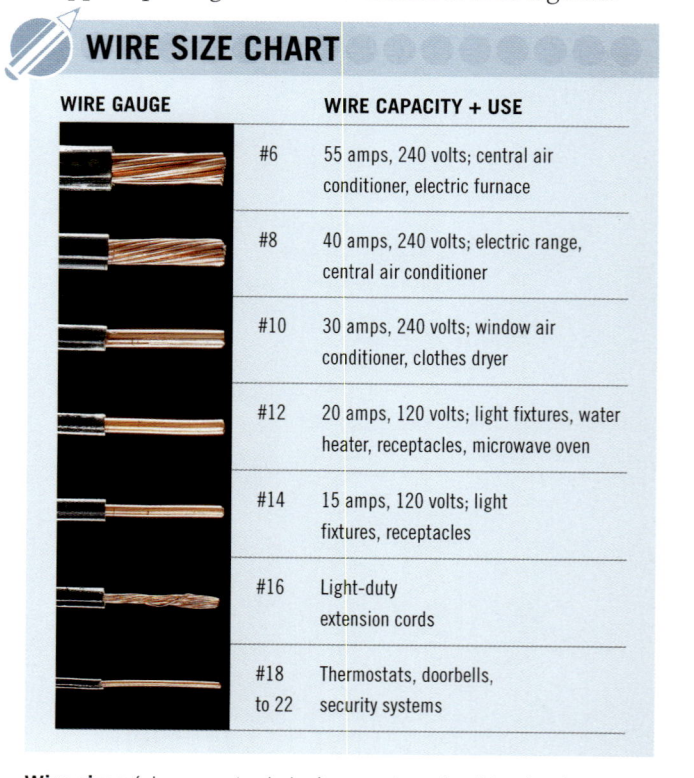

WIRE GAUGE		WIRE CAPACITY + USE
	#6	55 amps, 240 volts; central air conditioner, electric furnace
	#8	40 amps, 240 volts; electric range, central air conditioner
	#10	30 amps, 240 volts; window air conditioner, clothes dryer
	#12	20 amps, 120 volts; light fixtures, water heater, receptacles, microwave oven
	#14	15 amps, 120 volts; light fixtures, receptacles
	#16	Light-duty extension cords
	#18 to 22	Thermostats, doorbells, security systems

Wire sizes (shown actual size) are categorized by the American Wire Gauge system. The larger the wire size, the smaller the AWG number. The ampacities in this table are for copper wires in NM cable. The ampacity for the same wire in conduit is usually more. The ampacity for aluminum wire is less.

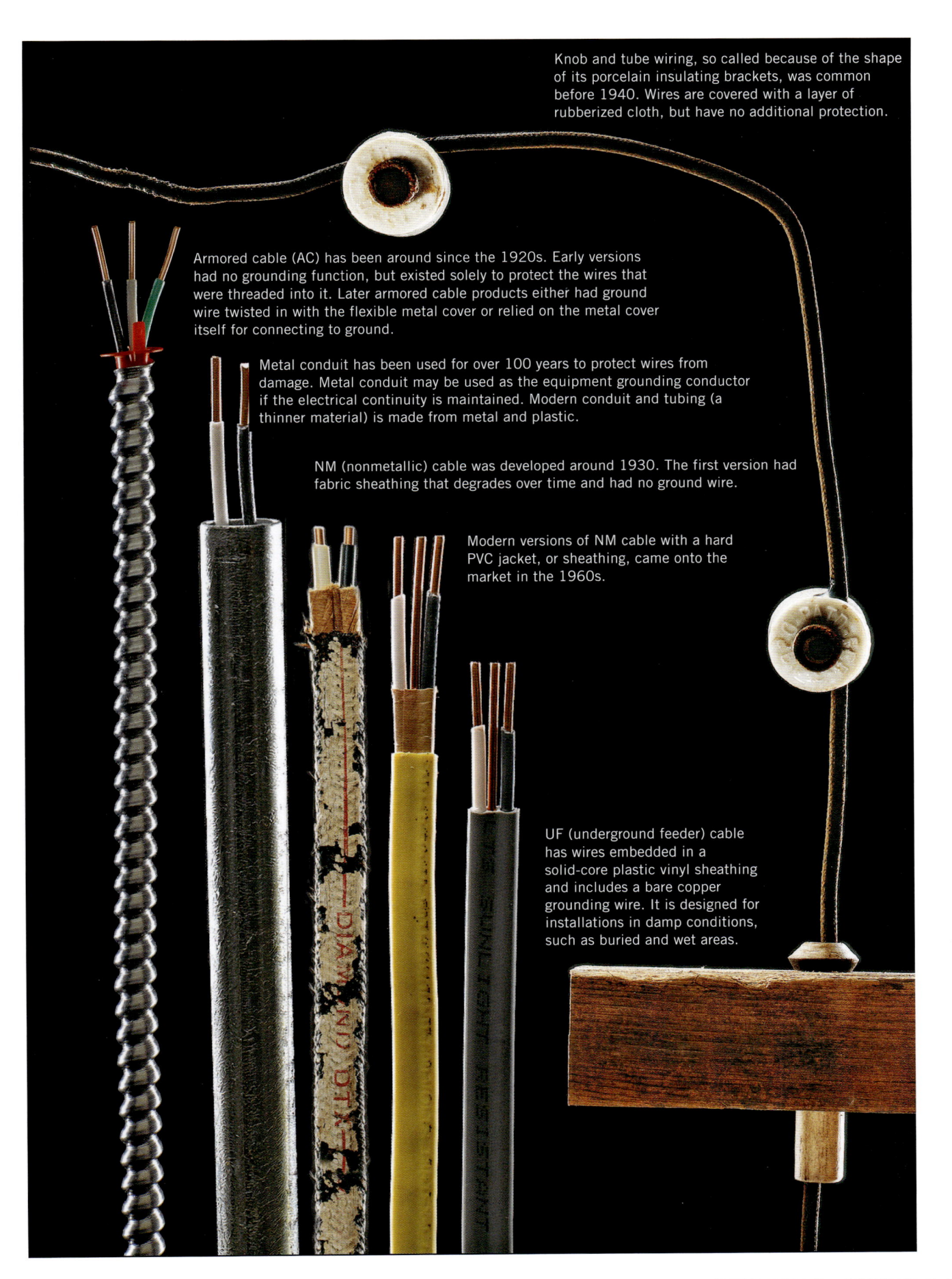

Knob and tube wiring, so called because of the shape of its porcelain insulating brackets, was common before 1940. Wires are covered with a layer of rubberized cloth, but have no additional protection.

Armored cable (AC) has been around since the 1920s. Early versions had no grounding function, but existed solely to protect the wires that were threaded into it. Later armored cable products either had ground wire twisted in with the flexible metal cover or relied on the metal cover itself for connecting to ground.

Metal conduit has been used for over 100 years to protect wires from damage. Metal conduit may be used as the equipment grounding conductor if the electrical continuity is maintained. Modern conduit and tubing (a thinner material) is made from metal and plastic.

NM (nonmetallic) cable was developed around 1930. The first version had fabric sheathing that degrades over time and had no ground wire.

Modern versions of NM cable with a hard PVC jacket, or sheathing, came onto the market in the 1960s.

UF (underground feeder) cable has wires embedded in a solid-core plastic vinyl sheathing and includes a bare copper grounding wire. It is designed for installations in damp conditions, such as buried and wet areas.

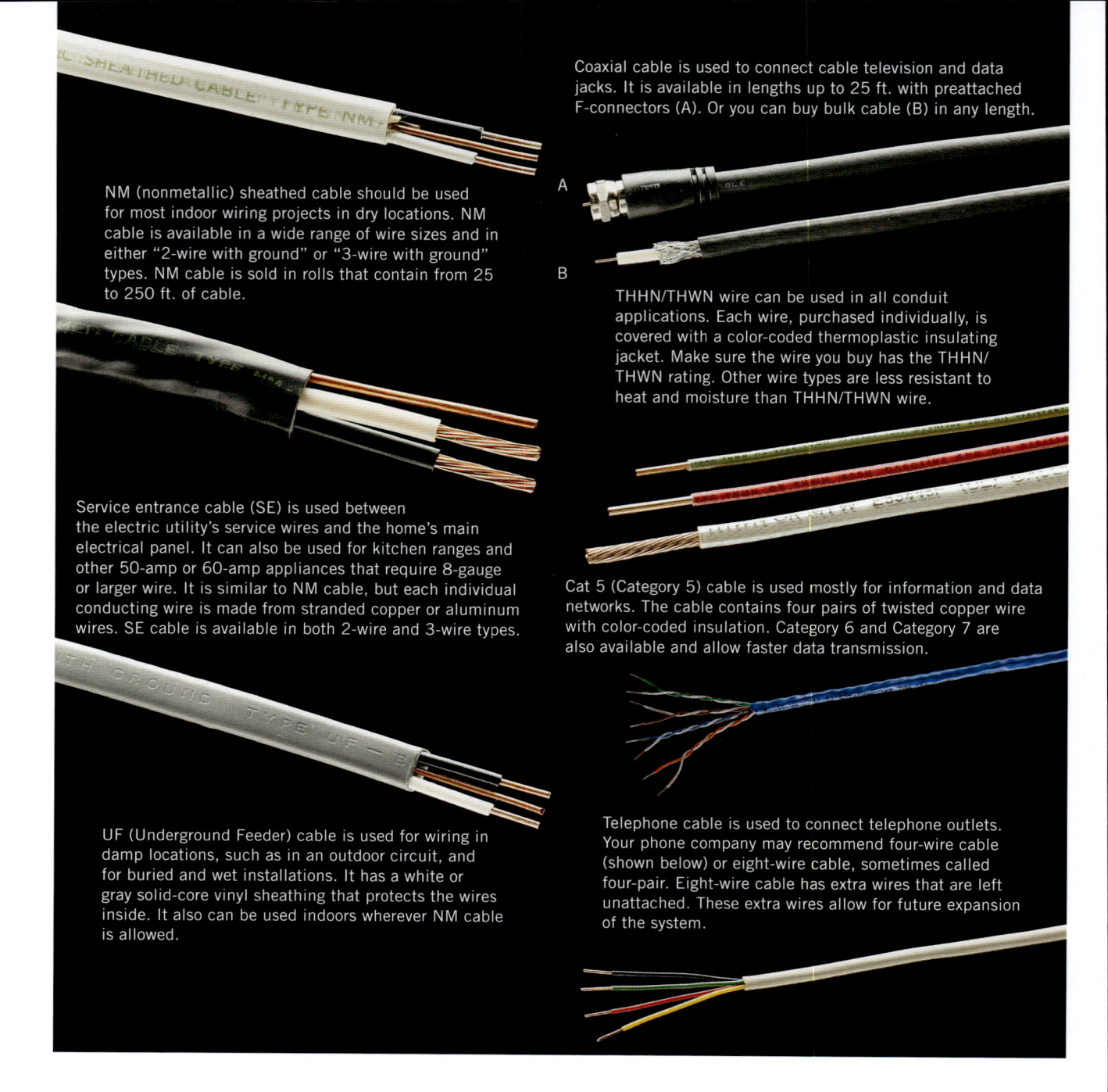

NM (nonmetallic) sheathed cable should be used for most indoor wiring projects in dry locations. NM cable is available in a wide range of wire sizes and in either "2-wire with ground" or "3-wire with ground" types. NM cable is sold in rolls that contain from 25 to 250 ft. of cable.

Service entrance cable (SE) is used between the electric utility's service wires and the home's main electrical panel. It can also be used for kitchen ranges and other 50-amp or 60-amp appliances that require 8-gauge or larger wire. It is similar to NM cable, but each individual conducting wire is made from stranded copper or aluminum wires. SE cable is available in both 2-wire and 3-wire types.

UF (Underground Feeder) cable is used for wiring in damp locations, such as in an outdoor circuit, and for buried and wet installations. It has a white or gray solid-core vinyl sheathing that protects the wires inside. It also can be used indoors wherever NM cable is allowed.

Coaxial cable is used to connect cable television and data jacks. It is available in lengths up to 25 ft. with preattached F-connectors (A). Or you can buy bulk cable (B) in any length.

THHN/THWN wire can be used in all conduit applications. Each wire, purchased individually, is covered with a color-coded thermoplastic insulating jacket. Make sure the wire you buy has the THHN/THWN rating. Other wire types are less resistant to heat and moisture than THHN/THWN wire.

Cat 5 (Category 5) cable is used mostly for information and data networks. The cable contains four pairs of twisted copper wire with color-coded insulation. Category 6 and Category 7 are also available and allow faster data transmission.

Telephone cable is used to connect telephone outlets. Your phone company may recommend four-wire cable (shown below) or eight-wire cable, sometimes called four-pair. Eight-wire cable has extra wires that are left unattached. These extra wires allow for future expansion of the system.

NM Sheathing Colors

The PVC sheathing for NM cable is coded by color so wiring inspectors can tell what the capacity of the cable is at a glance.

- Black = 6 or 8 AWG conductors
- Orange = 10 AWG conductors
- Yellow = 12 AWG conductors
- White = 14 AWG conductors
- Gray = UF cable (see photo above)

Reading NM (Nonmetallic) Cable

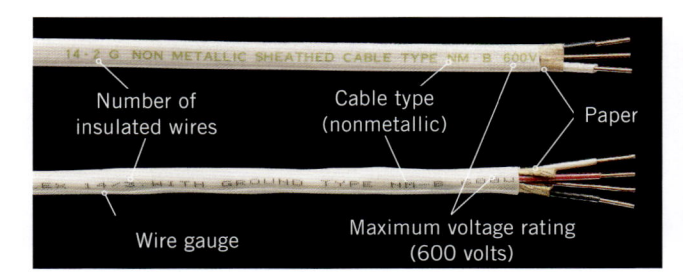

NM cable is labeled with the number of insulated wires it contains. The bare grounding wire is not counted. For example, a cable marked 14/2 G (or 14/2 WITH GROUND) contains two insulated 14-gauge wires, plus a bare copper grounding wire. Cable marked 14/3 WITH GROUND has three 14-gauge wires plus a grounding wire. NM cable also is stamped with a maximum voltage rating, as determined by Underwriters Laboratories (UL).

Reading Unsheathed, Individual Wire

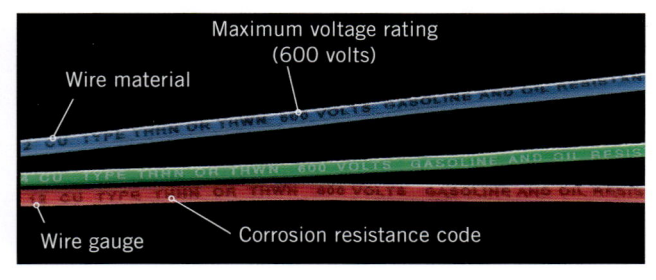

Unsheathed, individual wires are used for conduit and raceway installations. Wire insulation is coded with letters to indicate resistance to moisture, heat, and gas or oil. Code requires certain letter combinations for certain applications. T indicates thermoplastic insulation. H stands for heat resistance, and two Hs indicate high resistance (up to 194°F). W denotes wire suitable for wet locations. Wire coded with an N is impervious to damage from oil or gas.

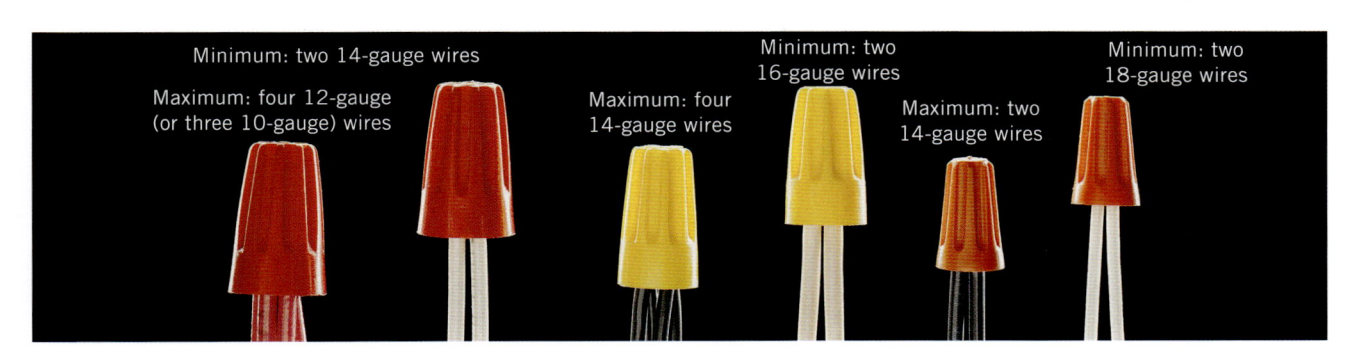

Use wire connectors (nuts) rated for the wires you are connecting. Wire connectors are color-coded by size, but the coding scheme varies according to manufacturer. The wire connectors shown above come from one major manufacturer. To ensure safe connections, each connector is rated for both minimum and maximum wire capacity. These connectors can be used to connect both conducting wires and grounding wires. Green wire connectors are used only for grounding wires.

TIPS FOR WORKING WITH WIRE

WIRE GAUGE		AMPACITY	MAXIMUM WATTAGE LOAD
	14-gauge	15 amps	1,440 watts (120 volts)
	12-gauge	20 amps	1,920 watts (120 volts) 3,840 watts (240 volts)
	10-gauge	30 amps	2,880 watts (120 volts) 5,760 watts (240 volts)
	8-gauge	40 amps	7,680 watts (240 volts)
	6-gauge	55 amps	10,560 watts (240 volts)

Wire ampacity is a measurement of how much current a wire can carry safely. Ampacity varies by the size of the wires. When installing a new circuit, choose wire with an ampacity rating matching the circuit size. For dedicated appliance circuits, check the wattage rating of the appliance and make sure it does not exceed the maximum wattage load of the circuit. The ampacities in this table are for copper wires in NM cable. The ampacity for the same wire in conduit is usually more. The ampacity for aluminum wire is less.

How to Strip NM Sheathing + Insulation

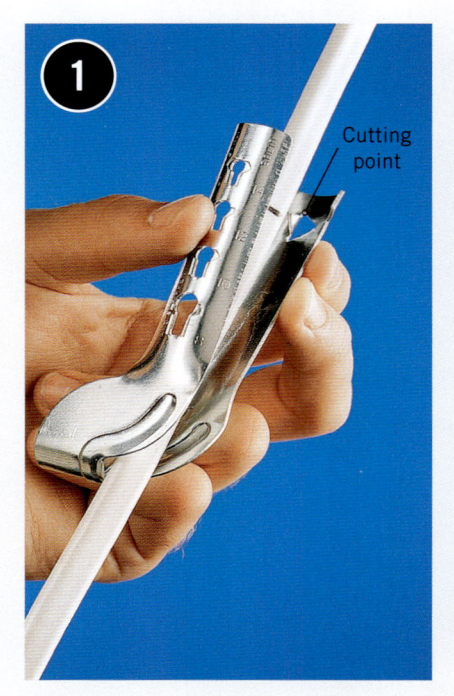

Cutting point

Measure and mark the cable 8" to 10" from the end. Slide the cable ripper onto the cable, and squeeze tool firmly to force the cutting point through the plastic sheathing.

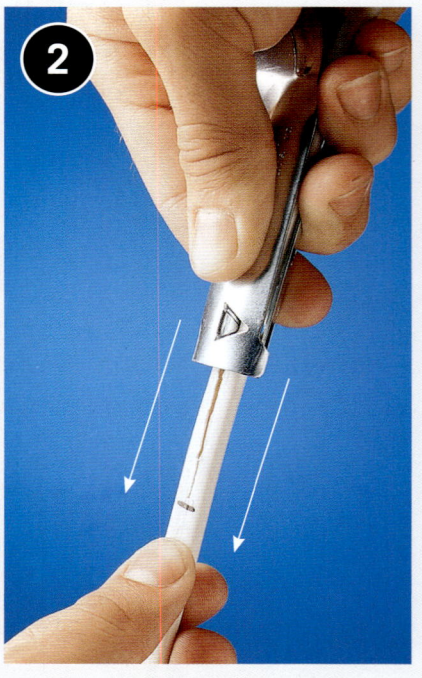

Grip the cable tightly with one hand, and pull the cable ripper toward the end of the cable to cut open the plastic sheathing.

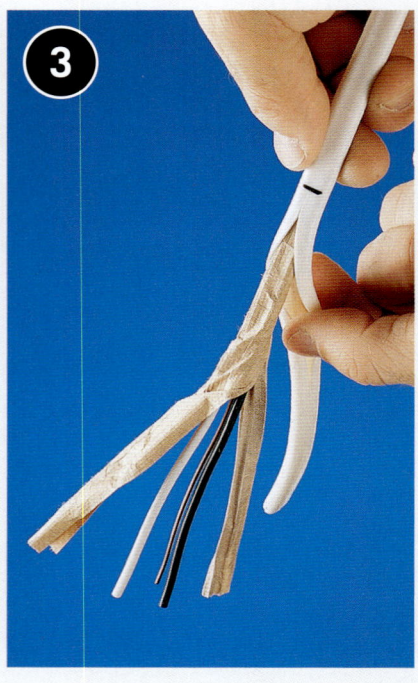

Peel back the plastic sheathing and the paper wrapping from the individual wires.

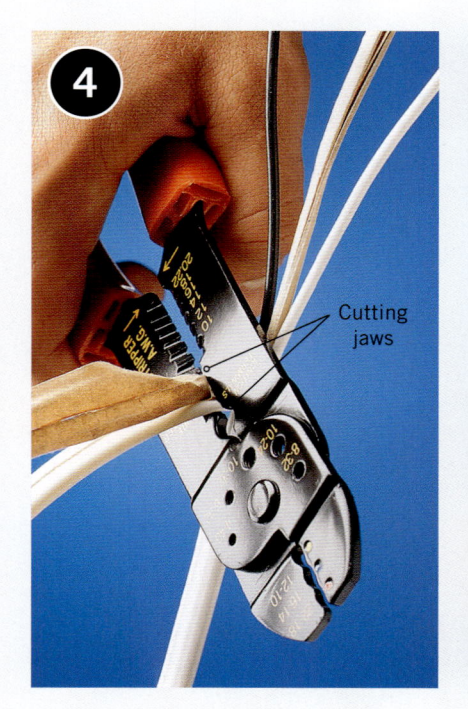

Cutting jaws

Cut away the excess plastic sheathing and paper wrapping using the cutting jaws of a combination tool.

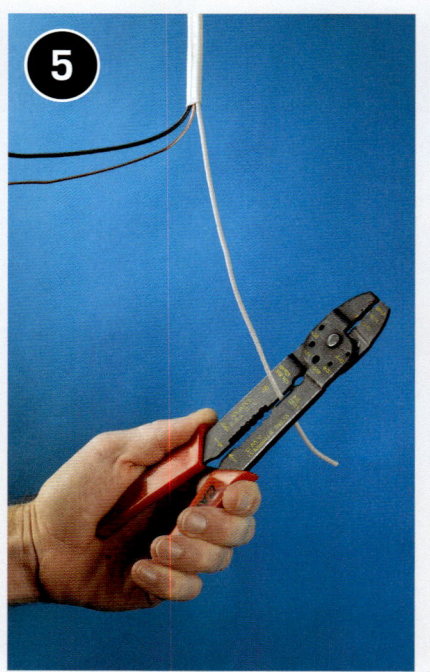

Cut individual wires as needed using the cutting jaws of the combination tool. Leave a minimum of 3" of wire running past the edge of the box.

Wire stripper openings

Strip insulation for each wire using the stripper openings. Choose the opening that matches the gauge of the wire, and take care not to nick or scratch the ends of the wires.

How to Connect Wires to Screw Terminals

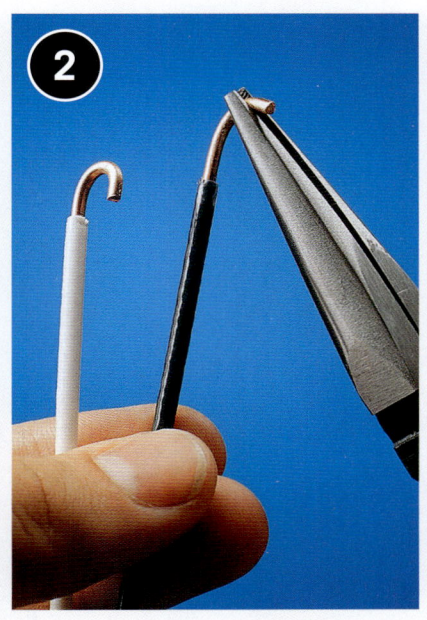

Strip about ¾" of insulation from each wire using a combination tool. Choose the stripper opening that matches the gauge of the wire, and then clamp the wire in the tool. Pull the wire firmly to remove plastic insulation.

Form a C-shaped loop in the end of each wire using a needlenose pliers or the hole of the correct gauge in a pair of wire strippers. The wire should have no scratches or nicks.

Hook each wire around the screw terminal so it forms a clockwise loop. Tighten the screw firmly. Insulation should just touch the head of the screw. Never place the ends of two wires under a single screw terminal. Instead use a pigtail wire (see page 33).

 ## CABLE STAPLES

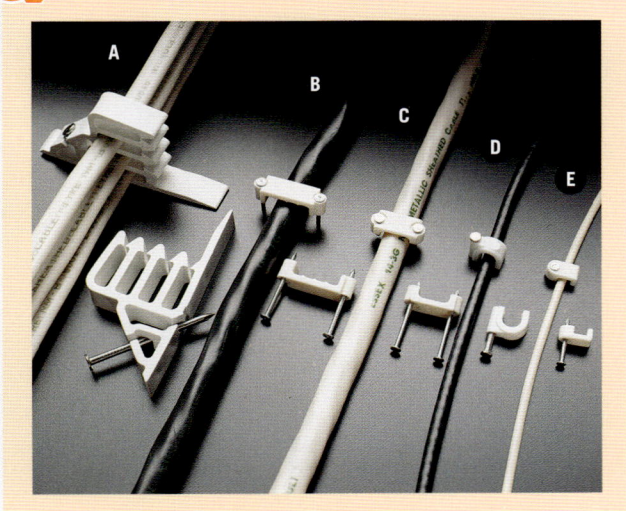

Use plastic cable staples to fasten cables. Choose staples sized to match the cables. Stack-It® staples (A) hold up to four 2-wire cables; ¾" staples (B) for 12/2, 12/3, and all 10-gauge cables; ½" staples (C) for 14/2, 14/3, or 12/2 cables; coaxial staples (D) for anchoring television and data cables; bell wire staples (E) for attaching telephone cables.

 ## PUSH-IN CONNECTORS

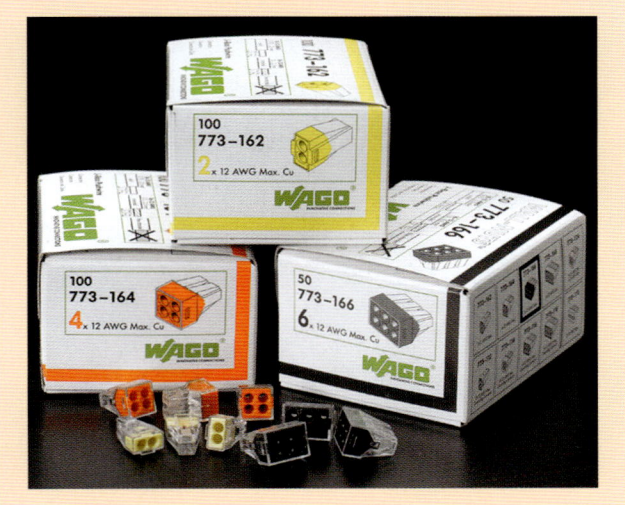

Push-in connectors are a relatively new product for joining wires. Instead of twisting the bare wire ends together, you strip off about ¾" of insulation and insert each into a hole in the connector. The connectors come with two to six holes sized for various gauge wires. These connectors are perfect for inexperienced DIYers, because they do not pull apart like a sloppy twisted connection can.

How to Join Wires with a Wire Connector

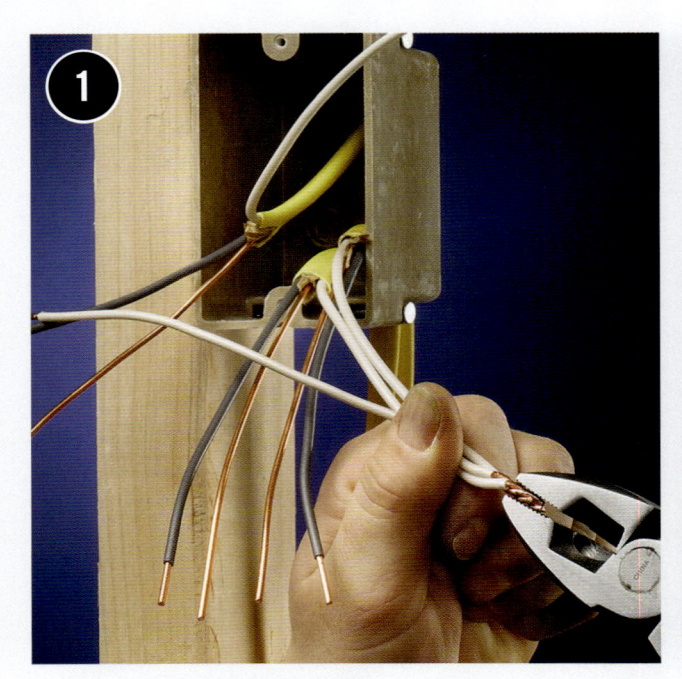

Ensure power is off and test for power. Grasp the wires to be joined in the jaws of a pair of linesman's pliers. The ends of the wires should be flush and they should be parallel and touching. Rotate the pliers clockwise two or three turns to twist the wire ends together.

Twist a wire connector over the ends of the wires. Make sure the connector is the right size (see page 29). Hand-twist the connector as far onto the wires as you can. There should be no bare wire exposed beneath the collar of the connector.

OPTION: Reinforce the joint by wrapping it with electrician's tape. By code, you cannot bind the wire joint with tape only, but it can be used as insurance. Few professional electricians use tape for purposes other than tagging wires for identification.

OPTION: Strip ¾" of insulation off the ends of the wires to be joined, and insert each wire into a push-in connector. Gently tug on each wire to make sure it is secure. Always read and follow the connector manufacturer's instructions.

How to Pigtail Wires

Cut a 6" length from a piece of insulated wire the same gauge and color as the wires it will be joining. Strip ¾" of insulation from each end of the insulated wire.

NOTE: Pigtailing is done mainly to avoid connecting multiple wires to one terminal, which is a code violation.

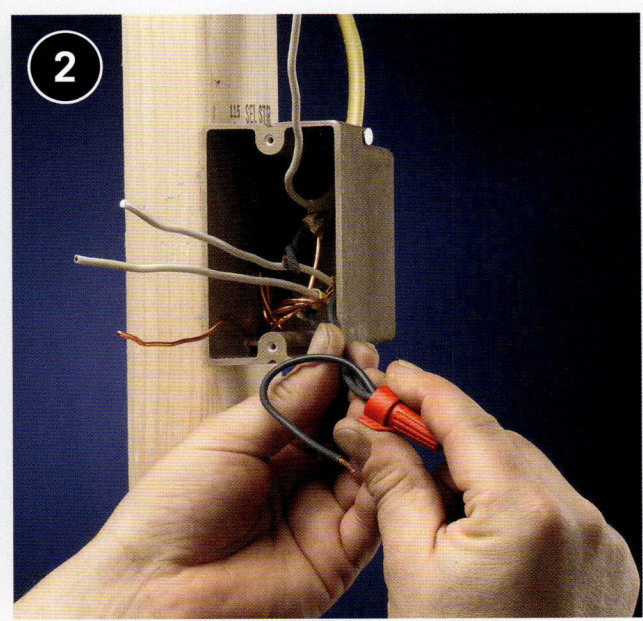

Join one end of the pigtail to the wires that will share the connection using a wire nut.

ALTERNATIVE: If you are pigtailing to a grounding screw or grounding clip in a metal box, you may find it easier to attach one end of the wire to the grounding screw before you attach the other end to the other wires.

Connect the pigtail to the appropriate terminal on the receptacle or switch. Fold the wires neatly and press the fitting into the box.

NM Cable

Non metallic (NM) cable is used for most indoor wiring projects except those requiring conduit and those in damp areas such as against concrete or masonry walls. Cut and install the cable after all electrical boxes have been mounted. Refer to your wiring plan to make sure each length of cable is correct for the circuit size and configuration.

Cable runs are difficult to measure exactly, so leave plenty of extra cable when cutting each length. Cable splices inside walls are not allowed by code. When inserting cables into an electrical panel, make sure the power is shut off.

After all cables are installed and all the ground wires spliced, call your electrical inspector to arrange for the rough-in inspection. Do not install wallboard or attach light fixtures and other devices until this inspection is done. Check with your building inspector before using NM cable. Some areas, such as the Chicago area, may not allow NM cable.

Pulling cables through studs is easier if you drill smooth, straight holes at the same height. Prevent kinks by straightening the cable before pulling it through the studs. Use plastic grommets to protect cables on steel studs (inset).

FRAMING MEMBER	MAXIMUM HOLE SIZE	MAXIMUM NOTCH SIZE
2 × 4 loadbearing stud	1$\frac{7}{16}$" diameter	$\frac{7}{8}$" deep
2 × 4 non-loadbearing stud	2$\frac{1}{8}$" diameter	1$\frac{7}{16}$" deep
2 × 6 loadbearing stud	2$\frac{3}{16}$" diameter	1$\frac{3}{8}$" deep
2 × 6 non-loadbearing stud	3$\frac{5}{16}$" diameter	2$\frac{3}{16}$" deep
2 × 6 joists	1$\frac{13}{16}$" diameter	$\frac{15}{16}$" deep
2 × 8 joists	2$\frac{1}{2}$" diameter	1$\frac{1}{4}$" deep
2 × 10 joists	3$\frac{1}{16}$" diameter	1$\frac{9}{16}$" deep
2 × 12 joists	3$\frac{3}{4}$" diameter	1$\frac{7}{8}$" deep

This framing member chart shows the maximum sizes for holes and notches that can be cut into studs and joists when running cables. When boring holes, there must be at least $\frac{5}{8}$" of wood between the edge of a stud and the hole and at least 2" between the edge of a joist and the hole. Joists can be notched only in the end third of the overall span; never in the middle third of the joist. If 1$\frac{1}{4}$" clearance cannot possibly be maintained, you may be able to satisfy code by installing a metal nail plate over the point of penetration in the stud or joist. Different rules apply to wood I-joists, metal-plate-connected trusses, engineered beams, and beams assembled from lumber. In general, you may not drill and notch trusses and assembled beams. Manufacturers of I-joists and engineered beams have limits about the size and location of holes.

TOOLS + MATERIALS

Drill and bits	Needlenose pliers	Cable staples	Wire connectors
Tape measure	Hammer	Masking tape	Eye protection
Cable ripper	Fish tape	Electrical tape	
Combination tool	NM cable	Grounding pigtails	
Screwdrivers	Cable clamps		

How to Install NM Cable

Drill ⅝" holes in framing members for the cable runs. This is done easily with a right-angle drill, available at rental centers. The edge of the hole must be set back at least 1¼" from the front face of the framing member, or the cable must be protected with a metal plate (page 116).

Where cables will turn corners (step 6, page 36), drill intersecting holes in adjoining faces of studs. Measure and cut all cables, allowing 2 ft. extra at ends entering the breaker panel and 1 foot for ends entering the electrical box.

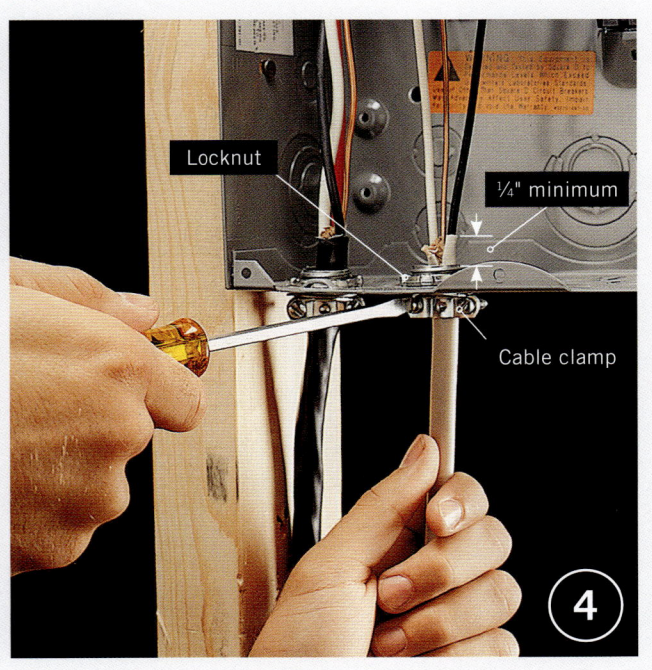

Locknut

¼" minimum

Cable clamp

Shut off power to the circuit breaker panel. Use a cable ripper to strip the cable, leaving at least ¼" of sheathing to enter the circuit breaker panel. Clip away the excess sheathing.

Open a knockout in the circuit breaker panel using a hammer and screwdriver. Insert a cable clamp into the knockout, and secure it with a locknut. Insert the cable through the clamp so that at least ¼" of sheathing extends inside the circuit breaker panel. Tighten the mounting screws on the clamp so the cable is gripped securely but not so tightly that the sheathing is crushed. *(continued)*

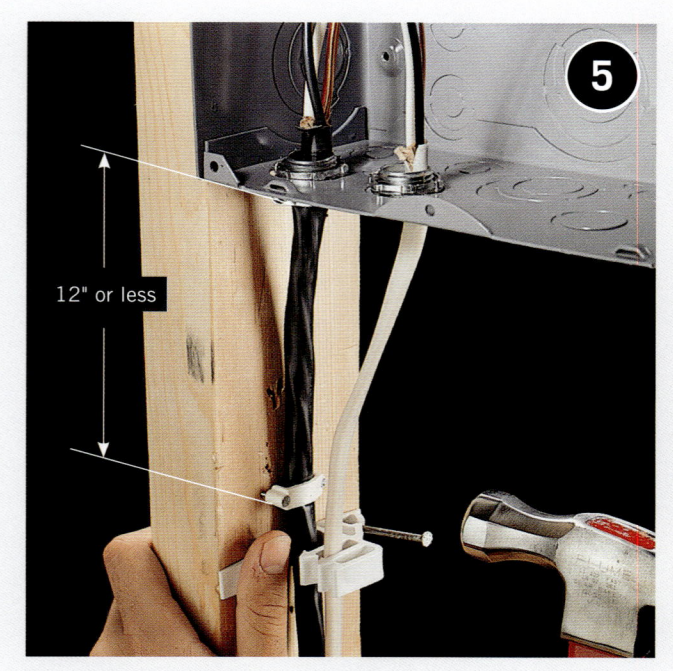

5

12" or less

Anchor the cable to the center of a framing member within 12" of the circuit breaker panel using a cable staple. Stack-It® staples work well where two or more cables must be anchored to the same side of a stud. Run the cable to the first electrical box. Where the cable runs along the sides of framing members, anchor it with cable staples no more than 4 ft. 6" apart.

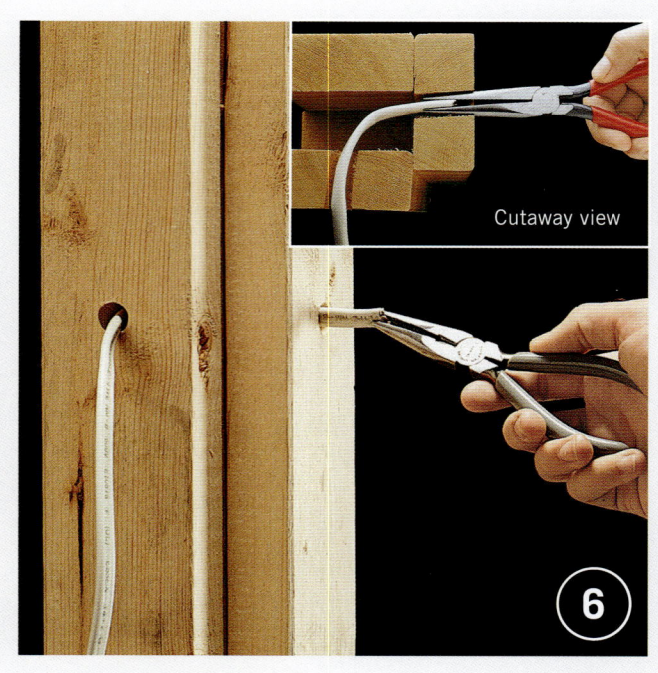

6

Cutaway view

At corners, form a slight L-shaped bend in the end of the cable and insert it into one hole. Retrieve the cable through the other hole using needlenose pliers (inset).

7

8"

¼"

Staple the cable to a framing member within 8" from where the sheathing ends in the box. Hold the cable taut against the front of the box, and mark a point on the sheathing ¼" past the box edge. Remove sheathing from the marked line to the end using a cable ripper, and clip away excess sheathing with a combination tool. Insert the cable through the knockout in the box.

¼"

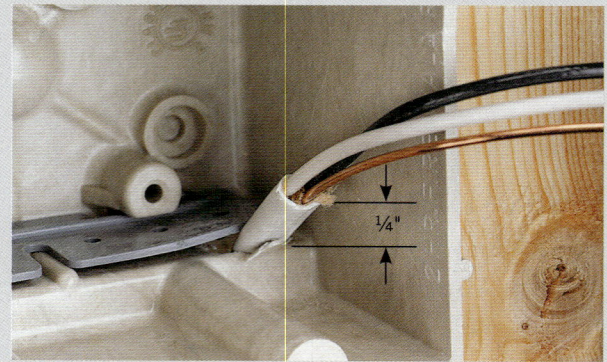

¼"

VARIATION: Different types of boxes have different clamping devices. Make sure cable sheathing extends ¼" past the edge of the clamp to ensure that the cable is secure and that the wire won't be damaged by the edges of the clamp. Clamp cable inside all boxes except single gang (2¼ × 4") boxes.

(8)

(9)

As each cable is installed in a box, clip back each wire so that at least 3" of workable wire extends past the front edge of the box.

Strip ¾" of insulation from each circuit wire in the box using a combination tool. Take care not to nick the copper.

(10)

(11)

Continue the circuit by running cable between each pair of electrical boxes, leaving an extra 1 ft. of cable at each end.

At metal boxes and recessed fixtures, open knockouts, and attach cables with cable clamps. From inside the fixture, strip away all but ¼" of sheathing. Clip back wires so there is 8" of workable length, and then strip ¾" of insulation from each wire. *(continued)*

12

For a surface-mounted fixture such as a baseboard heater or fluorescent light fixture, staple the cable to a stud near the fixture location, leaving plenty of excess cable. Mark the floor so the cable will be easy to find after the walls are finished.

Pigtail

13

At each recessed fixture and metal electrical box, connect one end of a grounding pigtail to the box using a grounding clip attached to the frame (shown above) or a green grounding screw. A grounding pigtail is not needed for plastic boxes.

Clamps

14

At each electrical box and recessed fixture, join grounding wires together with a wire connector. If the box has internal clamps, tighten the clamps over the cables.

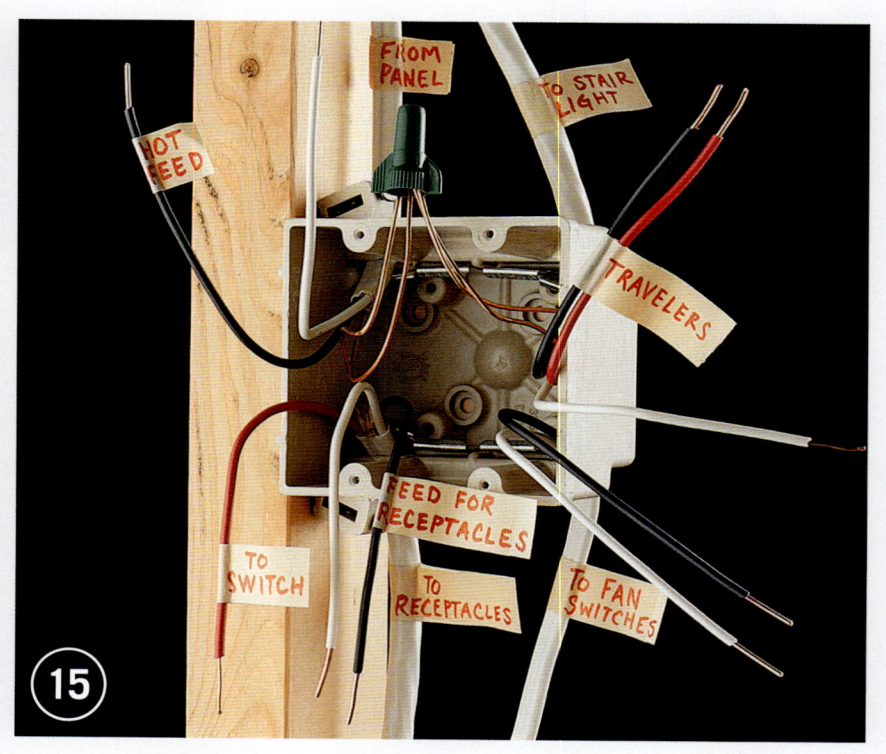

FROM PANEL

TO STAIR LIGHT

HOT FEED

TRAVELERS

FEED FOR RECEPTACLES

TO SWITCH

TO RECEPTACLES

TO FAN SWITCHES

15

Label the cables entering each box to indicate their destinations. In boxes with complex wiring configurations, also tag the individual wires to make final hookups easier. After all cables are installed, your rough-in work is ready to be reviewed by the electrical inspector.

How to Run NM Cable Inside a Finished Wall

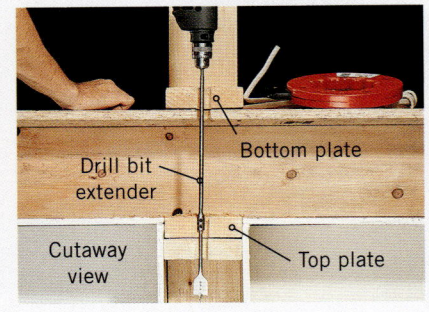

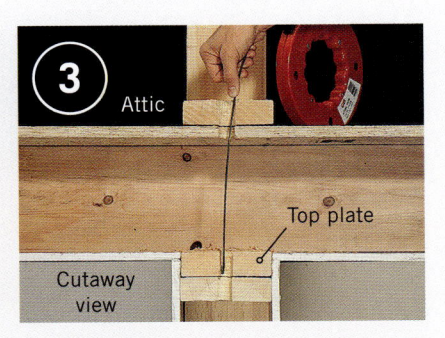
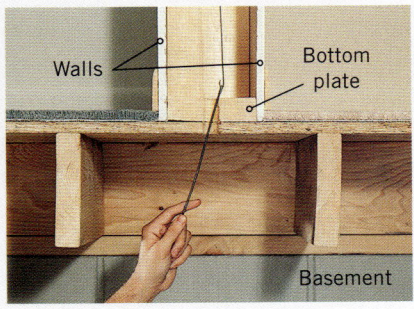

From the unfinished space below the finished wall, look for a reference point, such as a soil stack, plumbing pipes, or electrical cables, that indicates the location of the wall above. Choose a location for the new cable that does not interfere with existing utilities. Drill a 1" hole up into the stud cavity.

From the unfinished space above the finished wall, find the top of the stud cavity by measuring from the same fixed reference point used in step 1. Drill a 1" hole down through the top plate and into the stud cavity using a drill bit extender.

Extend a fish tape down through the top plate, twisting the tape until it reaches the bottom of the stud cavity. From the unfinished space below the wall, use a piece of stiff wire with a hook on one end to retrieve the fish tape through the drilled hole in the bottom plate.

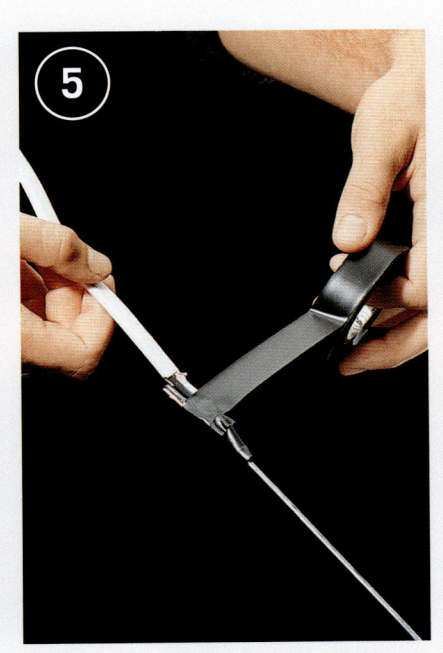

Trim back 2" of sheathing from the end of the NM cable, and then insert the wires through the loop at the tip of the fish tape.

Bend the wires against the cable, and then use electrical tape to bind them tightly. Apply cable-pulling lubricant to the taped end of the fish tape.

From above the finished wall, pull steadily on the fish tape to draw the cable up through the stud cavity. This job will be easier if you have a helper feed the cable from below as you pull.

Tips for Running Cable Inside Finished Walls

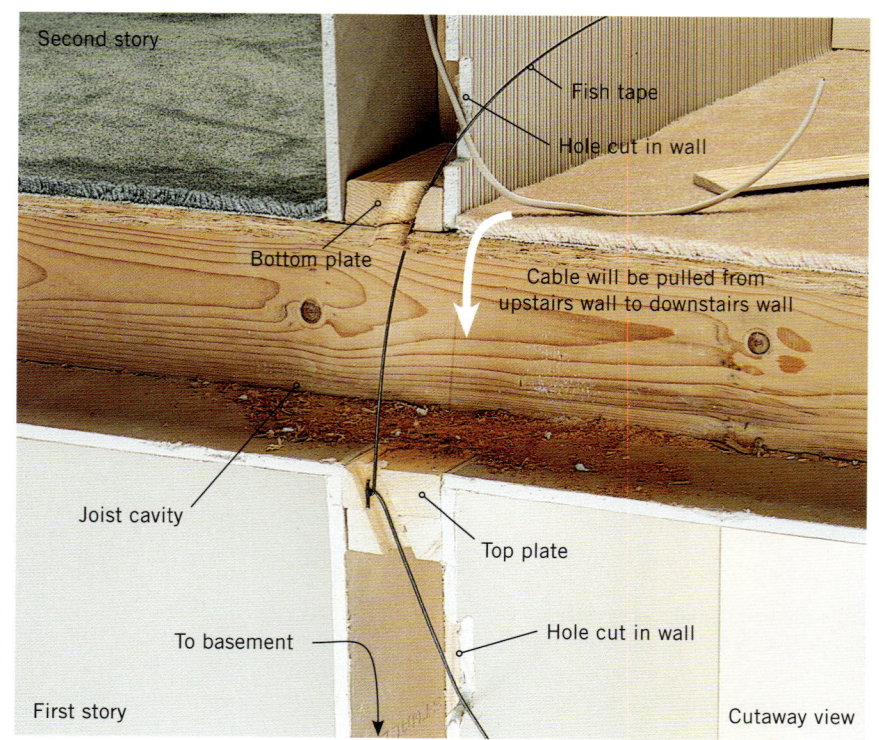
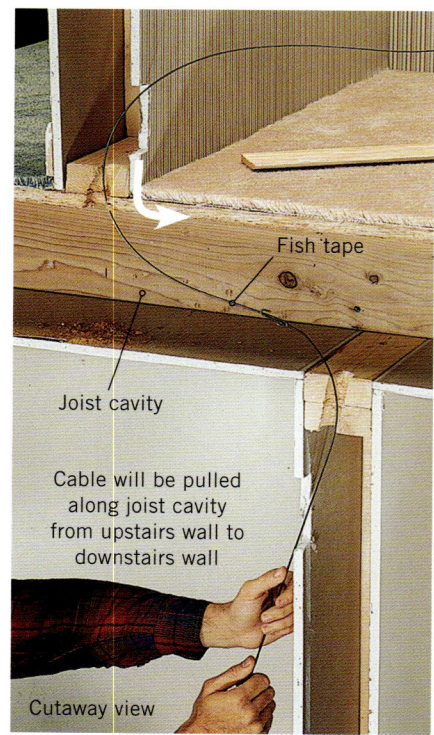

If there is no access space above and below a wall, cut openings in the finished walls to run a cable. This often occurs in two-story homes when a cable is extended from an upstairs wall to a downstairs wall. Cut small openings in the wall near the top and bottom plates, then drill an angled 1" hole through each plate. Extend a fish tape into the joist cavity between the walls and use it to pull the cable from one wall to the next. If the walls line up one over the other (left), you can retrieve the fish tape using a piece of stiff wire. If walls do not line up (right), use a second fish tape. After running the cable, repair the holes in the walls with patching plaster or drywall scraps and taping compound.

If you don't have a fish tape, use a length of sturdy string and a lead weight or heavy washer. Drop the line into the stud cavity from above, and then use a piece of stiff wire to hook the line from below.

Use a flexible drill bit, also called a bell-hanger's bit, to bore holes through framing in finished walls.

How to Install NM Cable in Finished Ceilings

If you don't have access to a ceiling from above, you can run cable for a new ceiling fixture from an existing receptacle in the room up the wall and into the ceiling without disturbing much of the ceiling. Be sure not to tap into a restricted circuit such as the kitchen countertop and bathroom receptacles. To begin, run cable from the receptacle to the stud cavity that aligns with the ceiling joists on which you want to install a fixture. Be sure to plan a location for the new switch. Remove short strips of drywall from the wall and ceiling. Make a notch in the top plates. Use a fish tape to pull the new cable up through the wall cavity and the notch in top plates. Next use the fish tape to pull the cable through the ceiling to the fixture hole. When you are finished pulling the cable, protect the notch with metal nail guards. After having your work inspected, replace the drywall and install the fixture and switch.

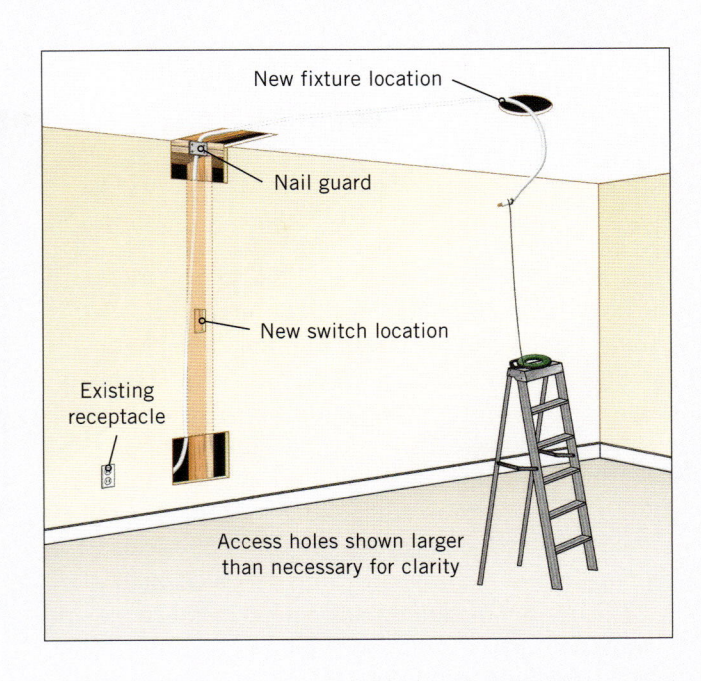

New fixture location

Nail guard

New switch location

Existing receptacle

Access holes shown larger than necessary for clarity

Plan a route for running cable between electrical boxes (see illustration above). Remove drywall on the wall and ceiling surface. Where cable must cross framing members, cut a small access opening in the wall and ceiling surface; then cut a notch into the framing with a wood chisel.

Fish a cable from the existing receptacle location up to the notch at the top of the wall. Protect the notch with a metal nail stop.

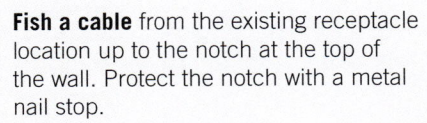

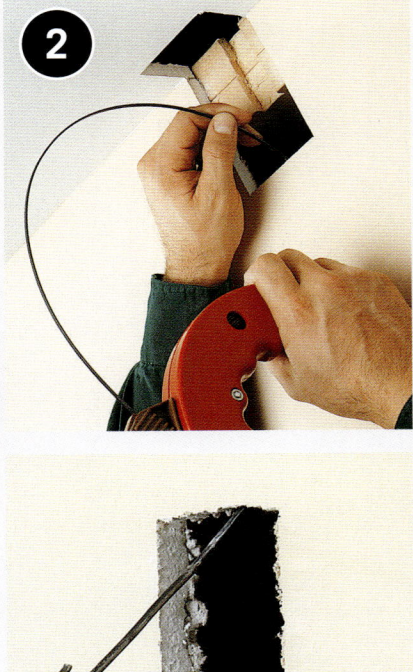

Fish the cable through the ceiling to the location of the new ceiling fixture. Install nail guards over the notches.

Electrical Bonding of Metal Conduit

Conduit

All individual wires (such as THHN/THWN) must be installed in conduit or in thinner material called tubing. Cables and wires that are subject to physical damage must be installed in conduit or some types of tubing to protect them. Whether a location is subject to physical damage depends on the judgment of the electrical inspector. Cables that are exposed and are within the reach of an adult and most cables installed outside are often considered subject to physical damage. Other exposed locations may also qualify.

The interior of conduit and tubing installed outside is considered a wet area. Don't install NM cable inside conduit being run outdoors. Use UF cable instead or pull individual wires rated for wet area use. Conduit and tubing installed outdoors must be rated for exterior use.

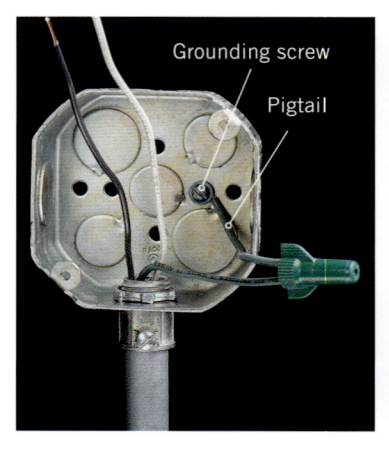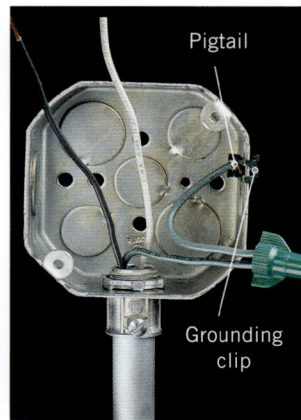

Grounding screw

Pigtail

Pigtail

Grounding clip

Install a green insulated grounding wire for any circuit that runs through metal conduit. Although code allows the metal conduit to serve as the grounding conductor, most electricians install a green insulated wire as a more dependable means of grounding the system. The grounding wires must be connected to metal boxes with a pigtail and grounding screw (left) or grounding clip (right).

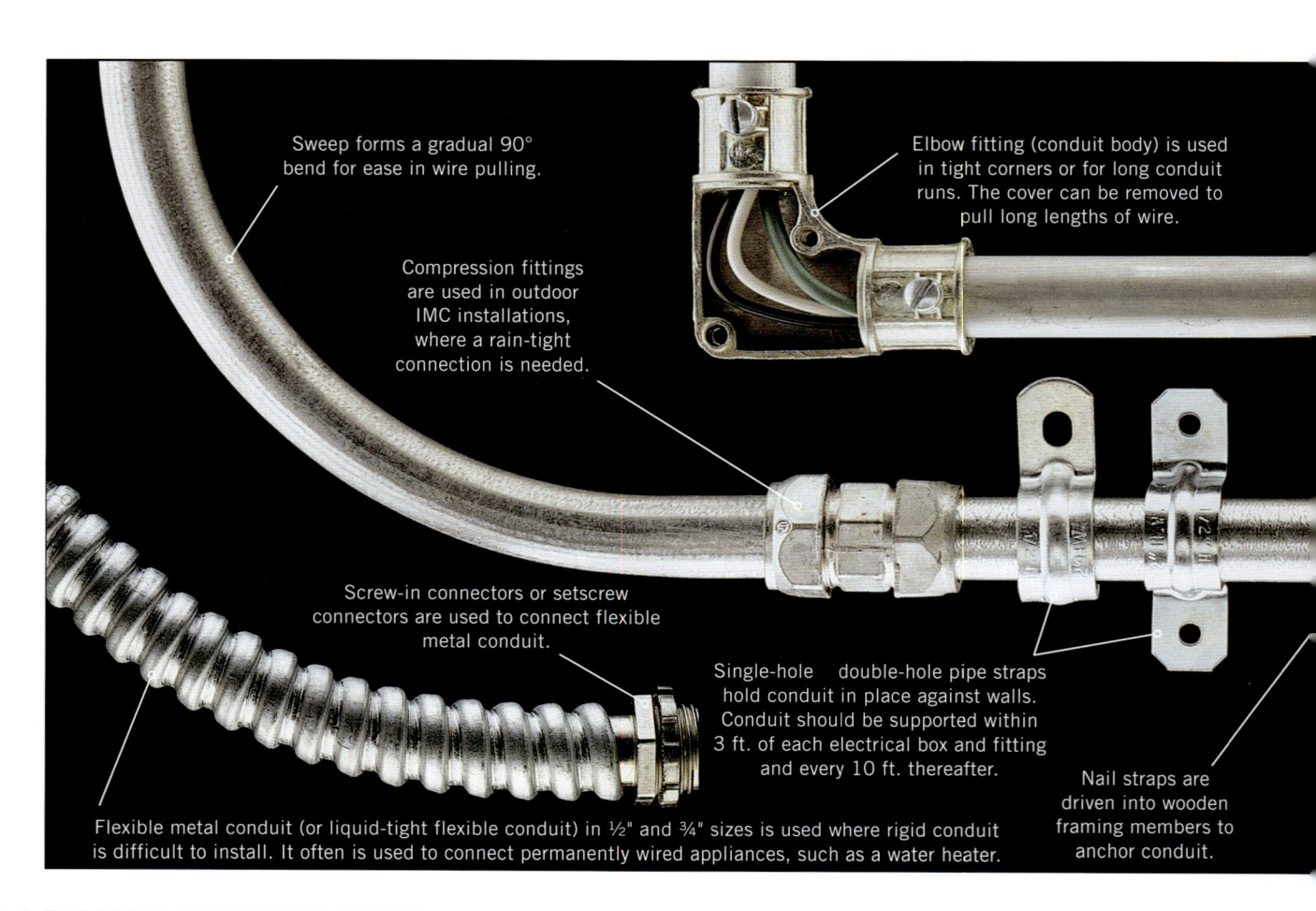

Sweep forms a gradual 90° bend for ease in wire pulling.

Elbow fitting (conduit body) is used in tight corners or for long conduit runs. The cover can be removed to pull long lengths of wire.

Compression fittings are used in outdoor IMC installations, where a rain-tight connection is needed.

Screw-in connectors or setscrew connectors are used to connect flexible metal conduit.

Single-hole   double-hole pipe straps hold conduit in place against walls. Conduit should be supported within 3 ft. of each electrical box and fitting and every 10 ft. thereafter.

Nail straps are driven into wooden framing members to anchor conduit.

Flexible metal conduit (or liquid-tight flexible conduit) in ½" and ¾" sizes is used where rigid conduit is difficult to install. It often is used to connect permanently wired appliances, such as a water heater.

Metal Conduit

EMT

IMC

Rigid metal conduit

EMT (electrical metallic conduit) is lightweight and easy to install. IMC (intermediate metallic conduit) has thicker galvanized walls and is a good choice for exposed outdoor use. Rigid metal conduit provides the greatest protection for wires, but it is more expensive and requires threaded fittings. EMT is the preferred metal material for home use.

Fill Capacity

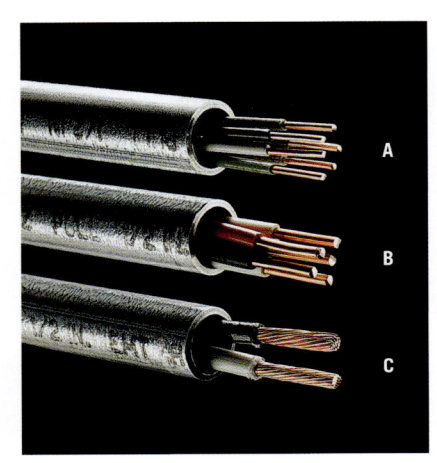

A

B

C

EMT ½" in diameter can hold up to twelve 14-gauge or nine 12-gauge THHN/THWN wires (A), five 10-gauge wires (B), or three 8-gauge wires (C). Use ¾" conduit for greater fill capacity.

Plastic Conduit

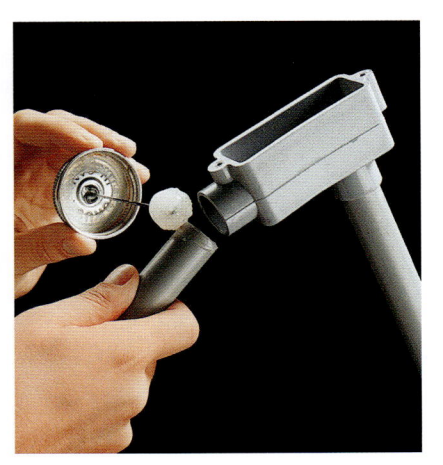

PVC conduit (schedule 80) is allowed by many local codes. It is assembled with solvent glue and PVC fittings that resemble those for metal conduit. When wiring with PVC conduit and tubing, always run a green grounding wire. Use material approved for use in electrical applications. Do not use PVC plumbing pipes.

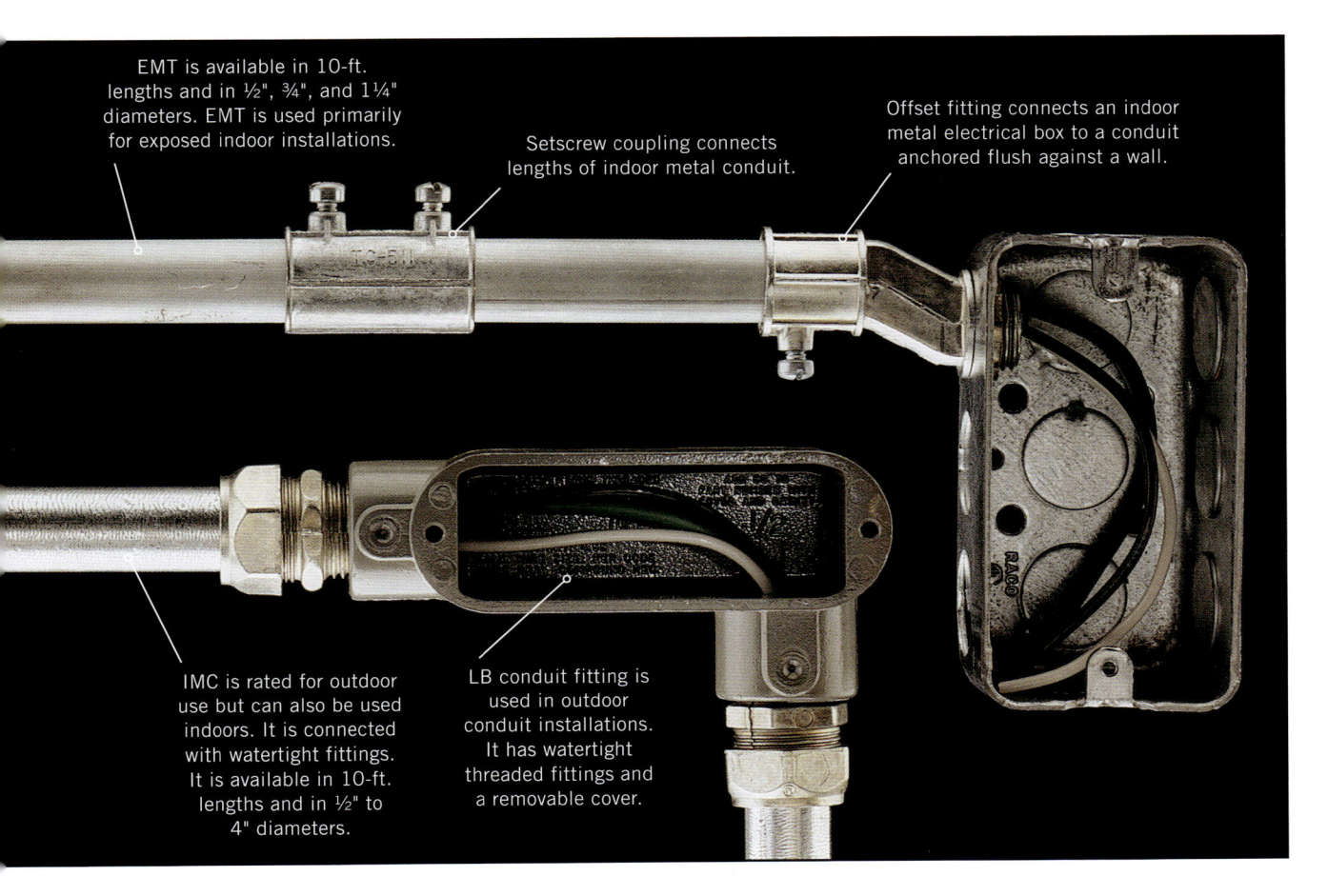

EMT is available in 10-ft. lengths and in ½", ¾", and 1¼" diameters. EMT is used primarily for exposed indoor installations.

Setscrew coupling connects lengths of indoor metal conduit.

Offset fitting connects an indoor metal electrical box to a conduit anchored flush against a wall.

IMC is rated for outdoor use but can also be used indoors. It is connected with watertight fittings. It is available in 10-ft. lengths and in ½" to 4" diameters.

LB conduit fitting is used in outdoor conduit installations. It has watertight threaded fittings and a removable cover.

Working with Conduit

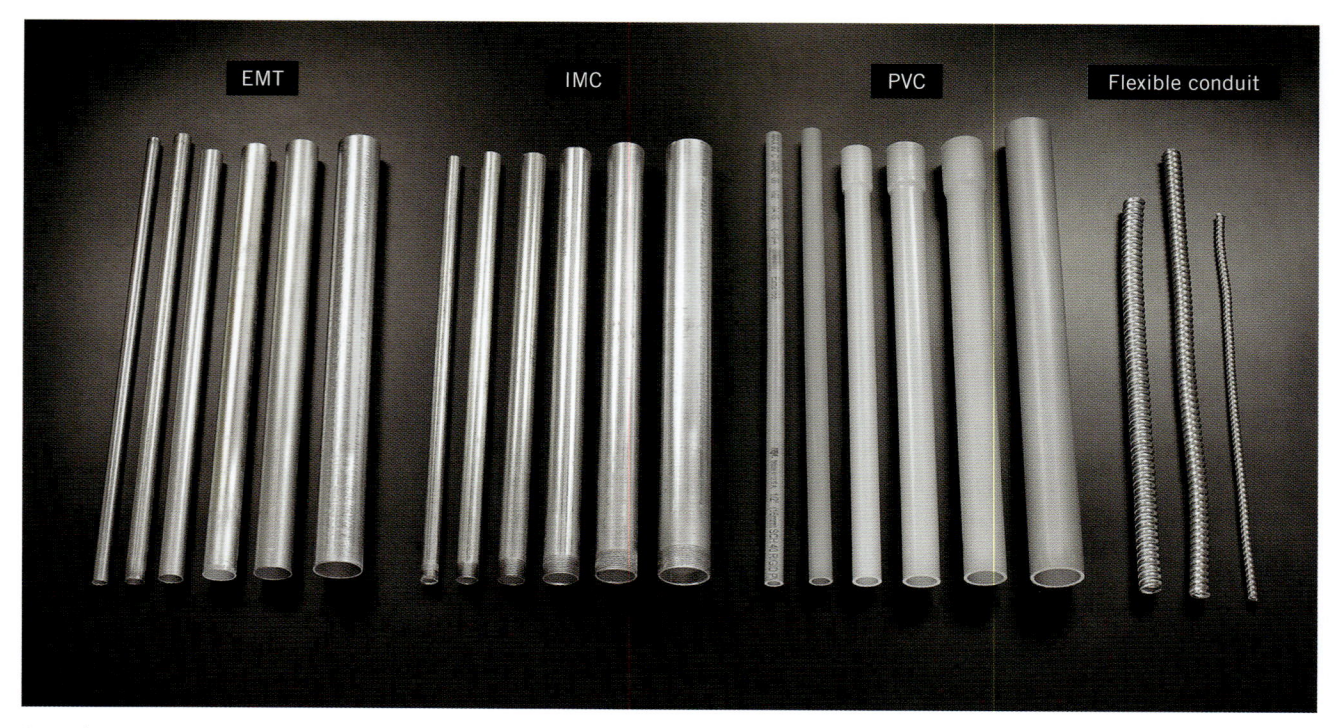

Conduit types used most in homes are EMT (electrical metallic tubing), IMC (intermediate metallic conduit), PVC (rigid nonmetallic conduit), and flexible metal conduit. The most common diameters are ½" and ¾", but larger sizes—which can carry more wires—are stocked at most building centers.

Nonmetallic conduit fittings typically are cemented to nonmetallic conduit, as opposed to metal conduit, which can be threaded and screwed into threaded fittings or attached with setscrews or compression fittings.

Liquid-tight flexible conduit (LFC) is used in outdoor applications, especially around pools and water features, at irrigation controllers, and in air-conditioning condensers.

How to Make Nonmetallic Conduit Connections

Cut the rigid nonmetallic conduit (PVC) to length with a fine-tooth saw, such as a hacksaw. For larger diameter (1½" and above), use a power miter saw with a fine-tooth or plastic cutting blade.

Deburr the cut edges with a utility knife or fine sandpaper such as emery paper. Wipe the cut ends with a dry rag. Also wipe the coupling or fitting to clean it.

Apply a coat of PVC cement to the end of the conduit and to the inside walls of the coupling (inset). Wear latex gloves to protect your hands. The cement should be applied past the point on the conduit where it enters the fitting or coupling.

Insert the conduit into the fitting or coupling and twist it a quarter turn to help spread the cement. Allow the joint to set undisturbed for 10 minutes.

How to Install Conduit + Wires on a Concrete Wall

Measure from the floor to position electrical boxes on the wall, and mark location for mounting screws. Boxes for receptacles in an unfinished basement or other damp areas are mounted at least 2 ft. from the floor. Laundry receptacles usually are mounted at 48".

Drill pilot holes with a masonry bit, then mount the box against the wall with masonry anchors, or use masonry anchors and panhead screws.

Open one knockout for each length of conduit that will be attached to the box. Attach an offset fitting to each knockout using a locknut.

Offset fitting

Measure the first length of conduit and cut it with a hacksaw. Remove any rough inside edges with a pipe reamer or a round file. Attach the conduit to the offset fitting on the box, and tighten the setscrew.

Anchor the conduit against the wall with pipe straps and masonry anchors. Conduit should be anchored within 3 ft. of each box and fitting and every 10 ft. thereafter.

Make conduit bends by attaching a sweep fitting using a setscrew fitting or compression fitting. Continue attaching additional lengths. You can also use a conduit bender (inset) to make your own sweeps and bends.

Use an elbow fitting in conduit runs that have many bends or in runs that require very long wires. The cover on the elbow fitting can be removed to make it easier to extend a fish tape and pull wires.

At the panel, turn the power off and then remove the cover and test for power. Open a knockout in the panel, attach a setscrew fitting, and install the last length of conduit.

Unwind the fish tape and extend it through the conduit from the circuit breaker panel outward. Remove the cover on an elbow fitting when extending the fish tape around tight corners.

Trim back 2" of outer insulation from the end of the wires, and then insert the wires through the loop at the tip of the fish tape.

Retrieve the wires through the conduit by pulling on the fish tape with steady pressure.

NOTE: Use extreme care when using a metal fish tape inside a circuit panel, even when the power is turned off.

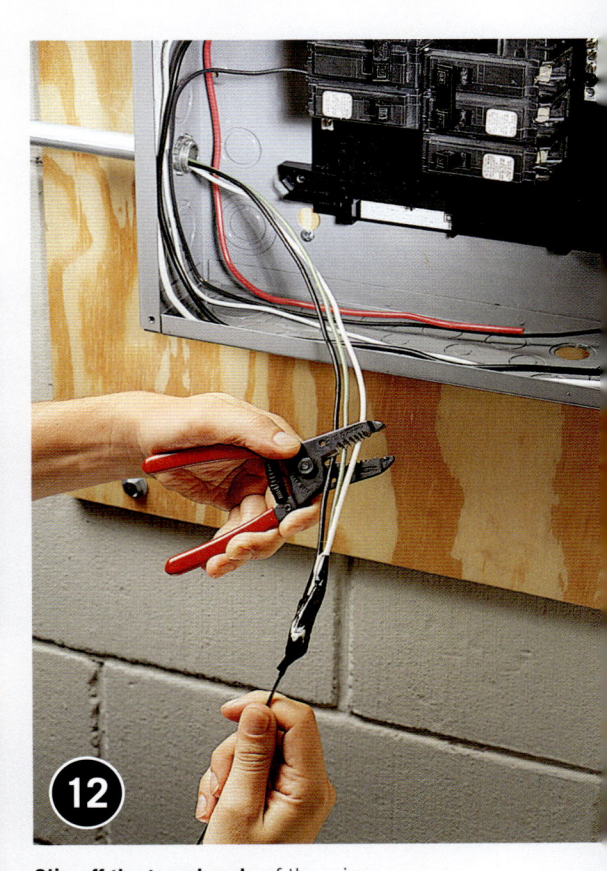

Clip off the taped ends of the wires. Leave at least 2 ft. of wire at the panel and 3" extending beyond the front edges at each electrical box.

Boxes + Panels

The electrical boxes used throughout your house are normally the points at which you most often interact directly with your electrical system. You must use the correct boxes for different situations and ensure that they are installed in the proper locations and in the correct way. This chapter will give you in-depth guidance on which to use when and, more importantly, why.

Electrical panels are more complex features and are essentially critical nerve centers distributing electricity throughout the various circuits in your home. There are actually two types of electrical panels in most homes: the primary panel that is the first inside connection to exterior power from the grid, and electrical breaker boxes. Electrical, or "service entrance" panels hold circuit breakers, a main power shutoff switch, bus bars, neutral and grounding bars, and potentially other features like GFCI breakers and surge-protection connections. Breaker boxes hold only circuit breakers. All of this becomes clearer the more you work with your system. The photos and diagrams in this chapter will also clarify the system for you.

In this chapter:
- Electrical Boxes
- Installing Boxes
- Electrical Panels

Electrical Boxes

The National Electrical Code requires that wire connections and cable splices be contained inside an approved metal or plastic box. The box shields framing members and other flammable materials from electrical sparks and protects people from being shocked.

Electrical boxes come in several standardized shapes. Rectangular and square boxes are used for switches and receptacles. Rectangular (2 × 3") boxes are used for single switches or duplex receptacles. Square (4 × 4") boxes are used any time it is convenient for two switches or receptacles to be wired, or "ganged," in one box. Octagonal electrical boxes contain wire connections for ceiling fixtures.

Electrical boxes are available in different depths. A box must be deep enough so a switch or receptacle can be removed or installed easily without crimping and damaging the circuit wires. The box must also be large enough to safely dissipate the heat from wires, switches, and receptacles. This is an important fire safety rule.

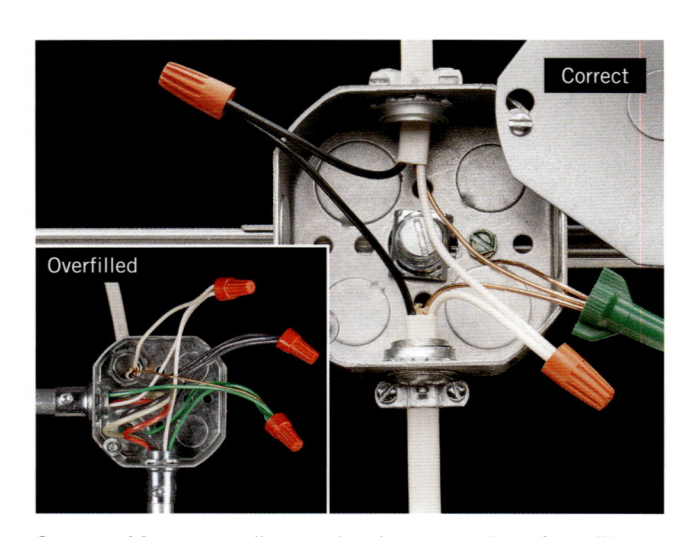

Octagonal boxes usually contain wire connections for ceiling fixtures. Because the ceiling fixture attaches directly to the box, the box should be anchored firmly to a framing member. A properly installed octagonal box should support a ceiling fixture weighing up to 50 pounds. Any box must be covered with a tightly fitting cover plate, and the box must not have open knockouts. Do not overfill the box (inset).

ELECTRICAL BOX FILL CHART

BOX SIZE AND SHAPE	MAXIMUM NUMBER OF CONDUCTORS PERMITTED (SEE NOTES BELOW)			
WIRE SIZE	8 AWG	10 AWG	12 AWG	14 AWG
JUNCTION BOXES				
4 × 1¼" R or O	4	5	5	6
4 × 1½" R or O	5	6	6	7
4 × 2⅛" R or O	7	8	9	10
4 × 1¼" S	6	7	8	9
4 × 1½" S	7	8	9	10
4 × 2⅛" S	10	12	13	15
4¹¹⁄₁₆ × 1¼" S	8	10	11	12
4¹¹⁄₁₆ × 1½" S	9	11	13	14
4¹¹⁄₁₆ × 2⅛" S	14	16	18	21
DEVICE BOXES				
3 × 2 × 1½"	2	3	3	3
3 × 2 × 2"	3	4	4	5
3 × 2 × 2¼"	3	4	4	5
3 × 2 × 2½"	4	5	5	6
3 × 2 × 2¾"	4	5	6	7
3 × 2 × 3½"	6	7	8	9
4 × 2⅛ × 1½"	3	4	4	5
4 × 2⅛ × 1⅞"	4	5	5	6
4 × 2⅛ × 2⅛"	4	5	6	7

NOTES:
- R = Round; O = Octagonal; S = Square or rectangular
- Each hot or neutral wire entering the box is counted as one conductor.
- Grounding wires are counted as one conductor in total—do not count each one individually.
- Raceway fittings and external cable clamps do not count. Internal cable connectors and straps count as either half or one conductor, depending on type.
- Devices (switches and receptacles mainly) each count as two conductors.
- When calculating total conductors, any nonwire components should be assigned the gauge of the largest wire in the box.
- For wire gauges not shown here, contact your local electrical inspections office.

Replace an undersized box with a larger box using the Electrical Box Fill Chart (above) as a guide. In addition to the maximum box fill allowed by the chart, the area of all wires, taps, and splices should not exceed 75 percent of the box area. The NEC also says that all electrical boxes must remain accessible. Never cover an electrical box with drywall, paneling, or wallcoverings.

Common Electrical Boxes

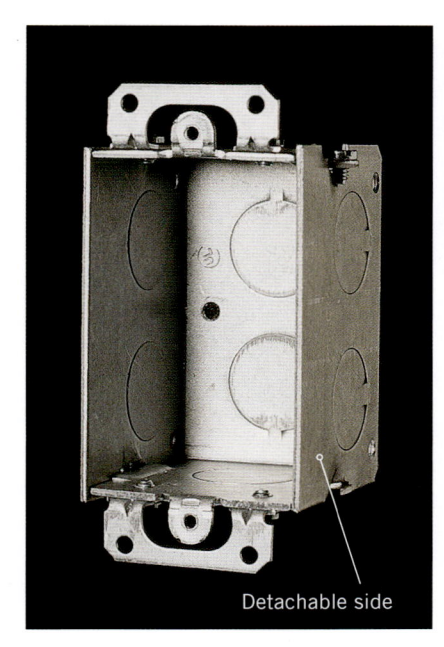

Detachable side

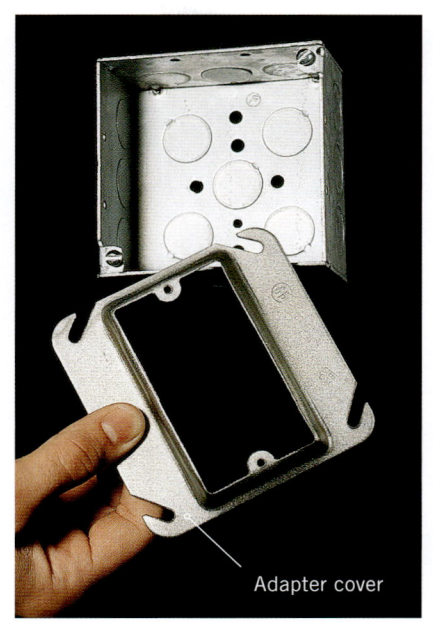

Adapter cover

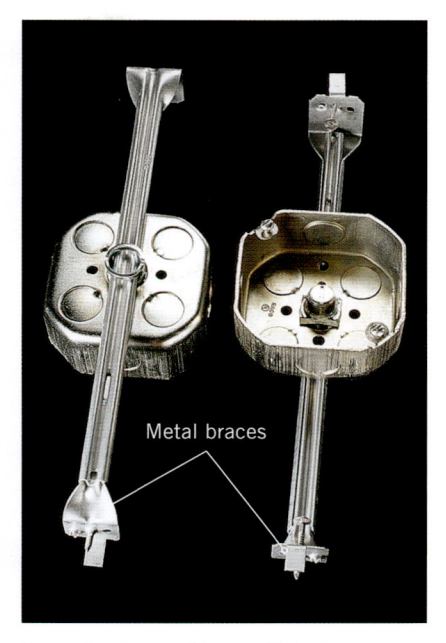

Metal braces

Rectangular boxes are used with wall switches and duplex receptacles. Single-size rectangular boxes (shown above) may have detachable sides that allow them to be ganged together to form double-size boxes.

Square 4" × 4" boxes are large enough for most wiring applications. They are used for cable splices and ganged receptacles or switches. To install one switch or receptacle in a square box, use an adapter cover.

Braced octagonal boxes fit between ceiling joists. The metal braces extend to fit any joist spacing and are nailed or screwed to framing members.

Foam gasket

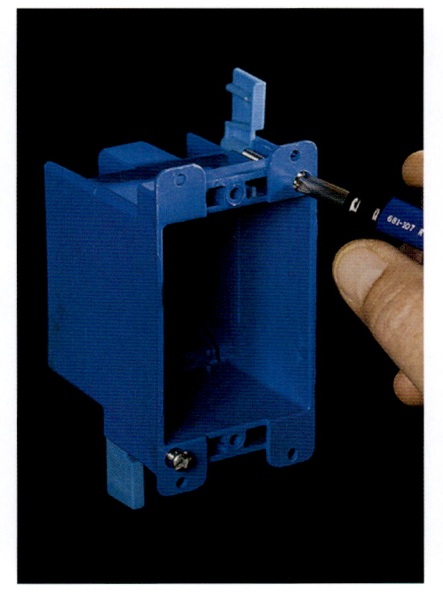

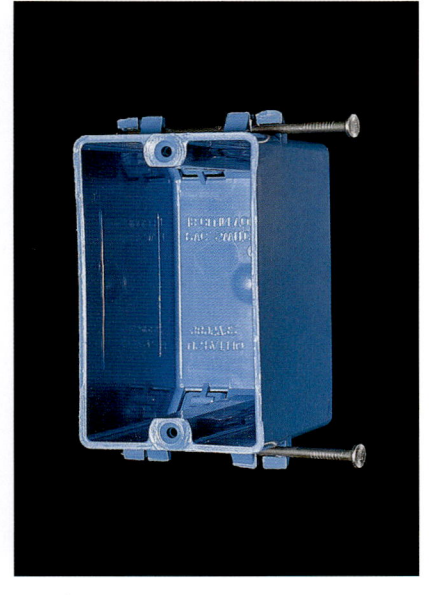

Outdoor boxes have sealed seams and foam gaskets to guard a switch or receptacle against moisture. Corrosion-resistant coatings protect all metal parts. Code-compliant models include a watertight hood that protects even when the outlet is in use.

Old work boxes can be installed to replace older boxes or to allow you to add new additional receptacles and switches. One type (above) has built-in clamps that tighten against the backside of the drywall and hold the box in place.

Plastic boxes are common in new construction. The box may include preattached nails for anchoring it to framing members. Wall switches must have grounding screws if installed in plastic boxes.

3½"-deep plastic boxes with preattached mounting nails are used for any wiring project protected by finished walls. Common styles include single-gang (A), double-gang (B), and triple-gang (C). Double-gang and triple-gang boxes require internal cable clamps. Metal boxes (D) should be used for exposed indoor wiring, such as conduit installations in an unfinished basement. Metal boxes also can be used for wiring that will be covered by finished walls. Plastic retrofit boxes (E) are used when a new switch or receptacle must fit inside a finished wall. Use internal cable clamps.

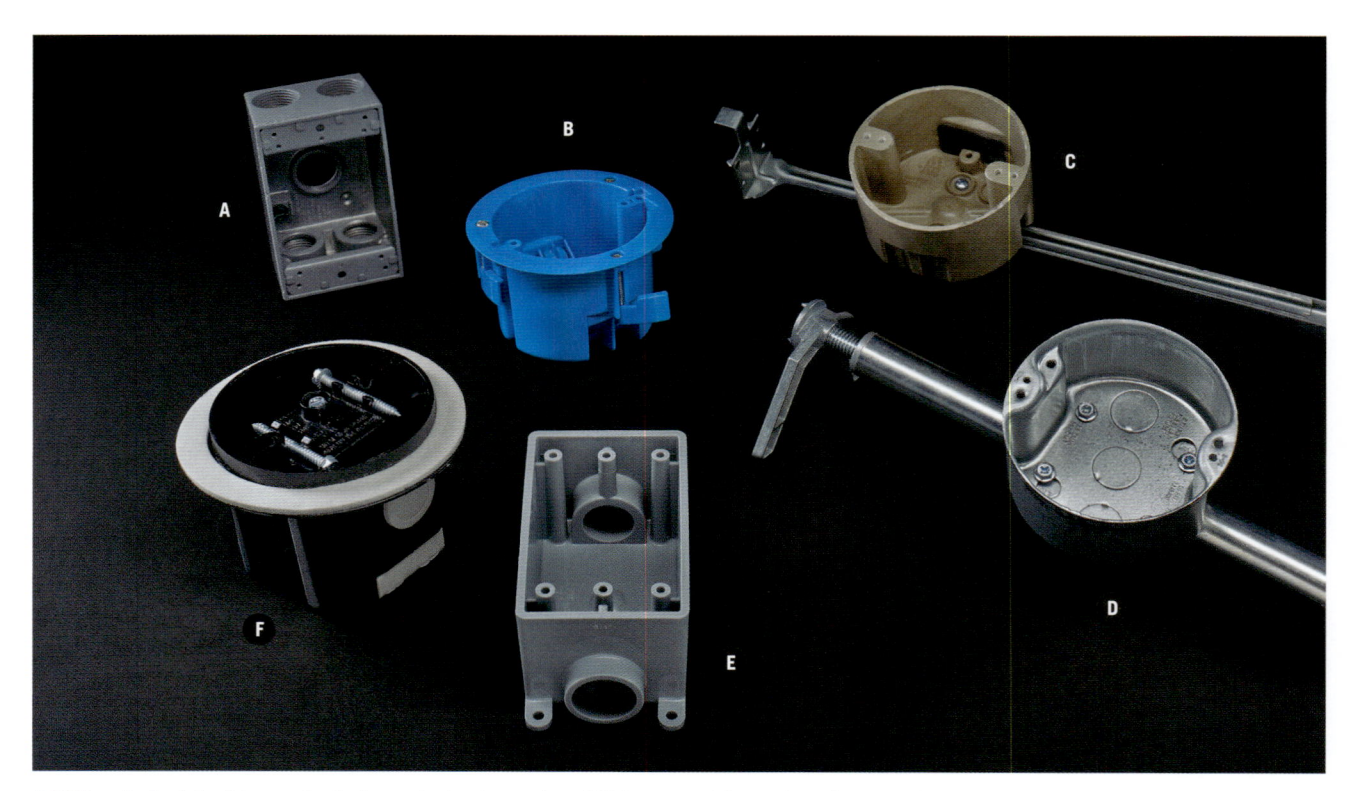

Additional electrical boxes include cast aluminum box (A) for use with outdoor fixtures, including receptacles that are wired through metal conduit (these must have in-use covers if they house receptacles); old work ceiling box (B) used for light fixtures; light-duty ceiling fan box (C) with brace that spans ceiling joists; heavy-duty retrofit ceiling fan box (D) designed for retrofit; PVC box (E) for use with PVC conduit in indoor or outdoor setting; vapor-proof ceiling box with foam gasket (F).

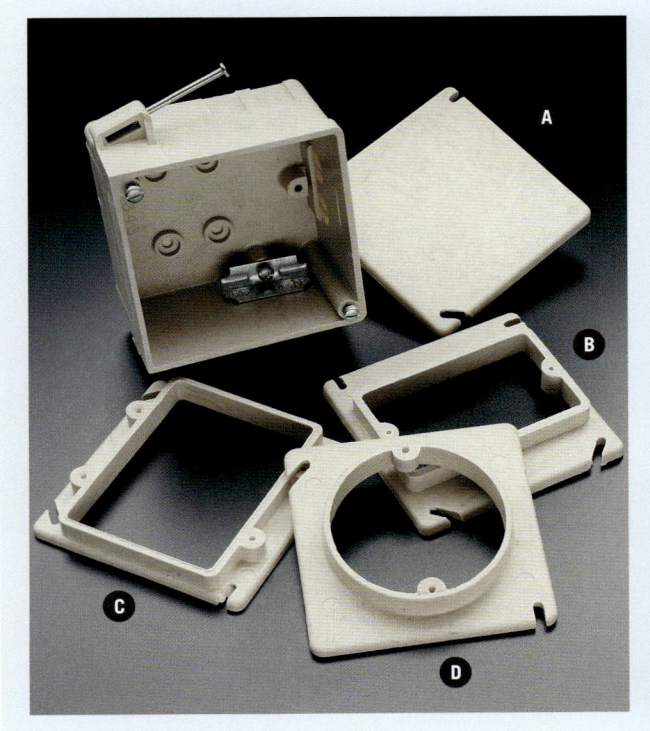

High-quality nonmetallic boxes are rigid and don't contort easily. A variety of adapter plates are available, including junction box cover plate (A), single-gang (B), double-gang (C), and light fixture (D). Adapter plates come in several thicknesses to match different wall constructions.

Boxes larger than 2 × 4" and all retrofit boxes must have internal cable clamps. After installing cables in the box, tighten the cable clamps over the cables so they are gripped firmly, but not so tightly that the cable sheathing is crushed.

Grounding screw

Pigtail

Metal boxes must be bonded to the circuit grounding system. Connect the circuit grounding wires to the box with a green insulated pigtail wire and wire connector (as shown) or with a grounding clip (page 42).

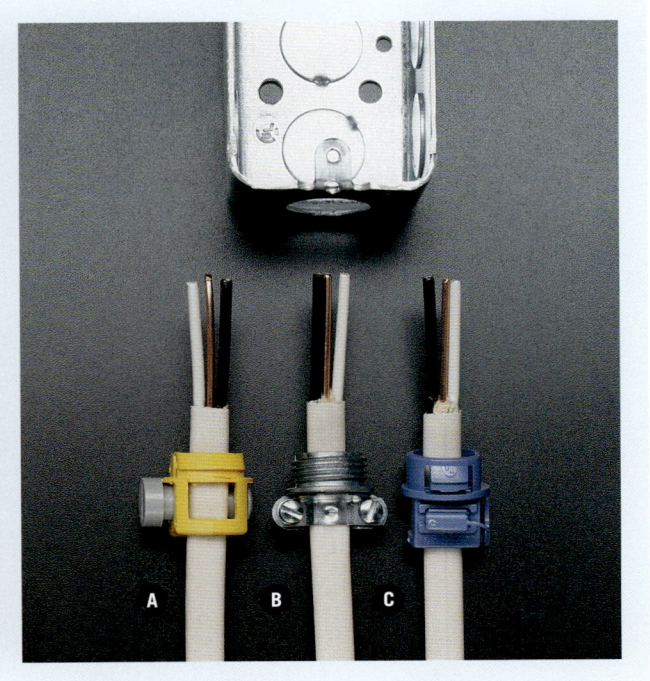

Cables entering a metal box must be clamped. A variety of clamps are available, including plastic clamps (A, C) and threaded metal clamps (B).

Nonmetallic Boxes

Nonmetallic electrical boxes have taken over much of the do-it-yourself market. Most are sold prefitted with installation hardware—from metal wings to 10d common nails attached at the perfect angle for a nail-in box. The bulk of the nonmetallic boxes sold today are inexpensive blue PVC. You can also purchase heavier-duty fiberglass or thermoset plastic models that provide a nonmetallic option for installing heavier fixtures such as ceiling fans and chandeliers.

In addition to cost and availability, nonmetallic boxes hold a big advantage over metal boxes in that their resistance to conducting electricity will prevent a sparking short circuit if a hot wire contacts the box. Nonmetallic boxes generally are not approved for exposed areas, where they may be susceptible to damage. Their lack of rigidity also allows them to compress or distort, which can reduce the interior capacity beyond code minimums or make outlets difficult to attach.

Low cost is the primary reason that plastic PVC nail-in boxes are so popular. Not only are they inexpensive, but they also feature built-in cable clamps. The standard plastic nail-in box is prefitted with a pair of 10d common nails for attaching to exposed wall studs.

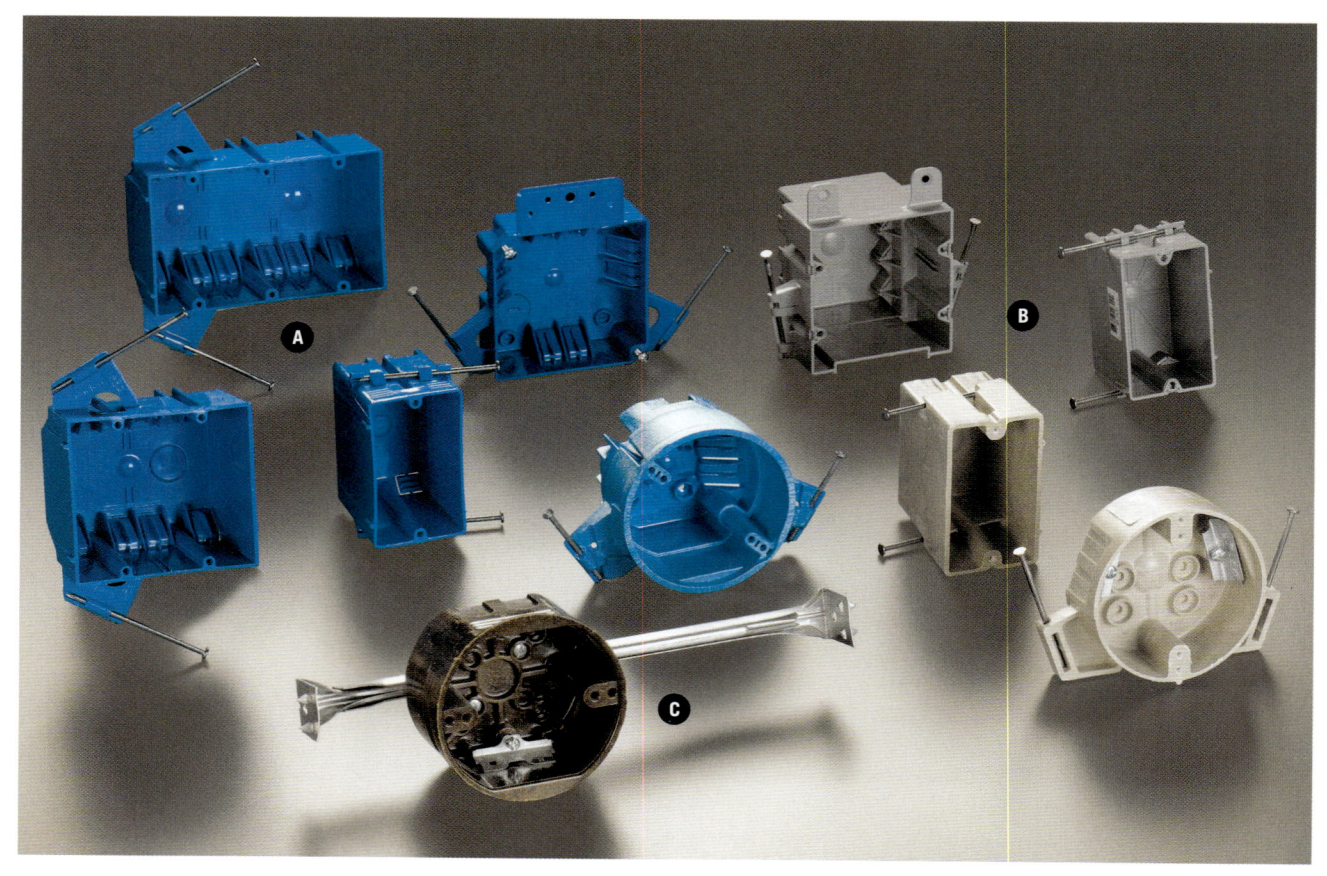

Nonmetallic boxes for home use include a single-gang, double-gang, triple gang, and quad boxes (A); thermoset and fiberglass boxes for heavier duty (B); and round fixture boxes (C) for ceiling installation (nail-in and with integral metal bracket).

Working with Nonmetallic Boxes

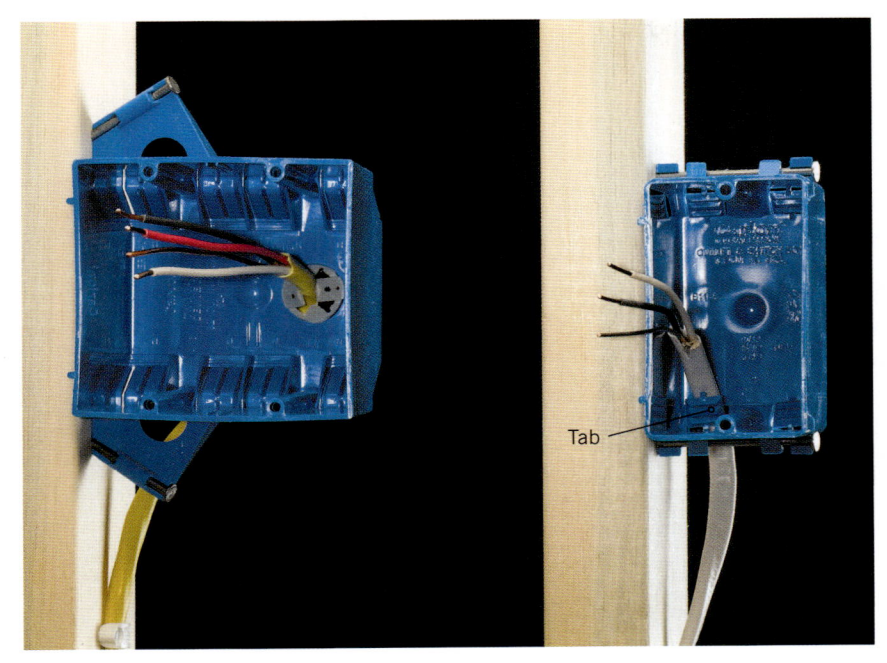

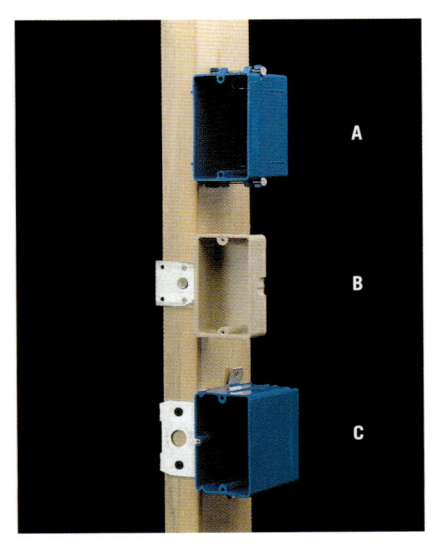

Tab

Do not break off the tabs that cover cable entry holes in plastic boxes. These are not knockouts as you would find in metal boxes. In single-gang boxes (right), the pressure from the tab is sufficient to secure the cable as long as it enters with sheathing intact and is stapled to the framing no more than 8" from the box. On larger boxes (left), you will find traditional knockouts intended to be used with plastic cable clamps that resemble metal cable clamps. Use these for heavier-gauge cable and cable with more than three wires.

Nail-in boxes (A) are prefitted with 10d nails that are attached perpendicular to the face of single-gang boxes and at an inward angle for better gripping power on larger boxes. Side-mount boxes (B) feature a nailing plate that is attached to the front of the stud to automatically create the correct setback; adjustable side-mount boxes (C) are installed the same way but can be moved on the bracket.

Ribs

Distortion can occur in nonmetallic boxes when nails or other fasteners are overdriven or installed at improper angles, or when the semiflexible boxes are compressed into improperly sized or shaped openings. This can reduce the box capacity and prevent devices and faceplates from fitting.

Integral ribs cast into many nonmetallic boxes are used to register the box against the wall studs so the front edges of the box will be flush with the wall surface after drywall is installed. Most are set for ½" drywall, but if your wall material will be a different thickness, or if you are going to install something like a mirror on the wall, you may be able to find a box with corresponding ribs. Otherwise, use a piece of the wallcovering material as a reference.

Installing Boxes

Install electrical boxes for receptacles, switches, and fixtures only after your wiring project plan has been approved by your inspector. Use your wiring plan as a guide, and follow all applicable height and spacing guidelines when laying out box positions.

Always use the deepest electrical boxes that are practical for your installation. Using deep boxes ensures that you will meet code regulations regarding box volume and makes it easier to make the wire connections.

Some electrical fixtures, such as recessed light fixtures, electric heaters, and exhaust fans, have built-in wire connection boxes. Install the frames for these fixtures at the same time you are installing the other electrical boxes. The box heights recommended on the following pages are for most situations. Box heights for Americans with Disabilities Act (ADA) compliance are different.

Electrical boxes in adjacent rooms should be positioned close together when they share a common wall and are controlled by the same circuit. This simplifies the cable installations and also reduces the amount of cable needed.

Fixtures That Do Not Need Electrical Boxes

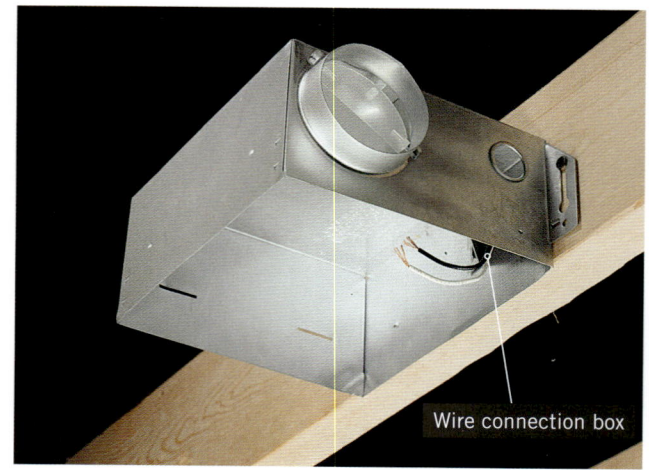

Wire connection box

Recessed fixtures that fit inside wall cavities have built-in wire connection boxes and require no additional electrical boxes. Common recessed fixtures include electric blower-heaters (left), bathroom exhaust fans (right), and recessed light fixtures. Install the frames for these fixtures at the same time you are installing the other electrical boxes along the circuit. Surface-mounted fixtures such as electric baseboard heaters (pages 232–235) also have built-in wire connection boxes. These fixtures are not installed until it is time to make the final hookups.

How to Install Electrical Boxes for Receptacles

Mark the location of each box on studs. Standard receptacle boxes should be centered 12" above floor level. GFCI receptacle boxes in a bathroom should be mounted so they will be about 10" above the finished countertop.

Position each box against a stud so the front face will be flush with the finished wall. For example, if you will be installing ½" drywall, position the box so it extends ½" past the face of the stud, plus the thickness of any additional material, such as tile or a mirror. Anchor the box by driving the mounting nails into the stud.

Adapter plate

If installing square boxes, attach the adapter plates before positioning the boxes. Use adapter plates that match the thickness of the finished wall. Anchor the box by driving the mounting nails into the stud.

Open one knockout for each cable that will enter the box using a hammer and screwdriver. Always introduce the new cable through the knockout that is farthest way from the wall stud.

Break off any sharp edges that might damage vinyl cable sheathing by rotating a screwdriver in the knockout.

How to Install Boxes for Light Fixtures

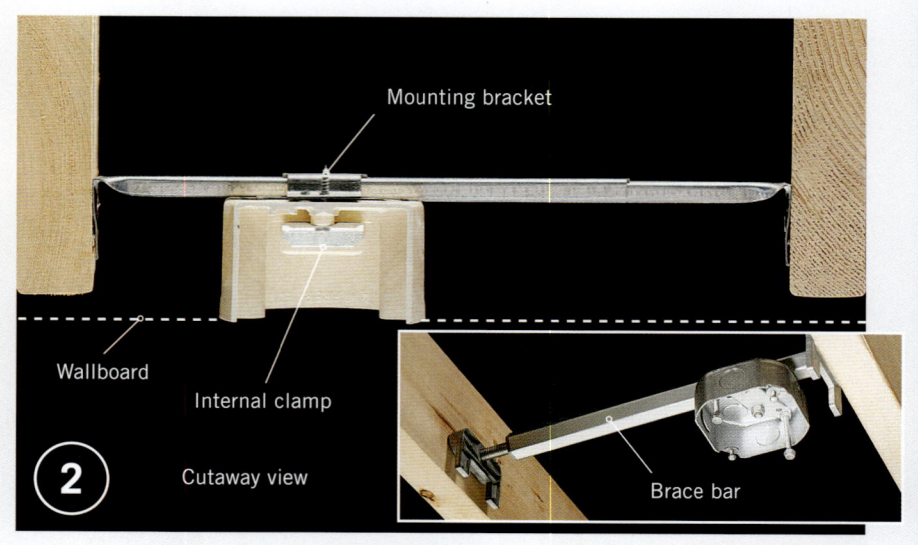

Position the light fixture box for a vanity light above the frame opening for a mirror or medicine cabinet. Place the box for a ceiling light fixture in the center of the room or as desired. Position each box against a framing member so the front face will be flush with the finished wall or ceiling, and then anchor the box by driving the mounting nails into the framing.

To position a light fixture between joists, attach an electrical box to an adjustable brace bar. Nail the ends of the brace bar to joists so the face of the box will be flush with the finished ceiling surface. Slide the box along the brace bar to the desired position, and then tighten the mounting screws. Use internal cable clamps when using a box with a brace bar.

NOTE: For ceiling fans and heavy fixtures, use a metal box and a heavy-duty brace bar rated for heavy loads (inset photo).

 # How to Install Boxes for Switches

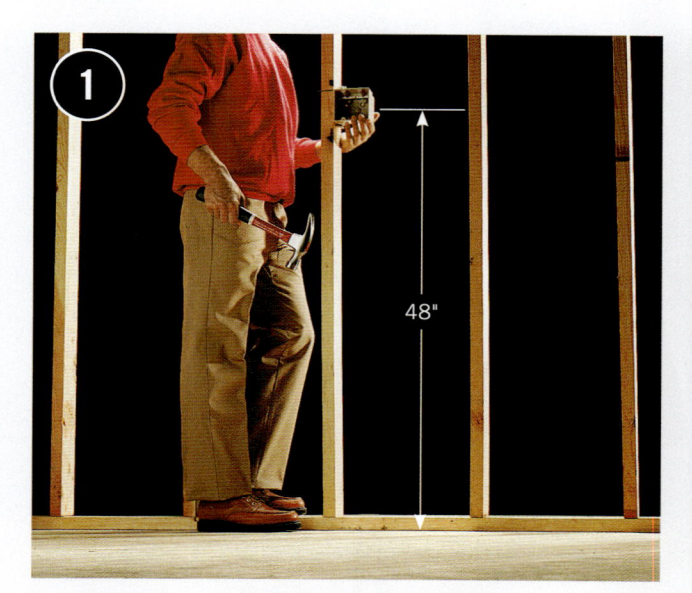

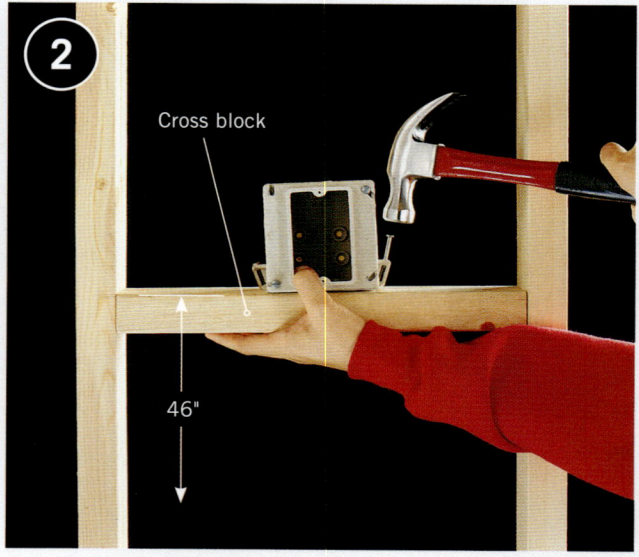

Install switch boxes at accessible locations, usually on the latch side of a door, with the center of the box 48" from the floor. The box for a thermostat is mounted at 48" to 60". Position each box against the side of a stud so the front face will be flush with the finished wall, and drive the mounting nails into the stud.

To install a switch box between studs, first install a cross block between studs, with the top edge 46" above the floor. Position the box on the cross block so the front face will be flush with the finished wall, and drive the mounting nails into the cross block.

How to Locate Electrical Boxes

Heights of electrical boxes vary depending on use. In the kitchen shown here, boxes above the countertop are 45" above the floor, in the center of 18" backsplashes that extend from the countertop to the cabinets. All boxes for wall switches also are installed at this height. The center of the box for the microwave receptacle is 72" off the floor. The centers of the boxes for the range and food disposer receptacles are 12" off the floor, but the center of the box for the dishwasher receptacle is 6" off the floor.

Typical Wallcovering Thickness

Consider the thickness of finished walls when mounting electrical boxes against framing members. Code requires that the front face of boxes be flush with the finished wall surface, so how you install boxes will vary depending on the type of wall finish that will be used. For example, if the walls will be finished with ½" drywall (A), attach the boxes so the front faces extend ½" past the front of the framing members. With ceramic tile and drywall or cementboard (B), extend the boxes ⅞" past the framing members. With ¼" Corian® over drywall (C), boxes should extend ¾"; and with drywall and laminate (D), boxes should extend ⅝".

Ceiling Boxes

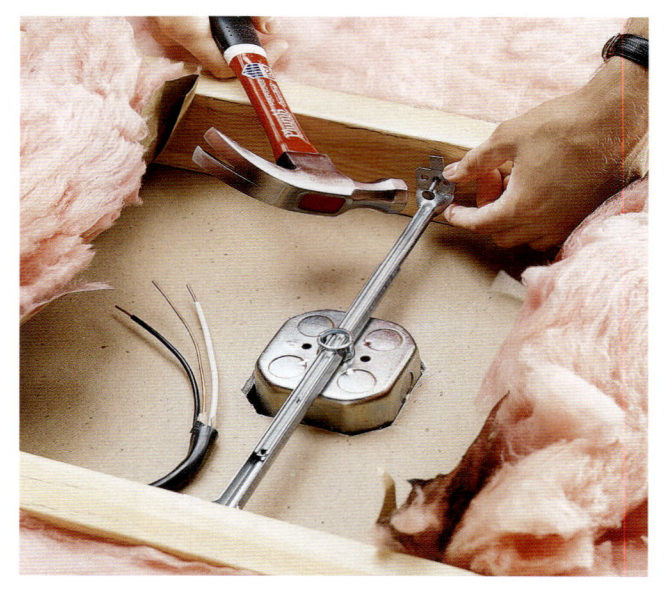

Shown cutaway

Brace

Joist

Ceiling boxes for lights are generally round or octagonal to fit typical lamp mounting plates. The easiest way to install one is by nailing the brace to ceiling joists from above. If the ceiling is insulated, pull the insulation away from the box if the fixture you're installing is not rated IC for insulation contact. Some codes require boxing the fixture with blocking members.

A heavy-duty brace is required for anchoring boxes that will support heavy chandeliers and ceiling fans. A remodeling brace such as the one seen here is designed to install through a small cutout in the ceiling (inset photo).

How to Install a Junction Box

1

Splices outside of a box are a code violation.

2

Knockout

Turn off power to circuit wires at the electrical panel. Test for power. Carefully remove any tape or wire connectors from the exposed splice. Disconnect the wires.

Open one knockout for each cable that will enter the box using a hammer and screwdriver. Any unopened knockouts should remain sealed.

Anchor the electrical box to a wooden framing member using screws or nails.

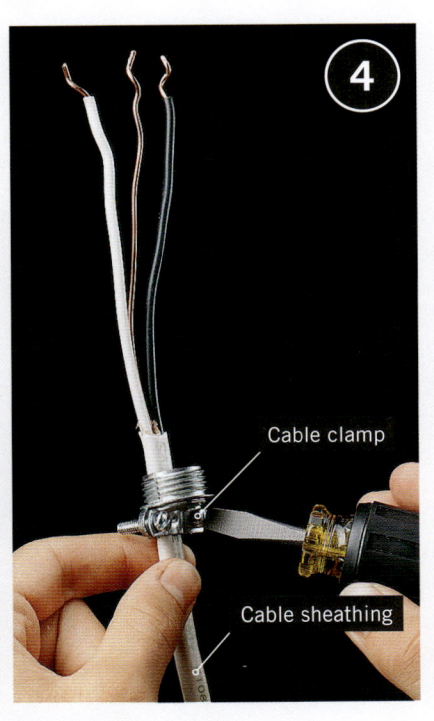

Cable clamp

Cable sheathing

Thread each cable end through a cable clamp. Tighten the clamp with a screwdriver. See if there is any slack in the cables so you can gain a little extra cable to work with.

Locknut

Insert the cables into the electrical box, and screw a locknut onto each cable clamp.

Locknut

Lugs

Tighten the locknuts by pushing against the lugs with the blade of a screwdriver.

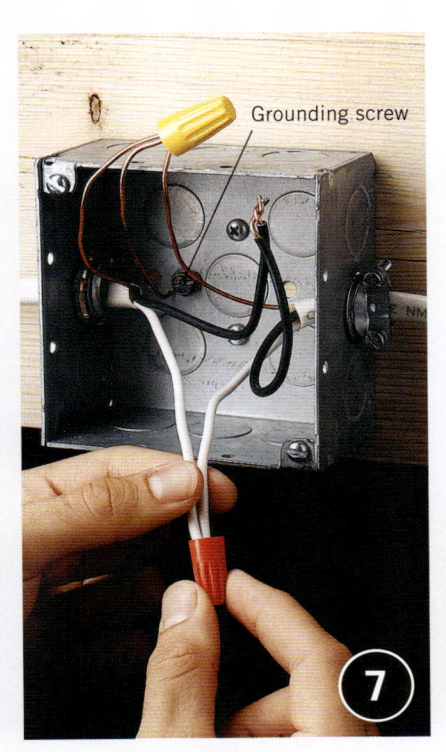

Grounding screw

Use wire connectors to reconnect the wires. Pigtail the copper grounding wires to the green grounding screw in the back of the box (required only for metal boxes).

Cover plate

Carefully tuck the wires into the box, and attach the cover plate. Turn on the power to the circuit at the main service panel. Make sure the box remains accessible and is not concealed by wall or ceiling finishes.

Installing Pop-In (Old Work) Retrofit Boxes

Attaching an electrical box to a wall stud during new construction is relatively easy (pages 54 to 57). The task becomes complicated, however, when you're working in finished walls during remodeling or repair. In most cases, it's best to use an electronic stud finder, make a large cutout in the wall, and attach a new box directly to a framing member or bracing (and then replace and refinish the wall materials). But there are occasions when this isn't possible or practical and you just need to retrofit an electrical box without making a large hole in the wall. You also may find that an older switch or receptacle box is too shallow to accommodate a new dimmer or GFCI safely. These situations call for a pop-in retrofit box (sometimes called an "old work" box).

A pop-in box typically has wings, tabs, or brackets that are drawn tight against the wall surface on the wall cavity side, holding the box in place. It can be either metal or plastic.

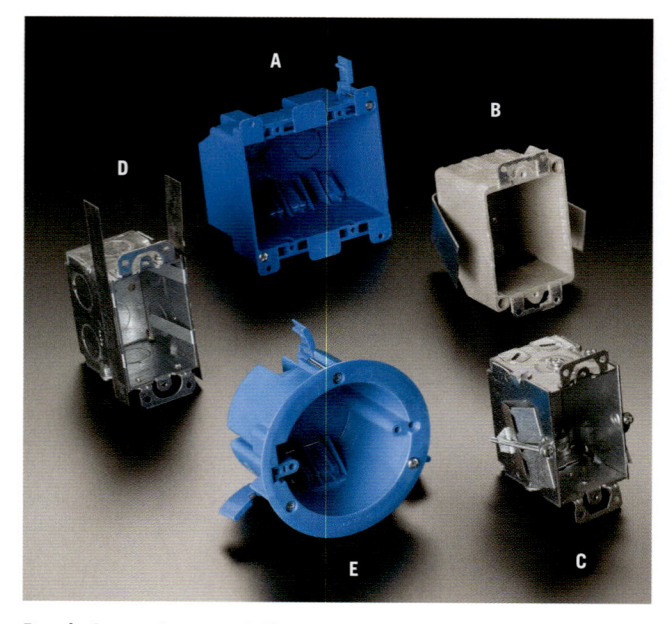

Pop-in boxes for remodeling come in a variety of styles. For walls, they include plastic retrofit boxes with flip-out wings (A), metal or plastic boxes with compression tabs or brackets (B), metal retrofit boxes with folding wings (C), and metal boxes with bendable brackets, also known as F-straps or Madison clips, (D). For ceilings, plastic fixture boxes with flip-out wings (E) are available.

TOOLS + MATERIALS

Screwdriver	Keyhole saw
Pencil	Template (if provided)
String	Plastic or metal pop-in box
Electrical tape	Eye protection

How to Replace an Electrical Box

To install a dimmer switch or GFCI receptacle, you may have to replace an old, overcrowded box. Shut off power and remove the old switch or receptacle. Identify the location of nails holding the box to the framing member and cut the nails with a hacksaw or reciprocating saw with a metal blade inserted between the box and the stud.

Bind the cable ends together and attach string in case they fall into the wall cavity when the old box is removed. Disconnect the cable clamps and slide the old box out. Install a new pop-in box (see opposite).

How to Install a Pop-In Box

1

Use a template to trace a cutout for the box at the intended location. If no template is provided, press the pop-in box against the wall surface and trace its front edges (but not the tabs on the top and bottom).

2

Puncture the drywall with the tip of a drywall saw or by drilling a small hole inside the lines, and make the cutout for the box.

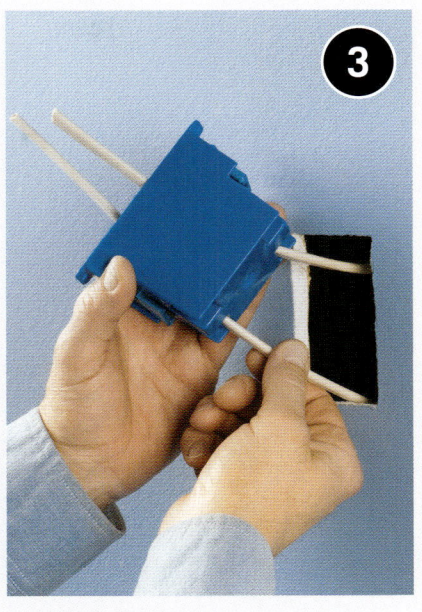

3

Pull NM cable through a knockout in the box (no cable clamp is required with a plastic box; just be sure not to break the pressure tab that holds the cable in place).

4

Insert the box into the cutout so the front flanges are flush against the wall surface. Tighten the screws that cause the flip-out wings to pivot (right) until the box is held firmly in place. Connect the switch or receptacle that the box will house.

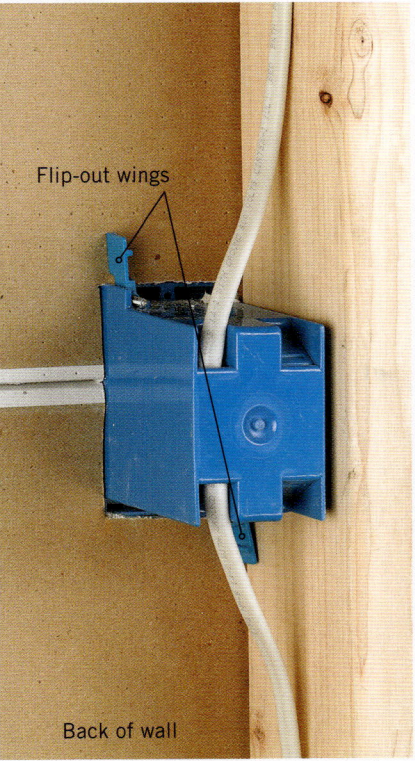

Flip-out wings

Back of wall

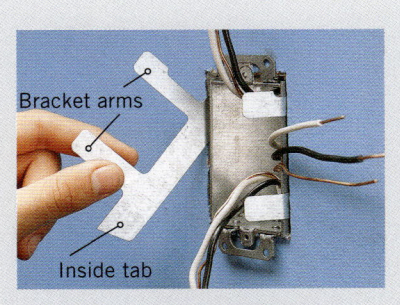

Bracket arms

Inside tab

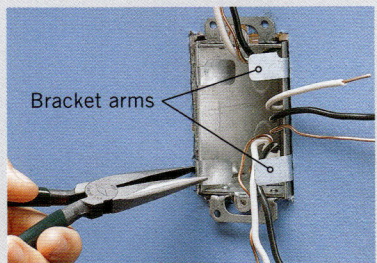

Bracket arms

VARIATION: Feed cable into the new box and secure it in the opening after clamping the cables. With this pop-in box, bracket arms are inserted at the sides of the box (top) and then bent around the front edges to secure the box in the opening (bottom).

Electrical Panels

Before making any repair to your electrical system, you must shut off power to the correct circuit at the main panel or at the subpanel where the circuit begins. Every circuit in every panel should be labeled (see page 22) so circuits can be identified easily.

Regardless of age, all panels have circuit breakers or fuses (see pages 66–69) that protect each circuit from overloads. In general, older service panels use fuses, while newer panels use circuit breakers.

In addition to the main panel, your electrical system may have one or more subpanels that protect some of the circuits in the home. A subpanel has its own circuit breakers or fuses.

The subpanel resembles the main panel but is usually smaller. It may be located near the main panel, or it may be found near the areas served by the new circuits. Garages and basements that have been updated often have their own subpanels. If your home has subpanels, make sure that their circuits are indexed correctly.

Panels vary in appearance, depending on the age of the system. Very old wiring may operate on 30-amp service that has only two circuits. New homes can have up to 400-amp service with 30 or more circuits. You can usually find the size of the service by reading the amperage rating printed on the main fuse block or main circuit breakers.

When handling fuses or circuit breakers, make sure the area around the panel is dry. Never remove the protective cover on the panel. After turning off a circuit to make electrical repairs, remember to always test the circuit for power before touching any wires.

200-Amp Service Panel

The main panel is the heart of your wiring system. As our demand for household energy has increased, the panels have also grown in capacity. Today, a 200-amp panel is often installed in new construction. Many homebuilders are installing dual 200-amp panels in larger houses.

100-Amp Service Panel

Protective (dead front) cover

Main circuit breaker

Panel index

Circuit breaker

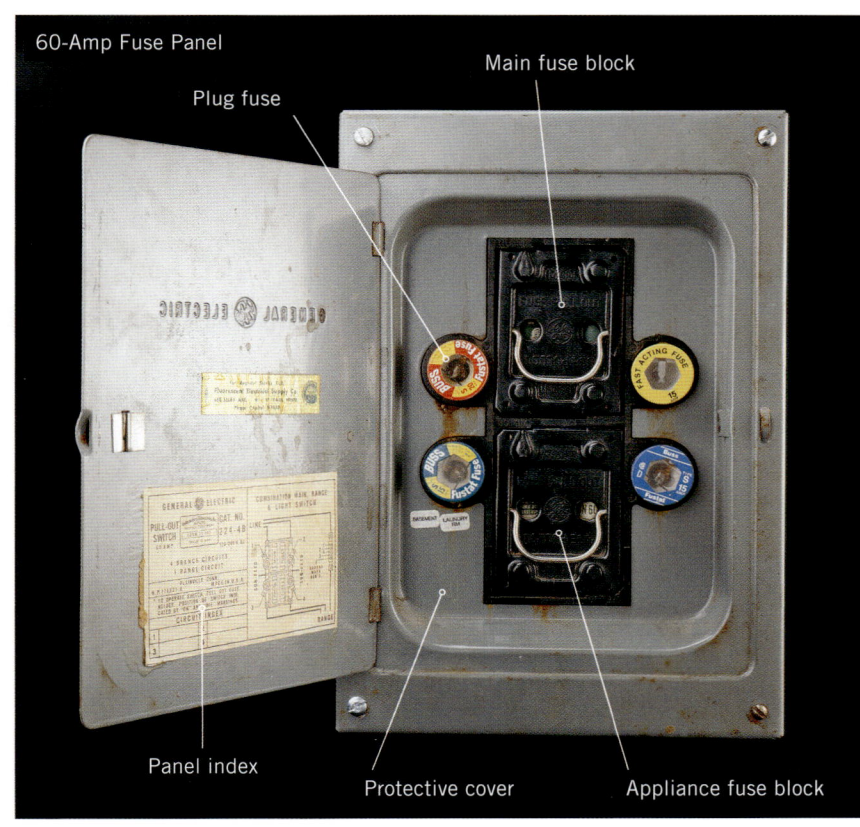

60-Amp Fuse Panel

Plug fuse

Main fuse block

Panel index

Protective cover

Appliance fuse block

A panel providing 100 amps or more of current is common in wiring systems installed during the 1960s and later. A main panel is housed in a gray metal cabinet that contains two rows of individual circuit breakers. You can often determine service size by reading the amperage rating of the main circuit breakers.

Larger new homes may have 300- or 400-amp service. These systems may have a single 300- or 400-amp panel or two 150- or 200-amp panels.

100-amp service is now the minimum standard for all new housing. It is adequate for a medium-sized house with no more than three major electric appliances. However, larger houses with more electrical appliances require a service panel that provides 150 amps or more.

To shut off power to individual circuits in a circuit breaker panel, flip the lever on the appropriate circuit breaker to the OFF position. To shut off the power to the entire house, turn the main circuit breaker(s) to the OFF position.

Some older homes may still have a 60-amp fuse panel. It usually is housed in a gray metal cabinet that contains four individual plug fuses, plus one or two pull-out fuse blocks that hold cartridge fuses. A 60-amp panel is considered undersized by current standards. This type of system should be upgraded for both convenience and safety. Insurance companies and mortgage lenders may require a complete electrical system upgrade before issuing a homeowner insurance policy or approving mortgage financing.

To shut off power to a circuit, carefully unscrew the plug fuse, touching only its insulated rim. To shut off power to the entire house, hold the handle of the main fuse block and pull sharply to remove it. Major appliance circuits are controlled with separate cartridge fuse blocks. Shut off an appliance circuit by pulling out its fuse block.

Circuit Breaker Panels

The circuit breaker panel is the electrical distribution center for your home. It divides the current into branch circuits that are carried throughout the house. Each branch circuit is protected by a circuit breaker that protects the wires from dangerous current overloads. When installing new circuits, the last step is to connect the wires to new circuit breakers at the panel. Follow basic safety procedures and always shut off the main circuit breaker and test for power before touching any parts inside the panel. **Never touch the service wire lugs.** If unsure of your own skills, hire an electrician to make the final circuit connections.

MAIN CIRCUIT BREAKER PANEL DISTRIBUTES THE POWER ENTERING THE HOME INTO BRANCH CIRCUITS.

Service lugs: Never touch these. They are always live unless the utility shuts off the service to the panel. The NEC requires protective covers (service barriers) on the two hot service lugs (see page 119).

Neutral service wire carries current back to the power source after it has passed through the home.

Main circuit breaker protects the panelboard from overloads and disconnects power to all circuits in the panel.

Neutral terminal bar has setscrew terminals for linking all neutral circuit wires to the neutral service wire.

Single-pole breaker connects to one hot bus bar to provide 120 volts to circuit.

Double-pole breaker connects to both hot legs of the bus bar to provide 240 volts.

120-volt branch circuits

Grounding conductor leads to metal grounding rods driven into the earth or to other grounding electrodes.

Two hot service wires each provide 120 volts of power to the main circuit breaker. These wires are always **hot**.

Grounding bus bar has terminals for linking grounding wires to the main grounding conductor. It is bonded to the neutral bus bar.

Two hot bus bars run through the center of the panel, supplying power to the circuit breakers. Each carries 120 volts.

Subpanel feeder breaker is a double-pole breaker. It is wired in the same way as a 120/240-volt circuit.

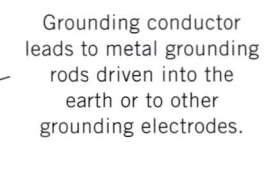

120/240-volt branch circuit

(If you have an older electrical service with fuses instead of circuit breakers, always have an electrician make these final hookups.)

If a circuit breaker panel does not have enough open slots for new full-size circuit breakers, you may be able to install ½-height (slimline) circuit breakers. Otherwise, you will need to install a subpanel.

Before installing any new wiring, evaluate your electrical service to make sure it provides enough current to support both the existing wiring and any new circuits. If your service does not provide enough current, you will need to upgrade to a panel with a higher amp rating and enough extra breaker slots for the new circuits you want to install.

CIRCUIT BREAKER SUBPANEL CAN BE INSTALLED WHEN THE MAIN CIRCUIT BREAKER PANEL DOES NOT HAVE ENOUGH SPACE TO HOLD CIRCUIT BREAKERS FOR NEW CIRCUITS YOU WANT TO INSTALL.

Neutral bus bar has setscrew terminals for linking neutral circuit wires to the neutral feed wire.

Single-pole circuit breaker transfers 120 volts of power from one hot bus bar to the black hot wire in a two-wire cable.

Grounding bus bar has setscrew terminals for connecting circuit grounding wires. In a circuit breaker subpanel, the grounding bus bar is not bonded to the neutral bus bar.

Two hot feeder wires supply 120 volts of power to the two hot bus bars.

Neutral feeder wire connects the neutral bus bar in the subpanel to the neutral bus bar in the main service panel.

120-volt branch circuit

120-volt isolated ground circuit

240-volt branch circuit

Feeder cable brings power from the main circuit breaker panel. A 30-amp, 240-volt subpanel requires a 10/3 feeder cable controlled by a 30-amp double-pole circuit breaker.

Two hot bus bars pass through the center of the service panel, supplying power to the individual circuit breakers. Each carries 120 volts of power.

Double-pole breaker wired for 240 volts transfers power from both hot bus bars to white and black hot wires in a two-wire cable. A 240-volt circuit has no neutral wire connection; the white wire is tagged with black tape to identify it as a hot wire.

🔧 EXERCISE YOUR BREAKERS

Your breakers (including the main) should be "exercised" once a year to ensure proper mechanical function. Simply turn them off and then back on. A convenient time to perform the exercise is at daylight saving time, when you'll need to reset all of your clocks anyway.

Circuit Breakers + Fuses

Circuit breakers and fuses are safety devices designed to protect the electrical system from short circuits and overloads. Circuit breakers and fuses are located in the main service panel and in subpanels.

Most panels installed before about 1965 rely on fuses to protect individual circuits. Screw-in plug fuses protect 120-volt circuits that power lights and receptacles. Cartridge fuses protect 240-volt appliance circuits and the main shutoff of the service panel.

Inside each fuse is a current-carrying metal alloy ribbon. If a circuit is overloaded, the metal ribbon melts and stops the current flow. A fuse must match the amperage rating of the circuit. Never replace a fuse with one that has a larger amperage rating.

In most panels installed after about 1965, circuit breakers protect individual circuits. Single-pole circuit breakers protect 120-volt circuits, and double-pole circuit breakers protect 240-volt circuits. Amperage ratings for circuit breakers range from 10 to over 200 amps.

Each circuit breaker has a permanent metal strip that heats up and bends when current passes through it. If a circuit is overloaded, the metal strip inside the breaker bends enough to "trip" the switch and stop the flow of power. Many circuit breakers are designed to trip only two times. After the second trip, a circuit breaker may not trip when it is supposed to. Consider replacing a circuit breaker that has tripped twice.

When a fuse blows or a circuit breaker trips, it may be because there are too many light fixtures and plug-in appliances drawing power through the circuit. Move some of the plug-in appliances to another circuit, and then replace the fuse or reset the breaker. If the fuse blows or the breaker trips again immediately, there may be a short circuit in the system. Call a licensed electrician if you suspect a short circuit.

Old-style fuse boxes can accept modern "S" type fuses if you use an Edison adapter. Be sure to screw the fuse into the adapter first, and then screw the assembly into the socket.

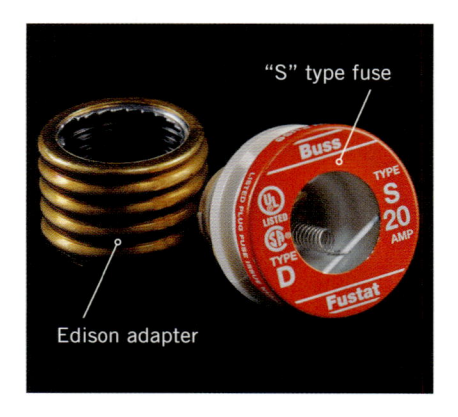

"S" type fuse

Edison adapter

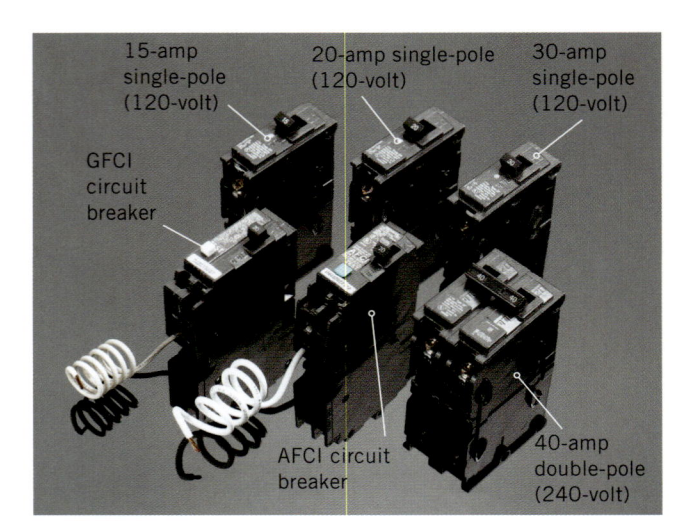

Circuit breakers are found in the majority of panels installed since the 1960s. Single-pole breakers control 120-volt circuits. Double-pole breakers rated for 20 to 60 amps control 240-volt circuits. Ground-fault circuit interrupter (GFCI) provides protection from shocks. Arc-fault circuit interrupter (AFCI) breakers provide protection from fire-causing arcs for the entire circuit.

15-amp single-pole (120-volt)

20-amp single-pole (120-volt)

30-amp single-pole (120-volt)

GFCI circuit breaker

AFCI circuit breaker

40-amp double-pole (240-volt)

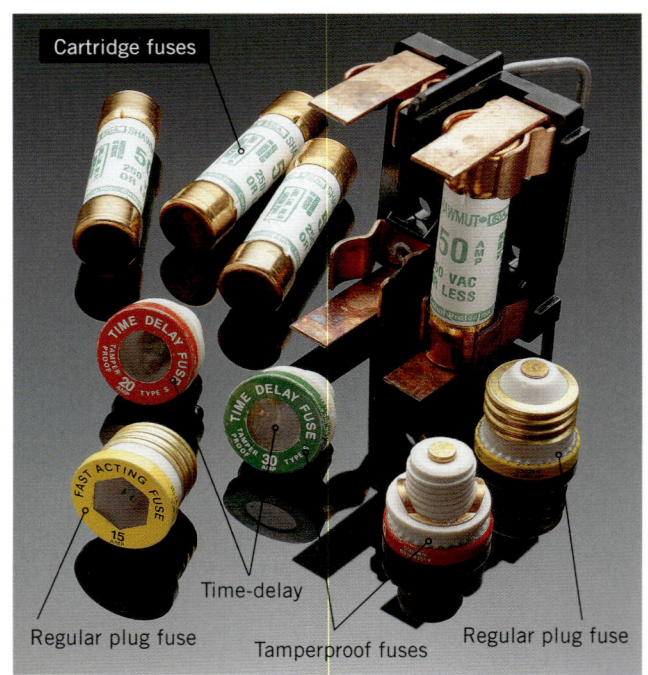

Cartridge fuses

Time-delay

Regular plug fuse

Tamperproof fuses

Regular plug fuse

Fuses are used in older panels. Plug fuses usually control 120-volt circuits rated for 15, 20, or 30 amps. Tamper-proof plug fuses have threads that fit only matching sockets, making it impossible to install a wrong-sized fuse. Time-delay fuses absorb temporary heavy power loads without blowing. Cartridge fuses control 240-volt circuits and range from 30 to 100 amps.

How to Identify + Replace a Blown Plug Fuse

Locate the blown fuse at the panel. If the metal ribbon inside is cleanly melted (left), the circuit was overloaded. If window is discolored (right), there was a short circuit.

Unscrew the fuse, being careful to touch only the insulated rim of the fuse. Replace it with a fuse that has the same amperage rating.

How to Remove, Test + Replace a Cartridge Fuse

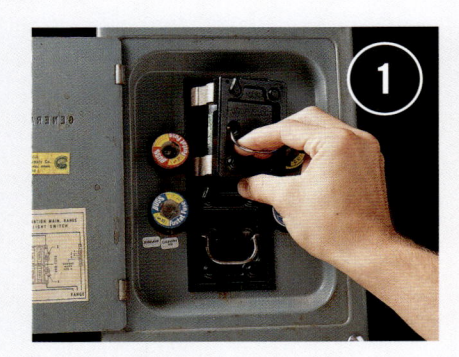

Remove cartridge fuses by gripping the handle of the fuse block and pulling out sharply.

Remove the individual cartridge fuses from the block using a fuse puller.

Test each fuse using a continuity tester. If the tester glows, the fuse is good. If not, install a new fuse with the same amperage rating.

How to Reset + Test a Circuit Breaker

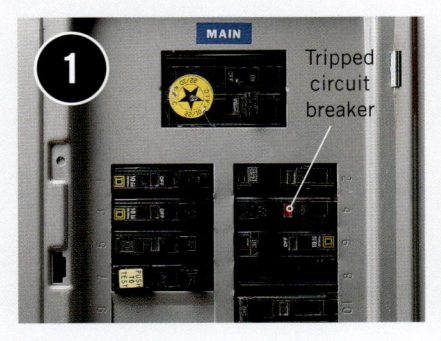

Open the panel and locate the tripped breaker. The lever on the tripped breaker will be either in the OFF position or in a position between ON and OFF.

Reset the tripped circuit breaker by pressing the circuit breaker lever all the way to the OFF position and then pressing it to the ON position.

Test AFCI and GFCI circuit breakers by pushing the TEST button. The breaker should trip to the OFF position. If not, the breaker is faulty and must be replaced.

Connecting Circuit Breakers

The last step in a wiring project is connecting circuits at the breaker panel. After this is done, the work is ready for the final inspection.

Circuits are connected at the main panel, if it has enough open slots, or at a circuit breaker subpanel (see pages 64–67). When working at a subpanel, make sure the feeder breaker at the main panel has been turned off, and test for power (see photo, right) before touching any parts in the subpanel.

Make sure the circuit breaker amperage does not exceed the ampacity of the circuit wires you are connecting to it. Also be aware that circuit breaker styles and installation techniques vary according to manufacturer. Use breakers approved by the panel manufacturer. You should install AFCI circuit breakers for most 15- and 20-amp, 120-volt circuits inside the home.

Test for current before touching any parts inside a circuit breaker panel. With the main breaker turned off but all other breakers turned on, touch one probe of a neon tester to the neutral terminal bar, and touch the other probe to each setscrew on one of the double-pole breakers (not the main breaker). If the tester does not light for either setscrew, it is safe to work in the panel.

NOTE: Noncontact voltage testers are preferred in most situations where you are testing for current because they're safer. But in some instances, you'll need a tester with individual probes to properly check for current.

TOOLS + MATERIALS

Screwdriver	Circuit tester
Hammer	Pliers
Pencil	Cable clamps
Combination tool	Single- and double-pole
Cable ripper	AFCI circuit breakers

 How to Connect Circuit Breakers

Shut off the main circuit breaker if you are working in a subpanel, shut off the feeder breaker in the main panel). Remove the panel cover plate, taking care not to touch the parts inside the panel. Test for power (photo, above right).

Open a knockout in the side of the circuit breaker panel using a screwdriver and hammer. Attach a cable clamp to the knockout.

Hold the cable across the front of the panel near the knockout, and mark the sheathing about ½" inside the edge of the panel. Strip the cable from the marked line to the end using a cable ripper. (There should be 18" to 24" of excess cable.) Insert the cable through the clamp and into the service panel, and then tighten the clamp.

Bend the bare copper grounding wire around the inside edge of the panel to an open setscrew terminal on the grounding terminal bar. Insert the wire into the opening on the terminal bar, and tighten the setscrew. Fold excess wire around the inside edge of the panel.

(Cable clamp)

For 120-volt circuits, bend the white circuit wire around the outside of the panel to an open setscrew terminal on the neutral terminal bar. Clip away excess wire, and then strip ½" of insulation from the wire using a combination tool. Insert the wire into the terminal opening, and tighten the setscrew.

Strip ½" of insulation from the end of the black circuit wire. Insert the wire into the setscrew terminal on a new single-pole circuit breaker, and tighten the setscrew.

Slide one end of the circuit breaker onto the guide hook, and then press it firmly against the bus bar until it snaps into place. (Breaker installation may vary, depending on the manufacturer.) Fold excess black wire around the inside edge of the panel.

Neutral terminal bar

120-volt circuit

240-volt circuit

For 120/240-volt circuit (top): Connect red and black wires to the double-pole breaker. Connect white wire to the neutral terminal bar, and the grounding wire to grounding terminal bar. For 240-volt circuits without a neutral (bottom), attach white and black wires to the double-pole breaker, tagging white wire with black tape. There is no neutral terminal bar connection on this circuit.

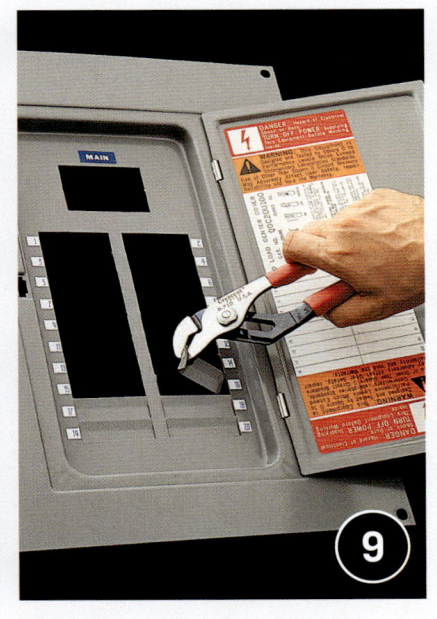

Remove the appropriate breaker tab on the panel cover plate to make room for the new circuit breaker. A single-pole breaker requires one tab, while a double-pole breaker requires two tabs. Reattach the cover plate, and label the new circuit on the panel door index.

Switches

Among wiring devices, switches fail with surprising frequency. If you've carefully wired a new circuit or a fixture and you know you got it right, but when you turn on the power it doesn't work, you should direct your attention to any switches in the line. Even brand-new switches can fail to function correctly. This is why most professional electricians will pay the extra couple of dollars to buy a quality switch out of the gate. It is also why most of them routinely test each switch for continuity before installing it (see pages 88–91).

The most basic switches for home wiring are single-pole switches, which control only one fixture and have only two screw (or push-in) terminals (not counting the grounding screw). Next, three-way switches and four-way switches have more installation possibilities and control circuits that are more complicated to wire. Dimmer switches, isolated ground switches, and motion-sensor switches are some of the other switch options.

Use caution when you handle switches. The wires are usually attached to screw terminals on the sides of the fitting, which makes them very easy to contact if you grab the switch. Always shut off the power to the switch before removing the switch cover plate. Also shut off the power at the panel if you will be working downstream from the switch—never count on a switch that is open to function as a breaker.

In this chapter:
- Wall Switches
- Types of Wall Switches
- Specialty Switches
- Testing Switches

Wall Switches

An average wall switch is turned on and off more than 1,000 times each year. Because switches receive constant use, wire connections can loosen and switch parts gradually wear out. If a switch no longer operates smoothly, it must be replaced.

The methods for replacing a switch vary slightly, depending on the switch type and its location along an electrical circuit. When working on a switch, use the photographs on pages 76–87 to identify your switch type and its wiring configuration. Individual styles may vary, but the basic switch types are universal.

It is possible to replace most ordinary wall switches with a specialty switch, such as a timer switch or an electronic switch. When installing a specialty switch, make sure it is compatible with the wiring configuration and size of the switch box.

NOTICE: Two changes in the NEC affect how new switch wiring should be installed. These changes do not affect existing switch wiring. The pictures and instructions in this book about replacing existing switches show wiring that does not comply with these new requirements. This is because you will probably see noncompliant wiring for many years to come. Pictures and instructions about installing new switch wiring show wiring that complies with these new requirements.

One change requires that a wire with white insulation should not supply current to a light or a switched receptacle, even when the wire is marked as hot. A black or red colored wire should supply current to the outlet. A white colored wire, marked as hot, may supply current to the switch when wiring 3-way and 4-way switches.

The other change requires that a neutral wire be available at switch boxes. An exception allows you to ignore this requirement if the switch box is accessible from above or below, such as from a basement, crawlspace, or attic. This new requirement is intended to allow easier installation of devices, such as intelligent switch controllers, that need power for controller operation. Instructions in this book show connecting wires to screw terminals of switched and receptacles. This the recommended method. Wire connections to many switches and receptacles can also be made using push-in terminals on the back of the switch and receptacle. If you elect to use push-in terminals, you may do so only on 15-amp circuits, and only with #14 AWG wires, unless the switch or receptacle is listed and marked for other types of wires.

A typical wall switch has a movable metal arm that opens and closes the electrical circuit. When the switch is ON, the arm completes the circuit and power flows between the screw terminals and through the black hot wire to the light fixture. When the switch is OFF, the arm lifts away to interrupt the circuit, and no power flows. Switch problems occur if the screw terminals are not tight or if the metal arm inside wears out.

NOTE: The switch at right has had part of its housing removed so the interior workings can be seen. Switches or fixtures that are not in original condition should never be installed.

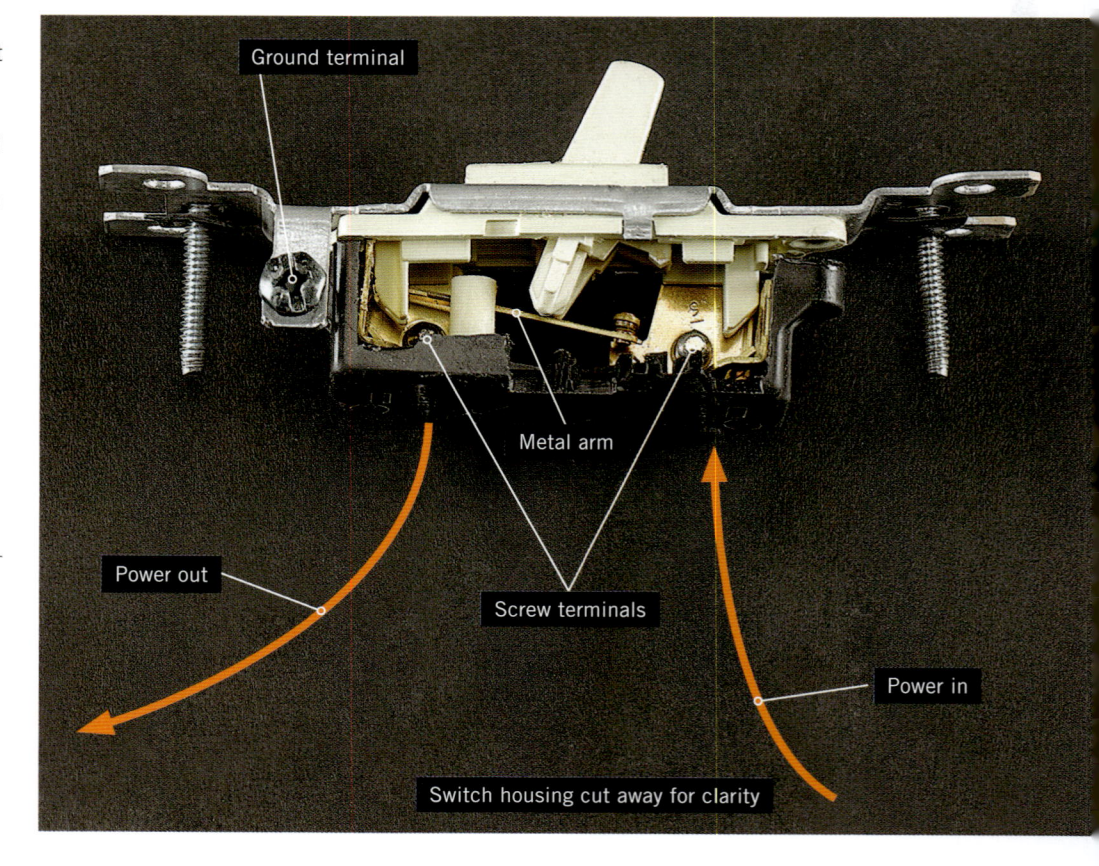

Ground terminal

Power out

Metal arm

Screw terminals

Power in

Switch housing cut away for clarity

Rotary snap switches are found in many installations completed between 1900 and 1920. The handle is twisted clockwise to turn light on and off. The switch is enclosed in a ceramic housing.

Push-button switches were widely used from 1920 until about 1940. Many switches of this type are still in operation. Reproductions of this switch type are available for restoration projects.

Toggle switches were introduced in the 1930s. This early design has a switch mechanism that is mounted in a ceramic housing sealed with a layer of insulating paper.

Toggle switches were improved during the 1950s and are now the most commonly used type. This switch type was the first to use a sealed plastic housing that protects the inner switch mechanism from dust and moisture.

Mercury switches became common in the early 1960s. They conduct electrical current by means of a sealed vial of mercury. No longer manufactured for home use, old mercury switches are considered a hazardous waste.

Electronic motion-sensor switches have an infrared eye that senses movement and automatically turns on lights when a person enters a room. Motion-sensor switches can provide added security against intruders.

Types of Wall Switches

Wall switches are available in three general types. To reconnect or replace a switch, it is important to identify its type.

Single-pole switches are used to control a set of lights from one location. Three-way switches are used to control a set of lights from two different locations and are always installed in pairs. Four-way switches are used in combination with a pair of three-way switches to control a set of lights from three or more locations.

Identify switch types by counting the screw terminals. Single-pole switches have two screw terminals, three-way switches have three screw terminals, and four-way switches have four. Most switches include a grounding screw terminal, which is identified by its green color.

When replacing a switch, choose a new switch that has the same number of screw terminals as the old one. The location of the screws on the switch body varies depending on the manufacturer, but these differences will not affect the switch operation.

Whenever possible, connect switches using the screw terminals rather than push-in fittings. Some specialty switches (pages 84–87) have wire leads instead of screw terminals. They are connected to circuit wires with wire connectors.

The recommended way to connect a wall switch to circuit wires is to the screw terminals. The push-in fittings on the back may be used, with restrictions. A switch may have a stamped strip gauge that indicates how much insulation must be stripped from the circuit wires to make the connections.

The switch body is attached to a metal mounting strap that allows it to be mounted in an electrical box. Several rating stamps are found on the strap and on the back of the switch. The abbreviation UL or UND. LAB. INC. LIST means that the switch meets the safety standards of the Underwriters Laboratories. Switches also are stamped with maximum voltage and amperage ratings. Standard wall switches are rated 15A or 125V. Voltage ratings of 110, 120, and 125 are considered to be identical for purposes of identification.

For standard wall switch installations, choose a switch that has a wire gauge rating of #12 or #14. For wire systems with solid-core copper wiring, use only switches marked COPPER, CU, or CO/ALR. For aluminum wiring, use only switches marked CO/ALR. Note that while CO/ALR switches and receptacles are approved by the National Electrical Code for use with aluminum wiring, the Consumer Products Safety Commission does not recommend using these. Switches and receptacles marked AL/CU can no longer be used with aluminum wiring, according to the National Electrical Code.

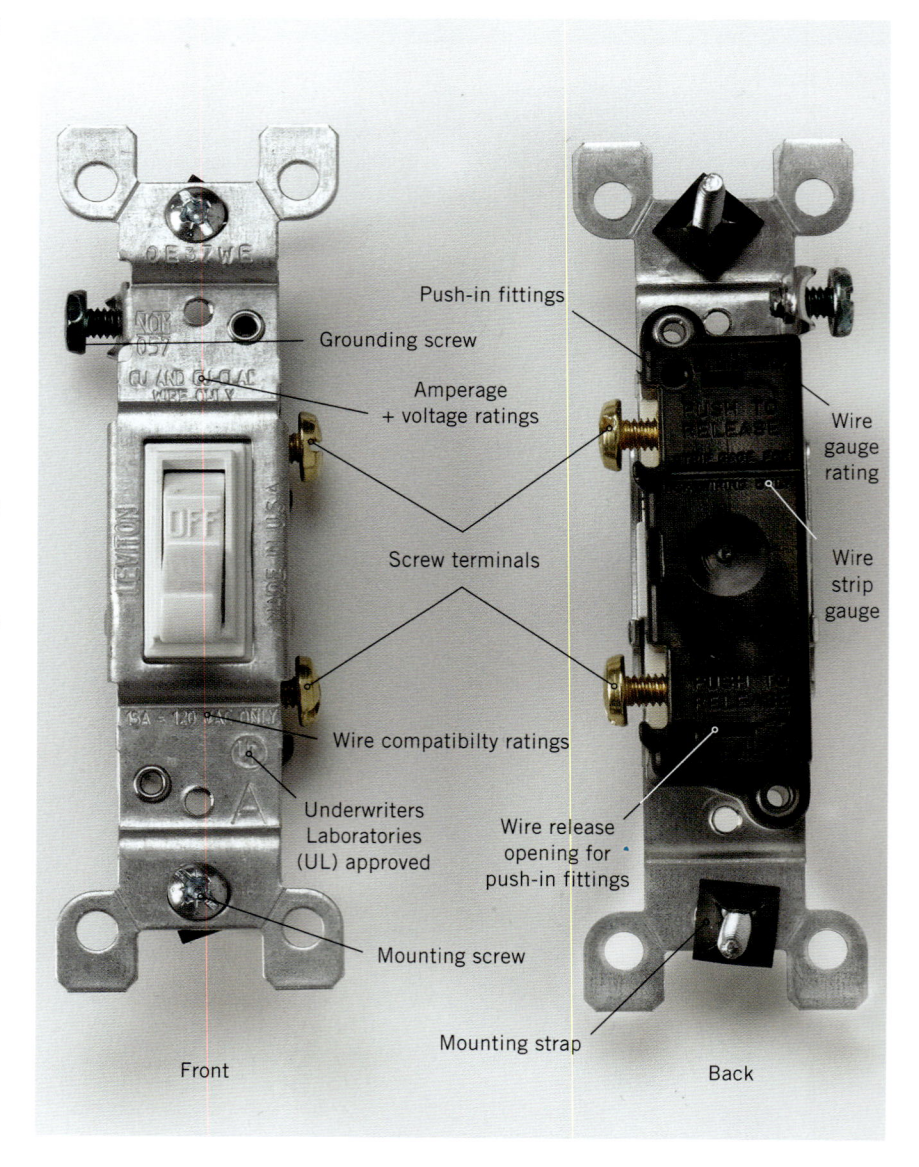

Push-in fittings

Grounding screw

Amperage + voltage ratings

Wire gauge rating

Screw terminals

Wire strip gauge

Wire compatibilty ratings

Underwriters Laboratories (UL) approved

Wire release opening for push-in fittings

Mounting screw

Mounting strap

Front

Back

Single-Pole Wall Switches

A single-pole switch is the most common type of wall switch. It has ON-OFF markings on the switch lever and is used to control a set of lights, an appliance, or a receptacle from a single location. A single-pole switch has two screw terminals and a grounding screw. When installing a single-pole switch, check to make sure the ON marking shows when the switch lever is in the up position.

In a correctly wired single-pole switch, a hot circuit wire is attached to each screw terminal. However, the color and number of wires inside the switch box will vary, depending on the location of the switch along the electrical circuit.

If two cables enter the box, then the switch lies in the middle of the circuit. In this installation, both of the hot wires attached to the switch are black.

If only one cable enters the box, then the switch lies at the end of the circuit. In this installation (sometimes called a switch loop), one of the hot wires is black, but the other hot wire usually is white. A white hot wire should be coded with black tape or paint.

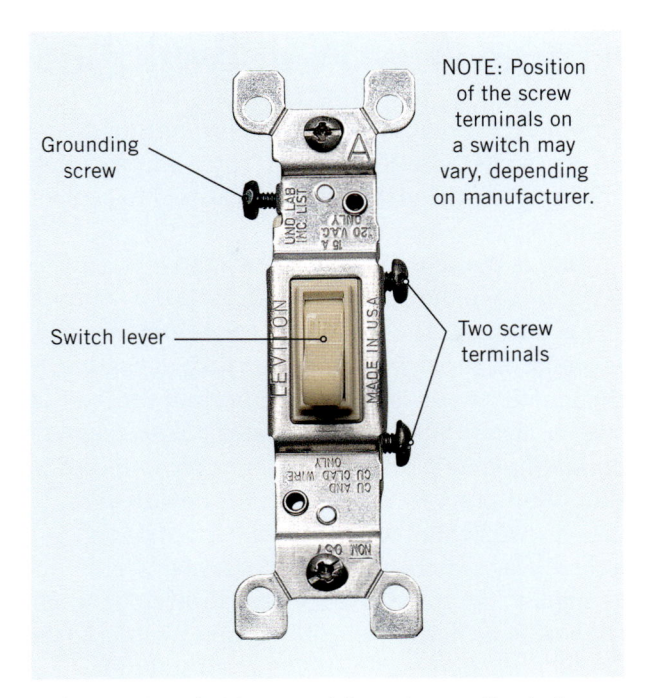

NOTE: Position of the screw terminals on a switch may vary, depending on manufacturer.

Grounding screw

Switch lever

Two screw terminals

A single-pole switch is essentially an interruption in the black power supply wire that is opened or closed with the toggle. Single-pole switches are the simplest of all home wiring switches.

Typical Single-Pole Switch Installations

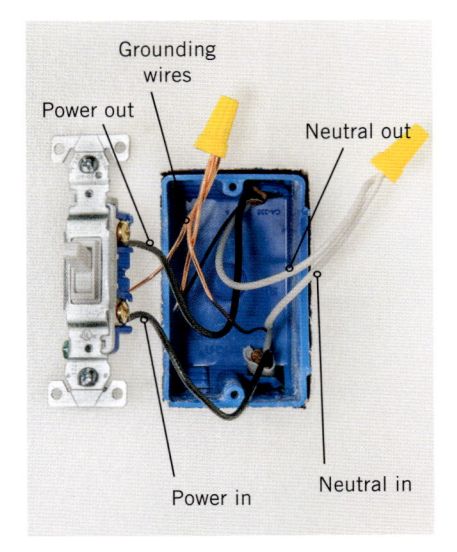

Grounding wires

Power out

Neutral out

Power in

Neutral in

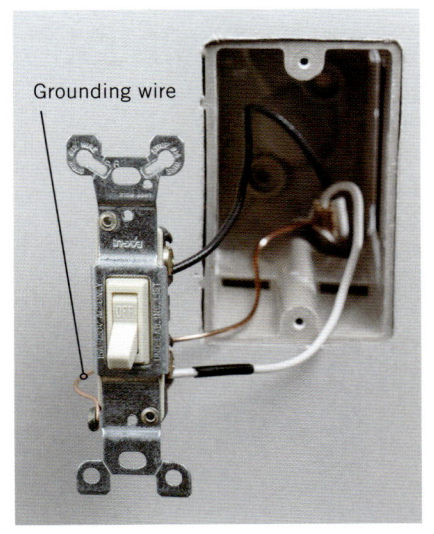

Grounding wire

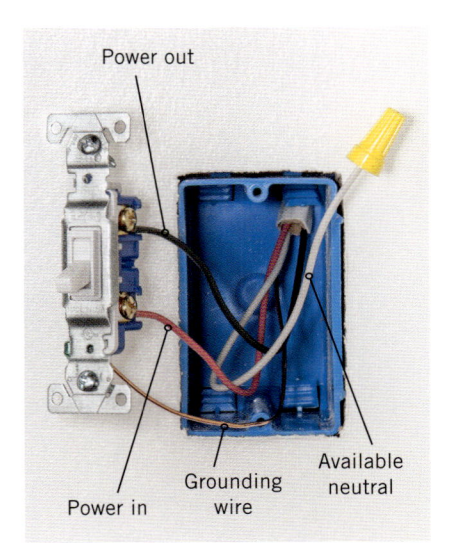

Power out

Power in

Grounding wire

Available neutral

Two cables enter the box when a switch is located in the middle of a circuit. Each cable has a white and a black insulated wire, plus a bare copper grounding wire. The black wires are hot and are connected to the screw terminals on the switch. The white wires are neutral and are joined together with a wire connector. Grounding wires are pigtailed to the switch.

Old method: One cable enters the box when a switch is located at the end of a circuit. In this installation, both of the insulated wires are hot. The white wire should be labeled with black tape or paint to identify it as a hot wire. The grounding wire is connected to the switch grounding screw.

New method: In new switch wiring, the white wire should not supply current to the switched device and a separate neutral wire should be available in the switch box.

Three-Way Wall Switches

Three-way switches have three screw terminals and do not have ON-OFF markings. Three-way switches are always installed in pairs and are used to control lights from two locations.

One of the screw terminals on a three-way switch is darker than the others. This screw is the common screw terminal. The position of the common screw terminal on the switch body may vary, depending on the manufacturer. Before disconnecting a three-way switch, always label the wire that is connected to the common screw terminal. It must be reconnected to the common screw terminal on the new switch.

The two lighter-colored screw terminals on a three-way switch are called the traveler screw terminals. The traveler terminals are interchangeable, so there is no need to label the wires attached to them.

Because three-way switches are installed in pairs, it sometimes is difficult to determine which of the switches is causing a problem. The switch that receives greater use is more likely to fail, but you may need to inspect both switches to find the source of the problem.

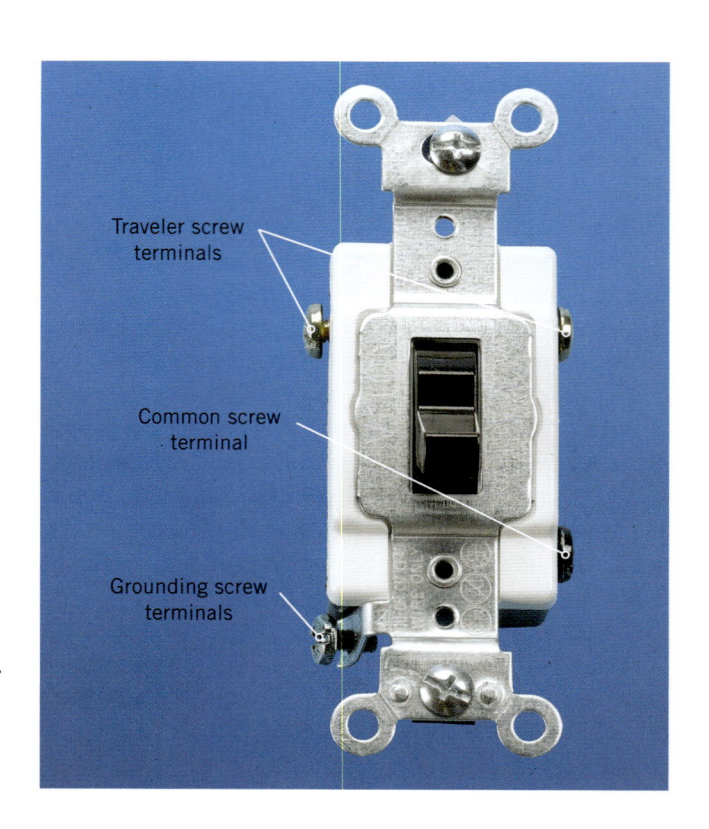

Traveler screw terminals

Common screw terminal

Grounding screw terminals

Typical Three-Way Switch Installation

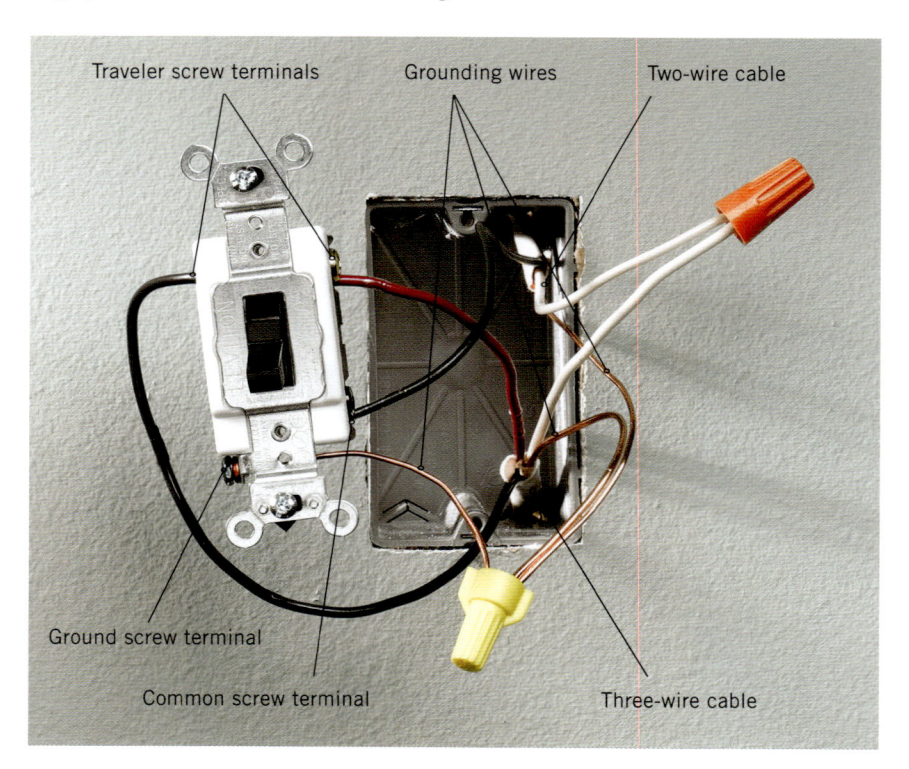

Traveler screw terminals

Grounding wires

Two-wire cable

Ground screw terminal

Common screw terminal

Three-wire cable

Two cables enter the box: One cable has two wires, plus a bare copper grounding wire; the other cable has three wires, plus a ground. The black wire from the two-wire cable is connected to the dark common screw terminal. The red and black wires from the three-wire cable are connected to the traveler screw terminals. The white neutral wires are joined together with a wire connector, and the grounding wires are pigtailed to the switch grounding terminal.

How to Replace a Three-Way Wall Switch

Turn off the power to the switch at the panel, and then remove the switch cover plate and mounting screws. Holding the mounting strap carefully, pull the switch from the box. Be careful not to touch the bare wires or screw terminals until they have been tested for power.

NOTE: If you are installing a new switch circuit, you must provide a neutral conductor at the switch.

Test for power by touching the probe of a noncontact voltage tester to each wire and screw terminal. Tester should not glow. If it does, there is still power entering the box. Return to the panel, and turn off the correct circuit, then test again for power.

Common screw terminal

Common screw terminal

Locate the dark common screw terminal, and use masking tape to label the "common" wire attached to it. Disconnect wires and remove switch. Test the switch for continuity. If it tests faulty, buy a replacement. Inspect wires for nicks and scratches. If necessary, clip damaged wires and strip them.

Connect the common wire to the dark common screw terminal on the switch. On most three-way switches, the common screw terminal is black. Or it may be labeled with the word COMMON stamped on the back of the switch. Reconnect the grounding screw, and connect it to the circuit grounding wires with a pigtail.

Connect the remaining two circuit wires to the screw terminals. These wires are interchangeable and can be connected to either screw terminal. Carefully tuck the wires into the box. Remount the switch, and attach the cover plate. Turn on the power at the panel.

Four-Way Wall Switches

Four-way switches have four screw terminals and do not have ON-OFF markings. Four-way switches are always installed between a pair of three-way switches. This switch combination makes it possible to control a set of lights from three or more locations. Four-way switches are common in homes where large rooms contain multiple living areas, such as a kitchen opening into a dining room. Switch problems in a four-way installation can be caused by loose connections or worn parts in a four-way switch or in one of the three-way switches (facing page).

In a typical installation, there will be a pair of three-wire cables that enter the box for the four-way switch. With most switches, the black and red wires from one cable should be attached to the bottom or top pair of screw terminals, and the black and red wires from the other cable should be attached to the remaining pair of screw terminals. However, not all switches are configured the same way, and wiring configurations in the box may vary, so always study the wiring diagram that comes with the switch.

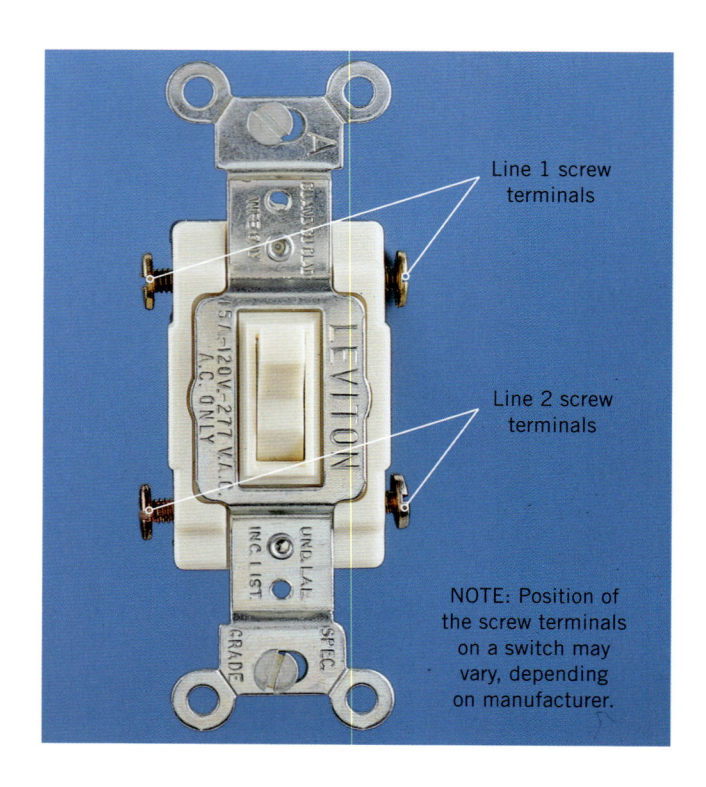

Line 1 screw terminals

Line 2 screw terminals

NOTE: Position of the screw terminals on a switch may vary, depending on manufacturer.

Common Four-Way Switch Installation

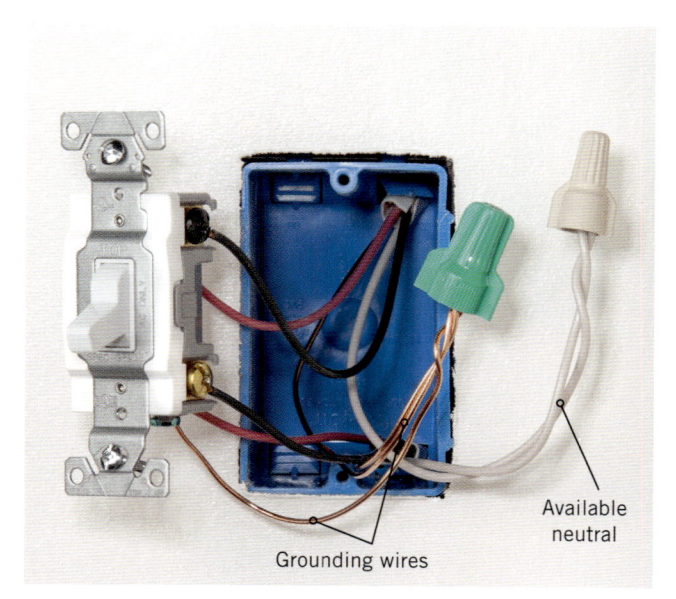

Available neutral

Grounding wires

Four wires are connected to a four-way switch. The black and red wires from one cable are attached to the top pair of screw terminals, while the black and red wires from the other cable are attached to the bottom screw terminals. In new switch wiring, the white wires are joined and bypass the switch but remain available for future use.

Switch variation: Some four-way switches have a wiring guide stamped on the back to help simplify installation. For the switch shown above, one pair of color-matched circuit wires will be connected to the screw terminals marked LINE 1, while the other pair of wires will be attached to the screw terminals marked LINE 2.

How to Replace a Four-Way Wall Switch

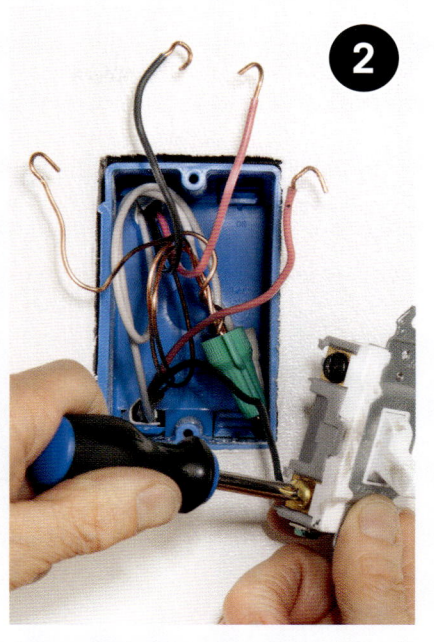

Turn off the power to the switch at the panel, and then remove the switch cover plate and mounting screws. Holding the mounting strap carefully, pull the switch from the box. Be careful not to touch any bare wires or screw terminals until they have been tested for power. Test for power by touching each wire and terminal with a noncontact voltage tester. The tester should not glow. If it does, there is still power entering the box. Return to the panel, and turn off the correct circuit.

Disconnect the wires and inspect them for nicks and scratches. If necessary, clip damaged wires and strip them. Test the switch for continuity (pages 88–91). Buy a replacement if the switch tests faulty.

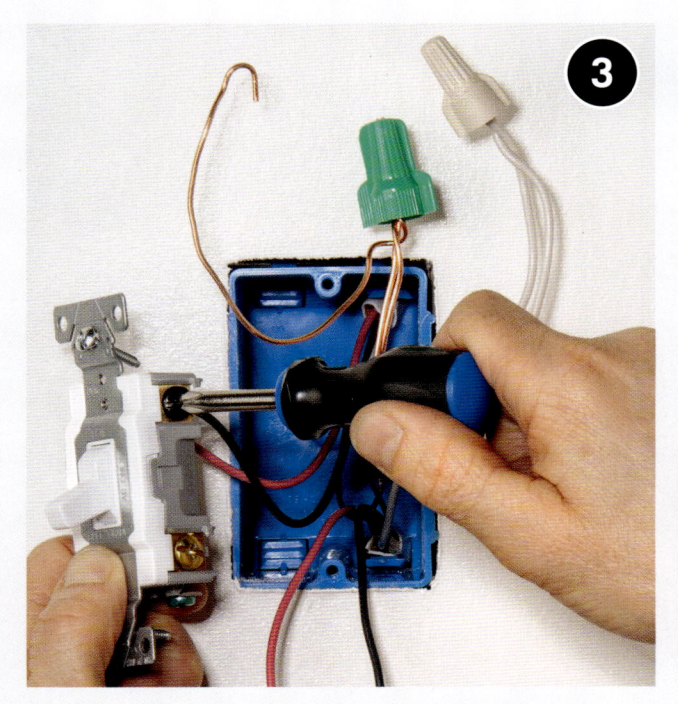

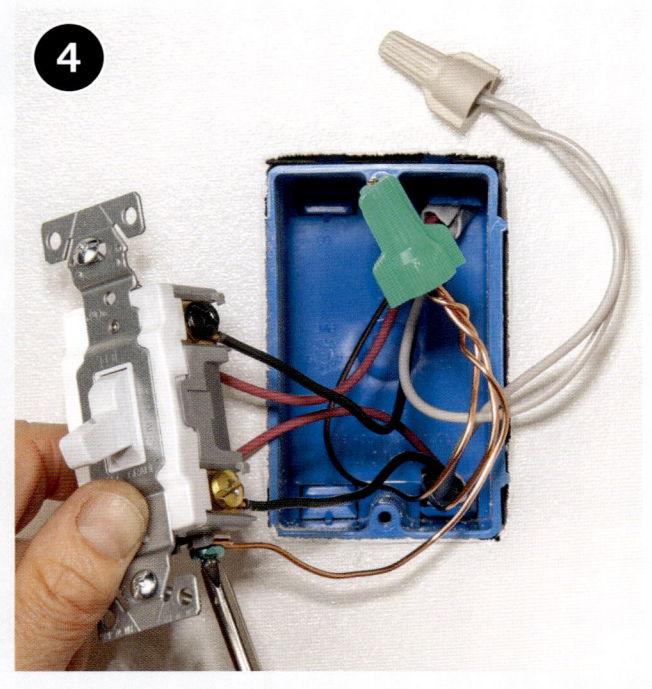

Connect two hot wires from one incoming cable to the top set of screw terminals.

Attach remaining hot wires to the other set of screw terminals. Pigtail the grounding wires to the grounding screw. Carefully tuck the wires inside the switch box, and then remount the switch and cover plate. Turn on power at the panel.

Double Switches

A double switch has two switch levers in a single housing. It is used to control two light fixtures or appliances from the same switch box.

In most installations, both halves of the switch are powered by the same circuit. In these single-circuit installations, three wires are connected to the double switch. One wire, called the feed wire (which is hot), supplies power to both halves of the switch. The other wires, called the switch leg, carry power out to the individual light fixtures or appliances.

In rare installations, each half of the switch is powered by a separate circuit. In these separate-circuit installations, four wires are connected to the switch, and the metal connecting tab joining two of the screw terminals is removed (see photo below).

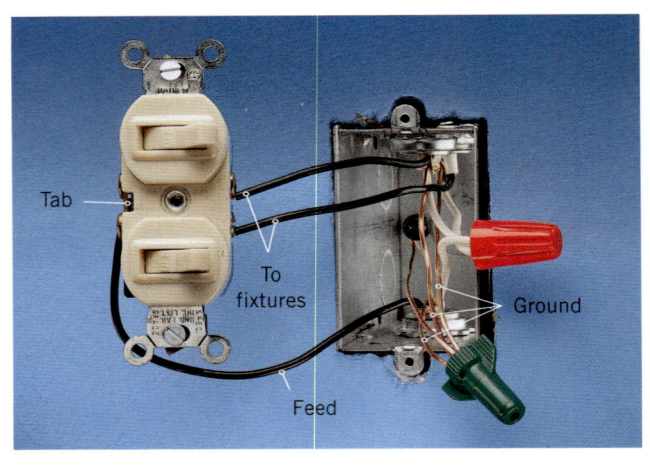

Single-circuit wiring: Three black wires are attached to the switch. The black feed wire bringing power into the box is connected to the side of the switch that has a connecting tab. The wires carrying power out to the light fixtures or appliances are connected to the side of the switch that does not have a connecting tab. The white neutral wires are connected together with a wire connector.

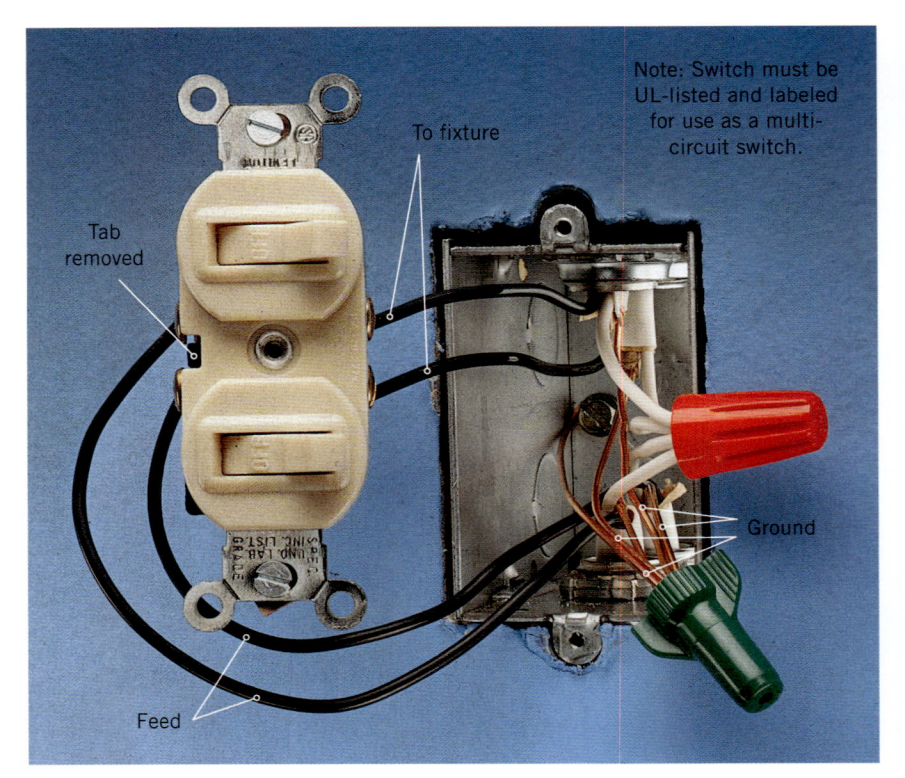

Separate-circuit wiring: Four black wires are attached to the switch. Feed wires from the power source are attached to the side of the switch that has a connecting tab, and the connecting tab is removed (photo, right). Wires carrying power from the switch to light fixtures or appliances are connected to the side of the switch that does not have a connecting tab. White neutral wires are connected together with a wire connector.

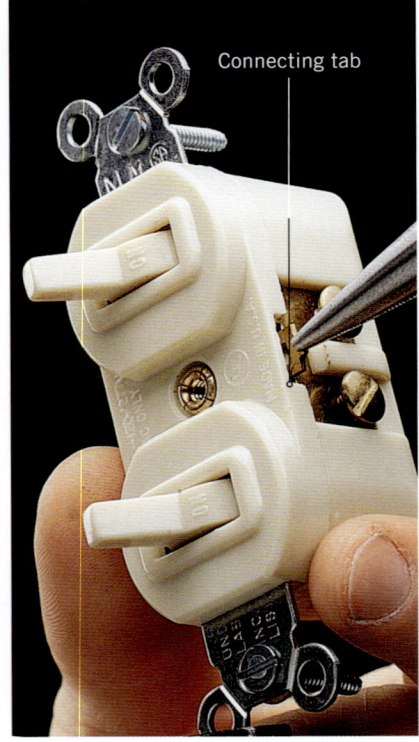

Remove the connecting tab on a double switch when wired in a separate-circuit installation. The tab can be removed with needlenose pliers or a screwdriver.

Pilot-Light Switches

A pilot-light switch has a built-in bulb that glows when power flows through the switch to a light fixture or appliance. Pilot-light switches often are installed for convenience if a light fixture or appliance cannot be seen from the switch location. Basement lights, garage lights, and attic exhaust fans frequently are controlled by pilot-light switches.

A pilot-light switch requires a neutral wire connection. A switch box that contains a single two-wire cable has only hot wires and cannot be fitted with a pilot-light switch.

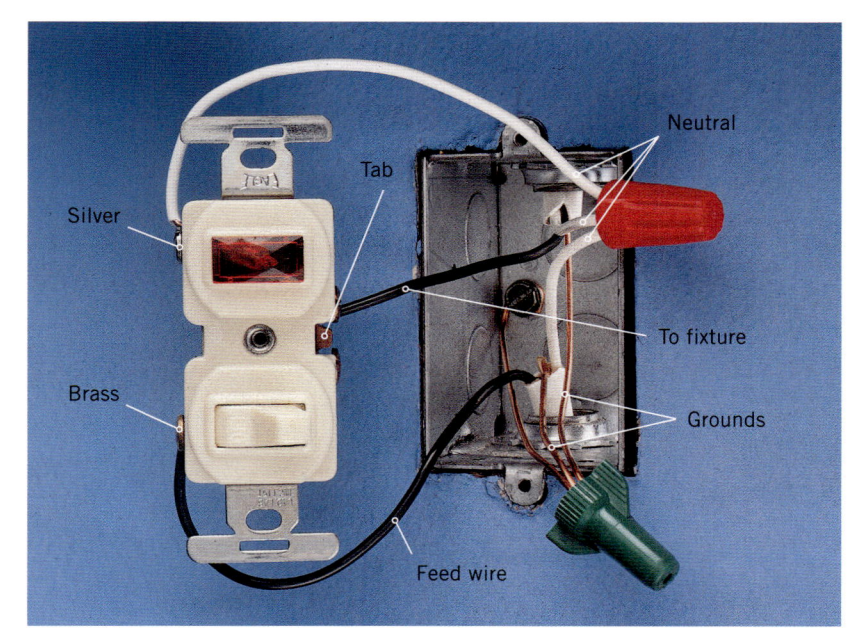

Pilot-light switch wiring: Three wires are connected to the switch. One black wire is the feed wire that brings power into the box. It is connected to the brass (gold) screw terminal on the side of the switch that does not have a connecting tab. The white neutral wires are pigtailed to the silver screw terminal. The black wire carrying power out to a light fixture or appliance is connected to the screw terminal on the side of the switch that has a connecting tab.

Switch/Receptacles

A switch/receptacle combines a grounded receptacle with a single-pole wall switch. In a room that does not have enough wall receptacles, electrical service can be improved by replacing a single-pole switch with a switch/receptacle.

A switch/receptacle requires a neutral wire connection. A switch box that contains a single two-wire cable has only hot wires and cannot be fitted with a switch/receptacle.

A switch/receptacle can be installed in one of two ways. In the most common installations, the receptacle is hot even when the switch is off (photo, right).

In rare installations, a switch/receptacle is wired so the receptacle is hot only when the switch is on. In this installation, the hot wires are reversed, so that the feed wire is attached to the brass screw terminal on the side of the switch that does not have a connecting tab.

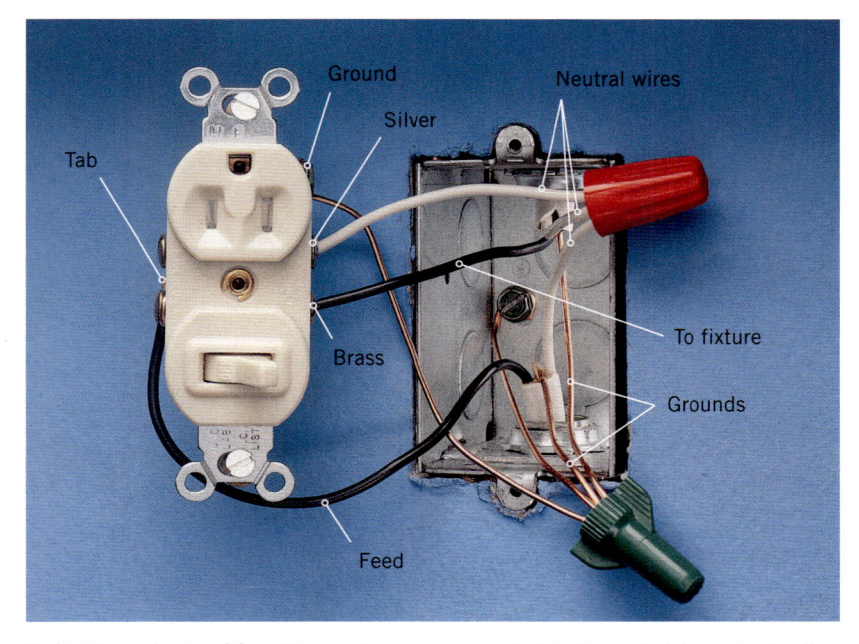

Switch/receptacle wiring: Three wires are connected to the switch/receptacle. One of the hot wires is the feed wire that brings power into the box. It is connected to the side of the switch that has a connecting tab. The other hot wire carries power out to the light fixture or appliance. It is connected to the brass screw terminal on the side that does not have a connecting tab. The white neutral wire is pigtailed to the silver screw terminal. The grounding wires must be pigtailed to the green grounding screw on the switch/receptacle and to the grounded metal box.

Specialty Switches

Your house may have several types of specialty switches. Dimmer switches (pages 86–87) are used frequently to control light intensity in dining and recreation areas. Timer switches and time-delay switches (below) are used to control light fixtures and exhaust fans automatically. Electronic switches provide added convenience and home security, and they are easy to install. Electronic switches are durable, and they rarely need replacement.

Most specialty switches have preattached wire leads instead of screw terminals and are connected to circuit wires with wire connectors. Some motor-driven timer switches require a neutral wire connection and cannot be installed in switch boxes that have only one cable with two hot wires. It is precisely due to the rise in popularity of "smart" switches that the NEC Code was changed in 2014 to require an available neutral wire in newly installed switch boxes.

If a specialty switch is not operating correctly, you may be able to test it with a continuity tester. Timer switches and time-delay switches can be tested for continuity, but dimmer switches cannot be tested. With electronic switches, the manual switch can be tested for continuity, but the automatic features cannot be tested.

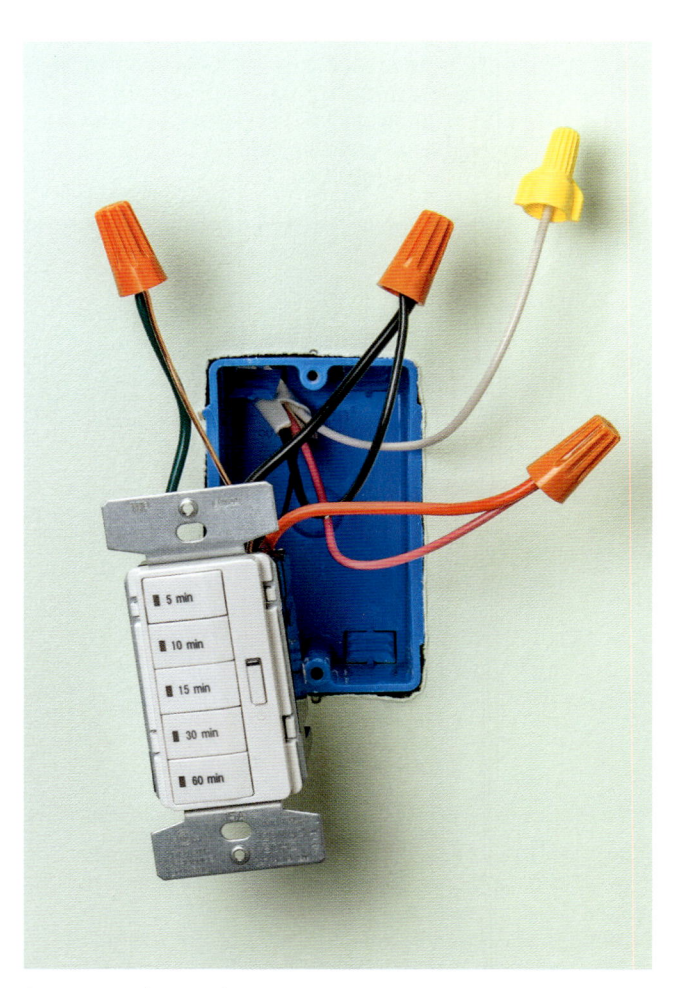

Countdown timer switch. This rocker-type switch gives you the option to easily program the switch to shut off after a specified time: from 5 to 60 minutes. Garage lights or basement lights are good applications: anywhere you want the light to stay on long enough to allow you to exit, but not to stay on indefinitely. These switches often are used to control exhaust fans.

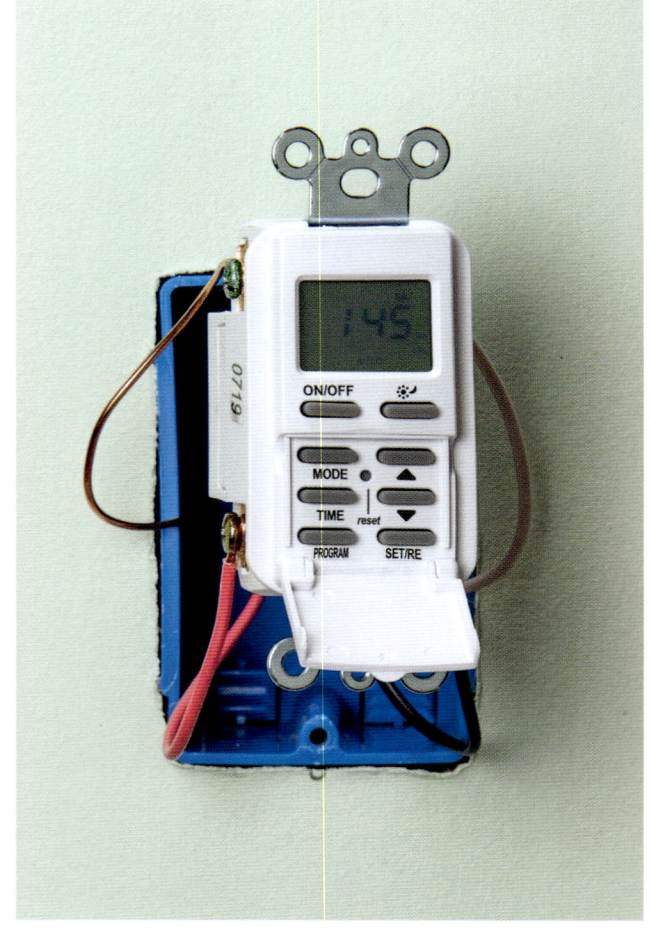

Programmable timer switch. A digital or dial-type timer allows you to program the switch to turn on for specific time periods at designated times of day within a 24-hour cycle. Security lights, space heaters, towel warmers, and radiant floors are typical applications.

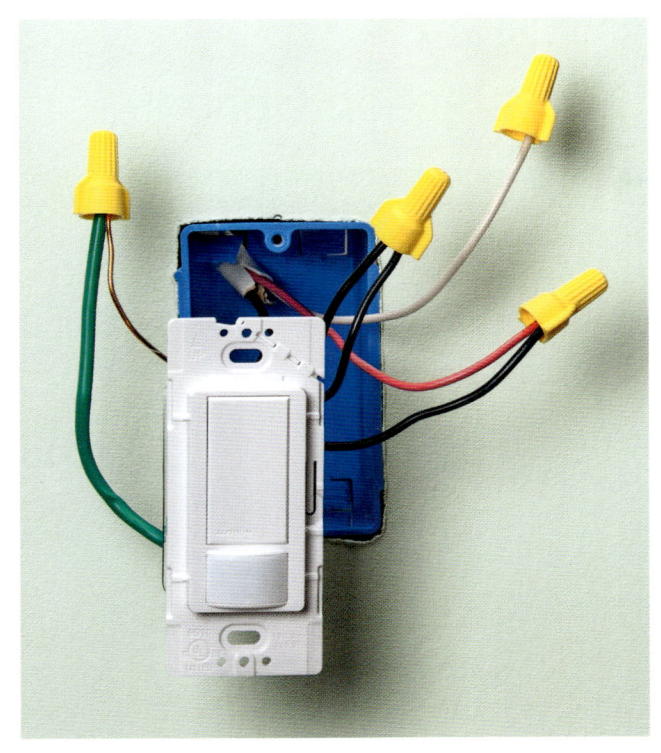

Occupancy sensor. Many smart switches incorporate a motion detector that will switch the lights on if they sense movement in the room and will also shut them off when no movement is detected for a period of time. The model shown above also has a dimmer function for further energy savings.

Spring-wound timer switch. A relatively simple device, this timer switch functions exactly like a kitchen timer, employing a hand-turned dial to and spring mechanism to shut the switch off in increments up to 15 minutes.

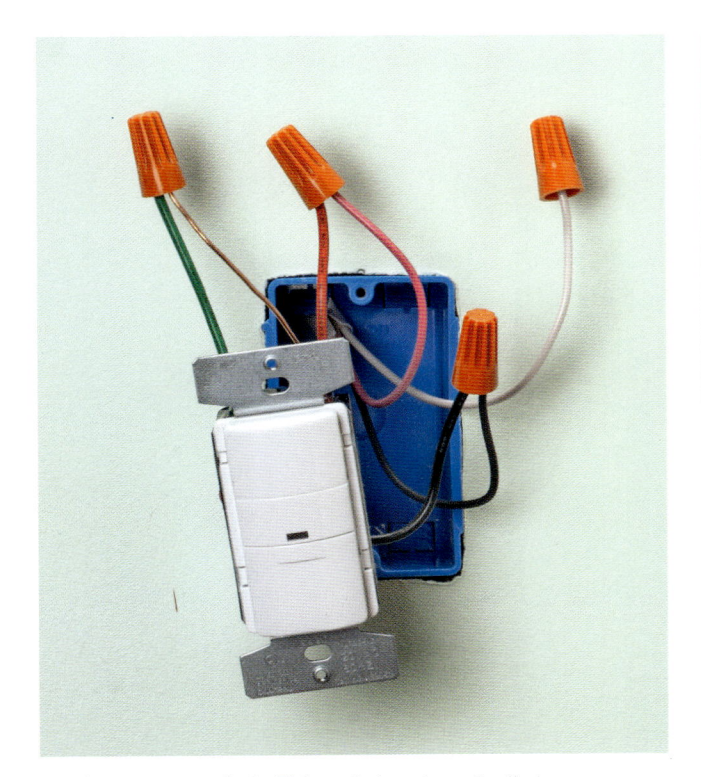

Daylight sensor switch. This switch automatically turns on when light levels drop below a proscribed level. It can also be programmed as an occupancy sensor to shut off when the room is vacant and turn on when the room is entered.

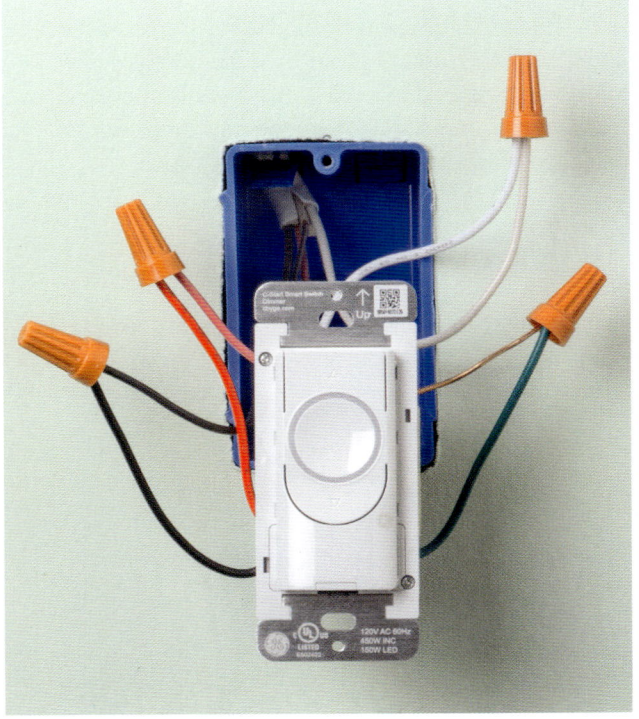

Smart switches let you control lights from a smart phone or other compatible device, such as a smart speaker, without the need for a central hub (a common requirement with early smart home systems).

Dimmer Switches

A dimmer switch makes it possible to vary the brightness of a light fixture. Dimmers are often installed in dining rooms, recreation areas, or bedrooms. Do not install a dimmer at stairway light switches unless you install a dimmer at all switches.

Any standard single-pole switch can be replaced with a dimmer, as long as the switch box is of adequate size. Dimmer switches have larger bodies than standard switches. They also generate a small amount of heat that must dissipate. For these reasons, dimmers should not be installed in undersized electrical boxes or in boxes that are crowded with circuit wires. Always follow the manufacturer's specifications for installation.

In lighting configurations that use three-way switches (pages 78–79), buy a packaged pair of three-way dimmers designed to work together.

Dimmer switches are available in several styles (see photo, right). All types have wire leads instead of screw terminals, and they are connected to circuit wires using wire connectors. Some types have a green grounding lead that should be connected to the grounded metal box or to the bare copper grounding wires. Until recently, dimmers were designed to work only with incandescent lamps. They may not work well, or may not work at all, with CFL and LED lamps. When replacing incandescent lamps with CFL and LED lamps, make sure the new lamps are designed to work with older dimmers. When replacing dimmers, make sure the new dimmers are designed to work with CFL and LED lamps.

TOOLS + MATERIALS

Screwdriver	Needlenose pliers	Wire connectors
Circuit tester		Masking tape

TIP: AUTOMATIC DIMMERS

An automatic dimmer has an electronic sensor that adjusts the light fixture to compensate for the changing levels of natural light. An automatic dimmer also can be operated manually. For another example, see page 85, lower left.

Switch Action Options

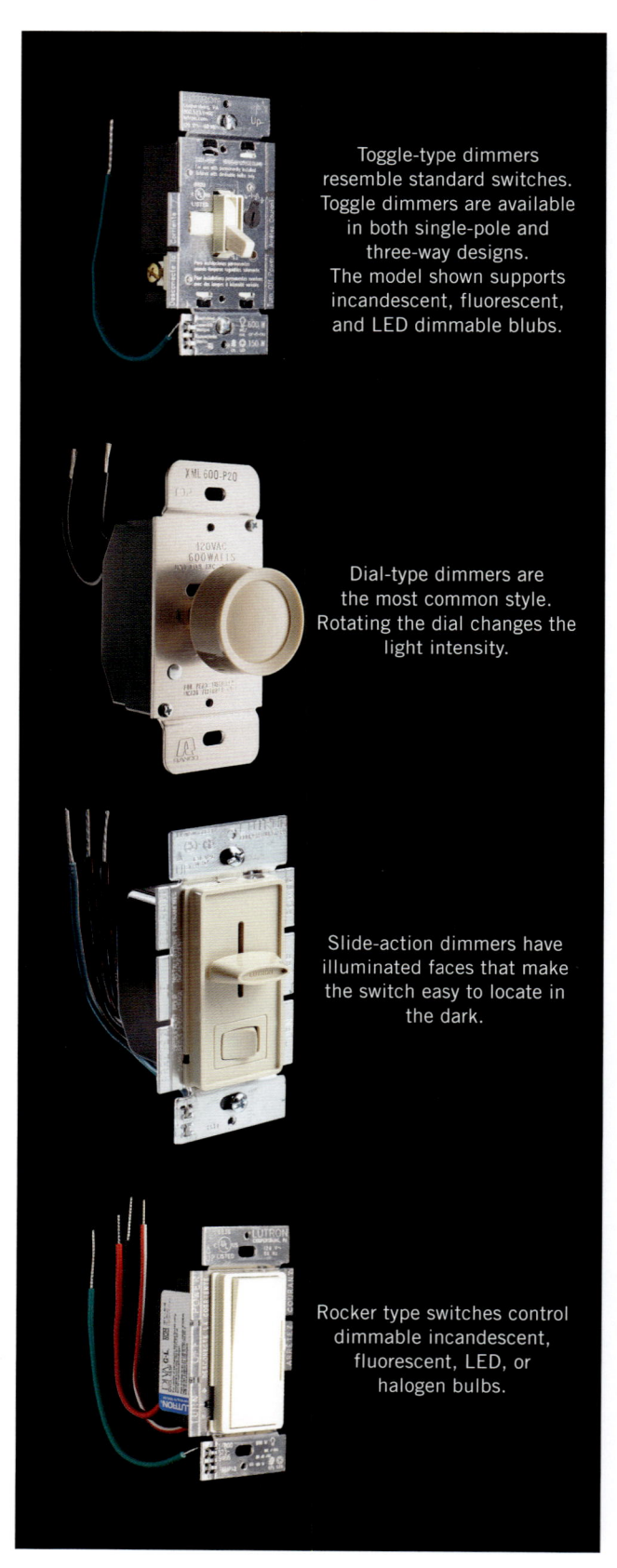

Toggle-type dimmers resemble standard switches. Toggle dimmers are available in both single-pole and three-way designs. The model shown supports incandescent, fluorescent, and LED dimmable blubs.

Dial-type dimmers are the most common style. Rotating the dial changes the light intensity.

Slide-action dimmers have illuminated faces that make the switch easy to locate in the dark.

Rocker type switches control dimmable incandescent, fluorescent, LED, or halogen bulbs.

How to Install a Dimmer Switch

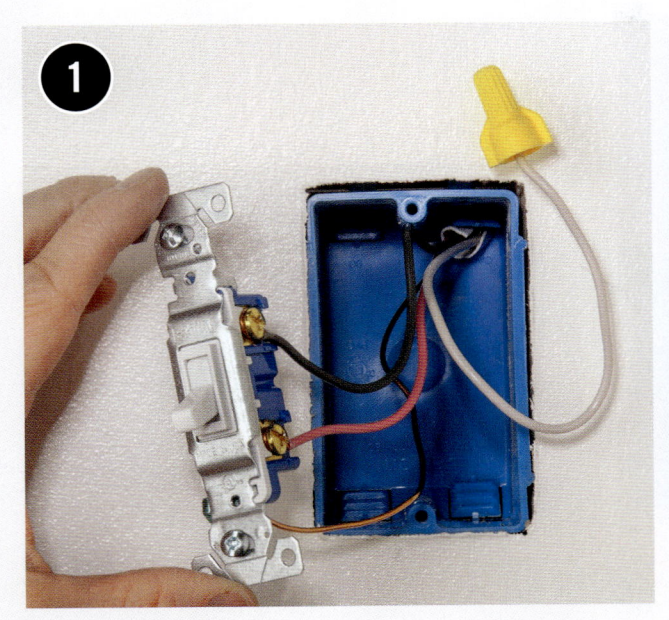

1 Turn off power to the switch at the panel, and then remove the cover plate and mounting screws. Holding the mounting straps carefully, pull the switch from the box. Be careful not to touch bare wires or screw terminals until they have been tested for power. In new switch wiring, the white wire should not supply current to the switched device, and a separate neutral wire should be available in the switch box.

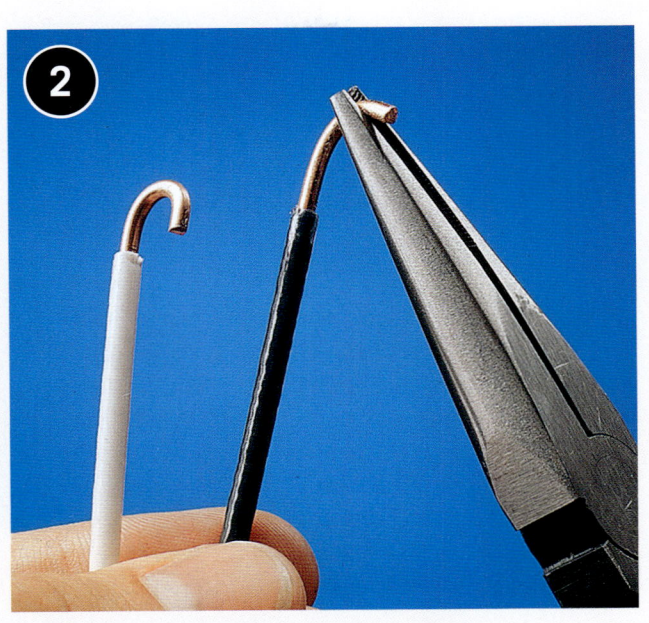

2 Disconnect the circuit wires and remove the switch. Straighten the circuit wires, and clip the ends, leaving about ½" of the bare wire end exposed.

3 Connect the wire leads on the dimmer switch to the circuit wires using wire connectors. The switch leads are interchangeable and can be attached to either of the two hot circuit wires.

4 A three-way dimmer has an additional wire lead. This "common" lead is connected to the common circuit wire. When replacing a standard three-way switch with a dimmer, the common circuit wire is attached to the darkest screw terminal on the old switch. In new switch wiring, the white wire should not supply current to the switched device, and a separate neutral wire should be available in the switch box.

Testing Switches

A switch that does not work properly may have worn or broken internal parts. Test switches with a battery-operated continuity tester. The continuity tester detects any break in the metal pathway inside the switch. Replace the switch if the continuity tester shows the switch to be faulty.

Never use a continuity tester on wires that might carry live current. Always shut off the power and disconnect the switch before testing for continuity.

Some specialty switches, such as dimmers, cannot be tested for continuity. Electronic switches can be tested for manual operation using a continuity tester, but the automatic operation of these switches cannot be tested.

How to Test a Single-Pole Wall Switch

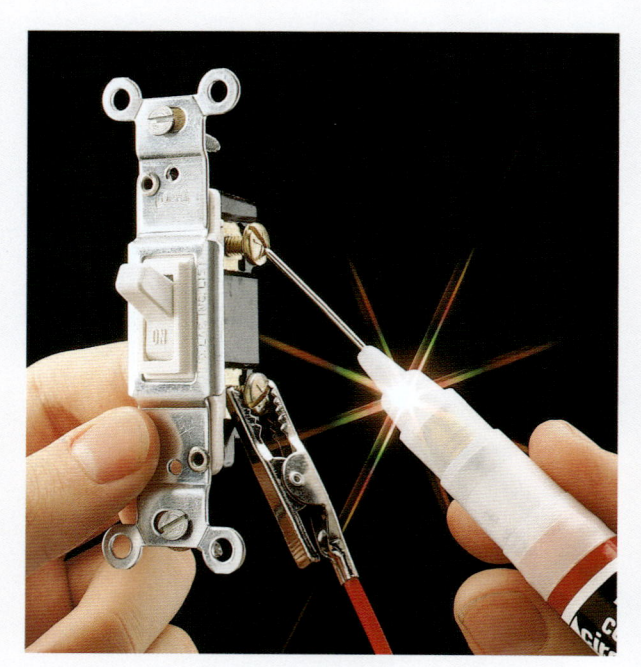

Attach the clip of the tester to one of the screw terminals. Touch the tester probe to the other screw terminal. Flip the switch lever from ON to OFF. If the switch is good, the tester glows when the lever is ON but not when it's OFF.

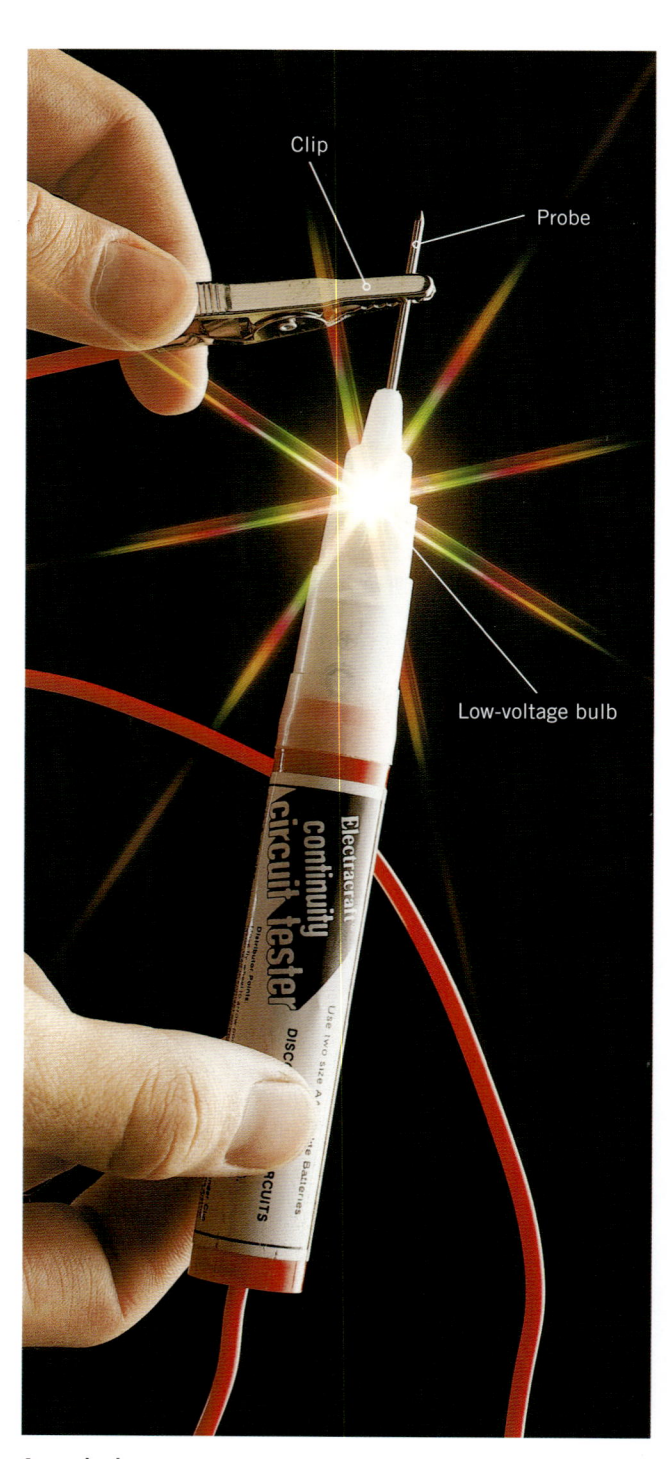

Clip

Probe

Low-voltage bulb

A continuity tester uses battery-generated current to test the metal pathways running through switches and other electrical fixtures. Always "test" the tester before use. Touch the tester clip to the metal probe. The tester should glow. If not, then the battery or lightbulb is dead and must be replaced.

How to Test a Three-Way Wall Switch

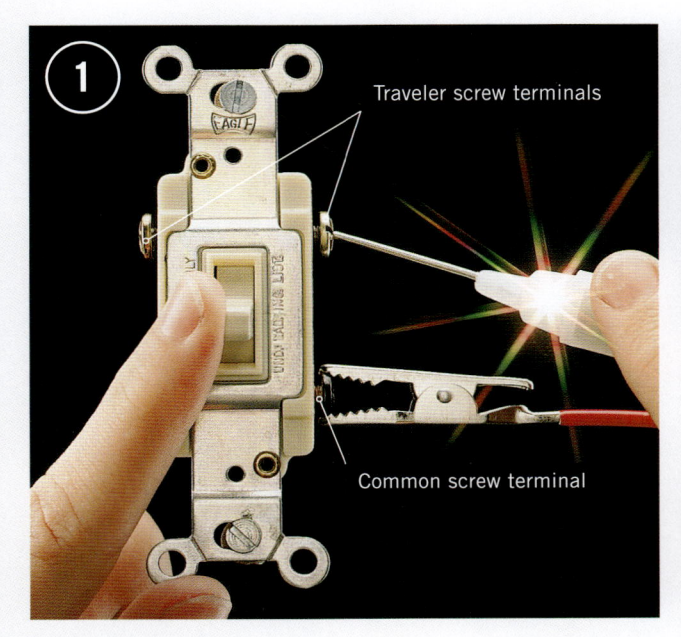

Traveler screw terminals

Common screw terminal

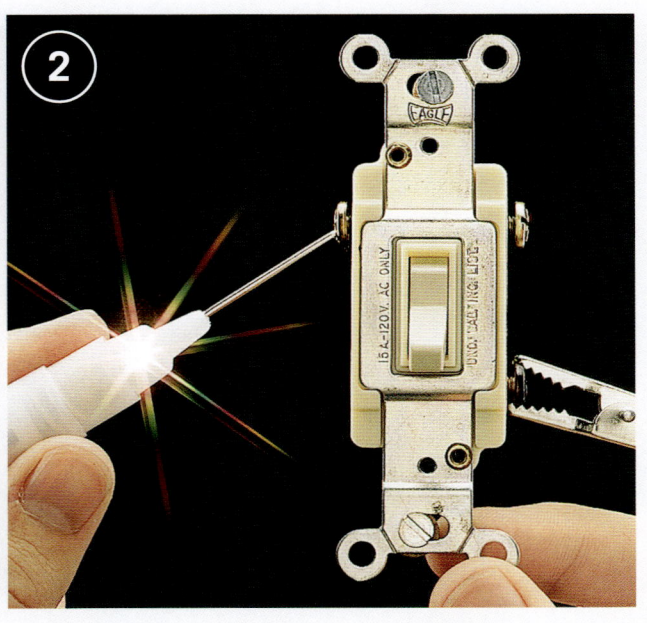

Attach the tester clip to the dark common screw terminal. Touch the tester probe to one of the traveler screw terminals, and flip the switch lever back and forth. If the switch is good, the tester should glow when the lever is in one position, but not both.

Touch the probe to the other traveler screw terminal, and flip the switch lever back and forth. If the switch is good, the tester will glow only when the switch lever is in the position opposite from the positive test in step 1.

 # How to Test a Four-Way Wall Switch

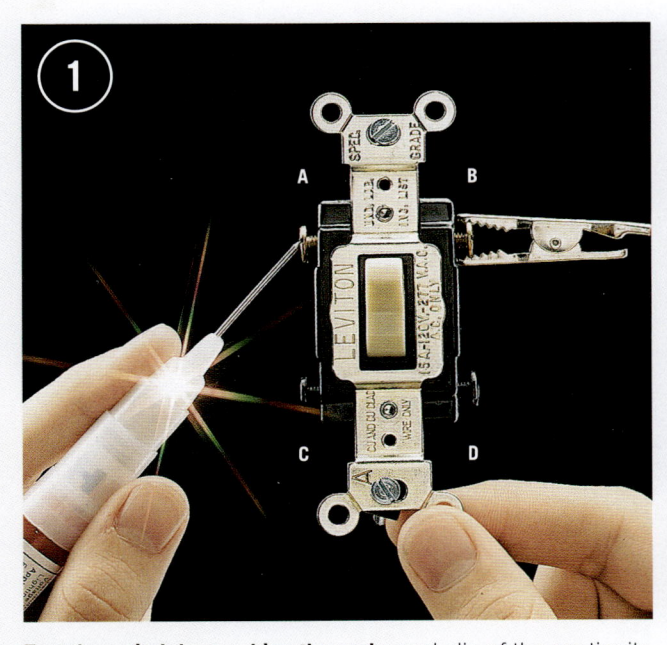

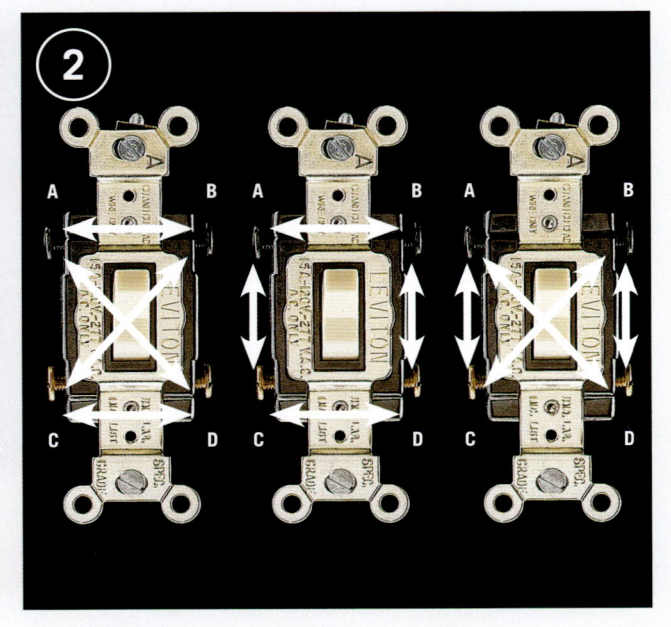

Test the switch by touching the probe and clip of the continuity tester to each pair of screw terminals (A-B, C-D, A-D, B-C, A-C, B-D). The test should show continuous pathways between the two different pairs of screw terminals. Flip the lever to the opposite position, and repeat the test. It should show continuous pathways between two different pairs of screw terminals.

If the switch is good, the test will show a total of four continuous pathways between screw terminals—two pathways for each lever position. If not, then the switch is faulty and must be replaced. (The arrangement of the pathways may differ, depending on the switch manufacturer. The photo above shows the three possible pathway arrangements.)

How to Test a Pilot-Light Switch

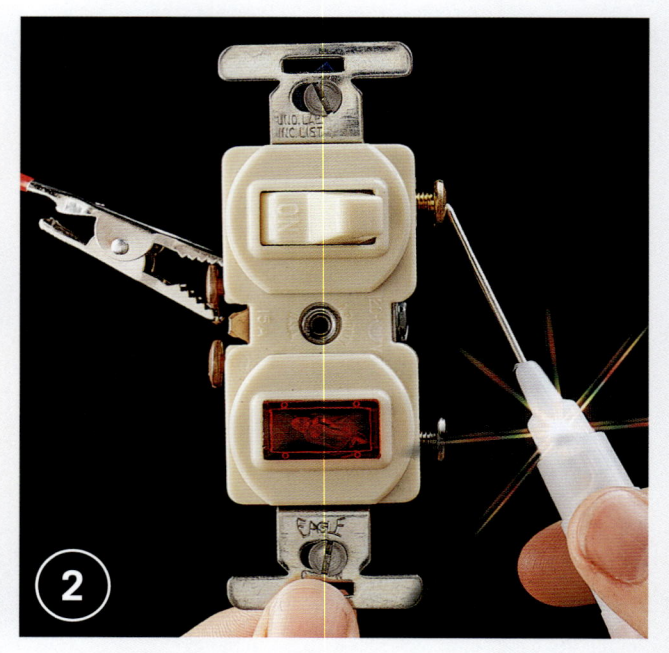

Test the pilot light by flipping the switch lever to the ON position. Check to see if the light fixture or appliance is working. If the pilot light does not glow even though the switch operates the light fixture or appliance, then the pilot light is defective and the unit must be replaced.

Test the switch by disconnecting the unit. With the switch lever in the ON position, attach the tester clip to the top screw terminal on one side of the switch. Touch the tester probe to the top screw terminal on the opposite side of the switch. If the switch is good, the tester will glow when switch is ON but not when OFF.

 # How to Test a Timer Switch

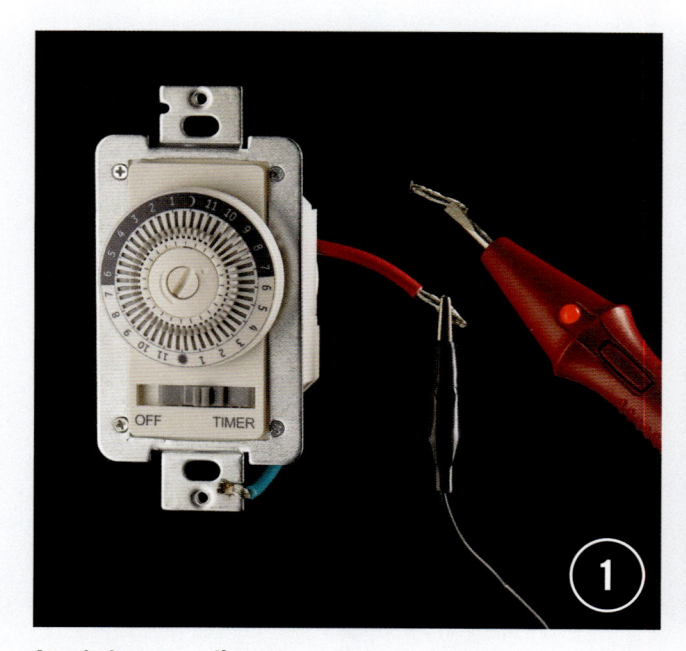
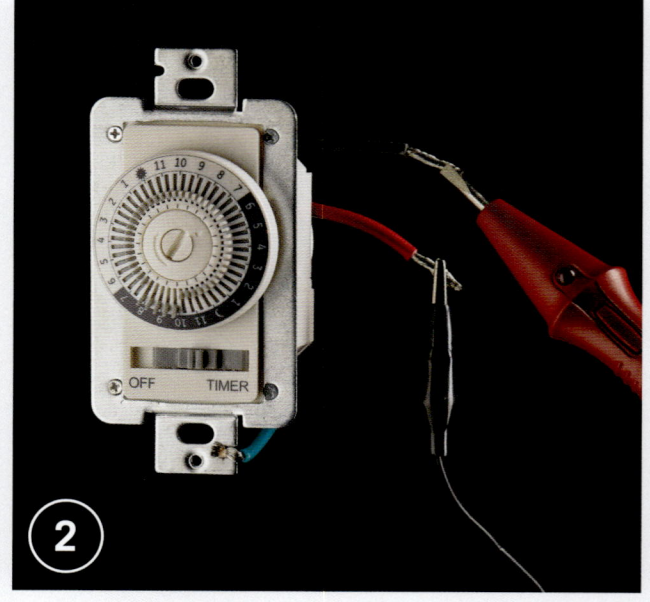

Attach the tester clip to the red wire lead on the timer switch, and touch the tester probe to the black hot lead. Rotate the timer dial clockwise until the ON tab passes the arrow marker. The tester should glow. If it does not, the switch is faulty and must be replaced.

Rotate the dial clockwise until the OFF tab passes the arrow marker. The tester should not glow. If it does, the switch is faulty and must be replaced.

How to Test a Switch/Receptacle

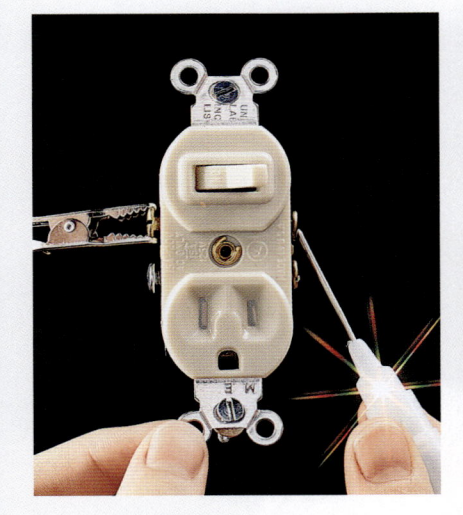

Attach the tester clip to one of the top screw terminals. Touch the tester probe to the top screw terminal on the opposite side. Flip the switch lever from ON to OFF position. If the switch is working correctly, the tester will glow when the switch lever is ON but not when it's OFF.

How to Test a Double Switch

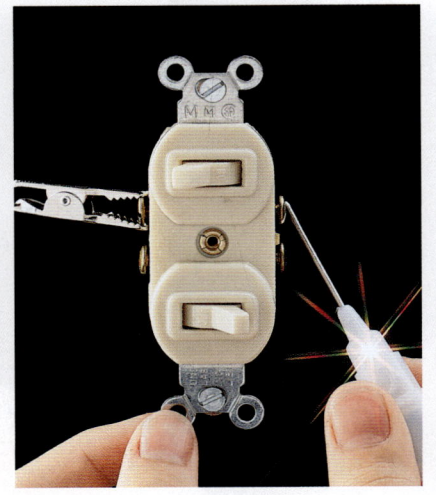

Test each half of the switch by attaching the tester clip to one screw terminal and touching the probe to the opposite side. Flip the switch lever from ON to OFF position. If the switch is good, the tester glows when the switch lever is ON but not when it's OFF. Repeat the test with the remaining pair of screw terminals. If either half tests faulty, replace the unit.

How to Test a Time-Delay Switch

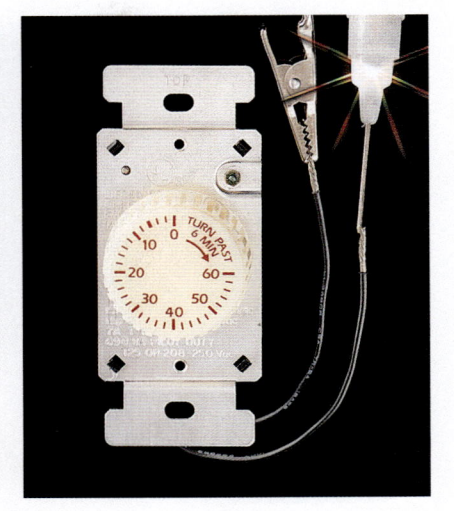

Attach the tester clip to one of the wire leads, and touch the tester probe to the other lead. Set the timer for a few minutes. If the switch is working correctly, the tester will glow until the time expires.

How to Test Manual Operation of Electronic Switches

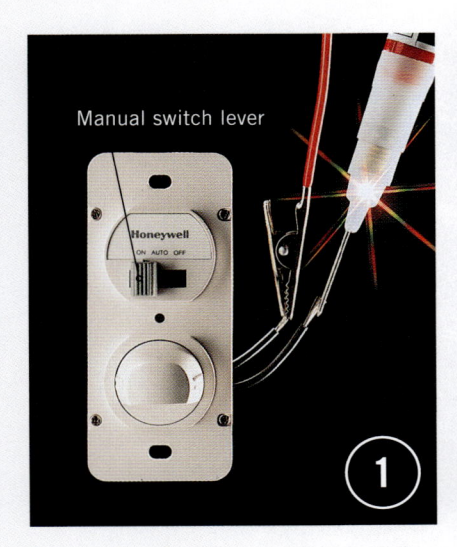

Manual switch lever

Automatic switch: Attach the tester clip to a black wire lead, and touch the tester probe to the other black lead. Flip the manual switch lever from ON to OFF position. If the switch is working correctly, the tester will glow when the switch lever is ON but not when it's OFF.

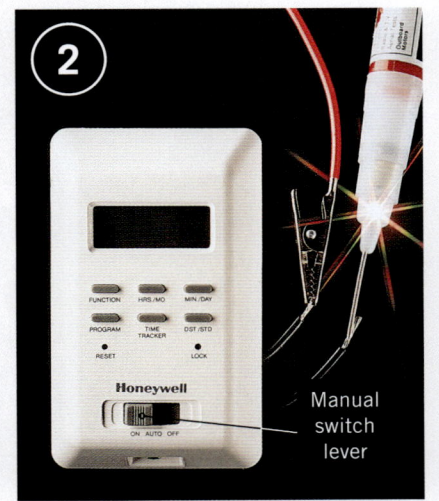

Programmable switch: Attach the tester clip to a wire lead, and touch the tester probe to the other lead. Flip the manual switch lever from ON to OFF position. If the switch is working correctly, the tester will glow when the switch lever is ON but not when it's OFF.

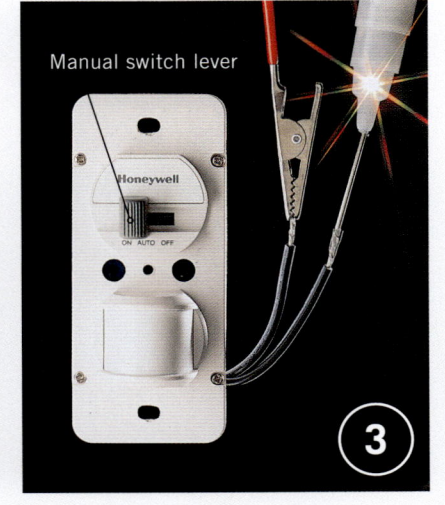

Manual switch lever

Motion-sensor switch: Attach the tester clip to a wire lead, and touch the tester probe to the other lead. Flip the manual switch lever from ON to OFF position. If the switch is working correctly, the tester will glow when the switch lever is ON but not when it's OFF.

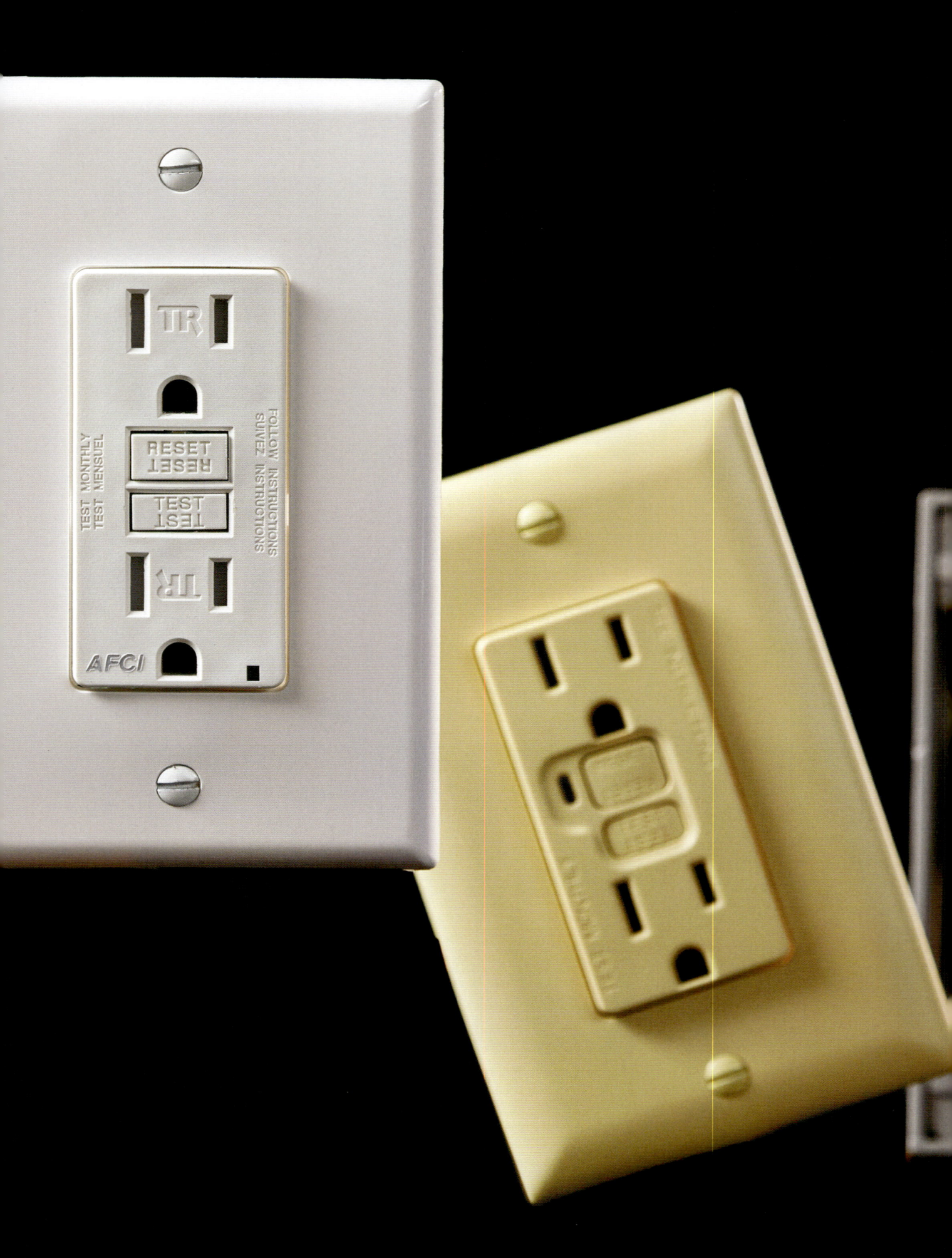

Receptacles

Whether you call them outlets, plug-ins, or receptacles, these important devices represent the point where the rubber meets the road in your home wiring system. From the basic 15-amp, 120-volt duplex receptacle to the burly 50-amp, 240-volt appliance receptacle, the many receptacles in your home do pretty much the same thing: transmit power to a load.

Learning the differences among receptacles does not take long. You need to know the amperage and voltage, and the number of devices on the circuit to select the correct receptacle. For circuits with one receptacle, match the circuit and receptacle amperage and voltage. A duplex receptacle (with a space for two plugs) counts as two receptacles. Use 15-amp receptacles on 15-amp circuits with multiple receptacles. Use either 15- or 20-amp receptacles on 20-amp circuits with multiple receptacles. Twenty-amp receptacles have the horizontal slot that forms a T with the large slot. Receptacles for 240-volt service have unique slot configurations so you can't accidentally plug in an appliance that's not rated for the amperage in the circuit. Some receptacles provide protection against dangerous situations such as ground faults and arc faults tripping themselves off if they detect a problem. Ground-fault (GFCI) and arc-fault (AFCI) receptacles are easy to identify by the *test* and *reset* buttons on their faces.

One last bit of information about receptacles: like switches, they vary quite a bit in quality. Paying the extra couple of dollars for a well made, durable device is worth the money.

In this chapter:

- Types of Receptacles
- Receptacle Wiring
- GFCI Receptacles
- Testing Receptacles

Types of Receptacles

Several different types of receptacles are found in the typical home. Each has a unique arrangement of slots that accepts only a certain kind of plug, and each is designed for a specific job.

Household receptacles provide two types of voltage: normal and high. Although voltage ratings have changed slightly over the years, normal receptacles should be rated for 110, 115, 120, or 125 volts. For purposes of replacement, these ratings are considered identical. High-voltage receptacles are rated at 220, 240, or 250 volts. These ratings are considered identical.

When replacing a receptacle, check the amperage rating of the circuit at the main service panel, and buy a receptacle with the correct amperage rating.

15 amps, 120 volts. Polarized two-slot receptacles are common in homes built before 1960. Slots are different sizes to accept polarized plugs.

15 amps, 120 volts. Three-slot grounded receptacles have two different-sized slots and a U-shaped hole for grounding, which is required in all new wiring installations.

20 amps, 120 volts. This three-slot grounded receptacle features a special T-shaped slot. It is installed for use with large appliances or portable tools that require 20 amps of current.

15 amps, 240 volts. This receptacle is used primarily for window air conditioners. It is available as a single unit or as half of a duplex receptacle, with the other half wired for 120 volts.

30 amps, 120/240 volts. This grounded receptacle is used for clothes dryers. It provides high-voltage current for heating coils and 120 volts to run lights and timers.

50 amps, 120/240 volts. This grounded receptacle is used for ranges. The high voltage powers heating coils, and the 120-volts run clocks and lights.

Older Receptacles

Older receptacles may look different from more modern types, but most will stay in good working order. Follow these simple guidelines for evaluating or replacing older receptacles:

- Never replace a receptacle with one of a different voltage or higher amperage rating.

- Do not replace a two-slot receptacle with a three-slot receptacle. Replace the two-slot receptacle with a polarized two-slot receptacle or with a GFCI receptacle.

- If in doubt, contact an electrician.

- Never alter the prongs of a plug to fit an older receptacle. Altering the prongs may remove the grounding or polarizing features of the plug.

The earliest receptacles were modifications of the screw-in light-bulb. This receptacle was used in the early 1900s.

Unpolarized receptacles have same-length slots. Modern plugs may not fit these receptacles. Never modify the prongs of a polarized plug to fit the slots of an unpolarized receptacle.

Surface-mounted receptacles were popular in the 1940s and 1950s for their ease of installation. Wiring ran behind hollowed-out base moldings. These receptacles are usually ungrounded.

Ceramic duplex receptacles were manufactured in the 1930s. They are polarized but ungrounded, and they are wired for 120 volts.

Twist-lock receptacles are designed to be used with plugs that are inserted and rotated. A small tab on the end of one of the prongs prevents the plug from being pulled from the receptacle.

This ceramic duplex receptacle has a unique hourglass shape. It is rated for 250 volts but only 5 amps and would not be allowed by today's electrical codes.

High-Voltage Receptacles

High-voltage receptacles provide current to large appliances such as clothes dryers, ranges, and air conditioners. The slot configuration of a high-voltage receptacle (page 94) will not accept a plug rated for 120 volts.

A high-voltage receptacle can be wired in one of two ways. In one type of high-voltage receptacle, voltage is brought to the receptacle with two hot wires, each carrying a maximum of 120 volts. No white neutral wire is necessary, but a grounding wire should be attached to the receptacle and to the receptacle box (if it is metal).

A clothes dryer or range also may require 120 volts to run lights, timers, and clocks. If so, a white neutral wire will be attached to the receptacle. The appliance itself will split the incoming electricity into a 120-volt circuit and a 240-volt circuit.

When replacing a high-voltage receptacle, it is important to identify and tag all wires on the existing receptacle so that the new receptacle will be properly wired.

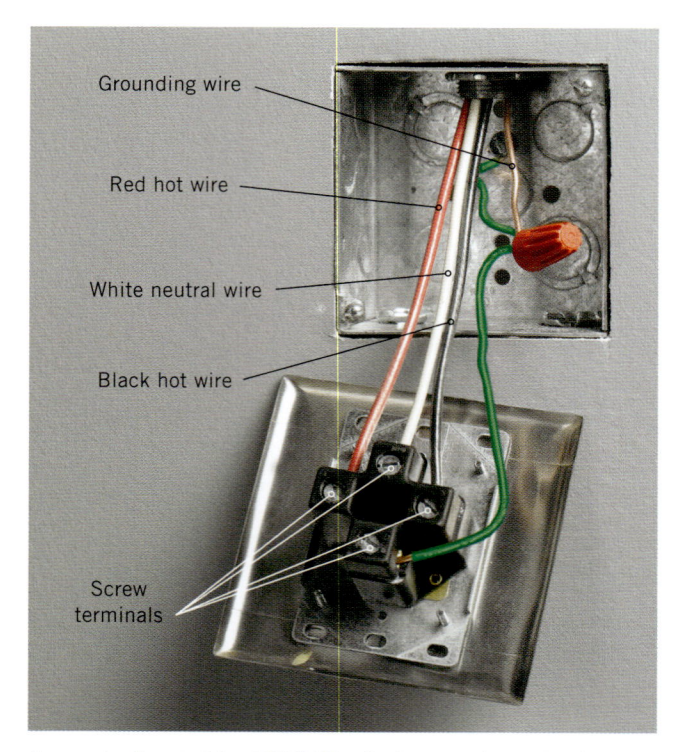

A receptacle rated for 120/240 volts has two incoming hot wires, each carrying 120 volts, a white neutral wire, and a copper grounding wire. Connections are made with setscrew terminals at the back of the receptacle.

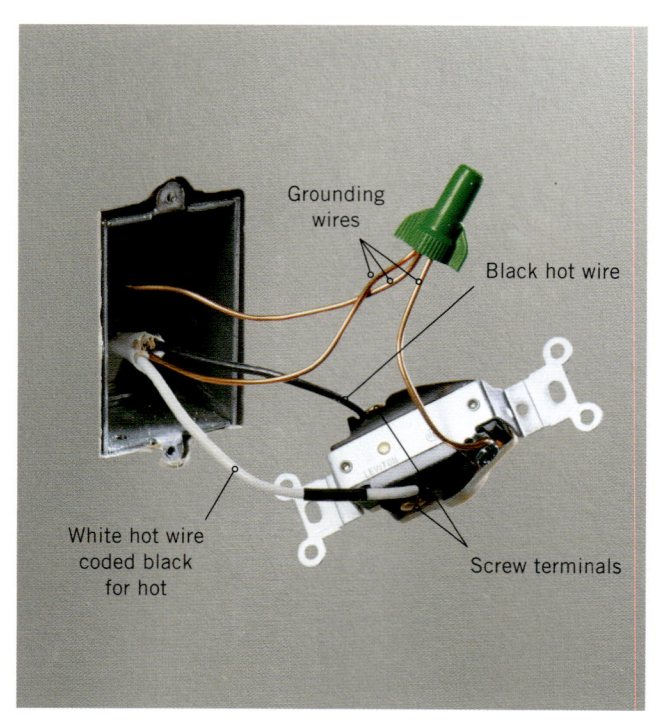

One type of receptacle rated for 240 volts has two incoming hot wires and no neutral wire. A grounding wire is pigtailed to the receptacle and to the metal receptacle box.

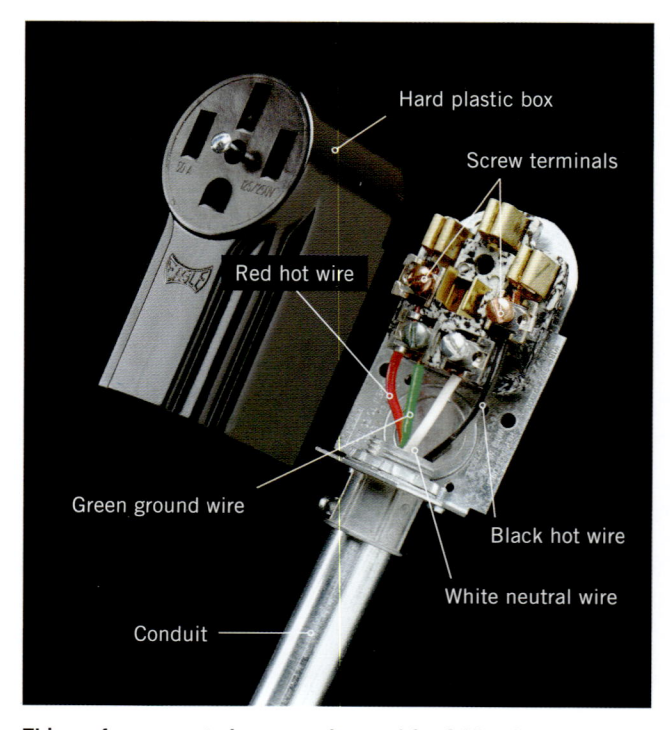

This surface-mounted receptacle rated for 240 volts has a hard plastic box that can be installed on concrete or block walls. Surface-mounted receptacles are often found in basements and utility rooms.

Childproofing

Tamper-resistant (TR) receptacles are now required in all new residential installations and when replacing an existing 3-slot receptacle. Tamper-resistant receptacles contain an internal safety device that prevents a child from inserting an object into the receptacle slots and getting a shock.

For standard existing receptacles, you can make them childproof or adapt them for special uses by adding receptacle accessories. Before installing an accessory, be sure to read the manufacturer's instructions.

Homeowners with small children should add inexpensive caps or covers to guard against accidental electric shocks.

Plastic caps do not conduct electricity and are virtually impossible for small children to remove. A receptacle cover attaches directly to the receptacle and fits over plugs, preventing the cords from being removed.

Tamper-resistant receptacles are labeled with "TR" on their faces. Use them for all new installations and replacements of 3-slot receptacles (including GFCI and AFCI types).

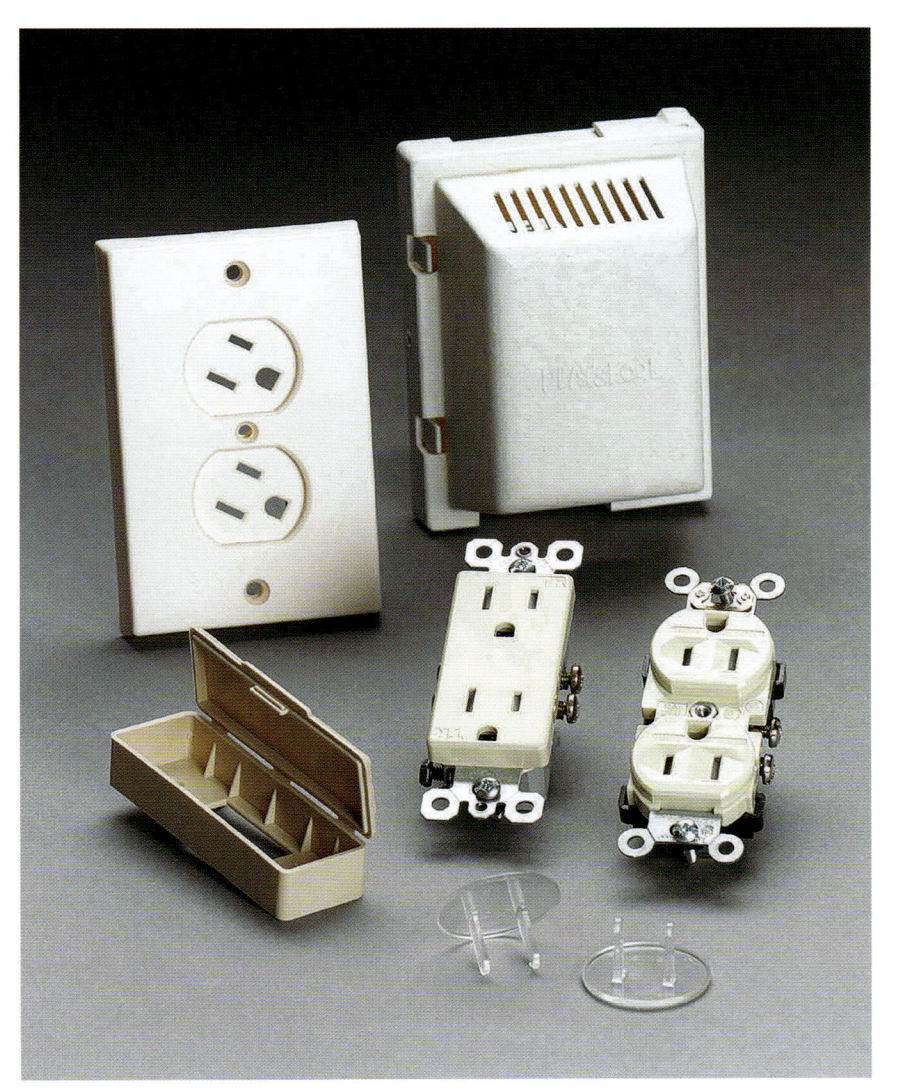

Standard receptacles present a real shock hazard to small children. Fortunately there are many products that make receptacles safer without making them less convenient.

Cover standard receptacles with childproofing plugs to prevent children from having access to the slots.

Duplex Receptacles

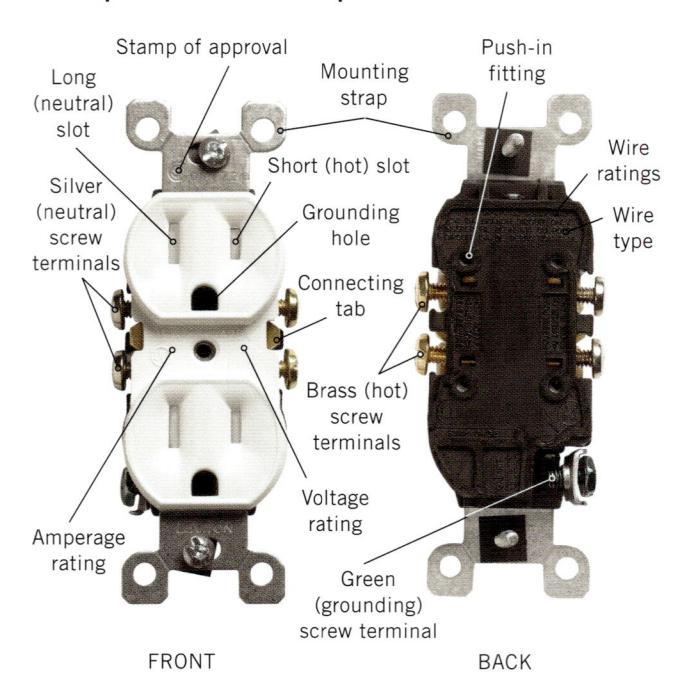

- Stamp of approval
- Long (neutral) slot
- Silver (neutral) screw terminals
- Mounting strap
- Short (hot) slot
- Grounding hole
- Connecting tab
- Brass (hot) screw terminals
- Voltage rating
- Amperage rating
- Push-in fitting
- Wire ratings
- Wire type
- Green (grounding) screw terminal

FRONT   BACK

The standard duplex receptacle has two halves for receiving plugs. Each half has a long (neutral) slot, a short (hot) slot, and a U-shaped grounding hole. The slots fit the wide prong, narrow prong, and grounding prong of a three-prong plug. This ensures that the connection between receptacle and plug will be polarized and grounded for safety.

The recommended way to connect to circuit wires is to use the screw terminals. Push-in fittings on the back may be used, with restrictions. A connecting tab between the screw terminals allows a variety of different wiring configurations. Receptacles also include mounting straps for attaching to electrical boxes.

Stamps of approval from testing agencies are found on the front and back of the receptacle. Look for the symbol UL or UND. LAB. INC. LIST to make sure the receptacle meets the strict standards of Underwriters Laboratories.

The receptacle is marked with ratings for maximum volts and amps. The common receptacle is marked 15A, 125V. Receptacles marked CU or COPPER are used with solid copper wire. Those marked CU-CLAD ONLY are used with copper-coated aluminum wire. Only receptacles marked CO/ALR may be used with solid aluminum wiring. Receptacles marked AL/CU no longer may be used with aluminum wire, according to code.

AFCI receptacles have integral protection against arc faults and may be required in some remodeling situations where AFCI protection cannot be provided at the panel.

The ground-fault circuit-interrupter, or GFCI, receptacle is a modern safety device. When it detects slight changes in current, it instantly shuts off power. The larger picture shows a modern GFCI with an alert bulb that lights when the device is tripped. The older but more familiar style is seen in the inset photo.

COMMON RECEPTACLE PROBLEMS

Household receptacles, also called outlets, have no moving parts to wear out and usually last for many years. Most problems associated with receptacles are actually caused by faulty lamps and appliances or their plugs and cords. However, the constant plugging in and removal of appliance cords can wear out the metal contacts inside a receptacle. Any receptacle that does not hold plugs firmly should be replaced. In addition, older receptacles made of hard plastic may harden and crack with age. They must be replaced when this happens.

A loose wire connection with the receptacle box is another possible problem. A loose connection can spark (called arcing), trip a circuit breaker, or cause heat to build up in the receptacle box, creating a potential fire hazard.

Wires can come loose for a number of reasons. Everyday vibrations caused by walking across floors, or from nearby street traffic, may cause a connection to shake loose. In addition, because wires heat and cool with normal use, the ends of the wires will expand and contract slightly. This movement also may cause the wires to come loose from the screw terminal connections. Another common cause is wires coming loose from push-in wire connections.

Not all receptacles are created equally. When replacing, make sure to buy one with the same amp rating as the old one. Inadvertently installing a 20-amp receptacle in replacement of a 15-amp receptacle is a very common error.

PROBLEM	REPAIR
Circuit breaker trips repeatedly or fuse burns out immediately after being replaced.	1. Repair or replace worn or damaged lamp or appliance cord. 2. Move lamps or appliances to other circuits to prevent overloads. 3. Tighten any loose wire connections. 4. Clean dirty or oxidized wire ends. 5. Bad AFCI, especially those from the early 2000s. Replace AFCI.
Lamp or appliance does not work.	1. Make sure the lamp or appliance is plugged in and that the circuit breaker or fuse is on. 2. Replace burned-out bulbs. 3. Repair or replace a worn or damaged lamp or appliance cord. 4. Tighten any loose wire connections. 5. Clean dirty or oxidized wire ends. 6. Replace any faulty receptacle.
Receptacle does not hold plugs firmly.	1. Repair or replace worn or damaged plugs. 2. Replace the faulty receptacle.
Receptacle is warm to the touch, buzzes, or sparks when plugs are inserted or removed.	1. Move lamps or appliances to other circuits to prevent overloads. 2. Tighten any loose wire connections. 3. Clean dirty or oxidized wire ends. 4. Replace the faulty receptacle.

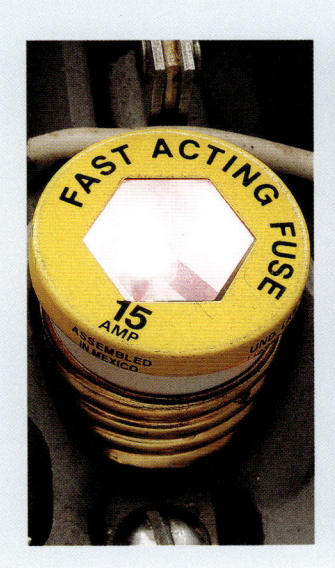   

Receptacle Wiring

A 120-volt duplex receptacle can be wired to the electrical system in several ways. The most common are shown on these pages.

Extending a branch circuit or adding a new branch to install new receptacles, lights, or switches requires a permit. The electrical inspector may require that you install arc-fault protection on the entire circuit. Check with the electrical inspector before starting such projects.

Wiring configurations may vary slightly from these photographs, depending on the kind of receptacles used, the type of cable, or the technique of the electrician who installed the wiring. To make dependable repairs or replacements, use masking tape and label each wire according to its location on the terminals of the existing receptacle.

Receptacles are wired as either end-of-run or middle-of-run. These two basic configurations are easily identified by counting the number of cables entering the receptacle box. End-of-run wiring has only one cable, indicating that the circuit ends. Middle-of-run wiring has two cables, indicating that the circuit continues on to other receptacles, switches, or fixtures.

A split-circuit receptacle is shown on the next page. Each half of a split-circuit receptacle is wired to a separate circuit. This allows two appliances of high current to be plugged into the same receptacle without tripping a breaker or blowing a fuse. This wiring configuration is similar to a receptacle that is controlled by a wall switch. Code requires a switch-controlled receptacle in most rooms that do not have a built-in light fixture operated by a wall switch.

Split-circuit and switch-controlled receptacles are connected to two hot wires, so use caution during repairs or replacements. Make sure the connecting tab between the hot screw terminals is removed.

Two-slot receptacles are common in older homes. There is no grounding wire attached to the receptacle, but the metal box may be grounded with armored cable or metal conduit.

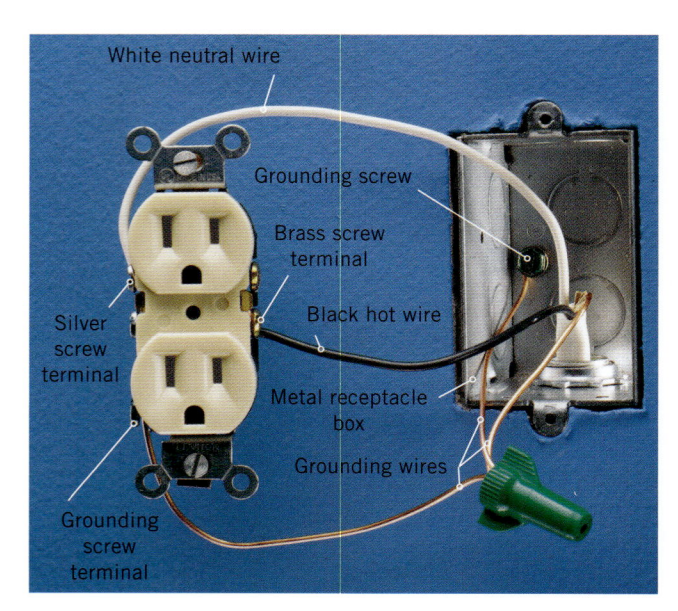

A single cable entering the box indicates end-of-run wiring. The black hot wire is attached to a brass screw terminal, and the white neutral wire is connected to a silver screw terminal. If the box is metal, the grounding wire is pigtailed to the grounding screws of the receptacle and the box. In a plastic box, the grounding wire is attached directly to the grounding screw terminal of the receptacle.

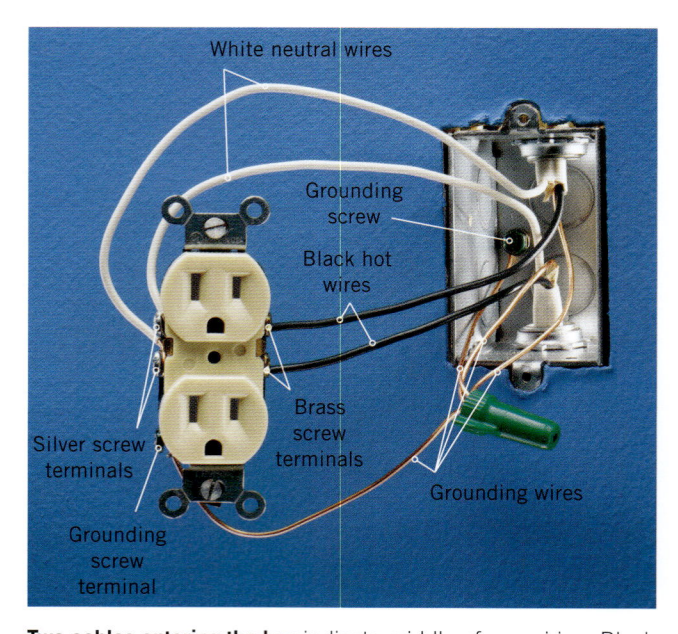

Two cables entering the box indicate middle-of-run wiring. Black hot wires are connected to brass screw terminals and white neutral wires to silver screw terminals. The grounding wire is pigtailed to the grounding screws of the receptacle and the box.

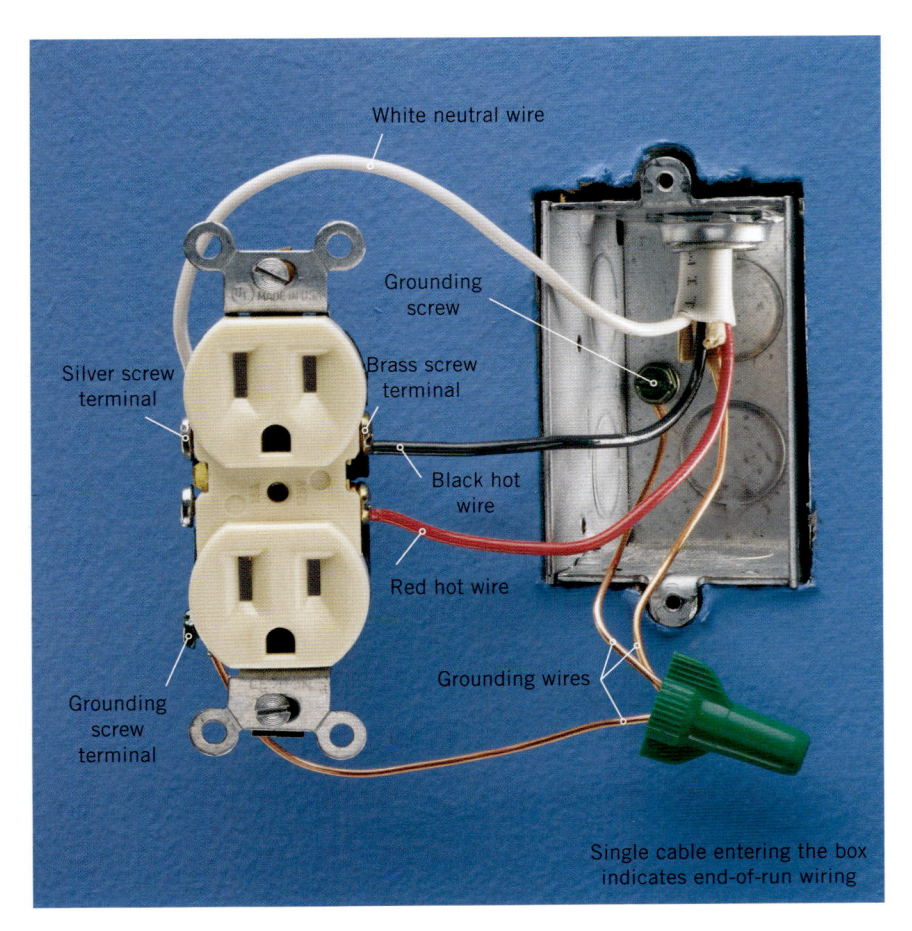

White neutral wire

Grounding screw

Silver screw terminal

Brass screw terminal

Black hot wire

Red hot wire

Grounding screw terminal

Grounding wires

Single cable entering the box indicates end-of-run wiring

A split-circuit receptacle (technically a multiwire branch circuit) is attached to a black hot wire, a red hot wire, a white neutral wire, and a bare grounding wire. The wiring is similar to a switch-controlled receptacle. The hot wires are attached to the brass screw terminals, and the connecting tab or fin between the brass terminals is removed. The white wire is attached to a silver screw terminal, and the connecting tab on the neutral side remains intact. The grounding wire is pigtailed to the grounding screw terminal of the receptacle and to the grounding screw attached to the box.

Note: A receptacle wired like this must be fed by a double-pole circuit breaker (with each hot wire connecting to a terminal on the breaker) or by two single-pole breakers connected with a handle tie. This ensures that both halves of the receptacle are always shut off at the same time, to prevent accidents.

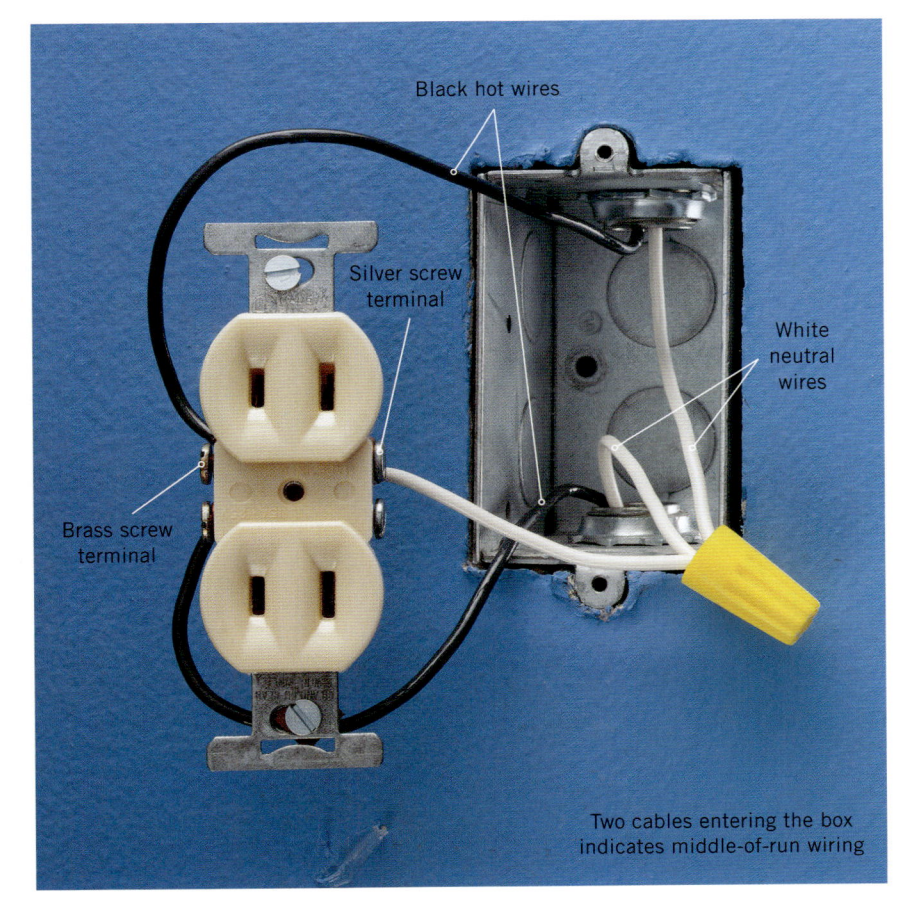

Black hot wires

Silver screw terminal

White neutral wires

Brass screw terminal

Two cables entering the box indicates middle-of-run wiring

A two-slot receptacle is often found in older homes. The black hot wires are connected to the brass screw terminals, and the white neutral wires are pigtailed to a silver screw terminal. Two-slot receptacles may be replaced with three-slot types, but only if a means of grounding exists at the receptacle box. In some municipalities, you may replace a two-slot receptacle with a GFCI receptacle as long as the receptacle has a label that reads "No equipment ground."

How to Install a New Receptacle

Position the new old-work box on the wall and trace around it. Consider the location of hidden utilities within the wall before you cut.

Remove baseboard between the new and existing receptacle. Cut away the drywall about 1" below the baseboard with a jigsaw, drywall saw, or utility knife.

Drill a ⅝" hole in the center of each stud along the opening between the two receptacles. A drill bit extender or a flexible drill bit will allow you a better angle and make drilling the holes easier.

Run the branch cable through the holes from the new location to the existing receptacle. Staple the cable to the stud below the box. Install a metal nail plate on the front edge of each stud that the cable routes through.

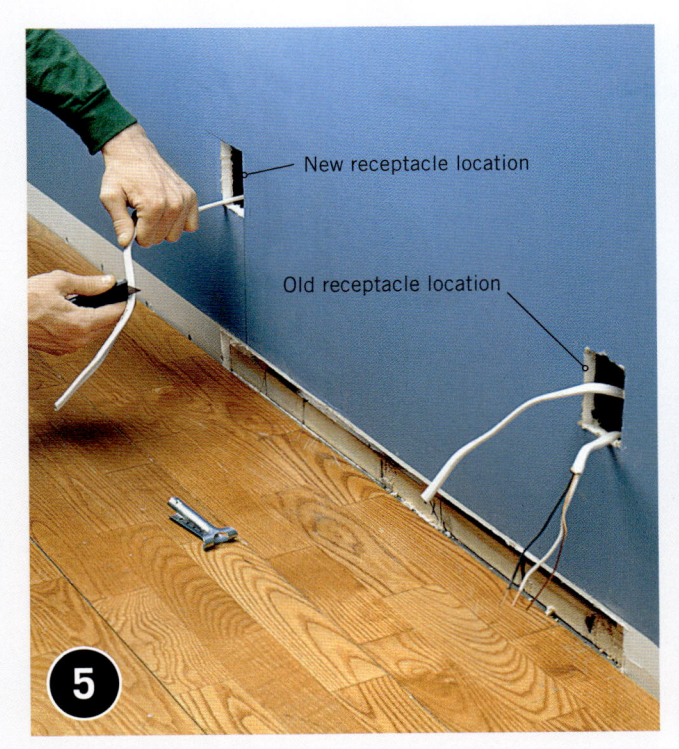

5 Turn off the power at the panel and test for power. Remove the old receptacle and its box, and pull the new branch cable up through the hole. Remove sheathing and insulation from both ends of the new cable.

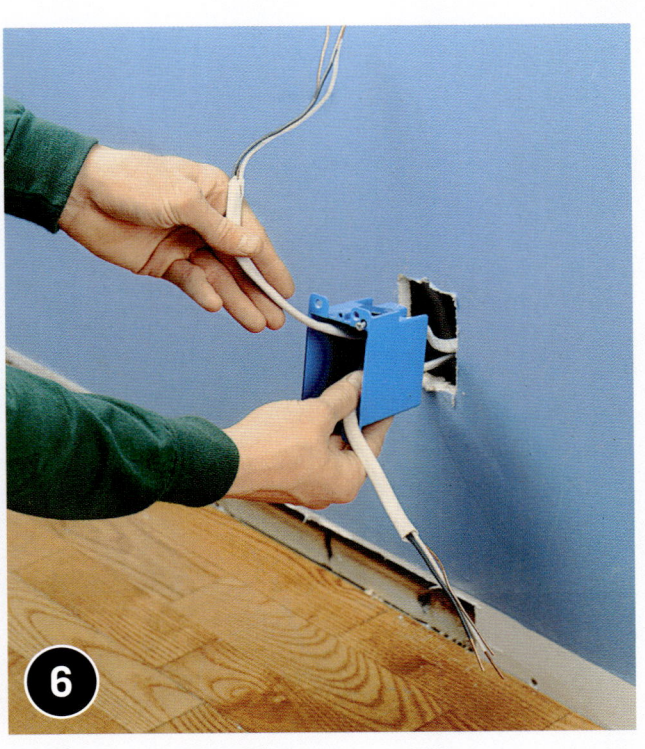

6 Thread the new and old cables into an old work box large enough to contain the added wires and clamp the cables. Fit the box into the old hole and attach it.

7 Reconnect the old receptacle using pigtails to connect the neutral, hot, and grounding wires from the new branch cable and the old cable.

8 Pull the cable through another old work box for the new receptacle. Secure the cable and install the box. Connect the new receptacle to the new branch cable. Insert the receptacle into the box and attach the receptacle and cover plate with screws. Patch the opening with drywall. Reattach the baseboard to the studs.

GFCI Receptacles

Aground-fault circuit-interrupter (GFCI) protects against electrical shock caused by a faulty appliance or a worn cord or plug. It senses small changes in current flow and can shut off power in as little as $\frac{1}{40}$ of a second. GFCIs can be a circuit breaker and protect the circuit from the panel. Often, however, they are receptacles that protect one receptacle and may protect other receptacles and light fixtures downstream.

GFCIs are now required in bathrooms, kitchens, within 6 feet of all sinks, garages, crawl spaces, basements, laundry rooms, and outdoor receptacle locations. Consult your local codes for any requirements regarding the installation of GFCIs. Most GFCI receptacles use standard screw terminal connections, but some have wire leads and are attached with wire connectors. Because the body of a GFCI receptacle is larger than a standard receptacle, small, crowded electrical boxes may need to be replaced with more spacious boxes.

Because the GFCI is so sensitive, it is most effective when wired to protect a single location. The more receptacles any one GFCI protects, the more susceptible it is to "nuisance tripping," shutting off power because of tiny, normal fluctuations in current flow. GFCI receptacles installed in outdoor locations must be rated for outdoor use and weather resistance (WR) along with ground fault protection.

Modern GFCI receptacles have tamper-resistant (TR) slots. Look for a model that's rated "WR" (for weather resistance) if you'll be installing it outdoors or in a wet location.

Noncontact voltage tester	Wire connectors
Screwdriver	Masking tape

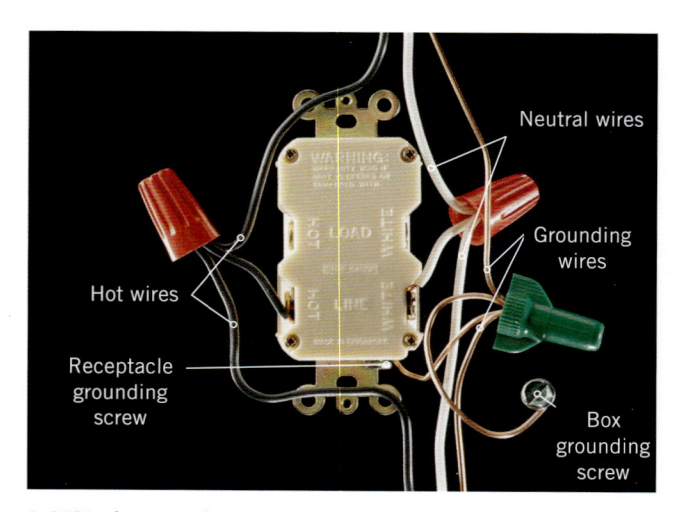

A GFCI wired for single-location protection (shown from the back) has hot and neutral pigtail wires connected only to the screw terminals marked LINE. A GFCI connected for single-location protection may be wired as either an end-of-run or middle-of-run configuration.

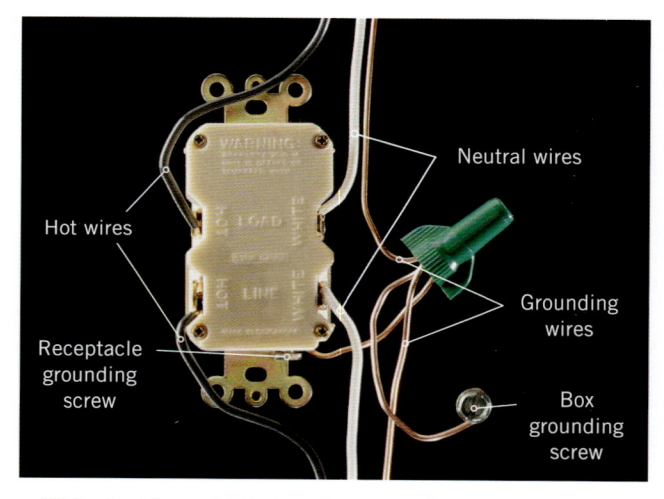

A GFCI wired for multiple-location protection (shown from the back) has one set of hot and neutral pigtail wires connected to the LINE pair of screw terminals and the other set connected to the LOAD pair of screw terminals. A GFCI receptacle connected for multiple-location protection may be wired only as a middle-of-run configuration.

How to Install a GFCI for Single-Location Protection

1

Shut off power to the receptacle at the panel. Test for power with a noncontact voltage tester. Be sure to check both halves of the receptacle.

2

Remove the cover plate. Loosen the mounting screws, and gently pull the receptacle from the box. Do not touch the wires. Confirm the power is off with the voltage tester.

3

Disconnect all wires from the receptacle terminals and remove the receptacle.

4

Pigtail all the white neutral wires together, and connect the pigtail to the terminal marked WHITE LINE on the GFCI (see photo on opposite page).

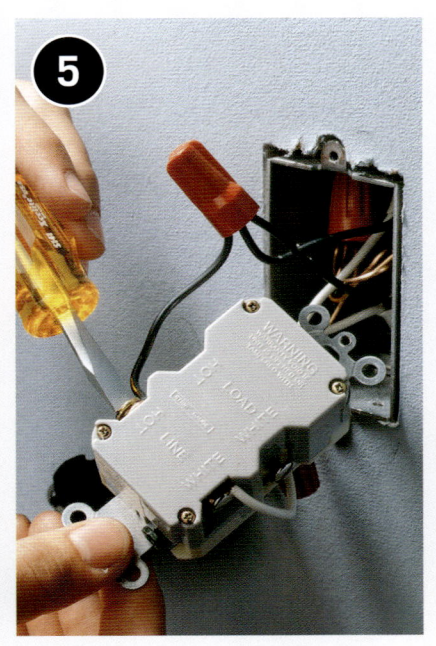

5

Pigtail the black wires together, and connect them to the terminal marked HOT LINE on the GFCI.

6

If a grounding wire is available, connect it to the green grounding screw terminal of the GFCI. Mount the GFCI in the receptacle box, and reattach the cover plate. Restore power and test the GFCI according to the manufacturer's instructions. If a grounding wire is not available, label the receptacle cover plate: NO EQUIPMENT GROUND.

How to Install a GFCI for Multiple-Location Protection

Use a map of your house circuits to determine a location for your GFCI. Indicate all receptacles that will be protected by the GFCI installation.

Turn off power to the correct circuit at the panel. Test all the receptacles in the circuit with a noncontact voltage tester to make sure the power is off. Always check both halves of each duplex receptacle.

Remove the cover plate from the receptacle that will be replaced with the GFCI. Loosen the mounting screws and gently pull the receptacle from its box. Take care not to touch any bare wires. Confirm the power is off with a non-contact voltage tester.

Disconnect all black hot wires. Carefully separate the hot wires and position them so that the bare ends do not touch anything. Restore power to the circuit at the panel. Determine which black wire is the feed wire by testing each black wire with the voltage tester. The feed wire brings power to the receptacle from the service panel.

USE CAUTION: This is a live wire test, during which the power is turned on temporarily.

When you have found the hot feed wire, turn off power at the panel. Identify the feed wire by marking it with masking tape.

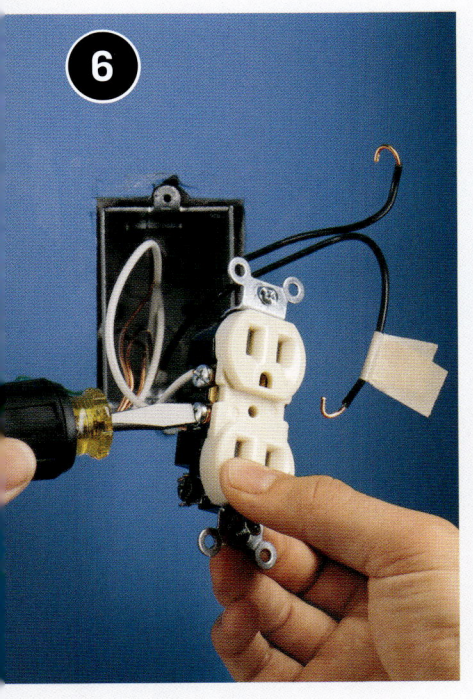

6

Disconnect the white neutral wires from the old receptacle. Identify the white feed wire and label it with masking tape. The white feed wire will be the one that shares the same cable as the black feed wire.

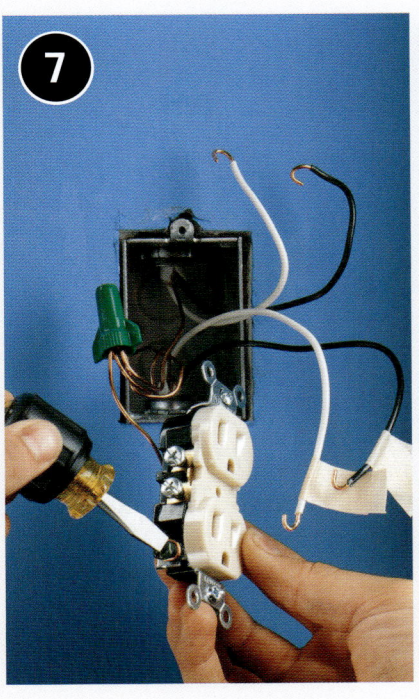

7

Disconnect the grounding wire from the grounding screw terminal of the old receptacle. Remove the old receptacle.

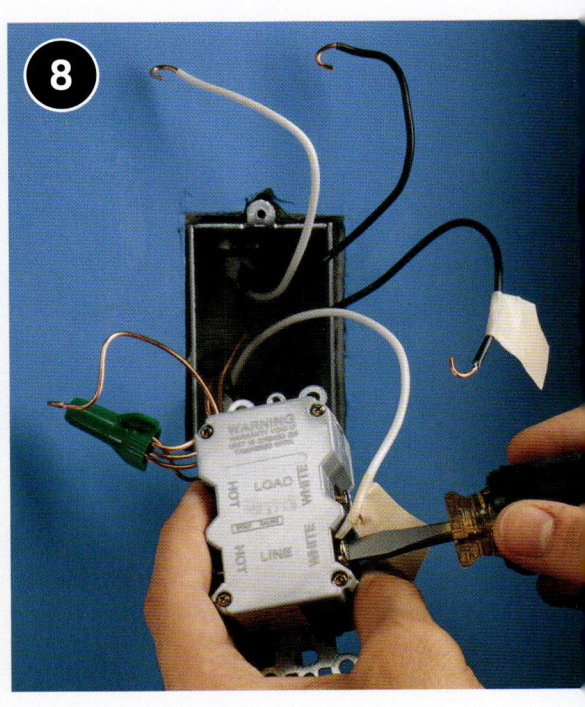

8

Connect the white feed wire to the terminal marked WHITE LINE on the GFCI. Connect the black feed wire to the terminal marked HOT LINE on the GFCI.

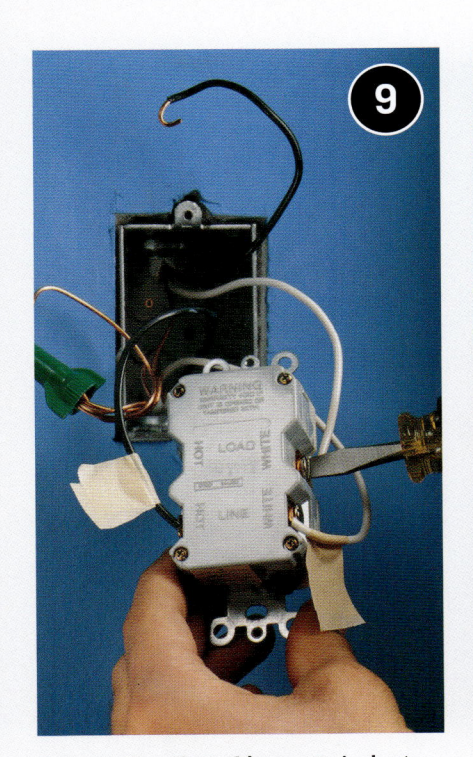

9

Connect the other white neutral wire to the terminal marked WHITE LOAD on the GFCI.

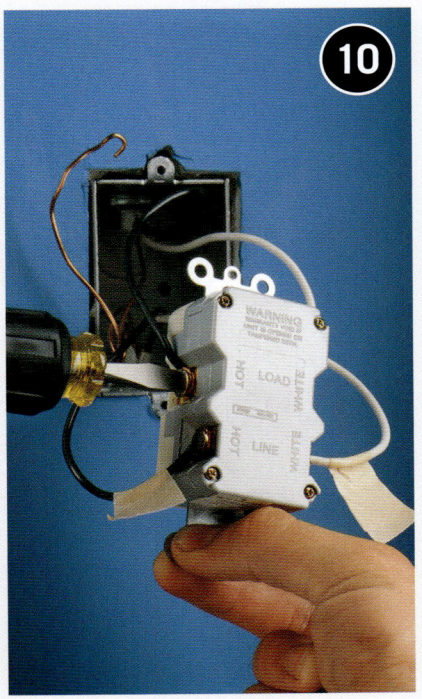

10

Connect the other black hot wire to the terminal marked HOT LOAD on the GFCI. Connect the grounding wire to the grounding screw terminal of the GFCI.

11

Carefully tuck all wires into the receptacle box. Mount the GFCI in the box and attach the cover plate. Turn on power to the circuit at the panel. Test the GFCI according to the manufacturer's instructions.

Testing Receptacles

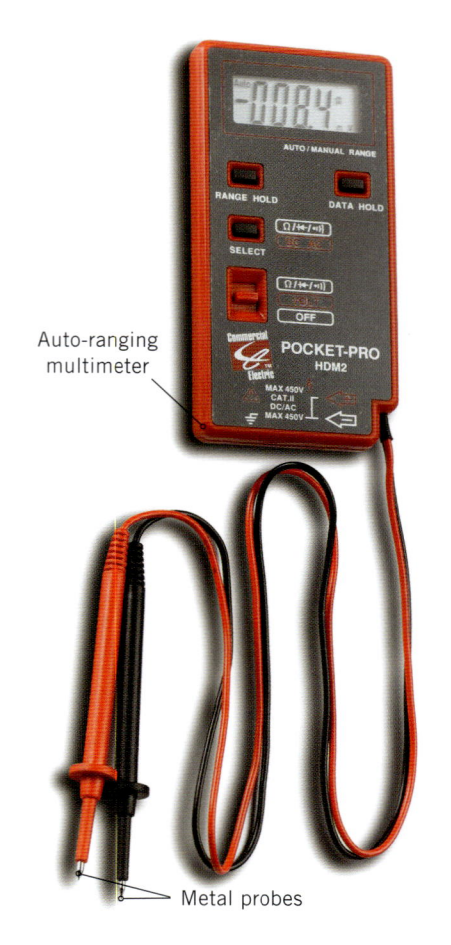

Auto-ranging multimeter

Metal probes

For testing receptacles and other devices for power, grounding, and polarity, neon circuit testers are inexpensive and easy to use. But they are less sensitive than auto-ranging multimeters. In some cases, neon testers won't detect the presence of lower voltage in a circuit. This can lead you to believe that a circuit is shut off when it is not—a dangerous mistake. The small probes on a neon circuit tester also force you to get too close to live terminals and wires. For a quick check and confirmation, a neon circuit tester (or a plug-in tester) is adequate. But for the most reliable readings, buy and learn to use a multimeter.

The best multimeters are auto-ranging models with a digital readout. Unlike manual multimeters, auto-ranging models do not require you to preset the voltage range to get an accurate reading. Unlike neon testers, multimeters may be used for a host of additional diagnostic functions such as testing fuses, measuring battery voltage, testing internal wiring in appliances, and checking light fixtures to determine if they're functional.

TOOLS + MATERIALS

| Multimeter | Noncontact voltage tester | Plug-in tester | Screwdriver |

How to Use a Plug-In Tester

Use a plug-in tester to test a three-slot receptacle. With the power on, insert the tester into the suspect outlet. The face of the tester has three colored lights that will light up in different combinations, according to the outlet's problem. A reference chart is provided with the tester, and there may be a chart on the tester itself. These testers are useful, but they do not test for all wiring errors.

How to Test Quickly for Power

Use a noncontact voltage tester to verify that power is not flowing to a receptacle. Using either a no-touch sensor or a probe-style circuit tester, test the receptacle for current before you remove the cover plate. Once the plate is removed, double-check at the terminals to make sure there is no current.

How to Test a Receptacle with a Multimeter

Set the selector dial for alternating-current voltage. Plug the black probe lead into the common jack (labeled COM) on the multimeter. Plug the red probe lead into the V-labeled jack.

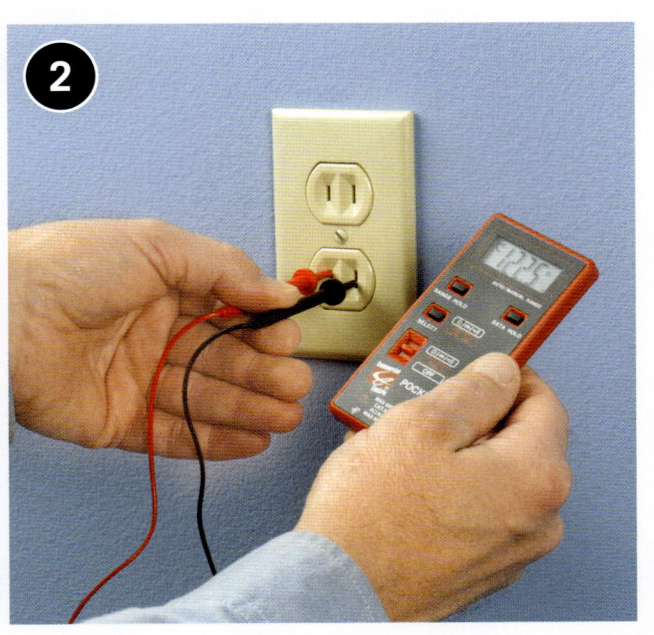

Insert each probe into one of the receptacle slots. It does not make a difference which probe goes into which slot as long as they're in the same receptacle. If power is present and flowing normally, you will see a voltage reading on the readout screen.

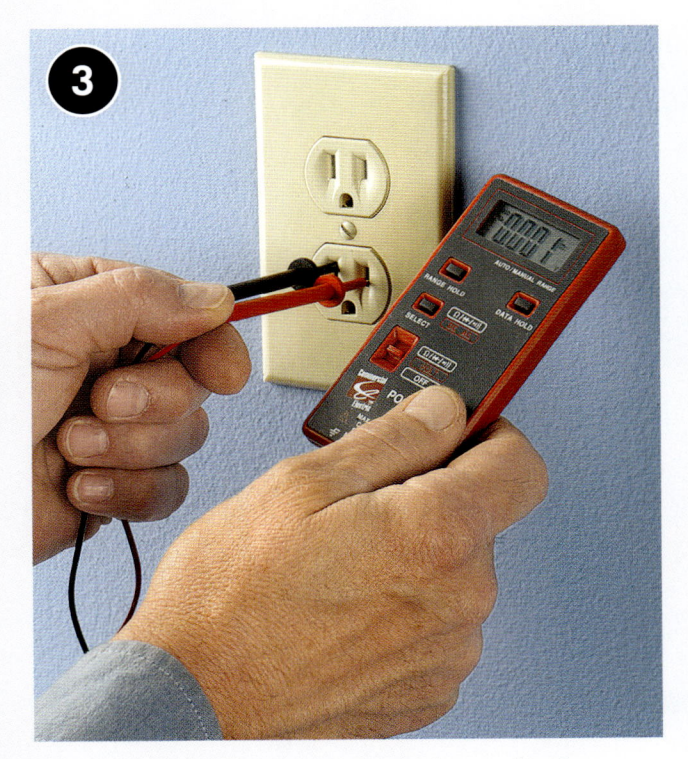

If the multimeter reads 0 or gives a very low reading (less than 1 or 2 volts), power is not present in the receptacle and it is safe to remove the cover plate and work on the device (although it's always a good idea to confirm your reading by touching the probes directly to the screw terminals on the receptacles).

OPTION: When a receptacle or switch is in the middle of a circuit, it is difficult to tell which wires are carrying current. Use a multimeter to check. With power off, remove the receptacle and separate the wires. Restore power. Touch one probe to the bare ground or the grounded metal box and touch the other probe to the end of each wire. The wire that shows current on the meter is hot.

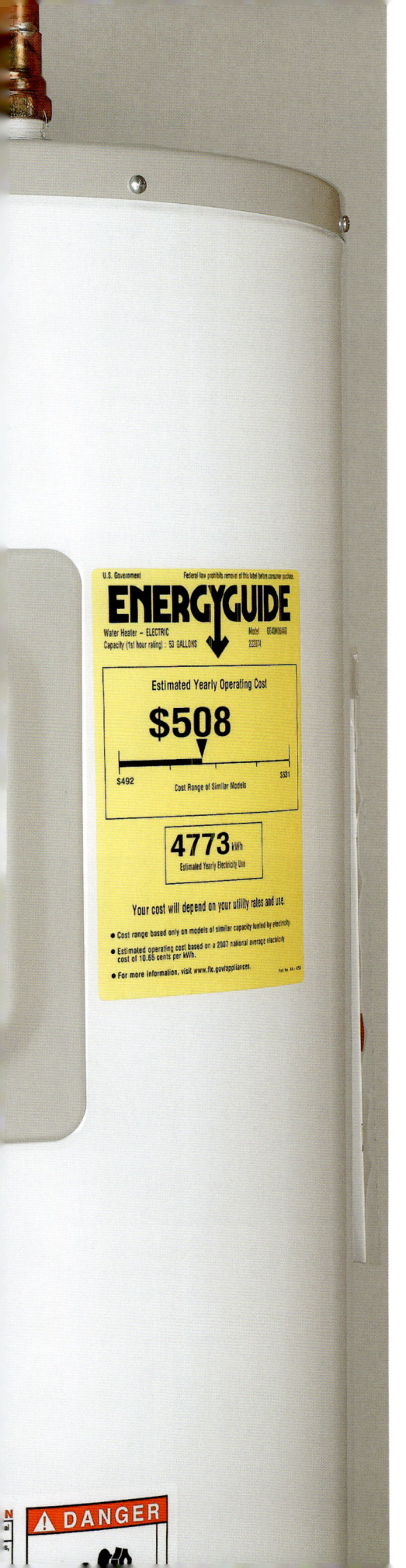

Planning + Prep

Given the importance of, and dangers posed by, your home's electrical system, carefully planning and prepping for any electrical work is essential. This begins with knowing what exactly you're dealing with anytime you modify existing circuits, fixtures, or fittings. A proper assessment of existing wiring, outlets, and boxes will go a long way toward ensuring success of any electrical project you tackle. It's the first crucial step in any electrical project, and certainly in creating accurate, workable plans.

The more detailed your plans, the better. In many cases, you'll need to deal with local building departments, permit processes, and electrical inspections. It's about more than just regulations. Developing clear plans and gathering all the background information you need will ensure smooth sailing through the whole process.

Don't fall into the trap of thinking that building and zoning department officials are simply nuisances to deal with only at inspections. They can be invaluable resources during the planning phase of an electrical project. Guidance about local codes—which can vary from region to region—can help you avoid costly, time-consuming mistakes once you begin a project.

In this chapter:
- Planning Your Project
- Draw a Diagram + Obtain a Permit
- Room-by-Room Wiring

Planning Your Project

Careful planning of a wiring project ensures you will have plenty of power for present and future needs. Whether you are adding circuits in a room addition, wiring a remodeled kitchen, or adding an outdoor circuit, consider all possible ways the space might be used, and plan for enough electrical service to meet peak needs.

For example, when wiring a room addition, remember that the way a room is used can change. In a room used as a spare bedroom, a single 15-amp circuit provides plenty of power, but if you ever choose to convert the same room to a family recreation space, you will need additional circuits.

When wiring a remodeled kitchen, it is a good idea to install circuits for an electric range or cooktop, even if you do not have these electric appliances. Installing these circuits now makes it easy to convert from gas to electric appliances at a later date.

A large wiring project adds a considerable load to your main electrical service. In about 25 percent of all homes, some type of service upgrade is needed before new wiring can be installed. For example, some homeowners will need to replace an older 60-amp electrical service with a new service rated for 100 amps or more. This is a job for a licensed electrician but it is well worth the investment. In other cases, the existing main service provides adequate power, but the main circuit breaker panel is too full to hold any new circuit breakers. In this case it is necessary to install a circuit breaker subpanel to provide room for hooking up added circuits. Installing a subpanel is a job most homeowners can do themselves (see pages 189–191).

This chapter gives an easy five-step method for determining your electrical needs and planning new circuits.

Five Steps for Planning a Wiring Project

Examine your main panel (see page 114). The amp rating of the electrical service and the size of the circuit breaker panel will help you determine if a service upgrade is needed.

Learn about codes (see pages 115–121). The National Electrical Code (NEC), and local electrical codes and building codes, provide guidelines for determining how much power and how many circuits your home needs. Your local electrical inspector can tell you which regulations apply to your job.

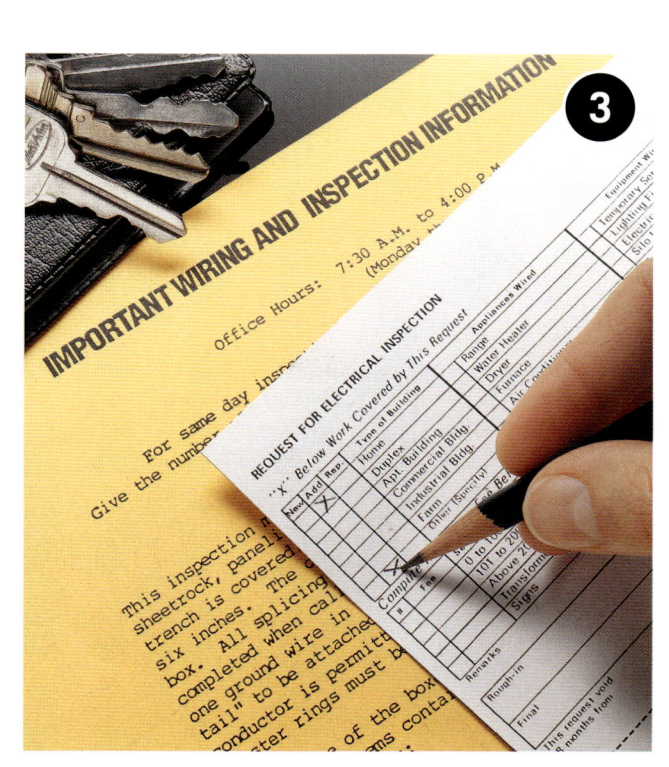

Prepare for inspections (see pages 130–131). Remember that your work must be reviewed by your local electrical inspector. When planning your wiring project, always follow the inspector's guidelines for quality workmanship.

Evaluate electrical loads (see pages 132–137). New circuits put an added load on your electrical service. Make sure that the total load of the existing wiring and the planned new circuits does not exceed the service capacity or the capacity of the panel.

Draw a wiring diagram and get a permit (see pages 132–133). This wiring plan will help you organize your work.

Examine Your Main Panel

The first step in planning a new wiring project is to look in your main (service equipment) panel and find the size of the service by reading the amperage rating on the main circuit breaker. As you plan new circuits and evaluate electrical loads, knowing the size of the main service helps you determine if you need a service upgrade.

Also look for open circuit breaker slots in the panel. The number of open slots will determine if you need to add a circuit breaker subpanel.

Find the service size by opening the main service panel and reading the amp rating printed on the main circuit breaker. This method works when there is one main circuit breaker or fuse block. Some houses have multiple services disconnects. In these cases, contact an electrician to determine your service size. In most cases, 100-amp service usually provides enough power to handle the added loads of projects such as the ones shown in this book. A service rated for 60 amps or less should be upgraded.

NOTE: In some homes the main circuit breaker is located in a separate box.

Older service panels use fuses instead of circuit breakers. Have an electrician replace this type of panel with a circuit breaker panel that provides enough power and enough open breaker slots for the new circuits you are planning.

Look for open circuit breaker slots in the main panel or in a subpanel, if your home already has one. You will need one open slot for each 120-volt circuit you plan to install and two slots for each 240-volt circuit. If your main panel has no open breaker slots, install a subpanel to provide room for connecting new circuits. Another option may be to install half-height circuit breakers, if allowed in the panel.

Learn About Codes

To ensure public safety, your community requires that you get a permit to install new wiring and have the work reviewed by an inspector. Electrical inspectors use the National Electrical Code (NEC) as the primary authority for evaluating wiring, but they also follow the local building code and electrical code standards.

Most communities use a version of the NEC that is not the most current version. Also, many communities make amendments to the NEC, and these amendments may affect your work.

As you begin planning new circuits, call or visit your local electrical inspector and discuss the project with him or her. The inspector can tell you which of the code requirements apply to your job and may give you a packet of information summarizing these regulations. Later, when you apply to the inspector for a work permit, he or she will expect you to understand the local guidelines as well as a few basic NEC requirements.

The NEC is a set of standards that provides minimum safety requirements for wiring installations. It is revised every three years. The national code requirements for the projects shown in this book are explained on the following pages. For more information, you can find copies of the current NEC, as well as a number of excellent handbooks based on the NEC, at libraries, bookstores, and online. Many city building departments and state authorities publish local code rules and updates online.

In addition to being the final authority of code requirements, inspectors are electrical professionals with years of experience. Although they have busy schedules, most inspectors are happy to answer questions and help you design well-planned circuits.

Basic Electrical Code Requirements

Electrical code requirements for living areas: Living areas need at least one 15-amp or 20-amp basic lighting/receptacle circuit for each 600 sq. ft. of living space and should have a dedicated circuit for each type of permanent appliance, such as an air conditioner or a group of baseboard heaters. Receptacles on basic lighting/receptacle circuits should be spaced no more than 12 ft. apart. Many electricians and electrical inspectors recommend even closer spacing. Any wall more than 24" wide also needs a receptacle. Every room should have a wall switch at the point of entry to control either a ceiling or wall-mounted light or plug-in lamp. Kitchens and bathrooms must have a ceiling or wall-mounted light fixture.

Selected NEC Standards + Tips

Measure the living areas of your home, excluding unconditioned spaces. You will need a minimum of one basic lighting/receptacle circuit for every 600 sq. ft. of living space. The total square footage also helps you estimate heating and cooling needs for new room additions.

Three-way switches

Stairways must have one or more light fixtures that are capable of lighting all stair treads and landings, including the top and bottom landings. The light fixture must be controlled by three-way switches at the top and bottom landings.

Kitchen and bathroom receptacles must be protected by a ground-fault circuit-interrupter (GFCI). Also, all outdoor receptacles and receptacles in basements, crawl spaces, and garages must be protected by a GFCI.

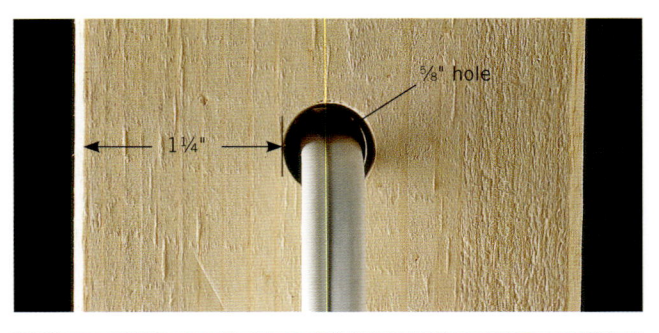

⅝" hole

1¼"

Nail guard

Furring strip

Cutaway view

Cables must be protected against damage by nails and screws by at least 1¼" of wood (top). When cables pass through 2" × 2" furring strips (bottom), protect the cables with metal nail guards. Nail guards also may be used to protect cable that cannot meet the 1¼" minimum of wood protection standard.

Walk-in closets and other storage spaces should have at least one light fixture that is controlled by a wall switch near the entrance. Prevent fire hazards by positioning the light fixtures so the outer globes are at least 12" away from all shelf areas.

NOTE: This suggestion is primarily for homeowner convenience and is not required by most codes.

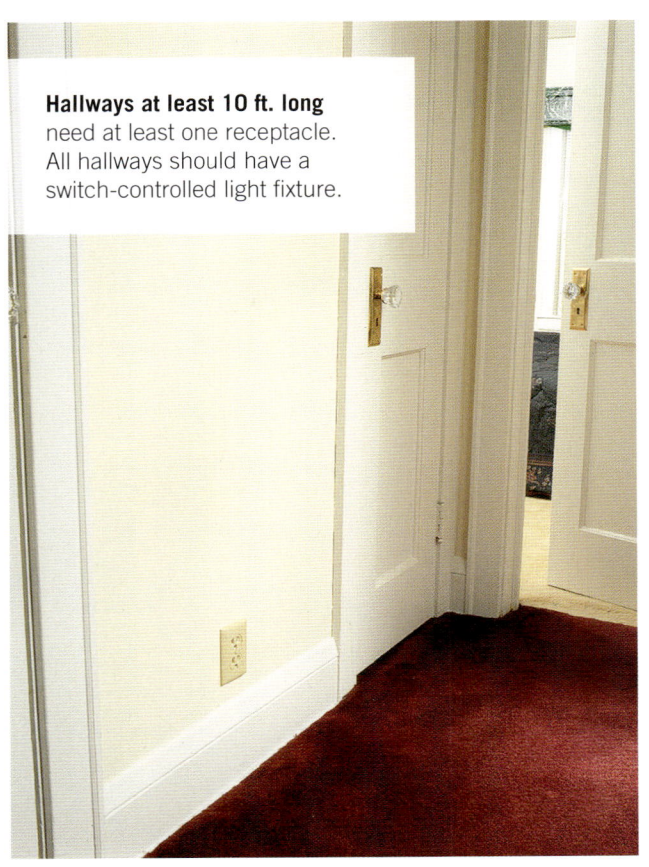

Hallways at least 10 ft. long need at least one receptacle. All hallways should have a switch-controlled light fixture.

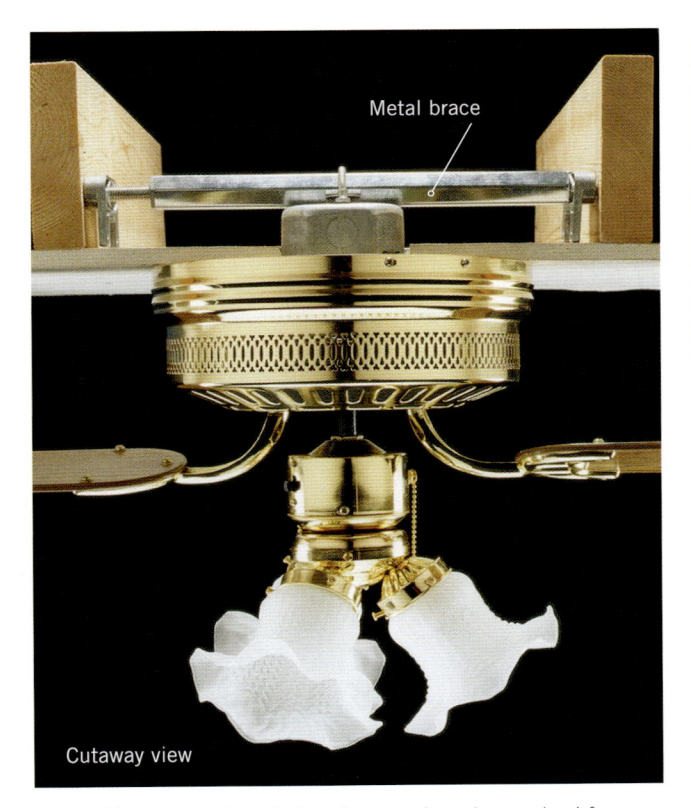

Metal brace

Cutaway view

A metal brace attached to framing members is required for ceiling fans and large light fixtures that are too heavy to be supported by an electrical box. All ceiling fans must be installed in a box that is fan-rated.

Label new circuits on an index attached to the circuit breaker panel door. List the rooms and appliances controlled by each circuit. Make sure the area around the panel is clean, well lighted, and accessible.

Selected NEC Standards + Tips

Light fixtures (luminaires) must be approved for their location. For example, in shower and tub areas, light fixtures must be rated for damp locations or, if they are subject to shower spray, for wet locations.

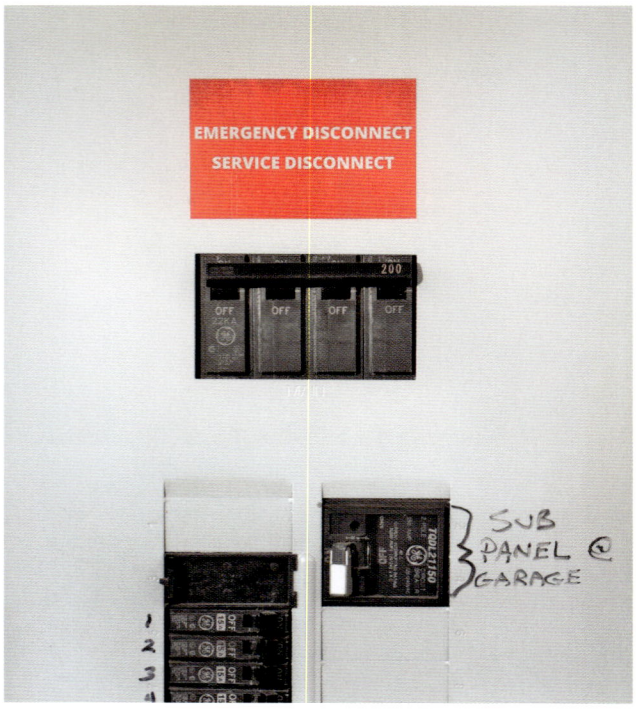

Electrical service to new homes must have disconnecting means located in an accessible outdoor location, and it must be labeled appropriately. This allows emergency responders to shut off the power before they enter the home.

Metal electrical boxes must be grounded with a machine screw or an approved grounding clip. Machine screws must be engaged with at least two threads into the box. Grounding screws are sold for this purpose. Drywall and sheet metal screws are not acceptable for grounding.

GFCI receptacles can be installed on circuits that do not have a ground wire. In this case, the receptacle face must be labeled "No Equipment Ground." The receptacle will provide GFCI protection but will not have a true ground connection. Most GFCI receptacles come with these sticker labels in the package.

Selected NEC Standards + Tips

Service lugs

Service lugs in the main service panel must be protected by approved barriers, sometimes called service barriers. This applies to any uninsulated, ungrounded conductor terminal or busbar in the service disconnect. Barriers are inexpensive, removable plastic covers.

SUITABLE FOR OUTDOOR USE ONLY

Transformers for low-voltage lighting systems must remain accessible. A transformer can be installed outdoors, indoors, or in a garage or outbuilding, depending on its rating. Consult the manufacturer's instructions for additional installation requirements.

Laundry rooms must have at least one 120-volt, 20-amp, GFCI-protected receptacle on a dedicated circuit, and it must be within 6 feet of any appliance it serves (such as a washing machine or a gas dryer). Electric dryers require a 30-amp (minimum), 120/240-volt, GFCI-protected receptacle on a dedicated four-conductor circuit (contains two hot wires, a neutral, and a ground). Existing three-conductor receptacle circuits are allowed to remain in use, if permitted by local code.

Panels

- Maintain a minimum 30" wide by 36" deep of clearance in front all electrical panels.
- Install a surge protective device when installing new electrical service and when changing or upgrading electrical service.
- Install an emergency disconnect device outside of the house when installing new electrical service and when changing or upgrading electrical service.
- Match the amperage rating of the circuit when replacing circuit breakers or fuses.
- Use handle ties on all 240-volt breakers and on 120-volt breakers protecting multiwire branch circuits.
- Close all unused panel openings.
- Label each fuse and circuit breaker clearly on the panel.

Electrical Boxes

- Use boxes that are large enough to accommodate the number of wires and devices in the box and panels.
- Install all junction boxes so they remain accessible.
- Leave no gaps greater than ⅛" between wall finish materials and the front of electrical boxes.
- Place receptacle boxes flush with combustible surfaces.
- Leave a minimum of 3" of usable cable or wire extending past the front of the electrical box.
- Ground metal electrical boxes.

Wires + Cables

- Use wires that are large enough for the amperage rating of the circuit (see Wire Size Chart, page 26).
- Drill holes at least 2" from the edges of joists. Do not attach cables to the bottom edge of joists.
- Do not run cables diagonally between framing members.
- Use nail plates to protect cable that is run through holes drilled or cut into studs less than 1¼" from the front edge of a stud.
- Do not crimp cables sharply.
- Contain spliced wires or connections entirely in a covered plastic or metal electrical box.
- Use approved wire connectors to join wires.
- Secure cables within 8" of an electrical box and every 54" along its run.
- Leave a minimum ¼" (maximum 1") of sheathing where cables enter an electrical box.
- Clamp cables and wires to electrical boxes with approved clamps. No clamp is necessary for one-gang plastic boxes if cables are secured within 8" of the box.

- Connect only a single wire to a single screw terminal. Use pigtails to join more than one wire to a screw terminal.

Switches

- Use a switch-controlled receptacle in rooms without a built-in light fixture operated by a wall switch.
- Use switches with grounding screws with plastic electrical boxes.
- Locate all wall switches within easy reach of the room entrance and not behind the door.
- Install a neutral wire in switch boxes.
- Use black or red wires to supply power to switched devices.

Receptacles

- Install a separate receptacle for an electric dryer, as applicable. This must be 30-amp (minimum), 240-volt, GFCI protected, and on a dedicated four-conductor circuit.
- Install receptacles on all walls at least 24" long.
- Install receptacles so a 6-foot cord can be plugged in from any point along a wall, or every 12 ft. along a wall.
- Include receptacles in living areas and any hallway that is 10 feet long or longer.
- Use three-slot, grounded receptacles for all 15- or 20-amp, 120-volt branch circuits.
- Install GFCI-protected receptacles in bathrooms, kitchens, garages, crawl spaces, basements, laundry rooms, and outdoors.
- Include GFCI protection for dishwashers and sump pumps.
- Install one 15-amp or 20-amp, 120-volt, GFCI-protected, receptacle for each parking space in a garage. Use the garage receptacle circuit only for receptacles in the garage and for receptacles located on garage exterior walls.
- Install at least one 120-volt receptacle in each unfinished basement area.
- Place each receptacle intended only for electric vehicle charging on a dedicated circuit.
- Install a 120-volt receptacle within 25 feet from HVAC equipment such as furnaces, boilers, and condensers.

Light Fixtures

- Use mounting straps that are anchored to the electrical boxes to mount ceiling fixtures.
- Keep non–IC-rated recessed light fixtures 3" from insulation and ½" from combustibles.
- Include at least one switch-operated lighting outlet in every habitable room, kitchen, bathroom, basement, hallway, stairway, attached garage, and attic and crawlspace area

that is used for storage or that contains equipment that requires service. This outlet may be a switched receptacle in areas other than kitchens and bathrooms.

- Do not install dimmer switches on interior stair lights unless a dimmer is installed on all switches controlling these lights.

AFCI and GFCI Protection

- Extending a branch circuit or adding a new branch to install new receptacles, lights, switches, or equipment requires a permit. The electrical inspector may require that you install arc-fault protection on the entire circuit and may require that you install GFCI protection where currently required. Check with the electrical inspector before starting such projects. GFCI protection may be required on 120-volt and 240-volt circuits.

Kitchens/Dining Rooms

- Install at least two 20-amp small-appliance receptacle circuits.
- Install dedicated 15-amp, 120-volt circuits for dishwashers and food disposals (required by many local codes). The dishwasher circuit should be GFCI protected.
- Install GFCI protection for all countertop receptacles; and for receptacles within 6 feet from the sink. The 6 feet from the sink rule includes all receptacles, such as a refrigerator receptacle, range receptacle, unused receptacles under the sink, and receptacles along walls.
- Position receptacles for appliances that will be installed within cabinets, such as microwaves or food disposals, according to the manufacturer's instructions.
- Install receptacles at countertops and work surfaces wider than 12".
- Space receptacles a maximum of 48" apart above countertops and closer together in areas where many appliances will be used.
- Locate receptacles on the wall above the countertop not more than 20" above the countertop.
- Do not connect lights to the small-appliance receptacle circuits.

Bathrooms

- Install a 20-amp circuit only for bathroom receptacles, or install a 20-amp circuit that serves receptacles and lighting in only one bathroom and no other rooms.
- Provide GFCI protection for all bathroom receptacles.
- Install a dedicated circuit for an exhaust fan with heater or other type of heating appliance, if required.

- Install at least one receptacle not more than 36" from each sink.
- Ensure light fixtures in tub/shower areas are rated for damp or wet locations, as required.

Laundry Rooms

- Install at least one 20-amp, GFCI-protected receptacle on its own circuit, located within 6 feet of a washing machine.
- Install approved conduit for wiring in unfinished rooms.
- Install a separate receptacle for an electric dryer, as applicable. This must be 30-amp (minimum), 240-volt, GFCI protected, and on a dedicated four-conductor circuit.

Living, Entertainment, Bedrooms

- Install at least one 15- or 20-amp lighting/receptacle circuit for each 600 sq. ft. of living space.
- Install a dedicated circuit for each permanent appliance, such as an air conditioner or group of electric baseboard heaters.
- Use electrical boxes listed and labeled to support ceiling fans in locations where ceiling fans are commonly installed.
- Space receptacles on walls in living and sleeping rooms a maximum of 12 feet apart.
- Check with your local electrical inspector about requirements for installing smoke and carbon monoxide alarms during remodeling.

Outdoors

- Check for underground utilities before digging.
- Use UF cable or other wiring approved for wet locations for outdoor wiring.
- Run cable and wires in approved conduit, as required by local code.
- Install in-use rated weatherproof receptacle covers.
- Bury cables and wires run in conduit at least 18" deep; cable not in conduit must be buried at least 24" deep.
- Use weatherproof electrical boxes with watertight covers.
- Provide GFCI protection for all outdoor receptacles.

Stairs/Hallways

- Use three-way switches at the top and bottom on stairways with six risers or more.
- Include receptacles in any hallway that is 10 feet long or longer.
- Position stairway lights so each step and landing is illuminated.

Prepare for Inspections

Electrical inspectors who issue the work permit for your wiring project will also visit your home to review the work. Make sure to allow time for these inspections as you plan the project. For most projects, inspectors make two visits.

The first inspection, called the rough-in, is done after the cables are run between the boxes but before the insulation, drywall, switches, and fixtures are installed. The second inspection, called the final, is done after the walls and ceilings are finished and all electrical connections are made.

When preparing for the rough-in inspection, make sure the area is neat. Sweep up sawdust and clean up any pieces of scrap wire or cable insulation. Before inspecting the boxes and cables, inspectors will check to make sure all plumbing and other mechanical work is completed. Some electrical inspectors will ask to see your building and plumbing permits.

At the final inspection, inspectors check random boxes to make sure the wire connections are correct. If they see good workmanship at the selected boxes, the inspection will be over quickly. However, if they spot a problem, inspectors may choose to inspect every connection.

Inspectors have busy schedules, so it is a good idea to arrange for an inspection several days in advance. In addition to basic compliance with code, inspectors expect your work to meet their own standards for quality. When you apply for a work permit, make sure you understand what the inspectors will look for during inspections.

You cannot put new circuits into use legally until an inspector approves them at the final inspection. If you have planned carefully and done your work well, electrical inspections are routine visits that give you confidence in your own skills.

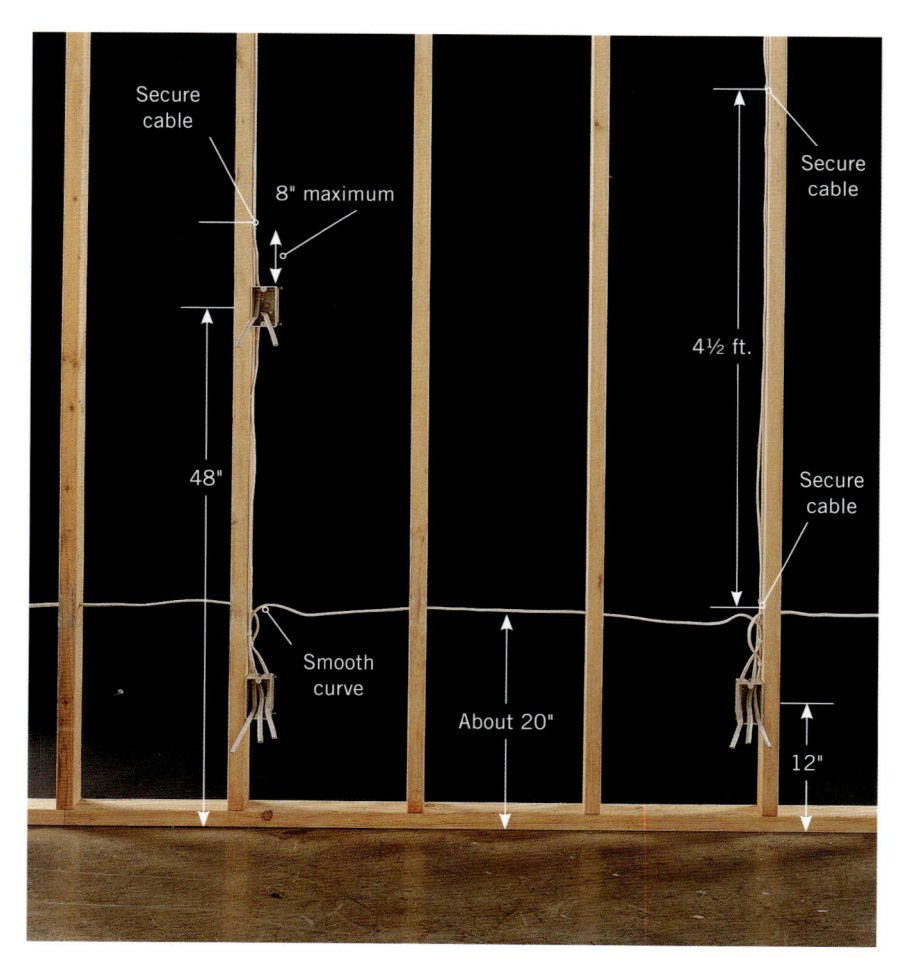

Secure cable

8" maximum

48"

Smooth curve

About 20"

Secure cable

4½ ft.

Secure cable

12"

Inspectors may measure to see that electrical boxes are mounted at consistent heights. Height may not be dictated by code, but consistency is a sign of good workmanship. Measured from the center of the boxes, receptacles in living areas typically are located 12" above the finished floor and switches at 48". For special circumstances, inspectors allow you to alter these measurements. For example, you can install switches at 36" above the floor in a child's bedroom, or set receptacles at 24" to make them more convenient for someone using a wheelchair.

Inspectors will check cables to see that they are secured within 8" of each box and every 4½ ft. thereafter when they run along studs. When bending cables, form the wire in a smooth curve. Do not crimp cables sharply or install them diagonally between framing members. Some inspectors specify that cables running between receptacle boxes should be about 20" above the floor.

What Inspectors Look For

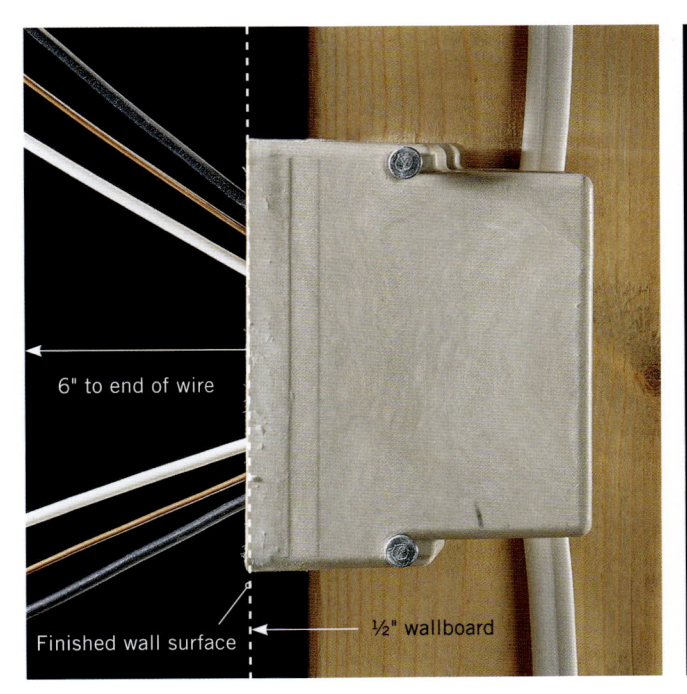

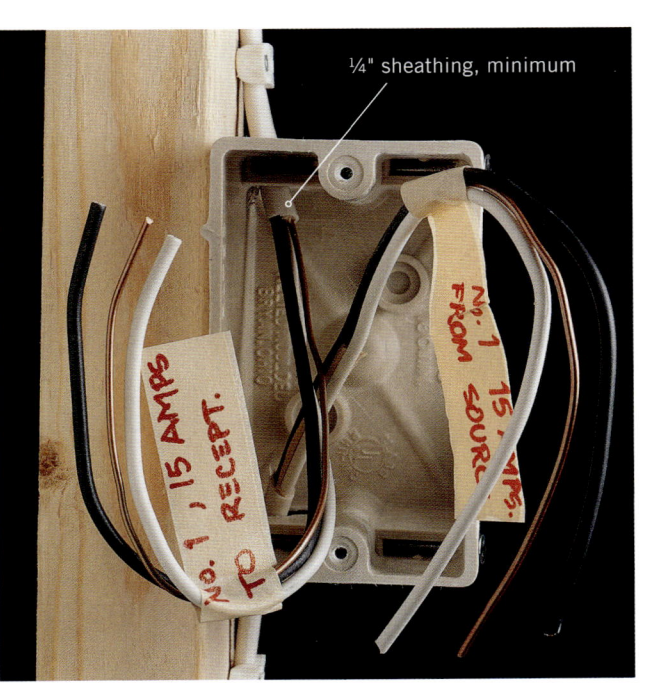

¼" sheathing, minimum

6" to end of wire

½" wallboard

Finished wall surface

Electrical box faces should extend past the front of framing members so the boxes will be flush with finished walls (left). Inspectors will check to see that all boxes are large enough for the wires they contain. Cables should be cut and stripped back so that at least 3" of usable length extends past the front of the box and so that at least ¼" of sheathing reaches into the box (right). Label all cables to show which circuits they serve: inspectors recognize this as a mark of careful work. The labels also simplify the final hookups after the drywall is installed.

IS YOUR RECEPTACLE SPACING CORRECT?

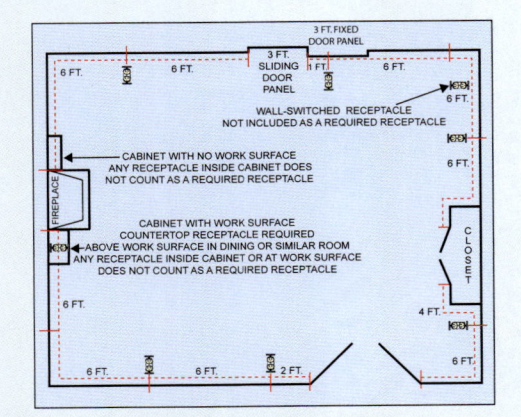

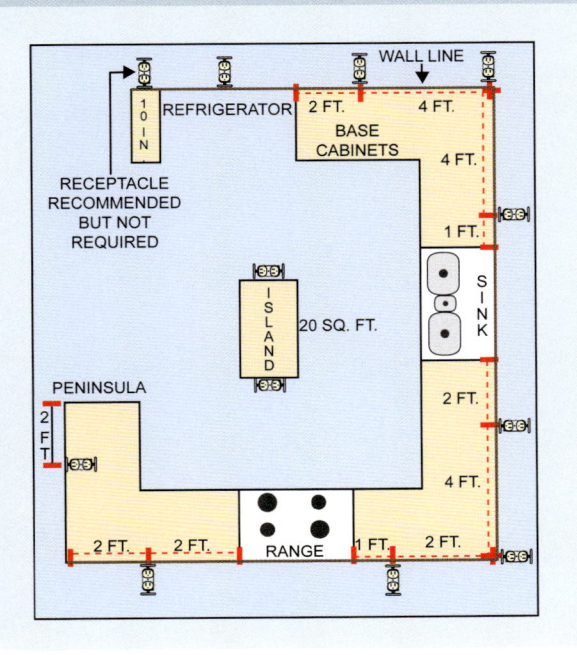

Example of receptacle spacing requirements in a typical room. Measure receptacle spacing distance along the wall line. Install receptacles along partial height walls and along balcony guards in lofts and similar areas.

Example of countertop receptacle spacing in a typical kitchen (right).

What Inspectors Look For

All wiring splices must be made with approved connectors. Common types include push-in connectors (left), standard wire connectors or "wire nuts" (center), and grounding-type wire connectors for ground wires (right).

Cable sheathing damage indicates the wiring inside (or its insulation) may be compromised. Damaged portions of cables and other wiring must be replaced to ensure safety.

Open, unused knockouts on boxes should be covered with knockout plugs to ensure that the box is fully enclosed.

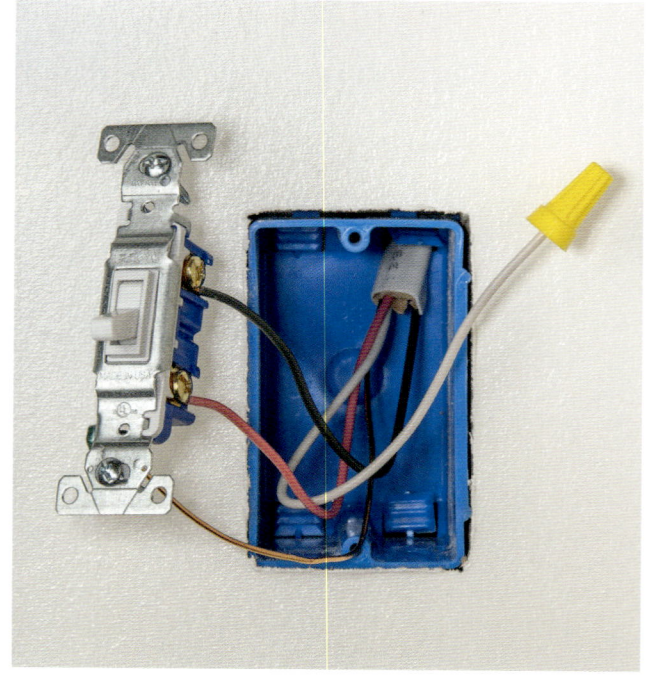

New switch installations should include a neutral conductor in the switch box. Most standard switches do not connect to neutral wires, but some "smart switches" with wireless control connect to a neutral because the switches need a small amount of current to receive wireless signals.

What Inspectors Look For

Circuits must be properly rated for the area(s) or appliance(s) they serve as well as for safe capacity. For example, a circuit for bathroom receptacles that is rated for less than 20 amps is an easy red flag during an inspection.

Closet light fixtures must be fully enclosed (over the bulb) and at least 12 inches from storage areas when the fixtures are surface-mounted. Recessed fixtures must be at least 6 inches from storage areas. Surface-mounted fixtures must be on the ceiling or on the wall above the door.

Smoke alarms are required in all bedrooms (sleeping rooms) and in areas adjoining sleeping rooms. In addition, each floor of the home must have at least one alarm, including basements and habitable attic areas. Smoke alarms and carbon monoxide alarms must be interconnected so activation of one alarm triggers all others. Check with the local code authority for specific installation details.

Carbon monoxide (CO) alarms are required in homes with fuel-fired systems (such as a gas furnace, water heater, or stove) and in homes with attached garages. Alarms are required outside of each sleeping area and inside any bedroom containing a fuel-fired appliance (such as a gas fireplace).

Estimate Electrical Loads

Before drawing a plan and applying for a work permit, make sure your home's electrical service provides enough power to handle the added load of the new circuits. In a safe wiring system, the current drawn by fixtures and appliances never exceeds the main service capacity.

To estimate electrical loads, use the work sheet on pages 130–131 or whatever method is recommended by your electrical inspector. Include the load for all existing wiring as well as that for proposed new wiring when making your evaluation.

Most of the light fixtures and plug-in appliances in your home are evaluated as part of general allowances for basic lighting/receptacle circuits and small-appliance circuits. However, appliances that are permanently installed usually require their own dedicated circuits. The electrical loads for these appliances are added in separately when evaluating wiring.

If your estimate shows that the load exceeds the service capacity, you must have an electrician upgrade the service before you can install new wiring. An electrical service upgrade is a worthwhile investment that improves the value of your home and provides plenty of power for present and future wiring projects.

AMPERAGE

AMPS × VOLTS	TOTAL CAPACITY	SAFE CAPACITY
15 A × 120 V =	1,800 watts	1,440 watts
20 A × 120 V =	2,400 watts	1,920 watts
25 A × 120 V =	3,000 watts	2,400 watts
30 A × 120 V =	3,600 watts	2,880 watts
20 A × 240 V =	4,800 watts	3,840 watts
30 A × 240 V =	7,200 watts	5,760 watts

Amperage rating can be used to find the wattage of an appliance. Multiply the amperage by the voltage of the circuit. For example, a 13-amp, 120-volt circular saw is rated for 1,560 watts.

Calculating Loads

Nameplate

Add 1,500 watts for each small-appliance circuit required by the local electrical code. In most communities, three such circuits are required—two in the kitchen and one for the laundry—for a total of 4,500 watts. No further calculations are needed for appliances that plug into small-appliance or basic lighting/receptacle circuits.

If the nameplate gives the rating in kilowatts, find the watts by multiplying kilowatts times 1,000. If an appliance lists only amps, find watts by multiplying the amps times the voltage—either 120 or 240 volts.

FIXED DEVICES

Do not connect one or more fixed devices that in total exceed 50 percent of a multiple outlet branch circuit's amperage rating. Fixed devices do not include light fixtures. This means that all fixed devices (such as a permanently wired disposal or hot water circulating pump) on a multiple outlet branch circuit may not exceed 7.5 amps (about 900 watts) on a 15-amp multiple outlet branch circuit and may not exceed 10 amps (about 1,200 watts) on a 20-amp multiple outlet branch circuit.

Air-conditioning and heating appliances are not used at the same time, so figure in only the larger of these two numbers when evaluating your home's electrical load.

Locating Wattage

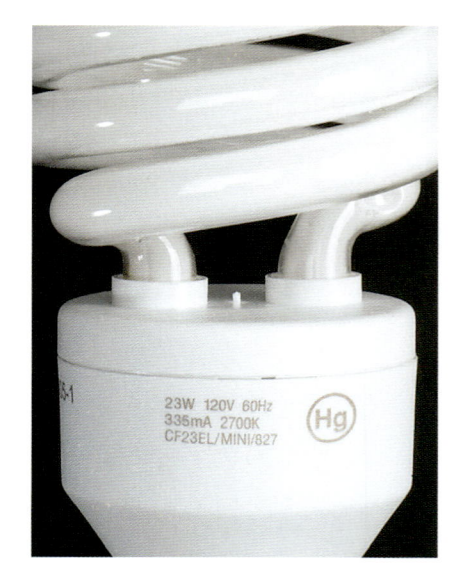

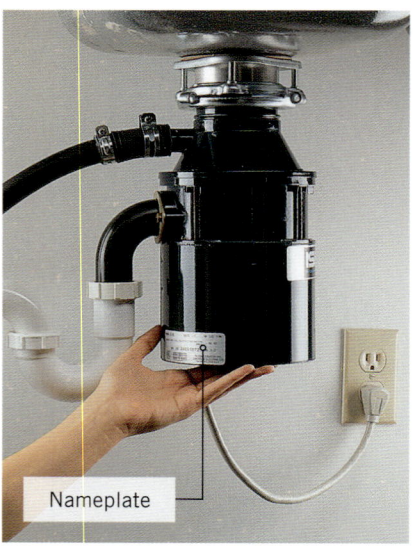

Lightbulb wattage ratings are printed on the base or top of the bulb. If a light fixture has more than one bulb, remember to add the wattages of all the bulbs to find the total wattage of the fixture.

Electric water heaters are permanent appliances that require their own dedicated 30-amp, 240-volt circuits. Most water heaters are rated between 3,500 and 4,500 watts. If the nameplate lists several wattage ratings, use the one labeled "Total Connected Wattage" when figuring electrical loads.

Food disposers are considered permanent appliances and may require their own dedicated 15-amp, 120-volt circuits. Most disposers are rated between 500 and 900 watts.

Dishwashers installed permanently under a countertop may need dedicated 15-amp, 120-volt circuits. Dishwasher ratings are usually between 1,000 and 1,500 watts. Portable dishwashers are regarded as part of small-appliance circuits and are not added in when figuring loads.

Electric ranges can be rated for as little as 3,000 watts or as much as 12,000 watts. They usually require dedicated 120/240-volt circuits. Find the exact wattage rating by reading the nameplate found inside the oven door or on the back of the unit.

Installed microwave ovens are regarded as permanent appliances. Add in its wattage rating when calculating loads. The nameplate is found on the back of the cabinet or inside the front door. Most microwave ovens are rated between 500 and 1,200 watts. A permanently installed microwave should be on a dedicated 20-amp, 120-volt circuit.

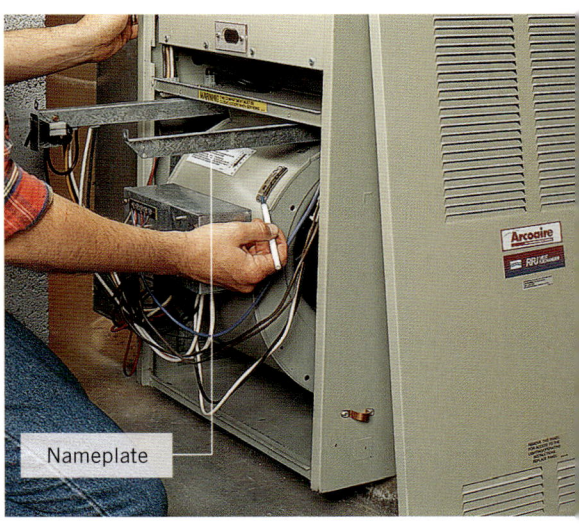

Freezers are appliances that may need a dedicated 15- or 20-amp, 120-volt circuits. Freezer ratings are usually between 240 and 480 watts. But combination refrigerator-freezers are plugged into small-appliance circuits and do not need their own dedicated circuits. The nameplate for a freezer is found inside the door or on the back of the unit, just below the door seal.

Electric clothes dryers are permanent appliances that need dedicated 30-amp, 120/240-volt circuits. The wattage rating is printed on the nameplate inside the dryer door. Use 5,000 watts as a minimum, regardless of the printed rating. Washing machines and gas-heat clothes dryers with electric tumbler motors do not need dedicated circuits. They plug into the 20-amp small-appliance circuit in the laundry room.

Forced-air furnaces and heat pump air handlers have electric fans and are considered permanent appliances. They require dedicated 15-amp, 120-volt circuits. Include the fan wattage rating, printed on a nameplate inside the control panel, when figuring wattage loads for heating. You should also include the wattage rating for heat pump backup heating coils.

A central air conditioner requires a dedicated 240-volt circuit. Estimate normal wattage use by multiplying the RLA (rated load amps) by 240 (volts).

Window air conditioners may be considered permanent appliances if they are connected to a dedicated circuit. Through-wall air conditioners are considered permanent appliances. The wattage rating, which can range from 500 to 2,000 watts, is found on the nameplate located inside the front grill. Include permanently installed through-wall air conditioners and window air conditioners that are connected to a dedicated circuit in your evaluation.

Electric baseboard heaters that are permanently installed require a dedicated circuit and must be figured into the load calculations. Use the maximum wattage rating printed inside the cover. In general, 240-volt baseboard-type heaters are rated for 180 to 250 watts for each linear foot.

How to Estimate Electrical Loads—with sample numbers

STEP	DESCRIPTION	QTY	UNITS	QTY	UNITS	LOAD (watts)
1.	**General lighting and receptacle circuits.** Multiply living area square footage by 3 watts per square foot. Include new and existing areas. Do not include garage and porches. Include parts of the basement that can be finished.	1,500	sq. ft.	3	watts/ sq. ft.	4,500
2.	**Kitchen and laundry circuits.** At least 3 circuits are required; 2 small-appliance circuits for the kitchen, dining, and breakfast areas, and 1 laundry circuit. Multiply the number of circuits by 1,500 watts per circuit. The refrigerator is included in the small-appliance circuits, not in the fixed appliance circuits. You may add an additional circuit for the refrigerator, if you wish.	3	circuits	1,500	watts/ circuit	4,500
3.	**Fixed appliance circuits.** Add the wattage ratings on the appliance labels. These appliances are often on a dedicated circuit. Examples are listed below.					
	Range	1	appliance	12,300	watts	12,300
	Surface cooking unit	0	appliance		watts	0
	Microwave oven	0	appliance		watts	0
	Wall oven	0	appliance		watts	0
	Disposer	1	appliance	800	watts	800
	Built-in dishwasher	1	appliance	1,200	watts	1,200
	Electric clothes dryer	1	appliance	5,000	watts	5,000
	Freezer	1	appliance	550	watts	550
	Heat pump air handler	0	appliance		watts	0
	Furnace	0	appliance		watts	0
	Electric water heater	0	appliance		watts	0
	Others (e.g., sump pump, well pump, pool pump)	0	appliance		watts	0
	Total fixed appliances					19,850
4.	**Add loads from steps 1, 2, and 3.**					28,850
5.	**Subtract 10,000 watts from Step 4.**					(10,000)
6.	**Adjusted load**					18,850
7.	**Calculated load.** Multiply the adjusted load (Step 6) by .40. This adjusts for all appliances not operating at the same time.					7,540

STEP	DESCRIPTION	QTY	UNITS	QTY	UNITS	LOAD (watts)
8.	**Cooling loads.** Include all heat pump or air conditioning condensers. Include all window air conditioners and through-wall air conditioners on dedicated circuits. Do not include window air conditioners connected to general lighting and receptacle circuits.					
	Condenser 1	*1*	*condenser*	*3,500*	*watts*	*3,500*
	Condenser 2	*0*	*condenser*	*0*	*watts*	*0*
	Window and through-wall air conditioners	*1*	*ac*	*1,100*	*watts*	*1,100*
	Total cooling loads					*4,600*
9.	**Heating loads.** Examples are listed below. This is a simplified procedure that will overestimate the heating loads.					
	Heat pump condenser 1	*0*	*condenser*		*watts*	*0*
	Heat pump condenser 2	*0*	*condenser*		*watts*	*0*
	Heat pump strip 1	*0*	*heat strips*		*watts*	*0*
	Heat pump strip 2	*0*	*heat strips*		*watts*	*0*
	Electric furnace/boiler	*1*	*appliance*	*1,200*	*watts*	*1,200*
	Electric baseboard heaters	*4*	*heaters*	*1,350*	*watts*	*5,400*
	Total heating loads					*6,600*
10.	**Enter the larger number from Steps 8 and 9.**					*6,600*
11.	**Add 10,000 watts to the calculated load from Step 7.**					*17,540*
12.	**Add Steps 10 and 11.**					*24,140*
13.	**Divide Step 12 by 240.** This is your estimated service current load in amps.					*101*
14.	**Enter your current service amperage.**					*150*
15.	**Compare the numbers in Steps 13 and 14.** If Step 13 is larger, you may need to upgrade your electric service. If Step 14 is larger, you are probably okay with your existing service.					

NOTICE: This is a service load calculation for the entire house. This is a simplified procedure that will usually overestimate the current load. Calculation of the feeder load for a subpanel is different. Contact your local electrical inspector or a licensed electrician for guidance about feeder load calculations.

Draw a Diagram + Obtain a Permit

Drawing a wiring diagram is the last step in planning a circuit installation. A detailed wiring diagram helps you get a permit, makes it easy to create a list of materials, and serves as a guide for laying out circuits and installing cables and fixtures. Use the circuit maps on pages 148–165 as a guide for planning wiring configurations and cable runs. Bring the diagram and materials list when you visit electrical inspectors to apply for a permit.

Never install new wiring without following your community's permit and inspection procedure. A permit is not expensive, and it ensures that your work will be reviewed by a qualified inspector. If you install new wiring without the proper permit, an accident or fire traced to faulty wiring could cause your insurance company to discontinue your policy and can hurt the resale value of your home.

When electrical inspectors look over your wiring diagram, they will ask questions to see if you have a basic understanding of the electrical code and fundamental wiring skills. Some inspectors ask these questions informally, while others give a short written test. Inspectors may allow you to do some, but not all, of the work. For example, they may ask that all final circuit connections at the circuit breaker panel be made by a licensed electrician, while allowing you to do all other work.

A few communities allow you to install wiring only when supervised by an electrician. This means you can still install your own wiring but must hire an electrician to apply for the work permit and to check your work before inspectors review it. The electrician is held responsible for the quality of the job.

Remember that it is the inspectors' responsibility to help you do a safe and professional job. Feel free to call them with questions about wiring techniques or materials.

A detailed wiring diagram and a list of materials is required before electrical inspectors will issue a work permit. If blueprints exist for the space you are remodeling, start your electrical diagram by tracing the wall outlines from the blueprint. Use standard electrical symbols (next page) to clearly show all the receptacles, switches, light fixtures, and permanent appliances. Make a copy of the symbol key and attach it to the wiring diagram for the inspector's convenience. Show each cable run, and label its wire size and circuit amperage.

How to Draw a Wiring Plan

Draw a scaled diagram of the space you will be wiring, showing walls, doors, windows, plumbing pipes and fixtures, and heating and cooling ducts. Find the floor space by multiplying room length by width, and indicate this on the diagram.

Mark the location of all switches, receptacles, light fixtures, and permanent appliances, using the electrical symbols shown below. Where you locate these devices along the cable run determines how they are wired. Use the circuit maps on pages 148–165 as a guide for drawing wiring diagrams.

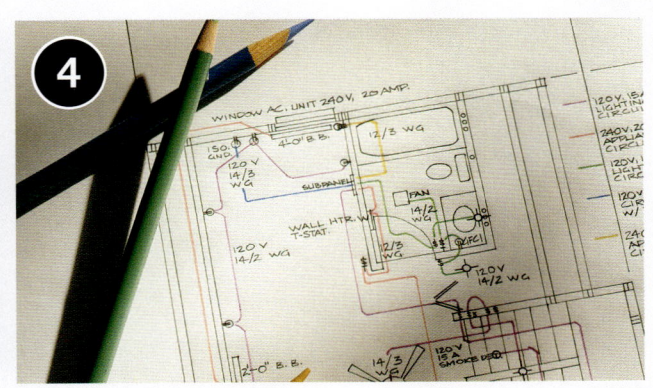

Draw in cable runs between devices. Indicate cable size and type and the amperage of the circuits. Use a different-colored pencil for each circuit.

Identify the wattages for permanent appliances and the type and size of each electrical box. On another sheet of paper, make a detailed list of all materials you will use.

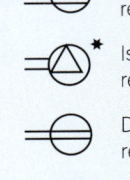 ## ELECTRICAL SYMBOL KEY (COPY THIS KEY AND ATTACH IT TO YOUR WIRING PLAN)

240-volt receptacle	Switched receptacle	J Junction box	CF Ceiling fan
Isolated ground receptacle	Weatherproof receptacle WP	S Ceiling pull switch	D Electric door opener
Duplex receptacle	S_{TH} Thermostat	Surface-mounted light fixture	BT Low-voltage transformer
240-volt dryer receptacle D	S_P Pilot-light switch	R Recessed light fixture	TV Television jack
Singleplex receptacle	S Single-pole switch	Fluorescent light fixture	Data Port
Fourplex receptacle	S_T Timer switch	Wall-mounted light fixture	D Smoke alarm
GFCI duplex receptacle GFCI	S_3 Three-way switch	WP Weatherproof light fixture	VF Exhaust fan

Room-by-Room Wiring

Most major home projects involve expansion or upgrading of existing wiring. For example, if you are remodeling a room of your house, and the plan calls for structural or significant cosmetic changes, it's probably also an ideal time to bring the wiring up to current standards. And when you pull a permit for the project, an electrical update will likely be required.

Updating the wiring for a remodeled space often includes adding new devices and fixtures (or replacing old ones) and, in many cases, adding new circuits.

Requirements vary considerably from room to room. A remodeled bedroom may need only a few added receptacles, some new light fixtures, and a ceiling fan, while a major kitchen renovation will likely require several new circuits if not a complete overhaul of the room's wiring.

One of the nice things about electrical systems is that their circuit layout makes them relatively compartmentalized. This means you can easily update one room without making major changes elsewhere, provided your service panel has enough capacity for any added circuits. And it makes good sense to bring the entire room up to current standards, whether it's required or not. Updating a room's wiring and devices not only adds convenience, it also enhances safety. If you remodel your laundry room, for instance, you now must provide GFCI protection for all of the receptacles—an important safety improvement for this often-wet area. And most areas of the house now must have AFCI protection.

Electrical code requirements cover all aspects of bathroom wiring, including receptacles, lighting, exhaust fans, and heaters. Most bathrooms need only one or two circuits, but those with jetted tubs or special heating systems will need more. Current requirements ensure that bathrooms have plenty of power for hair dryers, curling irons, and any other plug-in devices.

Kitchens

An updated kitchen with the usual suite of electric appliances will often have at least six individual circuits, but many kitchens have eight or more, depending on their size and the number of large appliances they have.

The most important things to watch out for in a kitchen wiring plan are GFCI protection and receptacle placement. All receptacles must be GFCI protected. In addition, any receptacle within 6 feet of a sink (measured from the sink's top inside edge) must have GFCI protection. This includes 240-volt receptacles for electric ranges and other large plug-in appliances. Circuits serving dishwashers also must be GFCI-protected, and all 15- and 20-amp circuits in the kitchen also must be AFCI-protected.

Placement of countertop receptacles follows the so-called "2-foot, 4-foot" rule: In short, this means that receptacles serving countertop areas are spaced no more than 4 feet apart, and that no countertop area (measured along the wall) is more than 2 feet from a receptacle. Receptacles are no longer required to be installed at islands and peninsulas. If a receptacle is not installed, the island or peninsula must be prewired on the kitchen small appliance branch circuit so a receptacle can be installed later. There are some exceptions and specific dimension requirements for applying the 2-foot, 4-foot rule, so check with the local code authority for details.

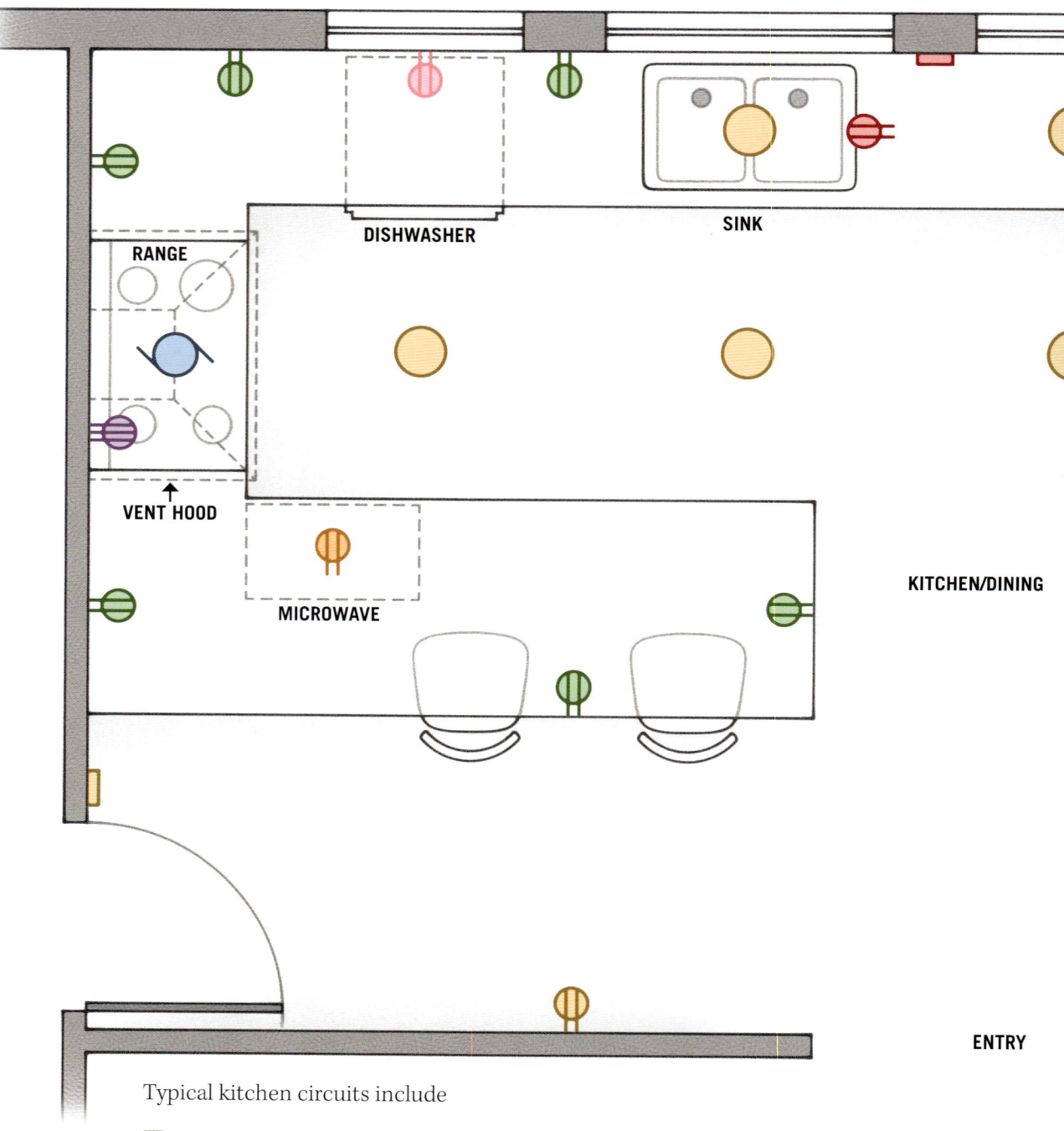

RANGE

DISHWASHER

SINK

VENT HOOD

MICROWAVE

KITCHEN/DINING

ENTRY

Typical kitchen circuits include

■ **Circuits #1 + #2: Small-Appliance Circuits**
The NEC requires at least two 120-volt, 20-amp circuits feeding receptacles in countertop areas and all wall (and floor) receptacles in the kitchen and adjacent pantry and dining areas. These are commonly called the "small-appliance" circuits because most of the receptacles feed plug-in countertop appliances. Lighting and fixed appliances may not connect to these circuits. However, receptacles for a plug-in clock or ignition on a gas stove may use these circuits. If the dining and/or pantry areas are large and contain a lot of wall receptacles, it's a good idea to include a separate 20-amp circuit for those receptacles.

■ **Circuit #3: Lighting**
One or more 120-volt, 15-amp circuit for all kitchen lighting, including overhead (ambient) lighting, task lighting (such as undercabinet lights), and accent lighting (pendant fixtures, lighting in or above cabinets, etc.). By code, the room must have at least one light fixture controlled by a wall switch. For large kitchens, it's a good idea to control general lighting in multiple locations with three-way and four-way switches. **Note:** Kitchen lighting can be on a general lighting circuit serving other rooms.

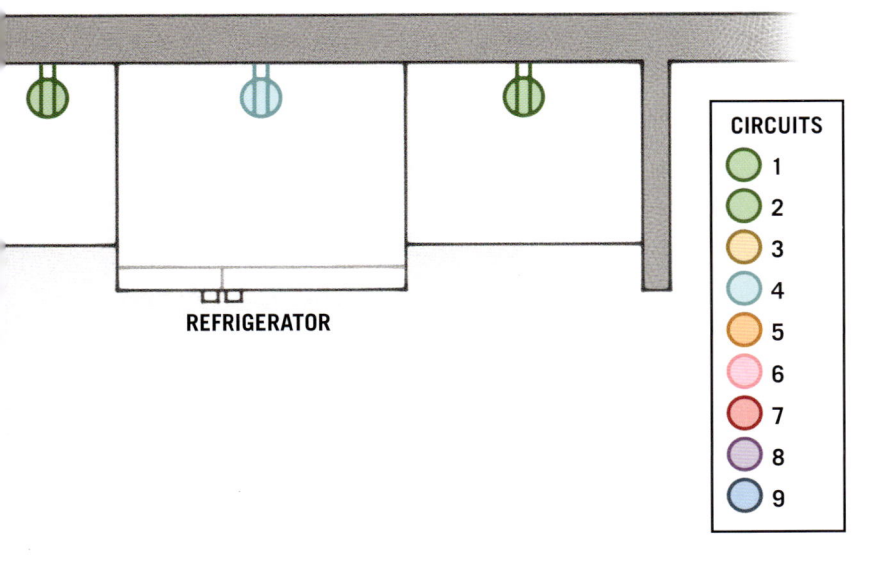

REFRIGERATOR

CIRCUITS

1
2
3
4
5
6
7
8
9

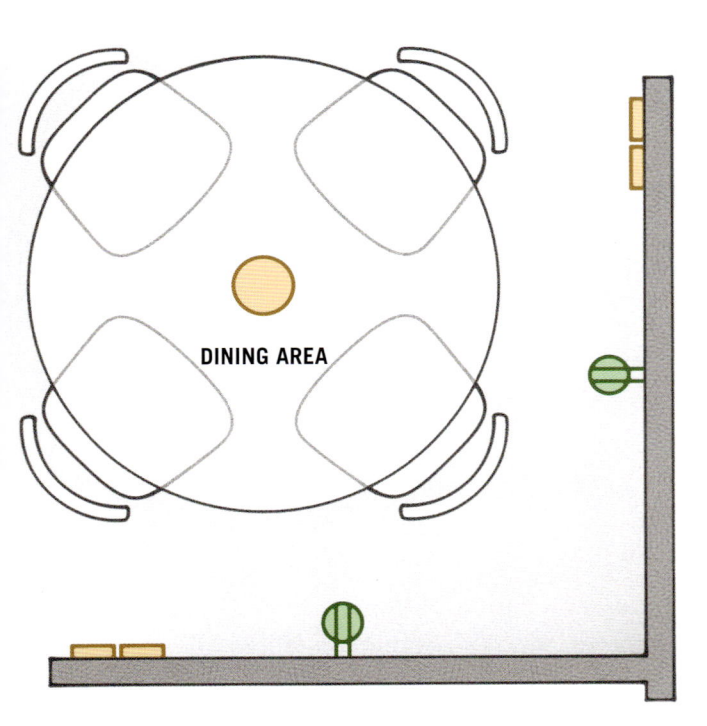

DINING AREA

Circuit #4: Refrigerator

Refrigerators are permitted by the NEC to plug into a receptacle on one of the small-appliance circuits (Circuits #1 + #2), but if you're remodeling the kitchen, it makes sense to include a dedicated 120-volt, 15- or 20-amp circuit for the refrigerator (this is required in some areas). If the fridge receptacle is within 6 feet of the sink, it must be GFCI protected.

Circuit # 5: Microwave

A portable plug-in microwave can be served by a countertop receptacle (there may be local restrictions on wattage), but as with the fridge, it's a good practice to include a dedicated 20-amp circuit for the microwave. Full-size microwaves draw 1,000 watts or more, which can strain a circuit's capacity when other high-wattage appliances, such as toaster ovens or hot-water kettles, are running at the same time.

Circuits #6 + #7: Dishwasher + Garbage Disposer

The NEC permits supplying a dishwasher and garbage disposer on a single circuit, but the combined wattage rating of both appliances must not exceed the safe capacity of the circuit. However, many local codes require separate circuits for these fixed appliances.

A dishwasher typically is fed by a 120-volt, 15- or 20-amp circuit, and it must be GFCI protected. A disposer circuit may be 15-amp or 20-amp, but 20-amp is generally recommended, especially when the circuit also feeds the dishwasher. Disposers are fed by a receptacle installed in the sink base cabinet, or they can be hardwired with liquid-tight flexible conduit. They are typically controlled by a switch installed on the wall near the sink.

Circuit #8: Electric Range, Cooktop, or Oven

An electric range, oven, or cooktop requires a dedicated 120/240-volt circuit with an insulated neutral. For a full-size range, it is best to install a 50-amp circuit, using 6-AWG copper wire. Freestanding ranges typically plug into a wall or floor receptacle, which must be four-slot (separate neutral and ground wires). Cooktops and built-in ovens typically are hardwired and may need a 30-, 40-, or 50-amp circuit, depending on the appliance wattage and the local code requirements.

Circuit #9: Range Hood

Range hoods, or kitchen exhaust fans, vary widely in size and wattage, so it's important to consult the manufacturer's recommendations for circuit capacity. For plug-in fans, the NEC requires a dedicated 120-volt circuit; local code may or may not have the same requirement for hardwired fans. When a dedicated circuit is not required, an exhaust fan may be served by a kitchen lighting circuit, provided the circuit capacity is not exceeded.

Bathrooms

Bathrooms are the second most complex rooms to wire (next to kitchens, of course), but they're much simpler than kitchens. As a bare minimum, the NEC requires a 120-volt, 20-amp, GFCI-protected receptacle within 3 feet of each sink as well as a light controlled by a wall switch near the entrance. If the bathroom does not have a window that opens, it must have an exhaust fan with a capacity of at least 50 CFM (cubic feet per minute).

Meeting just these minimum requirements may be suitable for a small powder room or half bath, but not anything bigger. A typical family bathroom may have two or more circuits, multiple receptacles, several lights, a large exhaust fan, and possibly a heater. A luxury primary bath may have all of that plus towel heaters, additional exhaust fans, a dedicated circuit for a whirlpool tub or a 240-volt circuit feeding a spa heater.

There are some special rules governing what you can put on a bathroom circuit, resulting in two basic approaches to the wiring plan:

1. A single 20-amp circuit feeds everything in a single bathroom, including receptacle(s), light(s), and exhaust fan. This circuit may not be used for any other room.

2. One or more 20-amp circuits feeds the receptacles in one or more bathrooms, but it must be used only for bathroom receptacles. In addition, a 15-amp or 20-amp lighting circuit feeds lights and exhaust fans in one or more bathrooms or lighting and/or receptacles in other rooms.

The first approach makes sense if you're wiring a single bathroom with relatively simple needs, as it can be fed with a single home run from the service panel. However, if there are any heaters involved—such as an exhaust fan with heat, an in-wall heater, or even a heater-type light fixture—additional circuits may be required.

The second approach makes more sense for everything else and it's better suited for bathrooms with potentially high demand. For example, in a busy bathroom for growing children, there may be multiple high-wattage appliances (hair dryers, curling irons, heaters, etc.) running at the same time; that's a lot of power draw for a single circuit. Separating the receptacles from the other loads in the room leaves more capacity for the receptacles.

Finally, there are some special rules for tub and shower areas:

- A light fixture directly above a tub or shower must be rated for wet locations if it will be subject to shower spray; otherwise, it must be rated for damp locations.

- The *bathing zone*—defined as the shower or tub area and 3 feet out from and 8 feet above the shower threshold or tub rim—can not have a paddle fan, hanging lights, track lights, or cord-connected fixtures.

A typical family bathroom might have the following circuits:

Circuit #1: Receptacles
120-volt, 20-amp circuit with a GFCI breaker or at least one GFCI receptacle (wired for multiple-location protection if there are additional receptacles; see page 106).

Circuit #2: Lighting and Ventilation
120-volt, 15- or 20-amp circuit for all lighting and a standard exhaust fan. If the exhaust fan includes a heater, it may need its own circuit, but it will surely need to be 20 amp.

Circuit #3: Heating
120-volt, 20-amp circuit for a small in-wall heater or an exhaust fan with a heater. For a larger heating unit, a 240-volt circuit may be required.

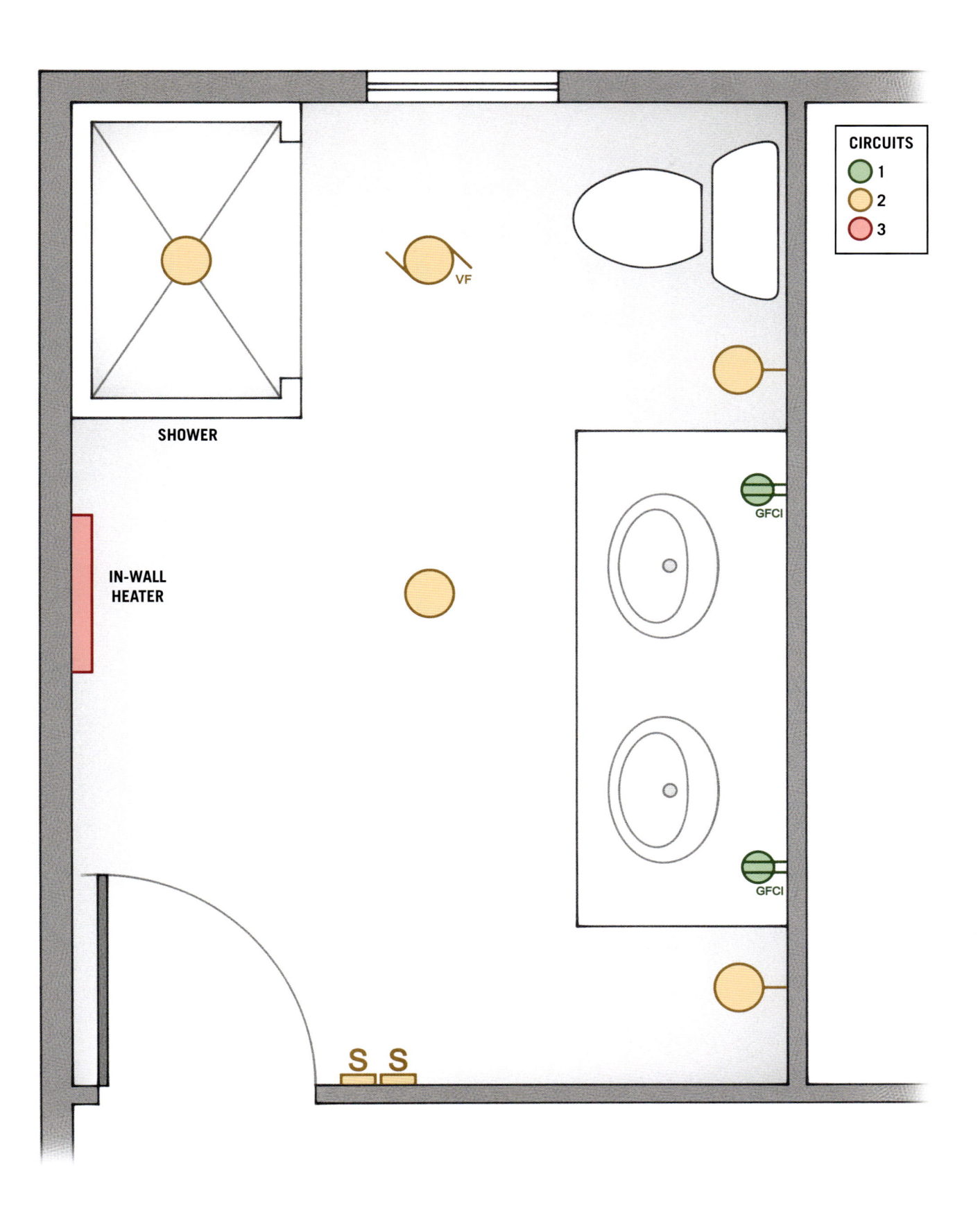

SHOWER

IN-WALL HEATER

CIRCUITS

1

2

3

VF

GFCI

GFCI

S S

Living + Dining Rooms

Living areas—including family rooms, TV rooms, rec rooms, living rooms, and dining rooms—generally need lighting and receptacles, and these may or may not be on the same circuit. Like all rooms in the house, each room in the living area must have a switch-controlled light or a switched receptacle (for plugging in a lamp that's controlled by a wall switch at the room's entrance). Receptacles follow the "6-foot, 12-foot" rule: Receptacles spaced no more than 12 feet apart so that no wall space is more than 6 feet from a receptacle. Any wall space 2 feet or longer must have a receptacle. All 120 volt, 15- and 20-amp circuits must be AFCI protected. In addition to these basic standards, there are plenty of easy upgrades that will help make rooms more functional and convenient:

- Full lighting control at all room entrances, with three-way or four-way switch configurations.

- Dimmer control for most or all fixed lighting.

- Braced, ceiling-fan-rated box and separate switch control for a ceiling fan.

- Dedicated circuits for window air conditioners or baseboard heaters.

- Receptacles closely flanking each window, fireplace, and built-in features.

- Recessed receptacle and data cable boxes for wall-mount TVs.

- Floor receptacles for furniture groupings in room centers.

- Lighting outlets for built-in cabinetry.

All circuits in living areas must be AFCI-protected. Dining rooms treated as living areas must not be connected to the kitchen small-appliance receptacle circuits. Breakfast and dining areas may be connected to the kitchen small appliance branch circuits.

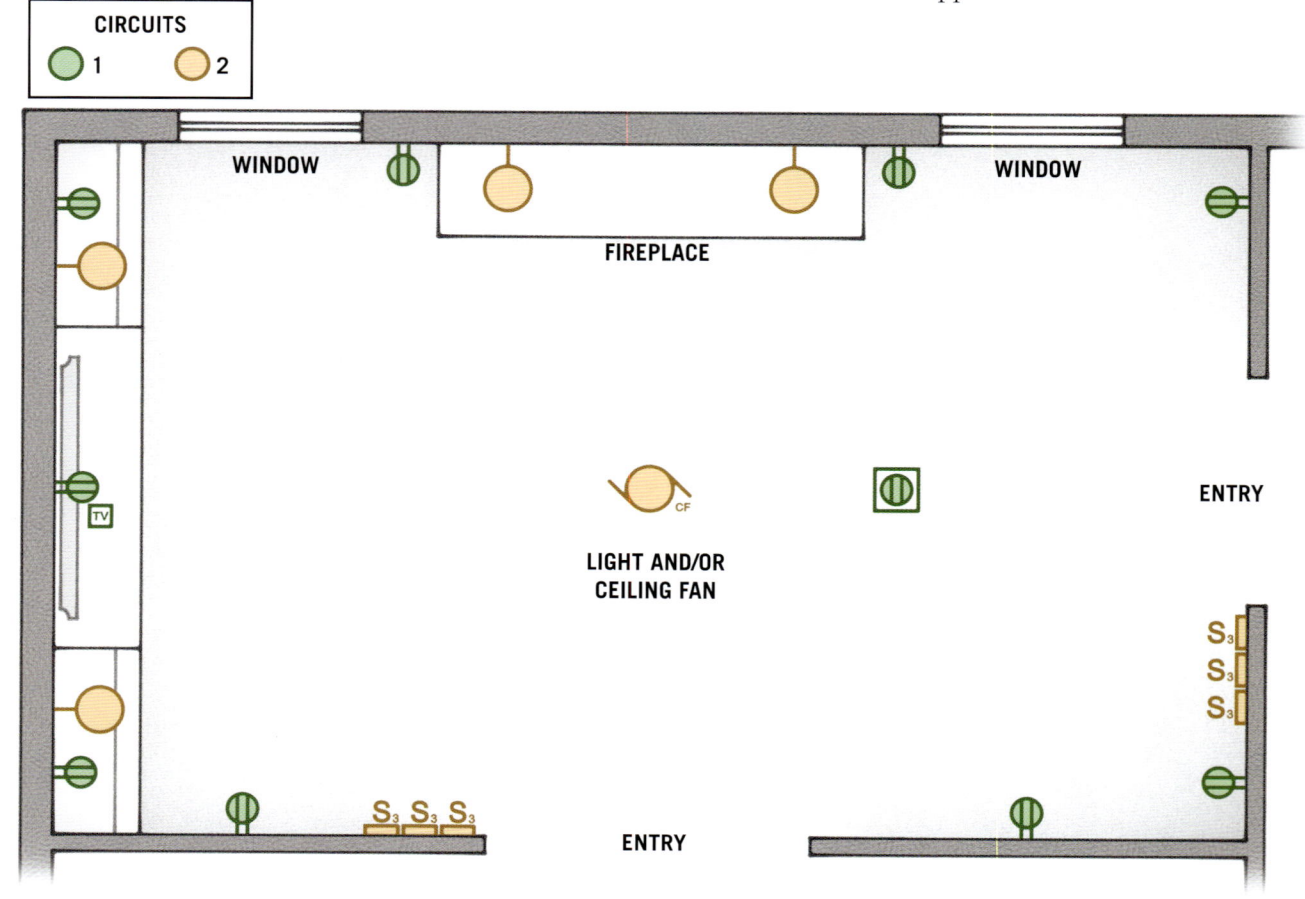

CIRCUITS
1
2

BED

CLOSET

WINDOW

LIGHT AND/OR
CELING FAN

Bedrooms

Bedrooms don't need much to meet code requirements and are typically supplied by one or two circuits. But as with living and dining areas, bedrooms can benefit greatly from additional receptacles and a thoughtful lighting and switch layout. The minimum requirements for bedrooms include a switch-controlled overhead light or a switched receptacle, and standard receptacles following the 6-foot, 12-foot rule. All bedroom circuits must be AFCI-protected and must include a smoke alarm (see page 218).

Adding more receptacles and switches can make a bedroom not only more user friendly, but it will also be more versatile, allowing for arranging (and rearranging) furniture any way you like. Consider the following upgrades in a bedroom plan:

- Include a receptacle about 2 feet from each wall corner, on both adjacent walls. This provides a convenient place to plug in lamps, electronics, or appliances regardless of the furniture arrangement. Consider making these two-receptacle (quad) outlets to allow for office equipment, such as monitors and printers.

- Add switched lighting at either side of the bed if you have established the bed location. Bedside switches can control a wall-mounted reading light on each side of the bed as well as control the room's overhead lighting and ceiling fan (as applicable).

- Install a braced, ceiling-fan-rated box at room's center for the overhead light and optional ceiling fan. Include separate switch control for a fan.

- Provide switch-controlled lighting in walk-in closets. Lighting is not required in reach-in closets, but it greatly improves usability. The best place for lights is the wall above the door; this keeps fixtures well away from storage areas (a code requirement; see page 125) and it prevents shadows beneath shelving. Provide cable TV and data ports where a television and a desk may be located.

Hallways, Stairways + Foyers

Hallways, stairs, foyers, and mudrooms typically are served by lighting and receptacle circuits (and often by a single circuit), in addition to service for smoke alarms and carbon monoxide alarms. Most code requirements are based on the size and/or layout of the space. As a simple upgrade to code minimums, you can always include more receptacles or switches for added convenience and, in the case of lighting, improved safety. All 120 volt, 15- and 20-amp circuits must be AFCI protected.

Hallways have one or more entrances, but all have at least two ends, and all must have adequate lighting controlled by one or more wall switches. A hallway with two entrances should have a three-way switch at each end. Those with a single entrance need a switch at the entrance. It's easy to add a switch based on convenience. For example, if there are two bedrooms at one end of a hallway, a switch on the wall between the bedroom doors provides convenient control for someone exiting either room. If the hallway is at least 10 feet long, it must have at least one receptacle but it can certainly have more.

All stairways need lighting that illuminates all landings and stair treads (the horizontal part of a step). If the staircase has at least six risers (the vertical part of a step), the lighting must be controlled by a three-way switch at the top and bottom of the staircase. Receptacles are not required on stairways— this is not a good place to leave plug-in appliances— but it adds convenience to include a receptacle on a wall area near the top and bottom of the stairs, for plugging in a vacuum cleaner.

Foyers and entryways that are larger than 60 square feet must have a receptacle on any wall that is at least 3 feet long. The door and any windows reaching to the floor do not count for this requirement. For convenience, safety, and aesthetics, most entryways have an overhead light fixture illuminating the entire area.

Mudrooms are entry areas that may be considered foyers, but if they are at least 7 × 10 feet (the minimum size for habitable space), they may be considered living areas. So it's important to check with the local authority for specific requirements.

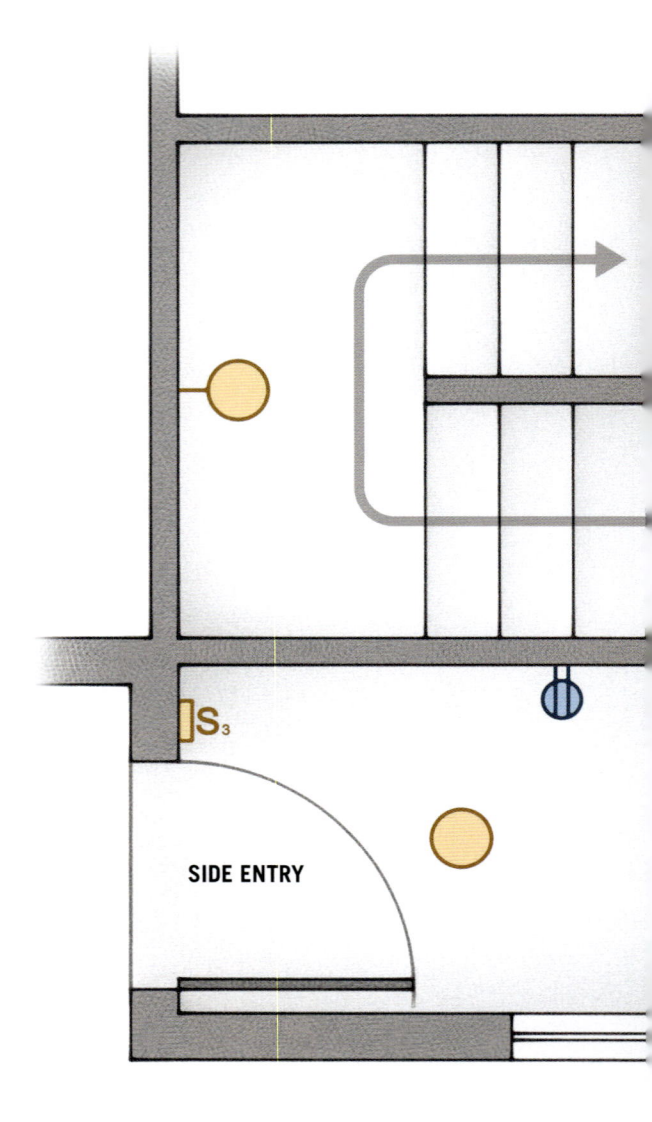

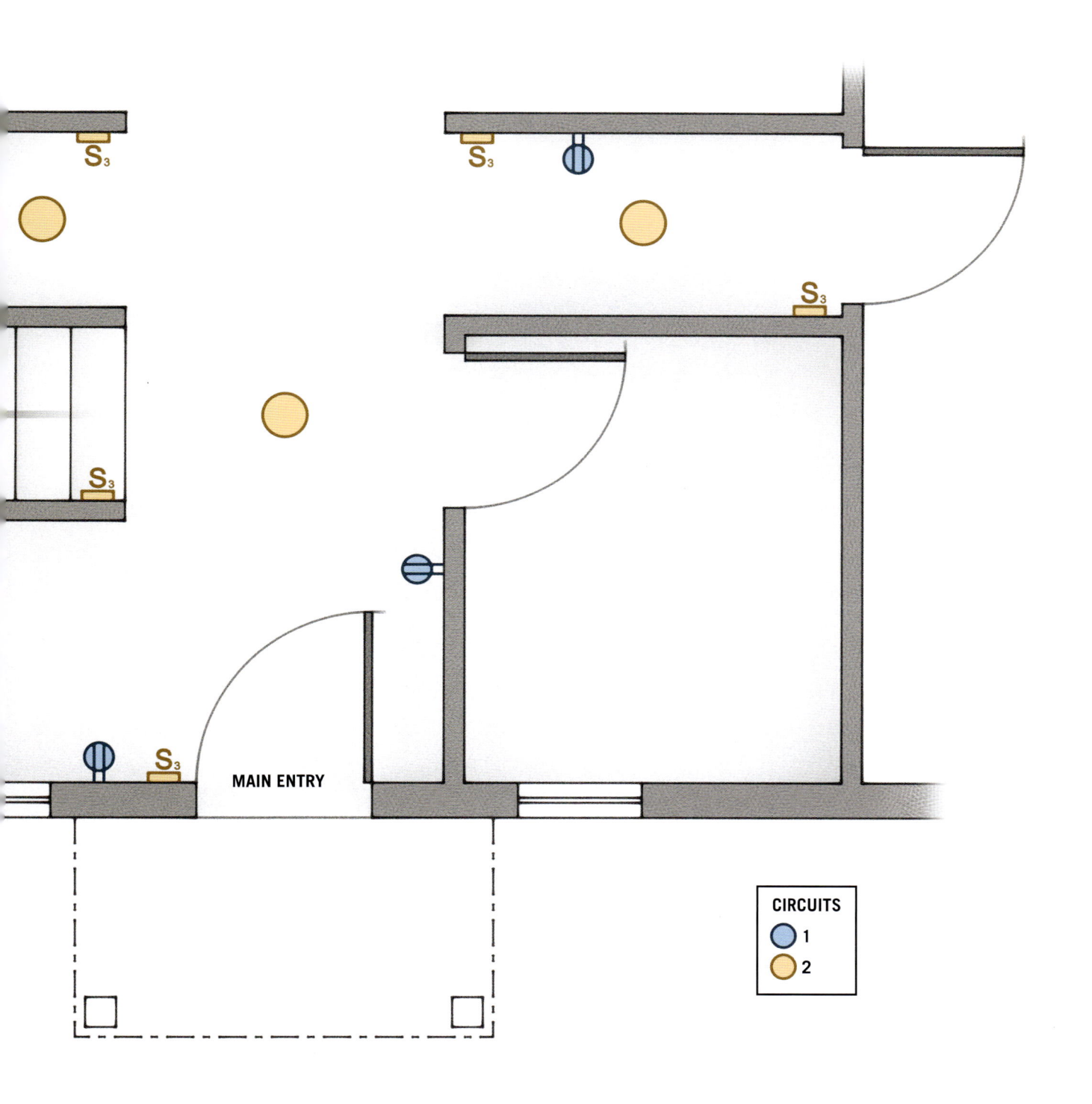

MAIN ENTRY

CIRCUITS
- 1
- 2

Laundry Room

Laundry rooms require at least one dedicated 120-volt, 20-amp receptacle circuit plus service from a separate lighting circuit. The lighting circuit may serve other rooms; the receptacle circuit may not. Only one 20-amp receptacle is required, and it must be located within 6 feet of the washing machine. A gas dryer can also use this receptacle or any others on the same circuit. If the room has any storage or work space, such as a counter area for ironing or folding clothes, it's a good idea to include one or more additional receptacles. Al 15- and 20-amp receptacles must be GFCI- and AFCI-protected.

If the laundry room contains an electric dryer, it needs a 30-amp (minimum), GFCI-protected receptacle fed by a four-conductor branch circuit.

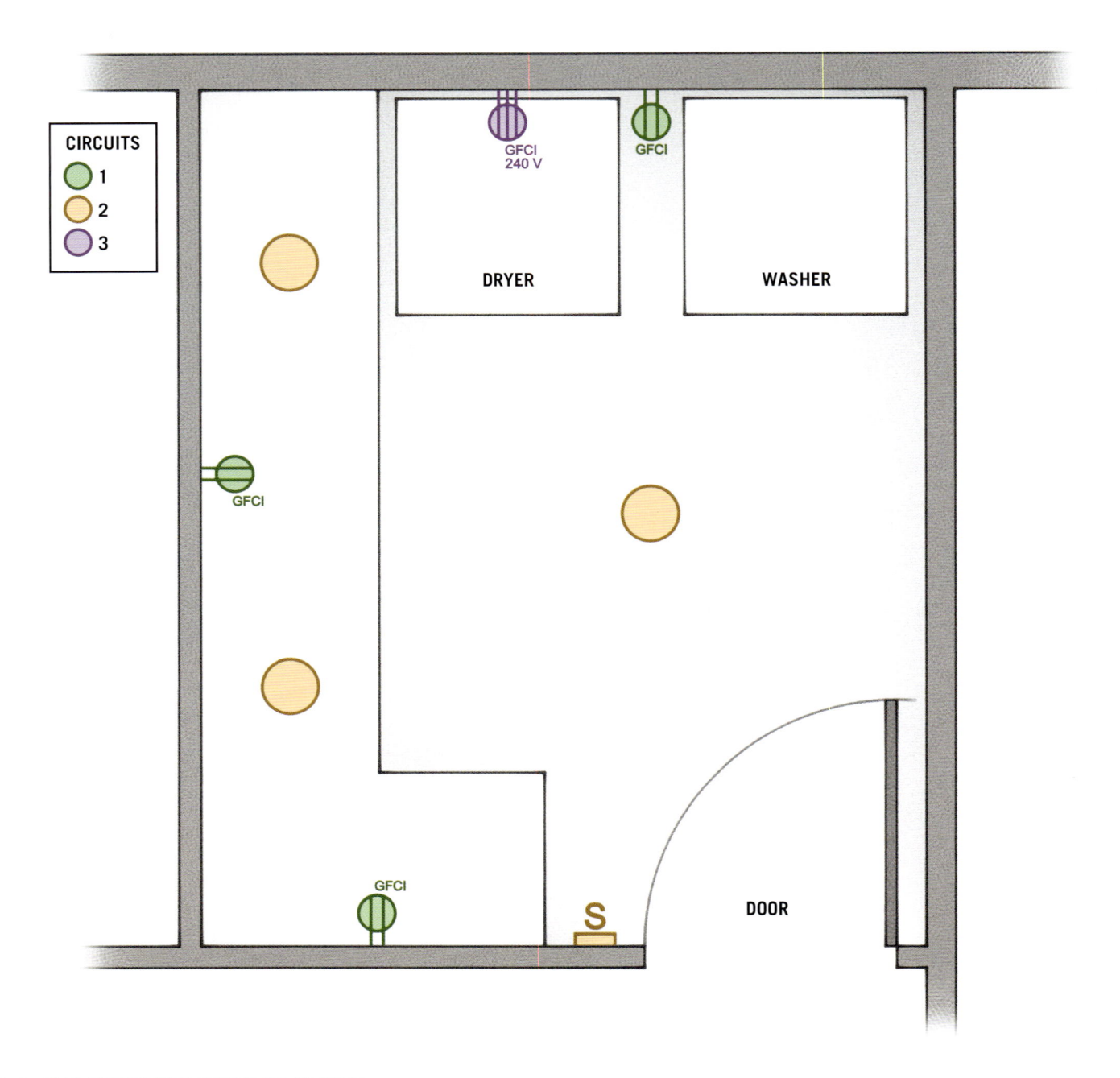

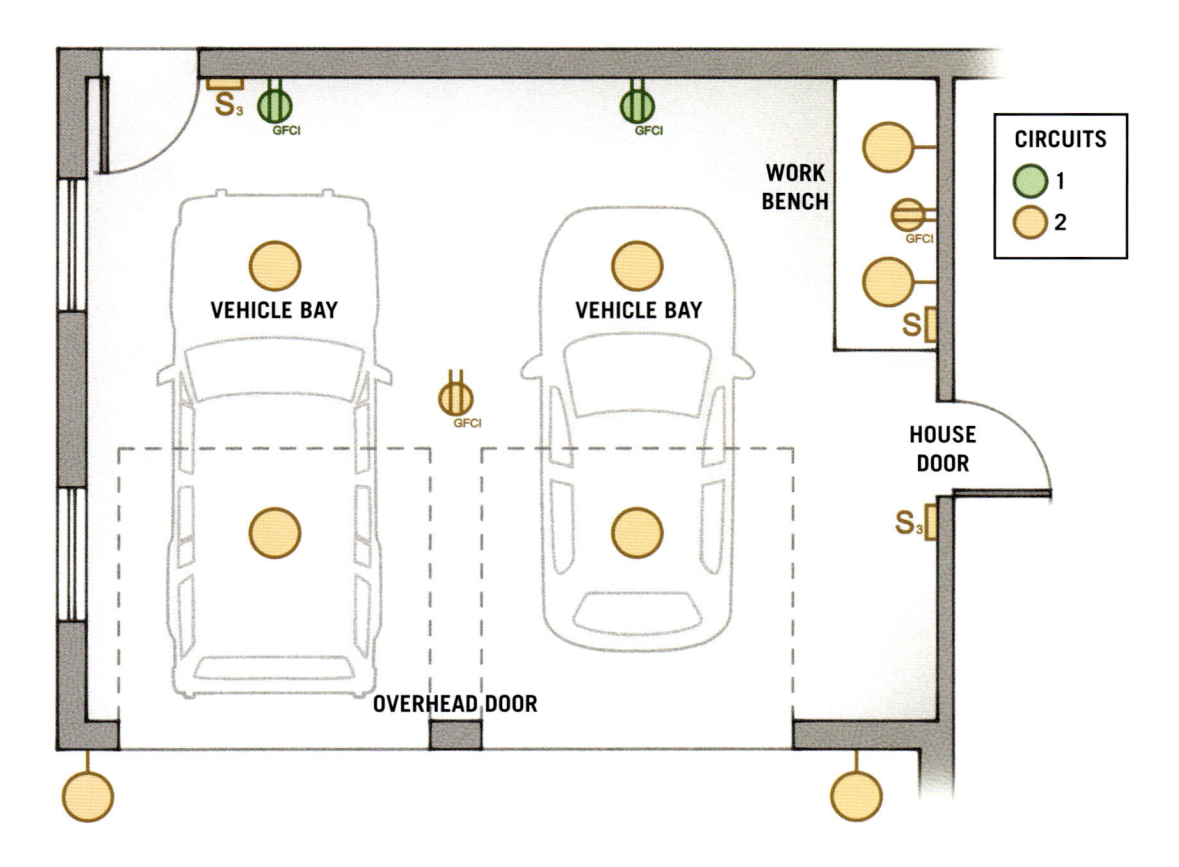

Garages + Basements

NEC requirements for garages apply to attached garages and detached garages with electrical power. In addition to lighting, a garage needs at least one 20-amp receptacle on a dedicated circuit. This receptacle requirement overlaps with the requirement for vehicle bays: Each bay must have one 20-amp receptacle located not more than 5½ feet above the floor. Therefore, a single-car garage needs at least one 20-amp receptacle, a two-car garage needs at least two; a three-car garage needs three, and so on. All receptacles in the garage must be GFCI protected. Each outlet provided for electric vehicle charging equipment should be on a dedicated circuit if the circuit is greater than 16 amps or 120 volts. Assume a continuous load when determining wire size.

Unfinished basements have similar minimum requirements to garages: switched lighting and at least one receptacle in each unfinished area. Lighting must illuminate any serviceable equipment, such as a furnace or water heater.

Finished basements are considered living space and thus are subject to all of the rules applied to living space elsewhere in the house with one important difference: All receptacles in the basement must be GFCI protected whether the basement is finished or unfinished.

There are several easy upgrades to the code minimum that will make a garage or unfinished basement safer and more convenient:

- Additional receptacles for work areas: These should be 20-amp and located at a convenient height for a work bench.

- A ceiling-mounted, GFCI-protected receptacle for each garage door opener.

- Ample overhead lighting controlled by a switch at each entrance (not counting any vehicle door).

- Task lighting for work areas; this could be on a separate switch or controlled by the main switch at the entrance(s).

Note: The garage wall that is shared with the house is an important fire barrier. Never install electrical boxes on the interior and garage sides of the wall so that the boxes are back to back. Instead, make sure they are in separate stud bays and offset them by at least 24 inches to maintain the fire barrier.

Crawlspaces + Attics

Circuit requirements for crawlspaces and unfinished attics vary by local code and whether or not the space houses serviceable equipment, such as a furnace or other HVAC appliances. These spaces also tend to be used for long-term storage, especially in homes without basements. All of this supports the need for adequate and convenient lighting in these unfinished spaces.

If serviceable equipment is present, there must be lighting for all equipment requiring service, and the lighting circuit must be GFCI protected in a crawlspace. The lighting must be controlled by a switch near the entrance. In addition, there must be a 15- or 20-amp receptacle located on the same level and within 25 feet of the equipment (this also must be GFCI protected in a crawlspace). The receptacle may not be connected to the load side (downstream) of the required branch circuit disconnect for the equipment.

Electrical service for HVAC equipment is specific to the equipment type and model; local code and the equipment manufacturer will determine what is required. As an example, a standard forced-air gas furnace needs a dedicated 15- or 20-amp circuit with an approved means of disconnect. Usually this includes a switch on or near the furnace so the furnace power can be easily shut off during repairs. In some cases, the circuit's breaker can serve as the disconnect.

If a crawlspace or attic does not house serviceable equipment, it's still a good idea to include lighting for all usable or accessible portions of the space. A general lighting circuit with a switch at the entrance to the space will suffice.

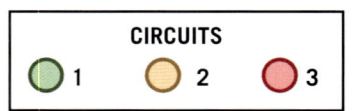

CIRCUITS

1   2   3

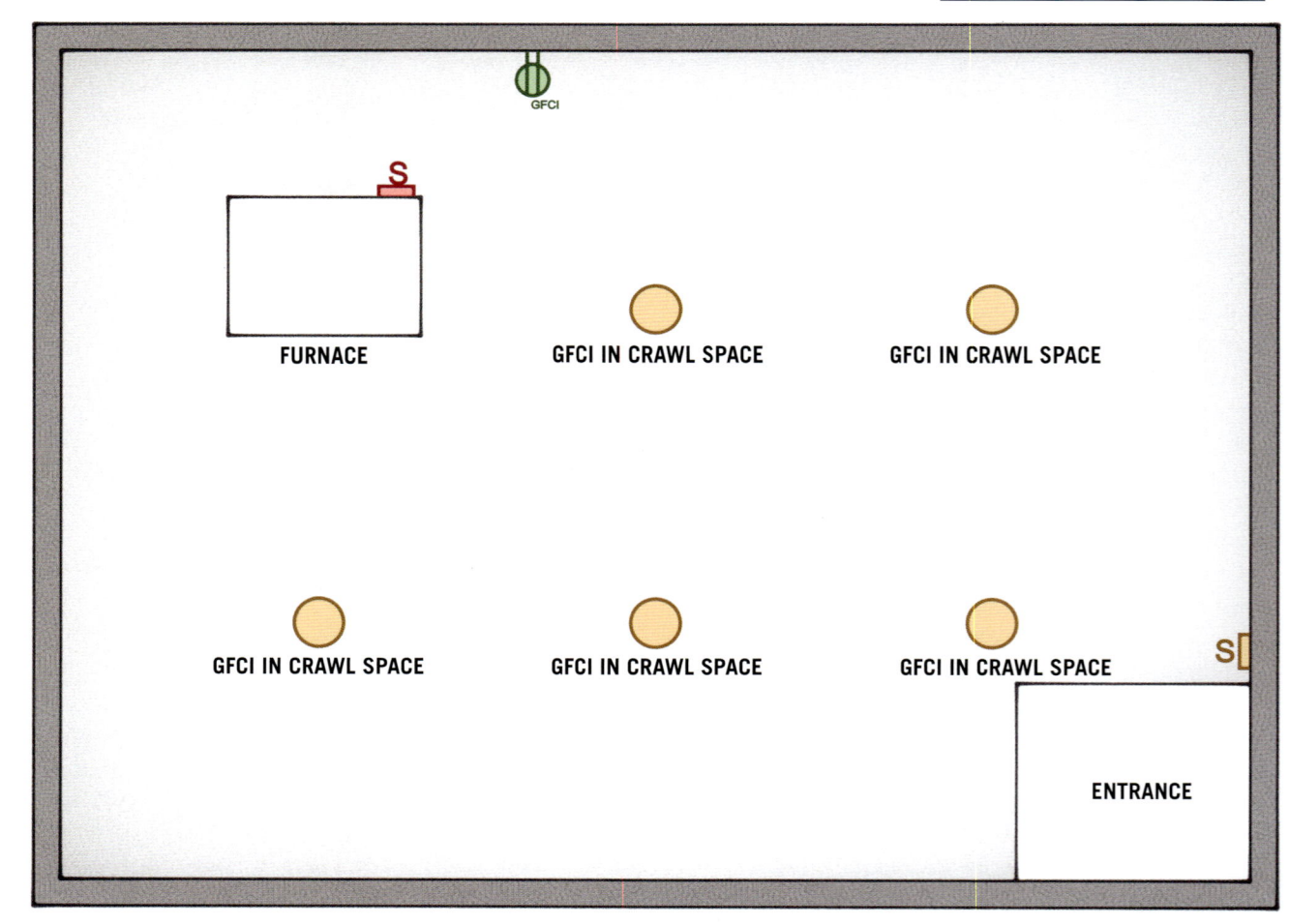

FURNACE

GFCI IN CRAWL SPACE   GFCI IN CRAWL SPACE

GFCI IN CRAWL SPACE   GFCI IN CRAWL SPACE   GFCI IN CRAWL SPACE

ENTRANCE

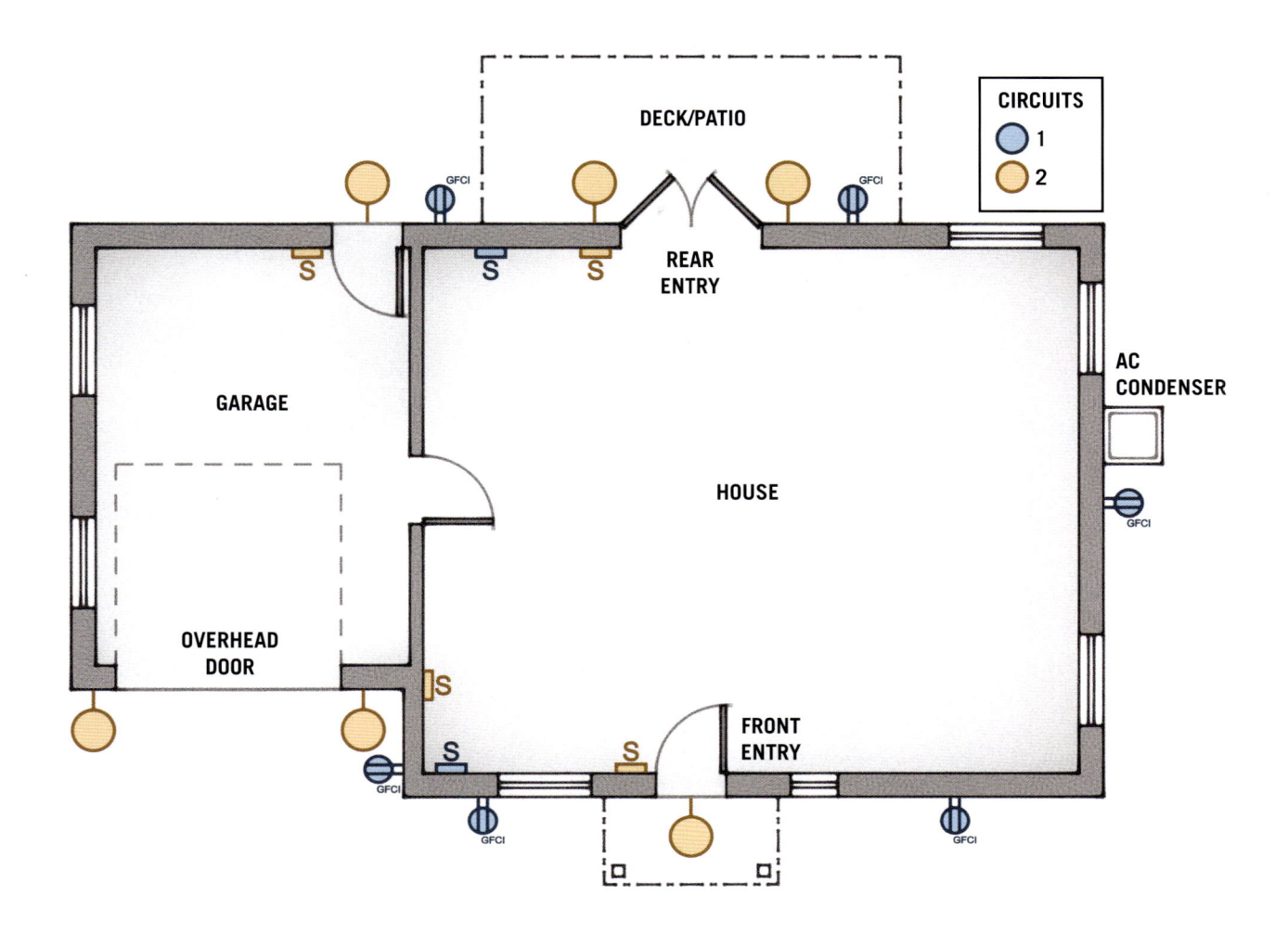

Outdoors

The minimum requirements for outdoor wiring are surprisingly simple. Homes need one receptacle at the front of the house and one at the back. Decks, balconies, and porches within 4 inches of the house also need a receptacle.

For lighting, each entry door at ground level needs a light (excluding garage doors for vehicles), as does a stairway landing that provides entrance to the house.

If there is outdoor air-conditioning equipment, there must be a 15- or 20-amp receptacle within 25 feet of the equipment and on the same level as the equipment.

All outdoor receptacles must be GFCI protected. The required front and rear receptacles may be no higher than 6½ feet above grade and receptacles on decks, balconies, or porches may be no more than 6½ feet above the walking surface. Outdoor receptacles and lighting can be served by circuits serving other areas, such as interior lighting and receptacle circuits or garage circuits not serving vehicle bays.

In addition to the minimum requirements, consider a few upgrades for improved safety or convenience:

- Receptacle in a convenient location for plugging in a low-voltage lighting transformer.

- Switch-controlled receptacle(s) for holiday lights.

- Extra wall receptacles and an outlet for a ceiling fan for a covered porch or patio (areas that tend to be used as indoor/outdoor spaces).

- Lighting above or at the sides of vehicle doors.

Note: Outdoor light fixtures and receptacles must be rated outdoor/weather-resistant (WR) type, and receptacles must have an approved cover (see page 198).

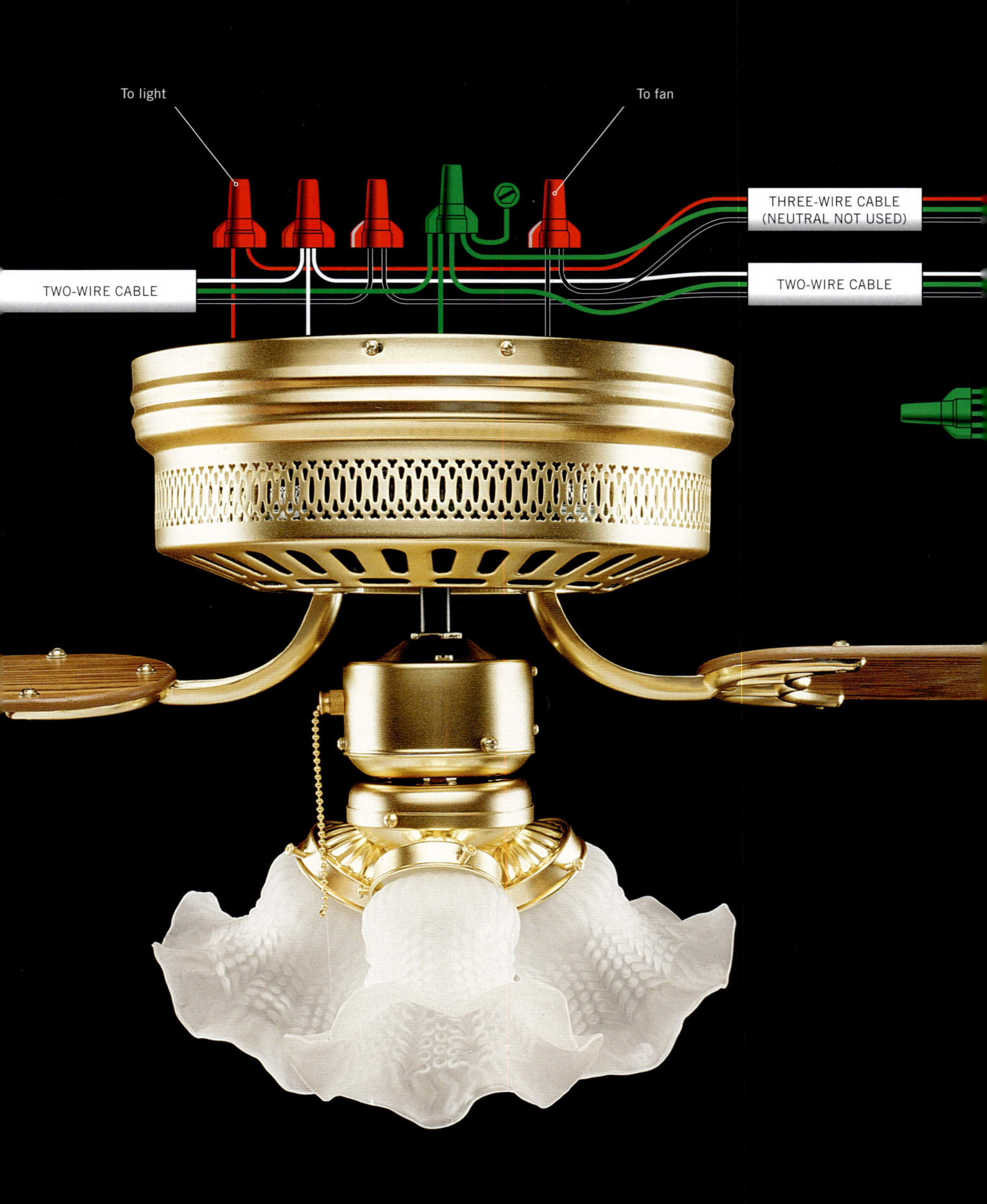

To light

To fan

THREE-WIRE CABLE
(NEUTRAL NOT USED)

TWO-WIRE CABLE

TWO-WIRE CABLE

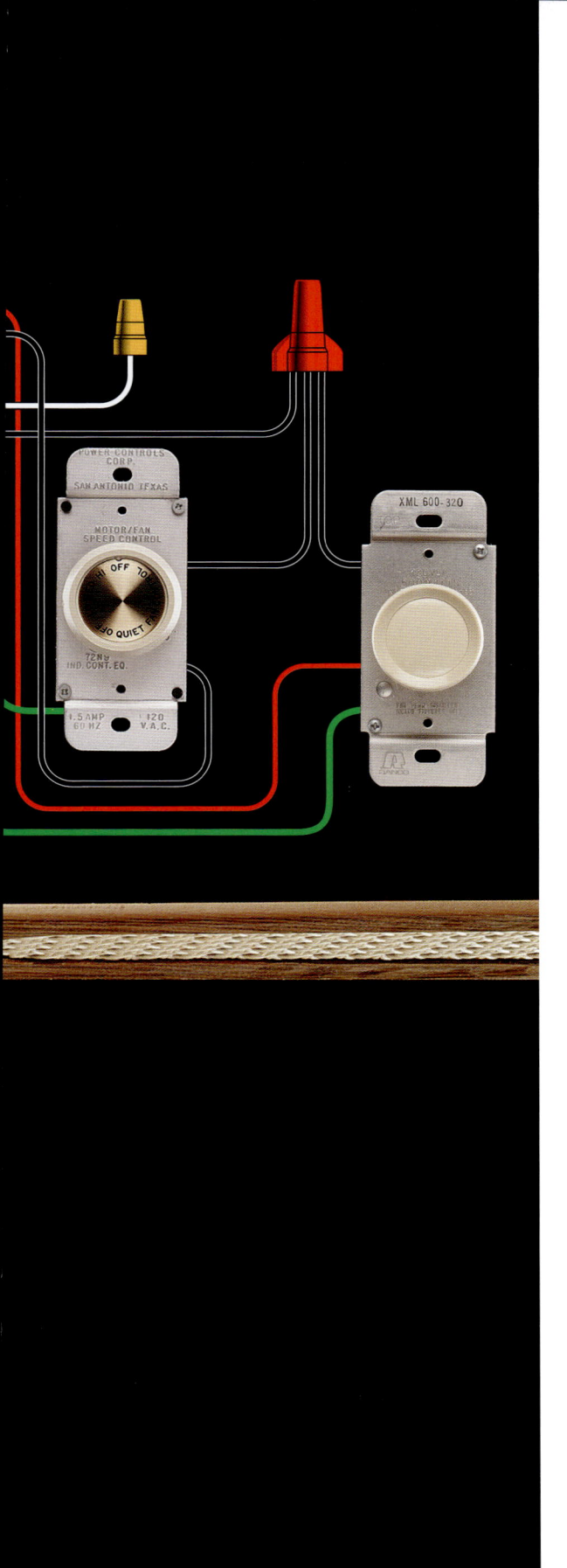

Circuit Maps

The circuit maps on the following pages show the most common wiring variations for typical electrical devices. Most new wiring you install will match one or more of the maps shown. Find the maps that match your situation and use them to plan your circuit layouts.

The 120-volt circuits shown on the following pages are wired for 15 amps using 14-gauge wire and receptacles rated at 15 amps. If you are installing a 20-amp circuit, substitute 12-gauge wires and use receptacles rated for 15 or 20 amps.

In configurations where a white wire serves as a hot wire instead of a neutral, both ends of the wire are coded with black tape to identify it as hot. In addition, each of the circuit maps shows a box grounding screw. This grounding screw is required in all metal boxes, but plastic electrical boxes do not need to be grounded.

You should remember two recent code requirements when wiring switches. (1) Provide a neutral wire at every switch box. This may require using 3-wire cable or two 2-wire cables where you may have used one 2-wire cable in the past. (2) Use a black or red wire to supply power from a 3-way or a 4-way switch to a light or switched receptacle.

NOTE: For clarity, all grounding conductors in the circuit maps are colored green. In practice, the grounding wires inside sheathed cables usually are bare copper.

In this chapter:
• Common Household Circuits

Common Household Circuits

1. 120-Volt Duplex Receptacles Wired in Sequence

Use this layout to link any number of duplex receptacles in a basic lighting/receptacle circuit. The last receptacle in the cable run is connected like the receptacle shown at the right side of the circuit map below. All other receptacles are wired like the receptacle shown on the left side. This configuration or layout requires two-wire cables.

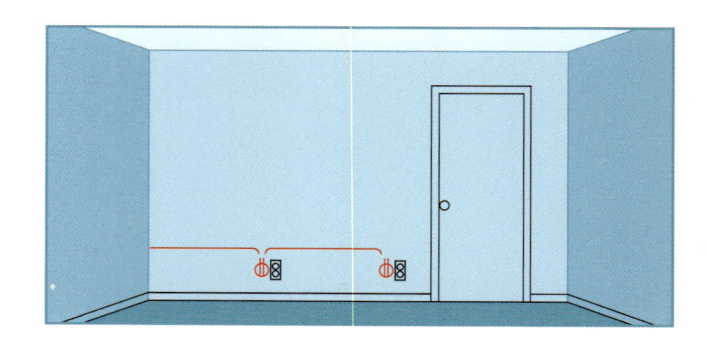

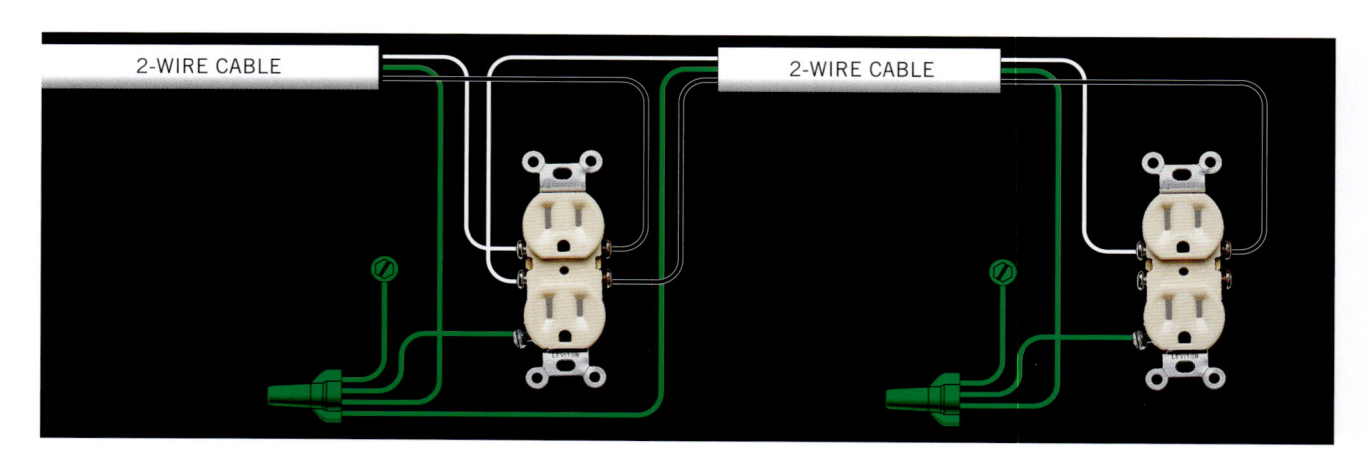

2-WIRE CABLE

2-WIRE CABLE

2. GFCI Receptacles (Single-Location Protection)

Use this layout when receptacles are within 6 ft. of a sink or water source, or any in kitchens and bathrooms. To prevent nuisance tripping caused by normal power surges, GFCIs should be connected only at the line screw terminal so they protect a single location, not the fixtures on the load side of the circuit. Requires two-wire cables. Where a GFCI must protect other fixtures, use circuit map 3. Remember that bathroom receptacles should be on a dedicated 20-amp circuit and that all bathroom receptacles must be GFCI protected.

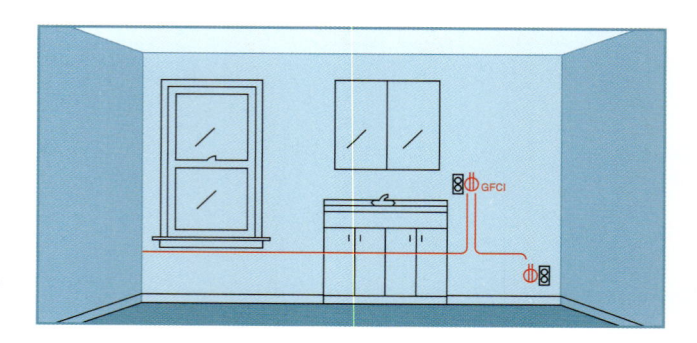

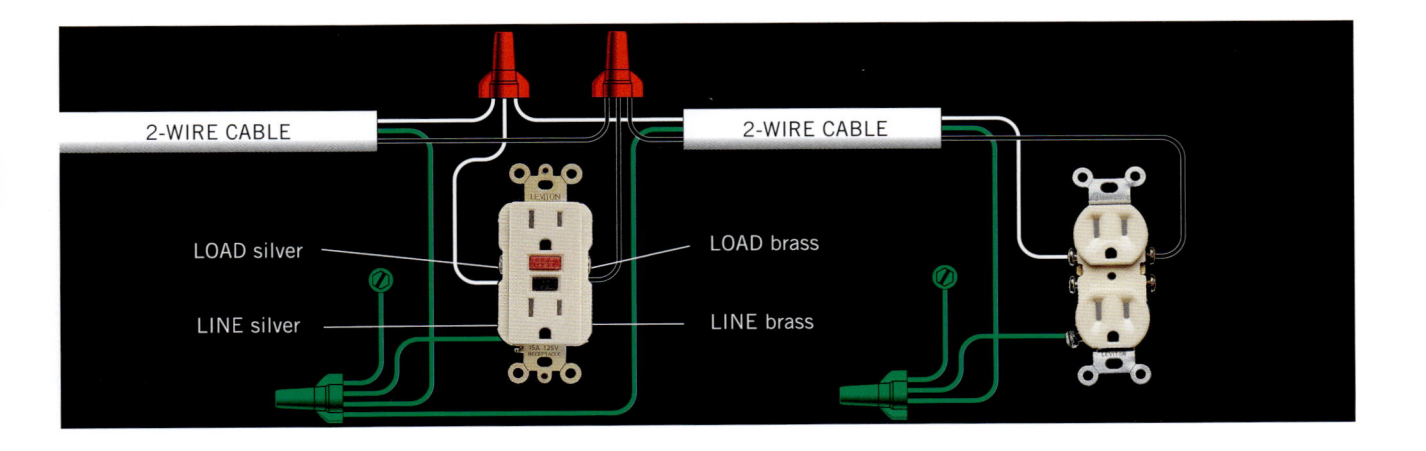

2-WIRE CABLE

2-WIRE CABLE

LOAD silver

LINE silver

LOAD brass

LINE brass

3. GFCI Receptacle, Switch + Light Fixture (Wired for Multiple-Location Protection)

In some locations, such as an outdoor circuit, it is a good idea to connect a GFCI receptacle so it also provides shock protection to the wires and fixtures that continue to the end of the circuit. Wires from the power source are connected to the line screw terminals; outgoing wires are connected to load screws. Requires two-wire cables.

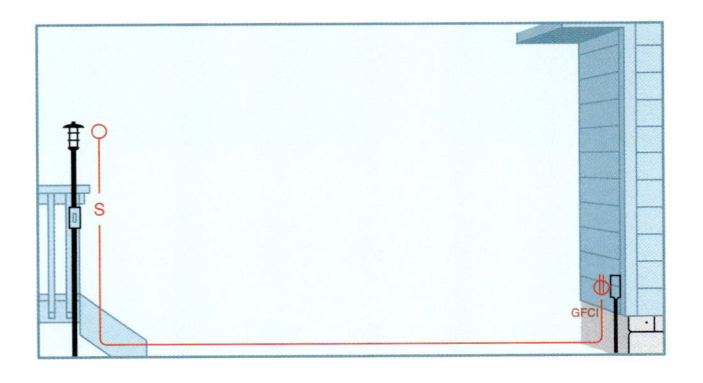

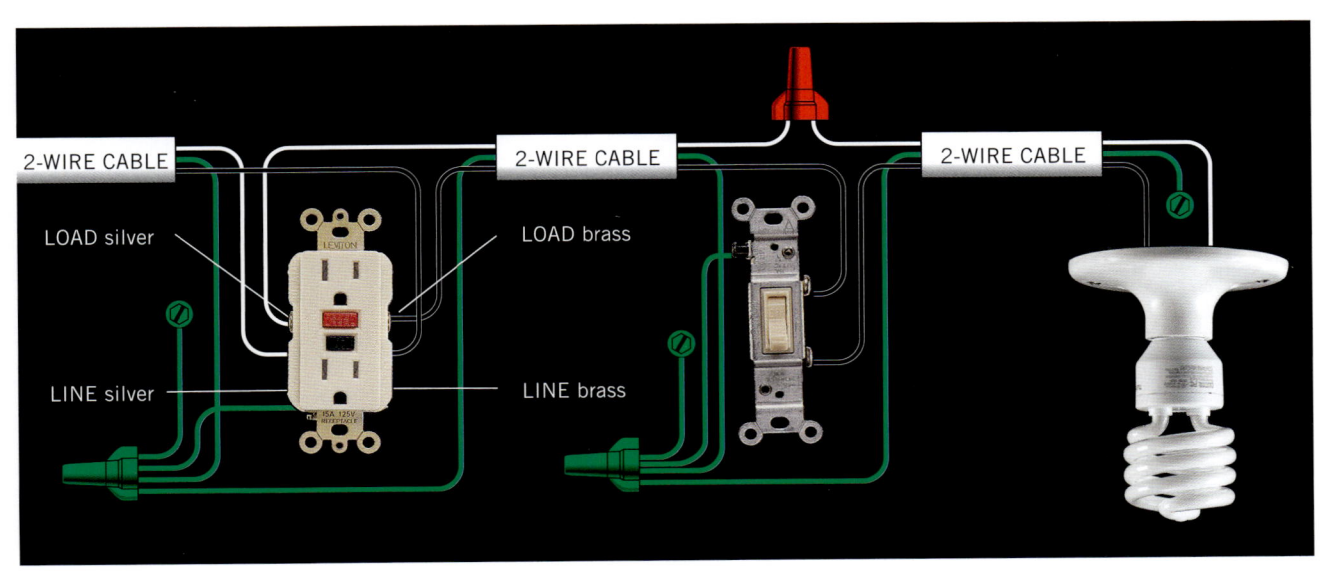

2-WIRE CABLE

2-WIRE CABLE

2-WIRE CABLE

LOAD silver

LINE silver

LOAD brass

LINE brass

4. Single-Pole Switch + Light Fixture (Light Fixture at End of Cable Run)

Use this layout for light fixtures in basic lighting/receptacle circuits throughout the home. It is often used as an extension to a series of receptacles (circuit map 1). Requires two-wire cables.

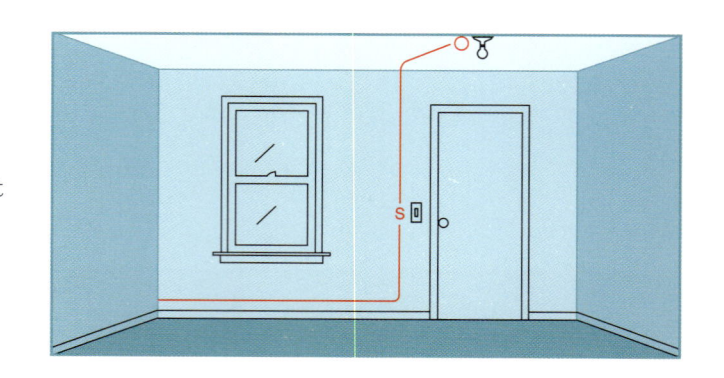

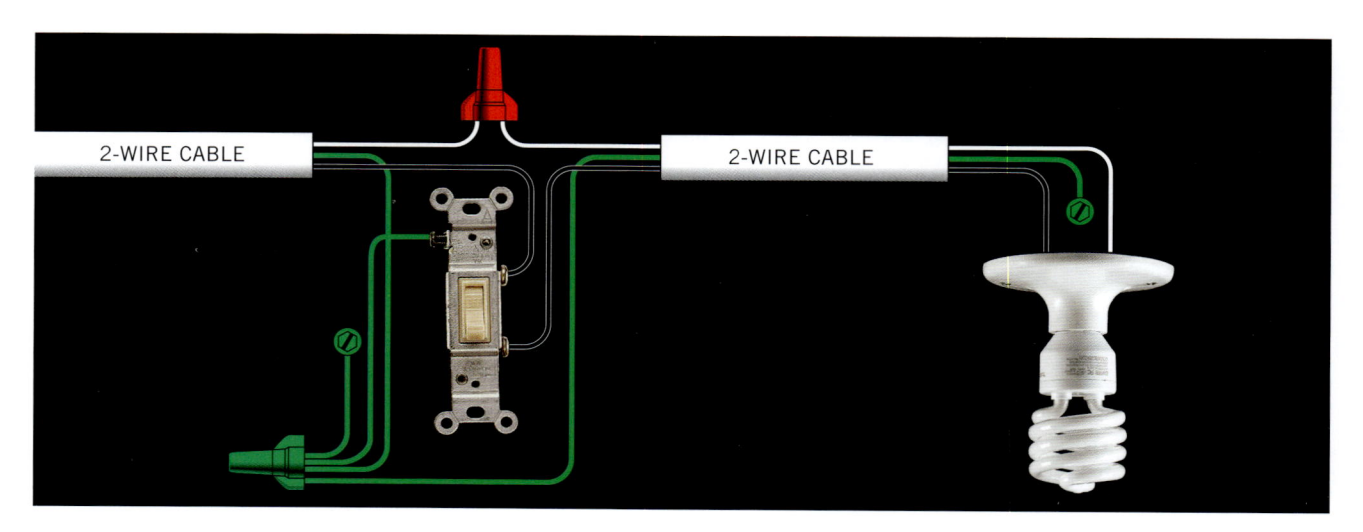

5. Single-Pole Switch + Light Fixture (Switch at End of Cable Run)

Use this layout, sometimes called a switch loop, where it is more practical to locate a switch at the end of the cable run. In the last length 3-wire cable is used to make a hot conductor available in each direction. Requires two-wire and three-wire cables.

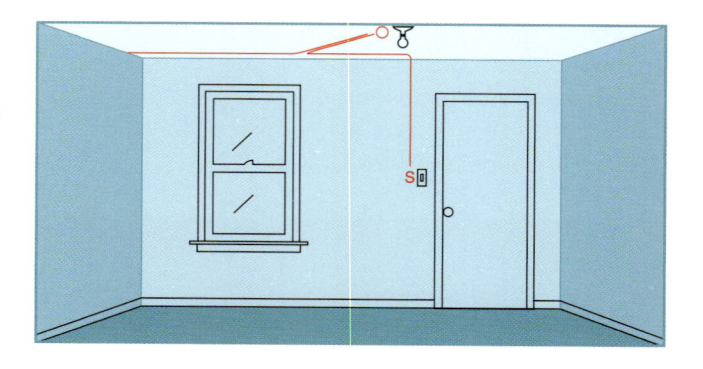

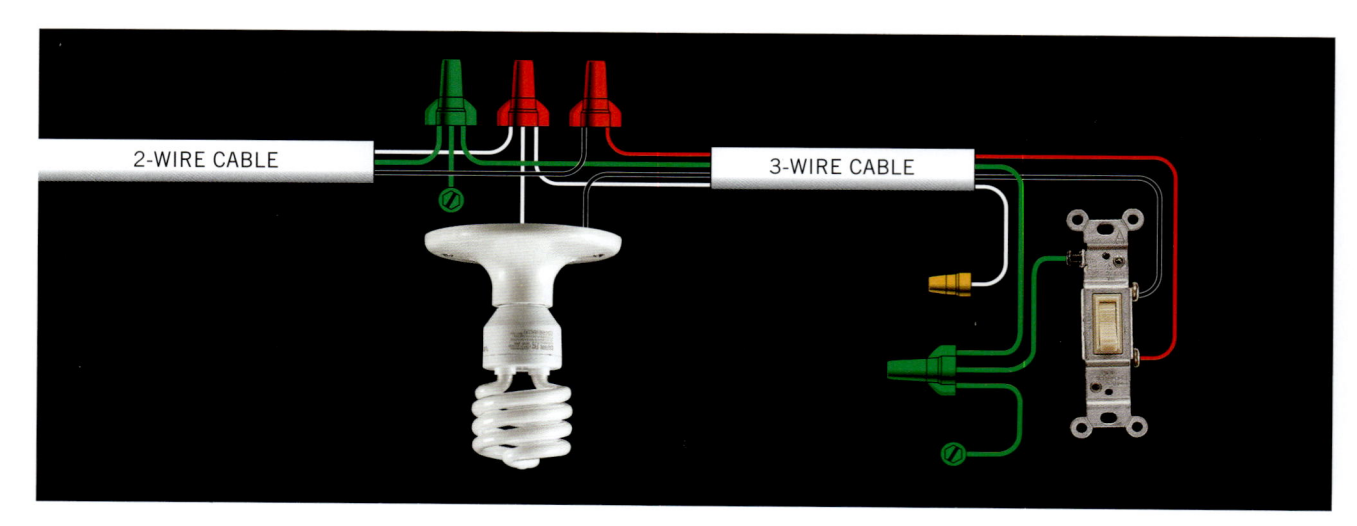

6. Single-Pole Switch + Two Light Fixtures (Switch Between Light Fixtures, Light at Start of Cable Run)

Use this layout when you need to control two fixtures from one single-pole switch and the switch is between the two lights in the cable run. Power feeds to one of the lights. Requires two-wire and three-wire cables.

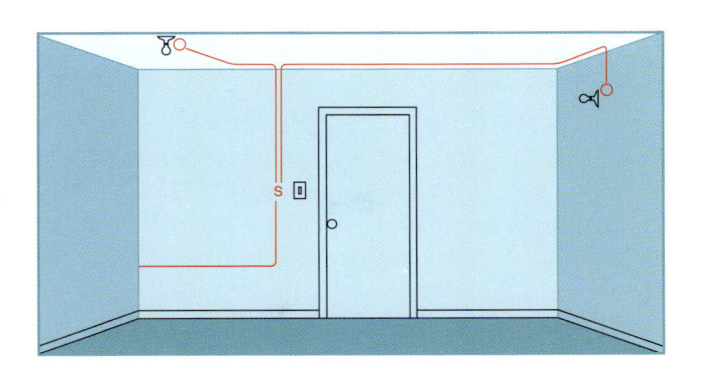

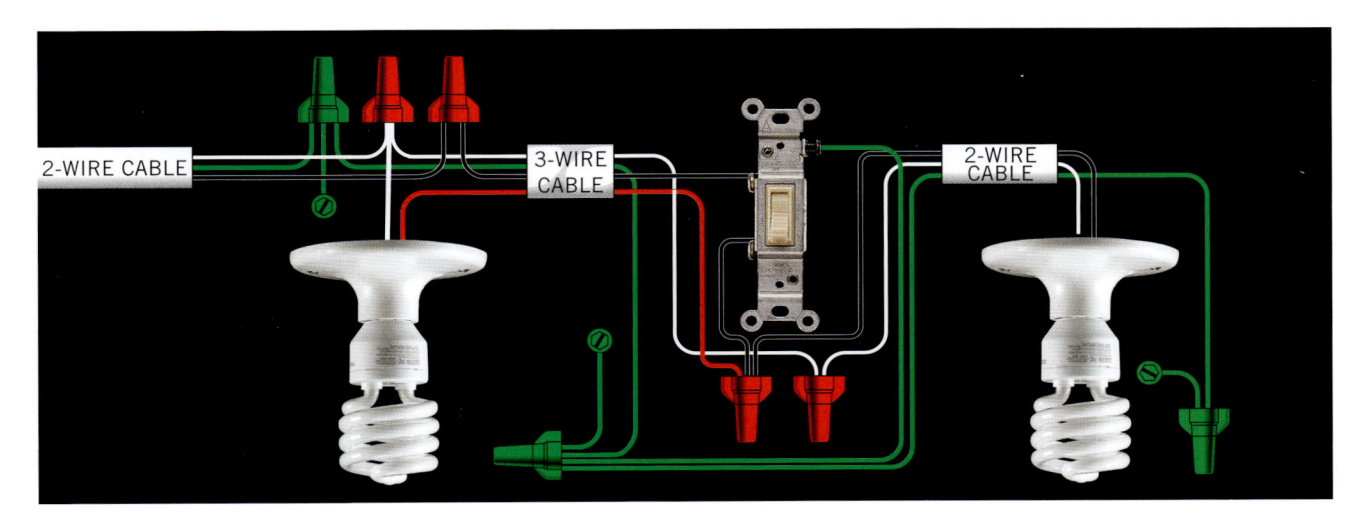

7. Single-Pole Switch + Light Fixture, Duplex Receptacle (Switch at Start of Cable Run)

Use this layout to continue a circuit past a switched light fixture to one or more duplex receptacles. To add multiple receptacles to the circuit, see circuit map 1. Requires two-wire and three-wire cables.

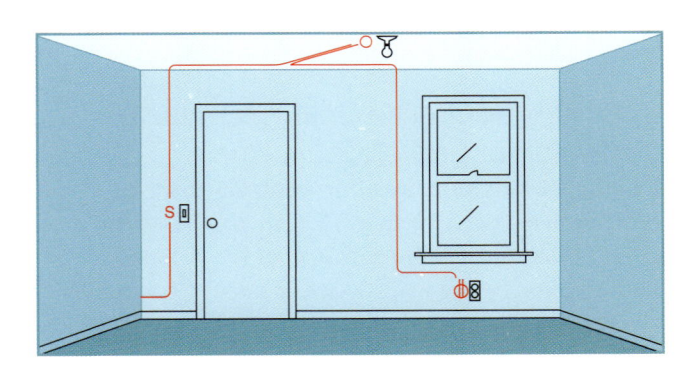

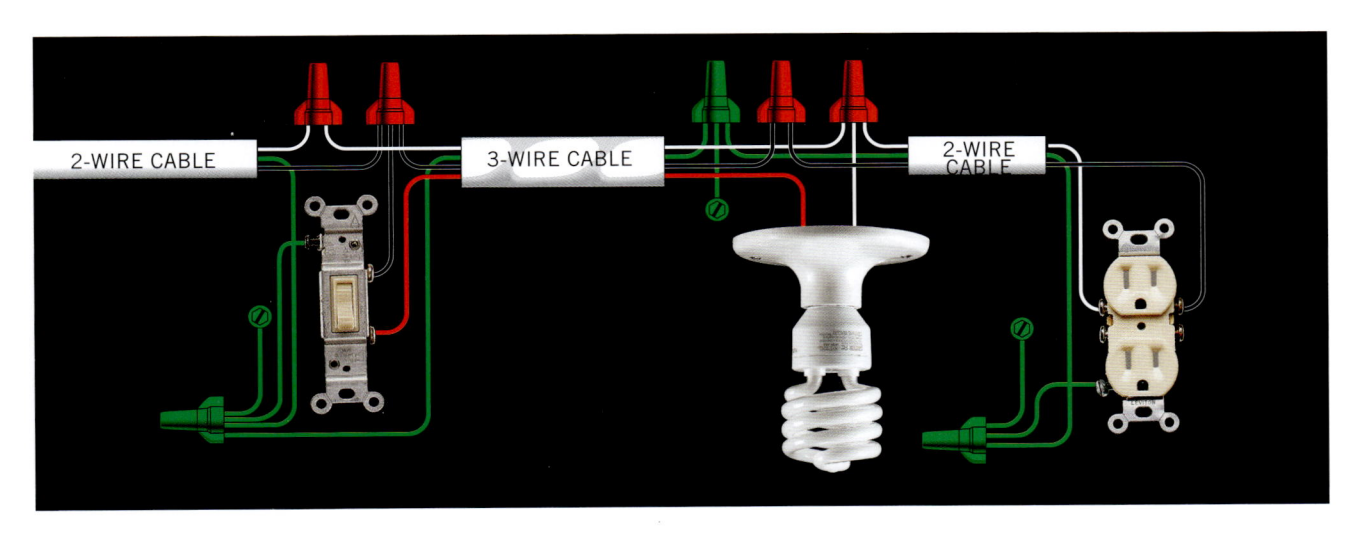

8. Switch-Controlled Split Receptacle, Duplex Receptacle (Switch at Start of Cable Run)

This layout lets you use a wall switch to control a lamp plugged into a wall receptacle. This configuration is required by code for any room that does not have a switch-controlled wall or ceiling fixture. Only the bottom half of the first receptacle is controlled by the wall switch; the top half of the receptacle and all additional receptacles on the circuit are always hot. Requires two-wire and three-wire cables. Some electricians help people identify switched receptacles by installing them upside down.

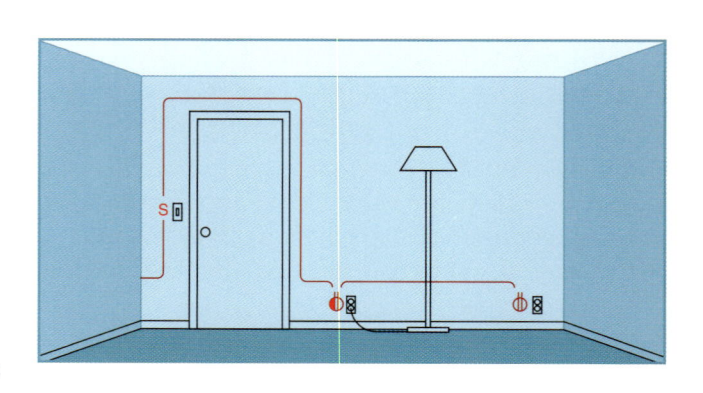

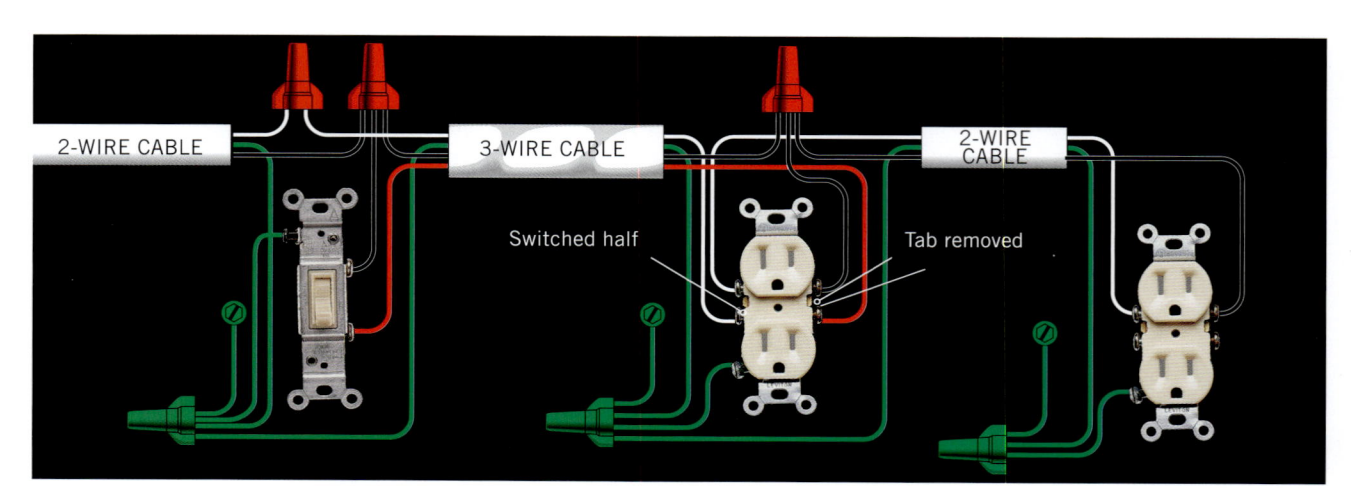

9. Switch-Controlled Split Receptacle (Switch at End of Cable Run)

Use this switch loop layout to control a split receptacle (see circuit map 7) from an end-of-run circuit location. The bottom half of the receptacle is controlled by the wall switch, while the top half is always hot. Requires two-wire and three-wire cable. Some electricians help people identify switched receptacles by installing them upside down.

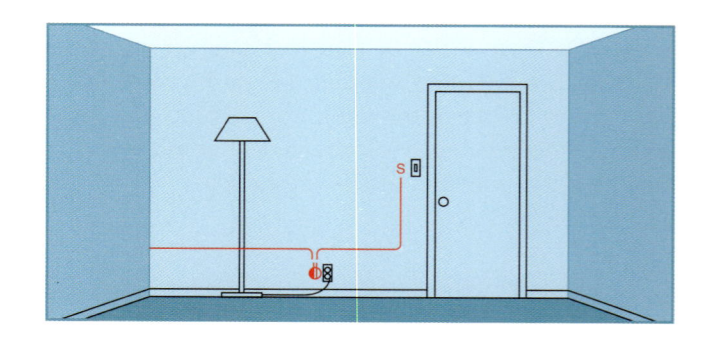

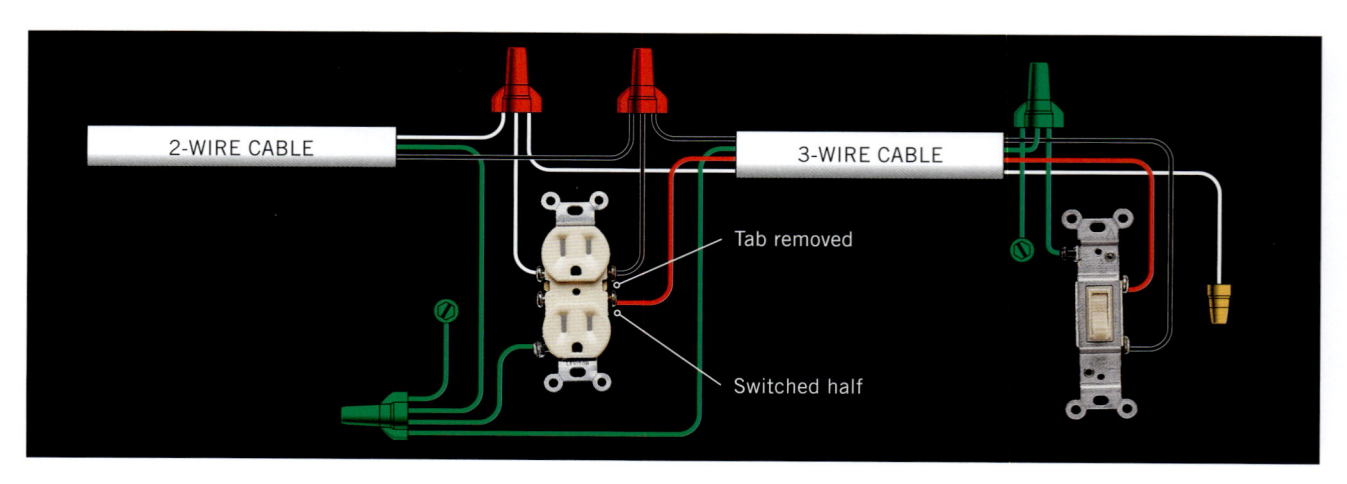

10. Switch-Controlled Split Receptacle, Duplex Receptacle
(Split Receptacle at Start of Run)

Use this variation of circuit map 7 where it is more practical to locate a switch-controlled receptacle at the start of a cable run. Only the bottom half of the first receptacle is controlled by the wall switch; the top half of the receptacle, and all other receptacles on the circuit, are always hot. Requires two-wire and three-wire cables. Some electricians help people identify switched receptacles by installing them upside down.

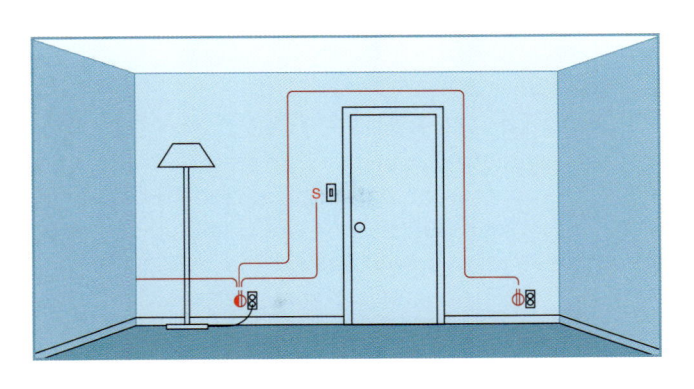

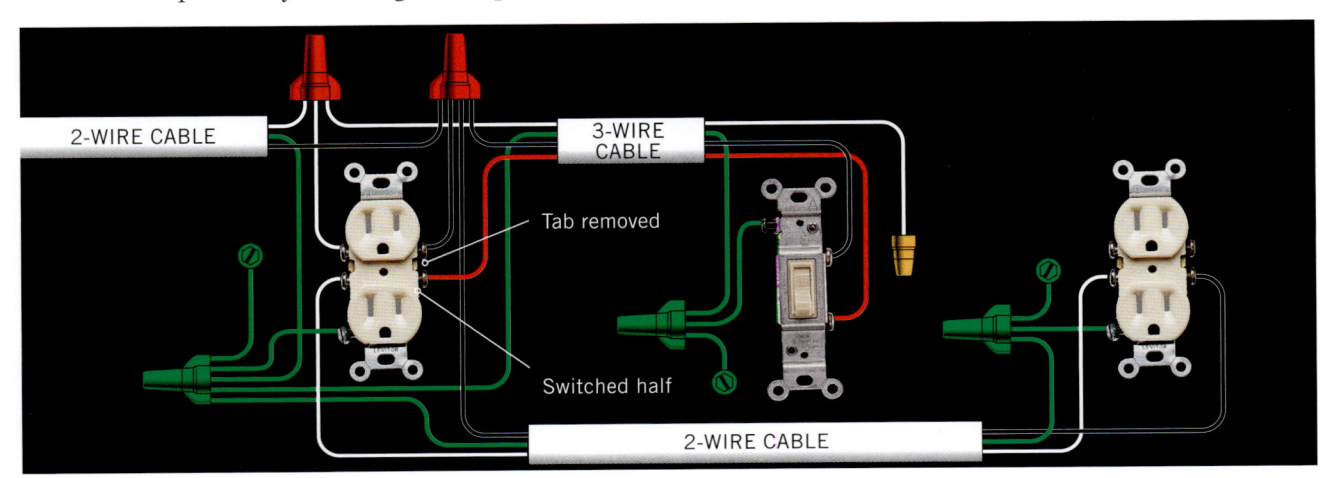

11. Double Receptacle Circuit
with Shared Neutral Wire
(Receptacles Alternate Circuits)

This layout features two 120-volt circuits wired with one three-wire cable connected to a double-pole circuit breaker. The black hot wire powers one circuit; the red wire powers the other. The white wire is a shared neutral that serves both circuits. When wired with 12/2 and 12/3 cable and receptacles rated for 20 amps, this layout can be used for the two small-appliance circuits required in a kitchen. Remember to use a GFCI circuit breaker if you use this circuit for kitchen countertop receptacles.

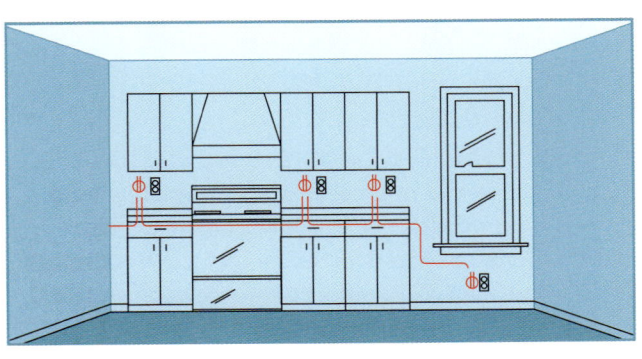

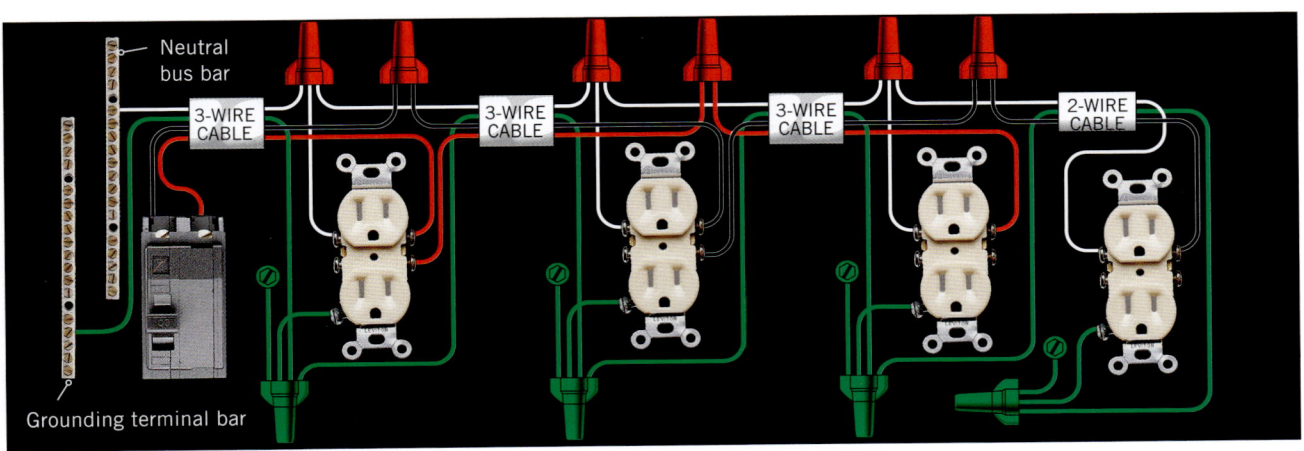

12. Double Receptacle Small-Appliance Circuit with GFCIs + Shared Neutral Wire

Use this layout variation of circuit map 10 to wire a double receptacle circuit when code requires that the receptacles be GFCIs. The GFCIs should be wired for single-location protection (see circuit map 2). Requires three-wire and two-wire cables. A GFCI circuit breaker is another option.

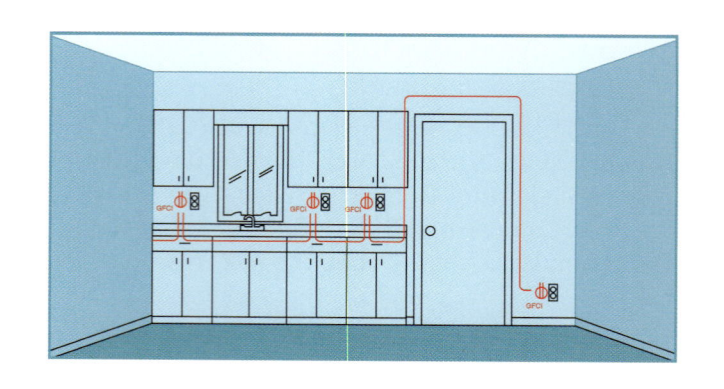

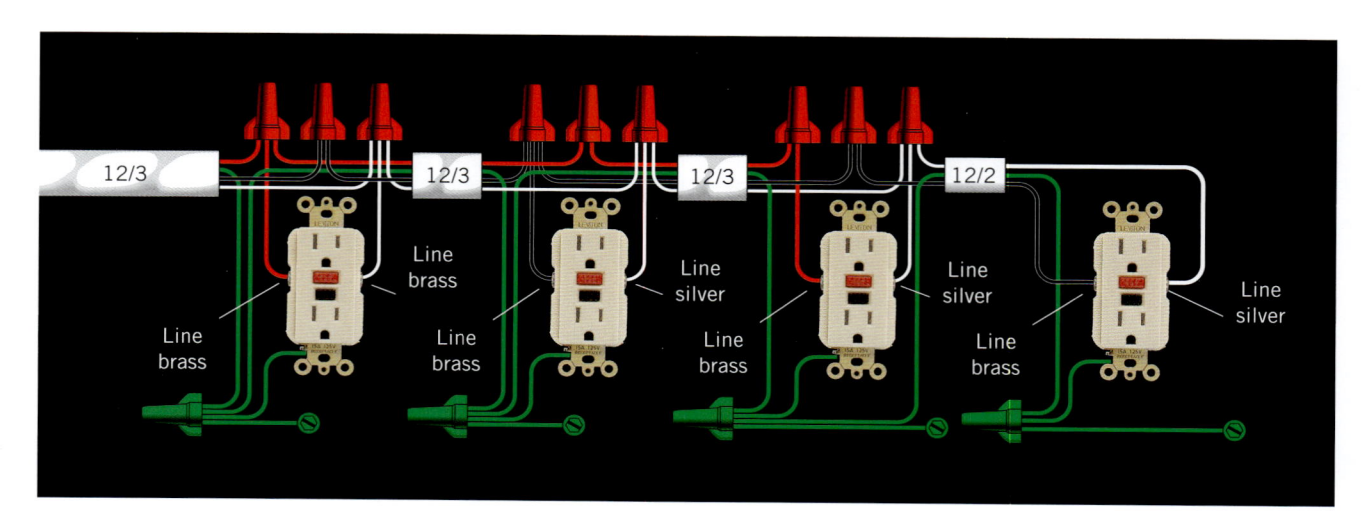

13. Double Receptacle Small-Appliance Circuit with GFCIs + Separate Neutral Wires

If the room layout or local codes do not allow for a shared neutral wire, use this layout instead. The GFCIs should be wired for single-location protection (see circuit map 2). Requires two-wire cable. A GFCI circuit breaker is another option.

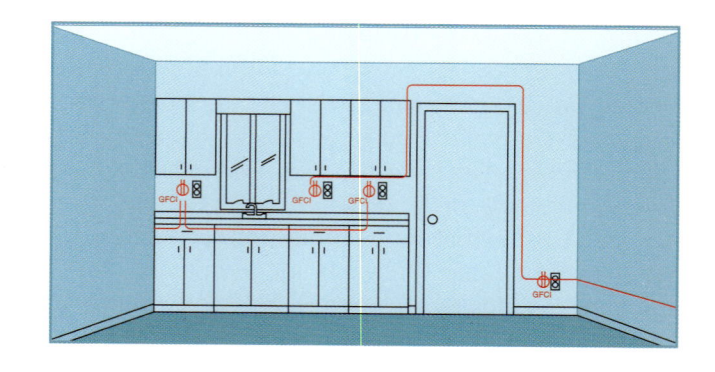

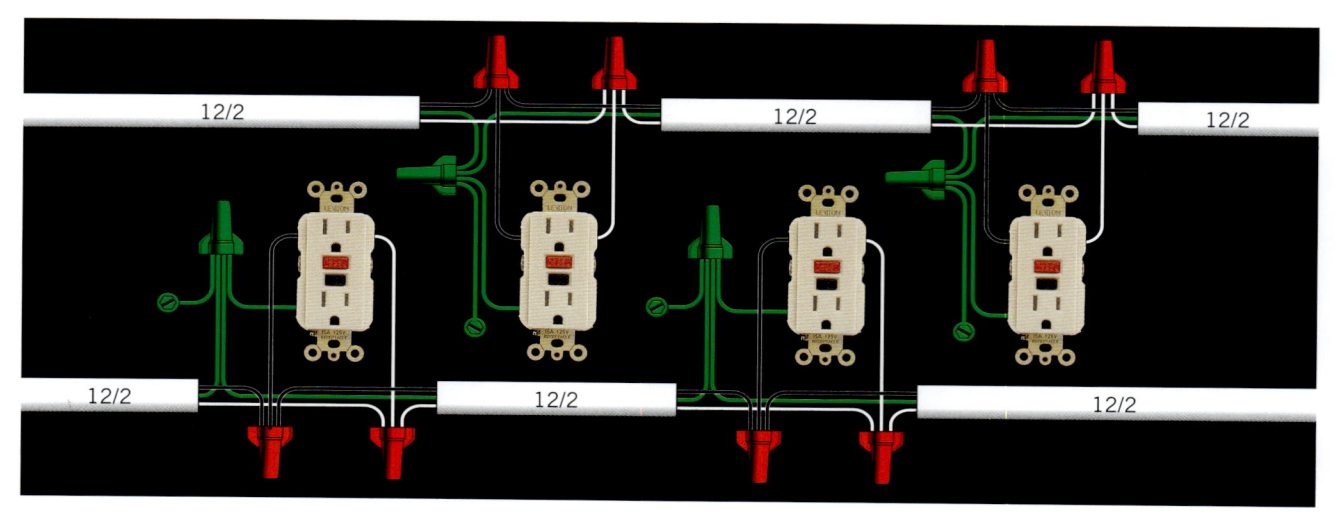

14. 120/240-Volt Range Receptacle

This layout is for a 40- or 50-amp, 120/240-volt dedicated appliance circuit wired with 8/3 or 6/3 cable, as required by code for a large kitchen range. The black and red circuit wires, connected to a double-pole circuit breaker in the circuit breaker panel, each bring 120 volts of power to the setscrew terminals on the receptacle. The white circuit wire attached to the neutral bus bar in the circuit breaker panel is connected to the neutral setscrew terminal on the receptacle. The receptacle must be GFCI protected.

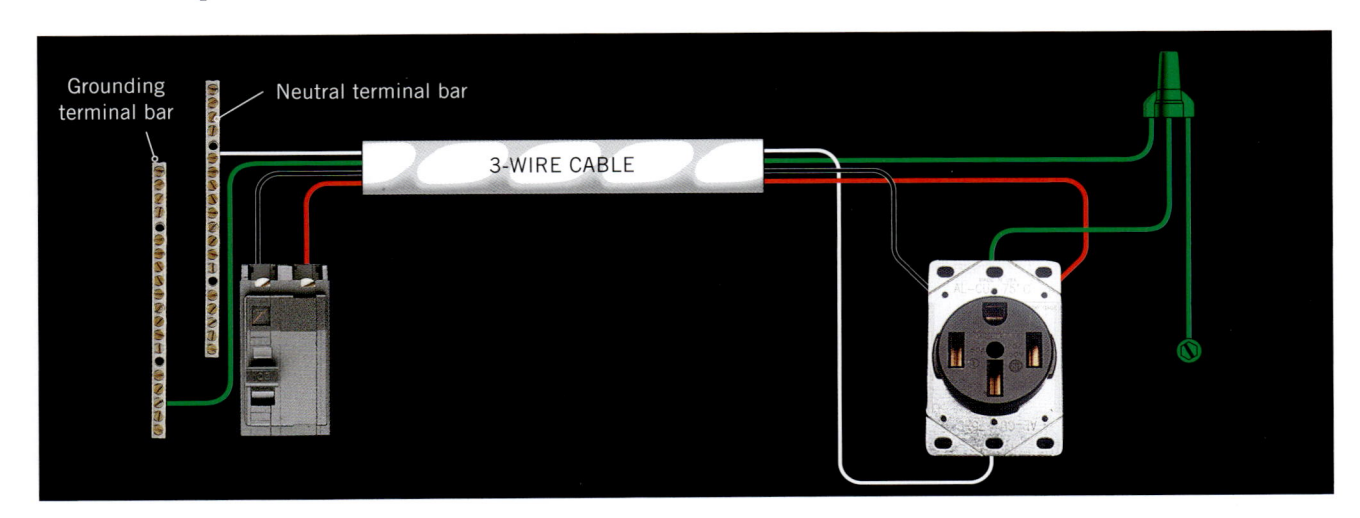

Grounding terminal bar

Neutral terminal bar

3-WIRE CABLE

15. 240-Volt Baseboard Heaters, Thermostat

This layout is typical for a series of 240-volt baseboard heaters controlled by a wall thermostat. Except for the last heater in the circuit, all heaters are wired as shown below. The last heater is connected to only one cable. The sizes of the circuit and cables are determined by finding the total wattage of all heaters. Requires two-wire cable.

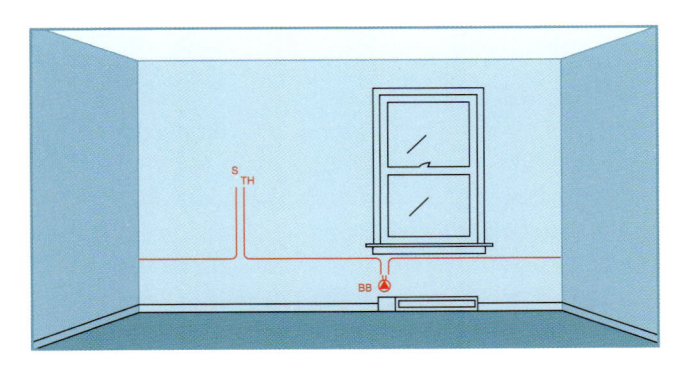

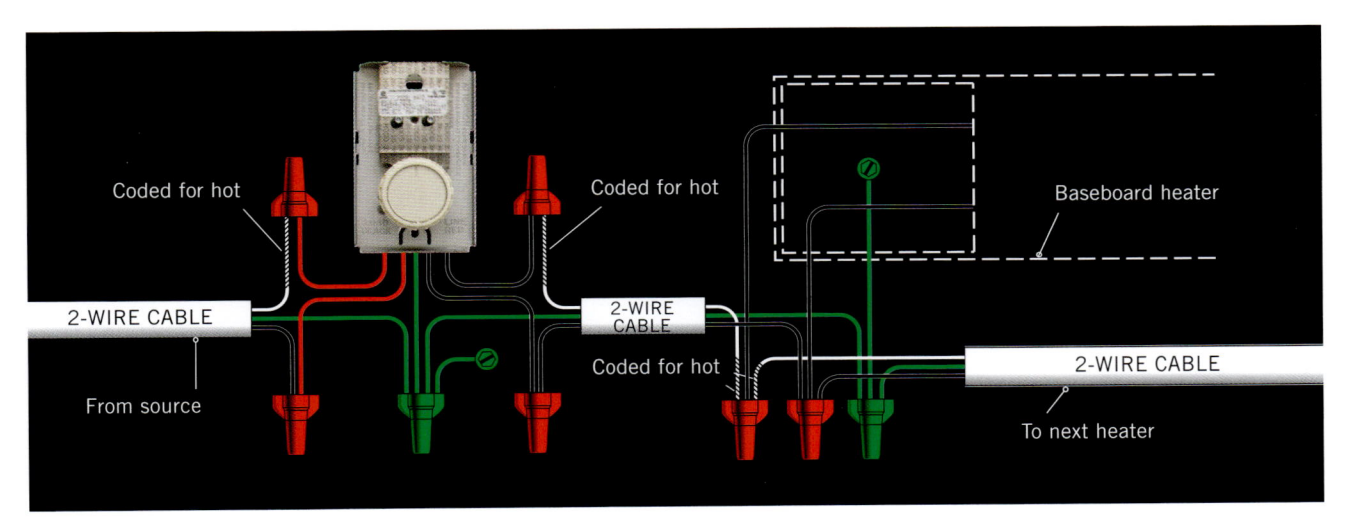

Coded for hot

Coded for hot

Baseboard heater

2-WIRE CABLE

2-WIRE CABLE

From source

Coded for hot

2-WIRE CABLE

To next heater

16. Dedicated 120-Volt Computer Circuit, Isolated-Ground Receptacle

This 15-amp isolated-ground circuit provides extra protection against surges and interference that can harm electronics. It uses 14/3 cable with the red wire serving as an extra grounding conductor. The red wire is tagged with green tape for identification. It is connected to the grounding screw on an isolated-ground receptacle and runs back to the grounding bus bar in the circuit breaker panel without touching any other house wiring.

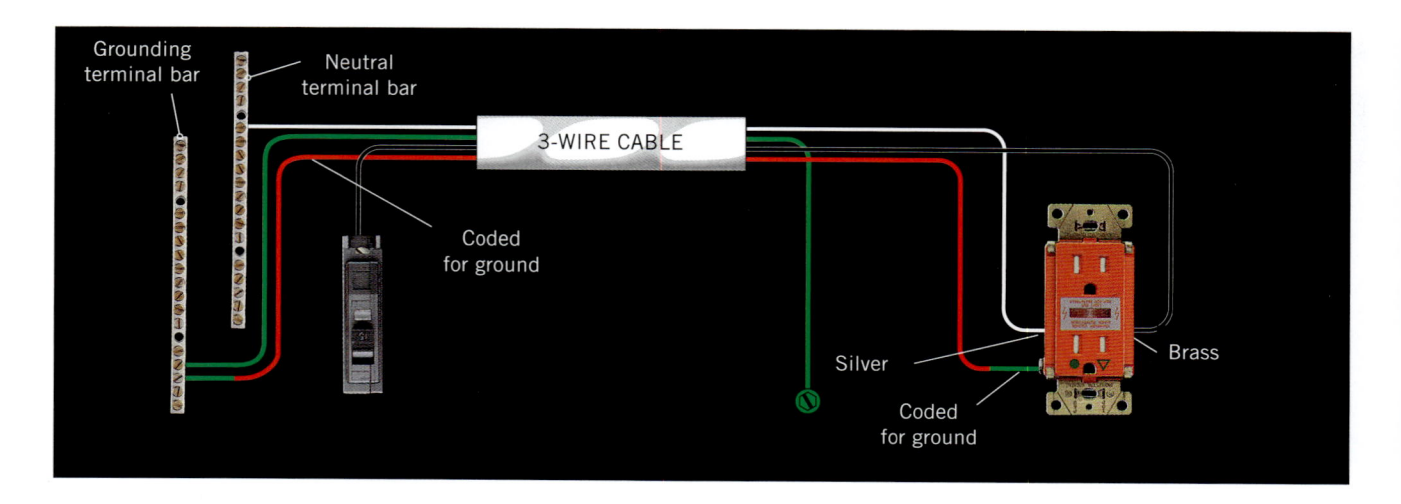

Grounding terminal bar

Neutral terminal bar

3-WIRE CABLE

Coded for ground

Silver

Brass

Coded for ground

17. 240-Volt Appliance Receptacle

This layout represents a 20-amp, 240-volt dedicated appliance circuit wired with 12/2 cable, as required by code for a large window air conditioner. Receptacles are available in both singleplex (shown) and duplex styles. The black and the white circuit wires connected to a double-pole breaker each bring 120 volts of power to the receptacle (combined, they bring 240 volts). The white wire is tagged with black tape to indicate it is hot.

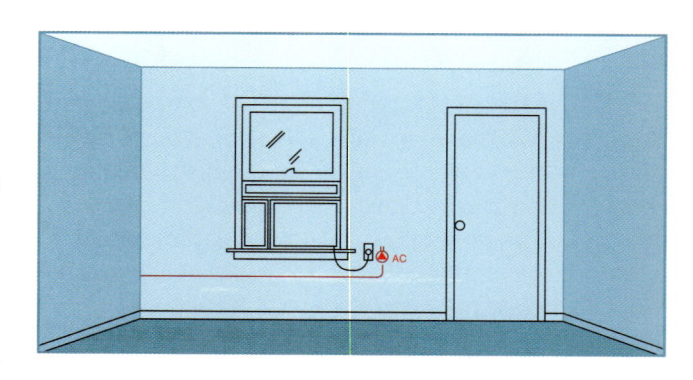

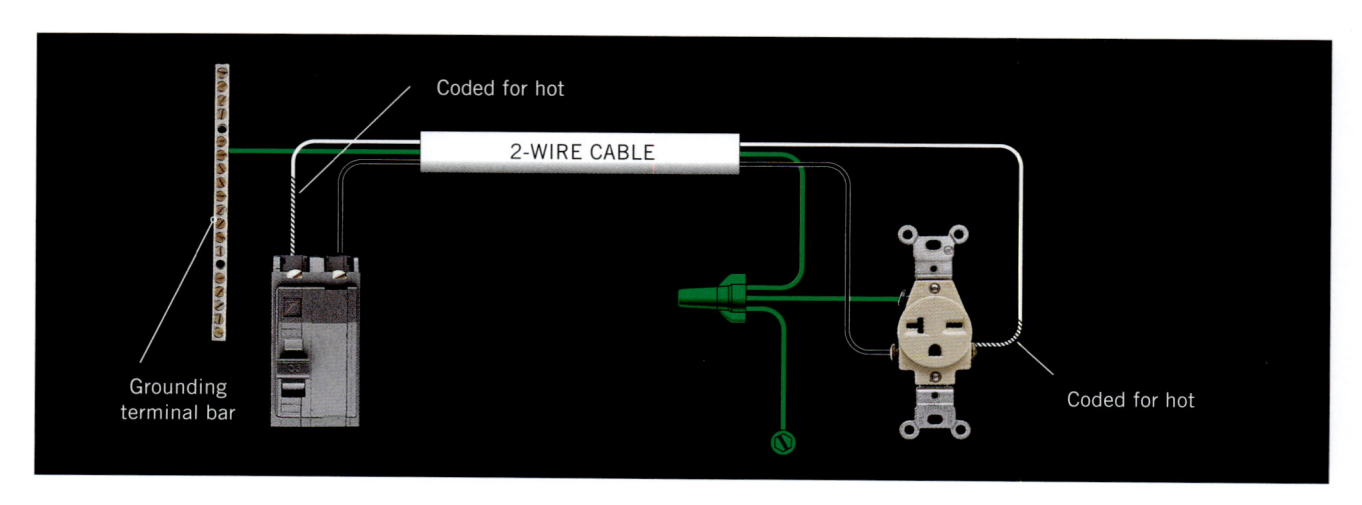

Coded for hot

2-WIRE CABLE

Grounding terminal bar

Coded for hot

18. Ganged Single-Pole Switches Controlling Separate Light Fixtures

This layout lets you place two switches controlled by the same 120-volt circuit in one double-gang electrical box. A single-feed cable provides power to both switches. A similar layout with two feed cables can be used to place switches from different circuits in the same box. Requires two-wire cable.

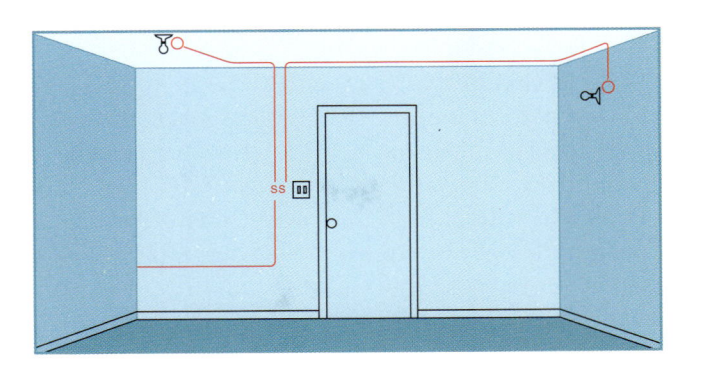

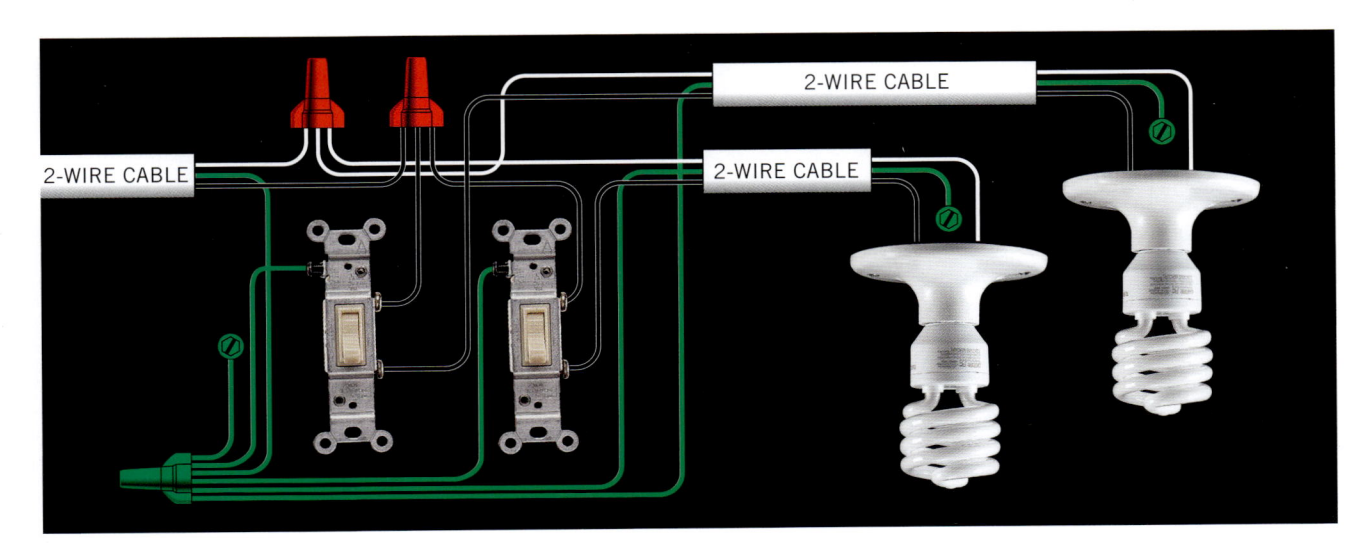

19. Ganged Switches Controlling a Light Fixture and an Exhaust Fan

This layout lets you place two switches controlled by the same 120-volt circuit in one double-gang electrical box. A single-feed cable provides power to both switches. A standard switch controls the light fixture, and a time-delay switch controls the exhaust fan.

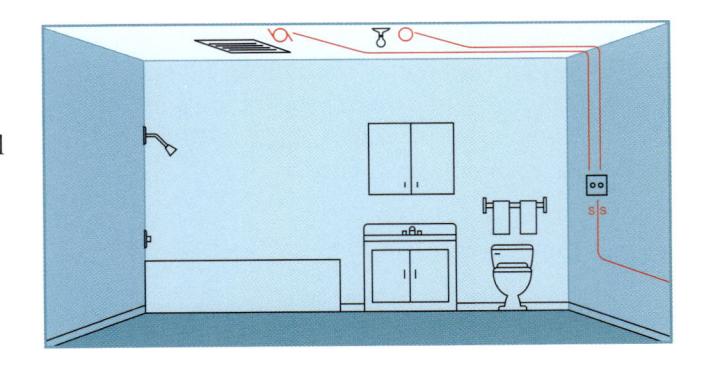

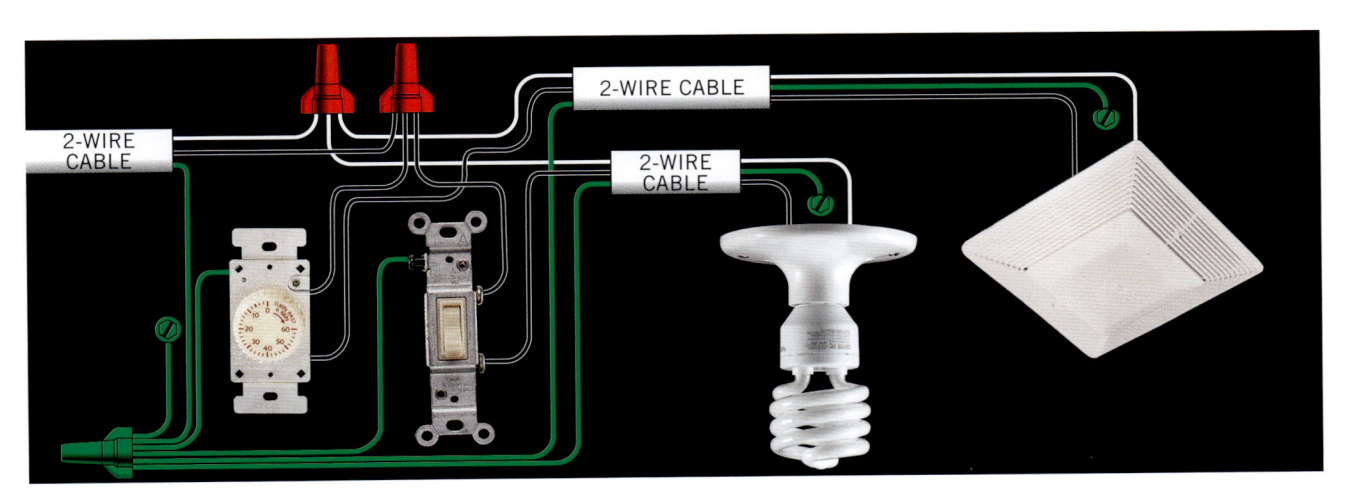

20. Three-Way Switches + Light Fixture (Fixture Between Switches)

This layout for three-way switches lets you control a light fixture from two locations. Each switch has one common screw terminal and two traveler screws. Circuit wires attached to the traveler screws run between the two switches, and hot wires attached to the common screws bring current from the power source and carry it to the light fixture. Requires parallel runs of 2-wire cable.

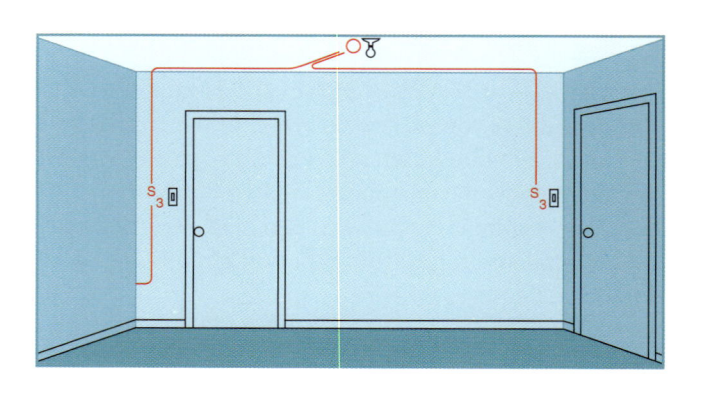

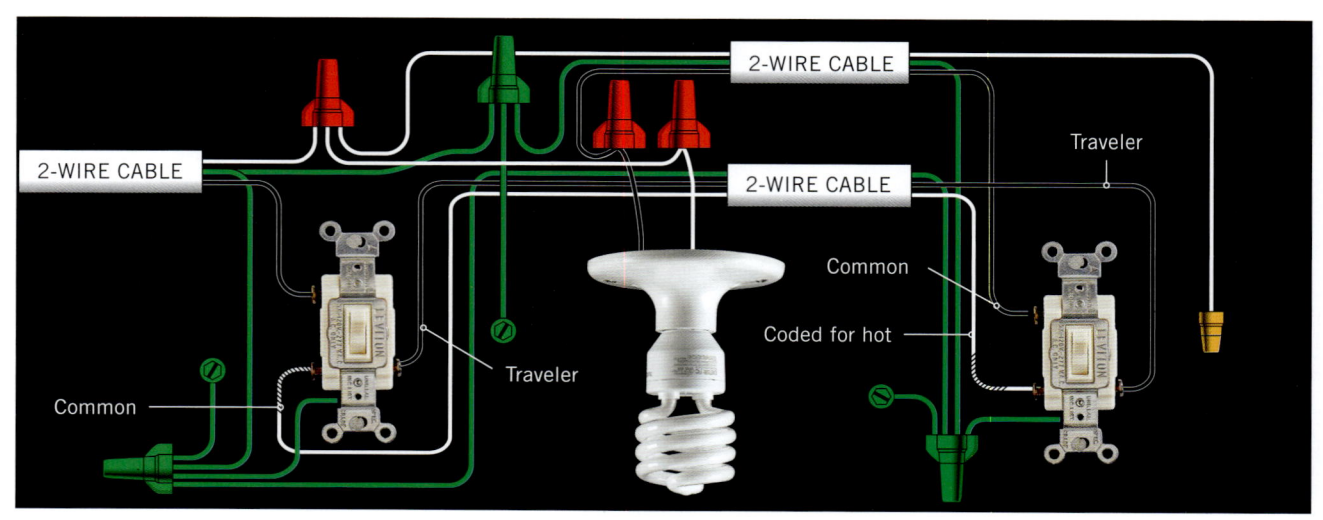

21. Three-Way Switches + Light Fixture (Fixture at Start of Cable Run)

Use this layout variation of circuit map 19 where it is more convenient to locate the fixture ahead of the three-way switches in the cable run. Requires two-wire and three-wire cables.

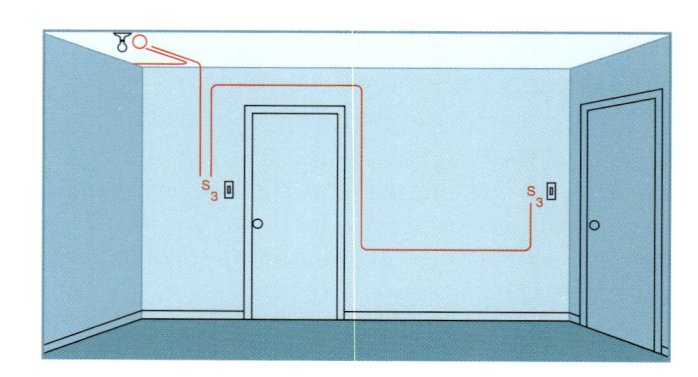

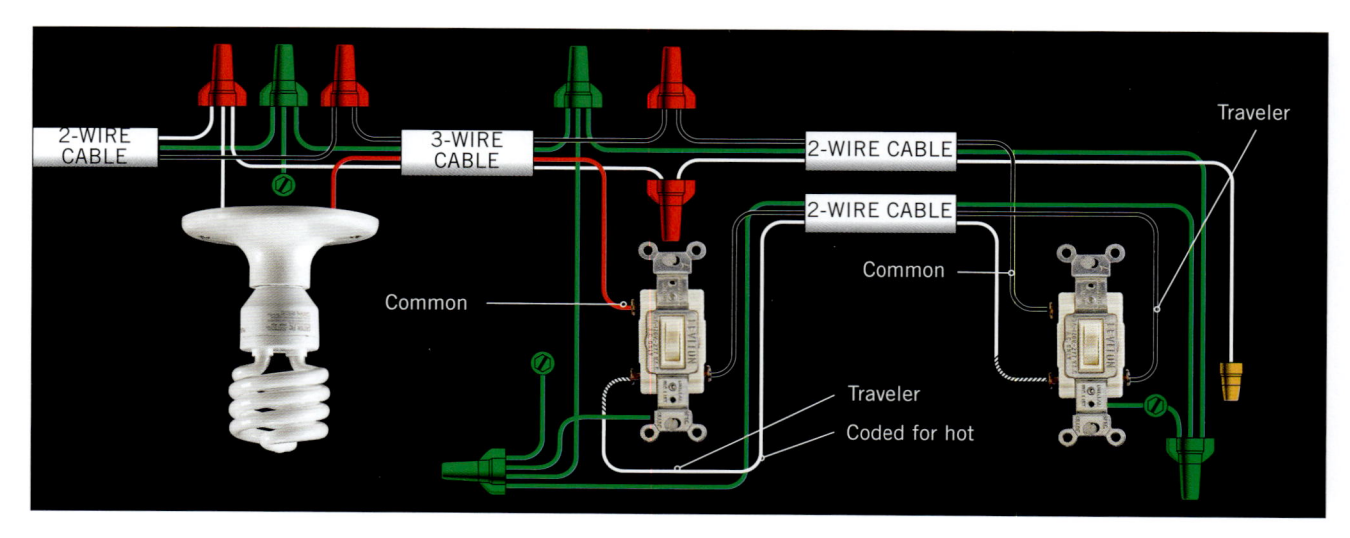

22. Three-Way Switches + Light Fixture (Fixture at End of Cable Run)

This variation of the three-way switch layout (circuit map 20) is used where it is more practical to locate the fixture at the end of the cable run. Requires two-wire and three-wire cables.

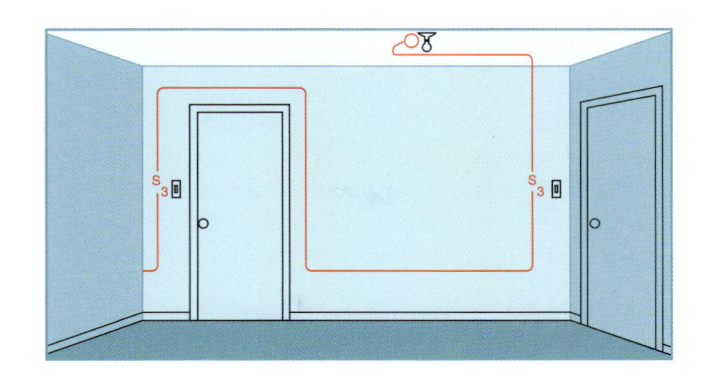

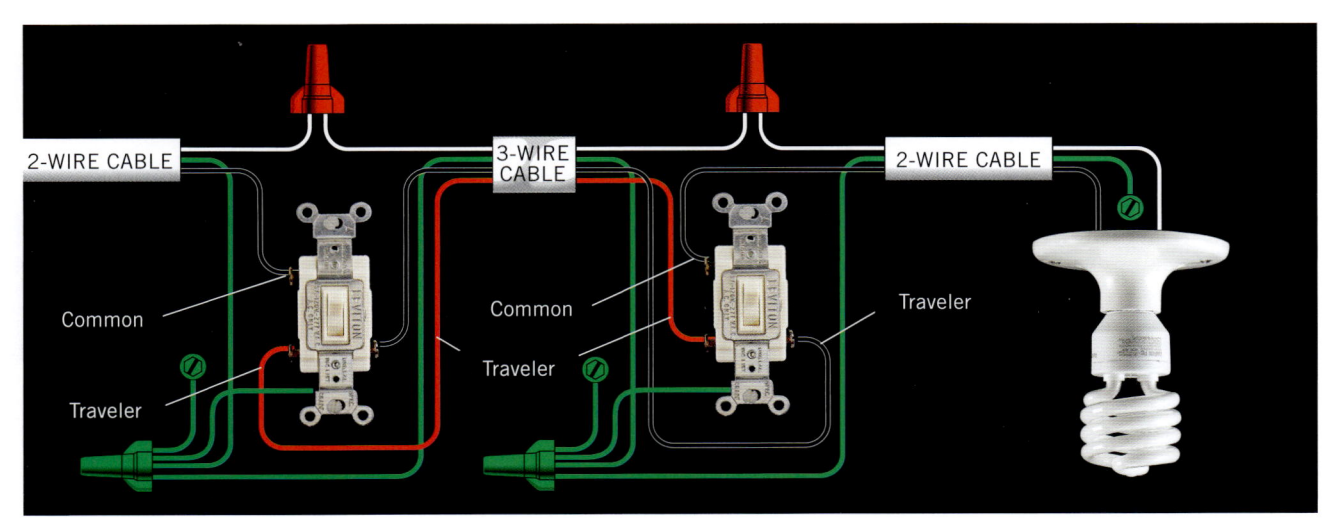

23. Three-Way Switches + Light Fixture with Duplex Receptacle

Use this layout to add a receptacle to a three-way switch configuration (circuit map 21). Requires two-wire and parallel runs of two-wire cables.

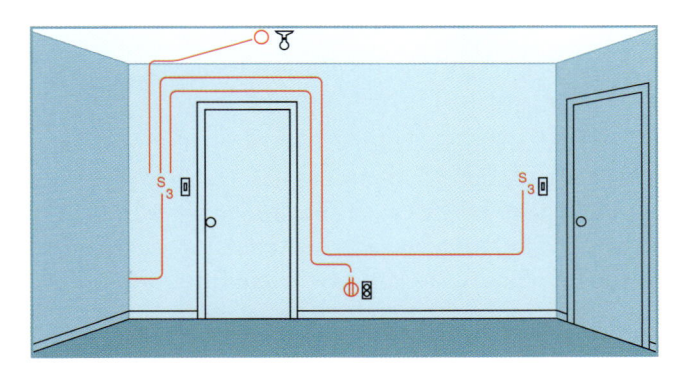

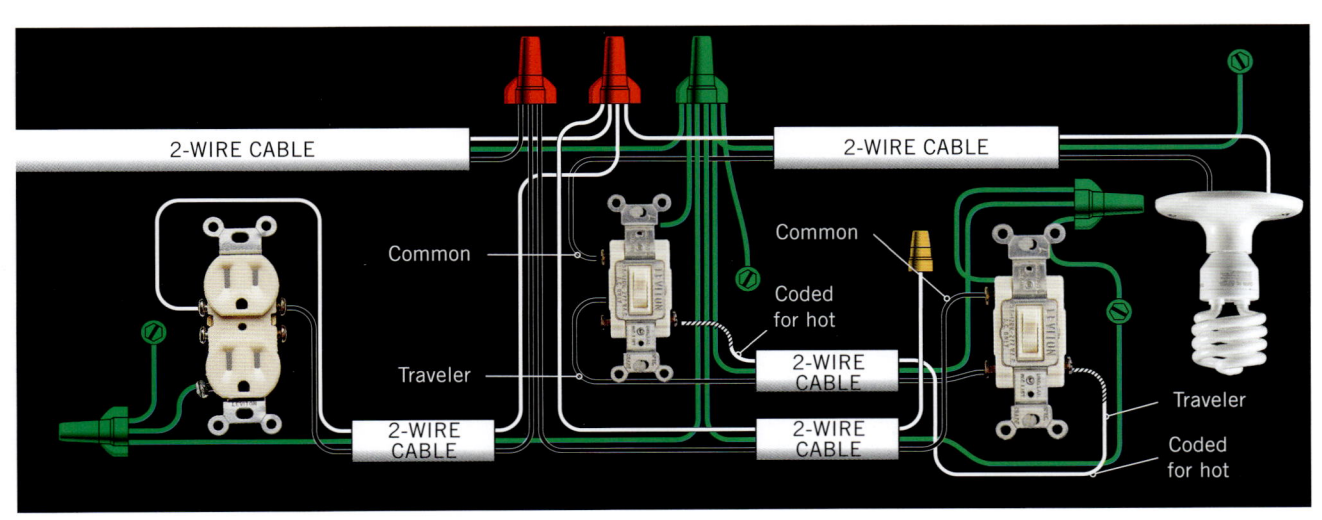

24. Three-Way Switches
+ Multiple Light Fixtures
(Fixtures Between Switches)

This is a variation of circuit map 20. Use it to place multiple light fixtures between two three-way switches where power comes in at one of the switches. Requires two- and three-wire cable.

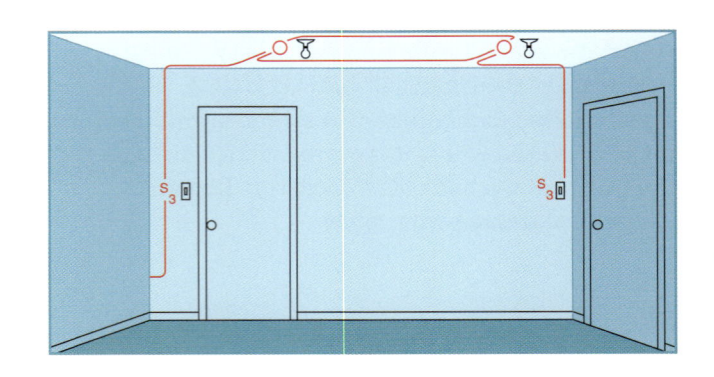

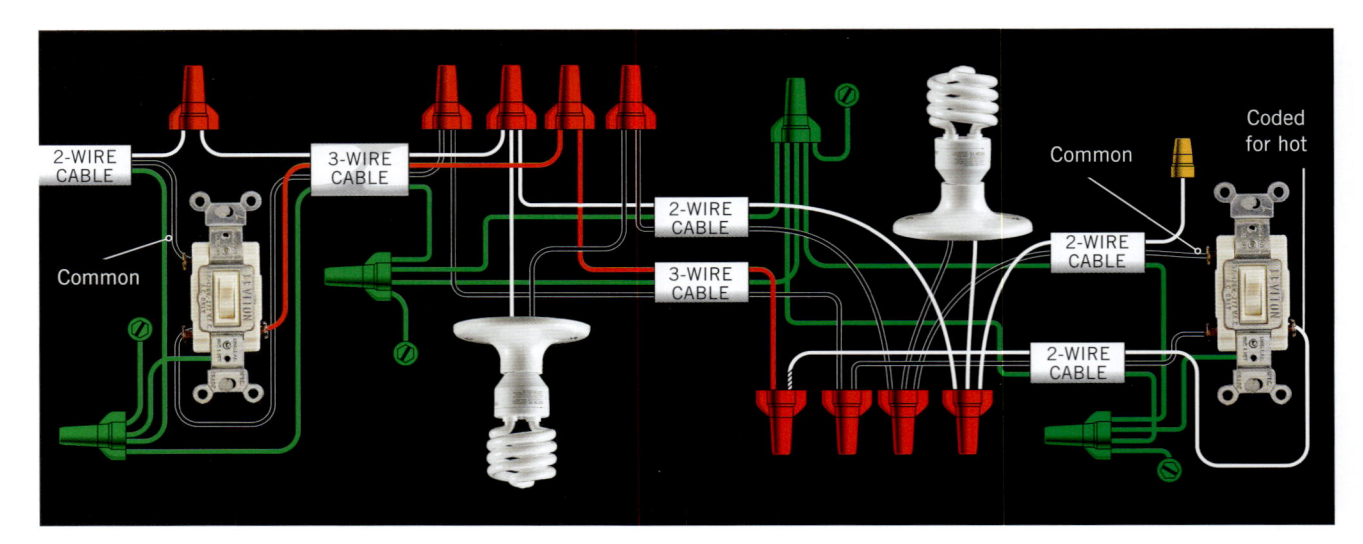

25. Three-Way Switches
+ Multiple Light Fixtures
(Fixtures at Beginning of Run)

This is a variation of circuit map 21. Use it to place multiple light fixtures at the beginning of a run controlled by two three-way switches. Power comes in at the first fixture. Requires two- and three-wire cable.

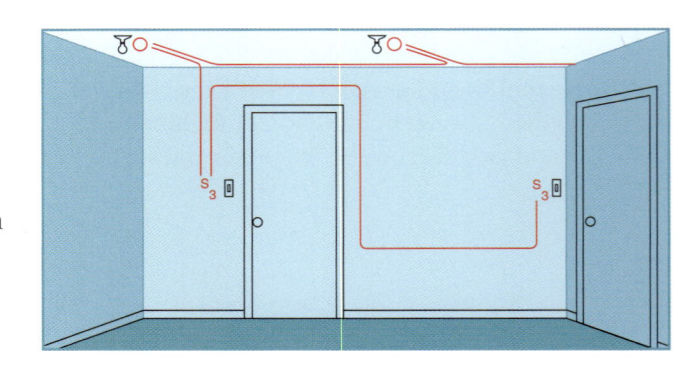

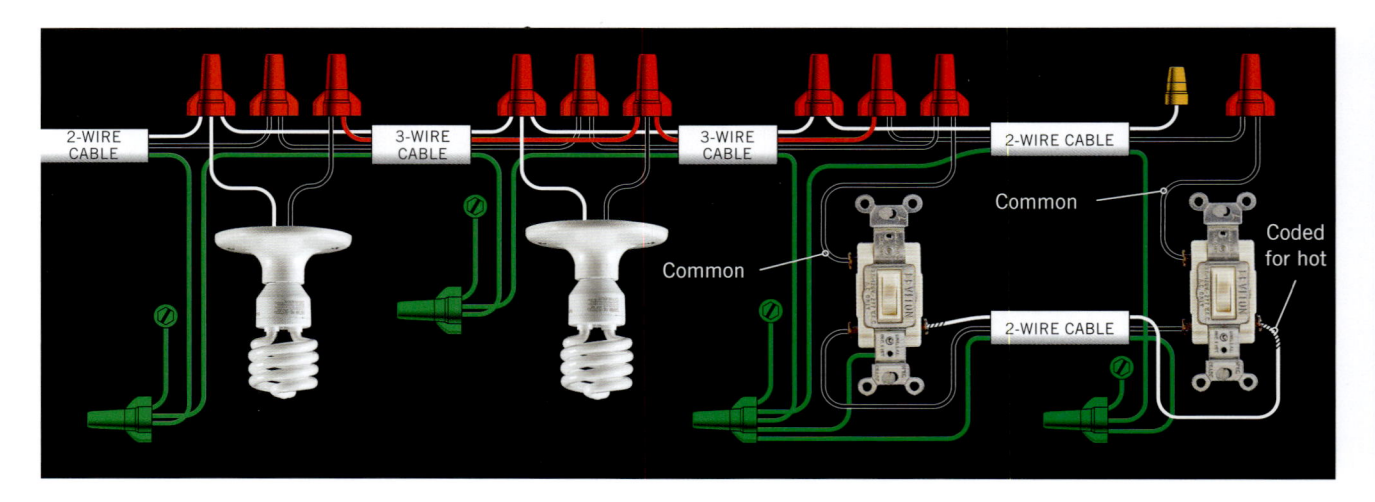

26. Four-Way Switch + Light Fixture
(Fixture at Start of Cable Run)

This layout lets you control a light fixture from three locations. The end switches are three-way, and the middle is four-way. A pair of three-wire cables enter the box of the four-way switch. The white and red wires from one cable attach to the top pair of screw terminals (line 1), and the white and red wires from the other cable attach to the bottom screw terminals (line 2). Requires two three-way switches and one four-way switch and two-wire and three-wire cables.

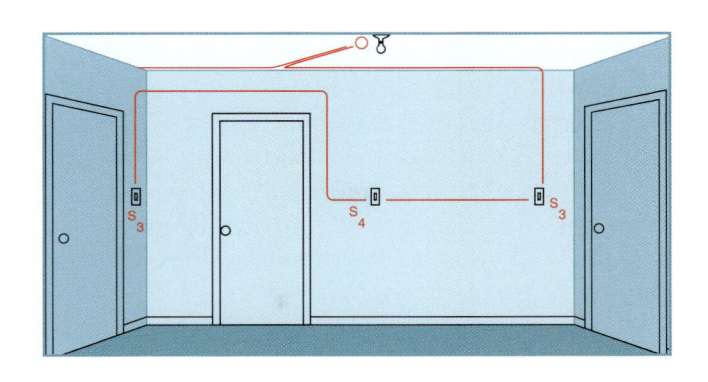

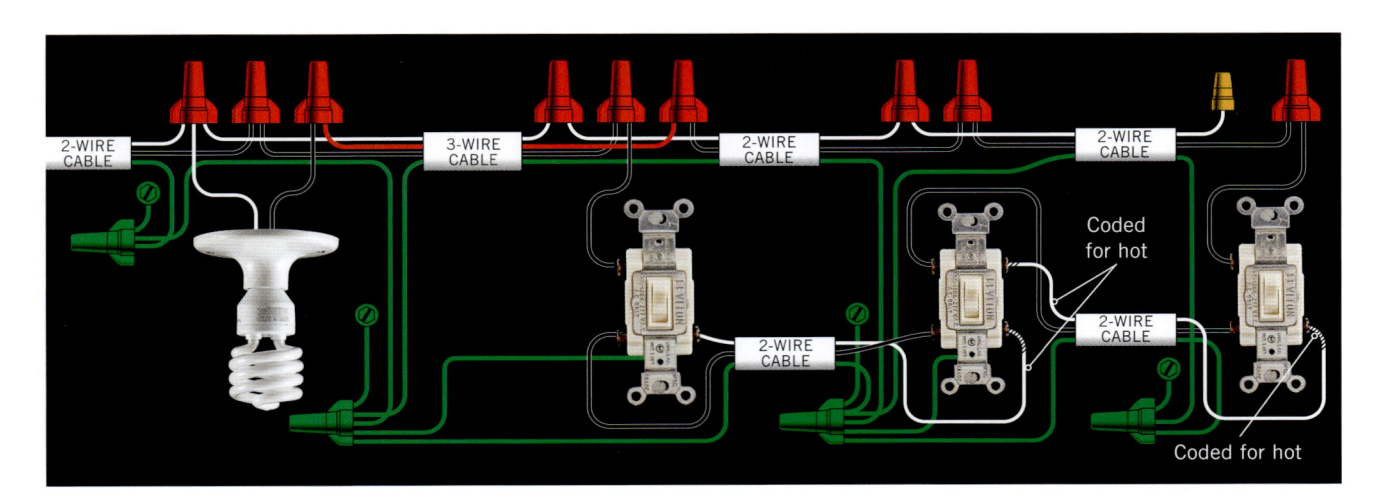

27. Four-Way Switch + Light Fixture
(Fixture at End of Cable Run)

Use this layout variation of circuit map 26 where it is more practical to locate the fixture at the end of the cable run. Requires two three-way switches and one four-way switch and two-wire and three-wire cables.

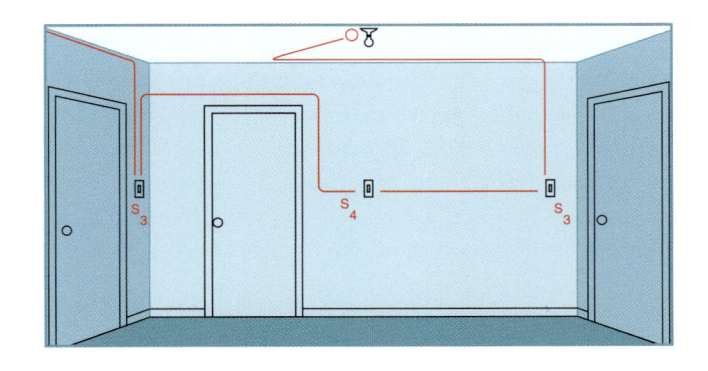

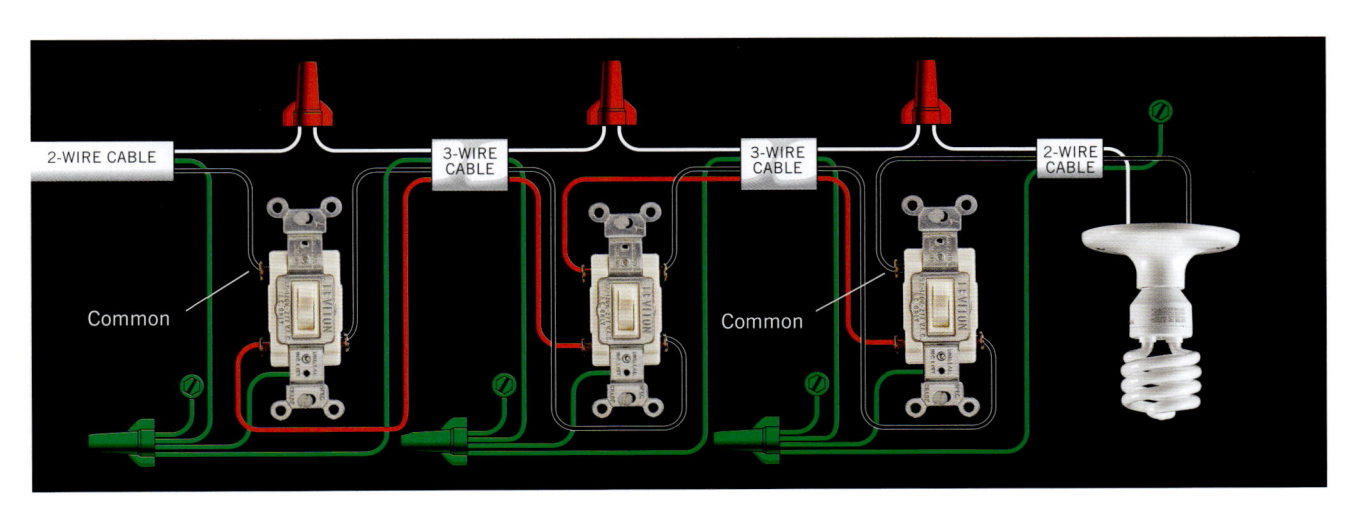

28. Multiple Four-Way Switches Controlling a Light Fixture

This alternate variation of the four-way switch layout (circuit map 27) is used where three or more switches will control a single fixture. The outer switches are three-way, and the middle are four-way. Requires two three-way switches and two four-way switches and two-wire and three-wire cables.

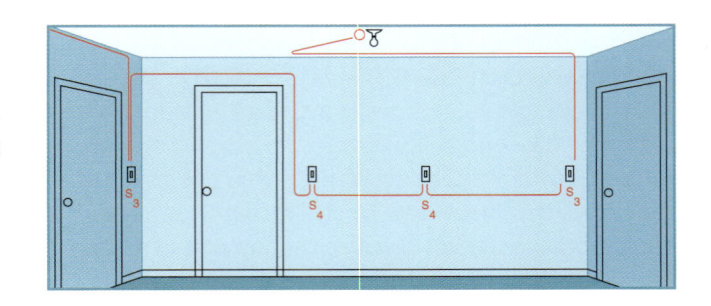

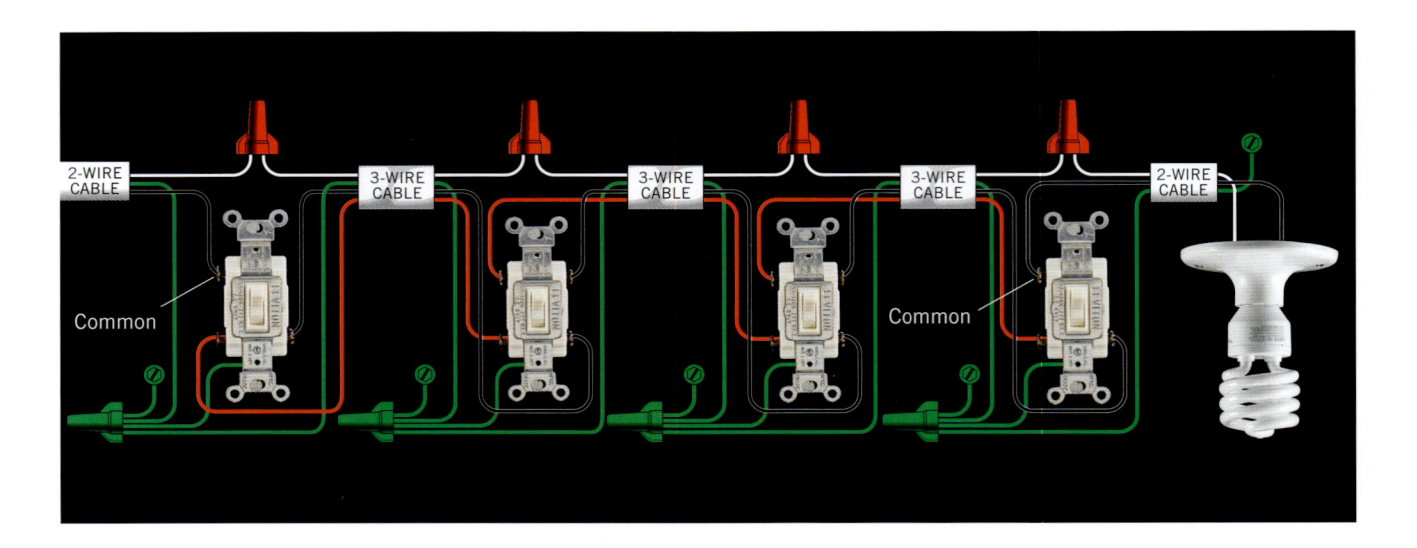

29. Four-Way Switches + Multiple Light Fixtures

This variation of the four-way switch layout (circuit map 26) is used where two or more fixtures will be controlled from multiple locations in a room. Outer switches are three-way, and the middle switch is a four-way. Requires two three-way switches and one four-way switch and two-wire and three-wire cables.

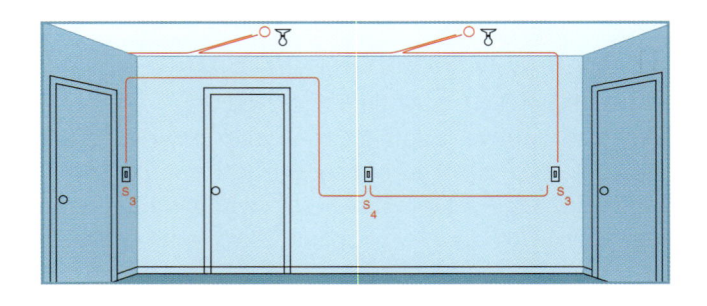

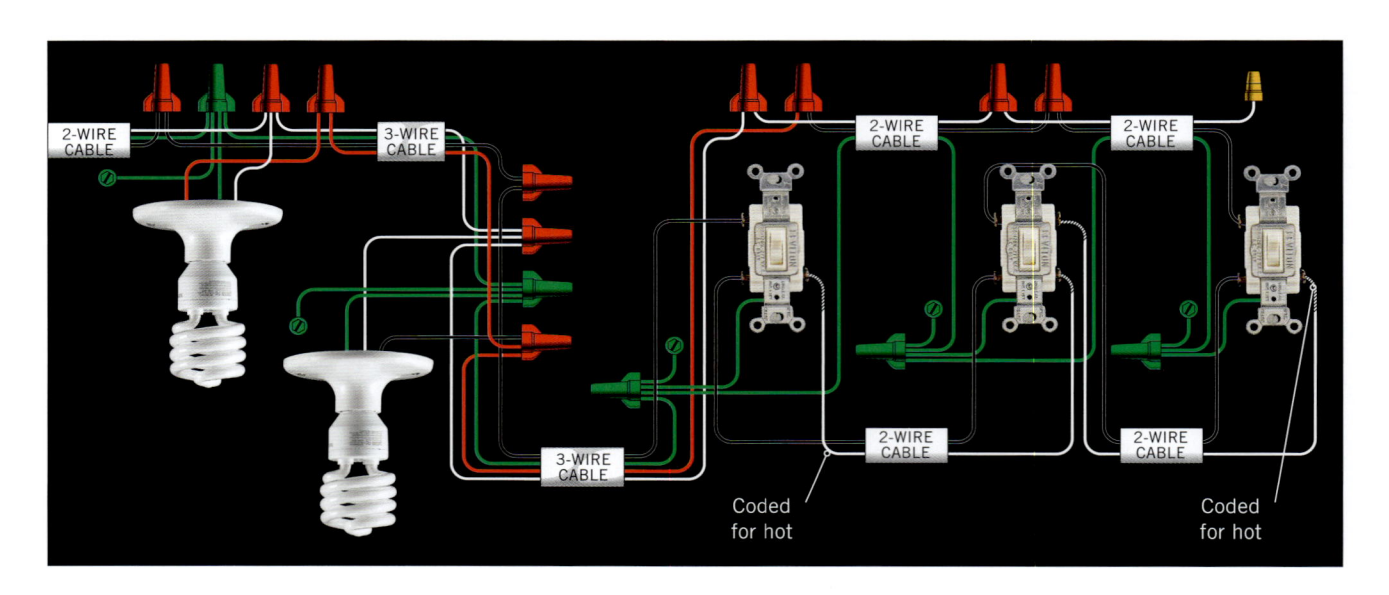

30. Ceiling Fan/Light Fixture Controlled by Ganged Switches
(Fan at End of Cable Run)

This layout is for a combination ceiling fan/light fixture controlled by a speed-control switch and dimmer in a double-gang switch box. Requires two-wire and three-wire cables.

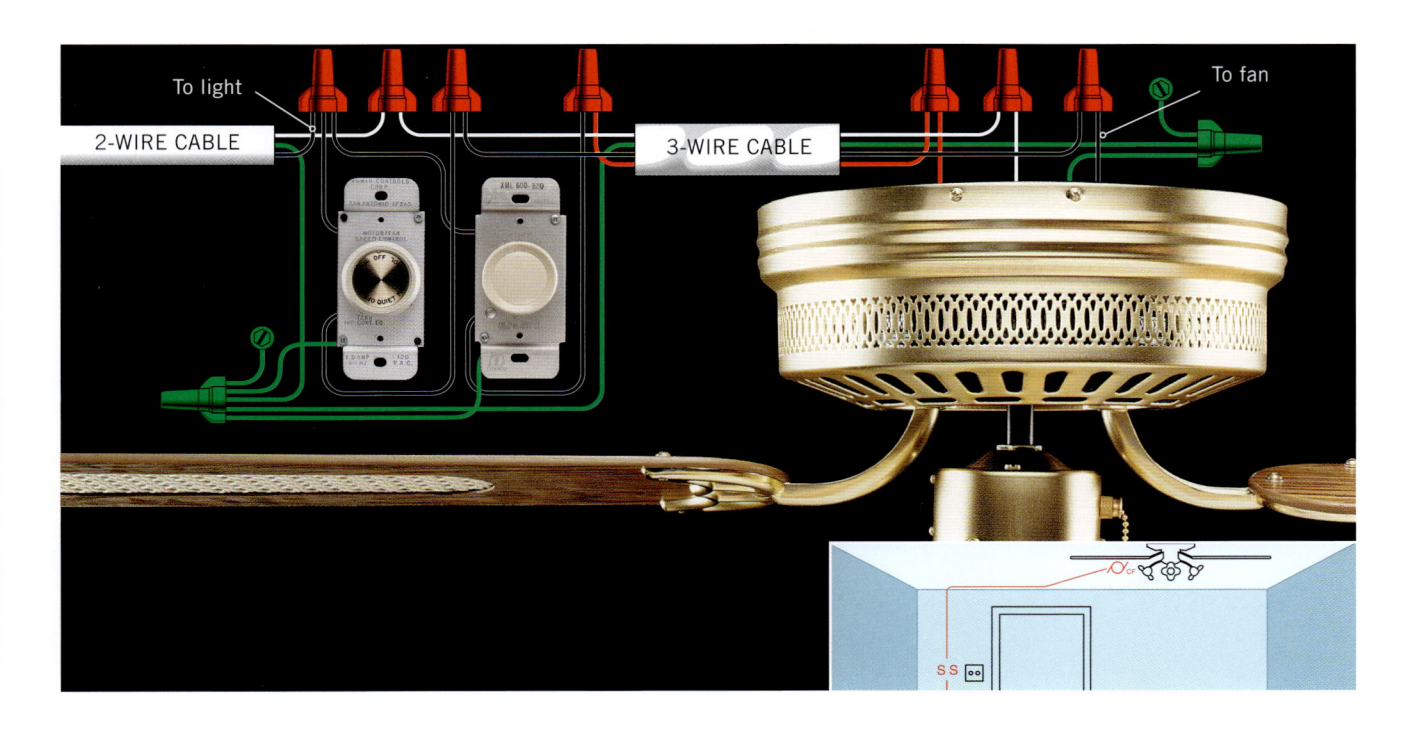

31. Ceiling Fan/Light Fixture Controlled by Ganged Switches
(Switches at End of Cable Run)

Use this switch loop layout variation when it is more practical to install the ganged speed control and dimmer switches for the ceiling fan at the end of the cable run. Requires two-wire and parallel runs of two-wire cables.

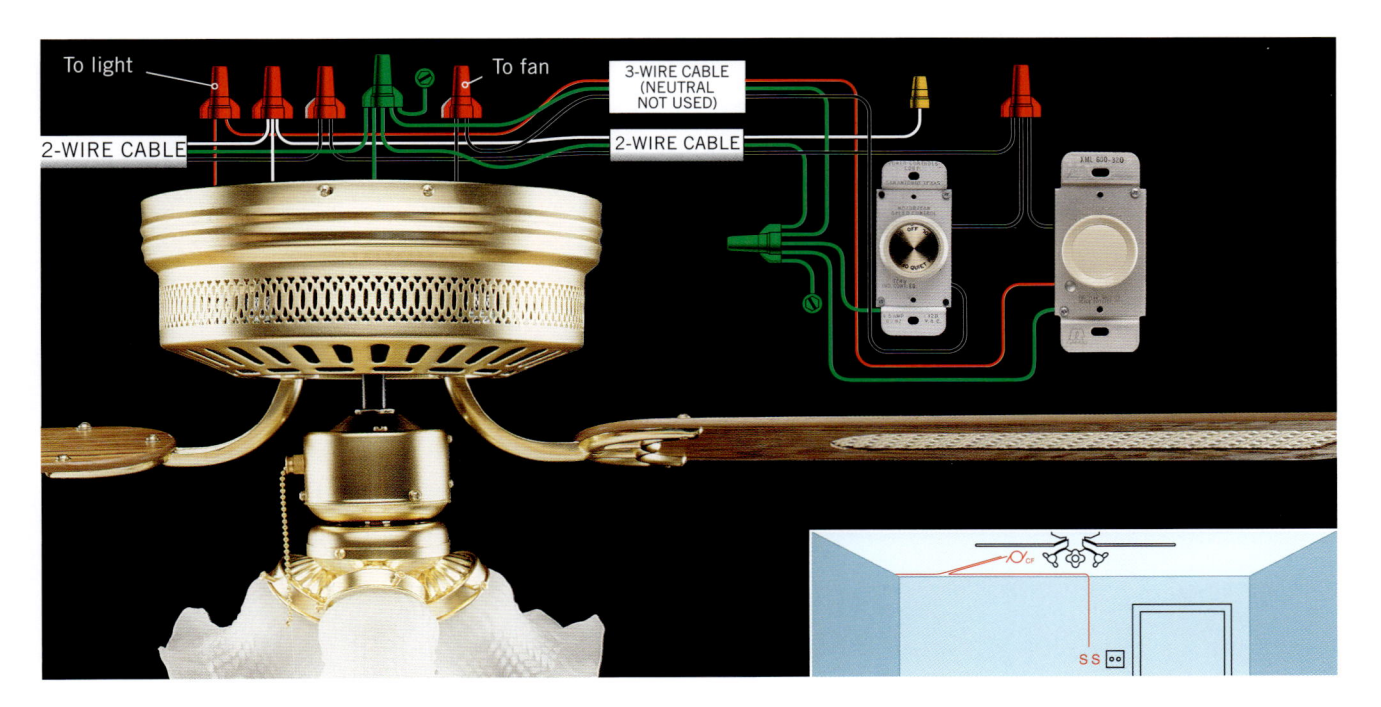

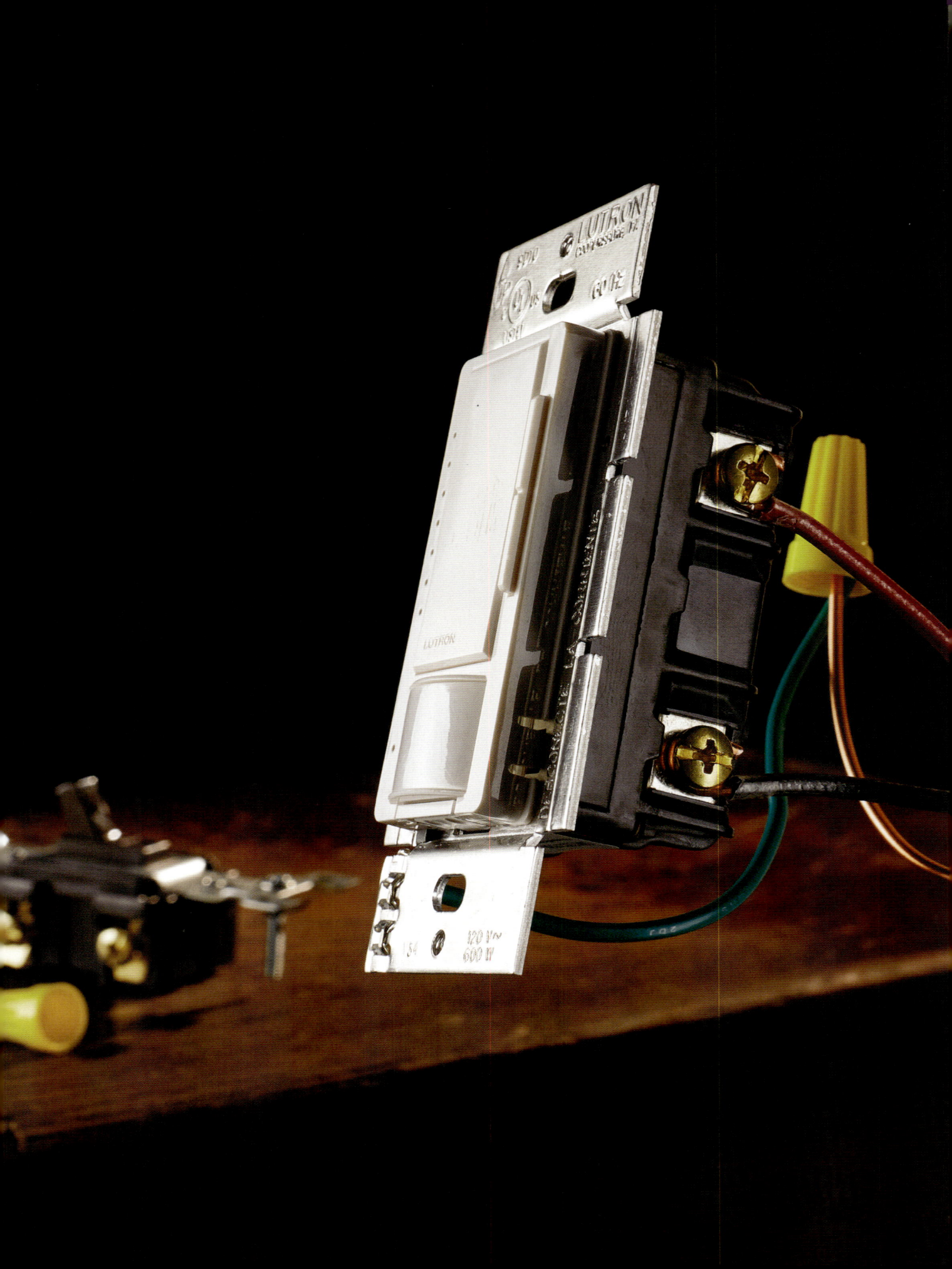

Common Wiring Projects

The instructions that follow show you how to accomplish the most popular home wiring projects. Refer to pertinent sections elsewhere in the book to find background information on tools and skills needed to get the job done.

In this chapter:

- GFCI + AFCI Breakers
- Surge-Protective Devices
- Service Panels
- Grounding + Bonding a Wiring System
- Subpanels
- 120/240-Volt Dryer Receptacles
- 120/240-Volt Range Receptacles
- Ceiling Lights
- Recessed Ceiling Lights
- Track Lights
- Undercabinet Lights
- Vanity Lights
- Low-Voltage Cable Lights
- Hardwired Smoke Alarms + CO Alarms
- Landscape Lights
- Doorbells

- Programmable Thermostats
- Wireless Switches
- Baseboard Heaters
- Wall Heaters
- Underfloor Radiant Heat Systems
- Ceiling Fans
- Remote-Control Ceiling Fan Retrofit
- Bathroom Exhaust Fans
- Range Hoods
- Backup Power Supply
- Installing a Transfer Switch
- Outbuildings
- Motion-Sensing Floodlights
- Standalone Solar Lighting System

GFCI + AFCI Breakers

Kitchen	AFCI + GFCI
Dishwasher	AFCI + GFCI
Microwave Oven	AFCI + GFCI
Dining Room	AFCI
Living Room	AFCI
Bedrooms	AFCI
Bathrooms	GFCI
Whirlpool/Jetted Bathtubs	GFCI
Basement	GFCI (also AFCI if finished)
Family Room	AFCI
Den	AFCI
Recreation Room	AFCI
Library	AFCI
Foyer	AFCI
Hallways	AFCI
Closets	AFCI
Laundry Area	AFCI + GFCI
Sunroom	AFCI
Garage	GFCI
Outdoors	GFCI
Crawl Space (lights + receptacles)	GFCI
Sump Pump	GFCI
Swimming Pool + Spa	GFCI

Understanding the difference between GFCI (ground-fault circuit-interrupter) and AFCI (arc-fault circuit-interrupter) is tricky for most homeowners. Essentially it comes down to this: Arc-fault interrupters keep your house from burning down; ground-fault interrupters keep people from being electrocuted. AFCIs and GFCIs may not be substituted for each other, and almost every room in the house requires one or both types of protection.

The National Electric Code (NEC) requires that an AFCI breaker be installed on most branch circuits that supply outlets or fixtures in newly constructed homes. The NEC also requires adding AFCI protection to select circuits when you add new circuits and modify or extend existing circuits. Because AFCI devices protect against faults that commonly lead to house fires, they are a prudent precaution in any home, especially if it has older wiring.

AFCI breakers will not interfere with the operation of GFCI receptacles, so it is safe to install an AFCI breaker on a circuit that contains GFCI receptacles. Where both AFCI and GFCI protection are required, the simplest and most protective solution is to install a dual-function GFCI/AFCI breaker, which provides ground-fault and arc-fault protection to the entire circuit.

GROUND-FAULT CIRCUIT-INTERRUPTERS

A GFCI is an important safety device that disconnects a circuit or device in the event of a ground fault (when current takes a path other than the neutral back to the panel). One common example demonstrating a ground-fault risk is the case of the faulty hair dryer: If a person is using a hair dryer that is not properly insulated or protected (most hair dryers today have their own GFCI protection) and the dryer has an internal fault (such as a loose wire), the case of the dryer can become energized, and that stray electrical current will seek the easiest path to ground. If the user touches water or a metal object with their free hand, they can create a path to ground (the metal or water), and the fault current can pass through the user's body—a potentially deadly event. A GFCI would detect this ground fault and shut off the power before the user is badly harmed.

On new construction and when adding or extending electrical circuits, GFCI protection is required for receptacles and equipment in any location that might involve moisture, such as by sinks, near kitchen and bath countertops, outdoors, in basements, and around swimming pools and spas; see the chart above for specific requirements. In general, it is a good practice to protect all receptacle and fixture locations that could encounter damp or wet conditions.

ARC-FAULT CIRCUIT INTERRUPTERS

As with a ground fault, an arc fault occurs when electrical current follows an unintended path. You've seen an example of minor arching when you unplug an appliance that is still running, and there's a small spark between the cord prong and the receptacle slot. While this arching is relatively harmless, arc faults that occur within house wiring can be very dangerous because they create intense heat that can melt wiring insulation and ignite combustible materials, such as wood framing.

There are two types of arc faults: serial and parallel. A serial, or series, arc fault can occur when there's a small break or gap in series with the electrical load. For example, if a hot wire has a break, an arc fault results from the electrical current jumping across the gap between the wire ends. A parallel arc fault occurs when a hot wire makes contact with another hot wire or a neutral or ground conductor. A metal staple piercing a cable can make a connection between the hot wire and another wire inside the cable, resulting in a parallel arc fault. AFCI breakers today are labeled "combination,"

Breakers designed for extra protection: 20-amp GFCI (A), 30-amp double-pole GFCI (B), 20-amp combination AFCI (C), and 20-amp dual-function GFCI/AFCI (D). GFCI and AFCI breakers are identifiable by two features: a white coiled neutral wire (which connects to the terminal bar in the panel) and a manual test button on the face of the breaker. While today's GFCI and AFCI devices include a self-monitoring feature that automatically tests for device failure, it is important to test the breakers manually (using the test button) as specified by the manufacturer.

meaning they protect against both serial and parallel arc faults.

AFCI protection is required for 15- and 20-amp, 120-volt circuits serving most areas of the house, except for bathrooms, garages, outdoors, and crawlspaces; see the chart on page 168 for specific requirements. The easiest way to provide AFCI protection for a circuit is to install an AFCI circuit breaker. The NEC permits several alternate methods of providing AFCI protection, but you should consult an electrician before using these alternate methods. You should use combination AFCI circuit breakers when installing new circuits that require AFCI protection. You should install either combination AFCI circuit breakers or AFCI receptacles when you modify, replace, or extend an existing circuit that requires AFCI protection.

DUAL-FUNCTION GFCI/ AFCI BREAKERS

Dual-function GFCI/AFCI circuit breakers provide GFCI and AFCI protection to an entire circuit from a single 15- or 20-amp breaker. Using a dual-function breaker is an easy way to meet the requirement for rooms that need both GFCI and AFCI protection, such as kitchens and basements. Dual-function breakers should not be confused with combination AFCI breakers, which do not provide GFCI protection. Dual-function is a GFCI plus a combination AFCI.

TOOLS + MATERIALS

Insulated screwdriver

Voltage tester

Combination tool

AFCI, GFCI, or dual-function GFCI/ AFCI circuit breaker

How to Install an AFCI, GFCI, or Dual-Function GFCI/AFCI Breaker

Locate the breaker for the circuit you'd like to protect. Turn off power to the panel. Remove the cover from the panel, and test to ensure that power is off (see page 70). Remove the breaker you want to replace from the panel. Remove the black wire from the LOAD terminal of the breaker.

Find the white wire on the circuit you want to protect, and remove it from the neutral terminal bar.

Verify that the new breaker is approved by the panel manufacturer. Flip the handle of the new AFCI or FCI breaker to OFF. Loosen both of the breaker's terminal screws. Connect the black circuit wire to the breaker terminal labeled LOAD POWER.

Connect the white circuit wire to the breaker terminal labeled PANEL NEUTRAL. Connect the new breaker's coiled white wire to the neutral terminal bar on the panel.

Make sure all the connections are tight. Snap the new breaker into the bus bar.

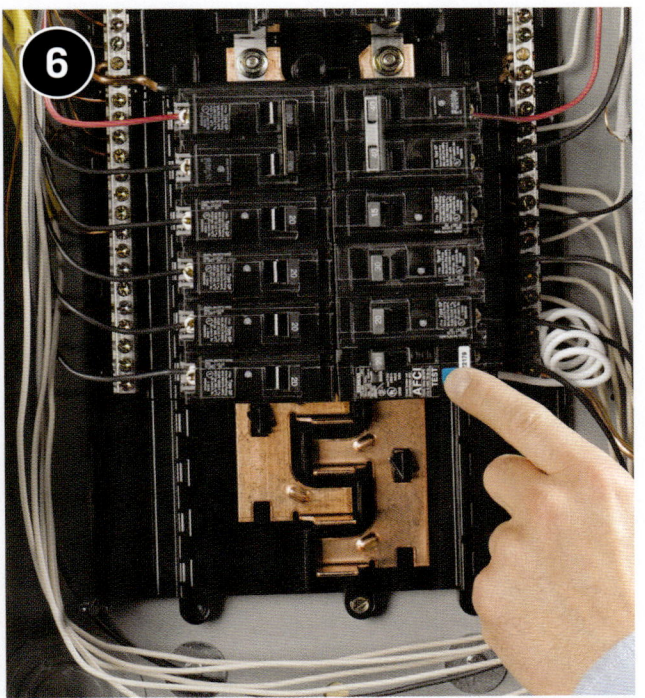

Turn the main breaker on. Turn off and unplug all fixtures and appliances on the AFCI or GFCI breaker circuit. Turn the AFCI or GFCI breaker on. Press the test button. If the breaker is wired correctly, the breaker trips open. If it doesn't trip, check all connections or consult an electrician. Replace the panel cover.

Surge-Protective Devices

Electrical surges caused by lighting or utility malfunctions can destroy or seriously damage sensitive electronics. Many homes contain tens of thousands of dollars worth of computers and home entertainment equipment protected by no more than a $10 plug-in surge suppressor. While these devices do afford a modest level of protection, they are no match for the voltage a lightning strike will push through a system. And they offer no protection for the wiring itself. Surge-protective devices (SPD), or whole-house surge arrestors, provide comprehensive protection for the wiring and devices attached to it. The NEC now requires surge protection for new and replacement services.

Surge-protective devices (SPD) are available in two basic types. Type I (SPD I) devices may be installed on the utility (line) side of the service equipment (main circuit breaker) or may be installed on the load side of the service equipment. Type II (SPD II) devices may be installed only on the load side of the service equipment. Do not attempt to install anything on the line side of the service equipment. Leave this work to a licensed electrician.

Manufacturers offer units that are housed in separate boxes (these look like a small subpanel) as well as models that are designed to replace a double-pole breaker in the panel itself. These install like standard breakers. Both types provide protection for the whole house. Freestanding models are also available with separate protection for phone, data, and cable-television lines—a wise addition if you need to protect networked computers or cable-TV receivers.

A whole-house surge arrestor is an inexpensive defense against expensive damage from high-voltage shocks caused by lightning strikes and power surges. Most models install next to the main panel.

Whatever style you choose, look for models with the Underwriters Laboratories 1449 rating and indicator lights showing that the system is protected. Most manufacturers also include a warranty against defect that covers a certain amount of property damage. This project may require a permit. Check with the electrical inspector before starting this project.

TOOLS + MATERIALS

Hammer	Whole-house surge arrestor
Combination tool	Conduit nipple and locknuts
Screwdrivers	
Cable ripper	Two 15- or 20-amp single-pole breakers
Linesman's pliers	
Circuit tester	Coaxial cable and terminators
Crimping tools	UTP cable and terminators

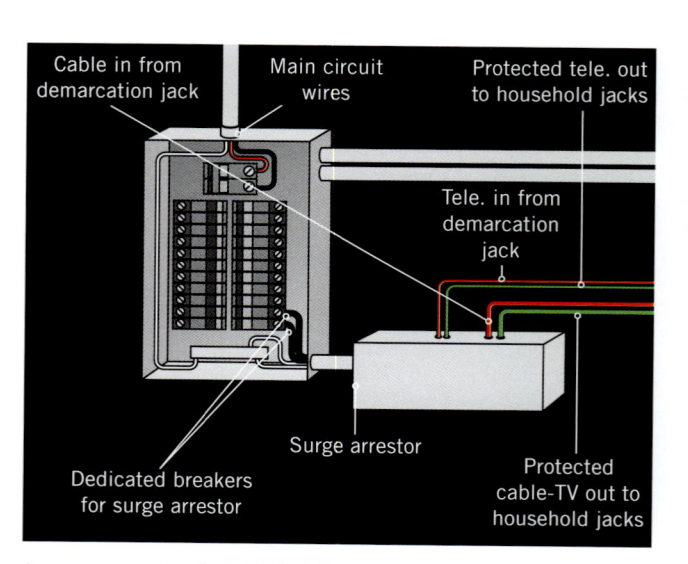

A surge protector installed at the panel protects all downstream connected devices and wires.

How to Install a Whole-House Surge Arrestor

Turn off power to the panel. Remove the cover, and test to make sure the power is off. Mount the arrestor near the service panel following the manufacturer's instructions. Typically the arrestor mounts on one side of the panel so its knockout lines up with a lower knockout on the panel. Remove the knockout on the panel. Install a conduit nipple on the arrestor, and thread the wires from the arrestor through the nipple and into the panel. Slip the other end of the nipple through the opening in the panel, and tighten the locknut. Secure the box to the wall with screws as directed.

Trim the wires as short as possible without making sharp bends. Connect the two black wires to two dedicated 15- or 20-amp breakers. Connect the white neutral wire to the neutral bar and the green grounding wire to the grounding bar. Keep wire lengths as short as possible. Snap the new breakers into the bus bar. Restore the power and carefully test that the voltage between the two black arrestor leads is 240 volts. Replace the panel cover and the arrestor cover. If the arrestor has indicator lights, they should glow, showing that the system is now protected.

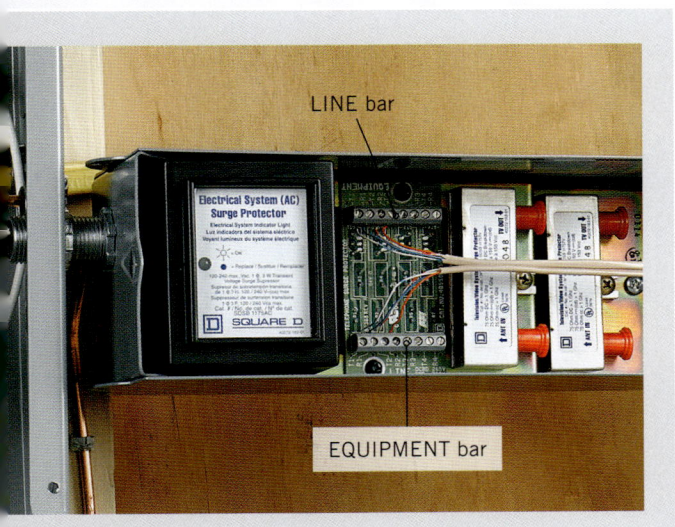

LINE bar

EQUIPMENT bar

VARIATION: If the arrestor has separate protection for the telephone circuits, remove the cable that runs from the phone demarcation jack to the junction box. Then remove a knockout in the arrestor and route a new UTP cable from the demarcation jack to the arrestor. Strip insulation from the wires and connect them to the terminals on the LINE bar (labeled IN on some models) on the phone protection module in the arrestor. Run a UTP cable from the EQUIPMENT bar (labeled OUT on some models) to the junction box. Strip and connect the wires from this cable to the appropriate terminals in the arrestor and the junction box.

VARIATION: If the arrestor has separate protection for a cable television circuit, remove the appropriate knockout from the arrestor and run a coaxial cable to the arrestor from the cable-TV demarcation jack. Connect the coaxial cable to the ANT-IN terminal on the cable-TV protection module. Run another coaxial cable from the TV-OUT terminal to the cable TV junction box or the distribution panel. Do not overtighten the connections.

TV-OUT terminal

ANT-IN terminal

Service Panels

Replacing an old 60- or 100-amp electrical service panel with a new 200-amp panel is an ambitious project that requires a lot of forethought. The first step is to obtain a permit. When you are ready to begin, you will need to have your utility company disconnect your house from electrical service at the transformer that feeds your house. When you schedule this, talk to your utility company about the size of your service drop or lateral. That may need to be upgraded too.

Also check with your utility company to make sure you know what equipment is theirs and what belongs to you. In most cases, the electric meter and everything on the street side belongs to the power company, and the meter base and everything on the house side is yours. Be aware that if you tamper with the sealed meter in any way, you likely will be fined. Utility companies will not re-energize your system without approval from your inspecting agency.

Note: The NEC requires outdoor emergency disconnects for home services in new construction, homes undergoing renovation, and all service replacements. An exterior disconnect allows emergency crews to shut off the power. Approved disconnects include
• Service disconnects
• Meter disconnects
• Listed disconnect switches or circuit breakers

Disconnects may be located before or after the meter base and may be in their own enclosure. They must be clearly labeled. Check with the local code authority for specific requirements.

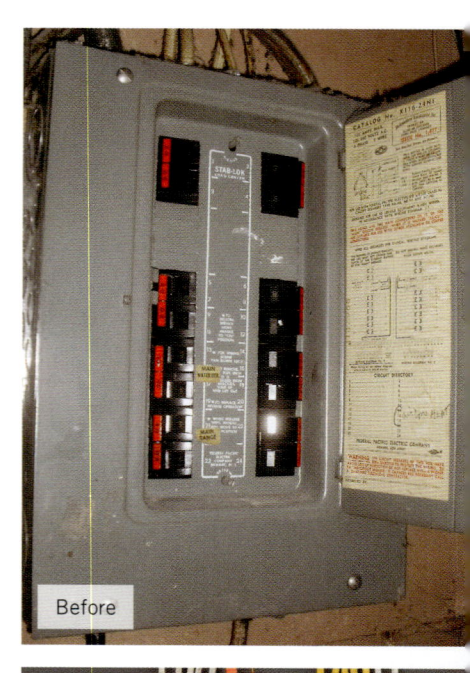

Before

After

Modern homeowners consume more power than our forebears, and it is often necessary to upgrade the electrical service to keep pace. While homeowners are not allowed to make the final electrical service connections, removing the old panel and installing the new panel and meter base yourself can save you hundreds or even thousands of dollars.

TOOLS + MATERIALS

200-amp service panel	Emergency disconnect	Drill/driver
200-amp bypass meter base	Weatherhead	Tape
Circuit breakers	Service cable	Allen wrench
Schedule 80 or RMC conduit and fittings	Circuit wires	Circuit tester
	Plywood backer board	Multimeter
	Screwdrivers	

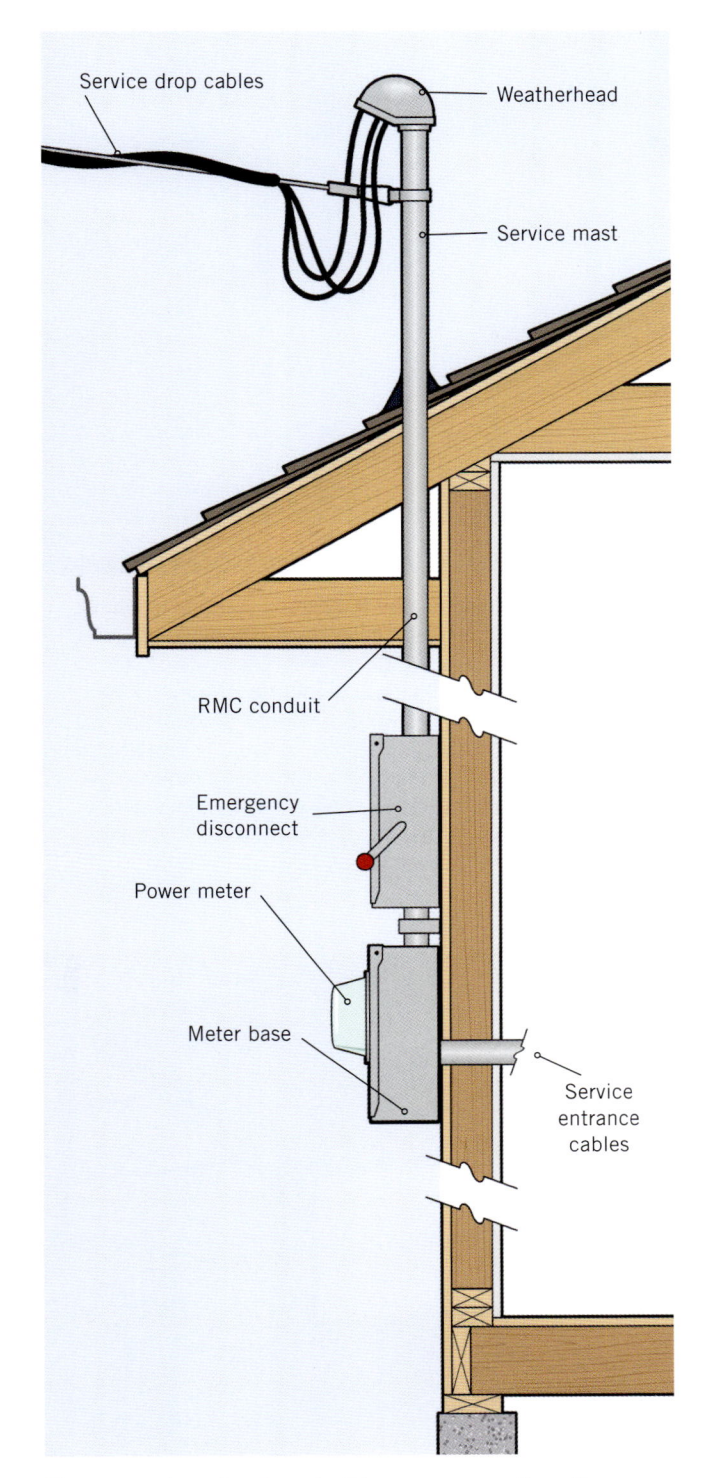

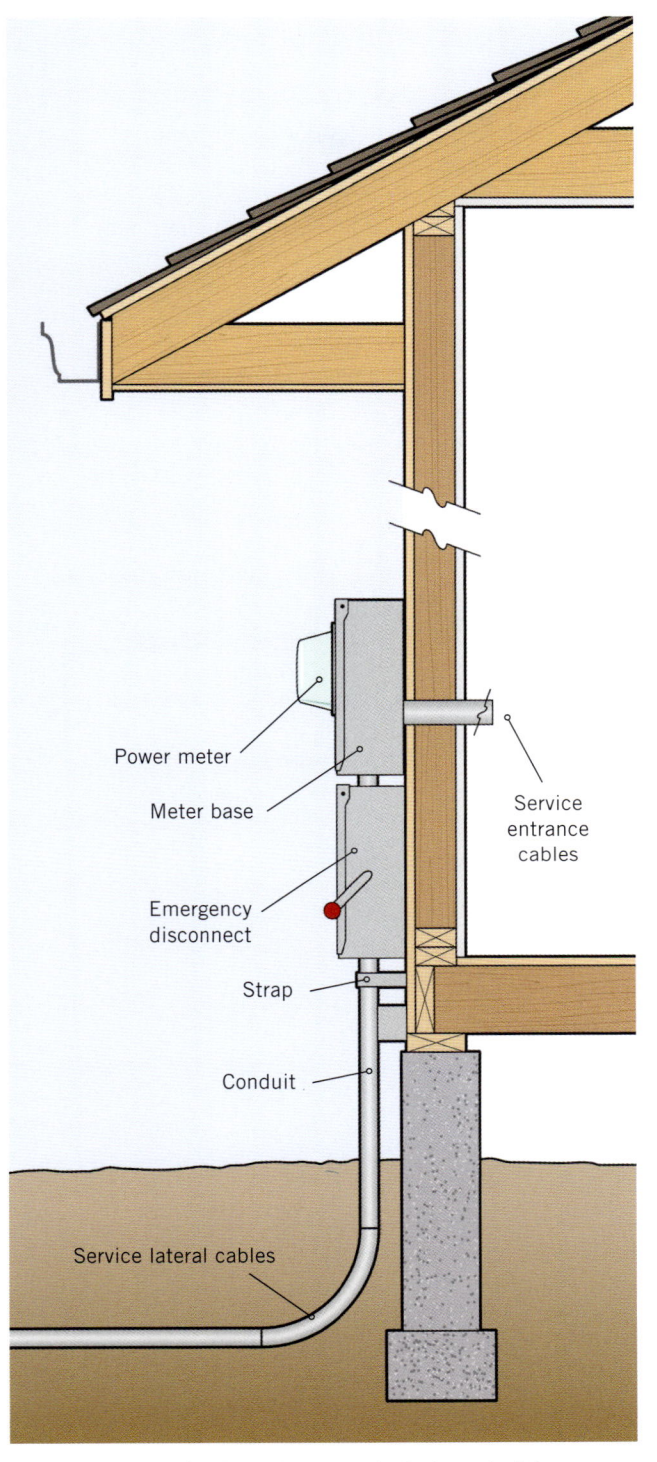

Aboveground service drop. In this common configuration, the service cables from the closest transformer (called the service drop) connect to service entrance wires near the weatherhead. This connection is called the service point and is where your property usually begins. The service entrance wires from the weatherhead are routed to a power meter that's owned by your utility company but is housed in a base that's considered your property. From the meter, the service entrance wires enter your house through the wall and are routed to the main service panel, where they are connected to the main circuit breaker.

Underground service lateral. Increasingly, homebuilders are choosing to have power supplied to their new homes underground instead of an overhead service drop. Running the cables in the ground eliminates problems with power outages caused by ice accumulation or fallen trees, but it entails a completely different set of cable and conduit requirements. For the homeowner, however, the differences are minimal, because the hookups are identical once the power service reaches the meter.

Local codes dictate where the main service panel may be placed relative to other parts of your home. Although the codes vary (and always take precedence), national codes stipulate that a service panel (or any other distribution panel) may not be located near flammable materials, in a bathroom, clothes closet or other area designated for storage, above stairway steps, or directly above a workbench or other permanent work station or appliance. The panel also can't be located in a crawl space. If you are installing a new service entry hookup, there are many regulations regarding height of the service drop and the meter. Contact your local inspections office for specific regulations.

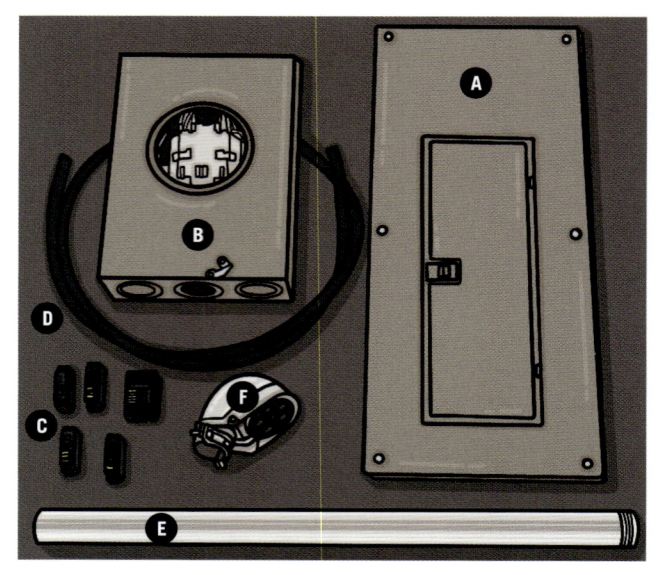

All the equipment you'll need to upgrade your main panel is sold at most larger building centers. It includes (A) a new 200-amp panel; (B) a 200-amp meter base (also called a socket); (C) individual circuit breakers; (D) new THW, THHW, THWN-2. RHW, RHW-2, XHHW 3/0 copper or 4/0 aluminum; (E) 2" dia. rigid metallic conduit; (F) weatherhead for mast. (E) and (F) are not necessary if you have underground service wires (a service lateral). An exterior service disconnecting means, as shown in the illustration below, will also be necessary.

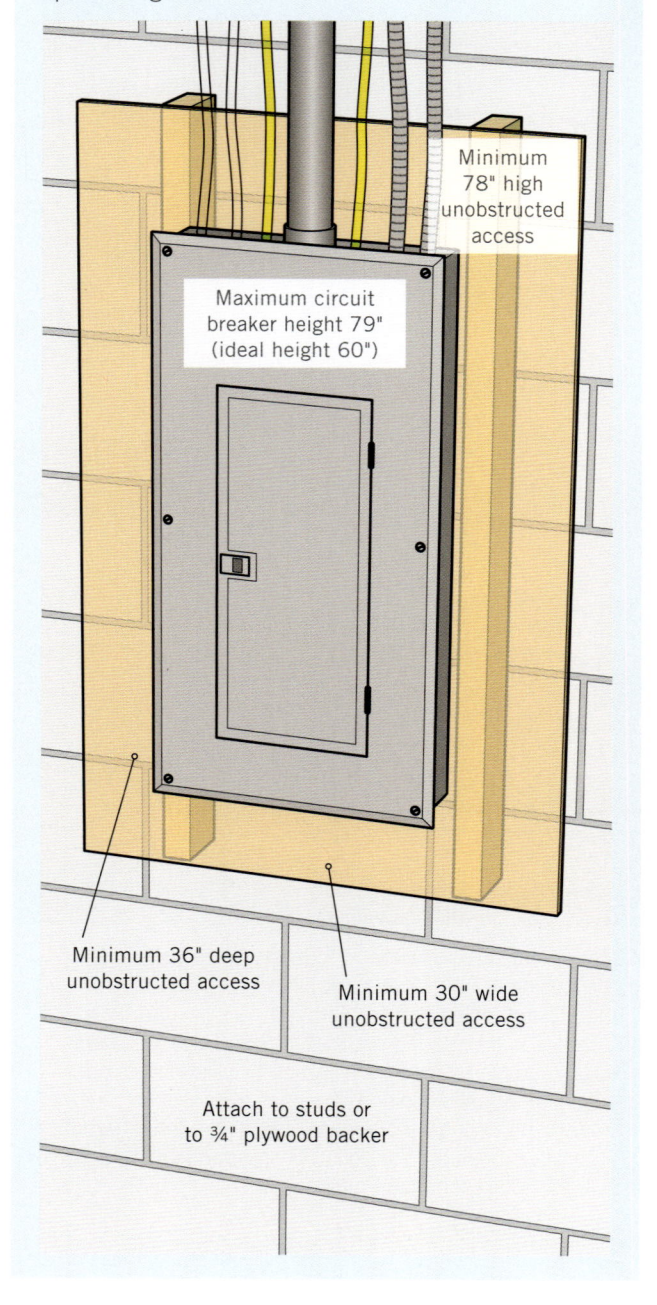

Minimum 78" high unobstructed access

Maximum circuit breaker height 79" (ideal height 60")

Minimum 36" deep unobstructed access

Minimum 30" wide unobstructed access

Attach to studs or to ¾" plywood backer

Meter

Shutoff switch

A means to disconnect electrical service must be located outside. This may be the main circuit breaker (service equipment), or it may be a separate switch or circuit breaker. This disconnecting means must be labeled as described in code.

How to Replace a Main Panel

1

Shut off power to the house at the transformer. This must be done by a technician who is certified by your utility company. Also have the utility worker remove the old meter from the base. It is against the law for a homeowner to break the seal on the meter.

2

Label all incoming circuit wires before disconnecting them. Labels should be written clearly on tape that is attached to the cables outside of the existing panel. Test the circuits before starting to make sure they are labeled correctly.

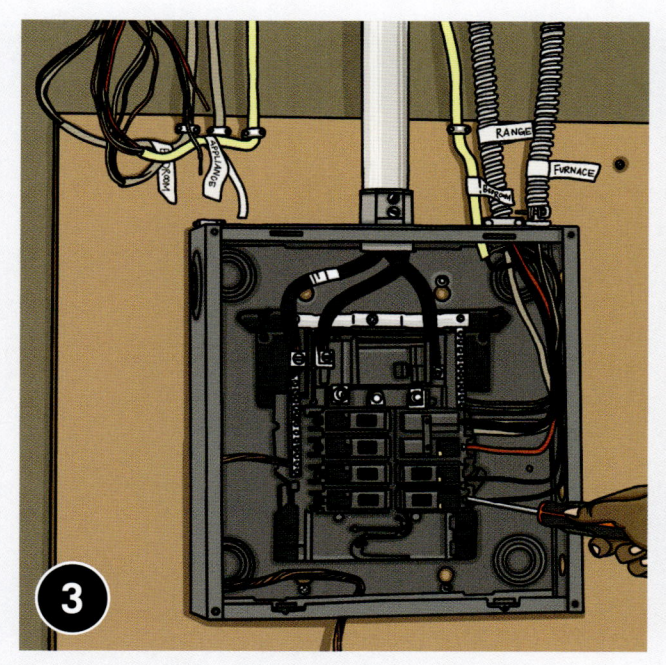

3

Disconnect incoming circuit wires from breakers, grounding bar, and neutral terminal bar. Also disconnect cable clamps at the knockouts on the panel box. Retract all circuit wires from the panel and coil them up neatly, with the labels clearly visible.

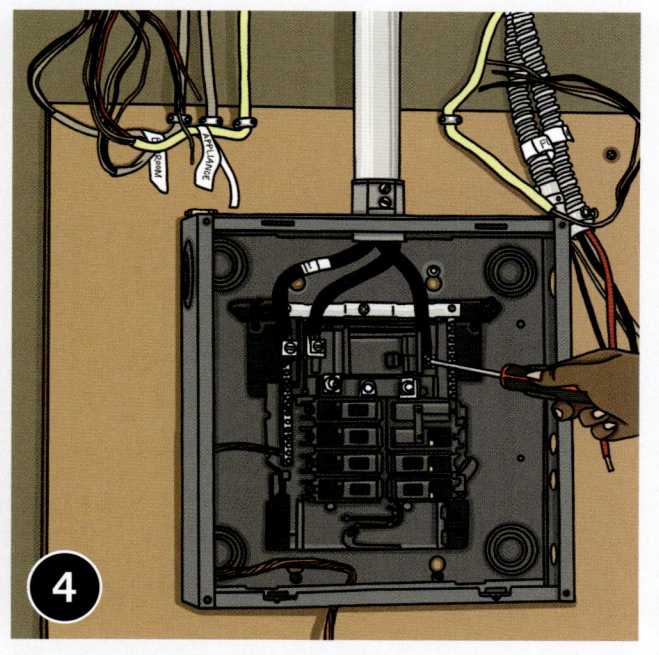

4

Unscrew the lugs securing the service entry cables at the top of the panel. For 240-volt service you will find two heavy-gauge SE cables, probably with black sheathing. Each cable carries 120 volts of electricity. A neutral service cable, usually of smaller gauge than the SE cables, will be attached to the neutral terminal bar. This cable returns current to the source.

(continued)

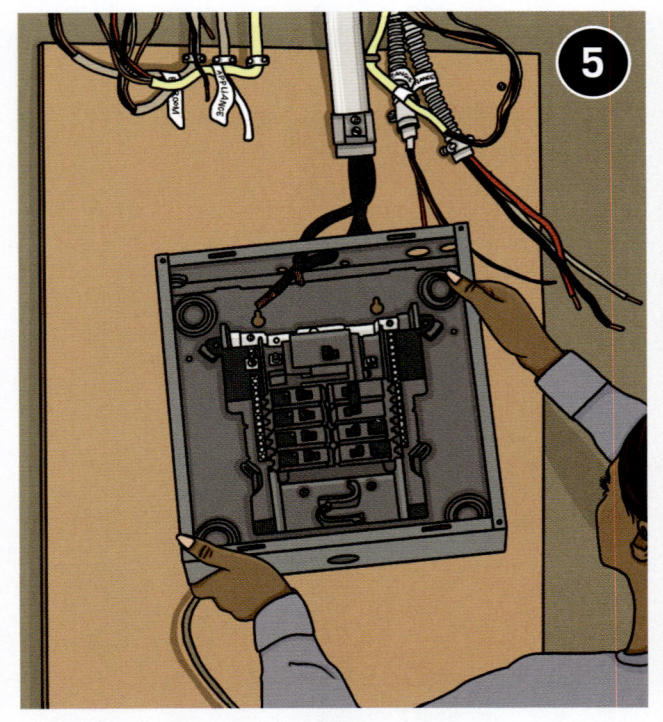

Remove the old service panel box. Boxes are rated for a maximum current capacity; and if you are upgrading, the components in the old box will be undersized for the new service levels. The new box will have a greater number of circuit slots as well.

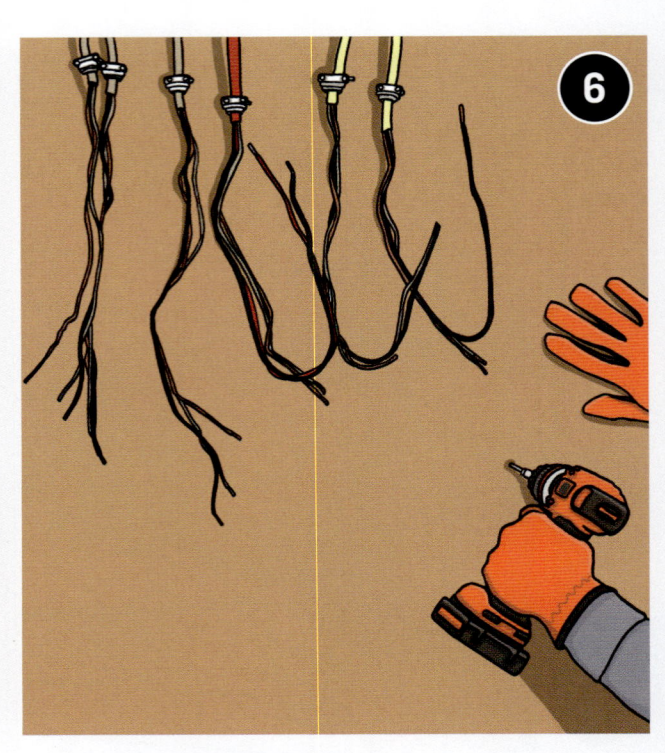

Replace the old panel backer board with a larger board in the installation area. A piece of ¾" plywood is typical. Make sure the board is well secured at wall framing members.

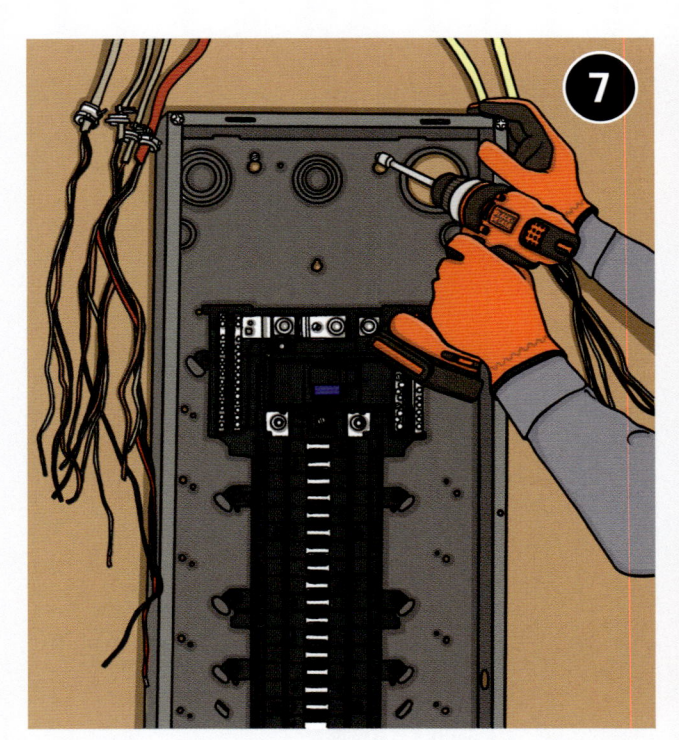

Attach the box to the backer board, making sure that at least two screws are driven through the backer and into wall studs. Drill clearance holes in the back of the box at stud locations if necessary. Use roundhead screws that do not have tapered shanks so the screwheads seat flatly against the panel.

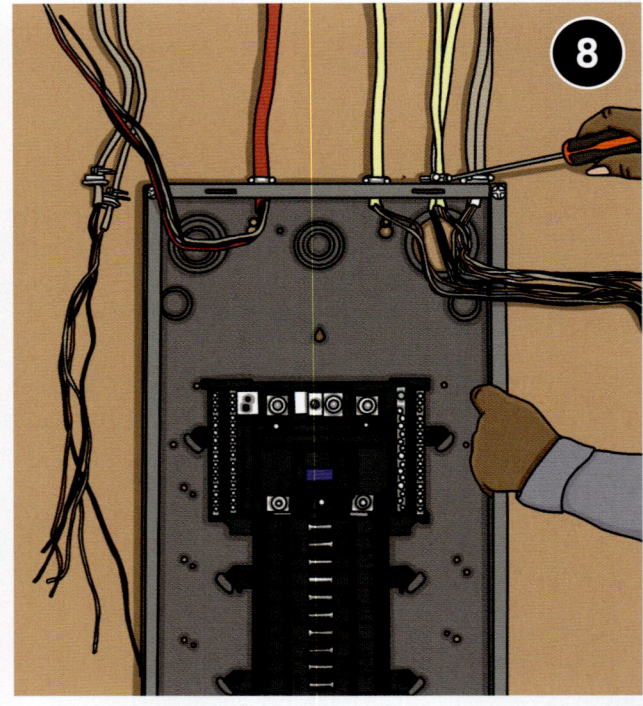

Attach properly sized cable clamps to the box at the knockout holes. Install one cable per knockout in this type of installation and plan carefully to avoid removing knockouts that you do not need to remove (if you do make a mistake, you can fill the knockout hole with a plug).

SPLICING IN THE BOX

Some wiring codes allow you to make splices inside the panel box if the circuit wire is too short. Use the correct wire cap and wind electrical tape over the conductors where they enter the cap. If your municipality does not allow splices in the panel box, you'll have to rectify a short cable by splicing it in a junction box before it reaches the panel and then replacing the cable with a longer section for the end of the run. Make sure each circuit line has at least 12" of slack.

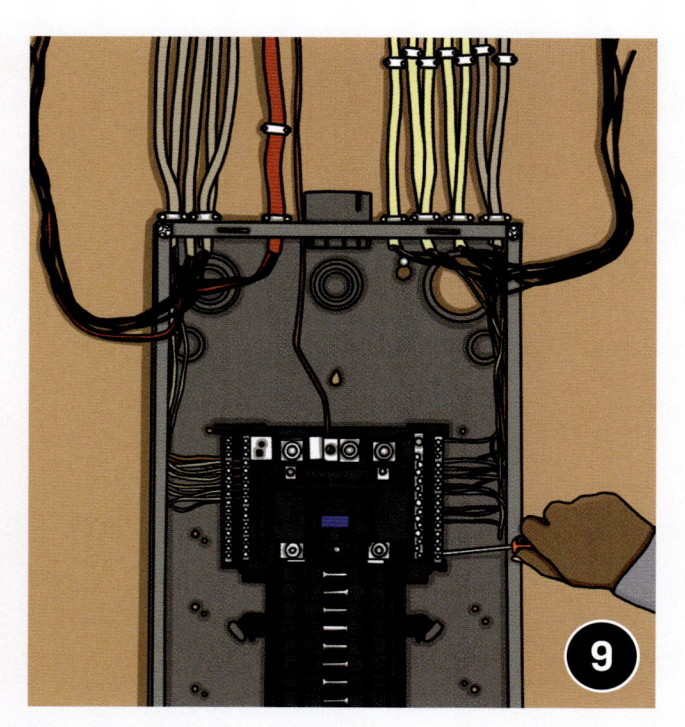

Attach the white neutral from each circuit cable to the neutral terminal bar. Most panels have a preinstalled neutral terminal bar, but in some cases you may need to purchase the bar separately and attach it to the panel back. The panel should also have a separate grounding bar that you also may need to purchase separately.

Note: For GFCI and AFCI breakers, the neutral circuit wire connects to the breaker, and the breaker's coiled neutral lead connects to the neutral terminal bar.

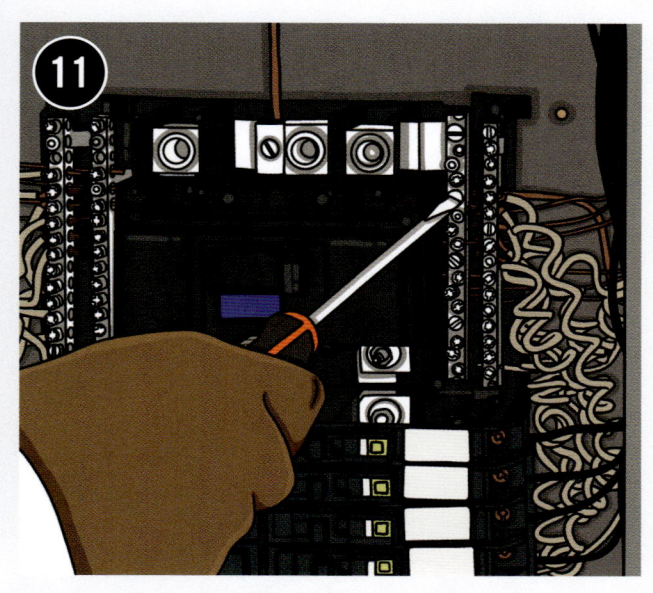

Attach the hot lead wire to the terminal on the circuit breaker, and then snap the breaker into an empty slot. When loading slots, start at the top of the panel and work your way downward. It is important that you balance the circuits as you go to equalize the amperage. For example, do not install all the 15-amp circuits on one side and all the 20-amp circuits on the other.

Install grounding conductors. Local codes are very specific about how the grounding and bonding needs to be accomplished. For example, some require multiple rods driven at least 6 ft. apart. Discuss your grounding requirements thoroughly with your inspector or an electrician before making your plan.

(continued)

Install service entrance wires from the weatherhead or the underground service lateral, where the connections to the service wires are made, to the meter main. Only your public utility company can make the hookup to the service wires.

Update the conduit that runs from your house to the bottom of the meter base. This should be 2" rigid conduit in good repair. Attach the conduit to the base and wall with the correct fittings. Rigid metal conduit is a good option, but Schedule 80 PVC is probably the best choice for housing the service entrance wires.

Install new feeder wires. Each wire carries 120 volts from the meter to the service wire lugs at the top of your service panel. Code is very specific about how these connections are made. In most cases, you'll need to tighten the terminal nuts with a specific amount of torque that requires a torque wrench to measure. Also attach the sheathed neutral wire to the neutral/ grounding lug.

Install service entrance wires from the emergency disconnect to the meter base.

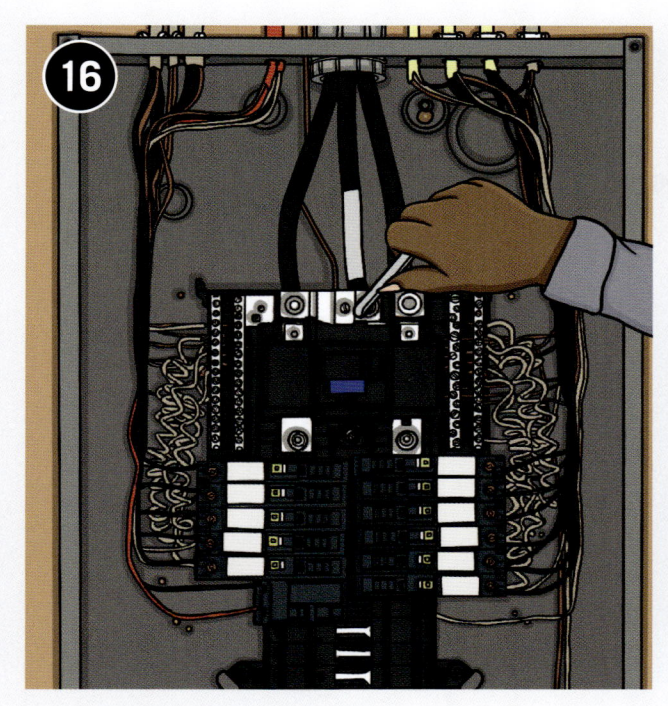

Attach the feeder wires to the lugs connected to the main breakers at the top of your service entry panel. Do not remove too much insulation on the wires—leaving the wires exposed is a safety hazard. The neutral service entry wire is attached either directly to the neutral terminal bar or to a metal bridge that is connected to the neutral bonding terminal bar. Install the green grounding screw provided with the panel.

Have the panel and all connections inspected and approved by your local building department, and then contact the public utility company to make the connections at the power drop. Once you have restored power to the new service panel, test out each circuit to make sure you don't have any surprises. With the main breakers on, shut off all individual circuit breakers, and then flip each one on by itself. Walk through your house and test every switch and receptacle to confirm the loads on that circuit.

 TALL MAST, SHORT ROOF

The service drop must occur at least 10 ft. above ground level, and as much as 14 ft. in some cases. Occasionally, this means that you must run the conduit for the service mast up through the eave of your roof and seal the roof penetration with a boot.

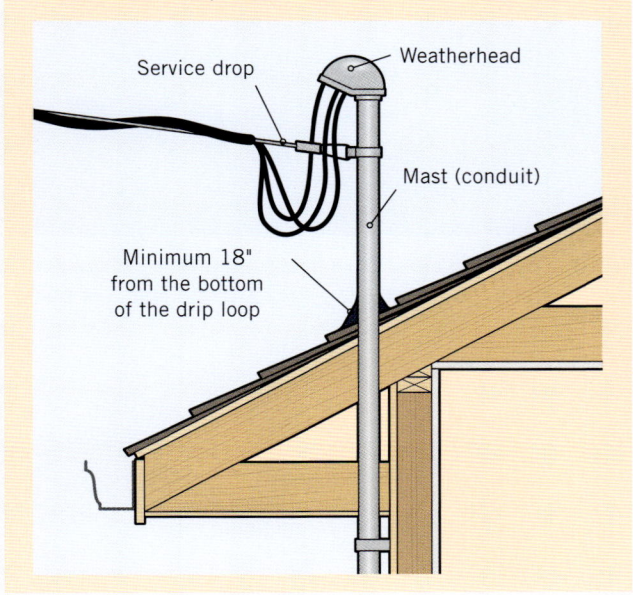

Service drop

Weatherhead

Mast (conduit)

Minimum 18" from the bottom of the drip loop

Create an accurate circuit index and affix it to the inside of the service panel door. List all loads that are on the circuit as well as the amperage.

Grounding + Bonding a Wiring System

All home electrical systems must be bonded and grounded according to code standards. This entails two tasks: the metal water and gas pipes must be connected electrically to create a continuous low resistance path back to the main electrical panel; and the main electrical panel must be grounded to a grounding electrode such as a ground rod or rods driven into the earth near the foundation of your house. Although the piping system is bonded to the ground through your main electrical service panel, the panel grounding and the piping bonding are unrelated when it comes to function. The grounding wire that runs from your electrical panel to grounding electrode helps even out voltage increases that often occur because of lightning and other causes. The wires that bond your metal piping are preventative, and they only become important in the unlikely event that an electrical conductor energizes the pipe. In that case, correct bonding of the piping system will ensure that the current does not remain in the system, where it could shock anyone who touches a part of the system, such as a faucet handle. Bonding is done relatively efficiently at the water heater, as the gas piping and water piping are typically located there.

Gas pipe in older homes is usually steel or copper. The bonding connection point for these pipes can be at any accessible location, such as at the water heater or at the gas meter. Gas pipe in some new homes is a flexible material called corrugated stainless-steel tubing (CSST). Refer to the manufacturer's instructions for bonding the CSST.

A pair of 8-ft.-long metal ground rods are driven into the earth next to your house to provide a path to ground for your home wiring system.

TOOLS + MATERIALS

Hammer	½" drill bit	3 pipe ground clamps	Grounding rods
Flat screwdriver	A length of ground wire	Eye protection	5-lb. maul
Drill	Wire staples	Work gloves	Caulk

How to Bond Metallic Piping

Determine the amperage rating of your electrical service by looking at your service equipment. (If you have an older system and are unsure about its amperage rating, consult an electrician.) The system amperage (usually 100 or 200 amps) determines the required gauge of the bonding wire you need. #6 copper wire is often sufficient for service not exceeding 200 amps. Always confirm the correct gauge with the local electrical inspector.

Run the bonding wire from a point near your water heater to an exit point where the wire can be bonded to the grounding wire that leads to the exterior grounding electrodes. This is frequently done at the service panel. Run this wire as you would any other cable, leaving approximately 6 to 8 ft. of wire at the water heater. If you are running this wire through the ceiling joists, drill a ½" hole as close to the center as possible to not weaken the joist. Staple the wire every 2 ft. if running it parallel to the joists.

Install pipe ground clamps on each pipe (hot water supply, cold water supply, gas), roughly 1 foot above the water heater. Do not install clamps near a union or elbow because the tightening of the clamps could break or weaken soldered joints. Also make sure the pipes are free and clear of any paint, rust, or any other contaminant that may inhibit a good clean connection. Do not overtighten the clamps. Use clamps that are compatible with the pipe so that corrosion will not occur. Use copper or brass clamps on copper pipe. Use brass or steel clamps on steel pipe.

Route the bonding wire through each clamp wire hole and then tighten the clamps onto the wire. Do not cut or splice the wire: the same wire should run through all clamps.

(continued)

5

6

At the panel, turn off the main breaker. Open the cover by removing the screws, and set the cover aside. Route the ground wire through a small ⅜" hole provided toward the rear of the panel on the top or bottom. You will usually have to knock the plug out of this hole by placing a screwdriver on it from the outside and tapping with a hammer. Make sure the ground wire will not come into contact with the terminal bars in the middle of the panel or any of the load terminals on the breakers.

Locate an open hole on your ground and neutral terminal and insert the ground wire. These holes are large enough to accommodate up to a #4 awg wire, but it may be difficult at times. If you're having trouble pushing the wire in, trim a little wire off the end and try with a clean cut piece. Secure the set screw at the lug. Replace the panel cover and turn the main breaker back on.

Tips for Grounding Service Panels

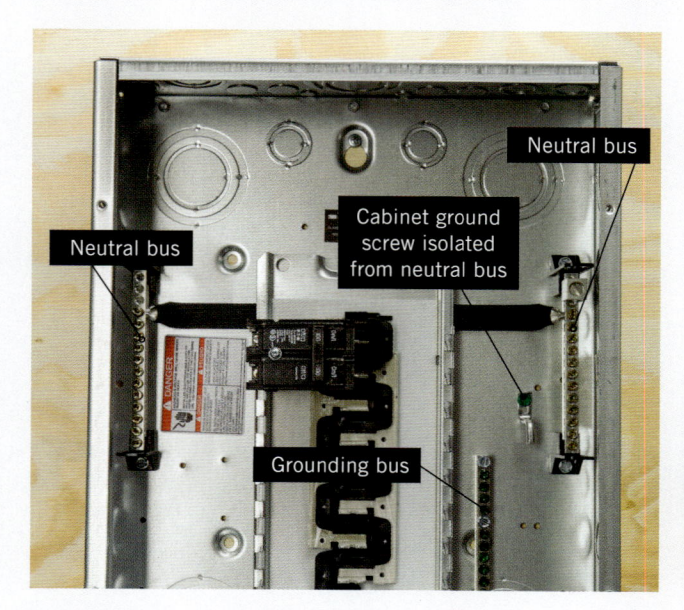

Neutral bus

Neutral bus

Cabinet ground screw isolated from neutral bus

Grounding bus

In a subpanel, the grounding terminal should be bonded to the subpanel cabinet. The neutral terminal should not be bonded to the subpanel cabinet.

Metallic conduit must be physically and electrically connected to panel cabinets. A bonding bushing may be required in some cases, where not all of a knockout is removed.

Ground Rod Installation

The ground rod is an essential part of the grounding system. Its primary function is to create a path to ground for electrical current, such as lightning, line surges, and unintentional contact with high voltage lines. If you upgrade your electrical service, you likely will need to upgrade your grounding wire and rods to meet current code.

Call before you dig! Make sure the area where you will be installing the ground rods is free and clear from any underground utilities.

NOTE: Different municipalities have different requirements for grounding, so be sure to check with the AHJ (Authority Having Jurisdiction) first before attempting to do this yourself.

TOOLS + MATERIALS

⅝" × 8' ground rods
Drill ¼"
⁵⁄₁₆" drill bit
Ladder

5-pound maul
Copper ground wire
  (size as required by
  local code)

Screwdriver
(2) brass (acorn) clamps
Pliers

Wire cutters
Caulk

How to Install a Grounding Electrode System

Begin by purchasing two copper-coated steel ground rods ⅝" diameter by 8' long. Grounding rods have a driving point on one end and a striking face on the other end.

Drill a ⁵⁄₁₆" hole in the rim joist of your house, as close as practical to the main service panel to the outside of the house above the ground level at least 6". *(continued)*

About 1 foot from the foundation of the house, pound one ground rod into the earth with a 5-lb. maul. If you encounter a rock or other obstruction, you can pound the ground rod at an angle as long as it does not exceed 45°. Drive until only 3" or 4" of the rod is above ground. Measure at least 6 ft. from the first ground rod and pound in another one.

Run copper ground wire from the ground bus in your main service panel through the hole in the rim joist and to the exterior of the house, leaving enough wire to connect the two ground rods together.

Using a brass clamp commonly referred to as an acorn, connect the wire to the first ground rod, pulling the wire taut so no slack exists. Continue pulling the wire to reach the second grounding rod, creating a continuous connection.

Connect the second ground rod with another acorn to the uncut grounding wire previously pulled through the first acorn. Trim the excess wire.

Dig out a few inches around each rod to create clearance for the 5-lb. maul. Creating a shallow trench beneath the grounding wire between the rods is also a good idea. Drive each rod with the maul until the top of the rod is a few inches below grade.

Inject caulk into the hole in the rim joist on both the interior and exterior side.

Tips for Grounding + Bonding

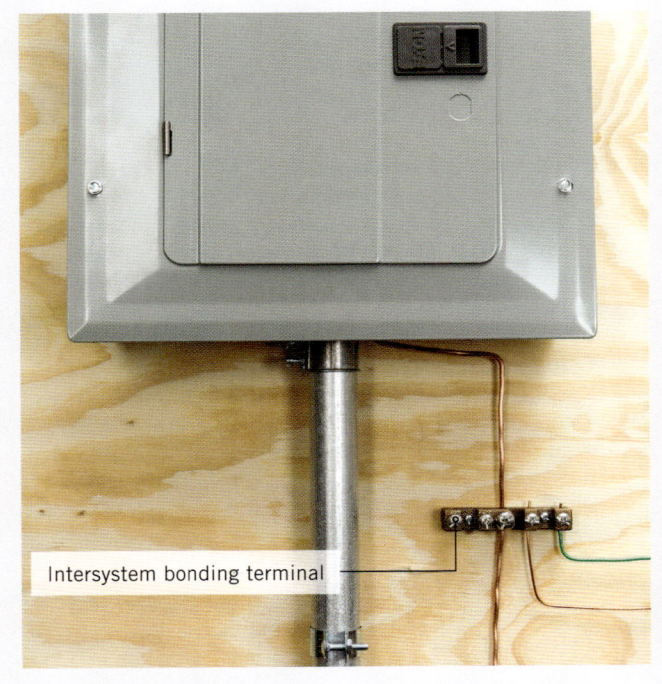

Intersystem bonding terminal

Use an intersystem bonding terminal to ground nonelectrical systems such as telephone and cable.

Grounding electrode

A piece of reinforcing bar encased in a concrete footing is a common grounding electrode in new construction. Called an ufer, the electrode must be No. 4 or larger rebar and at least 20 ft. long. (Shown prior to pouring concrete.)

Subpanels

Install circuit breaker subpanels if the main panel does not have enough open slots for the new circuits you are planning. Subpanels serve as additional distribution centers for connecting circuits. They receive power from a double-pole circuit breaker you install in the main circuit breaker panel.

If the main service panel is so full that there is no room for the double-pole subpanel breaker, you can reconnect some of the existing 120-volt circuits to special half-height breakers (see photo at right). You may be required to install AFCI breakers for the new circuits. AFCI breakers are full size breakers. Be sure to plan for this when estimating the space left in your existing main service panel and all subpanels.

Plan your subpanel installation carefully, making sure your electrical service supplies enough power to support the extra load of the new subpanel circuits. Assuming your main service is adequate, consider installing a subpanel that's a little larger than you need to provide enough extra amps to meet the needs of future wiring projects. The smallest panels have room for up to six single-pole breakers (or three double-pole breakers), while the largest models can hold 20 single-pole breakers or more.

Subpanels often are mounted near the main circuit breaker panel. Or, for convenience, they can be installed close to the areas they serve, such as in a new room addition. In a finished room, a subpanel can be painted or housed in a decorative cabinet so it is less of a visual distraction—just make sure it's accessible. This project requires a permit. The electrical inspector may require that you install arc-fault and ground-fault protection on new circuits. Check with the electrical inspector before starting this project.

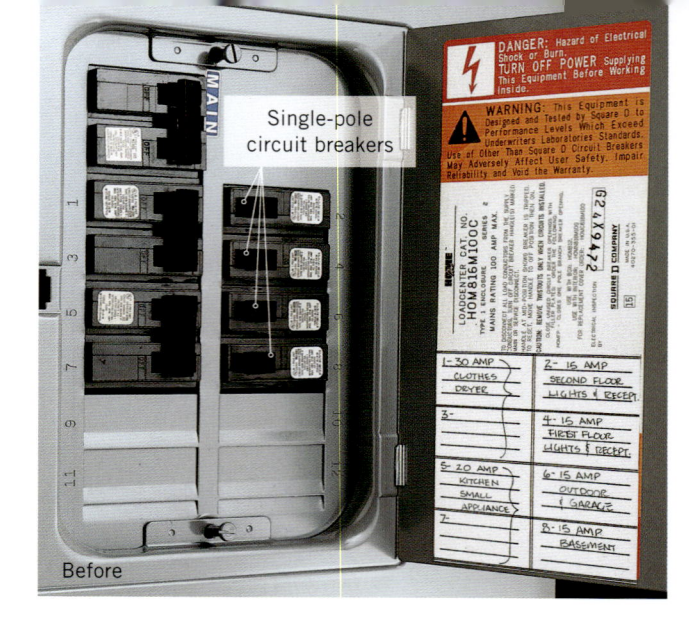

Single-pole circuit breakers

Before

Slimline breakers replace single-pole breakers

After

To conserve space in a service panel, you may be able to replace existing single-pole breakers with half-height breakers. These take up half the space of standard breakers, allowing you to fit two circuits into one single slot on the service panel. In the service panel shown above, four single-pole 120-volt breakers were replaced with slimline breakers to provide the double opening needed for a 30-amp, 240-volt subpanel feeder breaker. Use half-height breakers (if your municipality and the panel manufacturer allows them) with the same amp rating as the standard single-pole breakers you are removing. If your municipality and panel allow these breakers, there may be restrictions on the quantity and location where they may be installed on the panel.

TOOLS + MATERIALS

Hammer	Cable ripper	Cable clamps	Double-pole circuit breaker
Screwdriver	Combination tool	Three-wire NM cable	Circuit breaker subpanel
Voltage tester	Screws	Cable staples	Half-height circuit breakers

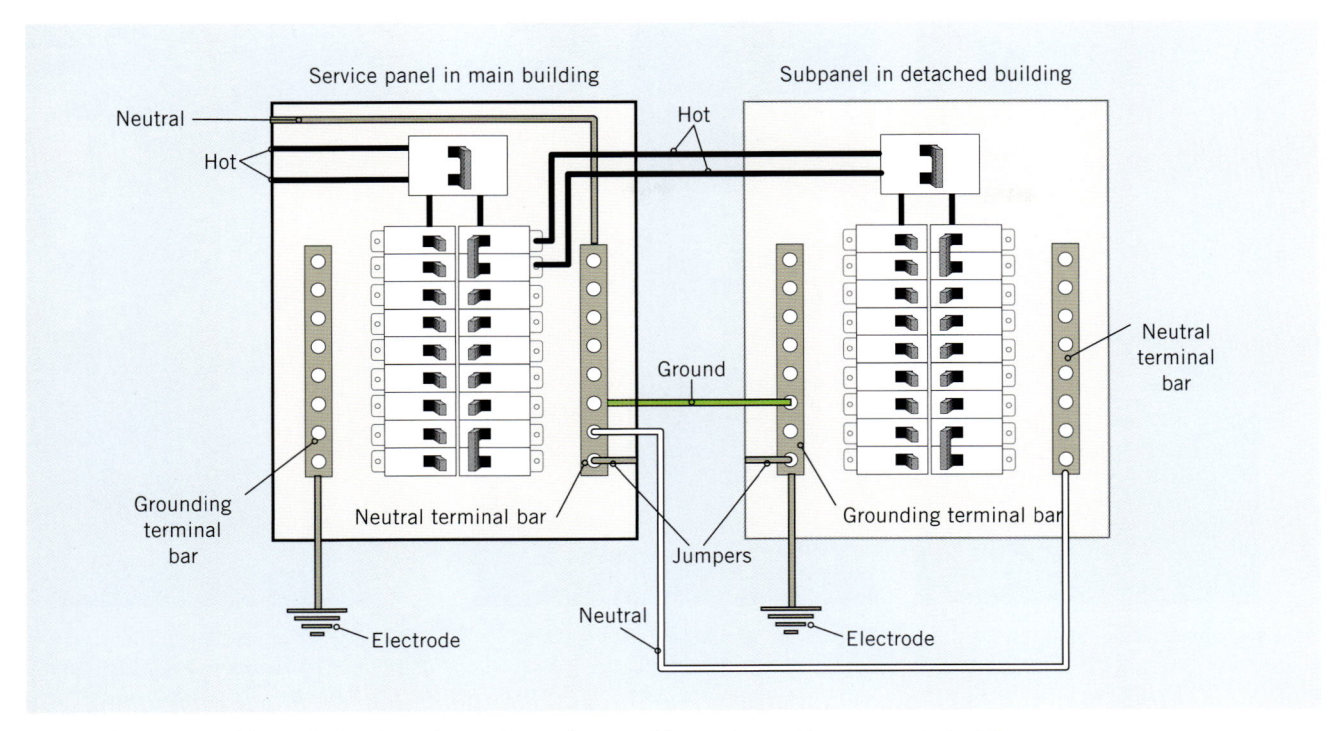

Wiring diagram for wiring a feeder from the main service panel to a subpanel in a separate building.

How to Install a Subpanel

Subpanels are subject to the same installation and clearance rules as service panels. The subpanel can be mounted to the sides of studs or to plywood attached between two studs. The panel shown here extends ½" past the face of studs so it will be flush with the finished wall surface. Follow the manufacturer's installation specifications.

Open a knockout in the subpanel using a screwdriver and hammer. Run the feeder cable from the main circuit breaker panel to the subpanel, leaving about 2 ft. of excess cable at each end. See page 40 if you need to run the cable through finished walls.

Attach a cable clamp to the knockout in the subpanel. Insert the cable into the subpanel, and then anchor it to framing members within 8" of each panel and every 54" thereafter.

(continued)

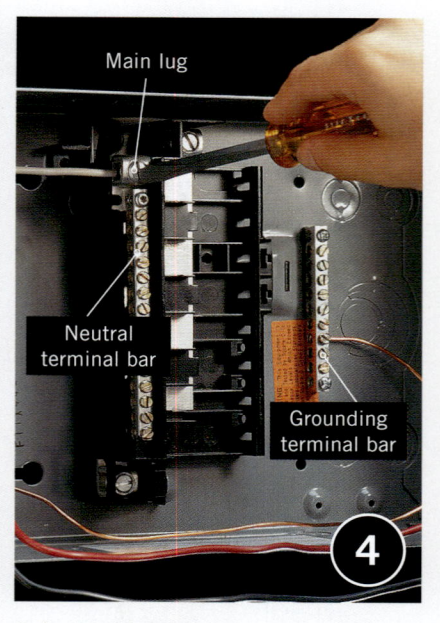

Main lug

Neutral terminal bar

Grounding terminal bar

Lug

Hot bus bars

Lug

Strip away outer sheathing from the feeder cable using a cable ripper. Leave at least ¼" of sheathing extending into the subpanel. Tighten the cable clamp screws so the cable is held securely, but not so tightly that the wire sheathing is crushed.

Strip ½" of insulation from the white neutral feeder wire, and attach it to the main lug on the subpanel neutral terminal bar. Connect the grounding wire to a setscrew terminal on the grounding terminal bar. Fold excess wire around the inside edge of the subpanel.

Strip away ½" of insulation from the red and the black feeder wires. Attach one wire to the main lug on each of the hot terminal bars. Fold excess wire around the inside edge of the subpanel.

Slimline breakers

At the main circuit breaker panel, shut off the main circuit breaker, and then remove the coverplate and test for power (page 80). If necessary, make room for the double-pole feeder breaker by removing single-pole breakers and reconnecting the wires to slimline circuit breakers. Open a knockout for the feeder cable using a hammer and screwdriver.

NOTE: Some panels do not allow slimline breakers and some restrict where slimline breakers can be installed. Read the instructions on the panel cover.

Strip away the outer sheathing from the feeder cable so that at least ¼" of sheathing will reach into the main service panel. Attach a cable clamp to the cable, and then insert the cable into the knockout, and anchor it by threading a locknut onto the clamp. Tighten the locknut by driving a screwdriver against the lugs. Tighten the clamp screws so the cable is held securely, but not so tightly that the cable sheathing is crushed.

8

Grounding terminal bar

Bend the bare copper wire from the feeder cable around the inside edge of the main circuit breaker panel, and connect it to one of the setscrew terminals on the grounding terminal bar.

9

Neutral terminal bar

Strip away ½" of insulation from the white feeder wire. Attach the wire to one of the setscrew terminals on the neutral terminal bar. Fold excess wire around the inside edge of the service panel.

10

Strip ½" of insulation from the red and the black feeder wires. Attach one wire to each of the setscrew terminals on the double-pole feeder breaker.

NOTE: If your subpanel arrived with a preinstalled grounding screw in the panel back, remove and discard it.

Guide hook pivot

11

Hook the end of the feeder circuit breaker over the guide hooks on the panel, and then push the other end forward until the breaker snaps onto the hot terminal bars (follow manufacturer's directions). Fold excess wire around the inside edge of the circuit breaker panel.

12

If necessary, remove two tabs from the cover plate where the double-pole feeder breaker will fit, and then reattach the cover plate. Label the feeder breaker on the circuit index. Turn the main breaker on, but leave the feeder breaker off until all subpanel circuits have been connected and inspected.

120/240-Volt Dryer Receptacles

Most electric dryers require both 120- and 240-volt power. If you are installing this type of electric dryer, you will need to install a 30-amp, 120/240-volt receptacle that feeds from a dedicated 30-amp double-pole GFCI breaker in your service panel. Verify your dryer's electrical requirements before wiring a new receptacle. Begin the installation by identifying a location for the dryer receptacle. Run 10/3 NM cable from the panel to the new receptacle. If you are mounting the dryer receptacle box on an unfinished masonry wall, run THNN wire in conduit and secure the box and conduit with straps and masonry screws. If you are mounting the receptacle box in a finished wall, cut a hole, fish the cable through, and mount the receptacle in the wall opening. Extending a branch circuit or adding a new branch for new receptacles, lights, or switches requires a permit. Check with the inspector before starting.

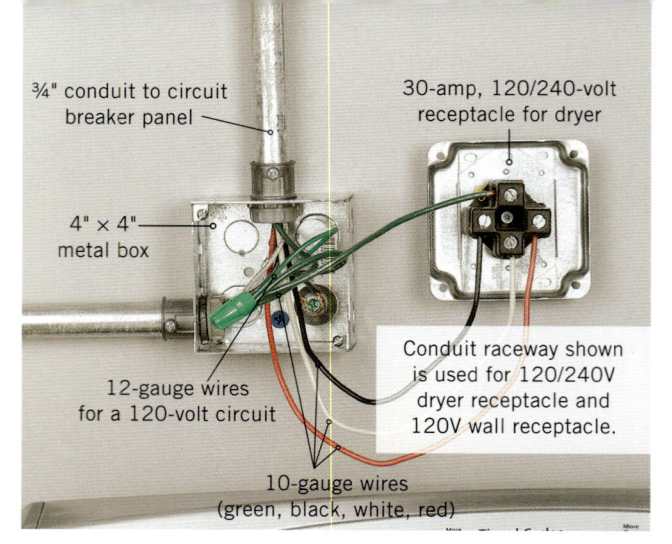

¾" conduit to circuit breaker panel

4" × 4" metal box

12-gauge wires for a 120-volt circuit

30-amp, 120/240-volt receptacle for dryer

Conduit raceway shown is used for 120/240V dryer receptacle and 120V wall receptacle.

10-gauge wires (green, black, white, red)

With a 120/240-volt installation, the dryer circuit's double-pole breaker contacts both 120-volt hot bus bars in the service panel.

TOOLS + MATERIALS

Combination tool	Screwdriver	Receptacle box	Conduit (where cable is exposed to physical damage)
Drill	30-amp double-pole GFCI breaker	10/3 NM cable or 10-gauge THHN/THWN	
Circuit tester	30-amp 120/240-volt dryer receptacle		
Hammer			

How to Install a 120/240-Volt Dryer Receptacle

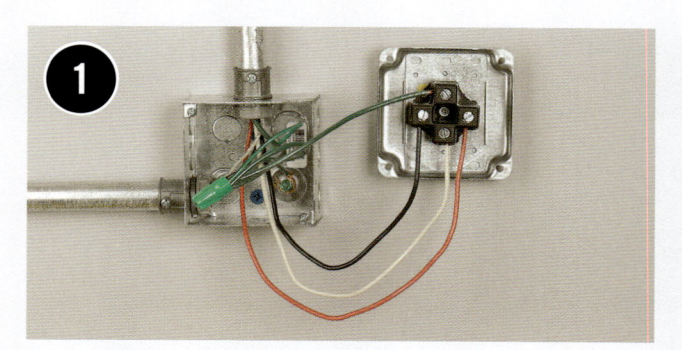

1

Connect the white neutral wire to the silver neutral screw terminal. Connect each of the black and the red wires to either of the brass screw terminals (the terminals are interchangeable). Connect the green ground wire to the receptacle grounding screw. Attach the cover plate.

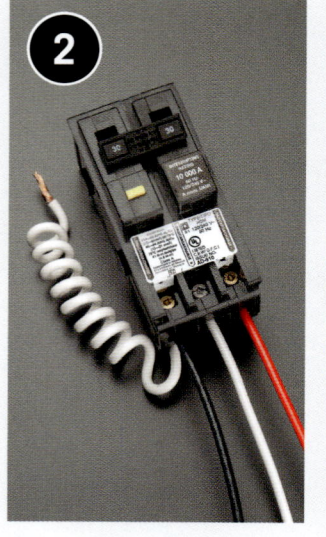

2

With the panel main breaker shut off, connect the dryer cable to a dedicated 30-amp double-pole GFCI breaker. Connect the ground wire to the panel grounding terminal bar. Connect the white neutral wire to the neutral bar. Connect the red and the black wires to the two brass screw terminals on the breaker. Connect the coiled white wire to the neutral terminal bar. Snap the breaker into the bus bar. Attach the panel cover. Restore power to the panel, and test the GFCI breaker and dryer receptacle.

120/240-Volt Range Receptacles

Many electric ranges require both 120- and 240-volt power and use a 40- or 50-amp 120/240-volt receptacle that feeds from a dedicated 40- or 50-amp breaker in the panel. Breaker amperage depends on the amount of current the range draws. Verify requirements before wiring a receptacle.

A range receptacle and breaker installation is no more complicated than wiring a single-pole breaker and outlet. The main difference is that the range circuit's double-pole breaker is designed to contact both 120-volt bus bars in the service panel. Together these two 120-volt circuits serve the range's heating elements with 240 volts of power. The range's electronics utilize the circuit's 120-volt power.

Modern range receptacles accept a four-prong plug. A four-conductor cable, containing three insulated wires and one ground, is required. The two hot wires might be black and red (shown below) or black and black with a red stripe. The neutral wire is generally white or gray. The grounding wire is green or bare. The size used for a kitchen range is usually 6/3 grounded NM aluminum or copper cable. The receptacle itself is generally surface mounted (shown below), though flush-mounted units are also available.

Note: If the range receptacle is in a kitchen, the circuit may need to be GFCI protected if the circuit is 150 volts or less. This is uncommon. Check the local building department for requirements.

TOOLS + MATERIALS

Combination tool	Range receptacle
Voltage tester	6/3 grounded NM cable
Screwdriver	40- or 50-amp double-pole
Drywall saw	circuit breaker
Fish tape	

How to Install a Kitchen Range Receptacle

Turn power off. Identify a location for the surface-mounted range receptacle. Cut a small hole in the wall. Fish the cable from the service panel into the wall opening. Thread the cable into a surface-mounted receptacle and clamp it. Strip insulation from the individual wires.

Wire the receptacle. Connect the bare copper ground wire to the receptacle grounding screw. Connect the white neutral wire to the silver neutral screw terminal. Connect each of the hot (black and red) wires to either of the brass screw terminals (the terminals are interchangeable). Mount the housing on the wall and attach the cover plate.

Wire the cable to a 40- or 50-amp breaker. With the main breaker off, remove the panel cover. Remove a knockout from the panel and feed the cable into the panel. Connect the ground to the grounding terminal bar. Connect the neutral wire from the cable to the neutral terminal bar. Connect the red and the black wires to the two brass screw terminals on the breaker. Snap it into the bus bar. Attach the panel cover. Turn the breakers on and test the circuit.

Dryer + Range Cords

Electric dryers and ranges typically are sold without power cords. This can be vexing for consumers, especially if their appliance dealer fails to advise them to buy a new cord before they leave the store. But this quirk exists for a very good reason. In 1996, the NEC began requiring that newly installed dryer and range receptacles must be designed for four-wire power cords. Prior to this change, most homes were built with receptacles for three-wire cords.

The code change continued trickling down to the local level well into the 2000s, and since dryers and ranges can easily last for 20 or 30 years, there are a lot of older appliances and receptacles out there with 3-wire configuration. Fortunately, the NEC allows homeowners to use existing three-wire receptacles. And that's why appliance manufacturers leave it up to the consumer to get the right cord for their home's dryer or range receptacle.

Installing a cord on a new appliance, or swapping out the cord on an older appliance, is a very easy job that takes just a few minutes. The important thing is to properly configure the appliance for a 3-wire or 4-wire cord, as needed. On the back of the dryer or range, there is a terminal block with three terminals: one neutral and two hots. There is also a ground screw that grounds the metal case of the appliance. A 4-wire, or 4-prong, cord has two hot wires, a neutral, and a separate ground wire. A 3-wire, or 3-prong, cord has two hots and a neutral—with no ground wire; it uses the neutral as a ground.

With a 4-wire configuration, the ground screw is isolated from the neutral terminal so that the ground and neutral are separate. With a 3-wire configuration, the ground screw is connected to the neutral with a metal ground strap. Some appliances have a small wire (usually with white insulation) that connects to the ground screw; this does the same thing as a metal strap. Once the appliance configuration is correct for your cord type, you simply connect each wire to its respective terminal (pages 196 and 197 show these setups clearly).

Cords for electric dryers and ranges are sold at appliance outlets and hardware and home improvement stores. They come in standard 4- to 6-foot lengths and usually include a strain-relief fitting for securing the cord to the appliance. Make sure any cord you use carries the UL stamp or similar certification to ensure that it meets industry safety standards.

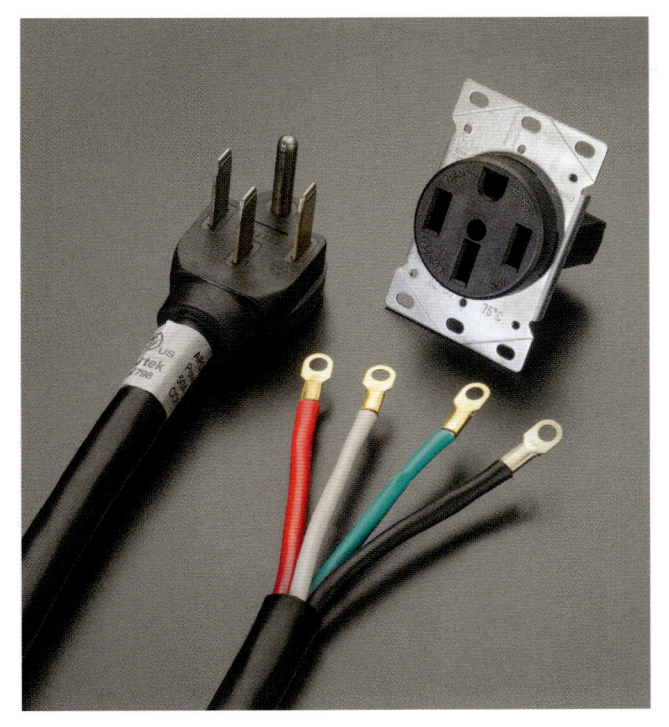

4-prong range cords have red and black hot wires, a white neutral wire, and a green ground wire. The hot wires carry 120 volts each and are interchangeable. These cords are typically rated for 50 amps and plug into a 4-slot NEMA 14-50 50-amp receptacle.

4-prong dryer cords have red and black hot wires, a white neutral wire, and a green ground wire. The hot wires carry 120 volts each and are interchangeable. They are typically rated for 30 amps. Dryer receptacles are identifiable by their L-shaped neutral slots.

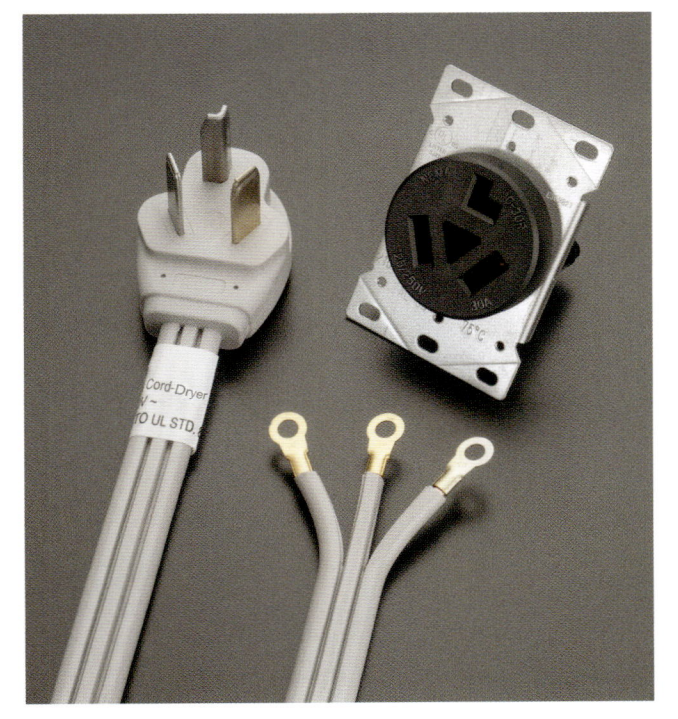

3-prong dryer cords are flat and do not have color-coded wires. The center wire is always neutral. The two outer wires are hot and carry 120 volts each; they are interchangeable. There is no separate ground wire. These cords typically are rated for 30 amps and must be used with matching NEMA 10-30R receptacles.

Strain-relief fittings are simple metal clamps that secure the cord to the appliance and protect the cord sheathing from damage. Strain reliefs for 4-prong cords (top) are rounded; strain reliefs for 3-prong cords (bottom) are flat. Always use an appropriate strain relief for the cord shape.

How to Install a Range or Dryer Cord

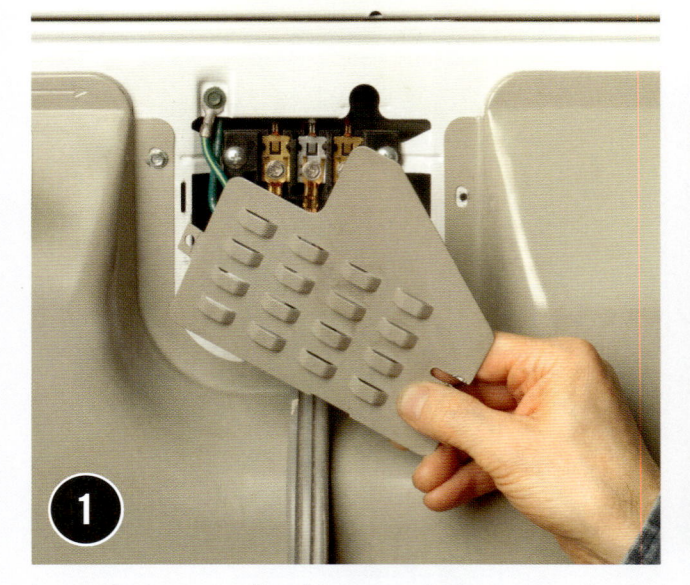

Loosen the screws on the wiring compartment cover on the back of the dryer or range, using a screwdriver or nut driver. Remove the cover and set it aside.

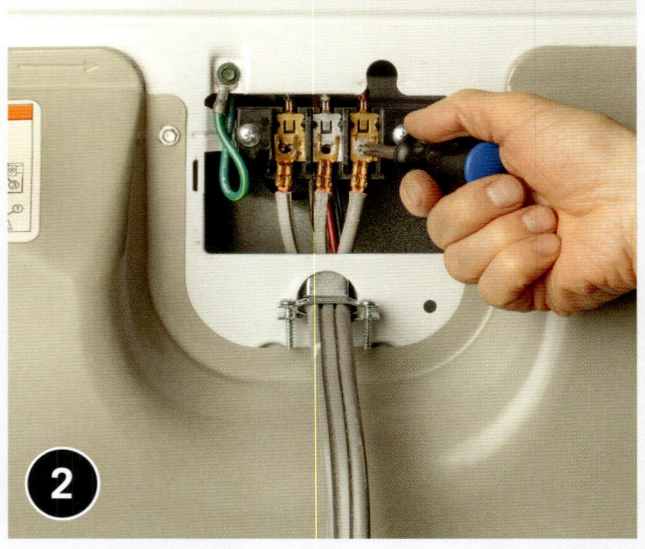

Remove each cord wire from its terminal on the terminal block (and ground screw, as applicable), if you're replacing an existing cord. Loosen the screws of the strain-relief fitting and remove the fitting. Pull the cord out through the hole in the back panel or bracket.

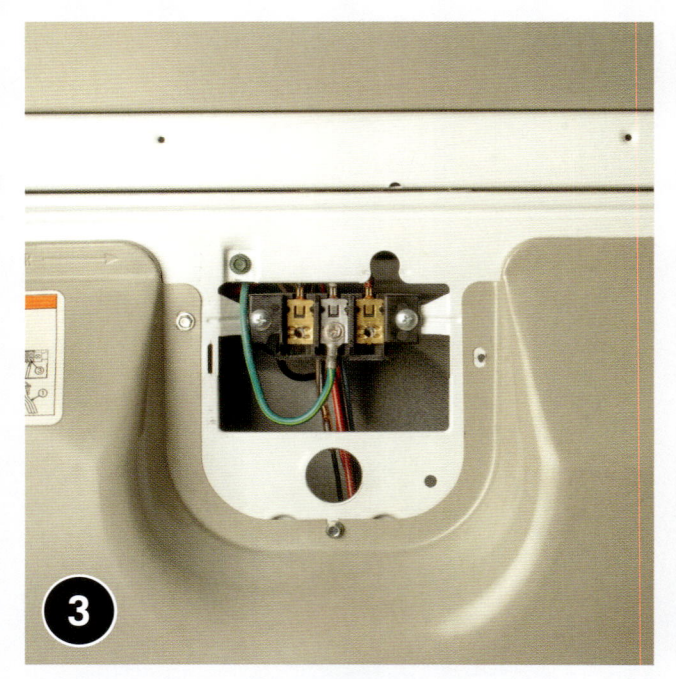

Configure the terminals for a 4-wire cord. Confirm that the ground screw is isolated from the neutral (center) terminal on the terminal block. If there is a metal strap between the ground and neutral, remove the strap from the neutral (you can leave it attached under the ground screw). If there is a white or green internal wire connected to the ground screw, move it to the neutral terminal; it will make a harmless neutral connection.

Connect a 4-wire cord. Secure the white cord wire under the neutral (center) terminal. Secure the black (hot) and red (hot) cord wires to the two outer terminals, connecting only one wire to each terminal (the hot terminals and wires are interchangeable). Connect the green ground wire to the ground screw. Make sure all connections are very tight.

VARIATION: Configure the terminals for a 3-wire cord.
Confirm that the ground screw is connected to the neutral (center) terminal on the terminal block. Make this connection with a metal ground strap between the ground screw and the neutral terminal. Alternatively, if there is a white or green wire extending from inside the appliance, make sure it is secured under the ground screw.

Note: If the dryer does not have a ground strap or wire, you can buy a new ground strap that is compatible with the dryer model.

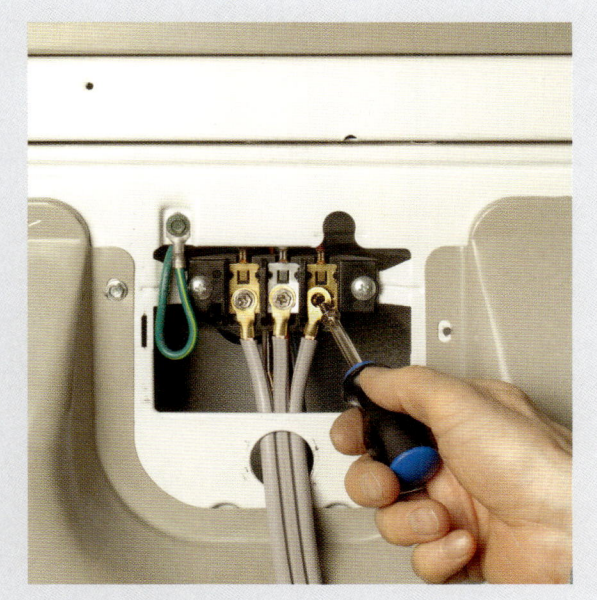

VARIATION: Connect a 3-wire cord. Secure the center (neutral) cord wire under the neutral (center) terminal. Secure each of the outer cord wires to one of the outer (hot) terminals, connecting only one wire to each terminal (the hot terminals and wires are interchangeable). Make sure all connections are very tight.

Note: This variation presents a very small risk of electric shock. It is better, if practical, to install a new 4-wire circuit with an equipment grounding wire.

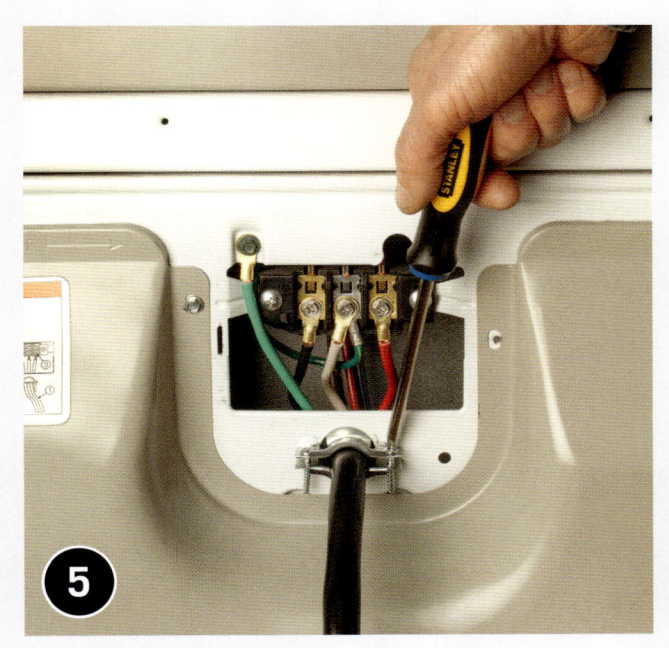

5

Install the strain relief by fitting the two halves together so they clamp onto the cord. Tighten the clamp screws so the cord is held securely but the clamp is not so tight that the cord is deformed.

6

Reposition the wiring compartment cover and secure its screws. The dryer or range is ready for use.

Adding an Outdoor Receptacle

Outdoor receptacles can be few and far between. The NEC requires only one receptacle on the front and back of the house, and while builders can go beyond the code requirement and install a few more, many homes have only the bare minimum. This leaves you with the chore and inconvenience of rolling out long extension cords to reach holiday lights, corded lawn tools, or outdoor equipment.

Since the interior sides of many house walls have a receptacle every 12 feet, at the most, there are plenty of places to tap into a receptacle circuit to power an outdoor receptacle. The easiest way to do this is to go straight out from the indoor box, extending the circuit to an outdoor box with a short length of NM cable.

Outdoor receptacles can be 15-amp or 20-amp, so most indoor receptacle circuits in living areas are suitable, provided the added receptacle doesn't overload the circuit. You cannot tap into a kitchen, bathroom, or laundry room receptacle circuit. Make sure the new receptacle has the correct amperage rating for the circuit; do not install a 20-amp receptacle on a 15-amp circuit.

Also make sure the new receptacle is GFCI protected, which is required for all outdoor receptacles. You can accomplish this by simply using a GFCI receptacle on the outdoor side. This will provide GFCI protection even if the circuit or indoor receptacle are not GFCI protected. The receptacle must be weather-resistant type (indicated by "WR" stamped on the receptacle's face) as well as tamper-resistant (indicated by a "TR" stamp).

The outdoor electrical box can be recessed or surface-mounted, depending on the box type. Surface-mounting requires a hole only for the new cable and clamp. This can greatly simplify the job when you're

Interior receptacles in ground-floor living areas typically are about 12 inches above the floor—a convenient height for adding a receptacle on the exterior side of the wall.

working with brick or stone siding. A recessed box installs flush to the wall and needs a hole cut out for the entire box. Recessing the box also means you can't go directly opposite the indoor box, since the wall cavity usually is not deep enough to accommodate two boxes back to back. The solution is to offset the boxes while staying within the same stud cavity.

Finally, the outdoor box needs a cover that's suitable for the location. Boxes that are protected from direct exposure to snow and rain, such as from a porch or patio roof, can have a cover rated for damp locations. Boxes that are exposed to moisture must have an "in-use" cover rated for wet locations. Extending a branch circuit or adding a new branch to install new receptacles, lights, or switches requires a permit. The inspector may require you install arc-fault protection on the entire circuit. Check with the inspector before starting.

TOOLS + MATERIALS

Noncontact voltage tester	Weatherproof exterior receptacle box with cover	Drill driver	Fish tape (as needed)
Screwdrivers	Cable clamp	Long ¼-inch drill bit	Wire strippers
3-foot length of 2-wire NM cable	Corrosion-resistant screws	1-inch spade bit	Caulking gun
	Exterior caulk	Spray foam insulation	Wire connectors

How to Add an Outdoor Receptacle

Shut off the power to the interior receptacle circuit. Remove the receptacle's cover plate and test each receptacle terminal and all wires in the box to confirm the power is off, using a noncontact voltage tester. Disconnect the wires and remove the receptacle.

Note: If the electrical box is small, this is a good time to replace it with a larger, old work retrofit box (see pages 62 to 63).

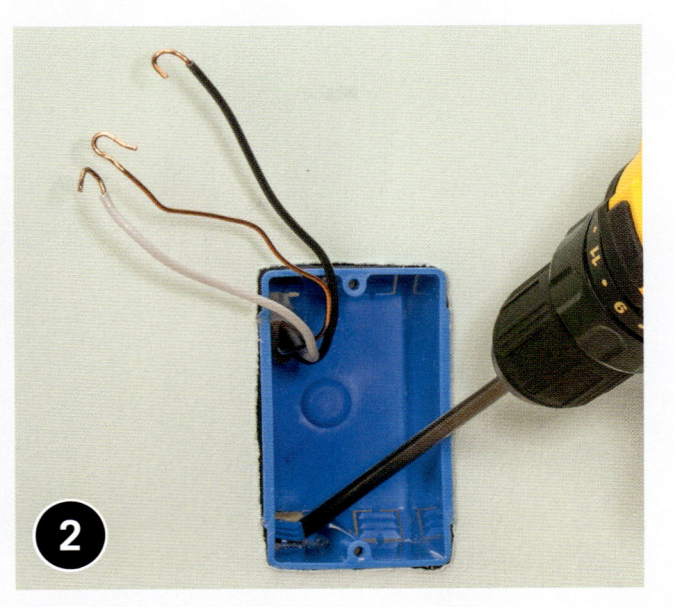

Drill through a cable-access hole in the box, using a long ¼-inch drill bit, drilling through the wall cavity and the sheathing and siding on the exterior side of the wall. Angle the drill bit as desired, based on where you want to install the exterior receptacle box.

Enlarge the hole on the exterior side of the wall, using a 1-inch spade bit (or as needed), drilling through the siding and sheathing to make room for the cable clamp.

Variation: To install a recessed box, trace the outline of the box body onto the wall, drill a ⅜-inch hole at each corner of the outline, then cut along the outline with a jigsaw.

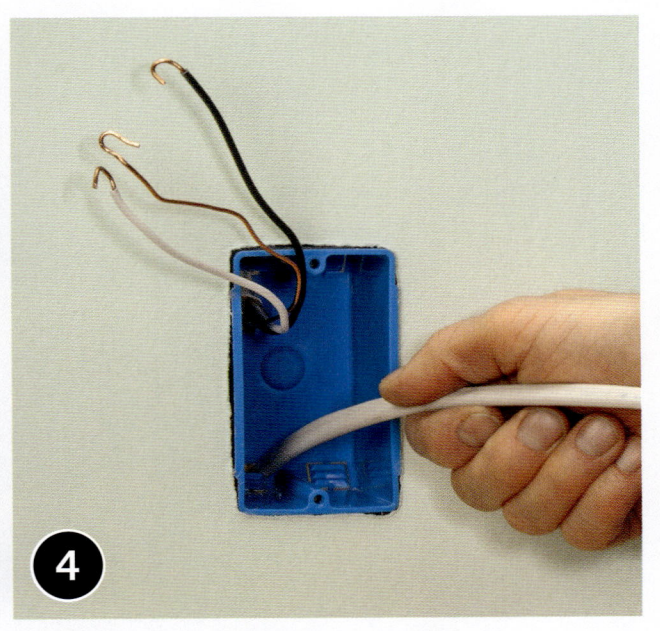

Cut a 2-foot length of 2-wire NM cable; this must have the same wire gauge as the cable of the receptacle circuit. Feed the cable through the hole in the interior box and out through the exterior hole. If necessary, use a fish tape to pull the cable through (see page 40).

Secure the cable to the exterior receptacle box with a cable clamp, leaving about 6 inches of cable extending from the front of the box.

Mount the exterior box to the wall siding, using corrosion-resistant screws. If necessary, drill pilot holes for the screws to prevent splitting the siding. Fill the wire hole with spray foam insulation to reduce air and water infiltration.

Note: If the receptacle box is metal, connect two grounding pigtails to the ground wire in the cable, using wire connectors. Connect one of the pigtails to the ground screw on the metal box.

Remove all but ½ inch of sheathing from the cable inside the box. Strip ¾ inch of insulation from each wire, using wire strippers. Connect the black (hot) wire to the HOT LINE (brass) terminal of the GFCI receptacle. Connect the white (neutral) wire to the WHITE LINE (silver) terminal and connect the ground wire to the receptacle's ground screw. Tuck the wires into the box and mount the receptacle to the box with the provided screws.

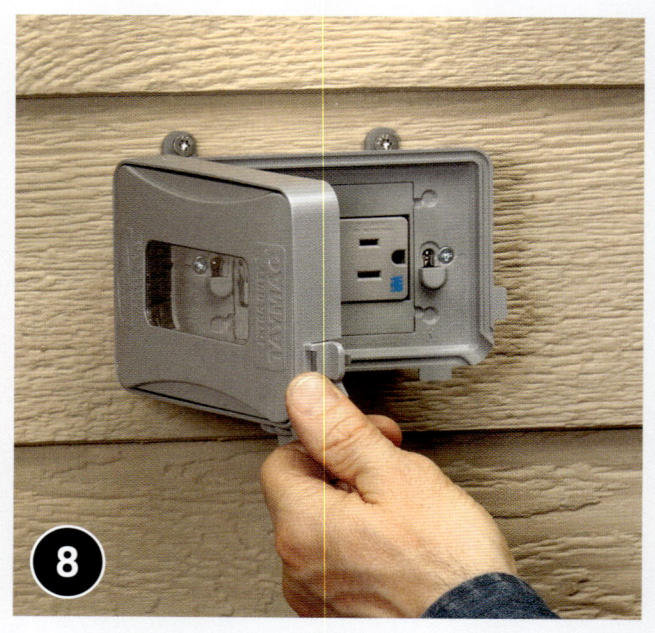

Install the box cover onto the front of the exterior box, following the manufacturer's instructions.

9

Apply a neat bead of exterior caulk along the top and sides of the exterior box, creating a watertight seal between the box and the siding. If desired, paint the caulk and box body (not the cover) to match the wall after the caulk cures completely.

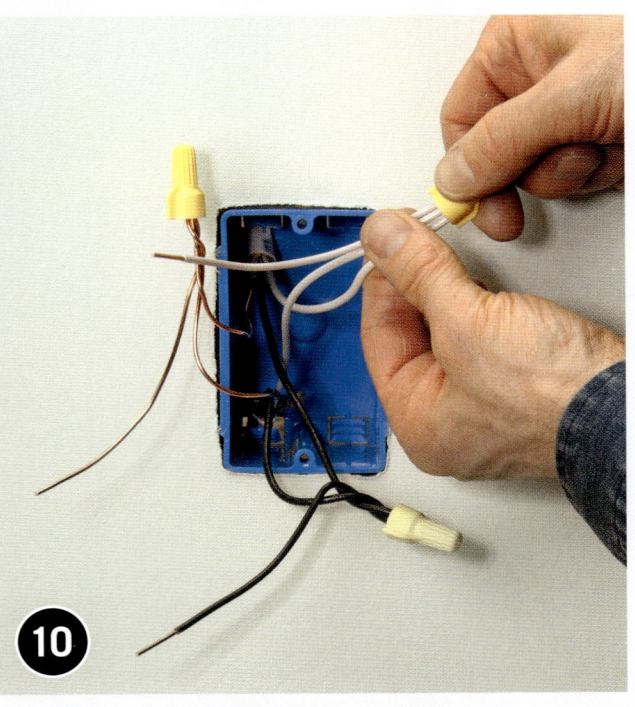

10

Cut a 6-inch length from the leftover NM cable. Remove the cable sheathing and strip both ends of the insulated wires to create pigtails (see page 33). Trim the NM cable so it extends about 6 inches beyond the front of the interior box and remove all but ½ inch of the cable sheathing. Connect the pigtails and original circuit wires to the wires of the new cable, using wire connectors.

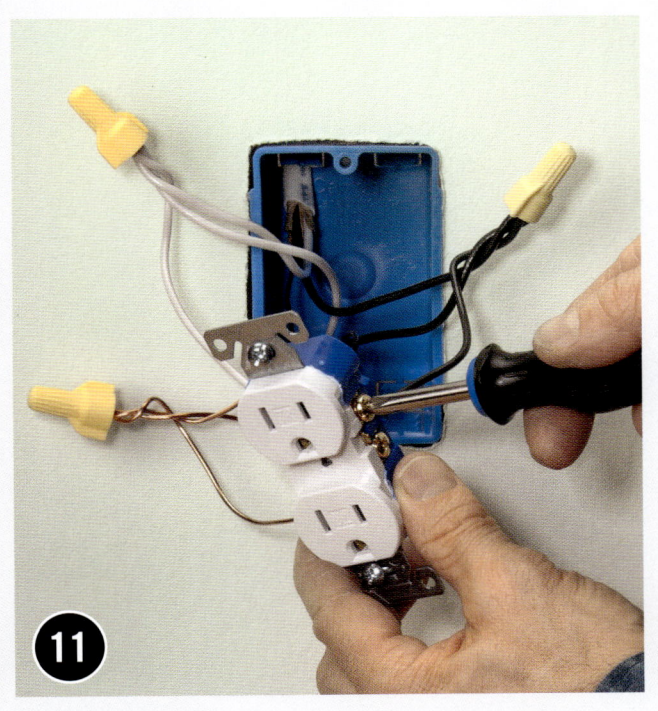

11

Connect the pigtail wires to the interior receptacle: black (hot) wire to the brass screw terminal, white (neutral) wire to the silver terminal, ground wire to the ground screw. Tuck the wires into the box and mount the receptacle to the box with the original screws.

12

Reinstall the cover plate on the interior receptacle. Restore power to the circuit and test the GFCI for proper operations, following the manufacturer's instructions.

Ceiling Lights

TOOLS + MATERIALS

Replacement light fixture	Insulated screwdrivers
Wire stripper	Wire connectors
Voltage tester	Eye protection

Ceiling fixtures don't have any moving parts, and their wiring is very simple, so, other than changing bulbs, you're likely to get decades of trouble-free service from a fixture. This sounds like a good thing, but it also means that the fixture probably won't fail and give you an excuse to update a room's look with a new one. Fortunately you don't need an excuse. Upgrading a fixture is easy and can make a dramatic impact on a room. You can substantially increase the light in a room by replacing a globe-style fixture with one with separate spot lights, or you can simply install a new fixture that matches the room's décor. Check the weight rating of the box to which you will attach your fixture. Older boxes may not handle a heavy fixture. If you are unsure how much weight the existing box can handle, consider changing the box. New light fixture boxes should handle fixtures up to 50 pounds. Support the fixture independently from the box if the fixture weighs more than 50 pounds.

Installing a new ceiling fixture can provide more light to a space, not to mention an aesthetic lift. It's one of the easiest upgrades you can do.

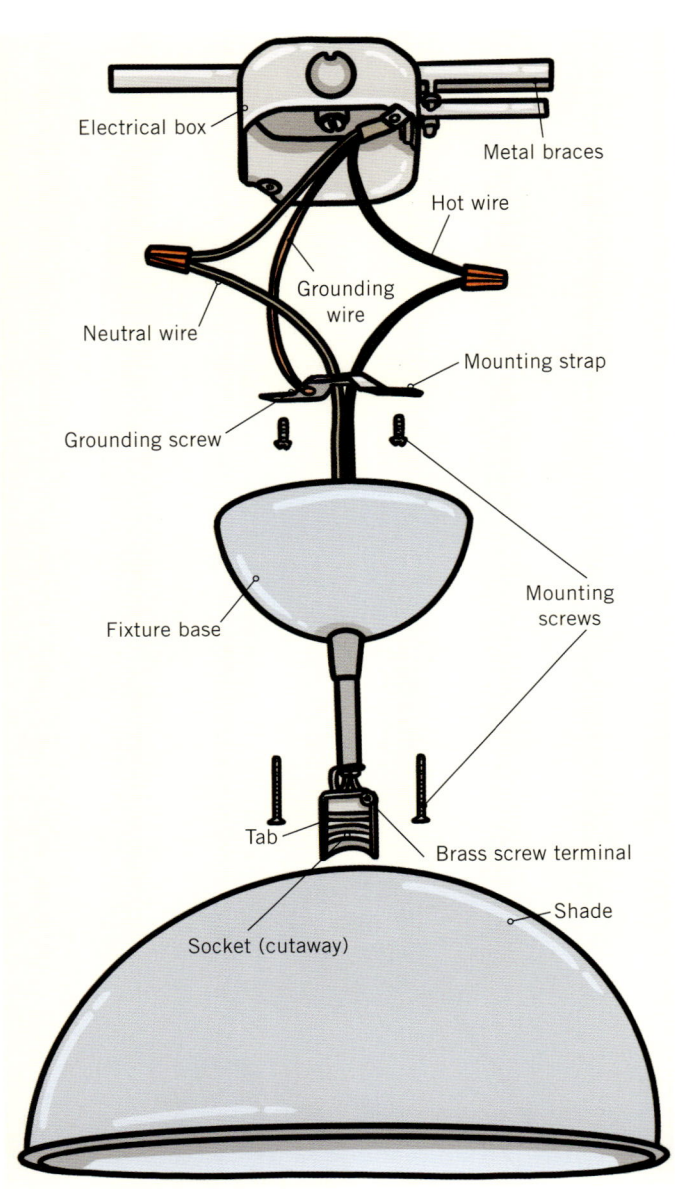

Electrical box

Metal braces

Hot wire

Neutral wire

Grounding wire

Grounding screw

Mounting strap

Fixture base

Mounting screws

Tab

Brass screw terminal

Socket (cutaway)

Shade

No matter what a ceiling light fixture looks like on the outside, they all attach in basically the same way. An electrical box in the ceiling is fitted with a mounting strap, which holds the fixture in place. The bare wire from the ceiling typically connects to the mounting strap. The two wires coming from the fixture connect to the black and the white wires from the ceiling.

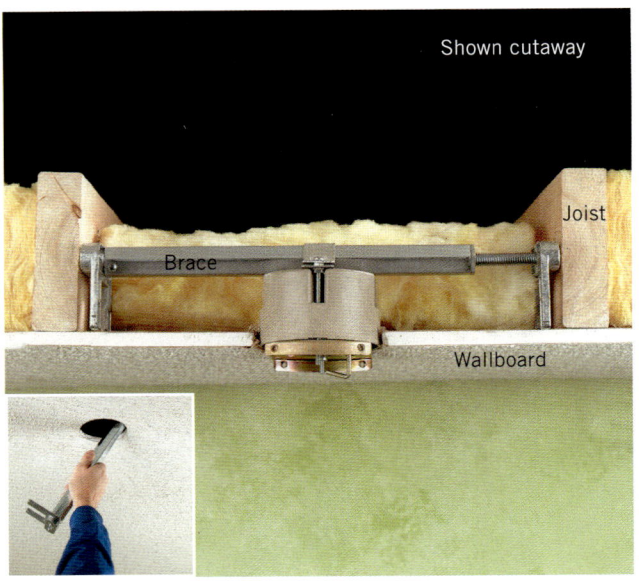

Shown cutaway

Joist

Brace

Wallboard

If the new fixture is much heavier than the original fixture, it will require additional bracing in the ceiling to support the electrical box and the fixture. The manufacturer's instructions should specify the size and type of box. If the ceiling is finished and there is no access from above, you can remove the old box and use an adjustable remodeling brace appropriate for your fixture (shown). The brace fits into a small hole in the ceiling (inset). Once the bracing is in place, install a new electrical box specified for the new fixture.

Inexpensive light fixtures have screw terminals mounted directly to the backside of the fixture plate. Often, as seen here, they have no grounding terminal. Some codes do not allow this type of fixture, but even if your hometown does approve them, it is a good idea to replace them with a better quality, safer fixture that is UL approved.

How to Replace a Ceiling Light

1

Shut off power to the ceiling light, and remove the shade or diffuser. Loosen the mounting screws and carefully lower the fixture, supporting it as you work (do not let light fixtures hang by their electrical wires). Use a voltage tester to make sure no power is reaching the connections.

2

Remove the twist connectors from the fixture wires or unscrew the screw terminals and remove the white neutral wire and the black lead wire (inset).

3

Before you install the new fixture, check the ends of the wires coming from the ceiling electrical box. They should be clean and free of nicks or scorch marks. If they're dirty or worn, clip off the stripped portion with your combination tool. Then strip away about ¾" of insulation from the end of each wire.

4

Attach a mounting strap to the ceiling fixture box if there is not one already present. Your new light may come equipped with a strap; otherwise you can find one for purchase at any hardware store.

5

Lift the new fixture up to the ceiling (you may want a helper for this), and attach the bare copper ground wire from the power supply cable to the grounding screw or clip on the mounting strap. Also attach the ground wire from the fixture to the screw or clip.

6

With the fixture supported by a ladder or a helper, join the white wire lead and the white fixture wire with a wire connector (often supplied with the fixture).

7

Connect the black power supply wire to the black fixture wire with a wire connector.

8

Position the new fixture mounting plate over the box so the mounting screw holes align. Drive the screws until the fixture is secure against the ceiling.

NOTE: Some fixtures are supported by a threaded rod or nipple in the center that screws into a female threaded opening in the mounting strap (inset).

Recessed Ceiling Lights

Recessed ceiling lights have long been a homeowner favorite and remain widely popular for new builds and remodeling projects alike. Although they're most often used in common areas like kitchens, dining rooms, and living rooms, they are just as effective in a bedroom. Damp or wet-rated units are natural lighting sources for bathrooms, and some homeowners even install exterior recessed lighting in soffits to increase security and add a design feature to the outside of the house.

Also known as "can lights" because of their housing structure, recessed ceiling lights can be used for new builds or retrofits. They come in many different sizes and mounting styles, although the most typical are 4-inch, 6-inch, and 8-inch diameters. Fixtures are rated "insulation compatible" (IC) or for "uninsulated" (non-IC) ceilings. Insulation-rated fixtures can be surrounded by attic insulation so that they don't become weak points in the thermal envelope of the house. They are usually further listed for use with specific types of insulation (for instance, most can lights cannot be used with blown-in insulation).

Always read labels and do your research, to make sure you purchase and install the correct version for your home and attic situation. A recessed fixture not meant for insulation can create a fire hazard if it comes in contact with ceiling insulation or other materials like boxes being stored in the attic.

It's important to note that incandescent bulbs have now been phased out, so avoid installing fixtures designed for use with incandescent bulbs. Trim kits and retrofit kits are available to make recessed lights airtight, and to convert them to LED lights. No retrofit can make a non-IC rated can IC rated.

Recessed ceiling lights often are installed in series to provide exacting control over the amount and direction of light. Spacing the canisters in every other ceiling joist bay is a common practice.

Rating symbol

This is an example of a traditional style can light, typical of those that were used with incandescent bulbs. Self-contained thermal switches shut of power if the unit gets too hot. A fixture like this one must be installed at least ½" from combustible materials. Newer fixtures are typically much lower profile.

Canless Fixtures

A relatively recent development, canless (or "wafer") recessed lighting fixtures were developed as easy-to-install retrofits in an existing, uninsulated ceiling. They have since become widely popular thanks to their ease of installation. These types do not need bridging supports and there is no concern about the weight of the fixture on the ceiling.

The fixtures are simple, all-in-one constructions. They incorporate the bulb (called a "lamp"), housing, supports, and trim into a single unit. Power is wired to a small junction box supplied with the fixture, and the junction box is screwed to the nearest joist. A push-fit cable connects the junction box to the fixture. The

TOOLS + MATERIALS

Recessed-lighting can for new construction or remodeling	Pliers
	Fish tape
Chalk line	Hack saw
Voltage tester	Drywall saw
Cable ripper	NM cable
Combination tool	Work gloves
	Eye protection

fixture is then secured into a precut ceiling hole with spring clamps.

Canless lights are currently offered only as LEDs (with the rare halogen exception). The integral bulbs are not replaceable; when the light burns out the entire fixture is replaced. Although that may sound dramatic, the reality is that the replacement simply involves unclipping the existing fixture from the ceiling and unhooking the connection to the junction box. The replacement is then just swapped in. In any case, it's a rare occurrence. LED bulbs last from 30,000 to as much as 50,000 hours of use. That can translate to a decade of service.

This specific type of lighting is bright, strong, and pure white as opposed to the soft warm glow of an incandescent source. (Many manufacturers also offer color-changing options.) The light is crisp and sharp and excellent at showing small interior details clearly.

However, some people find the light too harsh, and it's certainly not appropriate at full strength for all occasions and moods. That's why most homeowners use a dimmer switch with canless lights. This may require changing an existing switch, because you must use a dimmer switch rated for LEDs.

Most canless lights are sold in sets and they tend to be less expensive than can versions. They are usually installed as a series in specific joist bays, to make installation and wiring as straightforward as possible. They normally provide all the overhead ambient light the room will need.

Note: Extending a branch circuit or adding a new branch to install new lights or switches requires a permit. The electrical inspector may require that you install arc-fault protection on the entire circuit. Check with the electrical inspector before starting the project.

Traditional Recessed Can Lights

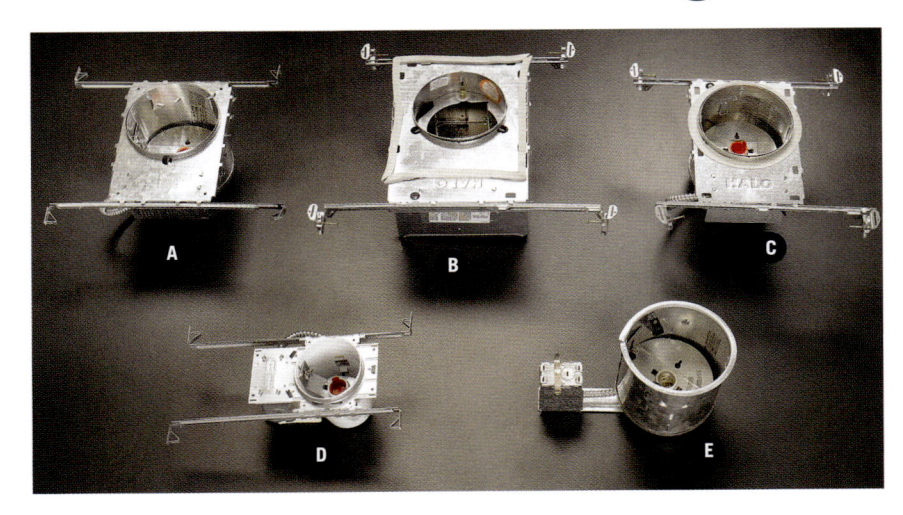

Recessed ceiling light housings come in many sizes and styles for various purposes and budgets. Some are sold with trim kits (below) included. Some common types are new construction recessed housing (sold in economical multipacks) (A); airtight recessed housings (for heated rooms below unheated ceilings) (B); shallow recessed housings (for rooms with 2 × 6 ceiling joists) (C); small-aperture recessed housing (D); recessed slope ceiling housing (for vaulted ceilings) (E).

Trim kits for recessed ceiling lights are often sold separately. Common types include open trim with reflective baffle (A); eyeball trim (B); baffle trim (black) (C); shower light trim (D); open trim (E); baffle trim (full reflective) (F).

How to Install Recessed Ceiling Lights

Mark the location for the light canister. If you are installing multiple lights, measure out from the wall at the start and end of the run, and connect them with a chalkline snapped parallel to the wall.

Install the housing for the recessed fixture. Housings for new construction (or remodeling installations where the installation area is fully accessible from either above or below) have integral hanger bars that you attach to each joist of the joist bay.

Run electric cable from the switch to each canister location. Multiple lights are generally installed in series. Make sure to leave enough extra cable at each location to feed the wire into the housing and make the connection.

Run the cables into the electrical boxes attached to the canister housings. You'll need to remove knockouts first and make sure to secure the cable with a wire staple within 8" of the entry point to the box.

5

Connect the circuit wires to the fixture wires inside the junction box. Twist the hot circuit wire together with the black fixture wire, as well as the hot circuit wire running to other fixtures further downline. Also connect the neutral white wires. Join the ground wires and pigtail them to the grounding screw or clip in the box. Finish the ceiling, as desired.

6

Attach your trim kit of choice. Normally these are hung with torsion spring clips from notches or hooks inside the canister. This should be done after the ceiling is installed and finished for new construction projects. With certain types of trim kits, such as eyeball trim, you'll need to install the lightbulb before the trim kit.

 # How to Install a Canless Ceiling Light Fixture

TOOLS + MATERIALS

LED canless light fixtures	⅜" clamp connectors
Stud finder	Wire nuts
Carpenter's pencil	Phillips screwdriver
Power drill and bits	Stepladder
6" hole saw and dust bowl	Flashlight (optional)
	Wire stripper tool
Tape measure	Cable ripper or utility knife
Fish tape	
Electrical tape	Push-fit connectors
Voltage tester	2-wire Romex cable
Multitool (optional)	Eye protection

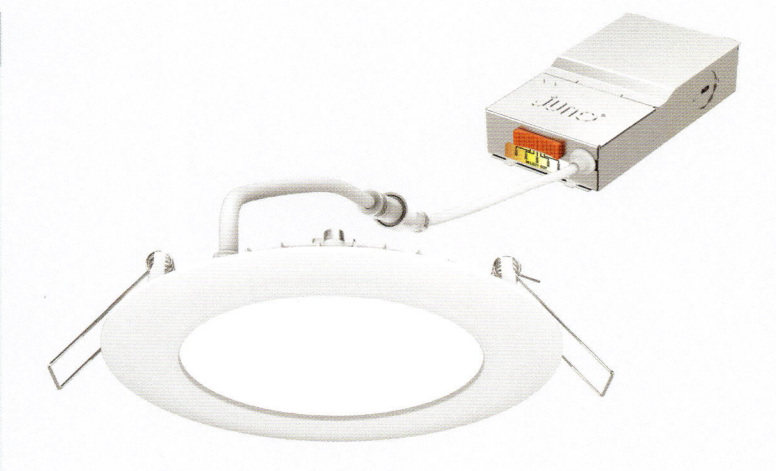

Canless fixtures are easily installed in groups, wired in series. They can replace traditional can lights or be entirely new remodeling elements.

Decide on the fixture's location. (In this project, the fixture is positioned near the switch that will control it, and draws power from that switch.) It should be centered between two joists. Determine the easiest path from the power source to the fixture. Ensure the room's circuit has enough capacity to accommodate the fixture or fixtures. Use the supplied template to mark the center of the fixture hole on the ceiling.

Center the hole saw's center drill on the mark and use the hole saw, equipped with a plastic dust shroud, to drill the hole for the light fixture. Wear eye protection while drilling.

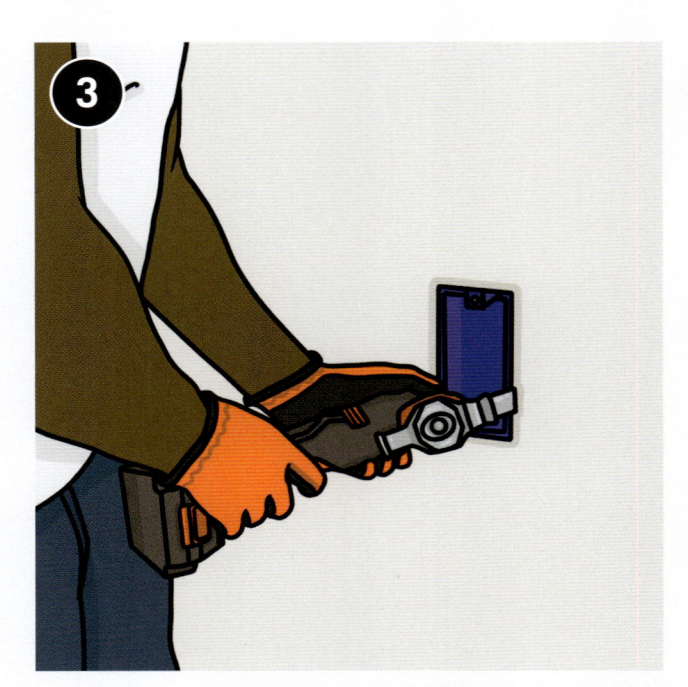

Unscrew and remove the wall switch faceplate. Unscrew the switch from the box and use a voltage tester to verify that the power is off. Pull the switch out and cut the wires to remove it. Remove the old electrical box. If it's the original box, you'll have to cut the nails holding it to the stud. Use a multitool to do this.

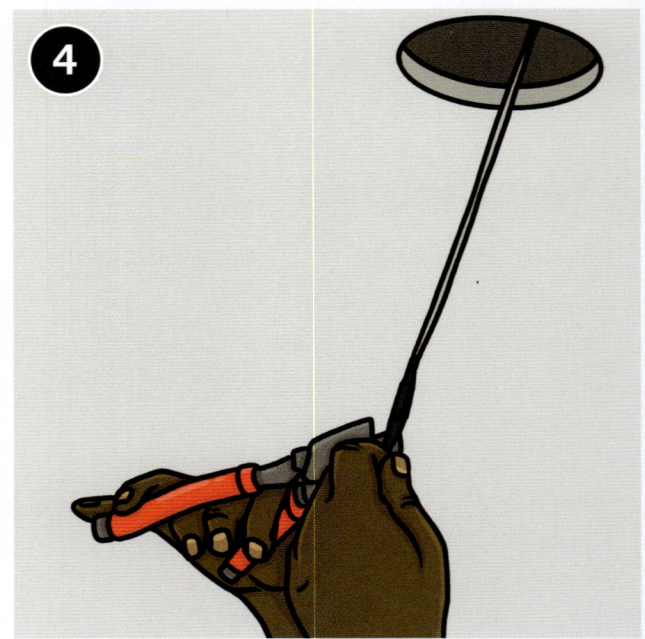

Use a flex bit to drill through the top plate of the wall to access the joist bay, working through the switch hole. (You may also need to drill holes in a joist or joists if they run parallel to the wall with the switch.) Guide fish tape up through the switch hole and drill holes to the ceiling hole for the light fixture. Securely crimp the end of a 14/2 Romex cable to the fish tape and pull it back down to the switch hole.

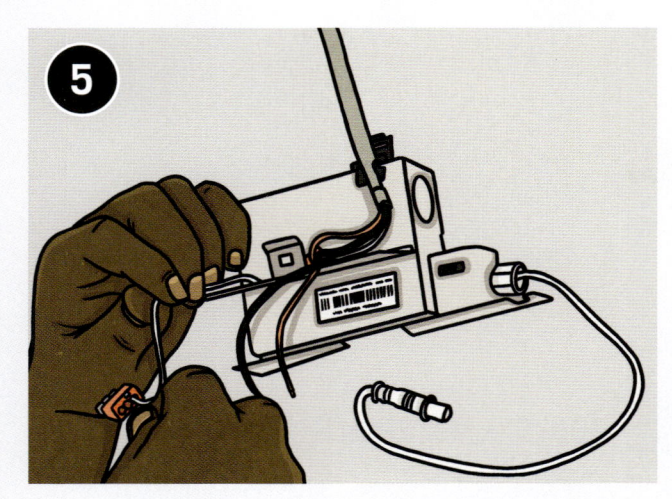

5

Remove a knockout in the side of the fixture's junction box. Feed the cable from the switch through the knockout using a ⅜" clamp connector. Strip the cable and cut the wires to length. Strip the wire ends. Connect the wires with the supplied push-fit connectors: white to white, black to black, and bare copper to copper.

Note: If you're wiring a series of fixtures, run 14/2 Romex cable from the first to the second. Strip the cable and wires in the first junction box and connect them like to like.

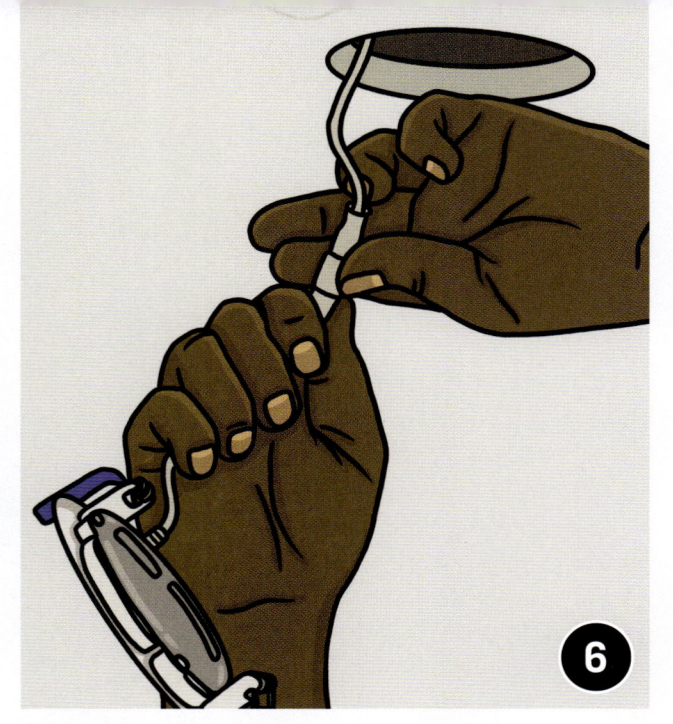

6

Secure the junction box cover and screw the box to the nearest joist. Fasten the junction box cable to the light fixture cable. Hold the spring clips closed to guide the fixture into the hole and then clip it securely to the ceiling.

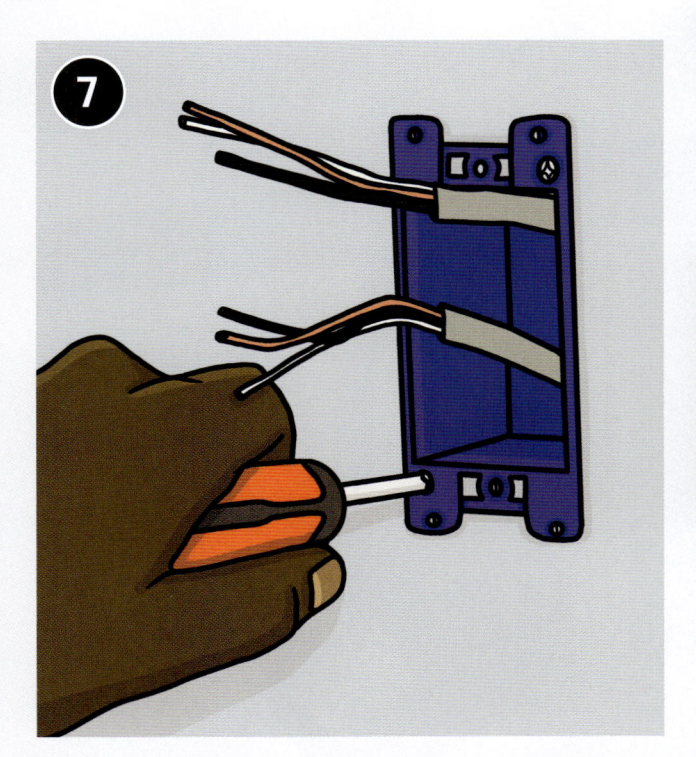

7

Feed the other end of the junction box power cable into a new old work box for the switch. Feed the existing power source cable wires through the second tab in the box. Secure the box in the wall opening.

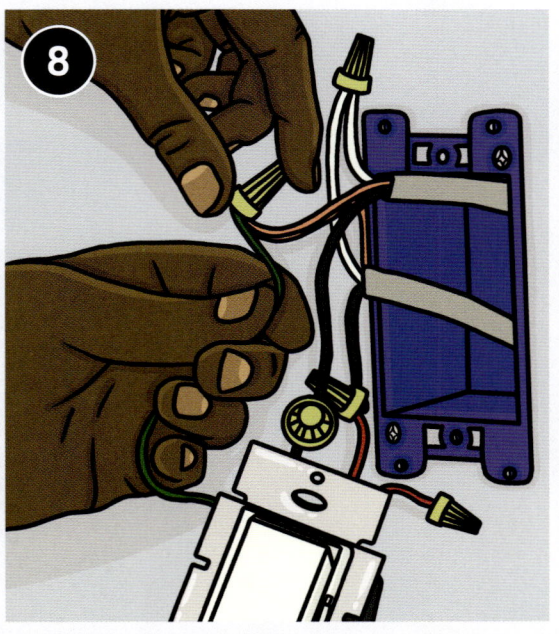

8

Install a dimmer switch (this project involves a single pole switch). Connect the dimmer's green wire to a pigtail from the two existing ground wires, with a wire nut. Connect the white wires from the power and light with a wire nut. Connect a black wire from the switch to a black wire in the box, and the solid red switch wire to the other black wire. Cap the remaining red wire from the switch with a wire nut. Push the wires into the box and screw the switch to the box. Turn on the power and test the switch. Fasten the faceplate to the box.

Note: The dimmer switch must be stamped for use with an LED fixture (or matching the type of fixture you've installed).

Track Lights

Track lighting offers a beautiful and functional way to increase the amount of light in a room or simply to update its look. A variety of fixture and lamp options let you control the shape, color, and intensity of the light. Installing track lighting in place of an existing ceiling-mounted light fixture involves basic wiring and hand-tool skills, but the connections are even easier to make than with traditional light fixtures. Once installed, the system is very easy to upgrade or expand in the future.

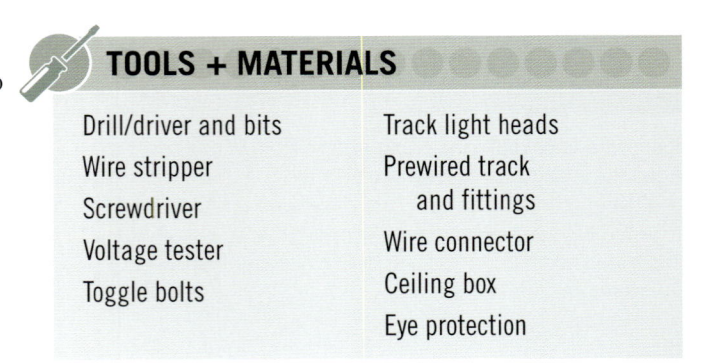

TOOLS + MATERIALS

Drill/driver and bits	Track light heads
Wire stripper	Prewired track and fittings
Screwdriver	Wire connector
Voltage tester	Ceiling box
Toggle bolts	Eye protection

If you currently have a ceiling-mounted light fixture that is not meeting your lighting needs, it's simple to replace it with a track-lighting fixture. With track lighting you can easily change the type and number of lights, their position on the track, and the direction they aim. These fixtures come in many different styles, including short 3-ft. track systems with just one or two lights up to 12-ft. systems with five or more lights.

How to Install Track Lighting

Shut off power to the circuit at the electrical panel. Remove the fixture globe and lightbulbs, then remove the fixture mounting screws. Carefully pull the fixture away from the ceiling without touching any wires.

Test the fixture wires with a voltage tester to make sure the circuit is dead. Support the fixture from below while you work—never allow a light fixture to hang by its electrical wires alone. Remove the wire connectors and pull the wires apart. Remove the old light fixture.

Attach the mounting strap for the new track light to the old ceiling box. If the mounting strap has a hole in the center, thread the circuit wires through the hole before screwing the strap to the box. The green or bare copper ground from the circuit should be attached to the grounding screw or clip on the strap or box.

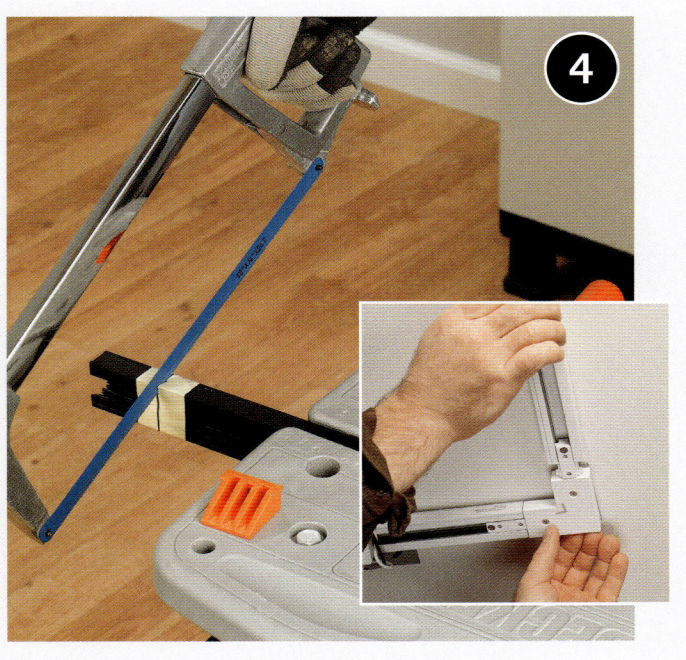

Cut the track section to length, if necessary, using a hacksaw. Deburr the cut end with a metal file. If you are installing multiple sections of track, assemble the sections with the correct connector fittings (sold separately from your kit). You can also purchase T-fittings or L-fittings (inset photo) if you wish to install tracks in either of these configurations. *(continued)*

Position the track section in the mounting saddle on the mounting strap and hold it temporarily in place in the location where it will be installed. The track section will have predrilled mounting holes in the back. Draw a marking point on the ceiling at each of these locations. If your track does not have predrilled mounting holes, remove it and drill a ³⁄₁₆" hole in the back every 16".

Insert the bolt from a toggle bolt or molly bolt into each predrilled screw location and twist the toggle or molly back onto the free end. These types of hardware have greater holding power than anchor sleeves. Drill a ⅝"-diameter access hole in the ceiling at each of the mounting hole locations you marked on the ceiling in step 5.

Insert the toggle or molly into the access hole far enough so it clears the top of the hole and the wings snap outward. Then tighten each bolt so the track is snug against the ceiling. If the mounting hole happens to fall over a ceiling joist, simply drive a #8 or larger, 2" or longer wood screw at that hole location.

Hook up wires from the track's power supply fitting to the circuit wires. Connect black to black and white to white. The grounding wire from the power supply fitting can either be pigtailed to the circuit ground wire and connected to the grounding screw or clip, or it can be twisted together with the circuit grounding wire at the grounding terminal. Snap the fitting into the track if you have not already done so.

9

Attach the protective cover that came with your kit to conceal the ceiling box and the electrical connections. Some covers simply snap in place; others require a mounting screw.

10

Dead end

Cap the open ends of the track with a dead end cap fitting. These also may require a mounting screw. Leaving track ends open is a safety violation.

11

Insert the light heads into the track by slipping the stem into the track slot and then twisting it so the electrical contact points on the head press against the electrified inner rails of the track slot. Tug lightly on the head to make sure it is secure before releasing it.

12

Arrange the track light heads so their light falls in the manner you choose, and then depress the locking tab on each fixture to secure it in position. Restore power and test the lights.

Vanity Lights

Many bathrooms have a single fixture positioned above the vanity, but a light source in this position casts shadows on the face and makes grooming more difficult. Light fixtures on either side of the mirror is a better arrangement.

For a remodel, mark the mirror location, run cable, and position boxes before drywall installation. You can also retrofit by installing new boxes and drawing power from the existing fixture.

The light sources should be at eye level; 66" is typical. The size of your mirror and its location on the wall may affect how far apart you can place the sconces, but 36" to 40" apart is a good guideline.

Extending a branch circuit or adding a new branch to install new receptacles, lights, or switches requires a permit. Check with your local electrical inspector before starting such projects.

Side-mounted vanity lights create a more real-world appearance and more natural skin tones, which aids in assessing how you look before you head out for the day.

TOOLS + MATERIALS

Drywall saw	Screwdrivers	Nail plates
Drill and bits	Hammer	Vanity light fixtures
Combination tool	Electrical boxes and braces	Wire connectors
Voltage tester	NM cable	Eye protection

How to Replace Vanity Lights in a Finished Bathroom

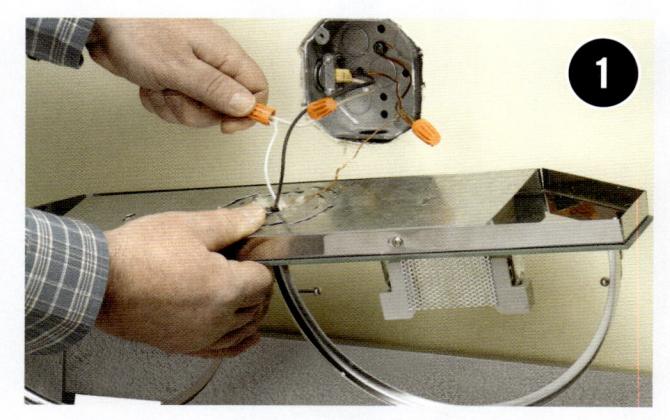

1

Turn off the power at the panel. Remove the old fixture from the wall, and test to make sure that the power is off. Then remove a strip of drywall from around the old fixture to the first studs beyond the approximate location of the new fixtures. Make the opening large enough that you have room to route cable from the existing fixture to the boxes.

2

Mark the locations for the fixtures, and install new boxes. Install the boxes about 66" above the floor and 18" to 20" from the centerline of the mirror (the mounting base of some fixtures is above or below the bulb, so adjust the height of the bracing accordingly). If the correct location is on or next to a stud, you can attach the box directly to the stud; otherwise you'll need to install blocking or use boxes with adjustable braces (shown).

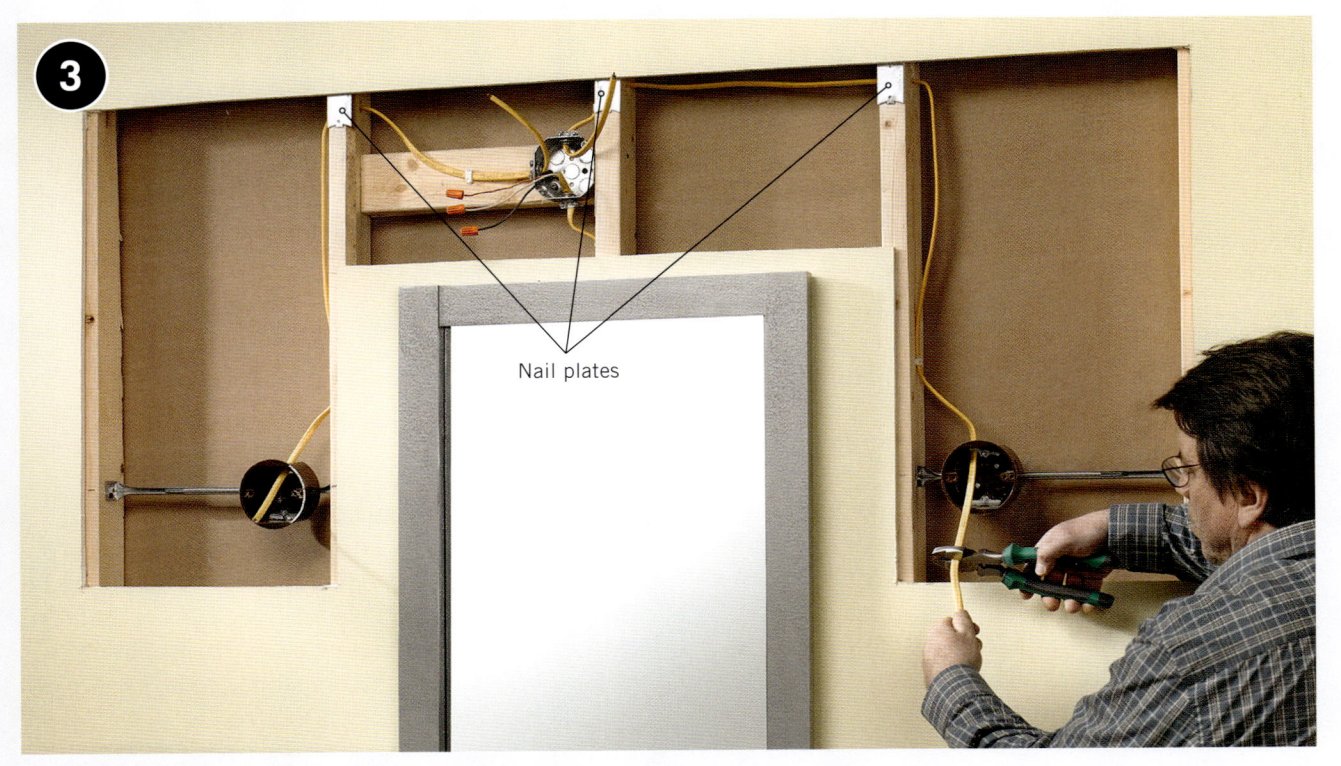

3

Nail plates

Open the side knockouts on the electrical box above the vanity. Then drill ⅝" holes in the centers of any studs between the old fixture and the new ones. Run two NM cables from the new boxes for the fixtures to the box above the vanity. Protect the cable with metal nail plates. Secure the cables with cable clamps, leaving 11" of extra cable for making the connection to the new fixtures. Remove sheathing, and strip insulation from the ends of the wires.

4

Connect the white wires from the new cables to the white wire from the old cable, and connect the black wires from the new cables to the black wire from the old cable. Connect the ground wires. Cover all open boxes, and then replace the drywall, leaving openings for the fixture and the old box. (Cover the old box with a solid junction box cover plate and leave it accessible.)

5

Install the fixture mounting braces on the boxes. Attach the fixtures by connecting the black circuit wire to the black fixture wire and connecting the white circuit wire to the white fixture wire. Connect the ground wires. Position each fixture over each box, and attach with the mounting screws. Restore power and test the circuit.

Hardwired Smoke + CO Alarms

Smoke alarms and carbon monoxide (CO) alarms are essential safety components of any living facility. All national fire-protection codes require that new homes have a hardwired smoke alarm in every sleeping room and on every level of a residence, including basements and habitable attics.

Three types of alarms exist that can alert you to a fire. Photoelectric alarms are better at detecting fires with lots of flames. Ionization smoke alarms are better at detecting smoldering fires. Heat alarms detect high temperature created by a fire.

Many experts recommend installing photoelectric alarms instead of the more common ionization alarms, or as an alternative, installing some of each type. Heat alarms may be installed in addition to smoke alarms but may not be substituted for them.

Smoke alarms have a limited service life of about 10 years. You should replace smoke alarms after 10 years regardless of whether the alarm sounds when you press the test button. The test button, especially

on older alarms, may only test the sounding device, not the smoke detection system.

Hardwired alarms operate on your household electrical current but have battery backups in case of a power outage. On new homes, all smoke alarms must be wired so that every alarm sounds regardless of the fire's location. When wiring alarms, be sure to use alarms of the same brand to ensure compatibility. Always check local codes before starting the job.

Smoke alarms installed on the ceiling should be at least 4" from the wall. Smoke alarms installed on the wall should be at least 4" and not more than 12" from the ceiling. As always, read and follow the manufacturer's instructions.

Smoke alarms and CO alarms are considered such important safety devices that national codes require updating these alarms to current code requirements during some types of remodeling projects. Enforcement of this requirement varies by jurisdiction, so check with your building department before remodeling.

Extending a branch circuit or adding a new branch to install new receptacles, lights, or switches requires a permit. The electrical inspector may require that you install arc-fault protection on the entire circuit. Check with the electrical inspector before starting such projects. In existing homes where it is impractical to install hardwired smoke alarms, battery-powered alarms are allowed. Use battery-powered smoke alarms that are interconnected by radio. Carbon monoxide alarms are required in homes that have fuel-burning appliances, including a fireplace. A CO alarm should be installed near sleeping rooms, so only one is necessary if all sleeping rooms are in one area. If more than one CO alarm is required, it should be hardwired and interconnected as a smoke alarm. Combination smoke alarm and carbon monoxide alarms are available, and may be installed instead of separate alarms. Note, however, that the typical service life of a CO alarm is 7 years, so combination alarms will need replacement more frequently.

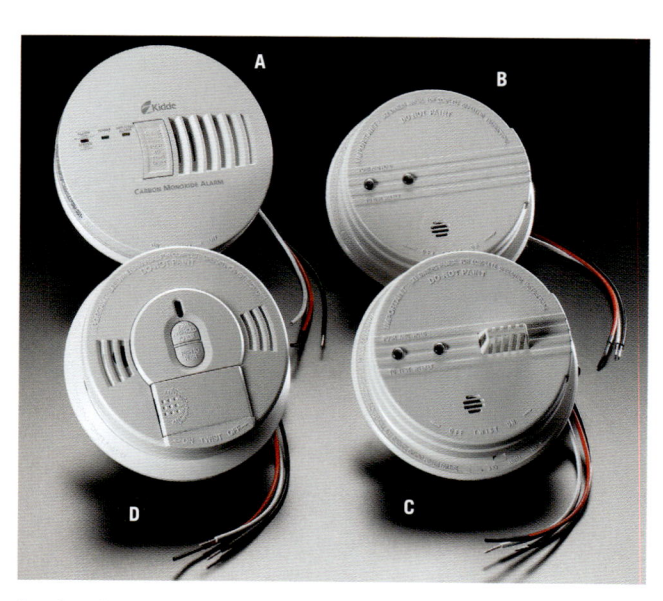

Smoke alarms and carbon monoxide (CO) alarms are required in new construction. Hardwired CO alarms (A) are triggered by the presence of carbon monoxide gas. Smoke alarms are available in photoelectric and ionizing models. In ionizing detectors (B), a small amount of current flows in an ionization chamber. When smoke enters the chamber, it interrupts the current, triggering the alarm. Photoelectric alarms (C) rely on a beam of light, which when interrupted by smoke triggers an alarm. Heat alarms (D) sound an alarm when they detect areas of high heat in the room.

How to Connect a Series of Hardwired Smoke Alarms

Three-wire cable to next detector in series

Two-wire cable from panel

1

Pull 14/2 NM cable from the panel into the first ceiling electrical box in the smoke alarm series. Pull 14/3 NM cable between the remaining alarm outlet boxes. Use cable clamps to secure the cable in each outlet box. Remove sheathing, and strip insulation from wires.

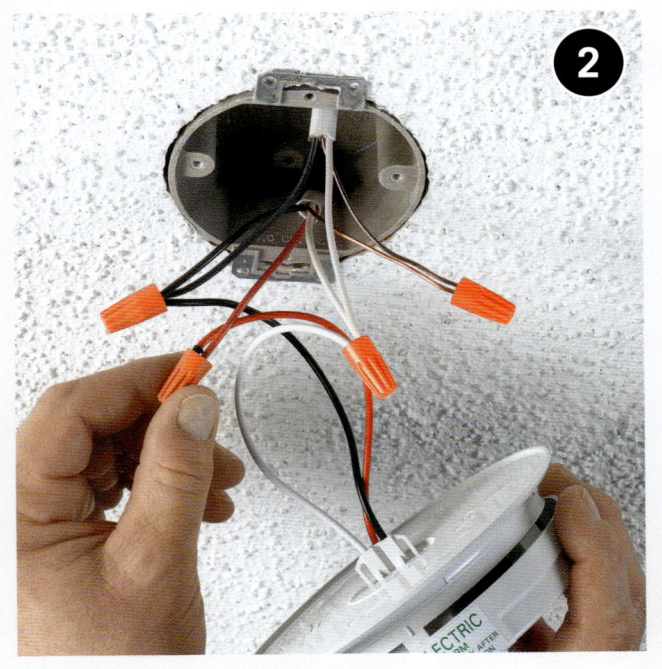

2

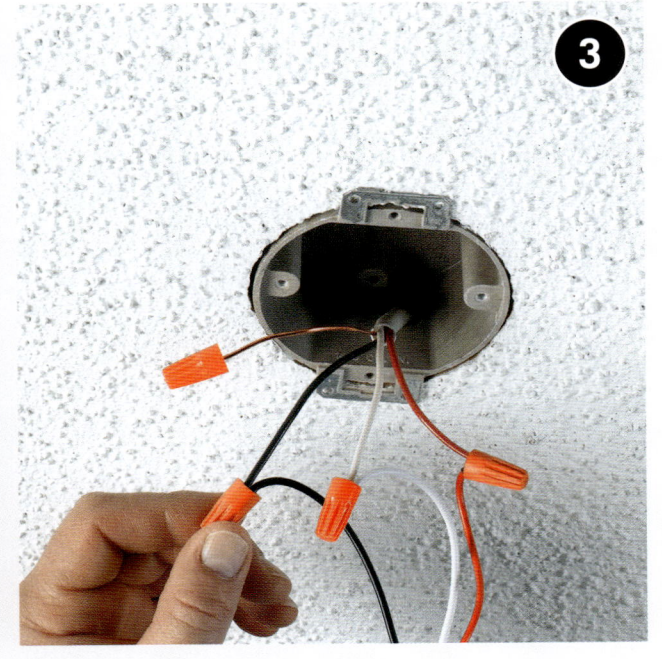

3

Ensure power is off, and test for power. Wire the first alarm in the series. Use a wire connector to connect the ground wires. Splice the black circuit wire with the alarm's black lead and the black wire going to the next alarm in the series. Splice the white circuit wire with the alarm's white wire and the white (neutral) wire going to the next alarm in the series. Splice the red traveler wire with the odd-colored alarm wire (in this case, also a red wire).

Wire the remaining alarms in the series by connecting the like-colored wires in each outlet box. Always connect the red traveler wire to the odd-colored (in this case, red) alarm wire. This red traveler wire connects all the alarms together so that when one alarm sounds, all the alarms sound. If the alarm doesn't have a grounding wire, cap the ground with a wire connector. When all alarms are wired, install and connect the new 15-amp AFCI breaker.

Low-Voltage Pathway + Patio Lighting

Patios are stages for relaxation, socializing, and pure enjoyment. That doesn't change after the Sun goes down. Lighting your nighttime patio is a way to extend its usefulness and ensure safety, especially if the patio is some distance from the natural ambient light cast by the interior of the house.

The wonderful thing about landscape lighting around a patio or along a walkway is that the fixtures and type of light they cast can be decorative elements as well as serving a functional purpose.

When it comes to this type of lighting, low-voltage systems are by far the most popular. These systems use a step-down transformer to convert household 120-volt current to a safer 12-volt current that powers what are often LED lighting boards in each fixture (called "integrated fixtures"). These fixtures often don't have actual bulbs. That means no bulb to replace, but also means that when the light stops functioning, the entire fixture must be replaced (you can avoid this by purchasing "lamp-ready" fixtures).

The popularity is due to the ease of installation, the relative safety of the system (you're unlikely to ever experience an electrical shock from these systems, and if you do, it will be modest and benign), their modest expense, and the vast selection of fixture styles and finishes. These are also energy efficient, so they won't add much to your electric bill.

There are few limitations on low-voltage lighting placement. You'll need to dig a trench for the power cable that is at least 6 inches deep, and the transformer needs to be plugged into the nearest outdoor receptacle. Other than that, the fixtures can be placed anywhere the underfoot surface is soft enough for the post to go down into.

TOOLS + MATERIALS

Low-voltage lighting kit	Drill and bits
Tape measure	Screwdriver
Chalk, lime, or landscape spray paint	Wire stripper/cutter
Carpenter's pencil or grease pencil	Electrical tape
	Torpedo level
Garden spade, drain spade, or trenching shovel	

Thoughtfully placed and appropriately spaced low-voltage lighting fixtures not only make the patio more attractive at night, they also serve as handy safety and security features.

Most landscapes and patios will benefit from a mix of lighting types. Here, uplight "spot lights" create dramatic silhouettes against the home's wall, while basic low-voltage fixtures add attractive ambient light that fills out the look.

Manufacturers offer different types of lighting fixtures in their low-voltage lighting kits. Choose the one that best serves your needs.

- **Spotlights.** These are usually directional and can often be adjusted to aim at the feature you intend to highlight. Spotlights include downlights and uplights, which create a sense of visual drama. They are also often used to showcase particular features such as a waterfall or specimen planting. Spotlights are usually bulb-equipped fixtures. That allows you change the bulb for special effects, such as using colored bulbs for holiday displays.

- **Area lights.** This is the most common type of backyard lighting for decks, patios, stairs, and walkways; and it is the type used in this project. Area lighting projects soft, diffuse ambient illumination, usually down around the fixture and sometimes in all directions. It's a good general lighting, and there is an emphasis on the fixtures themselves as design elements.

- **Floodlights.** These are meant to provide maximum light on a specific area or feature, such as the wall of a house or over a significant part of a yard. Floodlights are most often associated with security (most home motion-sensor lights are floodlights). The fixtures themselves are rarely considered decorative or stylish elements. They usually meant to just blend into the surface on which they are mounted.

- **Well lights.** These are specialized fixtures meant to be partially or completely concealed in landscaping or structural elements such as flush-mount deck step lights. They become apparent only when lit, and are used where a subtle effect is desired. The light projected is limited and is used for safety and decorative purposes.

How to Install Low-Voltage Lighting

Check that all the pieces you'll need have been included in the kit, as listed on the box. Measure and physically lay out the lights and electrical cables in position, along the patio edge you'll be illuminating. Mark the locations of each light fixture with chalk, lime, or landscape spray paint.

Move the lights and cable out of the way, and dig the cable trench. The trench should be 6" deep. Use a garden spade if you have to cut into sod, or a drain spade or trenching shovel to dig the trench out of dirt.

Alternative: Some manufacturers—and some installers—recommend laying the cable on top of the soil and connecting the fixtures before burying the cable in the trench. You can also simply leave the cable on the ground if the walkway or patio edge is raised above ground level, or cover it with mulch or stone. However, burying the cable ensures it won't be disturbed.

Carefully cover the cable with soil, but don't compact it. Leave a pinched half loop of cable pulled up and uncovered at each light fixture location. If you've removed sod, replace it, cutting an opening at each light location.

Position the transformer on the wall next to an exterior GFCI outlet and mark for the mounting screw holes. Drill holes at the marks and install anchors, if mounting on a masonry wall. Otherwise, screw the transformer in place using the supplied screws. *Note: Transformers must be mounted exactly as specified by the manufacturer to avoid fire or electrical failure risk. This usually entails mounting it with 1 ft. of clearance all around, and using a heat shield for units that produce a lot of heat and that will be mounted on flammable surfaces.*

Split the two sides of the cable end at the transformer box, and strip about 1" of insulation from the end of each wire. Screw or clamp the wire ends into the transformer terminals.

Connect each light fixture along the line by snapping the fixture's connectors onto the cable at the fixture location. Wrap the connection in electrical tape. Press the stake of the fixture support into the ground and check for level and plumb.

Plug in the transformer and check that all the lights work as intended. If the transformer includes a photo sensor, screw the bracket in place on the wall, secure the sensor end in the bracket, and plug the other end into the transformer. Otherwise, set the transformer timer.

Doorbells

The basic doorbell system in most homes is an exceptionally simple circuit. The doorbell switch is wired to a dedicated transformer. The transformer is hardwired into a household circuit and steps down the standard 120-volt current to a much more modest load of about 20 volts. The transformer is then wired to the doorbell chime. Push the button and the chime sounds.

Because the wiring is so simple and the technology so basic, doorbells tend to work for a long time without problems. When issues do occur, it can be a simple fix like the troubleshooting process described on the opposite page, or it can be an opportunity to upgrade. These days, most homeowners jump at the chance to improve their home security and add features to one of the most basic devices in the home. Of course, you don't have to wait for your doorbell to malfunction to enjoy the many benefits of upgrading.

Upgrading to a Video Doorbell

The meteoric rise of direct-to-home delivery of so many products has been mirrored by an explosion of package grab-and-run thefts (by what are widely known as "porch pirates"). Thankfully, homeowners have a reasonably priced security solution that does double duty in the home. Hardwired video doorbells are an easy and fairly inexpensive upgrade to existing doorbells, providing 24/7 security coverage.

These modern wonders transmit wireless video to a smart phone app, allowing homeowners to monitor their home and yard even when they aren't there.

You can even subscribe to a service that will upload and store date-stamped digital files of everything the doorbell records. The cameras in these doorbells are usually motion-activated and they often detect surprising activity.

Even better, many of these include a speaker. That gives you a chance to disrupt a package theft in progress or respond to potential burglars who often ring the doorbell just to see if anyone is at home.

Upgrading to a video doorbell is easy enough for even novice DIYers. The project shown here is hardwired into the home's electrical system, requiring only a couple of tools and less than an hour of your time. A battery-powered video doorbell is pricier but even easier to install. However, you will have to regularly recharge the battery. In either case, the faceplate is attached with specialized screws (installed with a supplied proprietary driver) that tamper-proofs the doorbell.

That all assumes a wood- or vinyl-sided home. Masonry surfaces like stucco or brick will require slightly more work. You'll need to use a carbide-tipped masonry drill bit to drill two mounting holes and you'll have to buy special masonry screw anchors to use with the supplied hardware.

There are several different makes of video doorbells on the market, but all work in roughly the same way. They are also installed in a similar fashion, regardless of brand. Depending on your home and property's exposure, you may want to upgrade a front, back, and even side door for increased coverage.

TOOLS + MATERIALS

- Phillips screwdriver
- Pliers
- Continuity tester
- Painter's tape
- Multimeter
- Cotton swab
- Alcohol

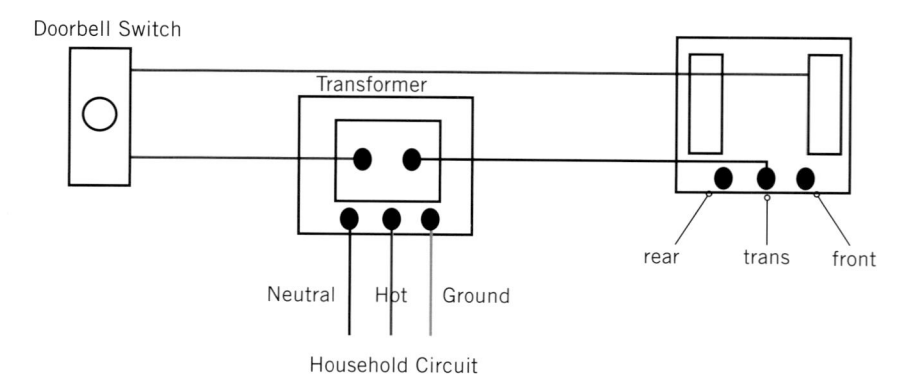

A doorbell circuit is basic and easy to track. The doorbell is a wired to a transformer that reduces the power from an existing circuit. The transformer is wired to a chime that is wired back to the doorbell. The main difference with a wired video doorbell is that a power feed is connected to the chime, powering the doorbell's wireless features.

How to Troubleshoot a Doorbell

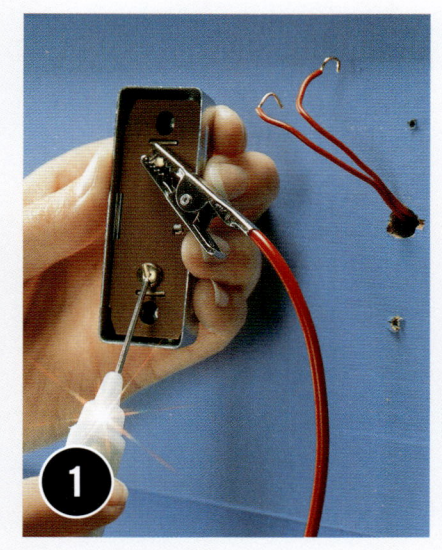

Unscrew the doorbell button and pull it away from the siding. Check the wires for secure connections and tighten if loose. If it still doesn't work, clip a continuity tester to one terminal and touch the probe to the other. If the tester doesn't glow, the switch is bad.

Twist the doorbell wires together. Locate the transformer. (It should be identifiable by the double-digit voltage rating listed on the transformer.) Turn off power to the circuit.

Open the cover to the junction box serving the transformer and test that the power is off. Check for loose wires or connections and resecure them. Replace the cover.

Tighten the wire connections on the transformer terminals and check for damage to the terminals or wires. Repair as necessary. Restore power, and check the transformer with a multimeter to determine the current flow; it should be within 2 volts of the rated voltage.

Remove the chime cover and tighten any loose connections. Check the chime terminals in the same way you did the transformer. If there is no voltage, there is broken wire between the transformer and chime. Replace the wires and test again.

Clean the chime components with a cotton swab and replace the cover. Replace the doorbell and test the switch. If it still does not work, the chime is faulty and should be replaced.

How to Upgrade to a Video Doorbell

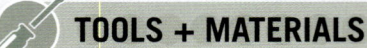
Check the package to ensure all the components have been included. Purchase masonry anchors and a masonry bit, if necessary. Turn off the power at the breaker box and press the doorbell to check that the power is off.

Find the doorbell transformer and check the ratings listed on the transformer against the minimum specifications for the doorbell. (For instance, the unit shown here requires: 10–24 VAC, 50/60 Hz, 10–40 VA.) If the transformer does not meet the specs required by the doorbell manufacturer, swap it with the recommended transformer; many manufacturers sell replacement transformers to match their doorbells.

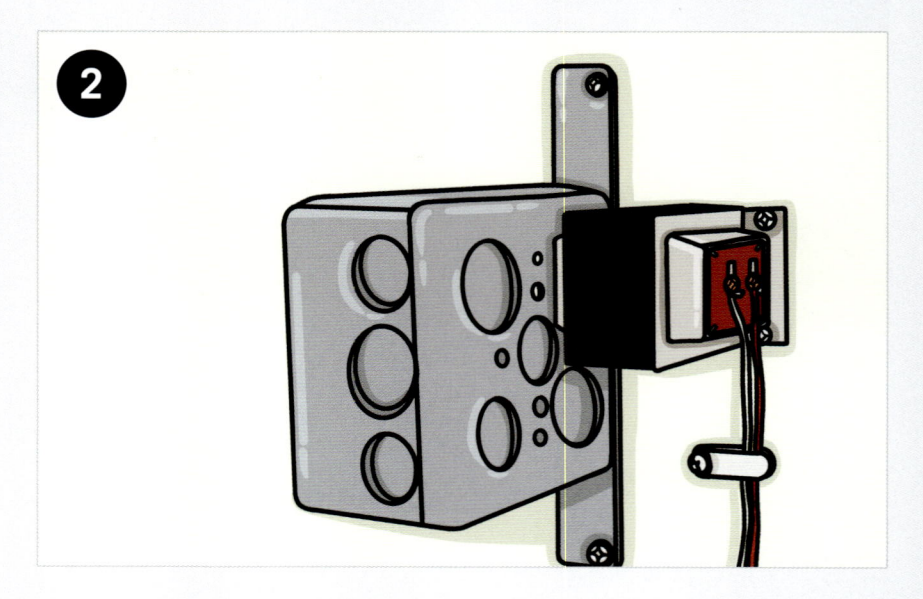

Find the chime unit inside your house and remove the housing. Loosen the screws marked "front" and "trans." Remove each wire and slip each into a separate push fit connector (supplied by the manufacturer). Slip one pigtail wire from each terminal wire on the new power source into the other side of each connector. Screw down the open end of each power source wire to the front and trans terminals. Use the attached adhesive pads to secure the power sources in the chime housing, leaving room for the cover. Replace the cover.

Unscrew and remove the existing doorbell button. Disconnect the wires and tape them to the wall to stop them from falling back into the hole. Remove the new doorbell's faceplate and use the base as a template to mark new screw holes on the wall (check level and plumb with a level to ensure the doorbell will be mounted correctly). Optional: For masonry surfaces, drill out the marked holes and use a masonry anchor to hold the supplied screws.

Attach the wires to the new doorbell's terminal screws, hooking them clockwise on the screw terminals. Tighten the screws.

Note: If the wires coming out of the wall are too short, use the wire extenders usually supplied with the new doorbell, or cut new wire extenders. Attach the extensions with wire nuts.

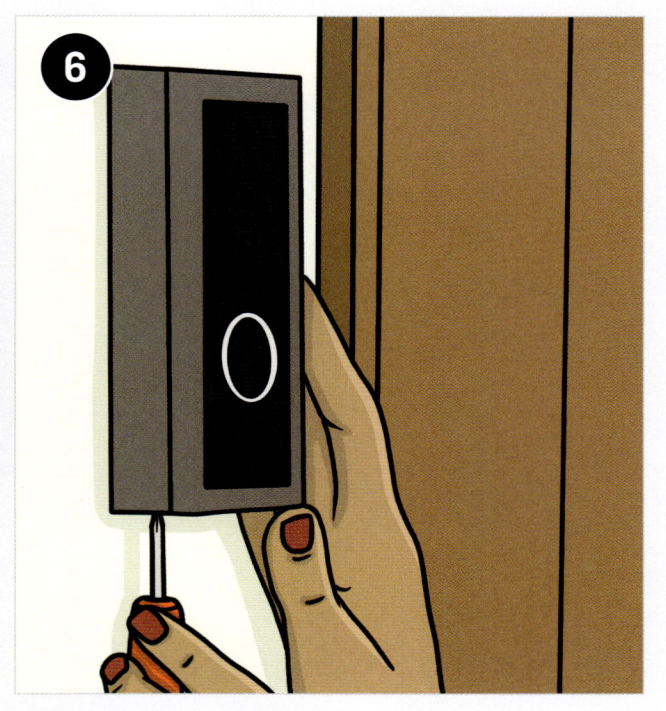

Screw the new doorbell to the wall, using the supplied screws. Turn the power back on at the breaker box. The doorbell face light or power indicator should light up. Slip the faceplate onto the doorbell. Secure the faceplate with the tamper-proof screws supplied. Sync the doorbell with the phone app using the set-up process.

Wireless Switches

Sometimes a light switch is just in the wrong place, or it would be more convenient to have two switches controlling a single fixture. Adding a second switch the conventional way generally requires hours of work and big holes in walls. (Electricians call this a three-way switch installation.) Fortunately wireless switch kits are available to perform basically the same function for a fraction of the cost and effort. There is a bit of real wiring involved here, but it's not nearly as complicated as the traditional method of adding a three-way switch installation.

The kits work by replacing a conventional switch with a unit that has a built-in radio frequency receiver that will read a remote device mounted within a 50-foot radius. The kits come with a remote, battery-powered switch (it looks like a standard light switch) that you can attach to a wall with double-sided tape.

Two other similar types of wireless switch kits are also available. One allows you to control a plugged-in lamp or appliance with a remote light switch. The second type allows you to control a conventional light fixture remotely, but instead of replacing the switch, the receiver screws in below the lightbulb. This is particularly useful if you want to control a pull-chain light from a wall switch.

TOOLS + MATERIALS

Voltage tester
Screwdrivers
Wire connectors

Wireless switch transmitter + receiver/switch

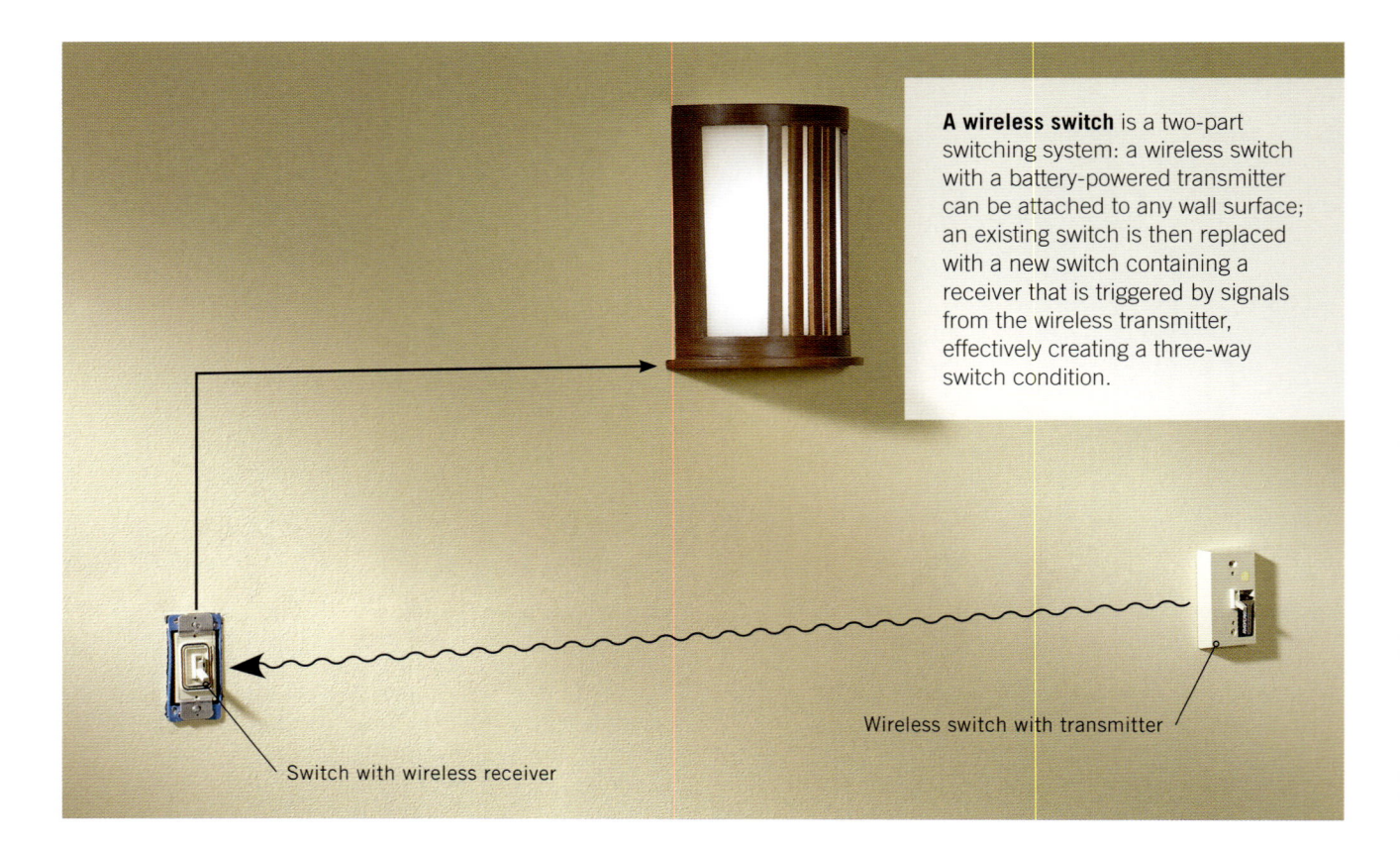

A wireless switch is a two-part switching system: a wireless switch with a battery-powered transmitter can be attached to any wall surface; an existing switch is then replaced with a new switch containing a receiver that is triggered by signals from the wireless transmitter, effectively creating a three-way switch condition.

Switch with wireless receiver

Wireless switch with transmitter

Wireless kits are available to let you switch lights on and off remotely in a variety of ways: at the switch, at the plug, or at the bulb socket.

The remote switch is a wireless transmitter that requires a battery. The transmitter switch attaches to the wall with adhesive tape or velcro strips.

A receiver with a receptacle can be plugged into any receptacle to give it wireless functionality. The switch is operated with a remote control transmitter.

A radio-controlled light fixture can be threaded into the socket of any existing light fixture so it can be turned on and off with a remote control device.

How to Install a Wireless Wall Switch

Get rid of the old switch. Shut off power to the switch circuit, and then disconnect and remove the old switch.

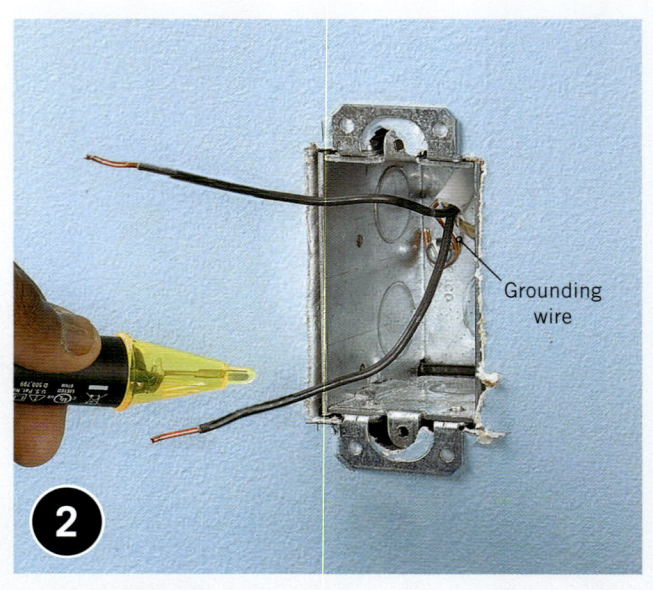

Grounding wire

Identify the lead wire. Carefully separate the power supply wires (any color but white or green) in the switch box so they are not contacting each other or any other surface. Restore power and test each lead wire with a noncontact voltage tester to identify which wire carries the power (the LINE) and which is headed for the fixture the switch controls (the LOAD). Shut power back off, and then label the wires.

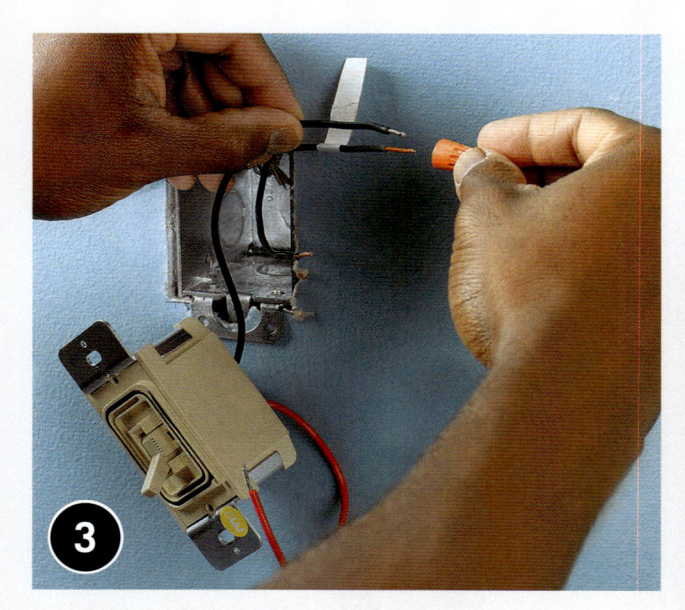

Connect the LINE wire to the LINE terminal or wire on the switch. Connect the LOAD wire (or wires) to the LOAD terminal or wire. The neutral whites (if present) and green grounding wires should be twisted together with a connector. The green wires should be grounded to the grounding clip or terminal in the box.

NOTE: Some switch boxes, such as the one above, are wired with NM2 cable that has two blacks and a green wire and no white.

Once the wires are connected, you can attach the switch to the box. Tuck the new switch and wires neatly back into the box. Then drive the two long screws that are attached to the new switch into the two holes in the electrical box.

Attach the cover plate to the new wireless switch. Turn the power service back on, and test to make sure the switch operates normally.

Install a new 9-volt battery (or other type as required) in the box, and connect it to the switch transmitter terminals. Remove the backing from the adhesive pads on the back of the wireless switch transmitter box.

Stick the transmitter box to the wall at the desired location. The box should be no more than 50 ft. from the receiver switch (see manufacturer's instructions). The box should be at the same height (usually 48") as the other switch boxes.

Test the operation of both switches. Each switch should successfully turn the light fixture on and off. You've just successfully created a three-way switch installation without running any new wires.

Baseboard Heaters

Baseboard heaters are a popular way to provide additional heating for an existing room or primary heat to a converted attic or basement. Extending a branch circuit or adding a new branch to install new receptacles, lights, switches, or equipment requires a permit. The electrical inspector may require that you install arc-fault protection on the entire circuit. Check with the electrical inspector before starting such projects.

Heaters are generally wired on a dedicated 240-volt circuit controlled by a thermostat. Several heaters can be wired in parallel and controlled by a single thermostat (see circuit map 15, page 157).

Baseboard heaters are generally surface-mounted without boxes, so in a remodeling situation, you only need to run cables before installing wallboard. Be sure to mark cable locations on the floor before installing drywall. Retrofit installations are also not difficult.

You can remove existing baseboard and run new cable in the space behind. Baseboard heaters (and other heating equipment) get very hot and can ignite nearby combustible materials. Maintain the manufacturer's recommended distance between the heater and materials such as curtains, blinds, and wood.

TOOLS + MATERIALS

Drill/driver	240-thermostat (in-heater or in-wall)
Wire stripper	
Cable ripper	12/2 NM cable
Drywall saw	Electrical tape
Baseboard heater or heaters	Basic wiring supplies

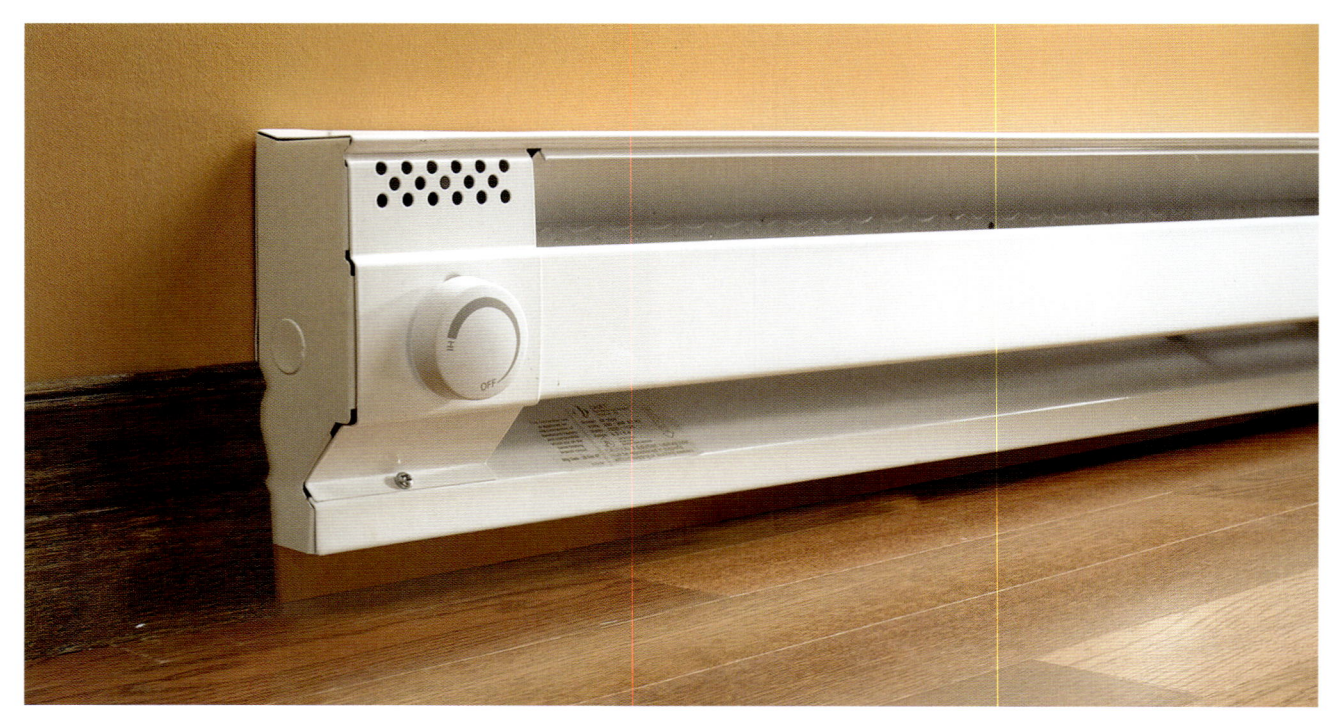

Baseboard heaters can provide primary or supplemental heat for existing rooms or additions. Install heaters with clear space between the heater and the floor.

Baseboard Thermostats

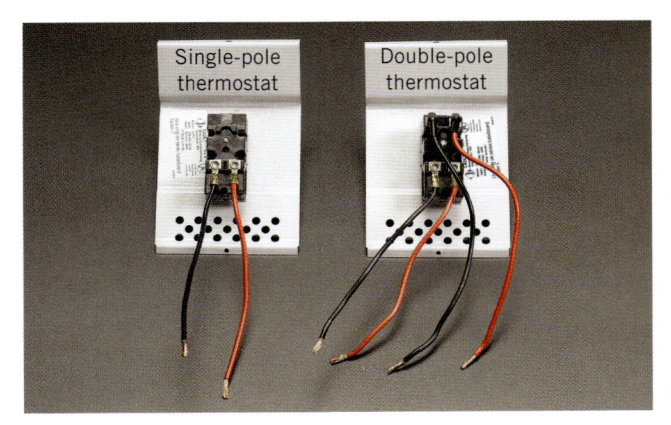

Single-pole and double-pole thermostats work in a similar manner, but double-pole models are safer. The single-pole model will open the circuit (causing shutoff) in only one leg of the power service. Double-pole models have two sets of wires to open both legs, lessening the chance that a person servicing the heater will contact a live wire.

In-heater and wall-mount are the two types of baseboard thermostats you can choose from. If you are installing multiple heaters, a single wall-mount thermostat is more convenient. Individual in-heater thermostats give you more zone control, which can result in energy savings.

HOW MUCH HEATER DO YOU NEED?

Here is a simple calculation get a rough idea of the lineal feet of baseboard a room requires. For a more accurate estimate, consult a professional.

1. Measure the area of the room in square feet (length × width): _____

2. Multiply the area by 10 to get the baseline minimum wattage: _____

3. Add 5% for each newer window or 10% for each older window: _____

4. Add 10% for each exterior wall in the room: _____

5. Add 10% for each exterior door: _____

6. Add 10% if the space below is not insulated: _____

7. Add 20% if the space above is not well insulated: _____

8. Add 10% if ceiling is more than 8 ft. high: _____

9. Total of the baseline wattage plus all additions: _____

10. Divide this number by 250 (the wattage produced per foot of standard baseboard heater): _____

11. Round up to a whole number. This is the minimum number of feet of heater you need. _____

NOTE: It is much better to have more feet of heater than is required than fewer. Having more footage of heater does not consume more energy; it does allow the heaters to work more efficiently.

PLANNING TIPS FOR BASEBOARD HEATERS

- Baseboard heaters require a dedicated circuit. A 20-amp, 240-volt circuit of 12-gauge copper wire may power up to 16 ft. of heater. Refer to the manufacturer's instructions for specific circuit load information.

- Do not install a heater beneath a wall receptacle. Cords hanging down from the receptacle are a fire hazard.

- Do not mount heaters directly on the floor. You should maintain at least 1" of clear space between the baseboard heater and the floor covering.

- Installing heaters directly beneath windows is a good practice.

- Locate wall thermostats on interior walls only, and do not install directly above a heat source.

How to Install a 240-Volt Baseboard Heater

At the heater locations, cut a small hole in the drywall 3" to 4" above the floor. Pull 12/2 NM (or the wire gauge specified by the heater manufacturer) cables through the first hole: one from the thermostat, the other to the next heater. Pull all the cables for subsequent heaters. Middle-of-run heaters will have two cables, while end-of-run heaters have only one cable. (See also circuit map 15, page 157.)

Remove the cover on the wire connection box. Open a knockout for each cable that will enter the box, and then feed the cables through the cable clamps and into the wire connection box. Attach the clamps to the wire connection box, and tighten the clamp screws until the cables are gripped firmly.

Anchor the heater against wall about 1" off floor by driving flathead screws through the back of the housing and into studs. Strip away cable sheathing so at least ½" of sheathing extends into the heater. Strip ¾" of insulation from each wire using a combination tool.

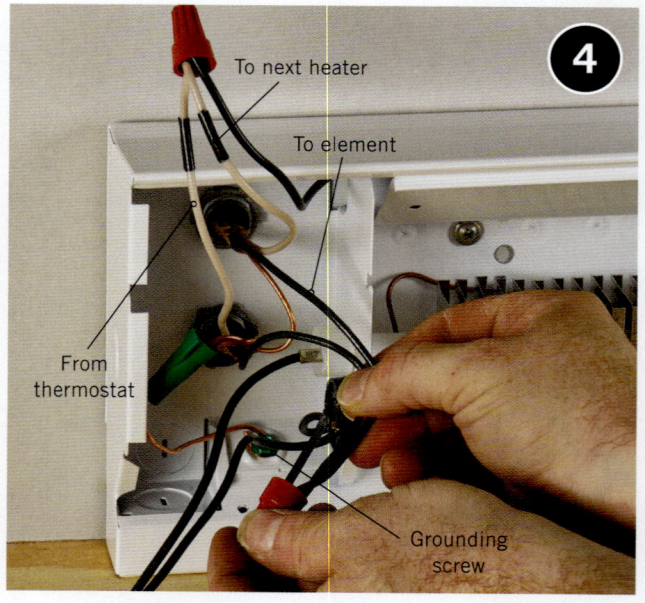

Make connections to the heating element if the power wires are coming from a thermostat or another heater controlled by a thermostat. See the next page for other wiring schemes. Connect the white circuit wires to one of the wire leads on the heater. Tag white wires with black tape to indicate they are hot. Connect the black circuit wires to the other wire lead. Connect a grounding pigtail to the green grounding screw in the box, and then join all grounding wires with a wire connector. Reattach the cover.

One heater with end-cap thermostat. Run both power leads (black plus tagged neutral) into the connection box at either end of the heater. If installing a single-pole thermostat, connect one power lead to one thermostat wire and connect the other thermostat wire, to one of the heater leads. Connect the other hot LINE wire to the other heater lead. If you are installing a double-pole thermostat, make connections with both legs of the power supply.

Multiple heaters. At the first heater, join both hot wires from the thermostat to the wires leading to the second heater in line. Be sure to tag all white neutrals hot. Twist copper ground wires together and pigtail them to the grounding screw in the baseboard heater junction box. This parallel wiring configuration ensures that power flow will not be interrupted to the downstream heaters if an upstream heater fails.

Wall-mounted thermostat. If installing a wall-mounted thermostat, the power leads should enter the thermostat first and then be wired to the individual heaters singly or in series. Hookups at the heater are made as shown in step 4. Be sure to tag the white neutral as hot in the thermostat box as well as in the heater box.

Underfloor Radiant Heat Systems

Floor-warming systems require very little energy to run and are designed to heat ceramic tile floors only; they generally are not used as sole heat sources for rooms. Extending a branch circuit or adding a new branch to install new receptacles, lights, switches, or equipment requires a permit. Check with the electrical inspector before starting such projects.

A typical floor-warming system consists of one or more thin mats containing electric resistance wires that heat up when energized, like an electric blanket. The mats are installed beneath the tile and are hardwired to a 120-volt GFCI circuit. A thermostat controls the temperature, and a timer turns the system off automatically.

The system shown in this project includes two plastic mesh mats, each with its own power lead that is wired directly to the thermostat. Radiant mats may be installed over a plywood subfloor, but if you plan to install floor tile, you should put down a base of cementboard first, and then install the mats on top of the cementboard.

A crucial part of installing this system is to use a multimeter to perform several resistance checks to make sure the heating wires have not been damaged during shipping or installation.

Electrical service required for a floor-warming system is based on size. A smaller system may connect to an existing circuit, but this may not be a bathroom receptacle circuit, and the system may not draw more than 50 percent of the circuit current capacity. A larger system will need a dedicated circuit; follow the manufacturer's instructions. These systems should be on a GFCI-protected circuit.

To order a floor-warming system, contact the manufacturer or dealer. In most cases, you can send them plans and they'll custom-fit a system for your project area.

TOOLS + MATERIALS

Vacuum cleaner
Multimeter
Tape measure
Scissors
Router/rotary tool
Marker
Electric wire fault indicator (optional)
Hot glue gun
Radiant floor mats
12/2 NM cable
Trowel or rubber float
Conduit
Thinset mortar
Thermostat with sensor
Junction box(es)
Tile or stone floorcovering
Drill
Double-sided carpet tape
Cable clamps

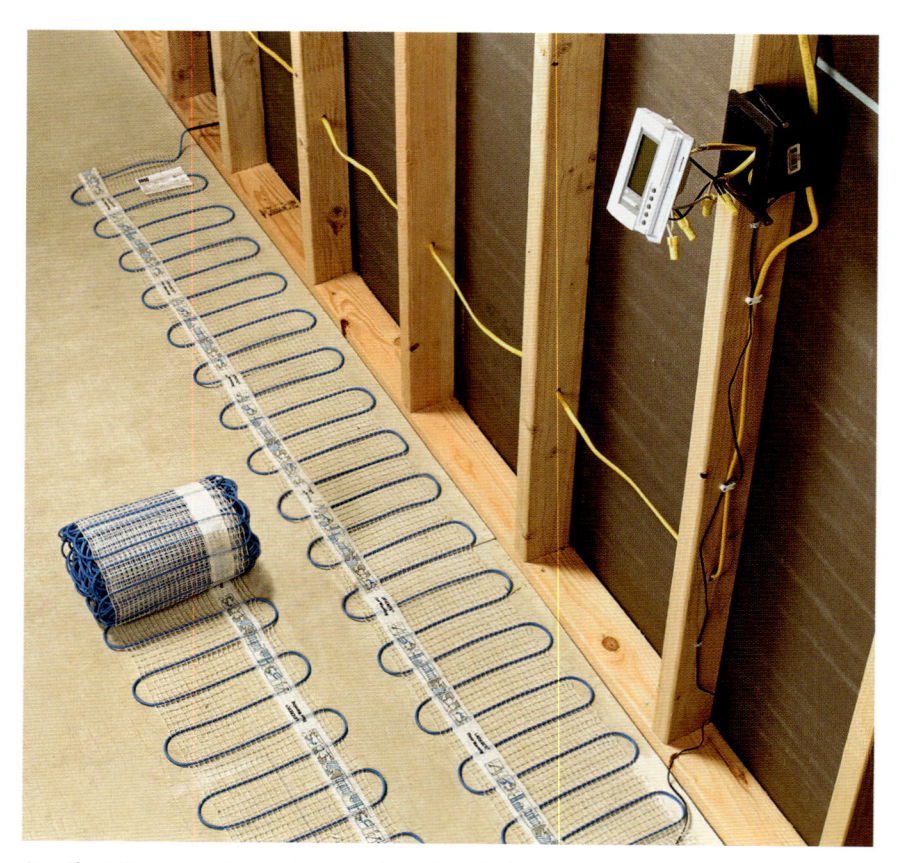

A radiant floor-warming system employs electric heating mats that are covered with floor tile to create a floor that's cozy underfoot.

Thermostat

Timer

Dedicated circuit cable

Thermostat sensor wire

Electrical conduit

Power leads

Heating mats

Floor tile

Thinset mortar

Heating mat

Concrete or cementboard underlayment

A floor-warming system requires a dedicated GFCI circuit to power and control its heating mats, thermostat, and timer.

- Each radiant mat must have a direct connection to the power lead from the thermostat, with the connection made in a junction box in the wall cavity. Do not install mats in series.

- Do not install radiant floor mats under shower areas.

- Do not overlap mats or let them touch.

- Do not cut heating wire or damage heating wire insulation.

- The distance between wires in adjoining mats should equal the distance between wire loops measured center to center.

Installing a Radiant Floor-Warming System

Floor-warming systems must be installed on a circuit with adequate amperage and a GFCI breaker. Smaller systems may tie into an existing circuit, but larger ones need a dedicated circuit. Follow local building and electrical codes that apply to your project.

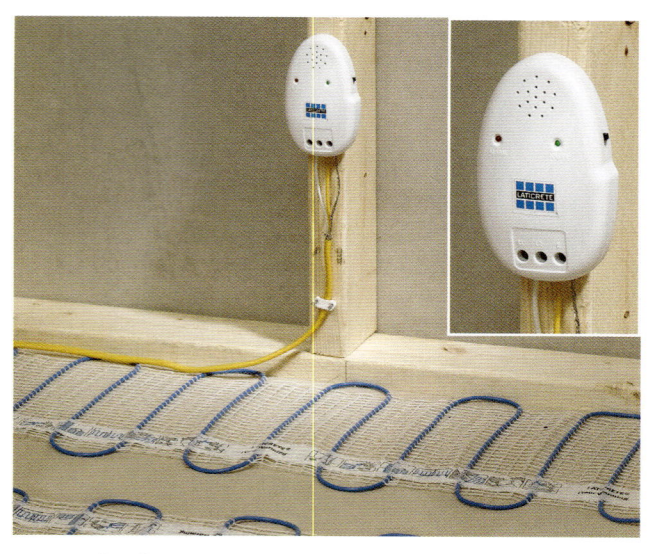

An electric wire fault indicator monitors each floor mat for continuity during the installation process. If there is a break in continuity (for example, if a wire is cut), an alarm sounds. If you choose not to use an indicator tool to monitor the mat, test for continuity frequently using a multimeter.

How to Install a Radiant Floor-Warming System

(1)

Install electrical boxes to house the thermostat and timer. In most cases, the box should be located 60" above floor level. Use a 4"-deep × 4"-wide double-gang box for the thermostat/timer control if your kit has an integral model. If your timer and thermostat are separate, install a separate single box for the timer.

(2)

Drill access holes in the sole plate for the power leads that are preattached to the mats (they should be over 10 ft. long). The leads should be connected to a supply wire from the thermostat in a junction box located in a wall near the floor and below the thermostat box. The access hole for each mat should be located directly beneath the knockout for that cable in the thermostat box. Drill through the sill plate vertically and horizontally so the holes meet in an L-shape.

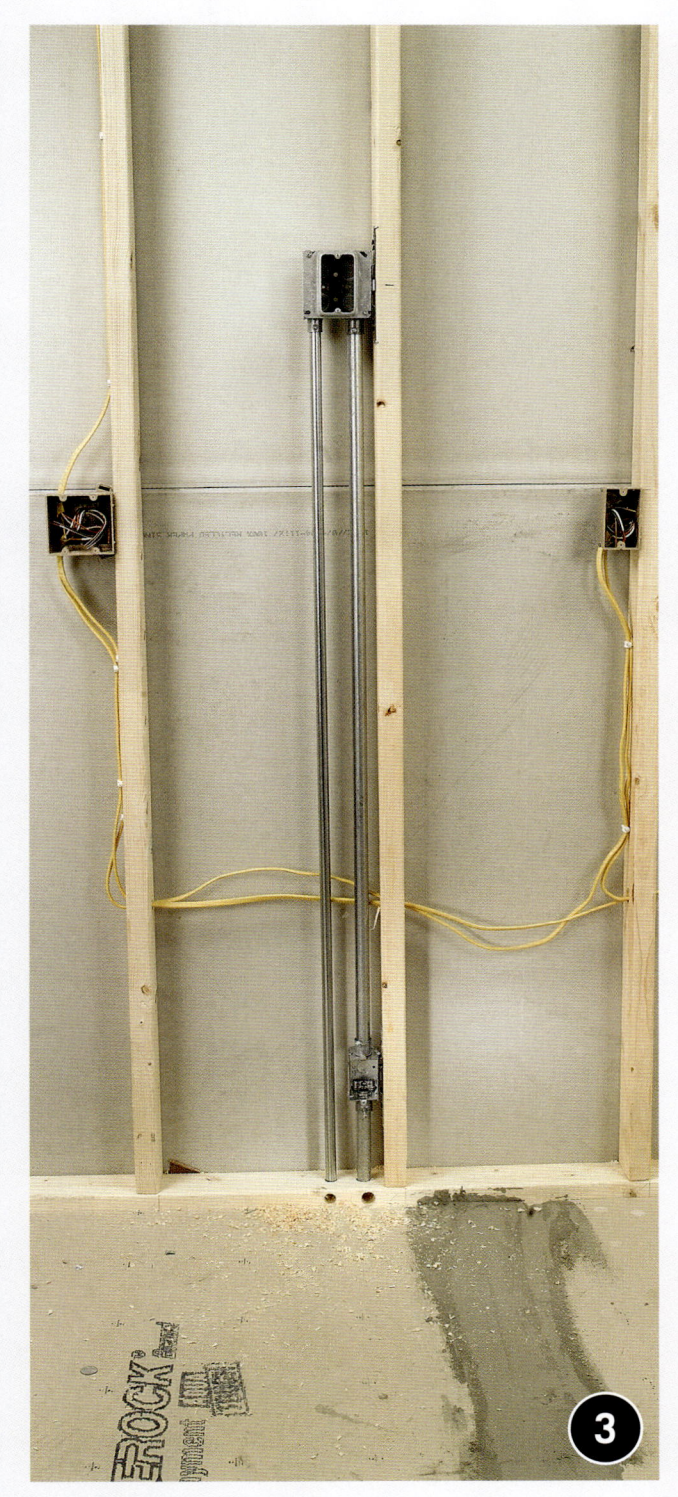

Clean the floor surface thoroughly to get rid of any debris that could potentially damage the wire mats. A vacuum cleaner generally does a more effective job than a broom.

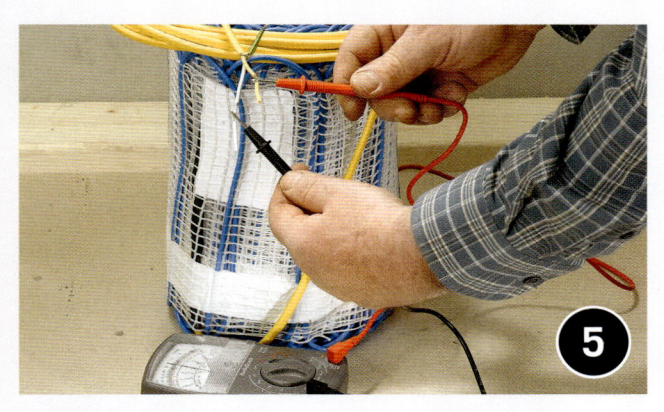

Test for resistance using a multimeter set to measure ohms. This is a test you should make frequently during the installation, along with checking for continuity. If the resistance is off by more than 10% from the theoretical resistance listing (see manufacturer's chart in installation instructions), contact a technical support operator for the kit manufacturer. For example, the theoretical resistance for the 1 × 50 ft. mat seen here is 19, so the ohms reading should be between 17 and 21.

Finalize your mat layout plan. Most radiant floor warming mat manufacturers will provide a layout plan for you at the time of purchase, or they will give you access to an online design tool so you can come up with your own plan. This is an important step to the success of your project, and the assistance is free.   *(continued)*

Run conduit from the electrical boxes to the sill plate. The line for the supply cable should be ¾" conduit. If you are installing multiple mats, the supply conduit should feed into a junction box about 6" above the sill plate and then continue into the ¾" hole you drilled for the supply leads. The sensor wire needs only ½" conduit that runs straight from the thermostat box via the thermostat. Unless you are tapping into an existing circuit, the mats should be powered by a dedicated 20-amp GFCI circuit of 12/2 NM cable run from your main service panel to the electrical box (this is for 120-volt mats—check your instruction manual for specific circuit recommendations).

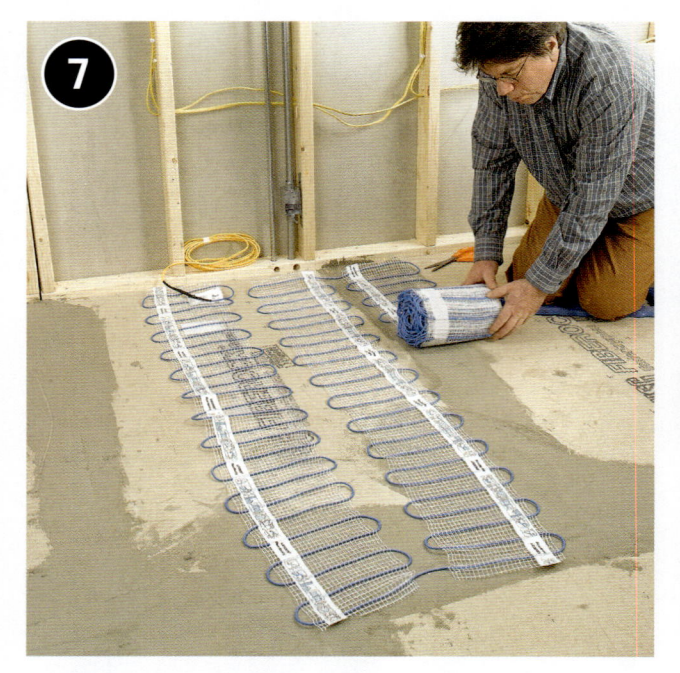

7

8

Unroll the radiant mat or mats and allow them to settle. Arrange the mat or mats according to the plan you created. It's okay to cut the plastic mesh so you can make curves or switchbacks, but do not cut the heating wire under any circumstances, even to shorten it.

Finalize the mat layout, and then test the resistance again using a multimeter. Also check for continuity in several different spots. If there is a problem with any of the mats, you should identify it and correct it before proceeding with the mortar installation.

9

Run the thermostat sensor wire from the electrical box down the ½" conduit raceway and out the access hole in the sill plate. Select the best location for the thermostat sensor, and mark the location onto the flooring. Also mark the locations of the wires that connect to and lead from the sensor.

VARIATION: If your local codes require it, roll the mats out of the way, and cut a channel for the sensor and the sensor wires into the floor or floor underlayment. For most floor materials, a spiral cutting tool does a quick and neat job of this task. Remove any debris.

Bond the mats to the floor. If the mats in your system have adhesive strips, peel off the adhesive backing and roll out the mats in the correct position, pressing them against the floor to set the adhesive. If your mats have no adhesive, bind them with strips of double-sided carpet tape. The thermostat sensor and the power supply leads should be attached with hot glue (inset photo) and run up into their respective holes in the sill plate if you have not done this already. Test all mats for resistance and continuity.

Cover the floor installation areas with a layer of thinset mortar that is thick enough to fully encapsulate all the wires and mats (usually around ¼" in thickness). Check the wires for continuity and resistance regularly, and stop working immediately if there is a drop in resistance or a failure of continuity. Allow the mortar to dry overnight.

Connect the power supply leads from the mat or mats to the NM cable coming from the thermostat inside the junction box near the sill. Power must be turned off. The power leads should be cut so about 8" of wire feeds into the box. Be sure to use cable clamps to protect the wires.

Connect the sensor wire and the power supply lead (from the junction box) to the thermostat/timer according to the manufacturer's directions. Attach the device to the electrical box, restore power, and test the system to make sure it works. Once you are convinced that it is operating properly, install floor tiles and repair the wall surfaces.

Note: Enclose the junction box with a blank cover. Do not cover it with drywall; it must remain accessible.

Ceiling Fans

Ceiling fans are installed and wired like ceiling fixtures. They always require heavy-duty bracing and electrical boxes rated for ceiling fans.

Most standard ceiling fans work with a wall switch functioning as master power for the unit. Pull chains attached to the unit control the fan and lights. In these installations, it's fairly simple to replace an existing ceiling fixture with a fan and light.

If you will be installing a new circuit for the fan, use three-wire cable so both the light and the motor can be controlled by wall switches (see circuit maps 30 and 31, page 165).

Because ceiling fans generally weigh more than ceiling lights and the motion of the blade creates more stress, it is very important that the ceiling box is securely mounted and is rated for ceiling fans. Ceiling boxes rated for ceiling fans are marked with the phrase "For ceiling fan support." If your existing ceiling box is not fan-rated, replace it with one that is. And be sure to inspect the manner in which the box is mounted to make sure it is strong enough.

Installation varies from fan to fan, so be sure to follow the manufacturer's instructions.

A ceiling fan helps keep living spaces cooler in the summer and warmer in the winter. Replacing an overhead light with a fan/light is an easy project with big payback.

Ceiling Fan Types

Bracket-mounted ceiling fans are hung directly from a mounting bracket that is attached to the ceiling box. A canopy conceals the motor and the connections.

Labels: Mounting bracket, Canopy, Motor, Fan blades, Pull chain, Switch housing, Bottom cap

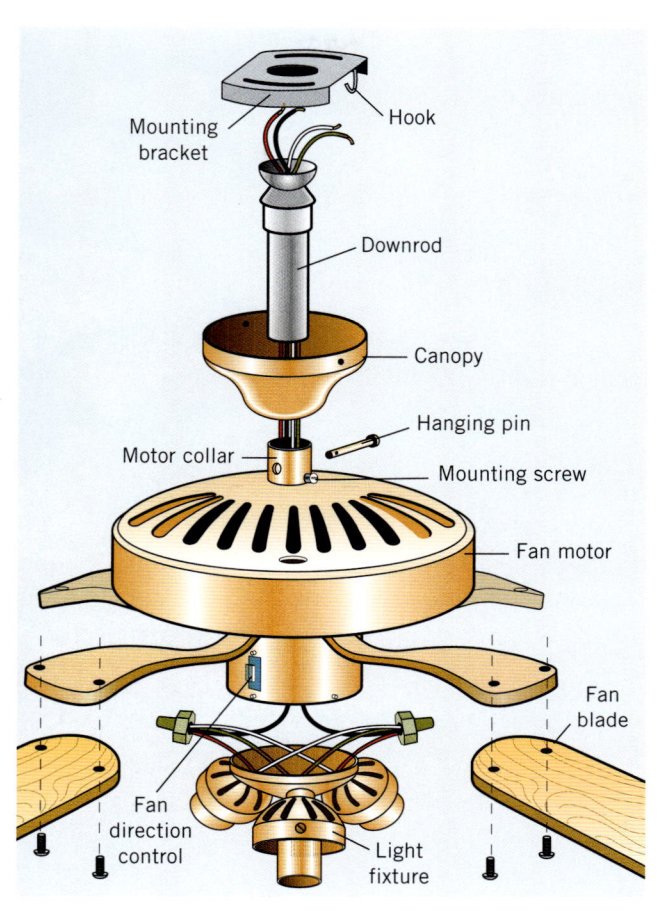

Downrod mounted ceiling fans are supported by a metal rod that's hung from the ceiling mounting bracket. The length of the rod determines the height of the fan. Downrod fans are used in rooms with ceilings 8 ft. high or higher. You may need to buy a longer downrod if you have a very high ceiling.

Labels: Mounting bracket, Hook, Downrod, Canopy, Hanging pin, Motor collar, Mounting screw, Fan motor, Fan blade, Fan direction control, Light fixture

FANS THAT HEAT

The first generation of ceiling fans did one job: they spun and moved air. As the technology advanced, light kits were added to replace the light source that is lost when a fan-only appliance is installed. Now, some ceiling fans are manufactured with electric heating elements that can produce up to 5,000 BTU of heat, comparable to a small space heater. Located in the fan canopy, the ceramic heat elements direct heat out the vents and force it down to the living area in the room, along with the heated air that naturally rises.

Fan-mounted heaters are relatively light duty, so they generally do not require a dedicated circuit. In most cases, you can supply power to the heater/fan with any 15-amp room light circuit that has extra capacity.

Supporting Ceiling Boxes

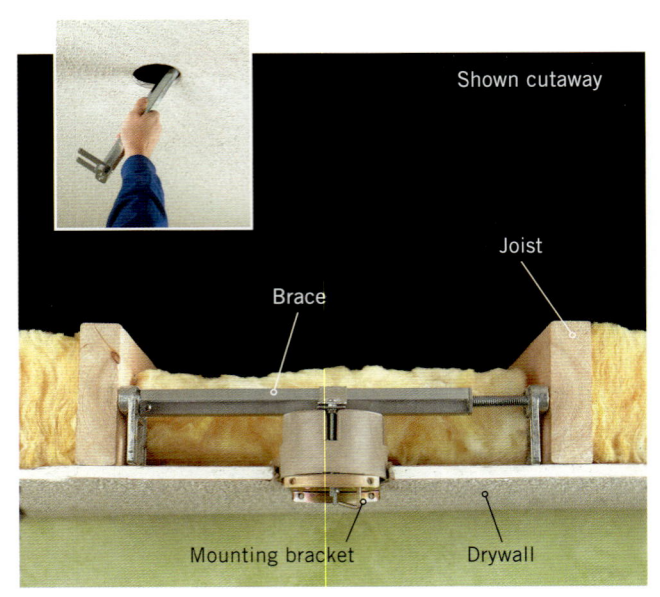

Add a wood brace above the ceiling box if you have access from above (as in an attic). Cut a 2 × 4 or deeper brace to fit and fasten it between the ceiling joists. Drive several deck screws through the ceiling box and into the brace. If the box is not fan rated, replace it with one that is.

Install an adjustable fan brace if the ceiling is closed and you don't want to remove the drywall. Remove the old light and the electrical box, and then insert the fan brace into the box opening (inset photo). Twist the brace housing to cause it to telescope outward. The brace should be centered over the opening and at the right height so the ceiling box is flush with the ceiling surface once it is hung from the brace.

Bracket-Mounted Fans

Direct-mount fan units have a motor housing with a mounting tab that fits directly into a slot on the mounting bracket. Fans with this mounting approach are secure and easy to install but difficult to adjust.

Ball-and-socket fan units have a downrod, but instead of threading into the mounting bracket, the downrod has an attached ball that fits into a hanger "socket" in the mounting bracket. This installation allows the fan to move in the socket and find its own level for quiet operation.

How to Install Downrod Ceiling Fans

Shut off the power to the circuit at the panel. Unscrew the existing fixture and carefully pull it away from the ceiling. Test for power with a voltage tester to confirm the power is off. Disconnect and remove the old fixture.

Canopy

Rod hanger pipe

Run the wires from the top of the fan motor through the canopy and then through the rod hanger pipe. Slide the rod hanger pipe through the canopy and attach the pipe to the motor collar using the included hanging pin. Tighten the mounting screws firmly.

Hanging pin

Hang the motor assembly by the hook on the mounting bracket. Connect the wires according to manufacturer's directions, using wire connectors to join the fixture wires to the circuit wires in the box. Gather the wires together and tuck them inside the fan canopy. Lift the canopy and attach it to the mounting bracket.

Light kit housing

Attach the fan blades with the included hardware. Connect the wiring for the fan's light fixture according to the manufacturer's directions. Tuck all wires into the switch housing, and attach the fixture. Install lightbulbs. Restore power and test the fan.

Remote-Control Ceiling Fan Retrofit

Ceiling fan remote control switches offer an easy way of controlling both the lighting and fan function of your ceiling fan. They are commonly used when there are only a hot and neutral at the fan location or where the ability to switch two different functions is not present in the wiring.

The remote can save you the need to install another switch and/or the need to pull another wire to your ceiling fan. Many different remotes on the market can be used with different manufacturer ceiling fans, so you are not limited to the brand of fan you are using.

TOOLS + MATERIALS

Ceiling fan remote kit	Screwdrivers	Needlenose pliers	Voltage tester
Wire connectors	Pliers	Wire strippers	Eye protection

A retrofit remote control kit lets you take the hassle (and the pull chains) out of operating just about any ceiling fan and light.

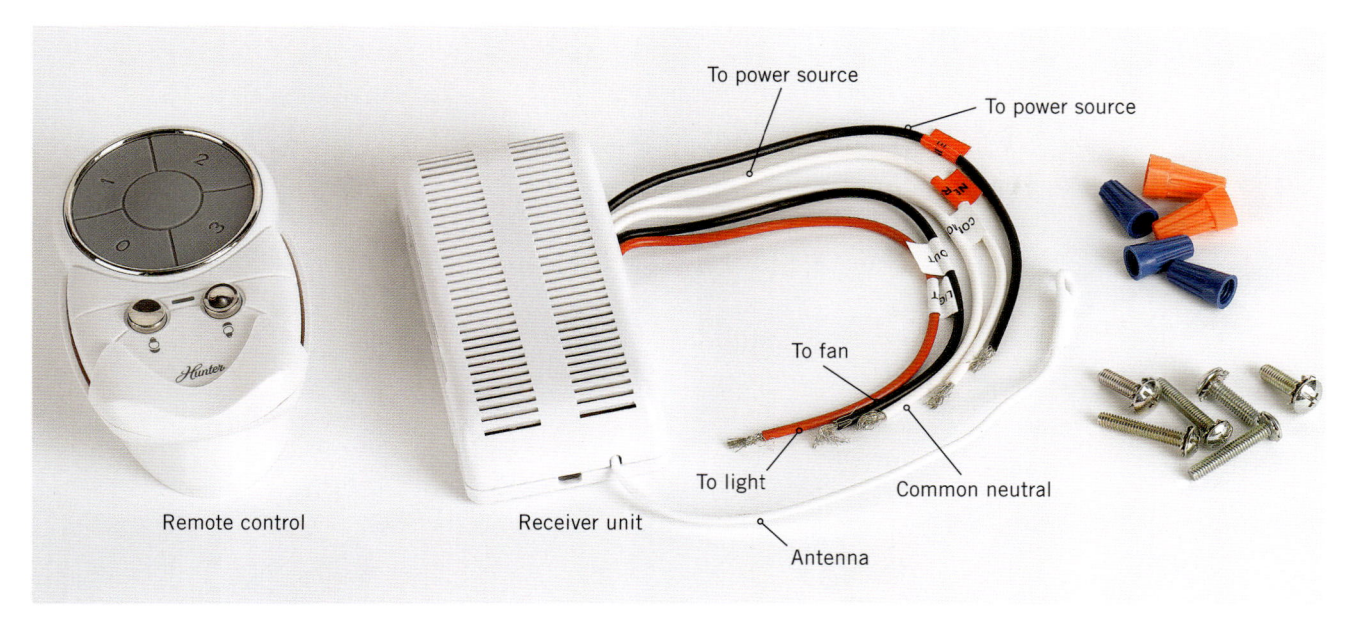

Parts of an aftermarket remote control kit for a ceiling fan usually include the remote control unit (some come with a cradle) and the receiver unit. Your unit may come with color-coded wire connectors and mounting hardware as well.

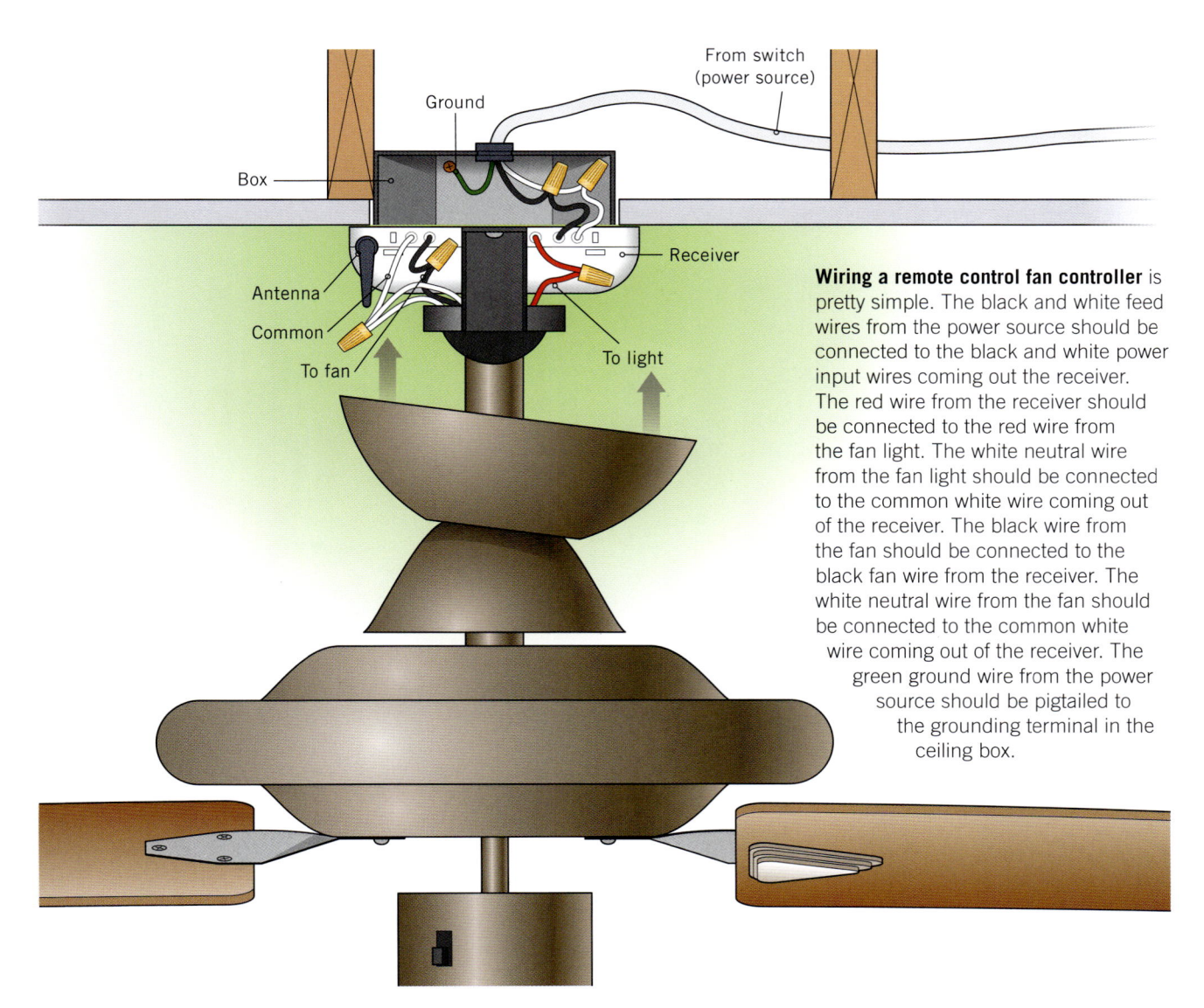

Wiring a remote control fan controller is pretty simple. The black and white feed wires from the power source should be connected to the black and white power input wires coming out the receiver. The red wire from the receiver should be connected to the red wire from the fan light. The white neutral wire from the fan light should be connected to the common white wire coming out of the receiver. The black wire from the fan should be connected to the black fan wire from the receiver. The white neutral wire from the fan should be connected to the common white wire coming out of the receiver. The green ground wire from the power source should be pigtailed to the grounding terminal in the ceiling box.

How to Retrofit a Remote Control to a Ceiling Fan

Turn your fan on high speed and turn the lights on. Then, at the electrical panel, shut off the power to the circuit that supplies your ceiling fan.

Remove the fan blades, one at a time on opposite sides of one another, so as to not overweight a certain side, which could bend the shaft and create a wobble. There are generally two vertically installed Phillips head #10 screws that hold the blade bracket to the motor housing.

If a light kit was installed on the fan, remove it as well. First, remove the bulbs and any glass diffusers, and then remove the light kit itself. Usually you'll find three horizontally installed #6 Phillips head screws attached to the pan directly below the motor housing. Unplug the light kit from the fan wires and set aside.

If your fan has a downrod between the motor housing and the ceiling, remove the canopy on the top of the pipe connected to the mounting plate on the ceiling. You should find two to four horizontally installed #6 screws near the base of the canopy. Remove the screws, and slide the canopy down to expose the wiring.

Check all wires with a voltage tester to verify there is no power present.

Disconnect the black, red or blue, and white wires from the electrical box wires.

Install the receiving unit of the remote fan kit. Connect the black and white wires from the receiving unit input to the black and the white wires coming from the electrical box in the ceiling. If a red wire was used originally to feed the light portion of the fan, cap this wire with a wire nut and fold it into the box.

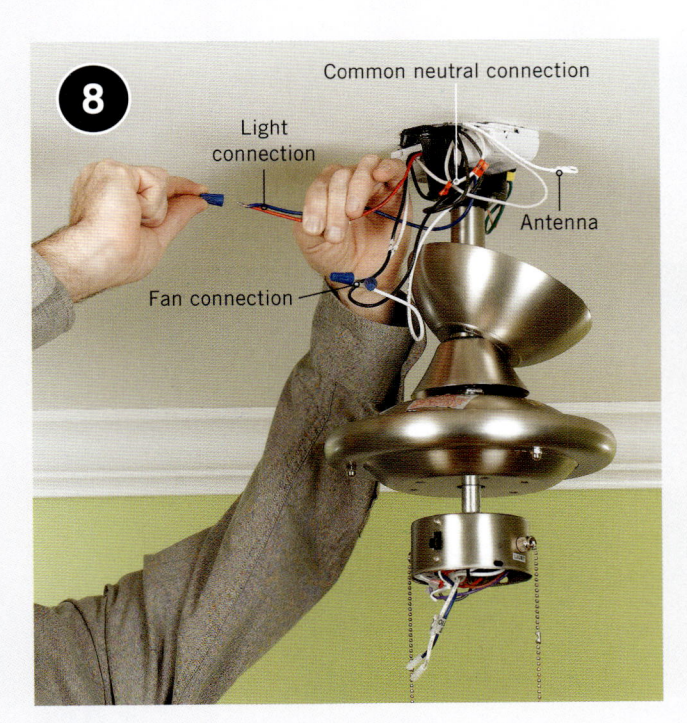

Common neutral connection

Light connection

Antenna

Fan connection

Connect the output of the receiving unit to the fan's associated wiring: black wire to black wire, white wire to white wire, and blue wire to blue wire (or red to red, or red to blue). If a downrod was used to hang the fan, place the receiving unit above the ball and flange portion of the mounting bracket.

Reinstall the canopy, fan blades, and light kit. Restore power. Install the batteries into the remote control sending unit, and test to make sure the fan is spinning on all three modes: Low, Medium, and High. Test the light switch to verify the light switch works as well. Disconnect and remove the pullchains.

Bathroom Exhaust Fans

Most exhaust fans are installed in the center of the bathroom ceiling or over the toilet area. A fan installed over the tub or shower area must be rated for use in wet areas. You can usually wire a fan that just has a light fixture into a main bathroom lighting circuit (but not into a dedicated bathroom receptacle circuit). Units with built-in heat lamps or blowers require separate circuits. Extending a branch circuit or adding a new branch to install new receptacles, lights, switches, or equipment requires a permit. Check with the electrical inspector before starting such projects.

If the fan you choose doesn't come with a mounting kit, purchase one separately. A mounting kit should include an exhaust hose (duct), a vent tailpiece, and an exterior terminal.

Three common places to terminate the exhaust are the roof, a soffit, or a sidewall. The instructions in this book are for a shingle roof covering. You should have a roofer install the exhaust termination if you have any other roofing material or if you are not comfortable walking on your roof.

A soffit exhaust involves routing the duct to a soffit (roof overhang) where it is connected to a terminal that directs the exhaust outside. While soffit exhausts are allowed, they are not recommended, because the moisture can be drawn back into the attic through the soffit vents. Check with the exhaust fan manufacturer for instructions about how to run and terminate the exhaust duct and to determine the required duct diameter and maximum length.

To prevent moisture damage, always terminate the exhaust duct outside your home—never into your attic.

Fan rating (cubic ft. per minute)

Sone rating

Check the information label attached to each exhaust fan unit. The minimum rating is 50 CFM; larger baths may need up to 100 CFM. The sone rating refers to quietness rated on a scale of 1 to 7; lower is quieter.

TOOLS + MATERIALS

Drill	NM cable (14/2, 14/3)
Jigsaw	Cable clamp
Combination tool	Hose clamps
Screwdrivers	Pipe insulation
Caulk gun	Roofing cement
Reciprocating saw	Self-sealing roofing nails
Pry bar	Shingles
Screws	Wire connectors
Double-gang retrofit electrical box	Switch and timer
	Eye protection

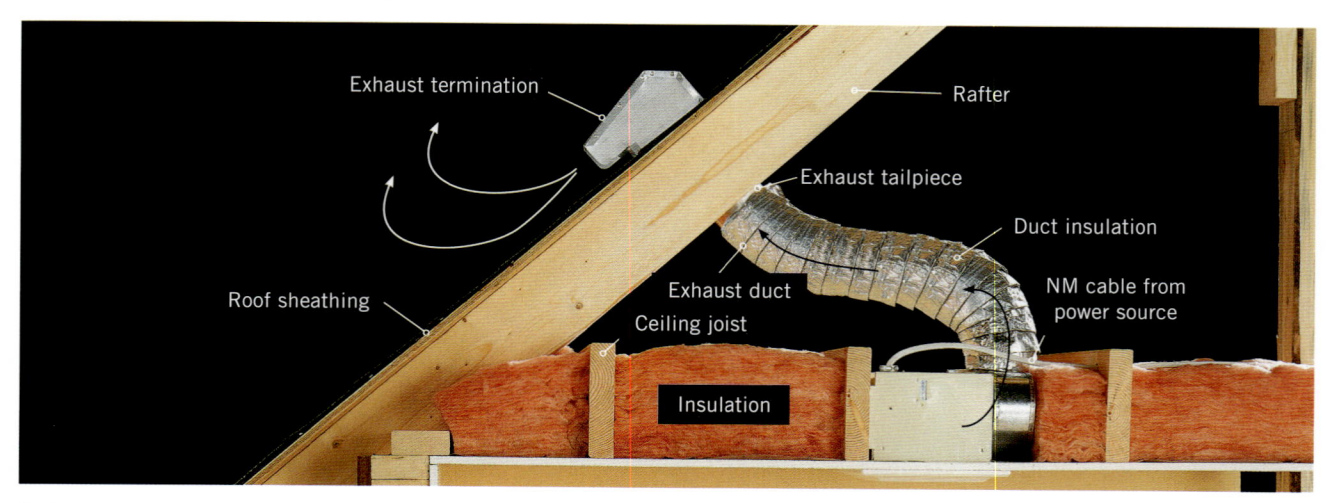

Bathroom exhaust fans must be exhausted to the outdoors, either through the roof or a wall. Three-inch-diameter flexible duct is not allowed for bathroom exhaust fans. Four-inch-diameter flexible duct is allowed for up to 56 feet without bends for 50 CFM fans. Use fan manufacturer's installation instructions for duct type and length. Use insulated duct in cold climates to reduce moisture damage from condensation on the duct.

How to Install a Bathroom Exhaust Fan

1

Position the fan unit against a ceiling joist. Outline the fan onto the ceiling surface. Remove the unit, drill pilot holes at the corners of the outline, and cut out the area with a jigsaw or drywall saw.

2

Remove the grille from the fan unit, and then position the unit against the joist with the edge recessed ¼" from the finished surface of the ceiling (so the grille can be flush mounted). Attach the unit to the joist using drywall screws.

VARIATION: For fans with heaters or light fixtures, some manufacturers recommend using 2× lumber to build dams between the ceiling joists to keep the insulation at least 6" away from the fan unit.

3

Switch box location

Mark and cut an opening for a double-gang box on the wall next to the latch side of the bathroom door, and then run a 14/3 NM cable from the switch cutout to the fan unit. Run a 14/2 NM cable from the power source to the cutout.

4

Strip 10" of sheathing from the ends of the cables, and then feed the cables into a double-gang retrofit switch box so at least ½" of sheathing extends into the box. Clamp the cables in place. Tighten the mounting screws until the box is secure.

5

Strip 10" of sheathing from the end of the cable at the unit, and then attach a cable clamp to the cable. Insert the cable into the fan unit. From the inside of the unit, screw a locknut onto the threaded end of the clamp.

(continued)

Exhaust termination flange

Exhaust tailpiece

Mark the exit location in the roof next to a rafter for the exhaust duct. Drill a pilot hole, and then saw through the sheathing and roofing material with a reciprocating saw to make the cutout for the exhaust tailpiece.

Remove a section of shingles from around the cutout, leaving the roofing paper intact. Remove enough shingles to create an exposed area that is at least the size of the exhaust termination flange.

Attach a hose clamp to the rafter next to the roof cutout about 1" below the roof sheathing (top). Insert the exhaust tailpiece into the cutout and through the hose clamp, and then tighten the clamp screw (bottom).

Slide one end of the exhaust duct over the tailpiece, and slide the other end over the outlet on the fan unit. Slip hose clamps or straps around each end of the duct, and tighten the clamps. Wrap the exhaust duct with pipe insulation. Insulation prevents moist air inside the duct from condensing and dripping down into the fan motor.

Apply roofing cement to the bottom of the exhaust termination flange, and then slide the termination over the tailpiece. Nail the termination flange in place with self-sealing roofing nails, and then patch in shingles around the cover.

(11)

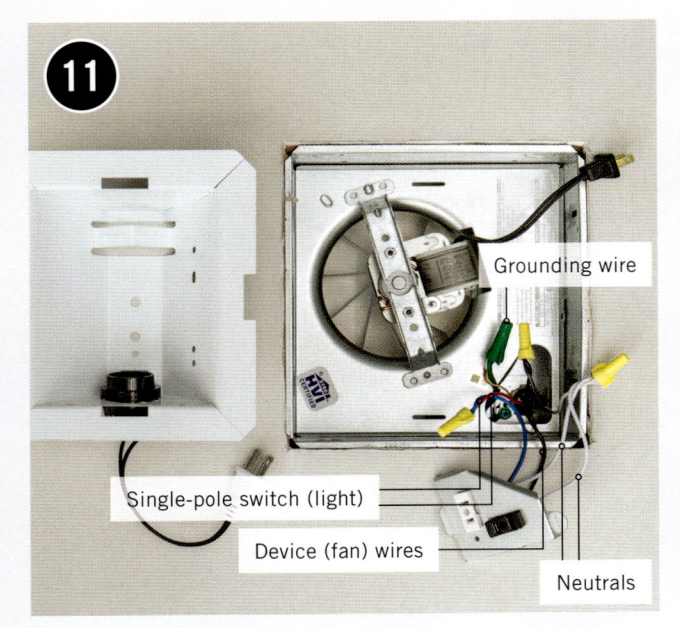

Grounding wire

Single-pole switch (light)

Device (fan) wires

Neutrals

Turn power off and test for power. Make the following wire connections at the fan unit: the black circuit wire from the timer to the wire lead for the fan motor; the red circuit wire from the single-pole switch (see step 14) to the wire lead for the light fixture in the unit; the white neutral circuit wire to the neutral wire lead; the circuit grounding wire to the grounding lead on the fan unit. Make all connections with wire connectors. Attach the cover plate over the unit when the wiring is completed.

(12)

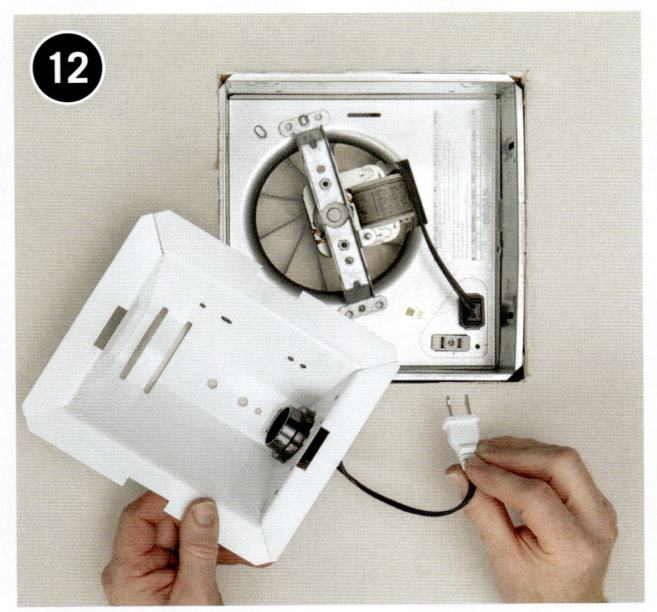

Connect the light plug to the built-in receptacle on the wire connection box. Attach the fan grille to the frame using the mounting clips included with the fan kit.

NOTE: If you removed the wall and ceiling surfaces for the installation, install new surfaces before completing this step.

(13)

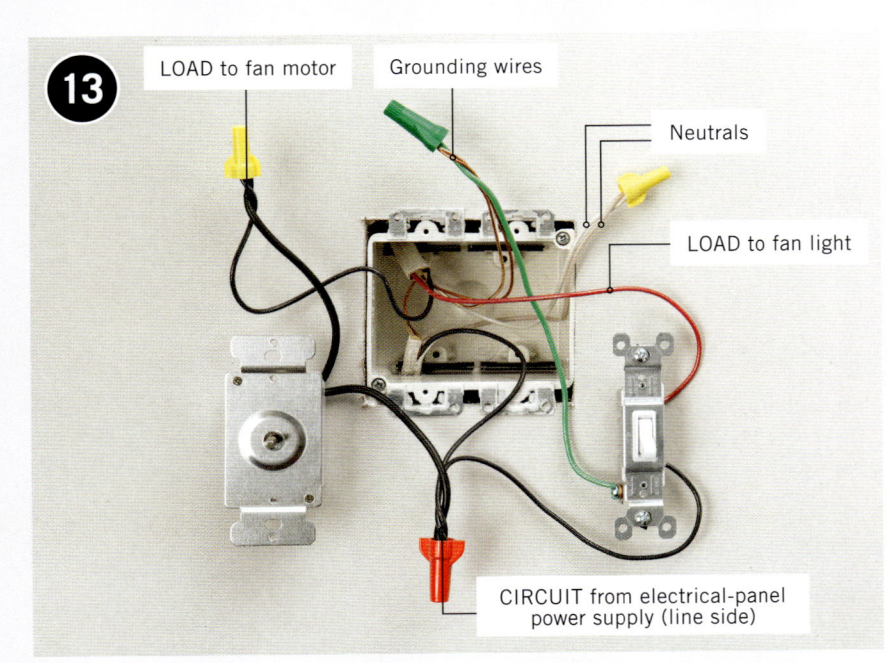

LOAD to fan motor

Grounding wires

Neutrals

LOAD to fan light

CIRCUIT from electrical-panel power supply (line side)

Test that the power to the switch circuit is off. At the switch box, add black pigtail wires to one screw terminal on the timer and to one screw terminal on the single-pole switch; add a green grounding pigtail to the groundling screw on the switch. Make the following wire connections: the black circuit wire from the power source to the black pigtail wires; the black circuit wire from the exhaust fan to the remaining screw on the timer; the red circuit wire from the exhaust fan to the remaining screw on the switch. Join the white wires with a wire connector. Join the grounding wires with a green wire connector.

(14)

Tuck the wires into the switch box, and then attach the switch and timer to the box. Attach the cover plate and timer dial. Turn on the power and test the fan.

Installing + Using a Whole-House Fan

As weather patterns change across the country, many areas that once saw mild summers now experience blistering heat for much of the season. Homeowners in other regions who once needed to open the windows only at night and close them during the day to stay cool, now have to find other means of keep their interior spaces from overheating.

Installing a new air-conditioning system, whether it's room-by-room minisplit units or more comprehensive central air, is out of the range of many homeowner budgets. Not only are those options exceptionally expensive to buy and install, they will also increase your seasonal utility costs significantly—sometimes doubling them in the summer, especially if it stays hot overnight or your home is not particularly well insulated.

They are also not feasible DIY projects for most people. And it doesn't stop with installation. Air conditioning compressors and filters require regular maintenance. Let that upkeep slip through the cracks and you face the threat of mold or other contaminants that can diminish indoor air quality and exacerbate allergies, asthma, and lung conditions.

All that is why a whole-house fan is a better answer for many homeowners. This basic technology uses simple airflow science to cool a home quickly and efficiently. When turned on, the fan draws cooler, cleaner outside air in through open windows, drawing warm stale indoor air up through the fan and exhausting it out of attic vents.

Americans have a long history of using whole-house fans, which were once noisy, single speed units that could easily be burned out if the homeowner closed the windows without shutting off the fan.

Today's whole-house fans are significantly quieter. Many, like the one in this project, are fabricated with a ceiling unit that is ducted to the actual fan placed higher up in the attic. Models like this can be amazingly quiet, often more so than even a modern bathroom exhaust fan. That's a big plus for any homeowner who is a light sleeper.

 **CRUCIAL CFM**

Ideally, a whole-house fan should replace the entire volume of air in the home every one to two minutes. This is key to buying the correct size and setting it up for success. You'll need to know the CFM that is right for you home and the total size of attic vent exposure that fan requires. Start with the CFM calculation:

Mountains/Coast = 2 × square footage of house
Inland Valley/Plain = 2.5 × square footage of house
Desert = 3 × square footage of house

* Increase size slightly if your ceilings are higher than 8 ft.

The critical factor is correct air movement in the attic will be the "net free vent area" (NVGA). The rule of thumb is 1 square foot of net free area for every 750 CFM of fan capacity. So, for instance, a 3,000 CFM fan requires attic vent area totaling 4 square feet. The attic vents can be gable, roof, soffit or ridge.

The calculation must account for the vent covering, such as screening or louvers. Here is the formula for calculating the feet of NFVA for the fan shown in this project.

Individual vent size: (L x W / 144) × .75 = Square feet of net free vent area
For a 24" × 24" vent: (24 x 24 / 144) × .75 = 3 square feet (or 432 square inches)

The formula for ridge vents is 13 percent of total length.
For a 12-foot vent ridge: 12 × .13 = 18.7 inches NFVA

Add up the numbers for all your attic vents and that's your total net free vent area.

Note: Different manufacturers use different formulas. Use your manufacturer's formula but double-check with the local building department to ensure your calculations and existing vents comply with local code.

As wonderful as they can be, whole-house fans are not appropriate for every location. They will be far less effective in areas that experience little cooling overnight or persistently high humidity, which impedes the cooling effect of this technology.

The fans are sized by the space they're meant to cool, rated in cubic feet per minute (CFM) of air they move. Some manufacturers also offer "zone" systems with fans installed in multiple rooms, allowing those spaces to be cooled individually.

If your vent area is inadequate for the size of whole-house fan you buy, you will need to install larger or more attic vents.

Wise Wiring

Wiring a new whole-house fan is fairly straightforward, but should always be focused on safety. The worst-case scenario is that windows are unintentionally left shut while the fan is running, overheating the motor and creating a fire danger. Many modern fans have an auto-shutoff feature for this situation, and most include a timer that is likely to help you prevent it. But suffice it to say, proper wiring is key to both fan performance and fire safety.

Leveraging the Technology

Getting the most from a new whole-house fan means using it correctly to exploit the science behind it. Although most homeowners simply open all the windows in the house and turn the fan on in the evening as the outside temperature begins to fall, experts recommend a more measured approach.

1. After sunset, when the outside air begins to cool, open the windows and turn on the fan to high.
2. When you go to bed, close the windows, except for the bedrooms (leave bedroom doors wide open).
3. If you're an early riser, get up and open the rest of the windows in the house.
4. Mid-morning, as the outside air begins to heat up, turn off the fan and close all the windows. It's wise to also close drapes or blinds on the southern and eastern sides of the house, or use awnings to cover the windows with those exposures.

TOOLS + MATERIALS

Whole-house fan kit	Flashlight (optional)
Carpenter's pencil	Drywall saw
Power drill and bits	Stepladder
Socket bit	Wire stripper tool
Tape measure	Cable ripper or utility knife
Large standard screwdriver	Wire nuts
Phillips screwdriver	Copper wire
Work gloves	3-wire Romex cable

Safety and Efficiency

Be aware that if the windows are not open, the fan can create a backdraft that extinguishes pilot lights and pulls carbon monoxide into the living space.

If the fan does not have a tight-fitting cover for the ceiling opening or attic side of the fan, you should buy or fabricate one. It's essential to stop heated air from leaking out during the winter. The cover must be operable or removable. Many modern fans come equipped with their own tight-sealing cover doors or shutters (including the one used in the project shown here).

How to Install a Whole-House Fan

Check with the local building department to determine what local codes apply to whole-house fan installation. Check the manufacturer's specifications for minimum attic ventilation area and add or increase vents as necessary. Unbox the fan. Check that all equipment and hardware are included and intact. Test that the fan blade spins freely.

Choose the fan location (ideally near the center of the home; there must be at least 30" of unobstructed space above the opening, to hang the fan). Use the supplied template to check on the attic side that the damper will sit between framing members. Use the template to drill tiny pilot holes at the corners of the opening. Return to the room and align the template with the holes. Use a carpenter's pencil to mark the fan hole outline on the ceiling.

Drill a starter hole in one corner of the outline and use a keyhole saw to cut the installation hole in the ceiling. Move the fan, motor housing, damper, and duct into the attic. Either move them through the attic access or disassemble them and pass them through the ceiling hole.

For 24"-on-center joists, use a large standard screwdriver to remove one of the damper box flanges (on the side that will butt the ceiling joist). If the joists are 16" on center, remove both damper box flanges.

Position the damper box over the hole, making sure to orient it correctly if you've only removed one flange (for a 24" on center mounting, as shown in this project). Fasten the rafter side directly to the rafter (left) and attach the flange side by driving the supplied screws through the ceiling into the flange (right). Screw the grill frame to the ceiling to cover the damper hole.

Position the motor head mounting strap locations on the rafter closest to the ceiling hole. Mark the mounting holes and drive the screws halfway in. Hang the motor head straps from the screws and tighten the screws down. The motor head electrical box must be on top of the head as mounted.

Note: The motor head must be 3 to 6 ft. above the damper; if there is no rafter close enough, you may have to install a cross brace over the ceiling damper hole.

Screw the opposite end of the duct to the top of the damper housing. Secure the duct into a gentle curve using the nylon support strap supplied.

How to Wire a Whole-House Fan

WIRING DIAGRAM FOR WALL SWITCH BOX

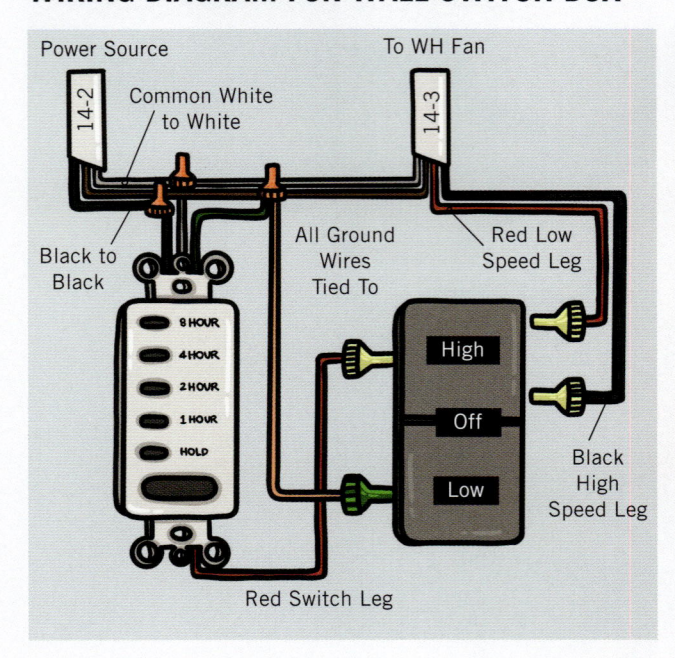

Power Source

To WH Fan

14-2

14-3

Common White to White

Black to Black

All Ground Wires Tied To

Red Low Speed Leg

8 HOUR
4 HOUR
2 HOUR
1 HOUR
HOLD

High

Off

Low

Black High Speed Leg

Red Switch Leg

1

Remove the cover from the junction box on the fan head. Remove the wire nut connectors and unfasten the wires. Unscrew the two ground wires from the ground screw, and then refasten the fan motor's ground wire to the ground screw.

2

Pull out the existing power cord (your fan may not have one if it does not have a plug-in option) by pushing out the cable box connector. Slip in the supplied connector clamp and push the end of the cable into the box so that about 10" of cable is on the box side. Use a cable ripper or utility knife to strip the cable.

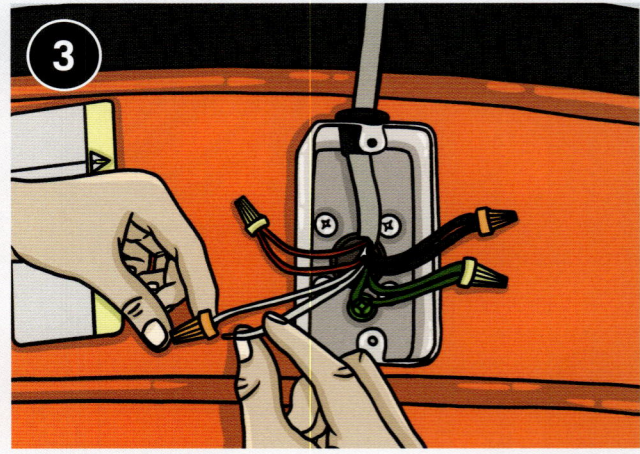

3

Cut the junction box green ground wire in half and strip both cut ends. Use a wire nut to connect both ends of the cut green wire with the cable's bare copper wire. Cut the cable's black, red, and white wires to length and strip the ends. Connect each wire with its like wire from the motor, using wire nuts. Check that the wire nuts are secure and push the wires into the junction box. Fasten the cover in place.

Choose the location for the double gang switch box. It should be on a wall as close as possible to the fan location, in a bay between two studs. The box should be placed 60" from the floor (the same height as a thermostat). Cut the new opening and route the fan junction box 14/3 cable and power source 14/2 cable into the stud cavity and secure them in the box.

Strip the sheathing from the cables. Cut the wires to length and strip the ends. Cut a piece of copper wire to length and join it with the two incoming copper wires and the green wire from the timer, securing them with a wire nut.

Connect the white wires from the cables with the white wire from the timer, using a wire nut. Strip the ends of the black and red wires on the timer. Connect the timer's black wire with the power source black wire, using a wire nut.

Use pliers to bend a loop in the free end of the loose copper wire you connected to the box's copper wires. Attach the loop to the green screw on the switch and tighten it down. Connect the red wire from the timer to the top left screw (above the green) on the switch and tighten it down. Connect the red and black from the fan junction box to the top right and bottom right switch screws respectively. Tighten them down.

Carefully push the wires into the box, and screw the timer and switch in place on the box. Screw the face plate over the timer and switch. Restore power to the circuit and check that each timer setting lights up, and that the fan-speed controls work correctly.

Range Hoods

Range hoods do more than just get rid of cooking odors. Their most important job is to reduce the amount of water vapor in the air that's generated by cooking. The pot of water that boils for 30 minutes creates a lot of water vapor. Usually the results are innocent enough. But prolonged periods of high moisture can lead to mildew and other molds that can possibly make family members sick.

The hardest part of adding a range hood is installing the ductwork between the hood and the outside of your house. Always use galvanized steel, copper, or stainless-steel ducts. Never use flexible duct, including flexible metal duct. If the range is located on an outside wall, the best choice is to run the duct from the back of the hood straight through the wall. If you have wood siding, this job is not difficult. But if you have brick or stone, plan on spending several hours to cut this hole.

If the range is on an interior wall, the preferred route is usually from the top of the hood through the roof. It's also possible to put the duct into the attic, then across the ceiling (between two rafters or trusses) and out through an overhanging soffit. Follow the hood manufacturer's instructions about the size and length of the duct. A duct that is too long or too small will not work well and may be a grease fire hazard.

TOOLS + MATERIALS

Hammer	Range hood
Jigsaw	Galvanized sheet metal ducts and fittings
Screwdrivers	Wire connectors
Drill/driver + bits	Sheet metal screws
Utility knife	Foil tape
Circular saw	Plastic roof cement
Caulk gun	Caulk
Exhaust exterior termination	Eye protection

Consult the local code and manufacturer's installation requirements. You may need to power the hood with a dedicated 20-amp circuit. If your range hood includes a microwave oven, be sure to read the installation instructions, preferably before you buy the microwave. You may need a different cabinet above the range. Inspectors may not approve microwaves that are too close to the range.

Extending a branch circuit, or adding a new branch to install new receptacles, lights, or switches requires a permit. The electrical inspector may require that you install arc-fault protection on the entire circuit. Check with the inspector before starting such projects.

A range hood captures steam and airborne food particles and draws them directly out of your house through an exhaust duct. For slide-in ranges, the hood usually is installed under a short cabinet that contains the ductwork connection.

Range Hoods

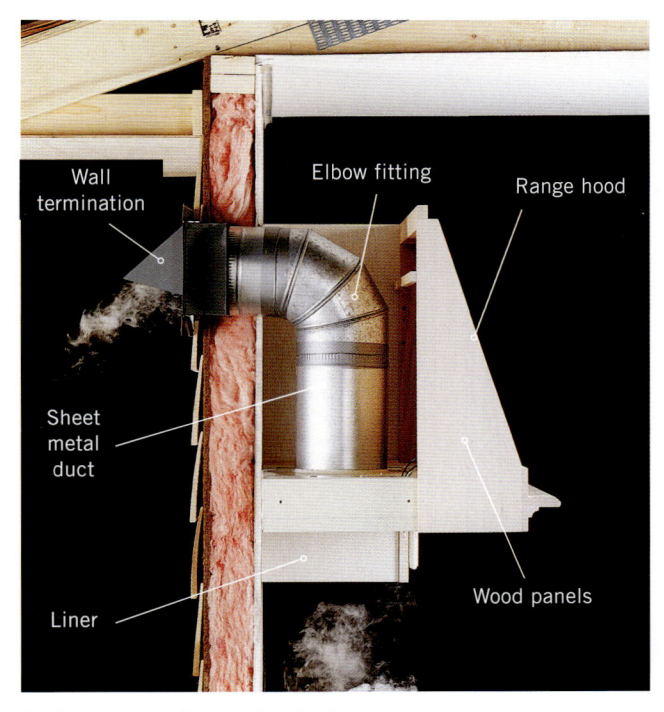

Cabinet-mounted range hoods draw steam upward and out of the house through a wall-mounted or roof-mounted termination.

Labels: Wall termination, Elbow fitting, Range hood, Sheet metal duct, Liner, Wood panels

Wall-mounted range hoods function in the same manner as cabinet mounted, but they are not integrated into the kitchen cabinet system.

Label: Blower unit

Downdraft exhaust pulls steam downward and exhausts it out through a wall exhaust. While leaving the space above the stovetop uncluttered, these exhausts are much less efficient (in large part because steam naturally rises).

Island exhausts hang down from ceiling-mounted ductwork and draw steam and odors up from stovetops that are installed in kitchen islands. They typically have a very contemporary appearance.

How to Install a Range Hood

Install the sheet metal duct in the wall first, and then cut a hole in the back of the range hood cabinet and mount the cabinet over the duct. Cut a hole in the bottom of the cabinet to match the opening on the top of the hood. The range hood often comes with templates to help you cut holes in the right place.

Make sure the circuit power is turned off at the service panel and test for power. Then join the electrical wires to the wires inside the range hood. Use wire connectors for this job.

Get someone to help lift the range hood into place and hold it there while you attach it. Drive two screws through both sides and into the adjacent cabinets. If the hood is slightly small for the opening, slip a shim between the hood and the walls, trying to keep the gaps even.

Run ductwork from the cabinet to the exhaust exit point. Use two 45° adjustable elbows to join the duct in the wall to the top of the range hood. Use sheet metal screws and foil tape to hold all parts together and keep them from moving. Connect the duct securely to the fan outlet, and connect all sections so they do not leak. A leaky connection can allow grease-laden air to collect on the wood and start a fire.

Exhaust Termination Locations

Wall termination: If the duct comes out through the sidewall of the house, install a vertical termination hood. Make sure to seal around the perimeter of the hood with exterior caulk. Don't locate the termination too close to a window, or the fumes will circulate back into the home. Comply with the siding manufacturer's instructions for flashing these wall terminations.

Masonry wall termination: You can run ductwork out through an exterior wall made of brick or stucco, but it is a lot of work. You need to cut an opening in the wall with a masonry saw or chip one with a cold chisel, and then attach the termination hood with masonry nails.

Soffit termination: If the duct goes through an overhang soffit, you'll need a transition fitting to connect the round duct to a short piece of rectangular duct. Once these parts are installed, add a protective grille to keep animals and insects from getting into the duct. Don't locate the termination near a soffit ventilation opening; the fumes and moisture will be drawn back into the attic.

Roof termination: For ducts that pass through the roof, cut an access hole through the roofing and sheathing, and then install a weatherproof cap on top of the duct and under the roofing shingles. Make a waterproof seal by caulking the cap with plastic roof cement. If you don't have much roofing experience, consult a roofing manual for some more information on this step. Have a roofer do this if you have a roof covering other than shingles or if your roof is steep or high.

Backup Power Supply

Installing a backup generator is an invaluable way to prepare your family for emergencies. The simplest backup power system is a portable gas-powered generator and an extension cord or two. A big benefit of this approach is that you can run a refrigerator and a few worklights during a power outage with a generator that can also be transported to remote job sites or on camping trips when it's not doing emergency backup duty. This is also the least expensive way to provide some backup power for your home. You can purchase a generator at most home centers and be up and running in a matter of hours. If you take this approach, it is critically important that you make certain any loads being run by your generator are disconnected from the utility power source.

The next step up is to incorporate a manual transfer switch for your portable generator. Transfer switches are permanently hardwired to your service panel. They are mounted on either the interior or the exterior of your house between the generator and the service panel. You provide a power feed from the generator into the switch. The switch is wired to selected essential circuits in your house, allowing you to power lights, furnace blowers, and other loads that can't easily be run with an extension cord. But perhaps the most important job a transfer switch performs is to disconnect the utility power. If the inactive utility power line is attached to the service panel, "backfeed" of power from your generator to the utility line can occur when the generator kicks in. This condition could be fatal to line workers who are trying to restore power. The potential for backfeed is the main reason many municipalities insist that only a licensed electrician hook up a transfer switch. Most also require a permit. Using a transfer switch not installed by a professional may also void the warranty of the switch and the generator.

Automatic transfer switches turn on the generator and switch off the utility supply when they detect a significant drop in line voltage. They may be installed with portable generators, provided the generator is equipped with an electric starter.

Large standby generators that resemble central air conditioners are the top of the line in backup power supply systems. Often fueled by home natural gas lines that offer a bottomless fuel source or in-yard propane tanks, standby generators are made in sizes with as much as 20 to 40 kilowatts of output—enough to supply all of the power needs of a 5,000-square-foot home.

NEC requirements for generators specify that the generator receptacles should be GFCI protected. The generator should be equipped with a means to shut it down in an emergency and render it incapable of restarting without a manual reset.

Generators have a range of uses. Large hardwired models can provide instant emergency power for a whole house. Smaller models (below) are convenient for occasional short-term backup as well as job sites or camping trips.

Choosing a Backup Generator

A 2,000- to 5,000-watt gas-powered generator and a few extension cords can power lamps and an appliance or two during shorter-term power outages. Appliances must not be connected to household wiring and the generator simultaneously. **Never plug a generator into an outlet. Never operate a generator indoors.** Run extension cords through a garage door.

A permanent transfer switch patches electricity from a large portable generator through to selected household circuits via an inlet at your service panel (inset), allowing you to power hardwired fixtures and appliances with the generator.

For full, on-demand backup service, install a large standby generator wired to an automatic transfer panel. In the event of a power outage, the household system instantly switches to the generator.

A Typical Backup System

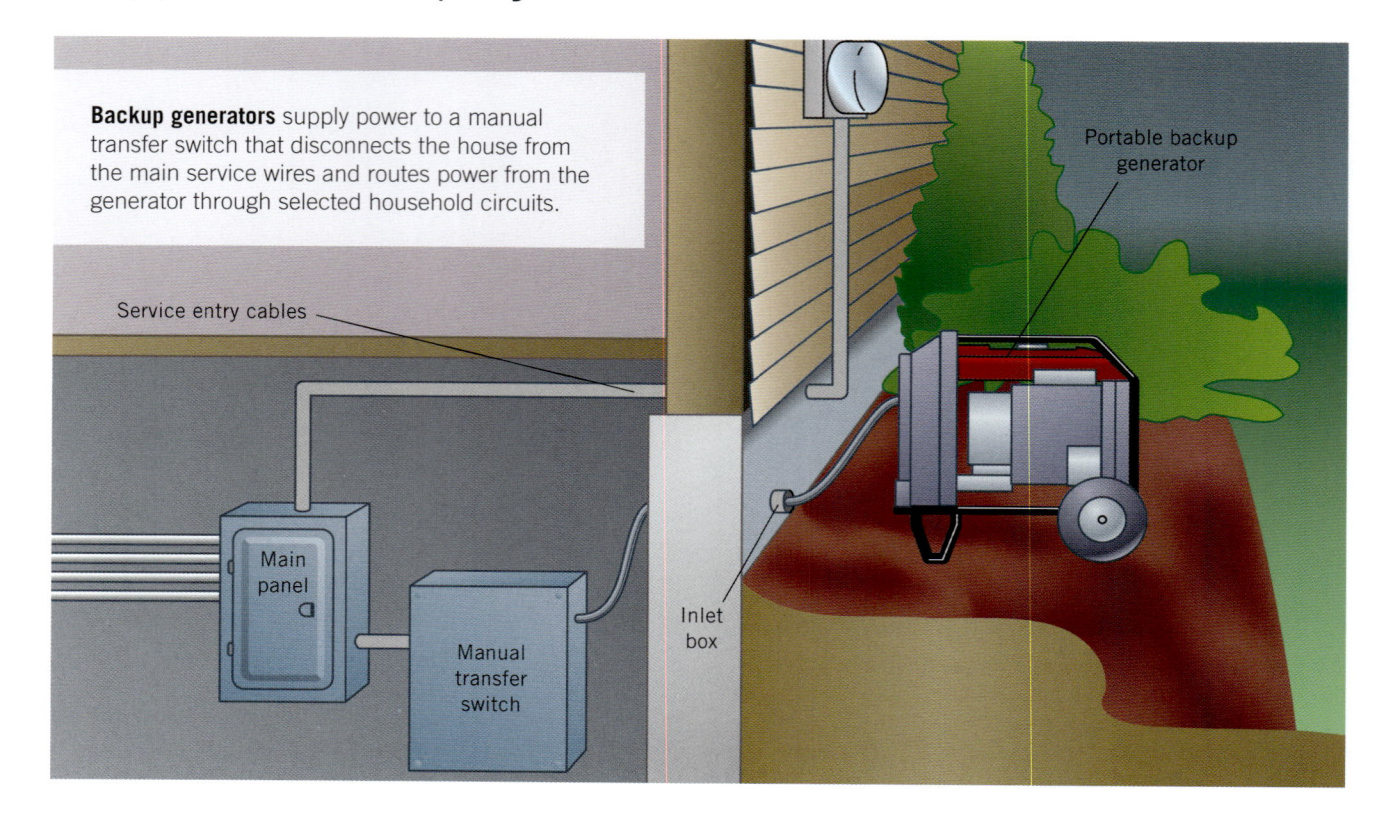

Backup generators supply power to a manual transfer switch that disconnects the house from the main service wires and routes power from the generator through selected household circuits.

Service entry cables

Main panel

Manual transfer switch

Inlet box

Portable backup generator

Choosing a Generator

Choosing a generator for your home's needs requires a few calculations. The chart below gives an estimate of the size of generator typically recommended for a house of a certain size. You can get a more accurate number by adding up the power consumption (the watts) of all the circuits or devices to be powered by a generator. It's also important to keep in mind that, for most electrical appliances, the amount of power required at the moment you flip the ON switch is greater than the number of watts required to keep the device running. For instance, though an air conditioner may run on 5,400 watts of power, it will require a surge of 7,200 watts at startup (the power range required to operate an appliance is usually listed somewhere on the device itself). These two numbers are called run watts (or Rated Load Amps, RLA) and surge watts (or Locked Rotor Amps, LRA). Generators are typically sold according to run watts (a 5,000-watt generator can sustain 5,000 watts). They are also rated for a certain number of surge watts (a 5,000-watt generator may be able to produce a

surge of 10,000 watts). If the surge watts aren't listed, ask, or check the manual. Some generators can't develop many more surge watts than run watts; others can produce twice as much surge as run wattage.

It's not necessary to buy a generator large enough to match the surge potential of all your circuits (you won't be turning everything on simultaneously), but surge watts should factor in your purchasing decision. If you will be operating the generator at or near capacity, it is also a wise practice to stagger startups for appliances.

You will need a large amount of gasoline to power a gasoline generator for more than a day or so. Gasoline goes bad over time, so you will need to stock up on gas before a long outage. Be sure to store gasoline well away from any living space. Portable generators powered by propane are available, and may be a better choice for some. Propane can last in a tank for years.

SIZE OF HOUSE (IN SQUARE FEET)	RECOMMENDED GENERATOR SIZE (IN KILOWATTS)
Up to 2,700	5–11
2,701–3,700	14–16
3,701–4,700	20
4,701–7,000	42–47

Types of Transfer Switches

When using a cord-connected switch, consider mounting an inlet box to the exterior wall. This will allow you to connect a generator without running a cord into the house.

Cord-connected transfer switches (shown above) are hard-wired to the service panel (in some cases they're installed after the service panel and operate only selected circuits). These switches contain a male receptacle for a power supply cord connected to the generator. Automatic transfer switches (not shown) detect voltage drop-off in the main power line and switch over to the emergency power source.

GENERATOR TIPS

If you'll need to run sensitive electronics such as computers or home theater equipment, look for a generator with power inverter technology that dispenses "clean power" with a stable sine wave pattern.

A generator that will output 240-volt service is required to run most central air conditioners. If your generator has variable output (120/240), make sure the switch is set to the correct output voltage.

Running + Maintaining a Backup System

Even with a fully automatic standby generator system fueled by natural gas or propane, you will need to conduct some regular maintenance and testing to make sure all systems are ready in the event of power loss. If you're depending on a portable generator and extension cords or a standby generator with a manual transfer switch, you'll also need to know the correct sequence of steps to follow in a power emergency. Switches and panels also need to be tested on a regular basis, as directed in your owner's manual. And be sure that all switches (both interior and exterior) are housed in an approved enclosure box.

Pull-cord starter

Smaller portable generators often use pull cords instead of electric starters.

Anatomy of a Portable Backup Generator

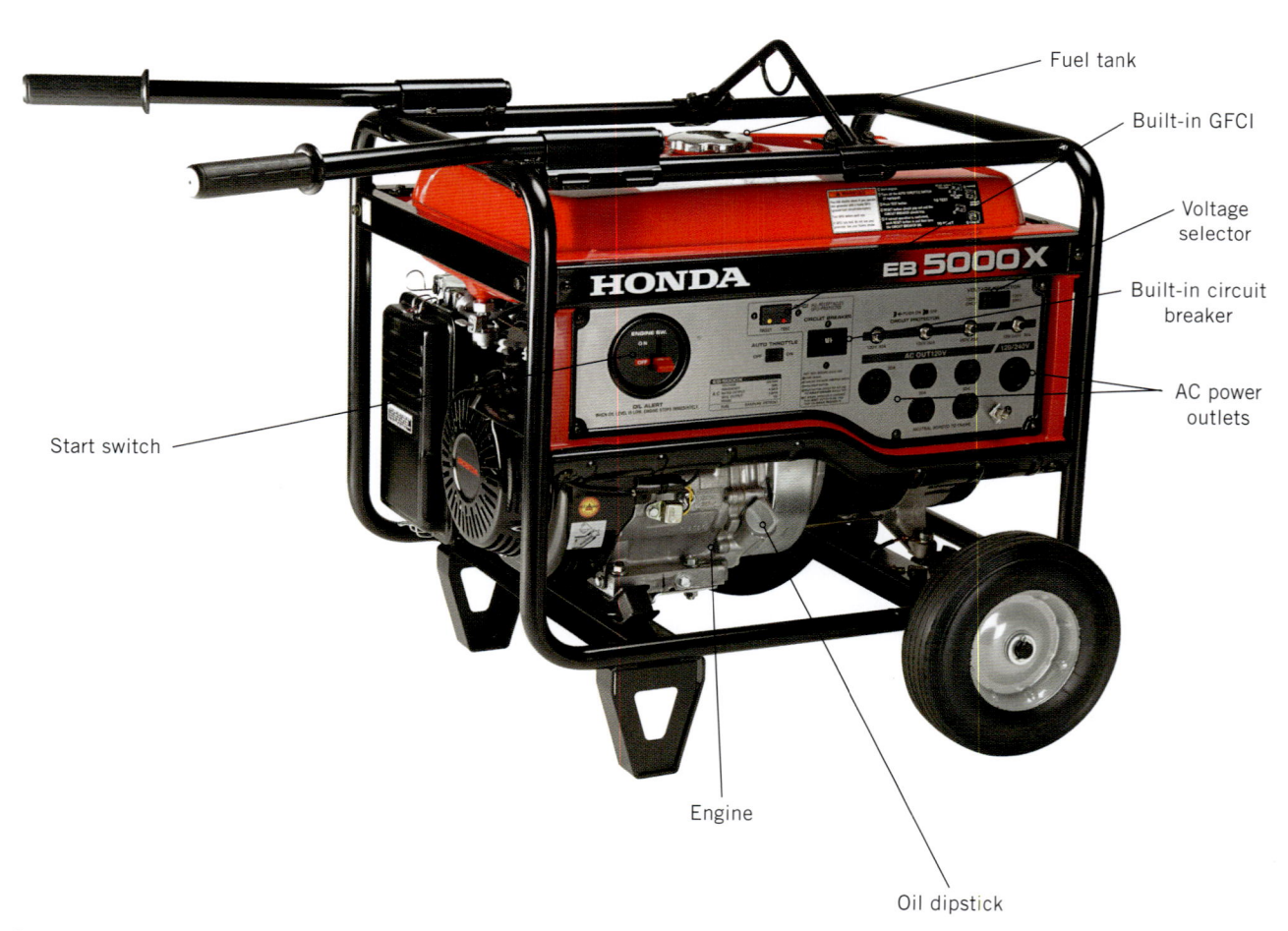

Fuel tank

Built-in GFCI

Voltage selector

Built-in circuit breaker

AC power outlets

Start switch

Engine

Oil dipstick

Portable generators use small gasoline engines to generate power. A built-in electronics panel sets current to AC or DC and the correct voltage. Most models will also include a built-in circuit breaker to protect the generator from damage in the event it is connected to too many loads. Better models include features such as built-in GFCI protection. Larger portable generators may also feature electric starter motors and batteries for push-button starts.

Operating a Manual System During an Outage

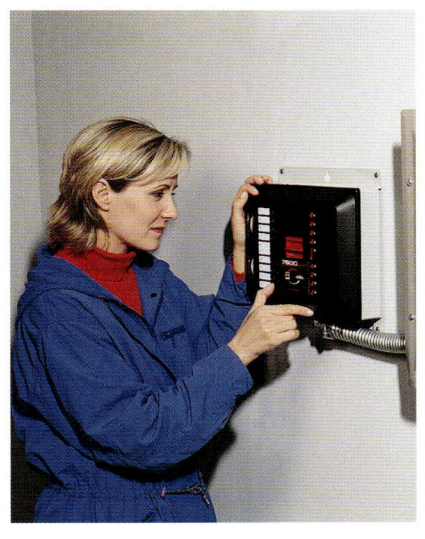

Plug the generator in at the inlet box. Make sure the other end of the generator's outlet cord is plugged into the appropriate outlet on the generator (120-volt or 120/240-volt AC) and the generator is switched to the appropriate voltage setting.

Start the generator with the pull cord or electric starter (if your generator has one). Let the generator run for several minutes before flipping the transfer switch.

Flip the manual transfer switch. Begin turning on loads one at a time by flipping breakers on, starting with the ones that power essential equipment. Do not overload the generator or the switch, and do not run the generator at or near full capacity for more than 30 minutes at a time.

Maintaining + Operating an Automatic Standby Generator

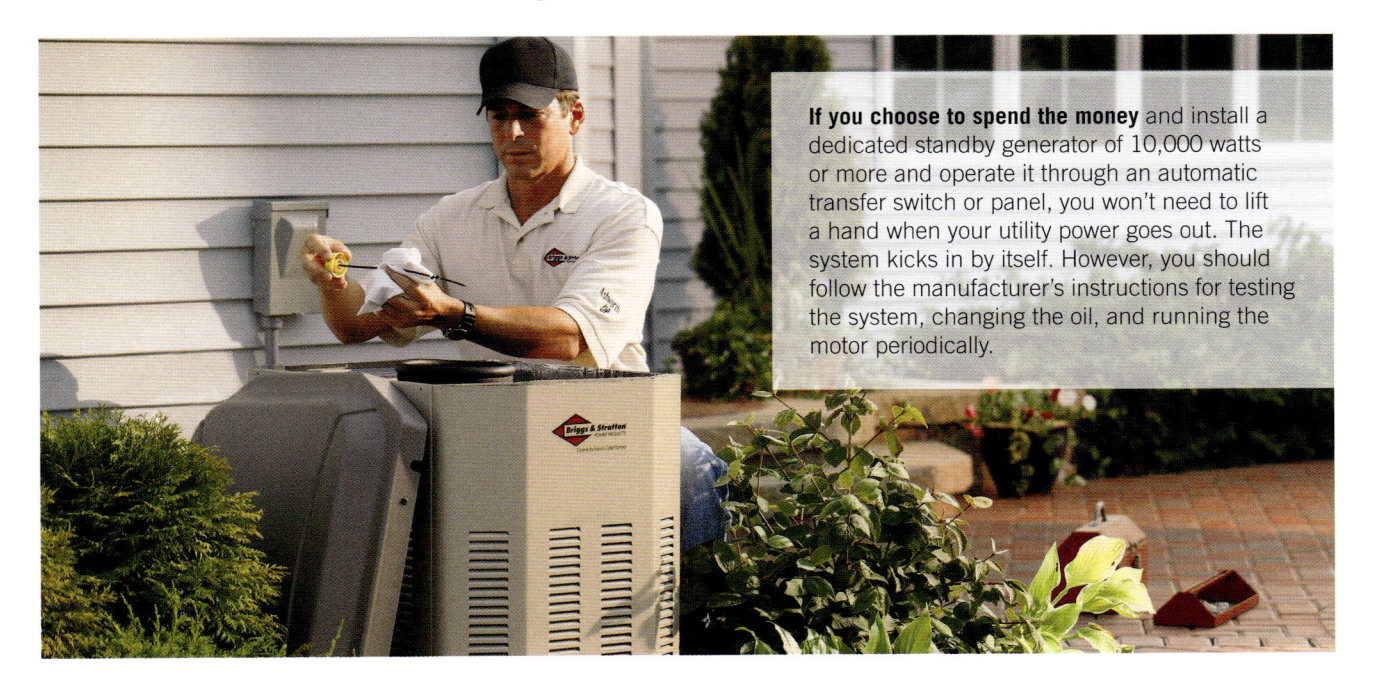

If you choose to spend the money and install a dedicated standby generator of 10,000 watts or more and operate it through an automatic transfer switch or panel, you won't need to lift a hand when your utility power goes out. The system kicks in by itself. However, you should follow the manufacturer's instructions for testing the system, changing the oil, and running the motor periodically.

Installing a Transfer Switch

A transfer switch is installed next to the main service panel to override the normal electrical service with power from a backup generator during a power outage. Manual transfer switches require an operator to change the power source, while automatic switches detect the loss of power, start the backup generator, and switch over to the backup power feed. Because the amount of electricity created by a backup generator is not adequate to power all of the electrical circuits in your house, you'll need to designate a few selected circuits to get backup current.

Note: This project requires a permit and inspection of all work.

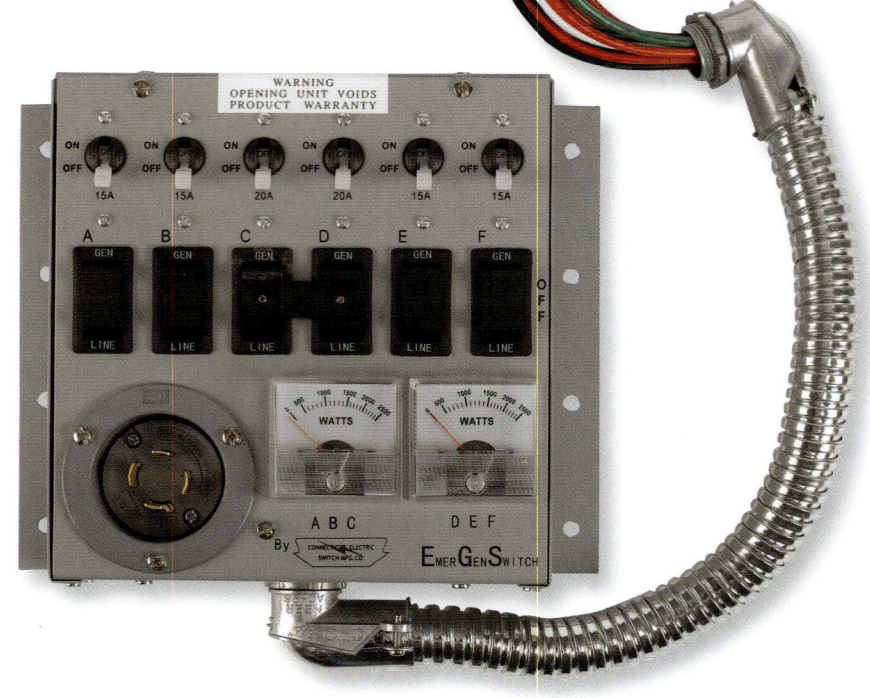

A manual transfer switch connects emergency circuits in your main panel to a standby generator.

TOOLS + MATERIALS

Voltage tester	Cable ripper	Wire connectors (yellow)
Drill/driver	Wire strippers	Standby power generator
Screwdrivers	Level	
Hammer	Manual transfer switch	
Wire cutters	Screws	

One flip of a switch reassigns the power source for each critical circuit so your backup generator can keep your refrigerator, freezer, and important lights running during a utility power outage.

Before you purchase a backup generator, determine which loads you will want to power from your generator in the event of a power loss. Generally you will want to power your refrigerator, freezer, and maybe a few lights. Add up the running wattage ratings of the appliances you will power up to determine how large your backup generator needs to be. Because the startup wattage of many appliances is higher than the running wattage, avoid starting all circuits at the same time—it can cause an overload situation with your generator. Here are some approximate running wattage guidelines (see pages 130–131 for more information on calculating electrical loads):

- Refrigerator: 750 watts
- Forced air furnace: 1,100 to 1,500 watts
- Incandescent lights: 60 watts per bulb (CFL and LED lights use less wattage)
- Sump pump: 800 to 1,000 watts
- Well pump: 2,000 to 5,000 watts
- Garage door opener: 550 to 1,100 watts
- Television: 300 watts

Add the wattage values of all the loads you want to power, and multiply the sum by 1.25. This will give you the minimum wattage your generator must produce. Portable standby generators typically output 5,000 to 7,500 watts. Most larger, stationary generators can output 10,000 to 20,000 watts (10 to 20 kilowatts).

How to Install a Manual Transfer Switch

Turn off the main power breaker in your electrical service panel. CAUTION: The service wires and terminals (lugs) that feed the main breaker remain live even when the main breaker is off.

Determine which household circuits are critical for emergency usage during a power outage. Typically this will include the refrigerator, freezer, furnace, and at least one light or small-appliance circuit. *(continued)*

3

Match your critical circuits with circuit inlet on your prewired transfer switch. Try to balance the load as best you can in the transfer switch: For example, if your refrigerator is on the leftmost switch circuit, connect your freezer to the circuit farthest to the right. Double-pole (240-volt) circuits will require two 120-volt circuit connections. Also make sure that 15-amp and 20-amp circuits are not mismatched with one another.

4

Select and remove a knockout at the bottom of the main service panel box. Make sure to choose a knockout that is sized to match the connector on the flexible conduit coming from the transfer switch.

5

Feed the wires from the transfer switch into the knockout hole, taking care not to damage the insulation. Note that each wire is labeled according to which circuit in the switch box it feeds.

6

Secure the flexible conduit from the switch box to the main service panel using a locknut and a bushing where required.

Attach the transfer switch box to the wall so the closer edge is about 18" away from the center of the main service panel. Use whichever connectors make sense for your wall type.

Remove the breaker for the first critical circuit from the main service panel box, and disconnect the hot wire lead from the lug on the breaker.

Locate the red wire for the switch box circuit that corresponds to the circuit you've disconnected. Attach the red wire to the breaker you've just removed, and then reinstall the breaker.

Locate the black wire from the same transfer switch circuit, and twist it together with the old feed wire, using a yellow wire connector. Tuck the wires neatly out of the way at the edges of the box. Proceed to the next circuit, and repeat the process.

(continued)

If any of your critical circuits are 240-volt circuits, attach the red leads from the two transfer switch circuits to the double-pole breaker. The two circuits originating in the transfer switch should be next to one another, and their switches should be connected with a handle tie. If you have no 240-volt circuits, you may remove the preattached handle tie and use the circuits individually.

Once you have made all circuit connections, attach the white neutral wire from the transfer switch to an opening in the neutral terminal bar of the main service panel.

Attach the green ground wire from the transfer switch to an open port on the grounding bar in your main service panel. This should complete the installation of the transfer switch. Replace the cover on the service panel box, and make sure to fill in the circuit map on your switch box.

Begin testing the transfer switch by making sure all of the switches on it are set to the LINE setting. The power should still be OFF at the main panel breakers.

Make sure your standby generator is operating properly and has been installed professionally. See page 265 for information on choosing a generator that is sized appropriately for your needs.

(15)

Before turning your generator on, attach the power cord from the generator to the switch box. Never attach or detach a generator cord with the generator running. Turn your standby power generator on, and let it run for a minute or two.

(16)

Flip each circuit switch on the transfer switch box to GEN, one at a time. Try to maintain balance by moving back and forth from circuits on the left and right side. Do not turn all circuits on at the same time. Observe the onboard wattage meters as you engage each circuit, and try to keep the wattage levels in balance. When you have completed testing the switch, turn the switches back to LINE, and then shut off your generator.

Outbuildings

Nothing improves the convenience and usefulness of an outbuilding more than electrifying it. Running a new underground circuit from your house to an outbuilding lets you add receptacles and light fixtures both inside the outbuilding and on its exterior. If you run power to an outbuilding, you are required to install at least one receptacle.

Adding one or two 120-volt circuits is not complicated, but every aspect of the project is strictly governed by local building codes. Therefore, once you've mapped out the job and have a good idea of what's involved, visit your local building department to discuss your plans and obtain a permit for the work.

This project demonstrates standard techniques for running a circuit cable from the house exterior to a shed, plus the wiring and installation of devices inside the shed. To add a new breaker and make the final circuit connections to your home's main service panel, see page 174.

First, determine how much current you will need. For basic electrical needs, such as powering a standard light fixture and small appliances or power tools, a 120-volt, 20-amp circuit should be sufficient. A small workshop may require one or two 120-volt, 20-amp circuits. If you need any 240-volt circuits or more than two 120-volt, 20-amp circuits, you will need to install at least a 60-amp subpanel with appropriate feeder wires. Installing a subpanel in an outbuilding is similar to installing one inside your home, but there are some important differences.

You may use #12 copper wire for one 120-volt, 20-amp circuit. Use #10 copper wire for two 120-volt, 20-amp circuits. Also, if the shed is more than 150 feet away from the house, you may need heavier-gauge cable to account for voltage drop.

Most importantly, don't forget to call before you dig. Have all utility and service lines on your property marked even before you make serious project plans. This is critical for your safety of course, and it may affect where you can run the circuit cable.

Adding an electrical circuit to an outbuilding such as this greatly expands the activities the building will support and is also a great benefit for home security.

TOOLS + MATERIALS

Spray paint

Trenching shovel (4"-wide blade)

4" metal junction box

Metal L-fittings (2) and conduit nipple for conduit

Wood screws

Conduit with watertight threaded and compression fittings

Wrenches

Hacksaw

90° sweeps for conduit (2)

Plastic conduit bushings (2)

Pipe straps

Silicone caulk and caulk gun

Double-gang boxes, metal (2)

One exterior receptacle box (with cover)

One 20-amp weather-resistant receptacle

One 20-amp receptacle

Single-pole switches (2)

Interior ceiling light fixture and metal fixture box

Exterior motion-detector fixture and plastic fixture box

EMT metal conduit and fittings for inside the shed

Utility knife

UF two-wire cable (12 gauge)

THNN wire (12 gauge)

20-amp GFCI circuit breaker

Wire strippers

Pliers

Screwdrivers

Wire connectors

Hand tamper

Schedule 80 conduit

Eye protection

Tape measure

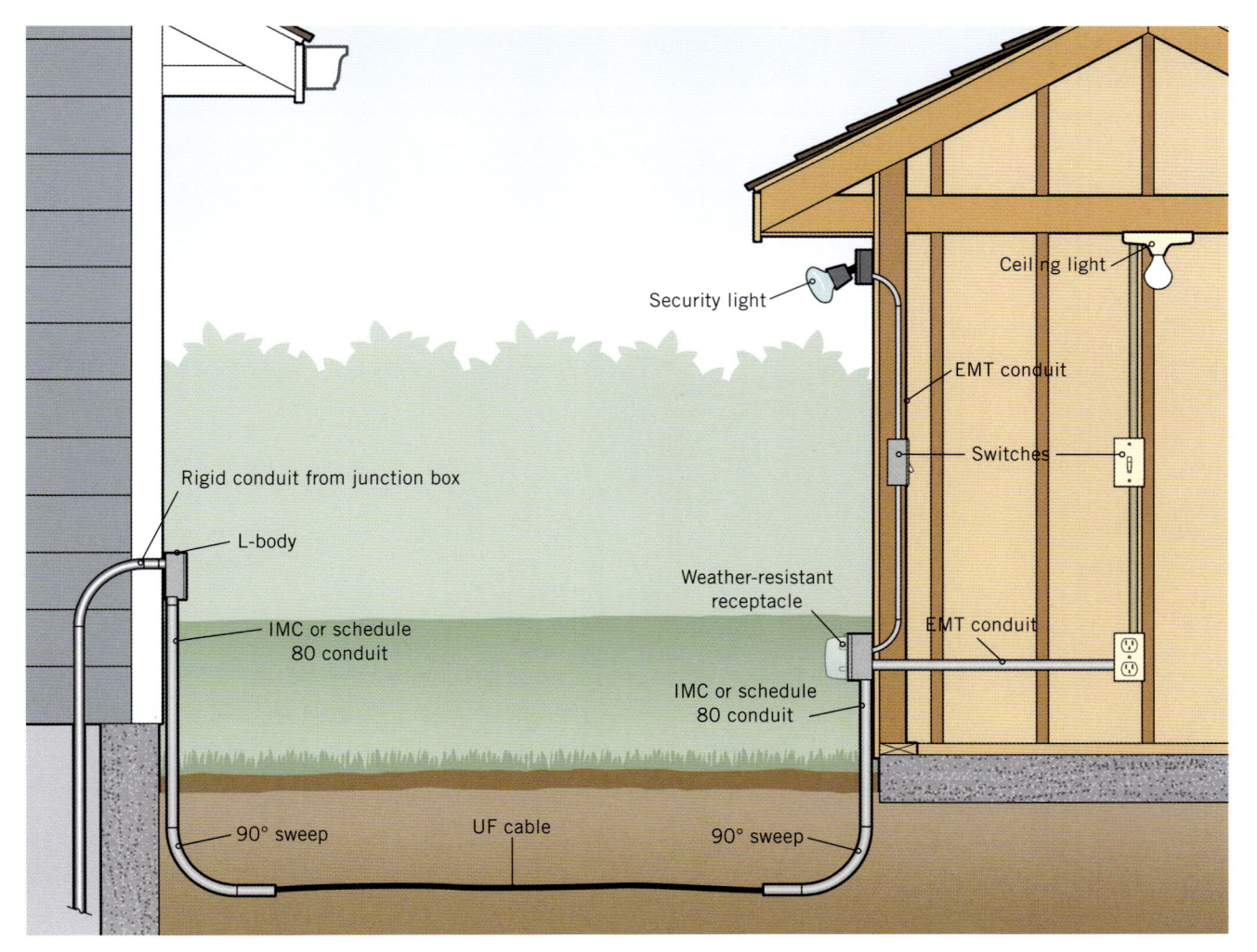

A basic outdoor circuit starts with a waterproof fitting at the house wall connected to a junction box inside. The underground circuit cable—rated UF (underground feeder)—runs in a 12"-deep trench and is protected from exposure at both ends by metal or PVC conduit. Inside the shed, standard NM cable runs through metal conduit to protect it from damage (not necessary if you will be adding interior wallcoverings). All receptacles must have GFCI protection; this is provided by a GFCI circuit breaker.

How to Wire an Outbuilding

Identify the circuit's exit point at the house and entry point at the shed and mark them. Mark the path of the trench between the exit and entry points using spray paint. Make the route as direct as possible. Dig the trench to the depth required by local code (typically 12" deep for a GFCI-protected circuit) using a narrow trenching shovel.

From outside, drill a hole through the exterior wall and the rim joist at the exit point for the cable (you'll probably need to install a bit extender or an extra-long bit in your drill). Make the hole just large enough to accommodate the L-body conduit fitting and conduit nipple.

Assemble the conduit and junction box fittings that will penetrate the wall. Here, we attached a 12" piece of ¾" PVC conduit and a sweep to a metal junction box with a compression fitting and then inserted the conduit into the hole drilled in the rim joist. The junction box is attached to the floor joist.

From outside, seal the hole around the conduit with expandable spray foam or caulk, and then attach the free end of the conduit to the back of a waterproof L-body fitting. Mount the L-body fitting to the house exterior with the open end facing downward.

Cut a length of PVC conduit to extend from the L-fitting down into the trench using a hacksaw. Deburr the cut edges of the conduit. Secure the conduit to the L-fitting, and then attach a 90° sweep to the bottom end of the conduit using compression fittings. Anchor the conduit to the wall with a corrosion-resistant pipe strap.

Inside the shed, drill a ¾"-diameter hole in the shed wall. On the interior of the shed, mount a junction box with a knock-out removed to allow the cable to enter through the hole. On the exterior side directly above the end of the UF trench, mount an exterior-rated receptacle box with cover. The plan (and your plan may differ) is to bring power into the shed through the hole in the wall behind the exterior receptacle.

Run conduit from the exterior box down into the trench. Fasten the conduit to the outbuilding with a strap. Add a 90° sweep and bushing, as before. Secure the conduit to the box with an offset fitting. Anchor the conduit with pipe straps, and seal the entry hole with caulk.

Run UF cable from the house to the outbuilding. Feed one end of the UF circuit cable up through the sweep and conduit and into the L-fitting at the house (the back or side of the fitting is removable to facilitate cabling). Run the cable through the wall and into the junction box, leaving at least 12" of extra cable at the end. *(continued)*

Lay the UF cable into the trench, making sure it is not twisted and will not contact any sharp objects. Roll out the cable, and then feed the other end of the cable up through the conduit and into the receptacle box in the shed, leaving 12" of slack.

Inside the outbuilding, install the remaining boxes for the other switches, receptacles, and lights. With the exception of plastic receptacle boxes for exterior exposure, use metal boxes if you will be connecting the boxes with metal conduit.

Connect the electrical boxes with conduit and fittings. Inside the outbuilding, you may use inexpensive steel EMT to connect the receptacle, switch, and fixture boxes. Once you've planned your circuit routes, start by attaching couplings to all of the boxes.

Cut a length of conduit to fit between the coupling and the next box or fitting in the run. If necessary, drill holes for the conduit through the centers of the wall studs. Attach the conduit to the fitting that you attached to the first box.

If you are surface-mounting the conduit or running it up or down next to wall studs, secure it with straps no more than 3 ft. apart. Use elbow fittings for 90° turns and setscrew couplings for joining straight lengths as needed. Make holes through the wall studs only as large as necessary to feed the conduit through.

THNN wire

Measure to find how much wire you'll need for each run, and cut pieces of THHN wire that are 1 or 2 feet longer than the measurements. Before making L-turns with the conduit, feed the wire through the first conduit run.

Feed the other ends of the wires into the next box or fitting in line. It is much easier to feed wire into 45° and 90° elbows if they have not been attached to the conduit yet. Continue feeding wire into the conduit and fitting until you have reached the next box in line.

Once you've reached the next box in line, coil the ends of the wires and repeat the process with new wire for the next run. Keep working until all of the wire is run and all of the conduit and fittings are installed and secured. If you are running multiple feed wires into a single box, write the origin or destination on a piece of masking tape and stick it to each wire end. *(continued)*

NOTE: Your code may require an in-use rated receptacle box cover (see page 51).

Make the wiring connections at the receptacles. Connect the receptacles with pigtails, including grounding pigtails for the receptacles and the metal boxes. Install the receptacles and cover plates.

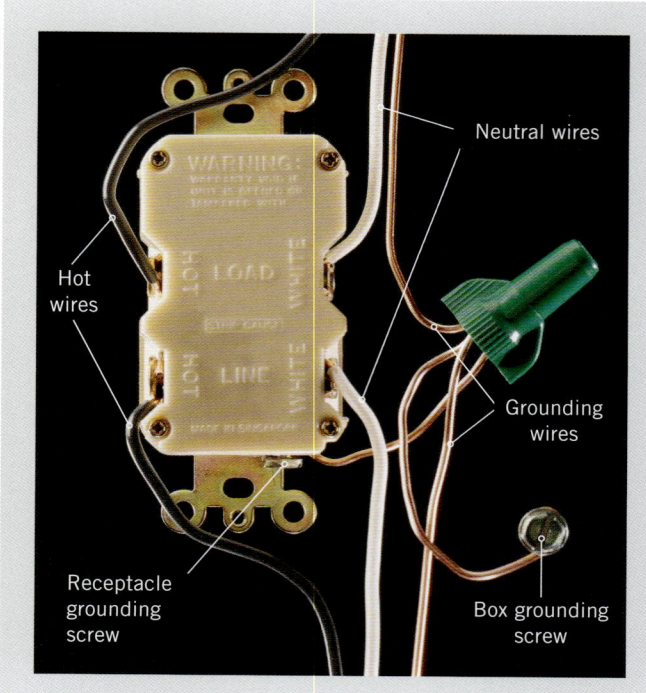

Neutral wires

Hot wires

Grounding wires

Receptacle grounding screw

Box grounding screw

VARIATION: Installing a GFCI breaker for the new circuit at the main service panel is the best way to protect the circuit and allows you to use regular receptacles in the building, but an alternative that is allowed in many areas is to run the service into a GFCI-protected receptacle and then wire the other devices on the circuit in series (see page 152). If you use this approach, only the initial receptacle needs to be a GFCI receptacle; however, the underground circuit cable will need to be at least 24" deep.

Run service from the last receptacle to the switch box for the light fixture or fixtures. (If you anticipate a lot of load on the circuit, you should probably run a separate circuit for the lights). Twist the white neutral leads and grounding leads together and cap them. Attach the black wires to the appropriate switches. Install the switches and cover plate.

Install the light fixtures. For this shed, we installed a caged ceiling light inside the shed and a motion-detector security light on the exterior side.

Run NM cable from the electrical box in the house at the start of the new circuit to the main service panel. Use cable staples if you are running the cable in floor joist cavities. If the cable is mounted to the bottom of the floor joists or will be exposed, run it through conduit.

At the panel, feed the NM cable in through a cable clamp. Arrange for your final electrical inspection before you install the breaker. Then attach the wires to a new GFCI circuit breaker, and install the breaker in an empty slot. Label the new circuit on the circuit map.

Turn on the new circuit, and test all of the receptacles and fixtures. If any of the fixtures or receptacles is not getting power, check the connections first, and then test the receptacle or switch for continuity with a multimeter. Backfill the trench.

Motion-Sensing Floodlights

Most houses and garages have floodlights on their exteriors. You can easily upgrade these fixtures so that they provide additional security by replacing them with motion-sensing floodlights. Motion-sensing floods can be set up to detect motion in a specific area—such as a walkway or driveway—and then cast light into that area. And there are few things intruders like less than the spotlight. These lights typically have timers that allow you to control how long the light stays on and photosensors that prevent the light from coming on during the day. Extending a branch circuit or adding a new branch to install new receptacles, lights, or switches requires a permit. Check with the electrical inspector before starting such projects.

A motion-sensing light fixture provides inexpensive and effective protection against intruders. It has an infrared eye that triggers the light fixture when a moving object crosses its path. Choose a light fixture with a photo cell to prevent the light from turning on in daylight, an adjustable timer to control how long the light stays on, and range control to adjust the reach of the motion-sensor eye.

An exterior floodlight with a motion sensor is an effective security measure. Keep the motion sensor adjusted to cover only the area you wish to secure—if the coverage area is too large, the light will turn on frequently.

TOOLS + MATERIALS

Voltage tester

Jigsaw

Fish tape

Screwdrivers

Wire cutter

Cable ripper

Wire stripper

Caulk gun

Motion-sensing floodlight fixture

Old work (retrofit) electrical box

NM cable

Wire connectors

Eye protection

How to Install a New Exterior Fixture Box

On the outside of the house, make the cutout for the motion-sensor light fixture. Outline the light fixture box on the wall, drill a pilot hole, and complete the cutout with a wallboard saw or jigsaw.

Estimate the distance between the indoor switch box and the outdoor motion-sensor box, and cut a length of NM cable about 2 ft. longer than this distance. Use a fish tape to pull the cable from the switch box to the motion-sensor box. See page 40 for tips on running cable through finished walls.

Mounting bracket

Retrofit box

Strip about 10" of outer insulation from the end of the cable using a cable ripper. Open a knockout in the retrofit light fixture box with a screwdriver. Insert the cable into the box so that at least ¼" of outer sheathing reaches into the box. Apply a heavy bead of silicone or polyurethane caulk to the flange of the electrical box before attaching it to the wall.

Mounting screws

Insert the box into the cutout opening, and tighten the mounting screws until the brackets draw the outside flange firmly against the siding. Follow the siding manufacturer's instructions about flashing this wall pentration.

How to Replace a Floodlight with a Motion-Sensor Light

Turn off power to the old fixture. To remove it, unscrew the mounting screws on the part of the fixture attached to the wall. There will probably be four of them. Carefully pull the fixture away from the wall, exposing the wires. Don't touch the wires yet.

Before you touch any wires, use a voltage tester to verify that the circuit is dead. With the light switch turned on, insert the tester's probe into the electrical box and hold the probe within ½" of the wires inside to confirm that there is no voltage. Disconnect the wire connectors, and remove the old fixture.

Examine the ends of the three wires coming from the box (one white, one black, and one bare copper). They should be clean and free of corrosion. If the ends are in poor condition, clip them off and then strip ¾" of wire insulation with a combination tool.

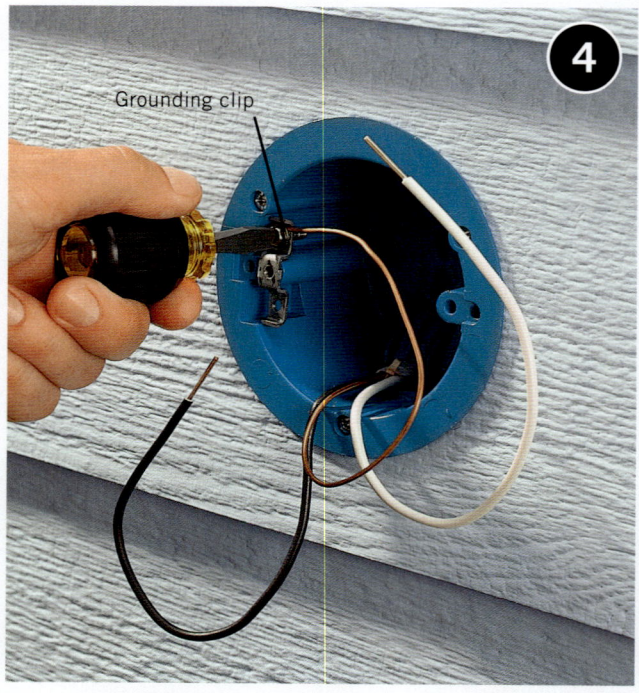

Grounding clip

If the electrical box is nonmetallic and does has a metal grounding clip, connect the circuit ground wire to the clip. Otherwise, connect the ground wire to the fixture base (if it has a grounding terminal), or connect the ground wire to the fixture's ground lead, using a wire connector.

Slide a rubber or foam gasket (usually provided with the fixture) over the wires and onto the flange of the box. Set the new fixture on top of a ladder or have a helper hold it while you make the wiring connections. There may be as many as three white wires coming from the fixture. Join all white wires, including the feed wire from the house, using a wire connector.

Next, join the black wire from the box and the single black wire from the fixture with a wire connector. You may see a couple of black wires and a red wire already joined on the fixture. You can ignore these in your installation.

Neatly tuck all the wires into the box so they are behind the gasket. Align the holes in the gasket with the holes in the box, and then position the fixture over the gasket so its mounting holes are also aligned with the gasket. Press the fixture against the gasket, and drive the four mounting screws into the box. Install exterior-rated lightbulbs and restore power.

Test the fixture. You will still be able to turn it on and off with the light switch inside. Flip the switch on and pass your hand in front of the motion sensor. The light should come on. Adjust the motion sensor to cover the traffic areas, and pivot the light head to illuminate the intended area.

Common Repair Projects, Wiring Problems + Solutions

Basic electrical repairs to lighting fixtures, fans, and power cords are easy DIY fixes that can save you a few bucks. However, these types of small repairs should always start with the question: Does the repair make sense, given the time and effort you'll put into it? For instance, incandescent lightbulbs have been banned now for years. As replacement supply runs out, you'll need to migrate to LED bulbs. Compact fluorescent bulbs (CFL) and fluorescent bulbs will likely be phased out federally in the near future. That means any fixture that can only use those bulbs will need to be replaced (and it's why this revised edition of *Wiring* no longer has a section on repairing fluorescent tube fixtures).

For more serious and potentially dangerous issues, you'll need to determine the extent of the problem and decide if you can fix it yourself or if you need an electrician. Any wiring or device that is not up to code carries the potential for problems. In addition, you may have trouble selling your home if it is not wired according to code-approved methods.

While this book cannot possibly identify all potential wiring problems in your house, we have identified some of the most common wiring defects here and will show you how to correct them. If you have questions regarding your home wiring system, consult an electrician or your local building department.

In this chapter:
- Troubleshooting Light Fixtures
- Repairing Chandeliers
- Repairing Ceiling Fans
- Replacing Plugs + Cords
- Replacing a Lamp Socket
- Service Panels + Grounding
- Cables + Wires
- Cords
- Receptacles + Switches

Troubleshooting Light Fixtures

Light fixtures are attached permanently to ceilings or walls. They include wall-hung sconces, ceiling-hung globe fixtures, recessed light fixtures, and chandeliers. Most light fixtures are easy to troubleshoot and can often be repaired using basic tools and inexpensive parts. However, depending on the issue, it may cheaper and easier to simply replace the fixture.

If a light fixture fails, always make sure the lightbulb is screwed in tightly and is not burned out. A faulty lightbulb is the most common cause of light fixture failure. If the light fixture is controlled by a wall switch, also check the switch as a possible source of problems.

Light fixtures can fail because the sockets or built-in switches wear out. Some fixtures have sockets and switches that can be removed for minor repairs. These parts are held to the base of the fixture with mounting screws or clips. Other fixtures have sockets and switches that are joined permanently to the base. If this type of fixture fails, purchase and install a new light fixture.

Damage to light fixtures often occurs because homeowners install lightbulbs with wattage ratings that are too high. Prevent overheating and light fixture failures by using only lightbulbs that match the wattage ratings printed on the fixtures.

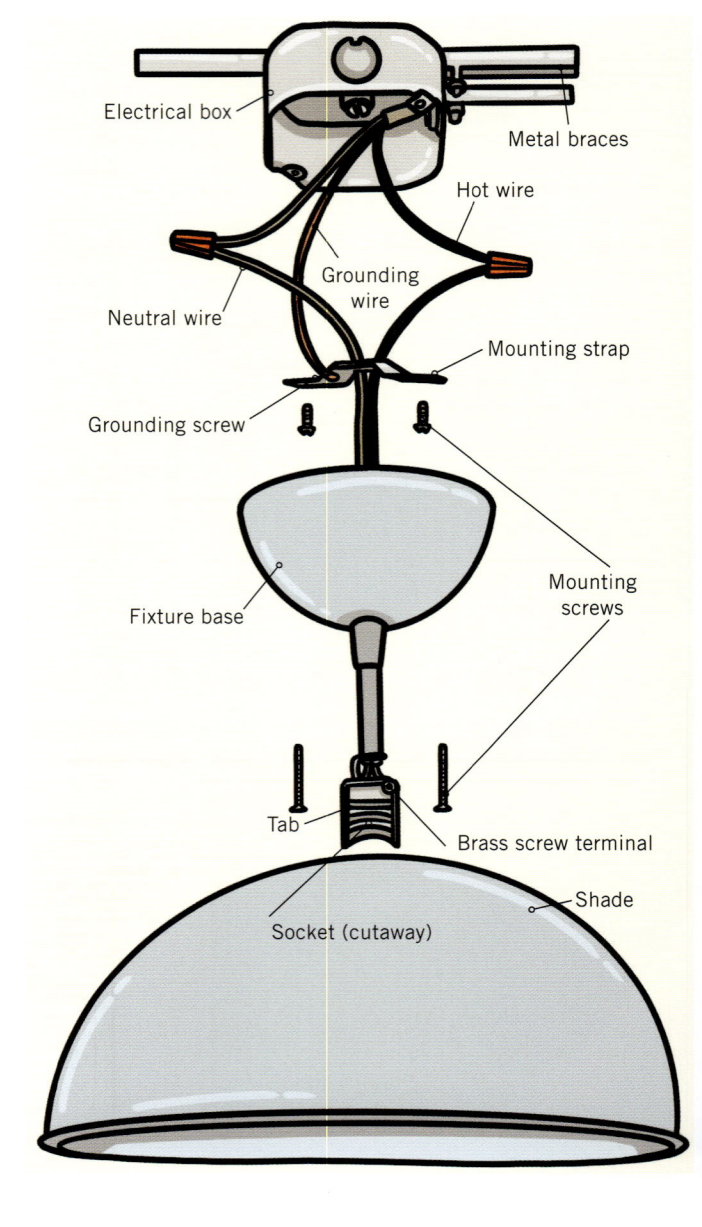

Electrical box · Metal braces · Hot wire · Grounding wire · Neutral wire · Mounting strap · Grounding screw · Fixture base · Mounting screws · Tab · Brass screw terminal · Socket (cutaway) · Shade

TOOLS + MATERIALS

Circuit tester	Combination tool
Screwdriver	Replacement parts, as needed
Continuity tester	

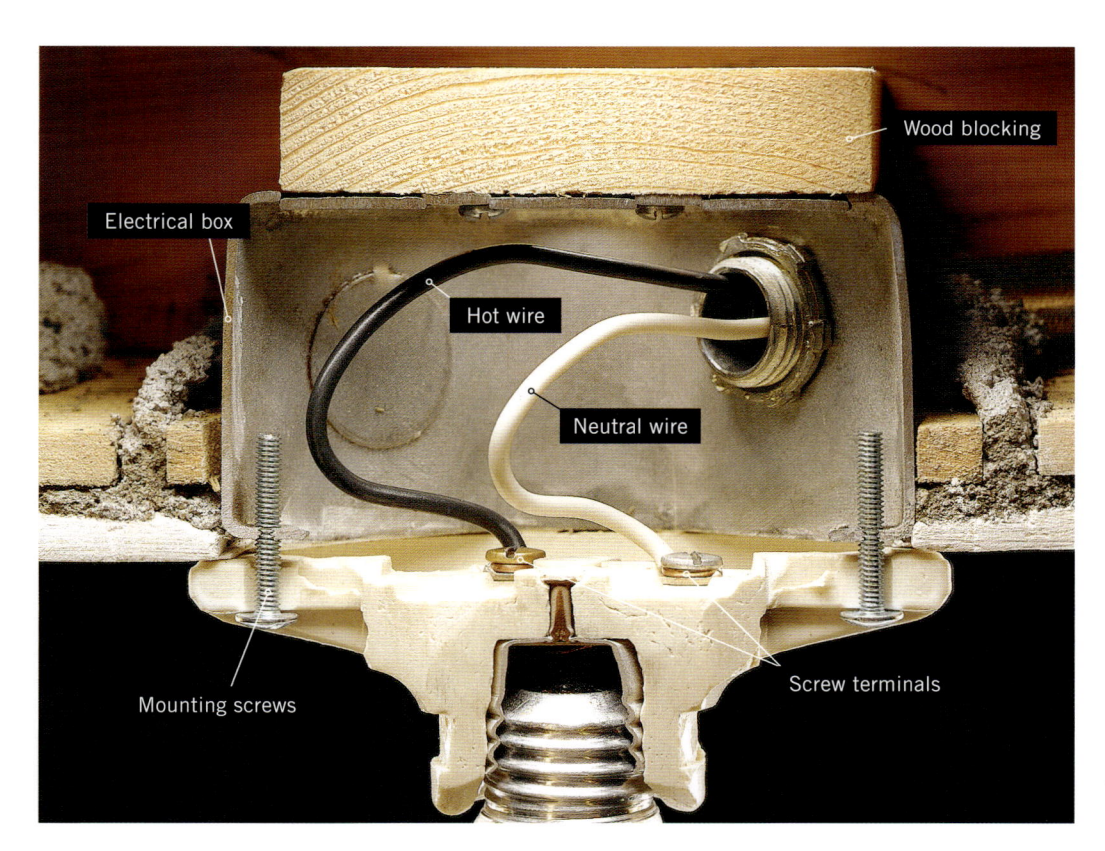

Wood blocking

Electrical box

Hot wire

Neutral wire

Mounting screws

Screw terminals

Before 1959, incandescent light fixtures (shown cutaway) often were mounted directly to an electrical box or to plaster lath. Electrical codes now require that fixtures be attached to mounting straps that are anchored to the electrical boxes. If you have a light fixture attached to plaster lath, install an approved electrical box with a mounting strap to support the fixture.

PROBLEM	REPAIR
Wall- or ceiling-mounted fixture flickers or does not light.	1. Check for faulty lightbulb. 2. Check wall switch and replace, if needed. 3. Check for loose wire connections in electrical box, and that the circuit breaker or fuse has not tripped or blown. 4. Replace light fixture.
Built-in switch on fixture does not work.	1. Check for faulty lightbulb. 2. Check that the circuit breaker or fuse has not tripped or blown. 3. Check for loose connections on the switch and replace as necessary. 4. Replace the fixture
Chandelier flickers or does not light.	1. Check for faulty lightbulb. 2. Check wall switch and replace, if needed. 3. Check for loose wire connections in electrical box, and that the circuit breaker or fuse has not tripped or blown. 4. Test sockets and fixture wires and replace, if needed.
Recessed fixture flickers or does not light.	1. Check for faulty lightbulb. 2. Check wall switch and replace, if needed. 3. Check for loose wire connections in electrical box, and that the circuit breaker or fuse has not tripped or blown. 4. Test fixture and replace, if needed. 5. Wait a few minutes. If light activates, fixture is overheating. Remove insulation from around fixture.

How to Remove a Light Fixture + Test a Socket

1

Turn off the power to the light fixture at the main panel. Remove the lightbulb and any shade or globe, then remove the mounting screws holding the fixture base and the electrical box or mounting strap. Carefully pull the fixture base away from the box.

Grounding screw

2

Test for power with a voltage tester. The tester should not glow. If it does, there is still power entering the box. Return to the panel and turn off power to the correct circuit.

3

Disconnect the light fixture base by loosening the screw terminals. If the fixture has wire leads instead of screw terminals, remove the light fixture base by unscrewing the wire connectors.

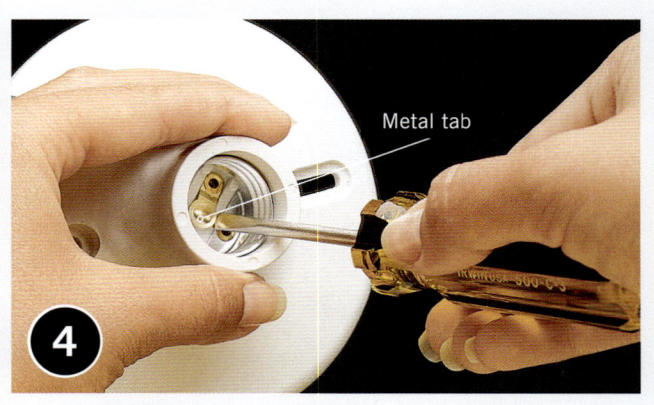

Metal tab

4

Adjust the metal tab at the bottom of the fixture socket by prying it up slightly with a small screwdriver. This adjustment will improve the contact between the socket and the lightbulb.

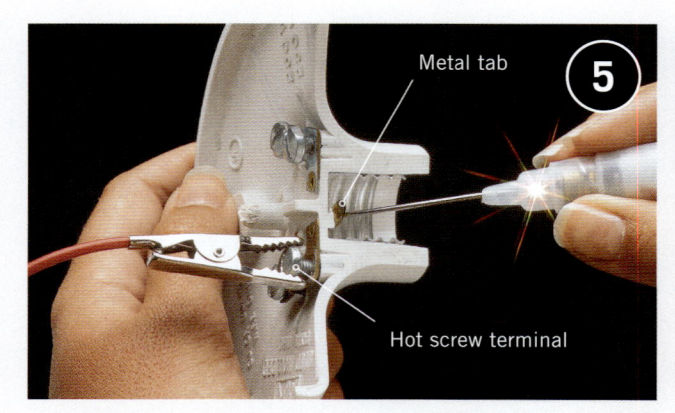

Metal tab

5

Hot screw terminal

Test the socket (shown cutaway) by attaching the clip of a continuity tester to the hot screw terminal (or black wire lead) and touching probe of the tester to the metal tab in the bottom of the socket. The tester should glow. If not, the socket is faulty and must be replaced.

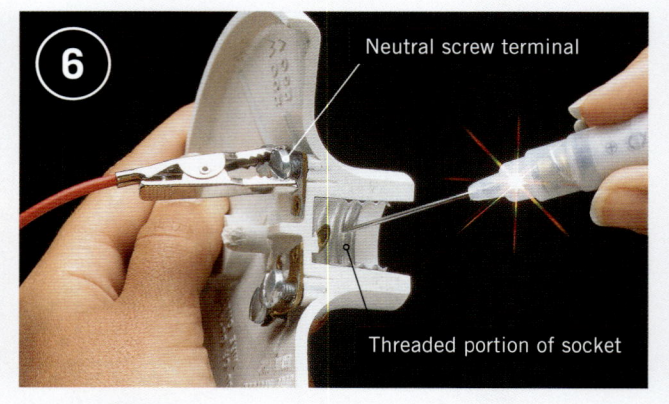

6

Neutral screw terminal

Threaded portion of socket

Attach the tester clip to the neutral screw terminal (or white wire lead), and touch the probe to the threaded portion of the socket. The tester should glow. If not, the socket is faulty and must be replaced. If the socket is permanently attached, replace the fixture.

How to Replace a Socket

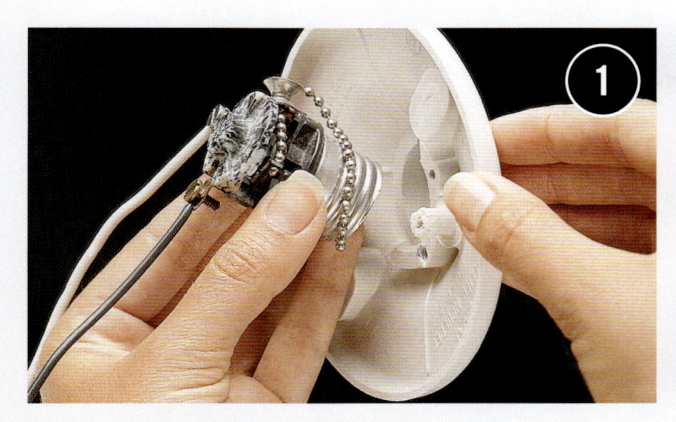

Remove the old light fixture. Remove the socket from the fixture. The socket may be held by a screw, clip, or retaining ring. Disconnect wires attached to the socket.

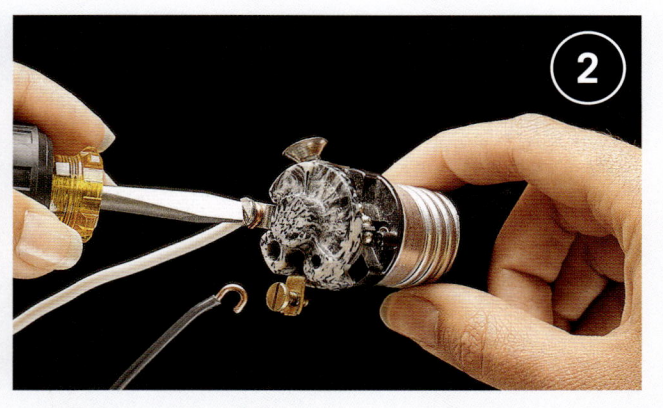

Purchase an identical replacement socket. Connect the white wire to the silver screw terminal on the socket, and connect the black wire to the brass screw terminal. Attach the socket to the fixture base, and reinstall the fixture.

How to Test + Replace a Built-In Light Switch

Retaining ring

Remove the light fixture. Unscrew the retaining ring holding the switch.

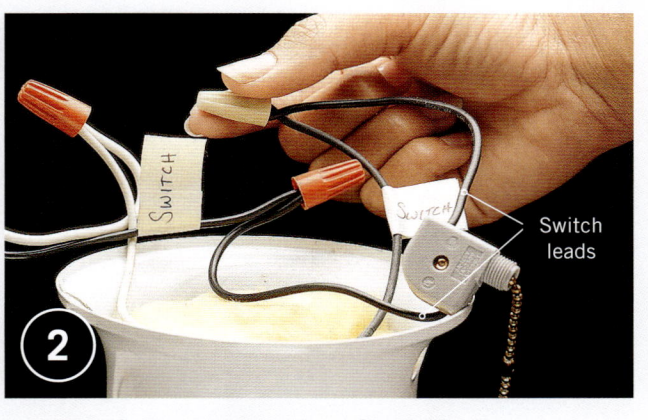

Switch leads

Label the wires connected to the switch leads. Disconnect the switch leads, and remove the switch.

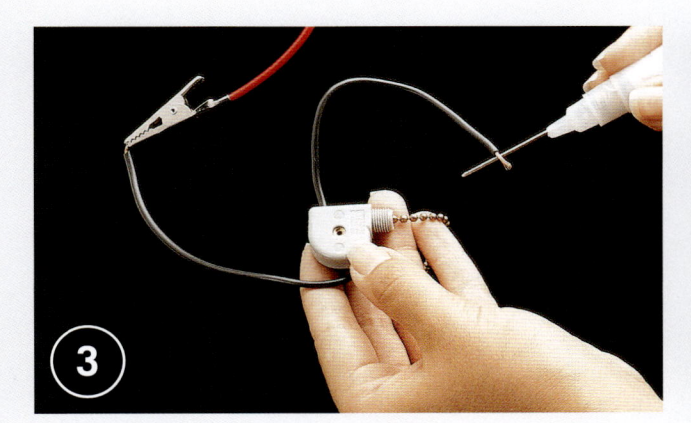

Test the switch by attaching the clip of the continuity tester to one of the switch leads and holding the tester probe to the other lead. Operate the switch control. If the switch is good, the tester will glow when the switch is in one position but not both.

If the switch is faulty, purchase and install a duplicate switch. Remount the light fixture, and turn on the power at the main service panel.

Repairing Chandeliers

Repairing a chandelier requires special care. Because chandeliers are heavy, it is a good idea to work with a helper when removing a chandelier. Support the fixture to prevent its weight from pulling against the wires.

Chandeliers have two fixture wires that are threaded through the support chain from the electrical box to the hollow base of the chandelier. The socket wires connect to the fixture wires inside this base.

Fixture wires are identified as hot and neutral. Look closely for raised ribs on one of the wires. This is the marked neutral wire that is connected to the white circuit wire and white socket wire. The other fixture wire is smooth or unmarked; it is hot and is connected to the black wires.

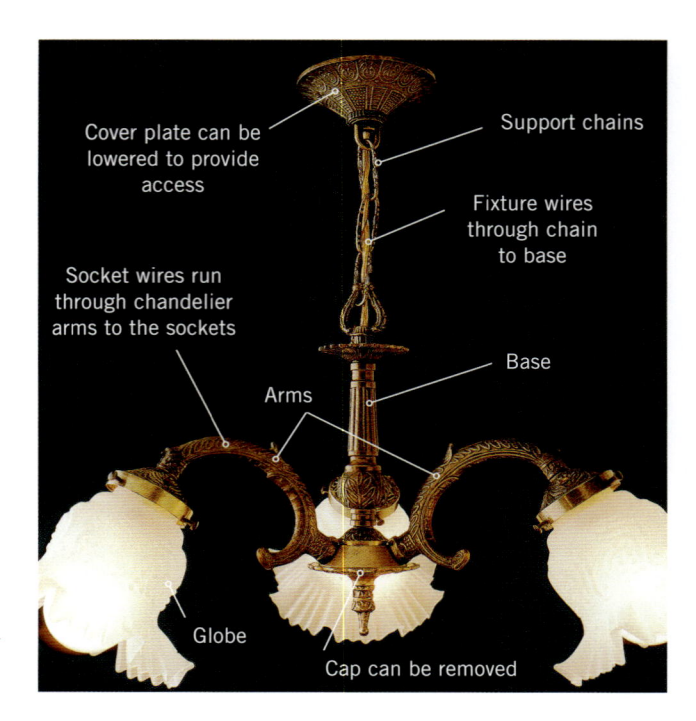

Cover plate can be lowered to provide access

Support chains

Fixture wires through chain to base

Socket wires run through chandelier arms to the sockets

Base

Arms

Globe

Cap can be removed

If you have a new chandelier, it may have a grounding wire that runs through the support chain to the electrical box. If this wire is present, make sure it is connected to the grounding wires in the electrical box.

How to Repair a Chandelier

1

Label any lights that are not working using masking tape. Turn off power to the fixture at the panel. Remove lightbulbs and all shades or globes.

2

Mounting strap

Threaded nipple

Cover plate

Retaining nut

Unscrew the retaining nut, and lower the decorative coverplate away from electrical box. Most chandeliers are supported by a threaded nipple attached to a mounting strap.

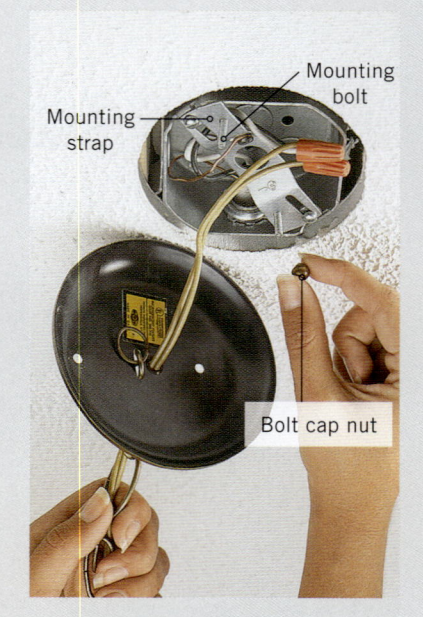

Mounting bolt

Mounting strap

Bolt cap nut

MOUNTING VARIATION: Some chandeliers are supported only by the cover plate that is bolted to the electrical box mounting strap. These types do not have a threaded nipple.

Test for power with a voltage tester. The tester should not glow. If it does, turn off power to the correct circuit at the panel.

Grounding screw

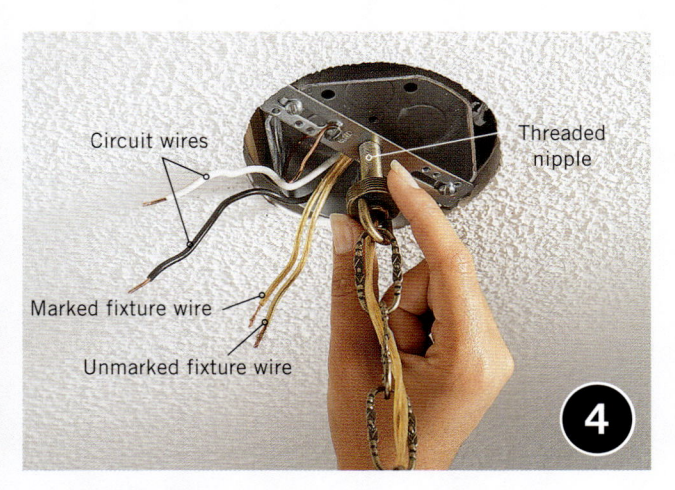

Disconnect fixture wires by removing the wire connectors. Unscrew the threaded nipple and carefully place the chandelier on a flat surface.

Circuit wires
Threaded nipple
Marked fixture wire
Unmarked fixture wire

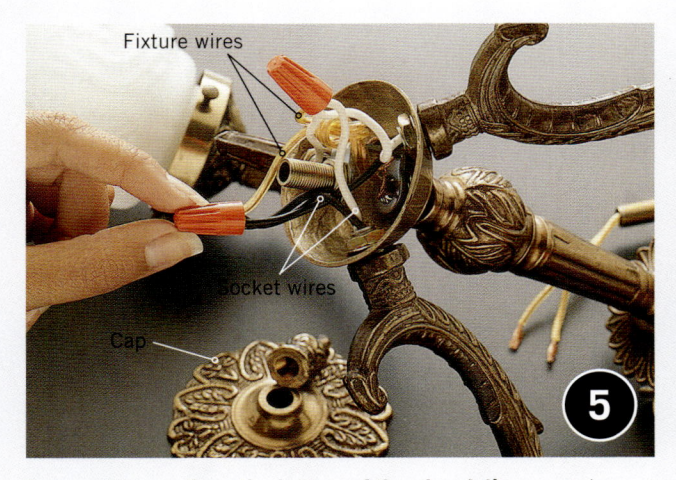

Remove the cap from the bottom of the chandelier, exposing the wire connections inside the hollow base. Disconnect the socket wires and fixture wires.

Fixture wires
Socket wires
Cap

Test the socket by attaching the clip of the continuity tester to the black socket wire and touching the probe to the tab in the socket. Repeat with the socket threads and the white socket wire. If the tester does not glow, the socket must be replaced.

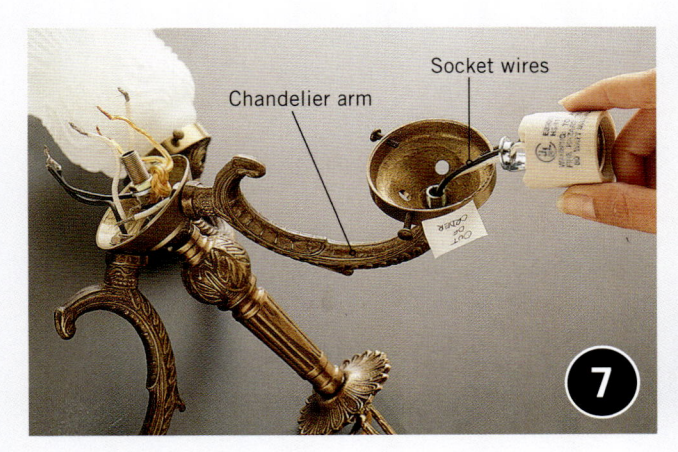

Remove a faulty socket by loosening any mounting screws or clips and pulling the socket and socket wires out of the fixture arm. Purchase and install a new chandelier socket, threading the socket wires through the fixture arm.

Socket wires
Chandelier arm

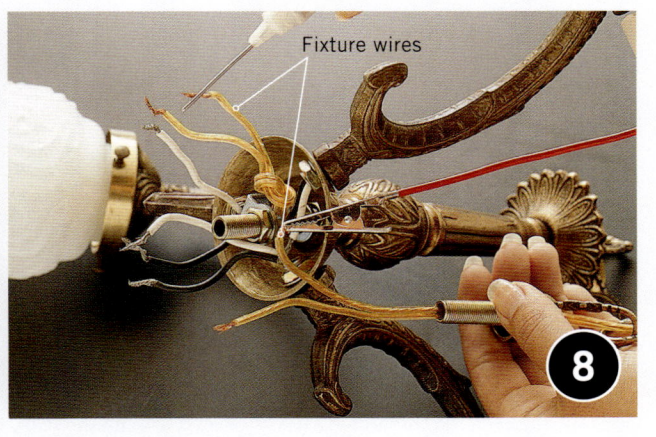

Test each fixture wire by attaching the clip of the continuity tester to one end of the wire and touching the probe to other end. If the tester does not glow, the wire must be replaced. Install new wires, if needed, then reassemble and rehang the chandelier.

Fixture wires

Repairing Ceiling Fans

Ceiling fans contain rapidly moving parts, making them more susceptible to trouble than many other electrical fixtures. Installation is a relatively simple matter, but repairing a ceiling fan can be very frustrating. The most common problems you'll encounter are balance and noise issues and switch failure, usually precipitated by the pull chain breaking. In most cases, both problems can be corrected without removing the fan from the ceiling. But if you have difficulty on ladders or simply don't care to work overhead, consider removing the fan when replacing the switch.

Ceiling fans are subject to a great deal of vibration and stress, so it's not uncommon for switches and motors to fail. Minimize wear and tear by making sure blades are in balance so the fan doesn't wobble.

TOOLS + MATERIALS

Screwdriver	Replacement switch
Combination tool	Voltage tester

 ## How to Troubleshoot Blade Wobble

Start by checking and tightening all hardware used to attach the blades to the mounting arms and the mounting arms to the motor. Hardware tends to loosen over time, and this is frequently the cause of wobble.

If wobble persists, try switching around two of the blades. Often this is all it takes to get the fan back into balance. If a blade is damaged or warped, replace it.

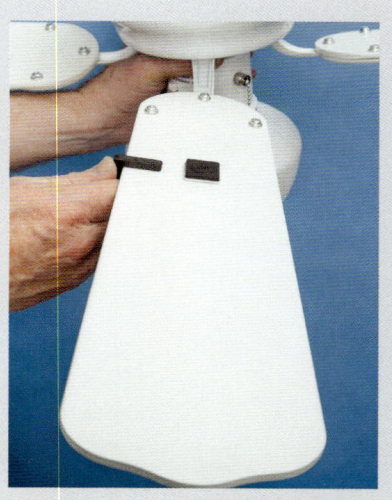

OPTION: Fan blade wobble also may be corrected using small weights that are affixed to the tops of the blades. For an easy DIY fix, you can use electrical tape and washer and some trial and error. You can also purchase fan blade weight kits for a couple of dollars. These kits include clips for marking the position of the weights as you relocate them as well as self-adhesive weights that can be stuck to the blade once you have found the sweet spot.

How to Fix a Loose Wire Connection

(1)

(2)

A leading cause of fan failure is loose wire connections. To inspect these connections, first shut off the power to the fan. Remove the fan blades to gain access, and then remove the canopy that covers the ceiling box and fan mounting bracket. Most canopies are secured with screws on the outside shell. Have a helper hold the fan body while you remove the screws so it won't fall.

Once the canopy is lowered, you'll see black, white, green, copper, and possibly blue wires. Hold a voltage tester within ½" of these wires with the wall switch that controls the fan in the ON position. The black and blue wires should cause the tester to beep if power is present.

(3)

(4)

Shut off power to the fan's circuit in the electrical panel, and test the wires by touching a voltage tester to each one. If the tester beeps or lights up, then the circuit is still live and is not safe to work on. When the tester does not beep or light up, the circuit is dead and may be worked upon.

When you have confirmed that there is no power, check all the wire connections to make certain each is tight and making good contact. You may be able to see that a connection has come apart and needs to be remade. But even if you see one bad connection, check them all by gently tugging on the wire connectors. If the wires pull out of the wire connector or the connection feels loose, unscrew the wire connector from the wires. Turn the power back on and see if the problem has been solved.

Replacing Plugs + Cords

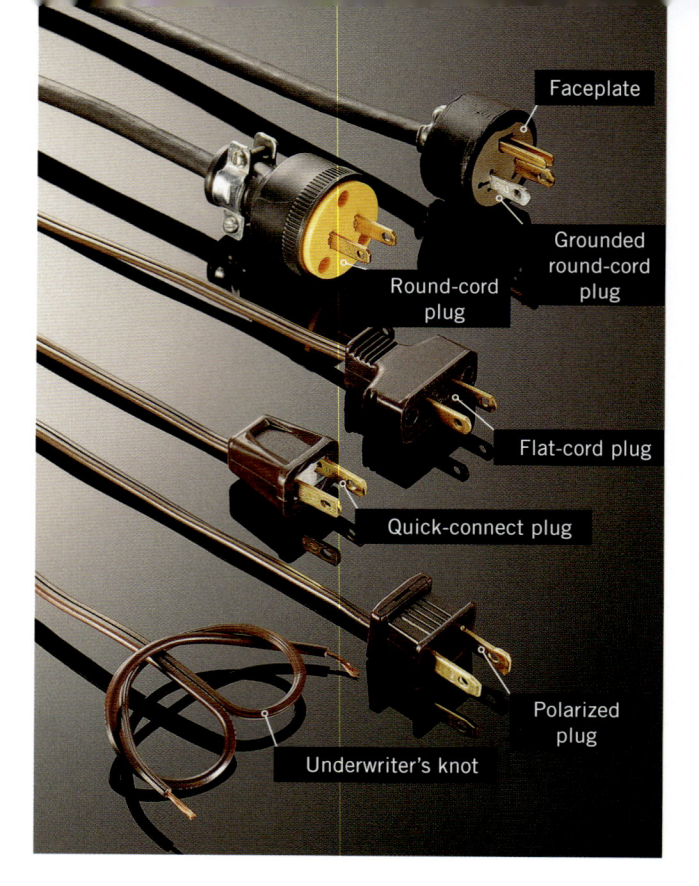

Faceplate

Grounded round-cord plug

Round-cord plug

Flat-cord plug

Quick-connect plug

Polarized plug

Underwriter's knot

Replace an electrical plug whenever you notice bent or loose prongs, a cracked or damaged casing, or a missing insulating faceplate. A damaged plug poses a shock and fire hazard.

Replacement plugs are available in different styles to match common appliance cords. Always choose a replacement that is similar to the original plug. Flat-cord and quick-connect plugs are used with light-duty appliances, such as lamps and radios. Round-cord plugs are used with larger appliances, including those that have three-prong grounding plugs.

Some tools and appliances use polarized plugs. A polarized plug has one wide (neutral) prong and one narrow (hot) prong, corresponding to the neutral and hot slots found in a standard receptacle.

If there is room in the plug body, tie the individual wires in an underwriter's knot to secure the plug to the cord (see photo, opposite page, top).

TOOLS + MATERIALS

Combination tool	Screwdriver
Needlenose pliers	Replacement plug

How to Install a Quick-Connect Plug

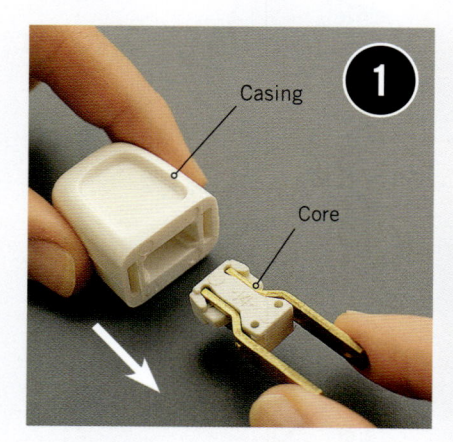

Casing

Core

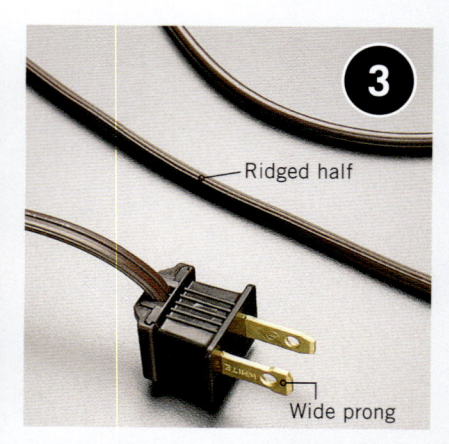

Ridged half

Wide prong

Squeeze the prongs of the new quick-connect plug together slightly, and pull the plug core from the casing. Cut the old plug from the flat-cord wire with a combination tool, leaving a clean cut end.

Feed unstripped wire through the rear of the plug casing. Spread the prongs, and then insert the wire into the opening in the rear of the core. Squeeze the prongs together; spikes inside the core penetrate the cord. Slide the casing over the core until it snaps into place.

When replacing a polarized plug, make sure that the ridged half of the cord lines up with the wider (neutral) prong of the plug.

How to Replace a Round-Cord Plug

Cut off the round cord near the old plug using a combination tool. Remove the insulating faceplate on the new plug and feed the cord through the rear of the plug. Strip about 3" of outer insulation from the round cord. Strip ¾" insulation from the individual wires.

Tie an underwriter's knot with the black and the white wires. Make sure the knot is located close to the edge of the stripped outer insulation. Pull the cord so that the knot slides into the plug body.

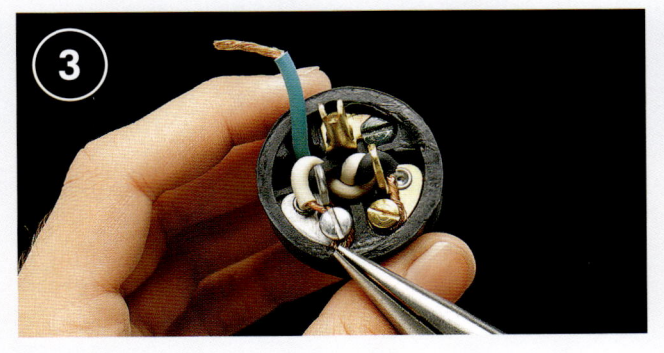

Hook the end of the black wire clockwise around the brass screw and the white wire around the silver screw. On a three-prong plug, attach the third wire to the grounding screw. If necessary, excess grounding wire can be cut away.

Tighten the screws securely, making sure the copper wires do not touch each other. Replace the insulating faceplate.

How to Replace a Flat-Cord Plug

Casing cover

Cut the old plug from cord using a combination tool. Pull apart the two halves of the flat cord so that about 2" of wire are separated. Strip ¾" insulation from each half. Remove the casing cover on the new plug.

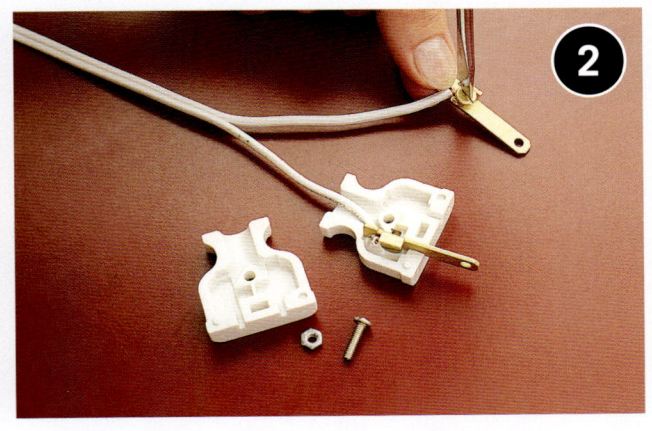

Hook the ends of the wires clockwise around the screw terminals, and tighten the screw terminals securely. Reassemble the plug casing. Some plugs may have an insulating faceplate that must be installed.

How to Replace a Lamp Cord

With the lamp unplugged, the shade off, and the bulb out, you can remove the socket. Squeeze the outer shell of the socket just above the base, and pull the shell out of the base. The shell is often marked "Press" at some point along its perimeter. Press there and then pull.

Under the outer shell there is a cardboard insulating sleeve. Pull this off and you'll reveal the socket attached to the end of the cord.

With the shell and insulation set aside, pull the socket away from the lamp (it will still be connected to the cord). Unscrew the two screws to completely disconnect the socket from the cord. Set the socket aside with its shell (you'll need them to reassemble the lamp).

Remove the old cord from the lamp by grasping the cord near the base and pulling the cord through the lamp.

5

Bring your damaged cord to a hardware store or home center and purchase a similar cord set. (A cord set is simply a replacement cord with a plug already attached.) Snake the end of the cord up from the base of the lamp through the top so that about 3" of cord is visible above the top.

6

Carefully separate the two halves of the cord. If the halves won't pull apart, you can carefully make a cut in the middle with a knife. Strip away about ¾" of insulation from the end of each wire.

7

Connect the ends of the new cord to the two screws on the side of the socket (one of which will be silver in color, the other brass colored). The neutral wire of the cord will have ribbing or markings along its length; wrap that wire clockwise around the silver (neutral) screw, and tighten the screw. The other half of the cord will be smooth; wrap it around the copper (hot) screw, and tighten the screw. Tie the two wires into an underwriter's knot (page 299) as applicable.

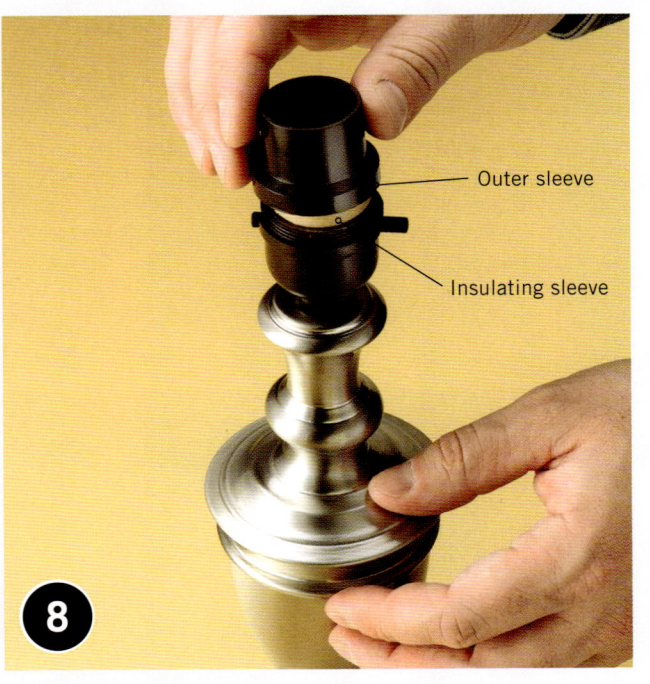

Outer sleeve

Insulating sleeve

8

Set the socket on the base. Make sure the switch isn't blocked by the harp—the part that holds the shade on some lamps. Slide the cardboard insulating sleeve over the socket so the sleeve's notch aligns with the switch. Now slide the outer sleeve over the socket, aligning the notch with the switch. It should snap into the base securely. Screw in a lightbulb, plug the lamp in, and test it.

Service Panels + Grounding

Problem: Rust stains are found inside the main service panel. This problem occurs because water seeps into the service head outside the house and drips down into the service panel.

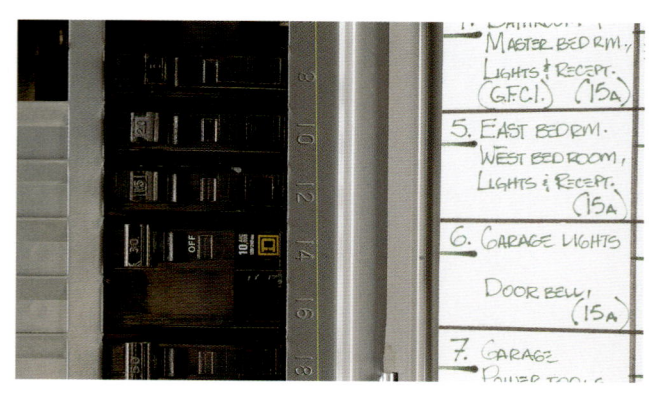

Solution: Have an electrician examine the service mast, weather head, service entrance cables, and the main panel. If the panel or service wires have been damaged, a new electrical service must be installed.

Problem: This problem is actually a very old and very dangerous solution. A penny or a knockout behind a fuse effectively bypasses the fuse, preventing an overloaded circuit from blowing the fuse. This is very dangerous and can lead to overheated wiring.

Solution: Remove the penny and replace the fuse. Have a licensed electrician examine the panel and circuit wiring. If the fuse has been bypassed for years, wiring may be dangerously compromised, and the circuit may need to be replaced. In addition, if you have the old Edison fuse socket, replace it with a new S-type fuse socket.

Problem: Two wires connected to one single-pole breaker is a sign of an overcrowded panel and also a dangerous code violation unless the breaker is approved for such a connection.

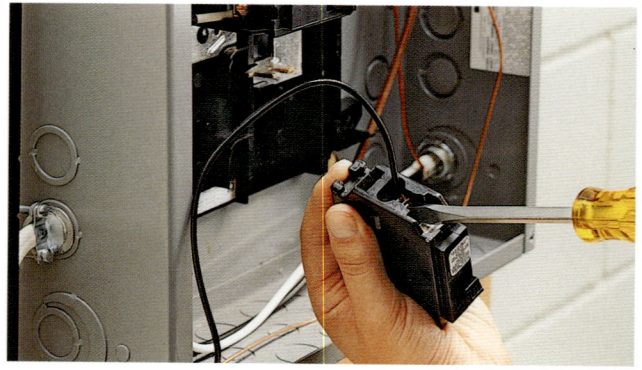

Solution: If there is room in the panel, install a separate breaker for the extra wire. If the panel is overcrowded, have an electrician upgrade the panel or install a subpanel. If the panel allows slimline (half-height) breakers, installing two of these may be an option.

Problem: Too much bare wire exposed at the breaker connection. This presents a short-circuit hazard.
Solution: With power off, trim the feed wire so no more than ½" of bare wire is exposed, and then reconnect.

Problem: There is no handle tie (or there is an improper handle tie) on breaker pair controlling a 240-volt circuit.
Solution: Install a handle tie approved by the circuit breaker manufacturer.

Problem: Conductor too small for breaker size. The #14 copper wires seen here are rated for 15-amp circuits. The 30-amp breaker allows too much current in the wires and could cause a fire. **Solution:** Replace the wires with wires approved for the circuit breaker size.

Problem: There is more than one neutral in a buss terminal. Sharing slots is fine for grounding wires, but each neutral wire should have its own terminal. **Solution:** Remove one of the wires and find an open neutral terminal for it.

Problem: Arc-fault protection (AFCI) circuit breakers may fail, especially if they are tripped with some frequency. **Solution:** Test each breaker as recommended by the manufacturer by depressing the "Test" button. If the breaker is functioning correctly, it will trip when the button is pushed.

Problem: GFCI circuit breakers may fail, especially if they are tripped with some frequency. **Solution:** Test each breaker as recommended by the manufacturer by depressing the "Test" button. If the breaker is functioning correctly, it will trip when the button is pushed.

Problem: There is a missing cable clamp at panel box. All NM cable entering a service panel (or any other box) needs protection from sharp edges that can cut sheathing. **Solution:** Disconnect the cable in the box, and retract and reinstall it with a cable clamp.

Problem: The shared hot terminal on the breaker is not wired correctly. **The example above is correct:** the conductors should be positioned on opposite sides of the terminal and held securely in the separate grooves by the terminal screw.

Cables + Wires

Problem: Cable running across joists or studs is attached to the edge of framing members. Electrical codes forbid this type of installation in exposed areas such as unfinished basements and crawl spaces.

Solution: Protect cable by drilling holes in framing members at least 2" from exposed edges and threading the cable through the holes.

Problem: Cable running along joists or studs hangs loosely. Loose cables can be pulled accidentally, causing damage to wires.

Solution: Anchor the cable to the side of the framing members at least 1¼" from the edge using plastic staples. NM cable should be stapled every 4½ ft. and within 8" of each electrical box.

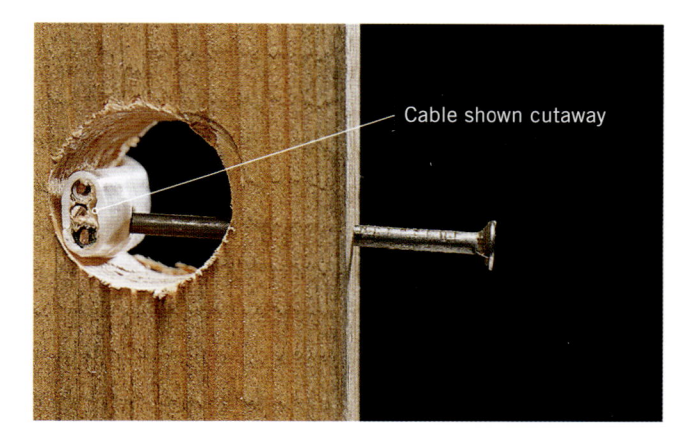

Cable shown cutaway

Problem: Cable threaded through studs or joists lies close to the edge of the framing members. NM cable (shown cutaway) can be damaged easily if nails or screws are driven into the framing members during remodeling projects.

Solution: Install metal nail guards to protect cable from damage. Nail guards are available at hardware stores and home centers.

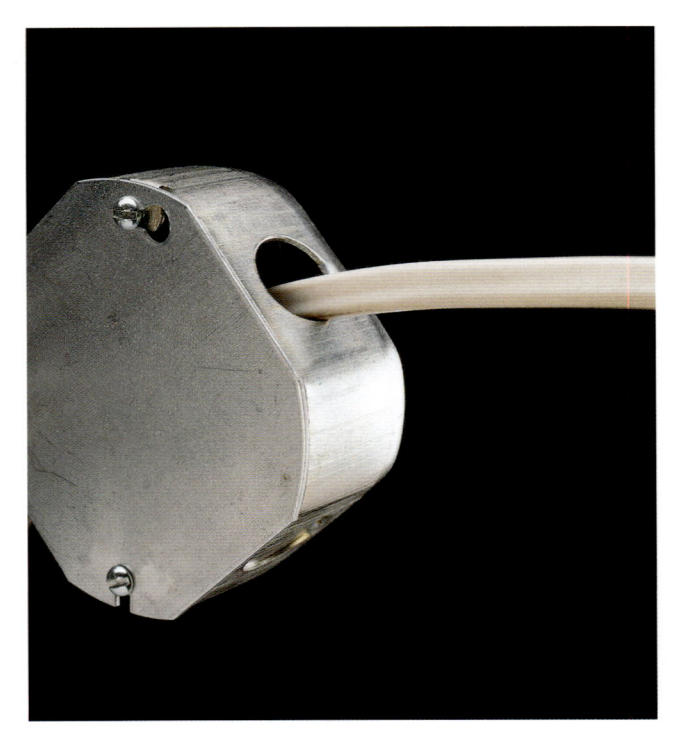

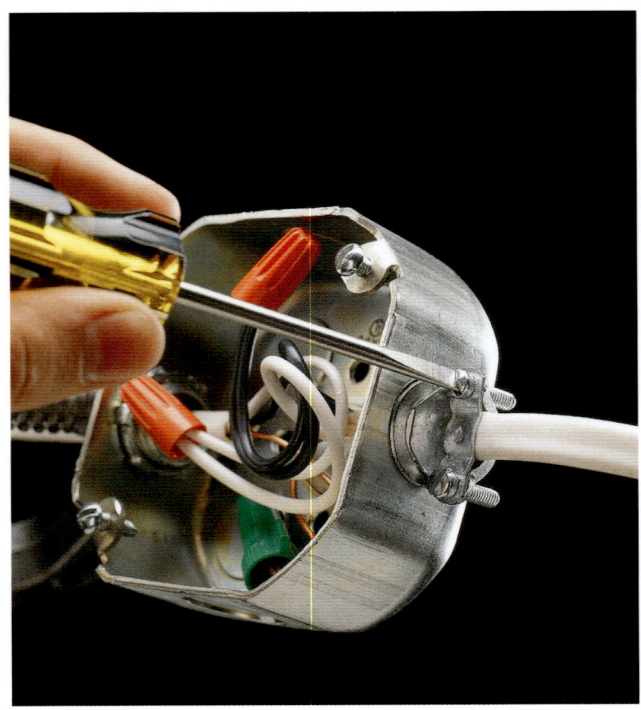

Problem: Unclamped cable enters a metal electrical box. Edges of the knockout can rub against the cable sheathing and damage the wires.

NOTE: With smaller plastic boxes, clamps are not required if cables are anchored to framing members within 8" of the box.

Solution: Anchor the cable to the electrical box with a cable clamp. Several types of cable clamps are available at hardware stores and home centers.

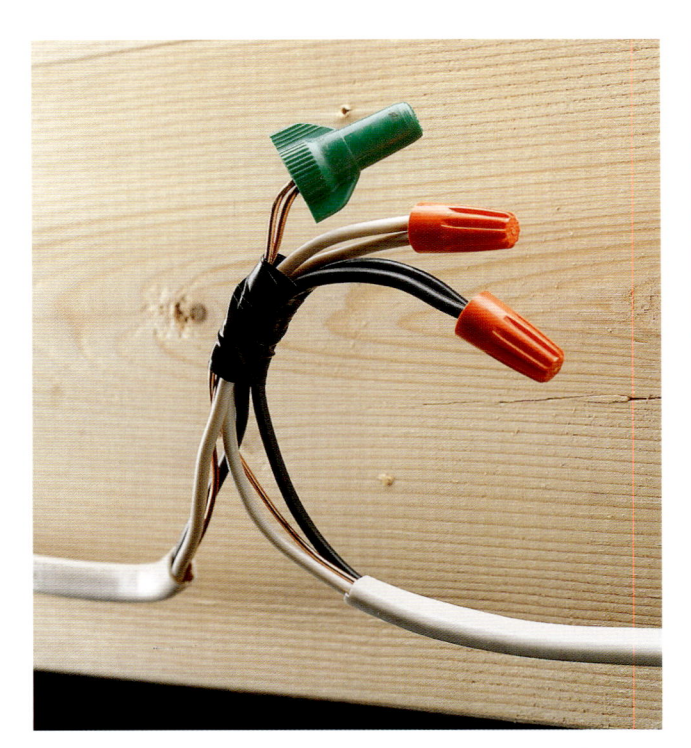

Problem: Cables are spliced outside an electrical box. Exposed splices can spark and create a risk of shock or fire.

Solution: Bring installation up to code by enclosing the splice inside a metal or plastic electrical box. Make sure the box is large enough to accommodate the number of wires it contains.

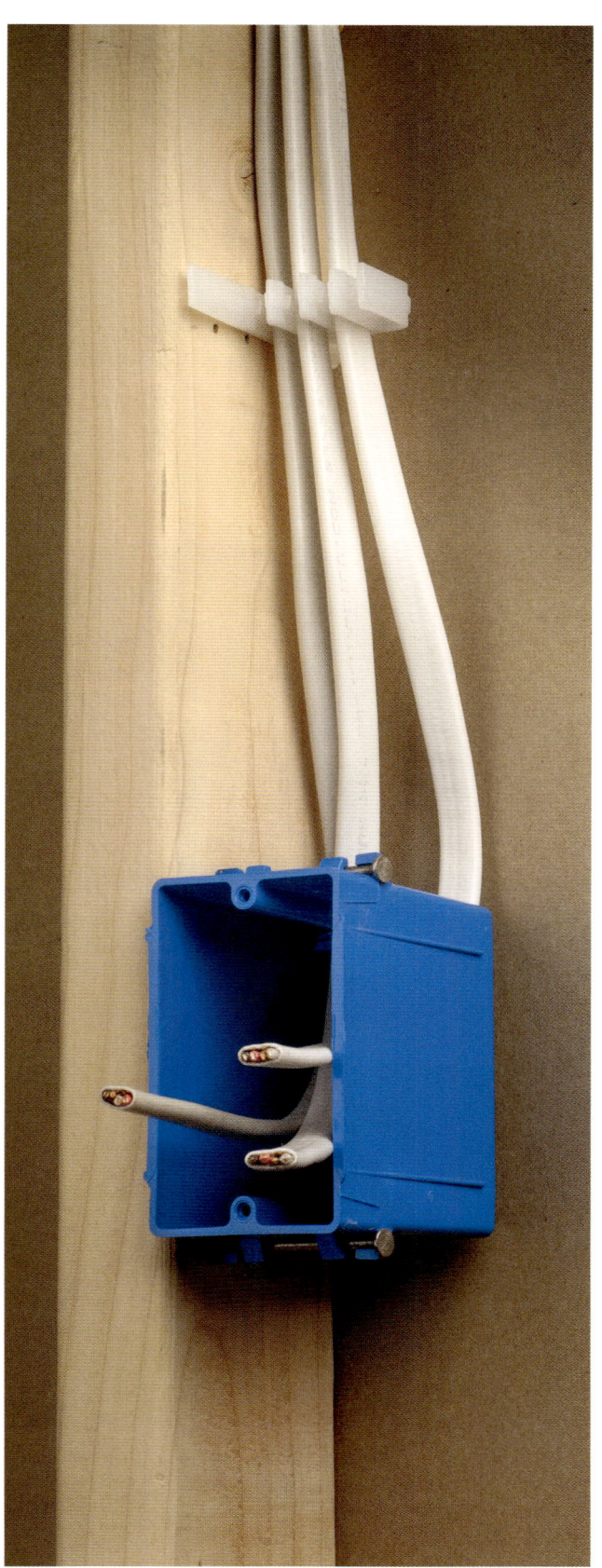

Problem: Standard cable staples are not rated for more than one cable; cables should not be stacked under a single staple. Stapling cables side by side usually violates the 1¼-inch minimum setback from the framing edge.

Solution: Secure multiple cables with an approved cable stacker device. These can hold up to four cables and are fastened with a single nail or screw. Install a cable stacker within 12 inches of the box.

Problem: Two or more wires are attached to a single-screw terminal. This type of connection is seen in older wiring but is now prohibited by the NEC.

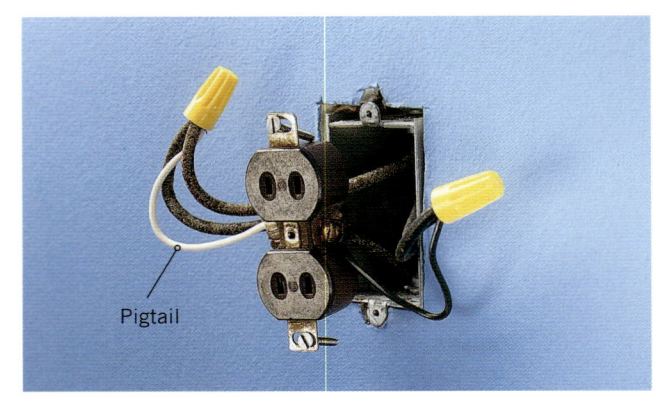

Pigtail

Solution: Disconnect the wires from the screw terminal, and then join them to a short length of wire (called a pigtail) using a wire connector. Connect the other end of the pigtail to the screw terminal.

Exposed wire

Problem: Bare wire extends past a screw terminal. Exposed wire can cause a short circuit if it touches the metal box or another circuit wire.

Solution: Clip the wire and reconnect it to the screw terminal. In a proper connection, the bare wire wraps completely around the screw terminal, and the plastic insulation just touches the screw head.

Problem: Wires are connected with electrical tape. Electrical tape was used frequently in older installations, but it can deteriorate over time, leaving bare wires exposed inside the electrical box.

Solution: Replace electrical tape with wire connectors. You may need to clip away a small portion of the wire so the bare end will be covered completely by the connector.

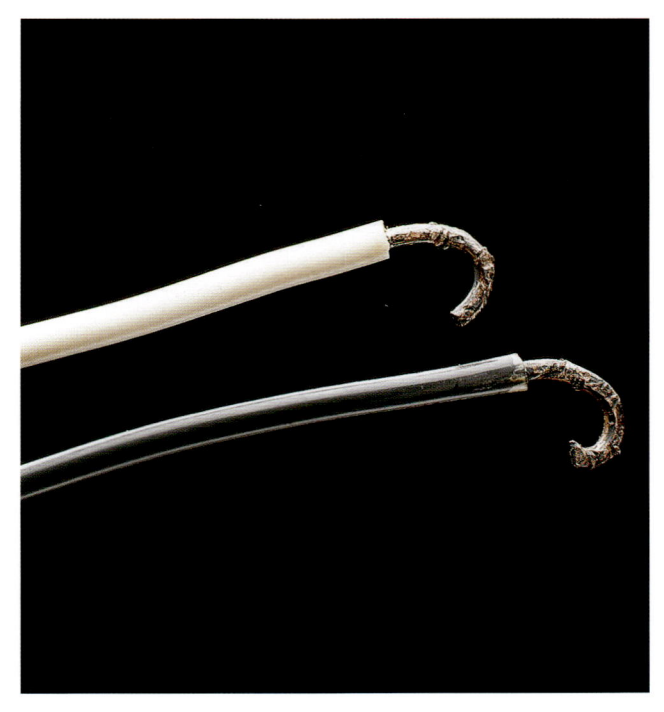

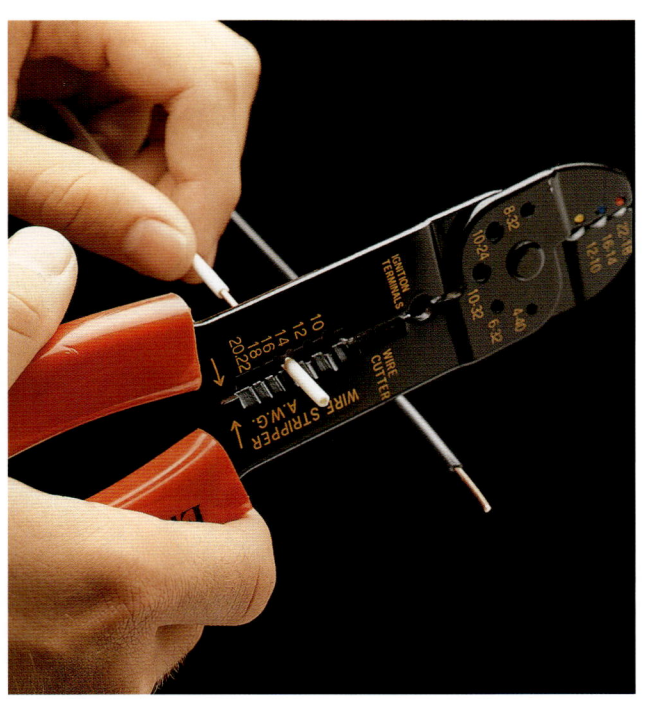

Problem: Nicks and scratches in bare wires interfere with the flow of current. This can cause the wires to overheat.

Solution: Clip away damaged portion of wire, restrip about ¾" of insulation, and reconnect the wire to the screw terminal.

Boxes

Problem: Insulation on wires is cracked or damaged. If damaged insulation exposes bare wire, a short circuit can occur, posing a shock hazard and fire risk.

Solution: Wrap damaged insulation temporarily with plastic electrical tape. Damaged circuit wires should be replaced by an electrician. *(continued)*

Problem: Open electrical boxes create a fire hazard if a short circuit causes sparks (arcing) inside the box.

Solution: Cover an open metal box with a solid metal cover plate. Cover an open plastic box with a plastic cover plate. Cover plates are available at any hardware store. Electrical boxes must remain accessible and cannot be sealed inside ceilings or walls.

Problem: Short wires are difficult to handle. The NEC requires that each wire in an electrical box have at least 3" of workable length from the front of the box.

Solution: Lengthen circuit wires by connecting them to short pigtail wires using wire connectors. Pigtails can be cut from scrap wire but should be the same gauge and color as the circuit wires and at least 3" long.

Problem: A recessed electrical box is hazardous, especially if the wall or ceiling surface is made from a flammable material, such as wood paneling. The NEC prohibits this type of installation.

Solution: Add an extension ring to bring the face of the electrical box flush with the surface. Extension rings come in several sizes and are available at hardware stores.

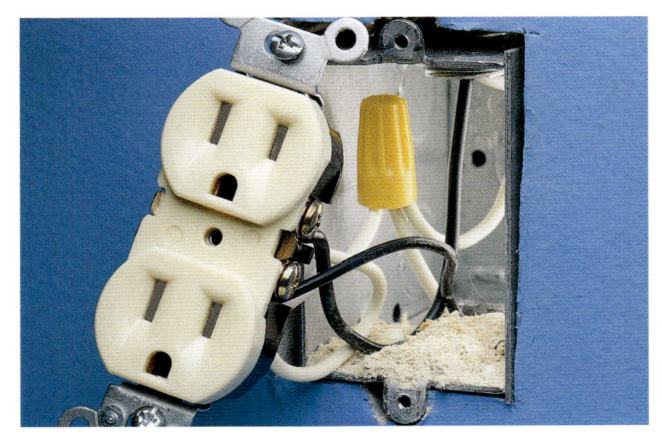

Problem: Open electrical boxes create a fire hazard if a short circuit causes sparks (dust and dirt in an electrical box can cause hazardous high-resistance short circuits). When making routine electrical repairs, always check the electrical boxes for dust and dirt buildup.

Solution: Vacuum the electrical box clean using a narrow nozzle attachment. Make sure power to the box is turned off at the panel before vacuuming.

Problem: A crowded electrical box (shown cutaway) makes electrical repairs difficult. This type of installation is prohibited, because the heat in the box can damage the wire or device and cause a fire.

Solution: Replace the electrical box with a deeper electrical box.

Problem: A light fixture is installed without an electrical box. This installation exposes the wiring connections and provides no support for the light fixture.

Solution: Install an approved electrical box to enclose the wire connections and support the light fixture.

Cords

Problem: A lamp or appliance cord runs underneath a rug. Foot traffic can wear off insulation, creating a short circuit that can cause fire or shock.

Solution: Reposition the lamp or appliance so that the cord is visible. Replace worn cords.

Problem: An older electric dryer or range has a three-prong cord that does not fit the four-slot receptacle in the house.

Solution: Replace the three-prong cord with a new, UL-listed four-prong cord that is properly rated for the appliance. See pages 196 to 197 for dryer/range cord installation.

Problem: A lamp or appliance plug is cracked, or an electrical cord is frayed near the plug. Worn cords and plugs create a fire and shock hazard.

Solution: Cut away damaged portions of wire, and install a new plug (see pages 298–299). Replacement plugs are available at appliance stores and home centers.

Problem: An extension cord is too small for the power load drawn by a tool or appliance. Undersized extension cords can overheat, melting the insulation and leaving bare wires exposed.

Solution: Use an extension cord with wattage and amperage ratings that meet or exceed the rating of the tool or appliance. Extension cords are for temporary use only. Never use an extension cord for a permanent installation.

Receptacles + Switches

Problem: Octopus receptacle attachments used permanently can overload a circuit and cause overheating of the receptacle.

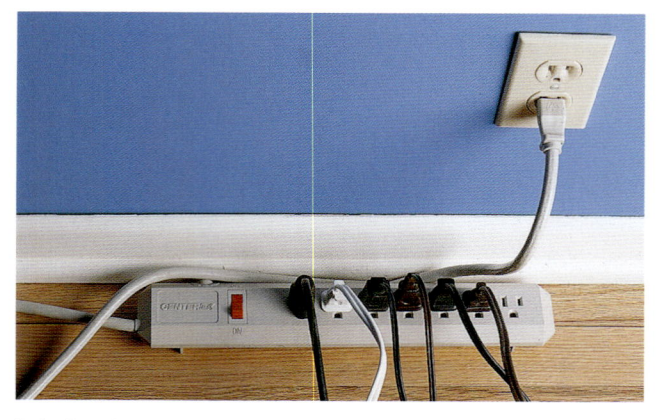

Solution: Use a multireceptacle power strip with built-in overload protection. This is for temporary use only. If the need for extra receptacles is frequent, upgrade the wiring system.

Problem: Scorch marks near screw terminals indicate that electrical arcing has occurred. Arcing usually is caused by loose wire connections.

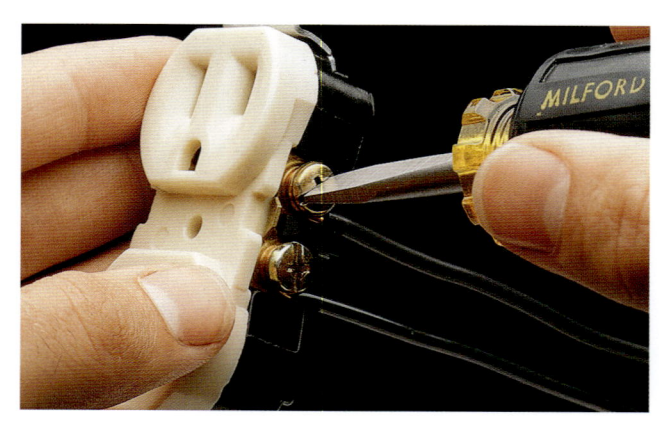

Solution: If the insulation is damaged, cut the wires back to intact insulation. Otherwise, clean the wires with fine grit sandpaper or steel wool. Replace the receptacle. Make sure wires are connected securely to screw terminals.

Problem: Two-slot receptacle in outdoor installation is hazardous because it has no grounding slot. In case of a short circuit, a person plugging in a cord becomes a conductor for current to follow to ground.

Solution: Replace the old receptacle with a weather-resistant GFCI receptacle to provide protection against ground faults. If the receptacle is exposed to the elements, be sure to include a cover rated for wet locations.

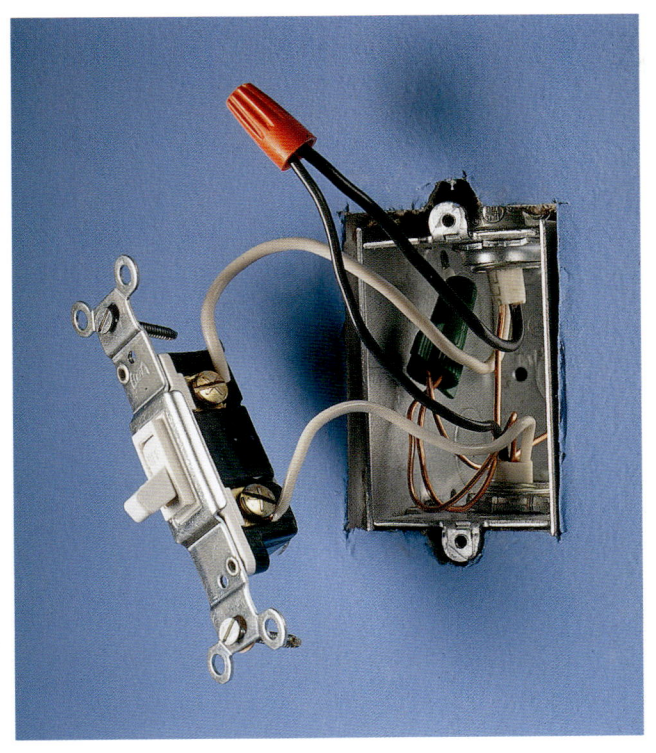

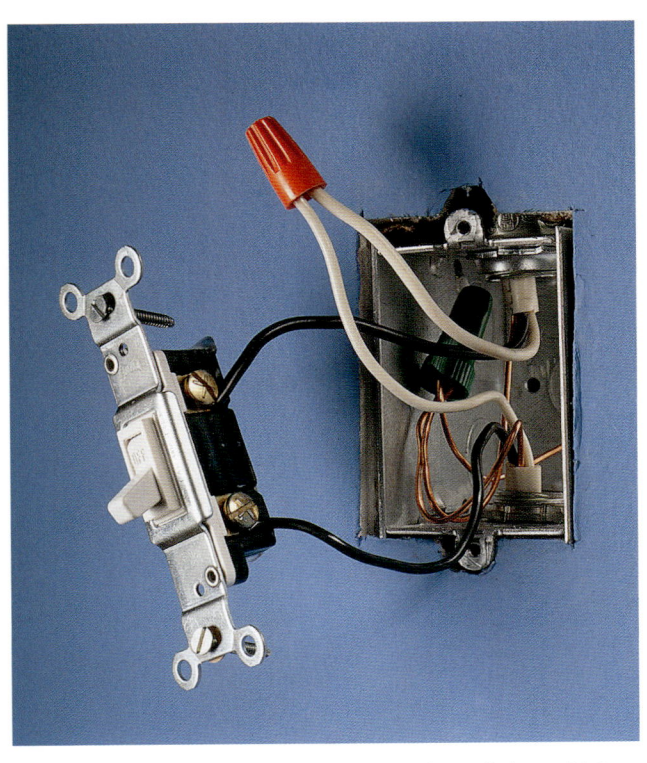

Problem: White neutral wires are connected to a switch. Although the switch appears to work correctly in this installation, it is dangerous because the light fixture carries voltage when the switch is off.

Solution: Connect the black hot wires to the switch, and join the white wires together with a wire connector.

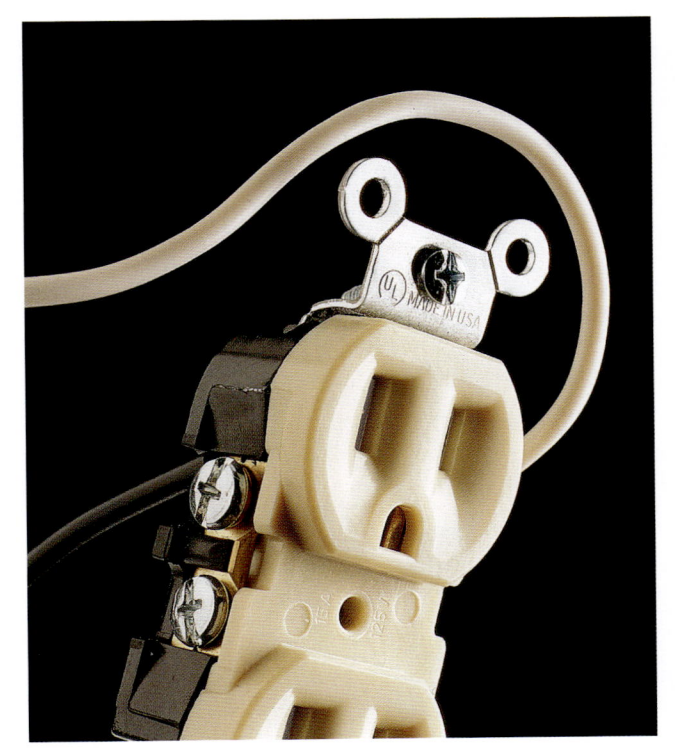

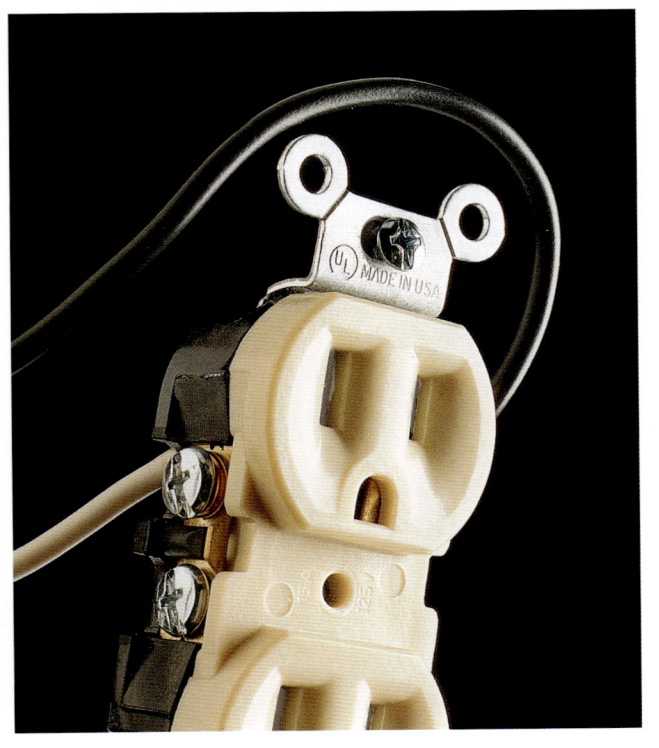

Problem: White neutral wires are connected to the brass screw terminals on the receptacle, and black hot wires are attached to silver screw terminals. This installation is hazardous because live voltage flows into the long neutral slot on the receptacle.

Solution: Reverse the wire connections so that the black hot wires are attached to brass screw terminals and white neutral wires are attached to silver screw terminals. Live voltage now flows into the short slot on the receptacle.

Conversions

METRIC EQUIVALENT

Inches (in.)	1/64	1/32	1/25	1/16	1/8	1/4	3/8	2/3	1/2	5/8	3/4	7/8	1	2	3	4	5	6	7	8	9	10	11	12	36	39.4
Feet (ft.)																								1	3	3 1/12
Yards (yd.)																									1	1 1/12
Millimeters (mm)	0.40	0.79	1		1.59	3.18	6.35	9.53	10	12.7	15.9	19.1	22.2	25.4	50.8	76.2	101.6	127	152	178	203	229	254	279	305	914	1,000
Centimeters (cm)					0.95	1	1.27	1.59	1.91	2.22	2.54	5.08	7.62	10.16	12.7	15.2	17.8	20.3	22.9	25.4	27.9	30.5	91.4	100		
Meters (m)																						.30	.91	1.00		

CONVERTING MEASUREMENTS

TO CONVERT:	TO:	MULTIPLY BY:
Inches	Millimeters	25.4
Inches	Centimeters	2.54
Feet	Meters	0.305
Yards	Meters	0.914
Miles	Kilometers	1.609
Square inches	Square centimeters	6.45
Square feet	Square meters	0.093
Square yards	Square meters	0.836
Cubic inches	Cubic centimeters	16.4
Cubic feet	Cubic meters	0.0283
Cubic yards	Cubic meters	0.765
Pints (U.S.)	Liters	0.473 (Imp. 0.568)
Quarts (U.S.)	Liters	0.946 (Imp. 1.136)
Gallons (U.S.)	Liters	3.785 (Imp. 4.546)
Ounces	Grams	28.4
Pounds	Kilograms	0.454
Tons	Metric tons	0.907

TO CONVERT:	TO:	MULTIPLY BY:
Millimeters	Inches	0.039
Centimeters	Inches	0.394
Meters	Feet	3.28
Meters	Yards	1.09
Kilometers	Miles	0.621
Square centimeters	Square inches	0.155
Square meters	Square feet	10.8
Square meters	Square yards	1.2
Cubic centimeters	Cubic inches	0.061
Cubic meters	Cubic feet	35.3
Cubic meters	Cubic yards	1.31
Liters	Pints (U.S.)	2.114 (Imp. 1.76)
Liters	Quarts (U.S.)	1.057 (Imp. 0.88)
Liters	Gallons (U.S.)	0.264 (Imp. 0.22)
Grams	Ounces	0.035
Kilograms	Pounds	2.2
Metric tons	Tons	1.1

Resources

Black + Decker
Portable power tools and more
www.blackanddecker.com

Broan-NuTone, LLC
Vent fans
www.broan-nutone.com

Generac Power Systems
Standby generators and switches
www.generac.com

Honda Power Equipment/American Honda Motor Company, Inc.
Standby generators
www.hondapowerequipment.com

Kohler
Standby generators
www.kohlergenerators.com

Pass + Seymour Legrand
Home automation products
www.legrand.us/pass-and-seymour

Red Wing Shoes Co.
Work shoes and boots shown throughout book
www.redwingshoes.com

Unistrut Metal Framing
Solar panel mounts
www.unistrut.us

Westinghouse
Ceiling fans, decorative lighting, solar outdoor lighting, + other lighting fixtures and bulbs
www.westinghouse.com

Index

Aboveground service drop, 175, 181
Adapters, receptacle, 19
AFCI breakers/receptacles, 68
    about, 68, 98, 168, 169–170
    code requirements, 121
    installing, 170–171
    problem and solution for, 304
    room-by-room wiring plans for, 135,
        140, 141, 144
Air conditioners, 127, 129, 158
Alarms, smoke and carbon monoxide,
    218–219
Amperage, 126
Ampere (amp), defined, 14
Appliances, 10, 65, 121, 126–129,
    135–136, 140, 156–158,
    See also specific appliances
Area lights, 221
Armored cable (AC), 14, 19, 27
Attics, 146
Automatic standby generators, 268, 269
Automatic switches, 86, 91, 264, 267

Backstabbing, 7
Backup power supplies, 264–275
Baseboard heaters.
    See Electric baseboard heaters
Basements, wiring overview for, 145
Bathrooms
    code requirements for, 116, 121
    exhaust fans in, 250–253
    vanity lights in, 216–217
    wiring, 138–139
Bedrooms
    code requirements for, 121
    smoke alarms in, 125
    wiring, 134, 141
Bonding, 18, 182–183, 184, 187
Boxes. *See* Electrical boxes; Junction boxes
Bracket-mounted ceiling fans, 243, 244
Built-in light switch, testing and
    replacing a, 293

Cable(s)
    about, 26
    code requirements for, 116, 120
    defined, 14
    inspections and, 122
    labeling, 38, 177
    problems and solutions for, 305–309
    running inside finished walls, 39–40
    types of, 27–28
Cable ripper, 20

Cable sheathing damage, 124
Cable staples, 31
Canless ceiling light fixture, 206–207,
    209–211
Can lights, traditional recessed, 207–208
Carbon monoxide (CO) alarms, 125, 218
Cartridge fuses, 69
Cat 5 (Category 5) cable, 28
Ceiling boxes, 60
Ceiling fans
    about, 242
    brace for, 58, 60
    bracket-mounted, 243, 244
    code requirements, 117
    downrod mounted, 243, 245
    with electric heating elements, 243
    remote control for, 246–249
    repairing, 296–297
    troubleshooting blade wobble on, 296
Ceiling lights
    about, 202–203
    canless, 206–207, 209–211
    chandeliers, repairing, 294–295
    recessed, 206–207, 208–209
    replacing, 204–205
Central air conditioners, 129
Chandeliers, 60, 294–295
Channel-type pliers, 20
Childproofing receptacles, 97
Circuit breaker panels
    about, 66–67
    labeling new circuits on an index
        attached to, 117
    replacing older service panels with, 114
    subpanel, 67
Circuit breakers, 64
    about, 68
    connecting, 70–71
    defined, 14
    exercising, 67
    resetting and testing, 69
    subpanels, 188–191
Circuit maps, 132, 149–165
Circuits
    defined, 14
    diagram, 16–17
    rated, 125
    understanding, 16
Closets
    code requirements, 117
    light fixtures in, 125, 141
Clothes dryers, 129, 144, 192, 194–197
CO/ALR switches, 76

Coaxial cable, 28
Codes
    See also National Electrical Code (NEC)
    learning about, 112, 115
    on location of main service panel, 176
    requirements, 115–119
Computer circuits, 158
Concrete walls, 46–47
Conductor, defined, 14
Conduits
    about, 42–43
    defined, 14
    electrical bonding of metal, 42
    installing on concrete walls, 46–47
    making nonmetallic connections, 45
    types of, 43, 44
Connectors, common types, 124
Consumer Products Safety Commission, 76
Continuity, defined, 14
Copper grounding wire, 26
Cord-connected transfer switches, 267
Cords
    dryer and range, 194–197
    problems and solutions for, 312–313
    replacing, 298–301
Countdown timer switches, 84
Countertop receptacles, 135
Crawlspaces, 146
Current, defined, 14

Daylight sensor switches, 85
Delivery system, 11
Diagnostic tools, 21
Diagrams. *See* Wiring diagrams/plans
Dial-type dimmer switches, 86
Dimmer switches, 86–87, 207
Dining areas
    code requirements for, 121
    wiring, 140
Dishwashers, 128, 135, 137
Doorbells, 224–227
Double-insulated tools, 19
Double receptacle circuit, 155–156
Double switches, 82, 91
Dual-function GFCI/AFCI breakers, 168,
    170–171
Ductwork, range hoods and, 260–263
Duplex receptacle
    about, 98
    defined, 14
    layouts for, 150, 154–155, 161

Edison adapter, 68
Elbow fitting, 47
Electrical boxes, 13
    ceiling, 60
    code requirements for, 120
    covered knockouts on, 124
    defined, 14
    fill chart, 50
    fixtures not needing, 56
    heights of, 59
    how to locate, 59
    how to replace, 62
    inspections and, 122, 123
    installing, 56–58
    installing a junction box, 60–61
    installing for light fixtures, 58
    installing for receptacles, 57
    installing for switches, 58
    installing pop-in, 62–63
    locating, 59
    nonmetallic, 54–55
    problems and solutions for, 309–311
    replacing, 62
    sizes and shapes of, 50, 51
    specifications, 53
    wallcovering thickness and, 59
Electrical circuits. See Circuits
Electrical loads
    calculating, 127
    estimating, 126, 130–131
    evaluating, 113
    how to estimate, 130–131
Electrical metal conduit (EMT), 43
Electrical metallic tubing (EMT), 44
Electrical symbol key, 132, 133
Electrical system, overview of, 10–13
    electrical terminology, 14
        Electrical transformers.
        See Transformers
Electric baseboard heaters, 129, 140, 157,
    232–235
Electric dryers. See Dryers, electric
Electric ranges, 137
    cords, 194–197
    hoods for, 137, 260–263
    receptacles for, 193
    wattage rating, 128
    wiring layout for, 157
Electric vehicle charging equipment
    (EVCE), 7
EMT (electrical metallic tubing), 44
Exhaust ducts, range hoods and, 260–263
Exhaust fans, 138, 250–253
Extension cords, 23, 313

Fans
    bathroom exhaust, 250–253
    ceiling fans, 242–249
    whole-house, 254–259
Final inspections, 122
Fish tape, 21, 47
Fixed devices, 127
Flat-cord plugs, 298, 299
Flexible metal conduit (FMC), 14, 44
Floodlights, 221, 284–287
Floor-warming systems, 236–241
Food disposers, 128
Forced-air furnaces, 129
Four-way switches, 76, 89, 163–164
Foyers, 142–143
Freezers, 129
Fuses, 23
    about, 68
    defined, 14
    electrical panels and, 64, 65
    identifying and replacing a blown, 69
    replacing with circuit breaker panel, 114

Garage door openers, 145
Garages, wiring, 145
Garbage disposals, 137
Gas pipes, 18
Generators, backup, 264–275
GFCI breakers, 68, 69, 168, 169, 304
GFCI receptacles
    about, 98, 104, 168
    AFCI breakers and, 168
    in bathrooms, 138
    code requirements for, 116, 118, 119, 121
    in crawlspaces and attics, 146
    in garages and basements, 145
    generators and, 264, 268
    installing, 62, 103, 105, 170–171
    in kitchens, 135, 137
    in laundry room, 144
    layouts for, 150, 151, 156
    NEC standards on, 118
    outdoors, 198
    updates on, 7
Greenfield, 14
Grounded wire. See Neutral wires
Grounding, 18–19, 182–187
Grounding conductors, 149, 179
Grounding electrode system, 185–187
Grounding wire, 12, 14
Ground rods, 182, 185–187, 1985

Hallways, 117, 121, 142–143
Heating appliances/systems
    baseboard heaters, 232–235
    bathroom wall heaters, 138

calculating electrical load and, 127
    underfloor radiant heat system, 236–241
Heat pump air handlers, 129
High-voltage receptacles, 96
Hot wire, defined, 14

IMC (intermediate metallic conduit), 44
Inspections/inspectors, 113, 122–125,
    132, 188
Insulator, defined, 14
Island exhausts, 261
Island (kitchen) receptacles, 7, 135
Isolated-ground receptacle, 158

Junction boxes, 60–61
    See also Electrical boxes

Kitchen island/peninsula receptacles, 7, 135
Kitchens
    code requirements for, 116, 121
    wiring for, 132, 135–137
Knob-and-tube wiring, 26, 27

Ladders, 23
Lamp cord, replacing a, 300–301
Lamp socket, replacing a, 293
Landscape lighting, 220–223
Laser level, 20
Laundry rooms
    code requirements for, 119, 121
    GFCI protection for, 104, 134
    wiring, 144
Lightbulbs
    LED, 207, 289
    light fixture failure and, 290
    wattage ratings, 128
Lighting and light fixtures, 12
    ceiling lights, 202–211
    circuits for kitchen, 136
    closet, 125
    code requirements for, 116, 117,
        120–121
    garages and basements, 145
    installing electrical boxes for, 58
    layouts for, 151, 152–153, 159–165
    motion-sensing floodlights, 284–287
    NEC standards for, 116, 117, 118
    pathway and patio, 220–223
    recessed, 206–211
    removing, 292
    replacing a lamp cord, 300–301
    stairways, 142
    track lights, 212–215
    troubleshooting and repairing, 290–295
    vanity lights, 216–217
    wiring for bathrooms, 138

wiring for bedrooms, 141
wiring for crawlspaces and attics, 146
wiring for garages and basements, 145
wiring for hallways, stairways and
    foyers, 142
wiring for kitchens, 136
wiring for living and dining rooms, 140
wiring for outdoor, 147
Linesman pliers, 20
Liquid-tight flexible conduit (LFC), 44
Living areas
    code requirements for, 115, 121
    wiring, 140
Low-voltage lighting, 220–223

Machine screws, 118
Main service panels
    about, 18, 65
    code requirements, 119
    in electrical system, 13
    examining, 112, 114
    how to replace, 177–181
    location of, 176
    shutting off, 22, 65
Masonry wall exhaust termination, 263
Measurement conversions, 316
Mercury switches, 75
Metal boxes, 53
Metal conduit, 27, 42–43, 44
Metallic piping, how to bond, 183–184
Meters, 11, 12, 14
Microwave ovens, 128, 137
Modern NM (nonmetallic) cable, 19
Motion-sensing floodlights, 284–287
Mudrooms, 142
Multimeter, 21, 108, 109

National Electrical Code (NEC), 112,
    115-121
National Fire Protection Agency (NEC), 7
Neutral wires, 10, 11, 18
    defined, 14
    separate, 156
    shared, 155, 156
Nonmetallic boxes, 53
Nonmetallic conduit fittings, 44
Nonmetallic sheathed cable
    about, 19, 27, 28
    defined, 14
    framing member chart for, 34
    how to strip, 30
    installing, 34–38
    installing in finished ceilings, 41
    reading, 29
    running inside a finished wall, 39
    sheathing colors, 28

Occupancy sensor, 85
Octagonal boxes, 50, 51
Outbuildings, 276–283
Outdoor boxes, types of, 51–52
Outdoors
    code requirements for, 121
    installing a new fixture box, 285
    landscape lighting, 220–223
    motion-sensing floodlights, 284–287
    receptacles, 198–201
    wiring overview, 147
Outlets. See Receptacles
Overload, defined, 14

Patio lighting, 220–223
Peninsula receptacles, 7, 135
Permits, 115, 132, 188
Pigtail wires, 14, 33
Pilot-light switches, 83, 90
Plastic boxes, 51, 52
Plastic conduit, 43
Pliers, 20
Plugs, repairing, 298–299
Polarized plugs/receptacles, 14, 19, 298
Pop-in retrofit boxes, installing, 62–63
Power, defined, 14
Power plants, 11, 13
Programmable timer switches, 84, 91
Project planning, 112–113
Push-in connectors, 31, 124
Push-in fittings, 76, 98
Push-in terminals, 74

Quick-connect plugs, 298

Range hoods, 137, 260–263
Receptacle adapter, 19
Receptacles, 13. See also GFCI receptacles
    120/240-volt dryer, 192
    120/240-volt range, 193
    about, 93
    in bathrooms, 138
    in bedrooms, 141
    changes in NEC 2023 code, 7
    childproof, 97
    code requirements for, 116, 117, 120
    common problems with, 99
    countertop, 135
    defined, 14
    duplex, 98
    in electrical system, 13
    for garages and basements, 145
    high-voltage, 96
    installing electrical boxes for, 57
    installing new, 102–103
    isolated-ground, 158
    in kitchens, 135, 136, 137

in laundry rooms, 144
in living and dining rooms, 140
older, 95
120/240-volt dryer, 192
120/240-volt range, 193
outdoors, 198–201
polarized, 14, 19
problems and solutions for, 314–315
spacing for, 123, 140
split, 154–155
switch-controlled, 154–155
switch/receptacles, 83, 91
tamper-resistant, 19, 97, 104
testing, 108–109
types of, 94
wired in sequence, 150
wiring for, 100–101
wiring layout for, 158
Recessed ceiling lights, 206–211
Refrigerators, 137
Remote-control ceiling fans, 246–249
Repair projects
    ceiling fans, 296–297
    chandeliers, 294–295
    light fixtures, 290–295
    plug and cord replacements, 298–301
Rocker type switches, 86
Romex, 14
Roof exhaust termination, 263
Room-by-room wiring, 134–147
    bathrooms, 138–139
    bedrooms, 141
    crawlspaces and attics, 146
    garages and basements, 145
    hallways, stairs, and foyers, 142
    kitchens, 135–137
    laundry room, 144
    living and dining rooms, 140
    outdoors, 147
Rotary snap switches, 75
Round-cord plugs, 298, 299
Rubber mats/rubber-soled shoes, 23

Safety issues
    with circuit breaker panels, 67
    whole-house fans and, 255
    wiring, 22–23
Screw terminals
    connecting wires to, 31
    defined, 14
Serial arc fault, 169
Service entrance cable (SE), 28
Service mast, 12
Service panels
    See also Main service panels
    about, 64–65
    code requirements for, 120

defined, 14
grounding, 184
locating, 176
problems and solutions for, 302–304
protected by service barriers, 119
replacing, 174–177
splicing in, 179
Shoes, rubber-soled, 23
Short circuit, defined, 14
Side cutters, 20
Single-pole wall switches, 77
    layouts for, 152–153
    testing, 88
Slide-action dimmer switches, 86
Smart switches, 85
Smoke alarms, 125, 218, 219
Sockets, 290, 292, 293–295
Specialty switches, 84–85
Split receptacles, 154–155
Spotlights, 221
Spring-wound timer switch, 85
Stairways
    code requirements, 121
    light fixtures in, 116
    wiring, 142–143
Strain-relief fittings, 194, 195
Subpanels, 64, 188–191
Substations, 13
Surge-protective devices, 172–173
Switches
    action options, 86
    code requirements for, 120
    defined, 14
    dimmer, 86–87
    double, 82
    in electrical system, 13
    four-way, 76, 80–81, 163–164
    ganged, 159, 165
    installations, 77, 78, 80, 87
    installing electrical boxes for, 58
    layouts for, 151–153, 159–165
    pilot-light, 83, 90
    problems and solutions for, 214–215,
        314–315
    replacing, 79, 81
    single-pole, 159

single-pole wall, 88
specialty, 84–85
testing, 88–91
testing and replacing a built-in light, 293
three-way, 76, 78, 89, 160–161, 162
timer, 84, 85
types of, 75, 76, 86
wall, 74–81
wireless, 228–231
Switch/receptacle, 83, 91

Tamper-resistant (TR) receptacles,
    19, 97, 104
Tape measure, 20
Telephone cable, 28
Thermostats, 157, 232, 233, 236,
    See also Heating appliances/systems
THHN/THWN wire, 28, 42
Three-way dimmer switches, 86, 87
Three-way wall switches, 76, 78–79, 89
Time-delay switches, 84, 91
Timer switches, 84, 85, 90
Toggle switches, 75
Toggle-type dimmers, 86
Tools
    double-insulated, 19
    home wiring, 20–21
Track lights, 212–215
Transfer switches, 264, 265, 267, 270–275
Transformers, 11, 13, 119, 220, 223,
    224–225, 226

UF (Underground Feeder) cable, 27, 28
UL (Underwriters Laboratories), 14
Underfloor radiant heat systems, 236–237
Underground service lateral, 175

Vanity lights, 216–217
Video doorbells, 224, 226–227
Voltage (volts), defined, 14
Voltage ratings, 11, 94
Voltage tester, 21

Walk-in closets, 117, 141
Wall heaters, 138

Wall-mount TVs, 140
Wall switches
    about, 74
    double, 82
    four-way, 80–81, 89
    how to replace, 79
    installing, 76, 77, 78
    pilot-light, 83
    single-pole, 88
    testing, 89
    three-way, 78, 89
    types of, 75
Water heaters, electric, 128
Wattage (watts)
    backup generators and, 271
    defined, 14
    identifying on wiring diagram, 133
    locating, 128–129
Well lights, 221
Wet-area receptacle covers, 7
Whole-house fan, 254–255
Whole-house surge arrestor, 172, 173
Window air conditioners, 129, 140
Wire(s)
    about, 26
    code requirements for, 120
    color chart for, 26
    connecting to screw terminals, 31
    fixing a loose connection, 297
    how to pigtail, 33
    installing on concrete walls, 46–47
    joining with a wire connector, 32
    problems and solutions for, 305–309
    reading unsheathed, 29
    size chart, 26
    tips for working with, 29
Wire ampacity, 29
Wire connectors
    about, 29
    defined, 14
    joining wires with, 32, 38
Wireless switches, 228–231
Wire strippers, 20
Wiring diagrams/plans
    drawing, 113, 132–133
    room-by-room, 134–147
    symbol key for, 132, 133